Lawfare

More praise for
LAWFARE
LAW AS A WEAPON OF WAR

"Law has become an important weapon in the strategic arsenal. In this remarkable book, Orde Kittrie gives us the first comprehensive examination of the techniques, promises, and perils of 'lawfare.' I believe Kittrie's book will long remain the best such examination of lawfare, for it unites a scholarly meticulousness with a pragmatic flair for policy proposals. This fine book is lucid and systematic, rich with valuable and pragmatic proposals. It will become a *vade mecum,* a manual kept close at hand, for a new generation of officials who must cope with the rise of market states—those decentralized ... networked post-industrial states that are at present emerging—and with the vulnerabilities that come with this development."

Philip C. Bobbitt, Herbert Wechsler Professor of Jurisprudence and Director of the Center for National Security, Columbia Law School

"With this seminal volume, Orde Kittrie opens a novel and exciting branch of scholarship and international practice. Alongside conventional tools— diplomacy, economic sanctions, covert action, and kinetic warfare—lawfare can now take its proper place both for offense and defense in the realm of international combat. The United States excels at deploying conventional tools, but it is far behind the curve in applying lawfare. Kittrie not only spells out the possibilities but also sounds a much needed wake-up call."

Gary Clyde Hufbauer, Reginald Jones Senior Fellow, Peterson Institute for International Economics, and former Deputy Assistant Secretary of the Treasury

"In the first comprehensive study of 'lawfare,' Orde Kittrie very ably analyzes how terrorists and insurgents around the world now use legal procedures and allegations of legal violations to hobble nations committed to the rule of law. While lawfare is generally an asymmetric threat—a tactic of conflict that is more effectively employed against developed nations than by them—Kittrie also describes emerging ways in which private parties have employed civil litigation to undermine terrorist organizations and their sponsors. This thorough volume is mandatory reading for scholars and policy makers in the field of counter terrorism."

Gregory E. Maggs, Professor of Law, The George Washington University Law School, and Colonel, Judge Advocate, U.S. Army Reserve

LAWFARE

Law as a Weapon of War

Orde F. Kittrie

OXFORD
UNIVERSITY PRESS

OXFORD
UNIVERSITY PRESS

Oxford University Press is a department of the University of Oxford. It furthers the University's objective of excellence in research, scholarship, and education by publishing worldwide.

Oxford   New York
Auckland   Cape Town   Dar es Salaam   Hong Kong   Karachi   Kuala Lumpur   Madrid
Melbourne   Mexico City   Nairobi   New Delhi   Shanghai   Taipei   Toronto

With offices in
Argentina   Austria   Brazil   Chile   Czech Republic   France   Greece   Guatemala   Hungary
Italy   Japan   Poland   Portugal   Singapore   South Korea   Switzerland   Thailand
Turkey   Ukraine   Vietnam

Oxford is a registered trademark of Oxford University Press in the UK and certain other countries.

Published in the United States of America by
Oxford University Press
198 Madison Avenue, New York, NY 10016

© Oxford University Press 2016

Library of Congress Cataloging-in-Publication Data
Kittrie, Orde F., author.
  Lawfare : law as a weapon of war / Orde F. Kittrie.
    pages cm
  Includes bibliographical references and index.
  ISBN 978-0-19-026357-7 (hardback)
1. Government liability (International law) 2. Actions and defenses—Political aspects. 3. Public interest law. 4. Malicious prosecution—Political aspects. 5. National security—Law and legislation. 6. Arab-Israeli conflict—Law and legislation. 7. United States.—Foreign relations—Law and legislation. I. Title.
  K967.K58 2016
  341.3—dc23
                                                                            2015020627

9 8 7 6 5 4 3 2 1
Printed in the United States of America on acid-free paper

Note to Readers

This publication is designed to provide accurate and authoritative information in regard to the subject matter covered. It is based upon sources believed to be accurate and reliable and is intended to be current as of the time it was written. It is sold with the understanding that the publisher is not engaged in rendering legal, accounting, or other professional services. If legal advice or other expert assistance is required, the services of a competent professional person should be sought. Also, to confirm that the information has not been affected or changed by recent developments, traditional legal research techniques should be used, including checking primary sources where appropriate.

(Based on the Declaration of Principles jointly adopted by a Committee of the American Bar Association and a Committee of Publishers and Associations.)

You may order this or any other Oxford University Press publication
by visiting the Oxford University Press website at www.oup.com

To my wife Liz for her support and encouragement

CONTENTS

FOREWORD BY R. JAMES WOOLSEY, JR.

My first introduction to international law was a class with Leon Lipson, a Yale professor who started the class with the following line: "This is the only class you'll take in law school in which there is a reasonable argument that the subject does not exist. The reason is that there's no sheriff."

In the Wild West, the vacuum caused by the lack of a sheriff was often filled by self-appointed lawmen, also known as vigilantes. As one scholar of the period put it, "self-constituted courts sprang up," "'Judge Colts' who made their own law often graced the frontier bench," "juries were easily influenced by friends or intimidated by foes," and "law enforcement … lagged behind violation of the law."[1] In addition, even when sheriffs did nominally exist, they were often not upstanding models of the rule of law. Wyatt Earp, Henry Plummer, and Bat Masterson, among others, served either simultaneously or alternately as lawmen and outlaws.[2]

Lawfare: Law as a Weapon of War, by Orde Kittrie, provides a fascinating analysis of how the vacuum caused by the lack of a sheriff is playing out today in the international legal arena. Many of the resulting phenomena are reminiscent of the Wild West. *Lawfare* describes foreign courts claiming "universal jurisdiction" over crimes allegedly committed by U.S. officials in third countries. It also details the International Criminal Court (ICC) claiming its own form of jurisdiction over U.S. officials notwithstanding the United States' refusal to join the ICC.

In addition, decisions by such international organizations and tribunals as do exist are largely the result of popularity contests manifested by nonaligned movement bloc voting. Meanwhile, international laws are routinely violated by many governments and non-state actors. Many of the most egregious violators simultaneously seek to sit in judgment of others. For example, the U.N. Human Rights Council features many of the world's worst human rights abusers—including the governments of China, Russia, and Saudi Arabia—hypocritically passing judgment on the human rights practices of governments with far better records.

As *Lawfare* convincingly illustrates, law is today, for many current and potential U.S. adversaries, a very useful weapon, wielded to oppress dissidents domestically and advance policy objectives internationally. In a jurisdiction subject to the rule of law, law would serve as a relatively fixed check on power. In a country like China or Russia, or in the international arena, which lacks an upstanding sheriff, law serves as a malleable instrument of power. Focused as it is on the international arena, the book provides numerous, painstakingly documented examples of how, in recent decades, both other governments and non-state actors have increasingly altered and deployed law both to augment their own power and constrain that of the United States and its allies.

However, while *Lawfare* does an outstanding job of diagnosing the role of law in the international arena, its greatest strength lies in its proposed antidotes—its balanced and practical recommendations for how the United States and its allies should respond. There are several options for how the United States and its allies might choose to deal with the absence of an upstanding sheriff and the fact that law-flouting rogue states and terrorists are today largely the source of international conflict—that is, that because of them, we still live, internationally, in a decidedly Hobbesian world.[3]

One approach might be to ignore our legal obligations as blithely as do our adversaries and potential adversaries. However, that would contribute to eroding the good that law does and could do in the international arena and bring us down to the level of our opponents; ignoring legal obligations would be beneath a country such as ours that prides itself on its values and commitment to the rule of law. *Lawfare* explicitly rejects such an approach. "This book's recommended approach to lawfare," writes Kittrie, "does not counsel violating either domestic or international law, or, as with the torture memos, developing convoluted arguments as to how an unlawful or morally reprehensible course of action can be portrayed as lawful."

A second approach is reflected in the reasoning of some in the United States and elsewhere who ignore the evidence that we live in a Hobbesian rather than a Lockean world and who insist that the United States must behave as if the Taliban, Hamas, and China are all genteel members of a collegial social contract. Those who take the second approach focus on holding the United States and its allies to standards that go far beyond the requirements of international law while ignoring clear-cut violations by our opponents. For example, *Lawfare* describes how various international bodies have ignored the illegality of the practice of militants attacking while dressed as civilians or hiding and firing weapons in or near schools, houses of worship, homes, and other civilian buildings. *Lawfare* also rejects this second approach.

The book also strikingly contrasts the white-glove, hyperdeferential practice of international law by the U.S. government with the pervasively instrumental and brass-knuckles approach to U.S. domestic law of attorneys within the United States. As an illustration of the latter, the book quotes Professor Robert W. Gordon's description of the "advocacy ideal," taught in U.S. law schools, as providing that while attorneys "should not tell outright lies to judges or fabricate evidence ... they may, and if it will serve their clients' interest must, exploit any gap, ambiguity, technicality or loophole, any not-obviously-and-totally-implausible interpretation of the law or facts,"[4] even if the result is a failure to "enforce[ ] the substantive law against its violators."[5] *Lawfare* notes that "it is surely a peculiarity of U.S. jurisprudence and its practicing attorneys that they, by and large, wield law more aggressively against each other than they do against the U.S.'s foreign adversaries."

A third approach for how the United States and its allies might choose to deal with the absence of an upstanding sheriff in a Hobbesian world is that advocated by Kittrie in *Lawfare*. The book recommends that the United States and its allies comply with their legal obligations while at the same time far more aggressively and creatively waging and defending against lawfare—in other words, deploying law as a weapon against our adversaries and countering their efforts to use it as a weapon against us.

Kittrie makes a compelling case for the benefits of this third approach. His book provides numerous remarkable examples of how U.S private sector attorneys, and occasionally U.S. government lawyers, have already impactfully waged lawfare against U.S. adversaries.

In light of the significant impact of lawfare waged by U.S. actors outside of the federal executive branch, readers will be surprised to learn that the U.S. executive branch is itself largely failing to wage lawfare as systematically as are some of our adversaries. For example, the book describes how the People's Republic of China has adopted lawfare as a major component of its strategic doctrine and is waging it aggressively and systematically across the maritime, aviation, space, cyber, and nonproliferation arenas. Indeed, while this is the first English-language book to provide an overview of lawfare, the Chinese People's Liberation Army has already published several such books.

Having worked for more than two decades as a private sector litigator, I found of particular interest the book's several case studies of impactful lawfare waged by private sector litigators. The most fascinating may be Kittrie's description and analysis of how private sector litigators won a judgment against Iran (and have seized some $2 billion in Iranian assets) on behalf of the families of the 241 U.S. Marines killed in the 1983 Marine barracks bombing. As the book discusses, the U.S. executive branch never retaliated against Iran for the attack—despite quickly acquiring strong evidence that the attack had been orchestrated by Iran. A plan to respond by bombing an Iranian base in Lebanon was developed but never implemented.

In 1994, more than a decade after the Marine barracks bombing, Secretary of Defense Casper Weinberger insisted that "we never had the fidelity on who perpetrated that horrendous act."[6] George Shultz, who was Secretary of State at the time, later criticized the lack of a response, stating: "We may never have the kind of evidence that can stand up in an American court of law, but we cannot allow ourselves to become the Hamlet of nations, worrying endlessly over whether and how to respond."[7]

As the book describes, it was, ironically, in an American court of law, on May 30, 2003, almost twenty years after the blast, that Iran was finally held accountable for the Marine barracks bombing. On that day, a U.S. district court judge ruled that Iran was responsible for the Marine barracks bombing and awarded $2.657 billion in compensation to its victims. In 2008, $2 billion in Iranian assets were seized as a result of the verdict. "For despots, taking their money away can be more important than dropping a few bombs and killing a few of their citizens, about whom they may not care very much," said Steve Perles, an American private sector lawyer who represented the plaintiffs in the Marine barracks bombing case.

The book goes on to provide a thoughtful analysis of why so much of the United States' most effective and creative lawfare is being waged not by the U.S. government but rather by private sector or other non-governmental attorneys. Kittrie describes how economic globalization, the information technology revolution, and the continued rigidity of the U.S. government bureaucracy have all in recent decades increased the ease and likelihood of effective ideas and implementation emerging from private sector and other non-governmental practitioners of lawfare, rather than from government attorneys.

Kittrie quotes John Hamre, a former Deputy Secretary of Defense who became head of CSIS, a Washington, D.C., think tank, putting it simply: "Big bureaucracies do not invent new ideas."[8] He also quotes Michele Flournoy, a former U.S. Under Secretary of Defense for Policy, recently questioning whether the United States' national security decision-making processes are "agile enough and responsive enough to … keep pace with the speed of the modern world."[9] "Sometimes it feels," said Flournoy, "like our interagency process is horribly slow and clunky compared to the demands being placed on it from the environment."[10]

Having served in the federal government in four different administrations, I am not unfamiliar with bureaucratic frustrations. As chairman of the Foundation for Defense of Democracies, I have enjoyed the opportunity to advise and participate in its efforts to nimbly develop, and implement or encourage implementation of, creative new ideas for lawfare against U.S. adversaries. Two of the organization's success stories—regarding Iranian gasoline imports and Iranian dependence on the SWIFT (Society for Worldwide Interbank Financial Telecommunications) financial transaction system—are detailed in this book, alongside similar case studies of creative lawfare waged by other NGOs.

As a former general counsel to the Senate Armed Services Committee, I also found very interesting the book's description of the tensions over private sector lawfare between the executive branch, which mostly considers it a bothersome interference in its foreign policy prerogatives, and Congress, which keeps passing new laws facilitating private sector litigation against state sponsors of terrorism and the like. As one analyst put it, "who could vote against … the belief in the law as the ultimate arbitrator of social justice; the reliance on the rights and energies of the individual; the emotional and moral draw of the common man taking on a dictatorial terrorist state in a courtroom showdown."[11]

The book explains that notwithstanding the Supreme Court's ruling in the recent case of *Zivotofsky v. Kerry*, the idea that the President speaks for the nation with one voice in dealing with other governments does not square with either the Constitution or U.S. practice. Aside from Congress exercising the considerable foreign policy powers provided to it in the Constitution, there is an extensive record of U.S. states, cities, and non-governmental actors undertaking lawfare-type actions to influence U.S. foreign policy.

These and other deployments of lawfare are wonderfully described in this thoroughly researched, thought-provoking, and compellingly readable book. *Lawfare* is both an invaluable work of scholarship and also a vitally important call to action. Both the U.S. government and the broader American legal community contain tremendous legal expertise. Their failure to engage with lawfare systematically, while our adversaries and potential adversaries are doing so, is a missed opportunity and is increasingly dangerous. U.S. and allied policymakers and lawyers should read this important book and heed its call to action.

ACKNOWLEDGMENTS

This book has benefited from the input and support of many people. I am grateful to Laurie Blank, Mark Dubowitz, Annie Fixler, Rob Kelner, Eugene Kontorovich, Alyza Lewin, Nat Lewin, Ed MacAllister, Josh Perles, Steve Perles, and Adam Smith for their comments on portions of the draft. A special thank you is due to David Weinberg for his comments on the entirety of the draft and especially the Conclusion. The book also benefited from interviews with the following experts whose generosity with their time and insights helped bring the chapters to life: Mkhaimar Abusada, Nitsana Darshan-Leitner, Mostafa Elostaz, Alyza Lewin, Nathan Lewin, Steven Perles, Daniel Reisner, Guy Roberts, Daniel Taub, and several government officials who agreed to speak only on condition of anonymity.

A particular thanks is due to the Foundation for Defense of Democracies, its president, Cliff May, and its executive director, Mark Dubowitz, for their inspiration, encouragement, and support. Thanks are also due to the John D. and Catherine T. MacArthur Foundation and Emma Belcher for their support of research that informed the portions of the book addressing nuclear trafficking. At Oxford University Press, Alden Domizio, John Louth, and Blake Ratcliff have been very helpful, encouraging, and patient guides along the publishing path. Cassie Tuttle copyedited the manuscript with great patience, thoroughness, and precision. Arun Kumar Vasu skillfully shepherded the manuscript during the production process. Thanks also to the Sandra Day O'Connor College of Law at Arizona State University, which has been my academic home for the past eleven years.

Last but not least, a very special hug of appreciation is due to my wife Liz and our two children—for their encouragement, support, and patience.

CHAPTER 1

A Conceptual Overview of Lawfare's Meaning, Variety, and Power

Lawfare is "the strategy of using—or misusing—law as a substitute for traditional military means to achieve a warfighting objective"

— Maj. Gen. Charles J. Dunlap, Jr., USAF (ret.)[1]

L aw is becoming an increasingly powerful and prevalent weapon of war. The reasons for this development include the increased number and reach of international laws and tribunals, the rise of non-governmental organizations (NGOs) focused on law of armed conflict and related issues, the information technology revolution, and the advance of globalization and thus economic interdependence.

The following are four recent illustrative examples of "lawfare," the use of law as a weapon of war:

- Palestinian Authority (PA) President Mahmoud Abbas wrote in a 2011 *New York Times* op-ed that UN recognition of Palestine as a member state "would pave the way for the internationalization of the conflict as a legal matter, not only a political one. It would also pave the way for us to pursue claims against Israel at the United Nations, human rights treaty bodies and the International Court of Justice."[2] Since then, the PA has joined dozens of international treaties and organizations, including the International Criminal Court. In addition, Palestinian and allied NGOs have filed lawsuits and insti- gated criminal prosecutions in Europe against companies accused of aiding alleged Israeli war crimes by supplying Israel with security technology or con- struction equipment. Some of these companies have felt compelled to stop doing business with Israel. As the PA advanced its lawfare strategy, the Israeli government became so concerned that it decided to trade the release of dozens of Palestinian prisoners who had murdered Israelis in exchange for a nine-month respite from PA lawfare. Thus, the Palestinian Authority has begun to win by "internationalization of the conflict as a legal matter" what it could not achieve through either armed force or negotiations.

- A Russian ship, the MV Alaed, was at sea in June 2012 carrying helicopter gunships bound for Syria's Assad regime. The U.K. wished to stop the shipment but understood that forcibly intercepting a Russian ship could have risked World War III. So the U.K. persuaded the ship's insurer, London's Standard Club, to withdraw the ship's insurance.[3] As a result, the ship and its deadly cargo turned around and returned to Russia.[4]

- The People's Republic of China (PRC) has explicitly adopted "legal warfare" as a major component of its strategic doctrine and is currently waging it in the maritime, aviation, space, cyber, and other arenas. For example, "China has," according to two U.S. Navy attorneys, "recently begun to engage in a resourceful legal warfare, or 'lawfare' strategy to deny access to its coastal seas to warships and aircraft of the United States, Japan, and other countries in the region."[5] A Naval War College professor calls this a part of "China's ongoing lawfare strategy to misstate or misapply international legal norms to accommodate its anti-access strategy."[6] According to another U.S. Navy lawyer, China's maritime lawfare strategy is "slowly proving effective . . . . [I]f successful, China will have achieved through the use of lawfare what it traditionally would have had to achieve almost solely through military force."[7]

- The Taliban have regularly placed military assets within or around schools, religious sites, and hospitals, in hopes of either deterring attacks or, if attacks do take place, accusing the United States and its allies of harming innocent civilians.[8] In response, the United States and its allies have adopted targeting standards more stringent than required by international law.[9] As U.S. Major General Charles Dunlap, Jr., put it, NATO's creation of restrictions beyond what is required by international law "creates for its adversary a substitute for conventional military weaponry . . . . [F]or the Taliban to survive it is not necessary for them to build conventional air defenses; rather, just by operating amidst civilians they enjoy a legal sanctuary . . . that is as secure as any fortress bristling with anti-aircraft guns."[10]

In recognition of law's increasing utility as a weapon of war, Dunlap, then a colonel in the U.S. Air Force Judge Advocate General's Corps, in November 2001 introduced the term "lawfare" into the mainstream legal and international relations literature.[11] He ultimately defined "lawfare" as the strategy of "using—or misusing—law as a substitute for traditional military means to achieve an operational objective."[12]

Despite the term having been coined by a U.S. government official, the U.S. government has only sporadically engaged with the concept of lawfare. It has no lawfare strategy or doctrine, and no office or interagency mechanism that systematically develops or coordinates U.S. offensive lawfare or U.S. defenses against lawfare.

In contrast, the People's Republic of China (PRC) has adopted the similarly defined concept of "legal warfare" as a major component of its strategic doctrine. In addition, law has become a preeminent weapon in the Israeli-Palestinian conflict, leading the Israeli government to create an office focused on waging and defending against lawfare.

The U.S. government's lack of systematic engagement with lawfare is a tremendous missed opportunity. Lawfare is not going to entirely or even largely replace traditional, kinetic warfare ("shooting warfare").[13] However, many of this book's case studies of impactful lawfare demonstrate that lawfare, deployed systematically and adeptly, could in various circumstances save U.S. and foreign lives by enabling U.S. national security objectives to be advanced with less or no kinetic warfare.

Lawfare is almost always less deadly than traditional warfare. "We have every reason to embrace lawfare," says Phillip Carter, an attorney and former U.S. Army officer, "for it is vastly preferable to the bloody, expensive, and destructive forms of warfare that ravaged the world in the 20th century."[14] As Carter wryly puts it, "I would far prefer to have motions and discovery requests fired at me than incoming mortar or rocket-propelled grenade fire."[15]

Lawfare is also almost always less financially costly than traditional warfare. Lawfare is thus a weapon eminently suitable for the U.S. public's aversion to casualties and the current U.S. focus on reducing government spending.

Lawfare can sometimes also be more effective than kinetic warfare. "For despots, taking their money away can be more important than dropping a few bombs and killing a few of their citizens, about whom they may not care very much," said Steve Perles, an American civil litigator who has, as described in Chapter 3, collected hundreds of millions of dollars in U.S. court judgments against state sponsors of terrorism.[16]

In addition, if some portion of warfare can be shifted from kinetic combat to the legal arena, that should be to the United States' great advantage. While the United States does have more sophisticated lethal weapons than do its adversaries, its advantage in sophisticated legal weapons has the potential to be even greater.[17] The United States is a far more law-oriented society, with a much higher percentage of its best minds going into the legal field and creatively using law to achieve their objectives than is, say, the PRC. Yet the PRC is currently waging lawfare much more diligently and systematically than is the United States.

Despite lawfare's advantages over traditional warfare, little scholarly attention has been paid to lawfare thus far. This is the first English-language book to provide a broad and systematic overview of "lawfare," defined here, as Dunlap defines it, as "the strategy of using—or misusing—law as a substitute for traditional military means to achieve a warfighting objective."[18]

This chapter, Chapter 1, analyzes lawfare conceptually. Section I of this chapter addresses the definition of lawfare, provides a brief overview of previous lawfare scholarship, and then discusses this book's goals, structure, and methodology. Section II of this chapter offers a lawfare typology. Section III provides an overview of the U.S. approach to lawfare thus far. Section IV, the final section of this chapter, analyzes why lawfare's impact and prevalence are increasing.

Each of this book's seven subsequent chapters focuses on lawfare waged by a distinct actor or set of actors: U.S. NGOs and individuals (Chapter 2); the U.S. government (Chapter 3); the PRC (Chapter 4); the PA (Chapter 5); Palestinian NGOs and their allies (Chapter 6); Hamas (Chapter 7); and Israel (Chapter 8). Each of these chapters uses case studies and other data to describe and analyze how and why lawfare has been waged and what the consequences have been for the wagers of lawfare, their adversaries, and other affected parties.

Chapters 2, 3, 4, 7, and 8 each conclude with a discussion of lessons learned and an assessment of how lawfare by the respective actor or set of actors may develop in the future. For Chapters 5 and 6 together, the discussion of lessons learned and potential future lawfare is contained at the conclusion of Chapter 6. The book's Conclusion highlights key opportunities for next steps in the study of lawfare, including by suggesting some ways in which future lawfare research could inform legal and international relations scholarship and vice versa.

I. THE MEANING AND STUDY OF LAWFARE

A. The Origins and Definition of Lawfare

While the concept of law as a weapon of war was first termed "lawfare" in an essay by Charles Dunlap, Jr., in November 2001, both the concept and the term preexisted Dunlap's linking of them. The use of law as a weapon of war arguably goes back all the way to Hugo Grotius, the "father of international law." During the first decade of the 1600s, European countries, including Grotius's Holland, were competing intensely over the control of seafaring trade routes.[19] Portugal was attempting to protect its lucrative spice trade by deploying its navy to exclude the Dutch East India Company (DEIC) from the Indian Ocean.[20] The DEIC hired Grotius to devise a theory under which "war might rightly be waged against, and prize taken from the Portuguese," on the grounds that the Portuguese had "wrongfully tried to exclude the Dutch."[21]

In response to the DEIC's commission, Grotius wrote his classic book, *Mare Liberum*, first published in 1609, in which he made the case that under the "Law of Nations," "the sea is common to all" and all nations are free to use it for sea-faring trade.[22] By the 1700s, "most states" had adopted Grotius's "idea of *mare liberum*—the freedom of the seas."[23] Thus, "Grotius used law to accomplish an objective that Dutch military power could not and thereby solidified the concept of freedom of the seas in modern international law."[24]

Grotius's success was so striking in part because it predated by some four hundred years many of the socioeconomic and technological factors that are making law a more powerful and prevalent weapon in twenty-first-century conflicts. These factors—which will be discussed in detail in Section IV of this chapter—had started to come to the fore by the mid-1990s. Thus, it is not surprising that during the five years before Dunlap's essay, a number of international legal and policy officials and analysts referred to the increasing power of law as a weapon of war, in many senses anticipating his argument—albeit without using the term "lawfare." For example, in 1996, PRC President Jiang Zemin advised a group of Chinese international law experts that China "must be adept at using international law as a weapon."[25]

In 1999, a book titled *Unrestricted Warfare*, which was written by two PRC colonels and published by the PRC military, repeatedly referenced the concept of using law as a weapon, sometimes referring to it as "legal warfare."[26] The book provided a list of "examples of non-military warfare," which included "establishing international laws that primarily benefit a certain country."[27] The list also included "the use of domestic trade law on the international stage," which the book asserted "can have a destructive effect that is equal to that of a military operation."[28]

Dunlap's seminal November 2001 essay, in which he first used the term "lawfare," was framed in part as an explicit response to an influential essay from the prior year by David Rivkin and Lee Casey. In their essay, Rivkin and Casey asserted that both U.S. allies and adversaries have "chosen to use" international law "as a means to check, or at least harness, American power."[29] Rivkin and Casey pointed to examples including the emerging International Criminal Court, with its ability to prosecute U.S. officials for violating international laws that are "ambiguous in their meaning and remarkably fluid in their application."[30] "If the trends of international law in the 1990s are allowed to mature," warned Rivkin and Casey, "international law may prove to be one of the most potent weapons ever deployed against the United States."[31]

"The good news," asserted Rivkin and Casey, "is that international law . . . can function as a positive force, capable of promoting a more stable international environment and advancing our national interest."[32] In order to achieve this, they urged that the United States "actively work to shape international law" as the Dutch did in employing Grotius to advocate for the freedom of the seas.[33] Rivkin and Casey noted that "as the world's pre-eminent power," the United States has "both the greatest opportunity and the most pressing need to shape international law."[34] They recommended that the United States could most effectively seize this opportunity if it were to integrate international law into "American statecraft," "consciously coordinate foreign policy and international law imperatives," and "approach the current problems posed by international law holistically, rather than one issue at a time."[35]

In contrast with the concept of law as a weapon of war, the word "lawfare" seems to have first appeared in 1975 in a paper on mediation by John Carlson and Neville Yeomans.[36] Expressing concern that the Western legal system had become too adversarial, Carlson and Yeomans wrote that "[l]awfare replaces warfare and the duel is with words rather than swords."[37] For Carlson and Yeomans, lawfare was clearly a portmanteau of—that is, a word whose form and meaning are derived from a blending of—the two distinct words "law" and "warfare."

The "lawfare" portmanteau coined by Carlson and Yeomans seems to have gone largely or entirely unnoticed by the international legal and policy arena until Dunlap married it in 2001 to the concept of law as a weapon of war. The November 2001 essay by Dunlap, then a colonel in the U.S. Air Force JAG Corps, both married the concept to the term and vaulted the term "lawfare" into wide circulation in the international legal and policy arenas.[38]

In his essay, Dunlap asserted that "'lawfare', that is, the use of law as a weapon of war, is the newest feature of 21st century combat."[39] He also offered a second, slightly different definition, stating that "lawfare describes a method of warfare where law is used as a means of realizing a military objective."[40] In subsequent essays, Dunlap adopted a third, and again slightly different definition, defining lawfare as "the strategy of using—or misusing—law as a substitute for traditional military means to achieve a warfighting objective."[41]

It is important to note that all three of these definitions of lawfare are value-neutral. Defined as such, lawfare is intrinsically neither good nor bad but can, as with most other weapons, be "wielded by either side in a belligerency"[42] and used "for good or bad purposes, depending on the mindset of those who wield it."[43] As Dunlap explained in a 2011 article, "lawfare . . . focuses principally on circumstances where law can create the same or similar effects as those ordinarily sought from conventional warmaking approaches."[44] Lawfare, said Dunlap, is "simply another kind of weapon, one that is produced, metaphorically speaking, by beating law books into swords."[45]

In contrast with his later value-neutral definition of the term lawfare, Dunlap's November 2001 essay described lawfare's impact as largely malign, at least from the perspective of U.S. national security. For instance, he wrote that "there is disturbing evidence that the rule of law is being hijacked into just another way of fighting (lawfare), to the detriment of humanitarian values as well as the law itself."[46] He also said that "foes of the United States" who are "no longer able to seriously confront—let alone defeat—America militarily . . . resort to a strategy that can be labeled 'lawfare.'"[47]

However, in subsequent essays, Dunlap provided numerous examples of lawfare having a beneficial impact on U.S. national security. He noted that many such "uses of 'legal weapons'... avoid the need to resort to physical violence" while being equally or more effective than traditional military means.[48] As illustrations, Dunlap included "establishing the rule of law"[49] in order to secure the population from insurgents, and "the use of legal processes to deconstruct terrorist financing."[50] As an example of the latter, Dunlap referenced the State Department officially designating the Pakistani Taliban as a "foreign terrorist organization," which "has the effect of criminalizing material support provided them."[51] Dunlap noted that while attacking the funding of terrorist groups "may be called 'financial warfare' rather than 'lawfare'" by some, "it nevertheless depends upon legal instruments and methodologies."[52]

Dunlap also included targeted trade sanctions as an example of where "actions that could be characterized as 'lawfare' have been carried out by the United States," noting that such "legal 'weaponry' can have effects utterly indistinguishable from those produced by their kinetic analogs."[53] As an illustration, during the 2003 invasion of Iraq by the United States, "the Iraqi Air Force found itself hobbled by a legal device—sanctions—as effectively as by any outcome from traditional aerial combat."[54] "By preventing the acquisition of new aircraft as well as spare parts for the existing fleet, Iraqi airpower was so debilitated," said Dunlap, "that not a single aircraft rose in opposition to the coalition air armada."[55]

As of 2015, "lawfare" is the only term widely used in English to describe the concept of law as a weapon of war. However, "lawfare" as defined by Dunlap is not the only usage of the term. Before proceeding, it is important to briefly address the other leading usages of "lawfare" and why this book adopts Dunlap's definition.

Lawfare: Hard National Security Choices is the title of a popular blog on U.S. national security law issues. The blog is not focused on lawfare as defined by Dunlap and this book, but rather addresses "that nebulous zone in which actions taken or contemplated to protect the nation interact with the nation's laws and legal institutions."[56] The founders of the blog explained their choice of name as follows: "The name Lawfare refers both to the use of law as a weapon of conflict and ... to the depressing reality that America remains at war with itself over the law governing its warfare with others."[57] The blog's founders explained that in titling theirs the Lawfare Blog, they adopted "[t]his latter sense of the word—which is admittedly not its normal usage."[58]

In addition, while both Dunlap and this book define lawfare to have neutral connotations, that is, "using—or misusing—law as a substitute for traditional military means to achieve a warfighting objective," some commentators define lawfare as carrying solely negative connotations. For instance, an advocacy group called the Lawfare Project asserts that lawfare denotes "the abuse of Western laws and judicial systems to achieve strategic military or political ends" and insists that lawfare "must be defined as a negative phenomenon to have any real meaning."[59]

In light of the somewhat confusing variety of other usages and definitions of "lawfare," this author briefly considered coining a new portmanteau for law as a weapon of war, say "juriscombat." However, in a nod to Dunlap, the author decided to stick with "lawfare."

This book is principally about the use of law as a weapon of war (rather than, for example, about the evolving use of the term lawfare). As this book will illustrate, law is an increasingly powerful yet understudied weapon of war. The book aims to shed light on the phenomenon. In doing so, the book will use the term "lawfare" as shorthand for "the use of law as a weapon of war," matching the term with the concept and ascribing to them the same meaning as Dunlap did.

In identifying examples of lawfare, the book will focus on both effects and intention. In order to qualify as lawfare, an action must therefore meet two tests: (1) the actor uses law to create the same or similar effects as those traditionally sought from conventional kinetic military action—including impacting the key armed force decision-making and capabilities of the target; and (2) one of the actor's motivations is to weaken or destroy an adversary against which the lawfare is being deployed.

The second test, inspired by a Merriam-Webster definition of warfare,[60] is designed to exclude from the definition of lawfare actions such as a scholar or organization advocating a new international law or interpretation for purposes that do not include weakening or destroying a particular state or non-state actor or actors. Although intent is notoriously difficult to discern, it is nevertheless a key element of many domestic and international crimes. If guilt or innocence of a criminal offense, with the accompanying stigma and punishment, can turn on the actor's intent, it seems reasonable that whether or not an action qualifies as lawfare, a value-neutral act, can also turn on the actor's intent.

The book uses the term "lawfare" in recognition of Dunlap's pioneering work on the topic of law as a weapon of war and because "lawfare" remains the only term widely used in English to describe the concept. The book ascribes neutral connotations to the concept and term because the author believes, as does Dunlap, that there is clear value in having a neutral term to describe the use of law as a weapon of war, while simultaneously being able to label some, but not all, uses of lawfare as "illicit lawfare." Ascribing neutral connotations to the concept is also consistent with the Chinese term *falu zhan* (most directly translated as "legal warfare"), which is a major component of the PRC's strategic doctrine, and is used in China's relatively advanced literature on the use of law as a weapon of war.

B. A Brief Overview of the Lawfare Literature

The existing English language literature about lawfare, defined as the use of law as a weapon of war, is still relatively thin. To this author's knowledge, there has been only one major scholarly conference on lawfare: the Lawfare! conference, conducted at the Case Western University School of Law in September 2010, which posed the threshold question of whether lawfare is a useful concept from a scholarly perspective. Based on the proceedings, the conference organizer, Professor Michael Scharf, concluded that "'lawfare' is a potentially powerful concept that reflects the importance of law in the conflicts of the 21st Century."[61] The author of this book participated in the conference, and his article titled *Lawfare and U.S. National Security* is included in a journal issue dedicated to the conference,[62] which is the only existing English-language, book-length scholarly treatment of the concept of lawfare.

Other than the Case Western journal issue and the several articles in which Dunlap defines (and then updates his definition of) lawfare,[63] the most significant grouping of American scholarly articles explicitly addressing lawfare (or the concept of law as a weapon of war) is a series of essays by U.S. Navy attorneys about Chinese maritime lawfare.[64]

There are also a handful of books focused on particular case studies, or other narrow slices, of lawfare. For example, LAWFARE: USE OF THE DEFINITION OF AGGRESSIVE WAR BY THE SOVIET AND RUSSIAN FEDERATION GOVERNMENTS (2010), by Christi Bartman, focuses narrowly on the use of the definition of aggressive war by the Soviet and Russian governments. ISRAEL AND THE STRUGGLE OVER THE INTERNATIONAL LAWS OF WAR (2012), by Peter Berkowitz, focuses on two case studies relating to Israeli defensive warfare. LAWFARE: THE WAR AGAINST FREE SPEECH: A FIRST AMENDMENT GUIDE FOR REPORTING IN AN AGE OF ISLAMIST LAWFARE (2011), by Brooke M. Goldstein and Aaron Eitan Meyer, focuses on advising journalists about how to protect themselves against what the book calls "'Islamist lawfare,' the use of the law as a weapon of war to silence and punish free speech about militant Islam, terrorism and its sources of financing." LAWFARE: THE COLOMBIAN CASE (2012), by Juan M. Padilla, focuses on the use of lawfare by non-state actors in Colombia.[65]

The closest English-language analog to this book in scope is probably the superb TREASURY'S WAR, a history of U.S. financial lawfare by Juan Zarate. Zarate served in the George W. Bush administration as Assistant Secretary of the Treasury for Terrorist Financing and Financial Crimes, and later as Deputy National Security Adviser for Combating Terrorism. Zarate's book covers some of the same ground as this book's chapter on U.S. financial lawfare against Iran. However, there is very little overlap between TREASURY'S WAR and the other seven chapters of this book.

As described in more detail in this book's Chapter 4 (on PRC lawfare), there are currently more books in Chinese that broadly address lawfare than there are in English. Over the last decade, the PRC's People's Liberation Army has published at least three books that broadly address *falu zhan*.[66] For example, ANALYSIS OF 100 CASES OF LEGAL WARFARE (2004), coauthored by leading Chinese jurist Cong Wensheng, describes and analyzes one hundred case studies of other countries, including the United States, using lawfare. LEGAL WARFARE IN MODERN WAR (2005), by Xun Hengdong, an attorney who is a high-ranking military officer, asserts and explains how the law of armed conflict should be treated not as an inviolable set of rules but rather as a weapon to achieve various objectives.[67] A PLA text titled UNDER INFORMATIZED CONDITIONS: LEGAL WARFARE (2007) defines its topic, "legal warfare," to include "activities conducted by using the law as the weapon."[68] Unfortunately, none of these books are publicly available in English, beyond relatively short quotations that have appeared in translation in various scholarly articles.

C. This Book's Goals, Structure, and Methodology

In this initial chapter, the book discusses and analyzes lawfare holistically. Each of the following seven chapters focuses on lawfare waged by a particular actor or set of actors. The protagonists were selected with an eye toward what the author considers to be the twenty-first century's most sophisticated, educational, impactful, and potentially precedent-setting lawfare deployments thus far. Lawfare waged by U.S. NGOs and individuals, the topic of Chapter 2, was selected because of its remarkable impact, creativity, and variety. The U.S. government's deployment of financial lawfare against Iran, the topic of Chapter 3, was selected because that has been the U.S. government's most systematic, sustained, and impactful deployment of lawfare thus far. The PRC's coordinated deployment of lawfare across the maritime, space, aviation, and nonproliferation arenas, the topic of Chapter 4, was selected because the PRC is the United States' leading rival for global primacy, and its lawfare in these arenas illustrates the PRC's comparatively more systematic and coordinated approach to lawfare.

Chapters 5 through 8 focus on wagers of lawfare in the Israeli-Palestinian conflict. Much as the Spanish Civil War served as a testing ground for weapons and tactics subsequently used in World War II,[69] the Israeli-Palestinian conflict is foreshadowing lawfare strategies and tactics that will inevitably be replicated in other conflicts. In light of the cutting-edge intensity, sophistication, and interplay of lawfare in the Israeli-Palestinian conflict, this book includes four chapters on lawfare in that conflict—one each on lawfare as waged by the PA, Palestinian NGOs and their allies, Hamas, and Israel.

While the book is far more wide-ranging than any previous English language book about lawfare, it is not meant to be either a comprehensive history or a comprehensive theoretical analysis of lawfare. Rather than seeking to catalog every case, or even every interesting case, of lawfare, the author decided to dig into a selection of cases that seemed to him to be particularly significant or indicative of lawfare's current state and future prospects.

Reflecting its pioneering nature, the book is designed to spur discussion and encourage further analysis by other authors. With regard to its case studies, the author has, wherever possible, relied on and cited to primary sources, including especially actual court filings rather than news media summaries. In order to facilitate future research by other scholars, the book is heavily endnoted, with the notes including links to those court filings and other primary documents the author was able to find online.

Some of the case studies include information derived from interviews. Because of the sensitivity of the lawfare deployments, many of which are ongoing, several interviewees (in particular government officials) were willing to be identified only on background (i.e., identified only by affiliation), and several others were willing to be interviewed only on deep background (i.e., not quoted or identified in any manner).[70]

II. A LAWFARE TYPOLOGY

Lawfare has thus far predominantly taken two interrelated forms: (1) "instrumental lawfare"—the instrumental use of legal tools to achieve the same or similar effects as those traditionally sought from conventional kinetic military action; and (2) "compliance-leverage disparity lawfare"—lawfare, typically on the kinetic battlefield, which is designed to gain advantage from the greater influence that law, typically the law of armed conflict, and its processes exerts over an adversary.

This book focuses largely on the first of these forms. As the book will illustrate, a vast range of actors—from international organizations to sovereign states to individual activists—have engaged in, and seem likely to in the future engage in, the instrumental use of legal tools to achieve the same or similar effects as those traditionally sought from conventional kinetic military action. Instrumental lawfare has been waged, and could in the future be waged, using a great variety of laws and forums, ranging from international laws in international forums to sub-national laws in sub-national forums. Instrumental lawfare is characterized by its remarkable variety and lends itself to exceptional creativity. It is also the type of lawfare that will typically be waged by Western state actors and Western non-state actors.

In contrast, a smaller set of actors are in position to take lawfare actions designed to gain advantage from the greater influence that law and its processes exerts over an adversary. Such compliance-leverage disparity lawfare is necessarily waged by state or non-state actors against adversaries over which law has significantly greater leverage or which otherwise feel more compelled to comply with the relevant type or provision of law.

For example, on the kinetic battlefield, such compliance-leverage disparity tactics typically have been used by terrorist groups and other non-state actors against Western state actors. As briefly discussed in Section II.B below, these battlefield tactics have been used to substantial effect by non-state actors including the Islamic State of Iraq and Levant (the Islamic State), Hamas, the Taliban, and Colombian rebel groups, and have received considerable media attention. Chapter 4 of this book provides an example of compliance-leverage disparity lawfare being waged in an arena outside of the kinetic battlefield. It describes the PRC's long history of gaming the international legal system by entering into legally binding nuclear nonproliferation obligations with which its rivals (including the United States, Japan, and South Korea) tend to comply, while China secretly violates those obligations by providing nuclear technology to its allies, often through proxies. While this book focuses less attention on compliance-leverage disparity lawfare than on instrumental lawfare, both are important and worthy of further study.

A. The Instrumental Use of Legal Tools

1. Types of Actors That Can Wage Instrumental Lawfare

This book provides examples of instrumental lawfare waged by:

- International organizations, including the Arab League and the European Union;
- Sovereign states, including Israel, the PRC, and the United States;
- Quasi-sovereign states, including the Palestinian Authority;
- U.S. states, including California, Florida, Massachusetts, and New York;
- U.S. cities, including Berkeley, California; Cambridge, Massachusetts; and New York City;
- Militias, including Hamas and Hezbollah;
- Advocacy networks and non-governmental organizations, including Al-Haq; the Boycott, Divestment, and Sanctions movement; the Foundation for Defense of Democracies; the Palestinian Centre for Human Rights; Shurat HaDin; the Sudan Divestment Task Force; and United Against Nuclear Iran; and
- Individual activists, such as Raphael Lemkin, and individual litigators, such as Gary Osen and Steven Perles.

2. Types of Laws and Forums That Can Be Used for Instrumental Lawfare

Instrumental lawfare can be waged using legal tools including international, national, and sub-national laws and forums, and different combinations thereof. The book includes the following varieties (with a salient example provided for each).

a. Using International Laws in International Forums

- *Creating new international laws designed to disadvantage an adversary.* For example, the Arab League successfully advocated insertion into the ICC statute of an offense designed to make a war crime out of Israeli settlements. This new international law proscribes settlements Israel believes serve its security needs, puts Israeli officials at risk of ICC prosecution, and serves as ammunition for lawfare steps in other fora. (Further details are provided in Chapter 5.)

- *Reinterpreting existing international laws so as to disadvantage an adversary.* The PRC is engaged in various initiatives to reinterpret in its favor the law of the sea, space law, and cyberlaw. If the PRC succeeds, the reinterpretations will considerably tilt future maritime, space, and cyber battlefields in favor of the PRC. (Chapter 4)

- *Generating international law criminal prosecutions in international tribunals.* The PA has joined the International Criminal Court and is acting to instigate prosecutions of Israeli officials for alleged war crimes relating to combat in Gaza and settlements in the West Bank. Israel was so concerned about the prospect of the PA joining the ICC that it released seventy-eight Palestinian prisoners, many of them convicted of murdering Israeli civilians, in exchange for the PA refraining for eight months from joining the ICC and other international organizations and treaties. (Chapter 5)

- *Using international law to generate intrusive and protracted investigations by international organizations.* The BDS (boycotts, divestment, and sanctions) movement generated a seventeen-month-long U.K. government investigation of G4S, a British vendor of security technology to Israel. The BDS complaint had asserted that G4S had contributed to alleged Israeli war crimes, in violation of guidelines issued by the Organization for Economic Cooperation and Development. The investigation contributed to G4S announcing its withdrawal from future business in Israel. (Chapter 6)

- *Generating international organization votes to disadvantage an adversary.* The PA and its allies successfully campaigned for passage of the U.N. General Assembly resolution that granted non-member observer state status to Palestine. The new status, as well as other provisions of the resolution, strengthened Palestine's claim to statehood and the legal rights that come with it without the PA having to make any concessions to Israel or defeat it on the kinetic battlefield. (Chapter 5)

- *Generating international law advisory opinions in international forums.* Arab states successfully campaigned for a General Assembly resolution requesting an International Court of Justice (ICJ) Advisory Opinion on the legal consequences of the construction by Israel of a security barrier separating it from much of the West Bank. The resulting Advisory Opinion declared both the security barrier and Israel's West Bank settlements to be in violation of international law. Despite assertions by Israeli officials and admissions by Hamas leaders that the security barrier hindered suicide bombing attacks against Israel, the ICJ concluded that Israel is "under an obligation" to dismantle the barrier. The ICJ's Advisory Opinion was the basis for subsequent actions in European courts against companies doing business with the settlements. (Chapter 5)

b. Using International Laws in National Forums

- *Using international law as grounds for "universal jurisdiction" prosecutions of third-country officials in national courts for alleged war crimes.* Iraqis brought "universal jurisdiction" prosecutions in Belgian courts against then Secretary of Defense Donald Rumsfeld and Secretary of State Colin Powell for allegedly committing war crimes in Iraq. After Rumsfeld threatened to withdraw NATO from Belgium, the law was changed and the prosecutions eliminated. However, many other countries still have such laws on their books, and former President George W. Bush cancelled a 2011 trip to Switzerland amid threats of legal action against him there for alleged mistreatment of suspected militants at Guantanamo. (Chapter 1)
- *Using international law as grounds for criminal prosecutions of domestic companies in national courts for alleged war crimes.* A Palestinian NGO generated a Dutch criminal investigation of the Dutch company Riwal for war crimes allegedly committed by Riwal's rental for sixteen days to Israel of equipment that Israel used in constructing the separation fence and settlements in the West Bank. The complaint referenced the ICJ's Advisory Opinion that the fence and settlements violated international law. The investigation lasted three years, included Dutch police raids of Riwal headquarters and officials' homes, and concluded without prosecution only after Riwal halted all activities anywhere in Israel. (Chapter 6)
- *Using international law as a defense to criminal prosecutions in national courts.* BDS activists twice broke into and damaged a Raytheon facility in Northern Ireland. Both times, they were acquitted after asserting as their defense that Raytheon supplies arms to Israel and that they were acting to prevent alleged Israeli war crimes against the people of Gaza and Lebanon. Citing the acquittals, Raytheon closed the facility. (Chapter 6)

c. Using National Laws in National Forums

- *Creating new national laws designed to put foreign vendors of strategic products to a choice between one's own market and that of an adversary.* A U.S. law in 2010 put foreign companies to a choice between providing gasoline to Iran and sanctions, including exclusion from the U.S. market. As a result, the United States managed to reduce Iran's gasoline imports as much as 90 percent without intercepting a single tanker or firing a single shot. (Chapter 2)

- *Creating new national laws enabling lawsuits against terrorist groups, their material supporters, and their state sponsors.* Stephen Flatow, the attorney father of a victim of Iranian-sponsored terrorism, successfully advocated for several amendments to U.S. law that enabled his subsequent successful lawsuit holding Iran accountable for his daughter's death. These amendments also facilitated numerous successful lawsuits by other plaintiffs against Iran and other state sponsors of terrorism including Cuba, Iraq, Libya, North Korea, and Syria. (Chapter 2)

- *National legislature actions other than passing new laws.* The mere prospect of either new legislation or implementation of existing legislation can sometimes be enough to have an impact. Eight members of the U.S. Congress sent a letter to the U.S. Export-Import Bank in 2008 asking it to review over $900 million in loan guarantees for Reliance Industries, an Indian company that was providing 10 percent of Iran's monthly gasoline consumption. On the first trading day after the letter was featured in the Indian press, shares in Reliance Industries dropped by over $1 billion on the Indian stock exchange. Reliance soon stopped supplying gasoline to Iran. In addition, the U.S. law that in 2010 required all foreign companies to choose between providing gasoline to Iran and exclusion from the U.S. market had a significant effect on gasoline exports to Iran even before enactment, with different companies halting their exports at different stages of the bill's progress toward passage. (Chapter 2)

- *National government criminal prosecutions of organizations that fund terrorist groups.* The U.S. government criminally prosecuted the Holy Land Foundation and several individuals for providing material support to Hamas. The prosecutions resulted in the imprisonment of several leading Hamas funders, contributed to the closure of the Holy Land Foundation, and helped significantly reduce Hamas fundraising in the United States. (Chapter 2)

- *National government criminal or civil enforcement actions against banks that provide financial services to rogue states or terrorist groups.* The U.S. government mounted a campaign of enforcement actions to discourage foreign banks from transacting with Iran and other rogue states. During the Obama administration's multiyear campaign to halt Iran's nuclear weapons program without bombing it, "the Treasury Department became Mr. Obama's favorite noncombatant command."[71] The U.S. government's enforcement efforts resulted in most of the world's top financial institutions halting or dramatically reducing their transactions with Iran. Iran's total foreign currency reserves dropped by as much as $110 billion, and the value of Iran's currency dropped by more than 50 percent. This economic pressure helped coerce Iran to make concessions regarding its nuclear program. (Chapter 3)

- *National permitting processes.* Shurat HaDin, an Israeli NGO, persuaded maritime insurers to stop insuring ships in a flotilla poised to sail to Gaza from Greece, then formally notified the Greek government that the ships had lost their insurance. The Greek officials confirmed the lack of insurance and prohibited the ships from sailing. (Chapter 8)
- *Civil lawsuits holding state sponsors of terrorism liable for terrorist acts against civilians.* A lawsuit in a U.S. federal court by three families of Brothers to the Rescue pilots shot down by the Cuban Air Force resulted in a $187.6 million judgment against Cuba. The families collected on the judgment by seizing $96.7 million in Cuban assets in the United States. (Chapter 2)
- *Civil lawsuits holding terrorist states liable for servicemen's deaths.* A lawsuit was brought against Iran in a U.S. court on behalf of victims and family members of victims of the 1983 Iranian-sponsored bombing of the U.S. Marine barracks in Beirut. In this and subsequent similar cases, Iran was ordered to pay over $9 billion to the barracks bombing victims. The plaintiffs succeeded in freezing some $2 billion in Iranian government funds when the U.S. government alerted them to the funds' location in a New York bank account. (Chapter 2)
- *Civil lawsuits holding organizations and individuals that fund foreign terrorist groups liable for the groups' terrorist acts.* A lawsuit in a U.S. court resulted in a $156 million judgment against several U.S.-based funders of Hamas on behalf of the family of a seventeen-year-old U.S. citizen killed by Hamas. The lawsuit and verdict helped shut down the Hamas fundraising network in the United States, contributed to U.S. executive branch action against the network, and set a precedent that has deterred other fundraising for terrorists and spurred a number of subsequent lawsuits against material supporters of terrorism. (Chapter 2)
- *Civil lawsuits holding banks that provide financial services to terrorist groups liable for the groups' terrorist acts.* A lawsuit in a U.S. court resulted in Arab Bank being held liable for damages suffered by victims and family members of victims killed or injured in terrorist attacks by Hamas. The amount of damages, to be set after this book goes to press, was estimated to be around $1 billion. The verdict was expected to set a precedent that would deter other banks from providing financial services to terrorist groups and spur subsequent lawsuits against such providers. (Chapter 2)
- *Civil lawsuits targeting multinational companies for their activities in third countries.* Shurat HaDin threatened that maritime insurers would be sued and held liable in U.S. courts for Hamas terrorist acts if they provided material support to Hamas by insuring boats departing from Greece to breach the Gaza blockade. As noted above, the insurers pulled their coverage, and the flotilla was prevented from departing. (Chapter 8)
- *Non-governmental organizations "naming and shaming" companies for running afoul of national law.* United Against Nuclear Iran has systematically

uncovered and publicized information about companies doing business with Iran in violation of U.S. sanctions. According to the *New York Times*, "companies frequently respond by cutting ties with Iran."[72] (Chapter 2)

d. Sub-national Laws in Sub-national Forums

- *Sub-national legislation.* At least twenty-four states (including most of the largest ones) divested from, and six states prohibited public contracts with, foreign companies with substantial investments in Iran's energy sector. State pension funds control about $2.7 trillion in total investments and oversee more than $1.7 trillion in spending each year. This economic pressure contributed to coercing Iran to make concessions regarding its nuclear program. (Chapter 2)
- *Sub-national executive discretion.* Minnesota Governor Tim Pawlenty threatened to block state infrastructure subsidies and perhaps even construction permits unless Essar, a prospective investor in Minnesota, withdrew from investing $5 billion in building a refinery in Iran. Essar promptly withdrew from the Iranian investment. This economic pressure helped sustain Iran's vulnerable dependence on importing refined petroleum and contributed to coercing Iran to make concessions regarding its nuclear program. (Chapter 2)
- *Sub-national civil enforcement actions against banks that provide financial services to rogue states or terrorist groups.* Enforcement action by the New York State Department of Financial Services (NYDFS) against London-based Standard Chartered Bank for providing prohibited financial services to Iran resulted in a $640 million penalty, a NYDFS monitor being installed inside the Bank, and the Bank exiting lines of business at high risk for Iranian transactions. In another case relating to transactions with Iran, the NYDFS reportedly used its leverage to insist that BNP Paribas fire thirteen senior employees. (Chapter 3)

B. Compliance-Leverage Disparity Lawfare

The second major type of lawfare is lawfare designed to gain advantage from the greater leverage that international law and its processes exert over an adversary. This subsection includes detailed analysis of the following: (1) compliance-leverage disparity lawfare on the kinetic battlefield, (2) the definition of compliance-leverage disparity lawfare, (3) factors that contribute to compliance-leverage disparity lawfare, and (4) compliance-leverage disparities and lawfare outside the kinetic battlefield.

In his 2001 article on lawfare, Dunlap provided the example of battlefield tactics, deployed by U.S. adversaries including the Taliban, which were designed to "make it appear that the U.S." was waging war in violation of the law of armed conflict.[73] Dunlap suggested that these tactics were designed to achieve two main objectives: (1) to cause U.S. armed forces to self-impose restraints that would render them less effective, and (2) to erode the American public's will to fight by making it appear that the United States was waging war in violation of the law of armed conflict.

On the kinetic battlefield, the same enemy act can accomplish both objectives.[74] For example, in June 2007, Taliban fighters fired at NATO forces while the Taliban fighters were positioned among civilians.[75] On this occasion, NATO forces fired back, and were heavily criticized for the resulting civilian deaths.[76] Australia's foreign minister, Alexander Downer, responded to the criticism by asserting that "the Taliban . . . make every effort to cause civilian casualties and to create situations where we might not be able to avoid civilian casualties."[77] Despite Downer and others holding the Taliban responsible for the civilian casualties, a NATO spokesman subsequently announced that its forces "would not fire on positions if it knew there were civilians nearby."[78]

A year later, the *Washington Post* reported that the Taliban were continuing to win "propaganda points by quickly denouncing and sometimes exaggerating the civilian deaths" that resulted from NATO airstrikes.[79] Brigadier General Richard Blanchette, chief spokesman for NATO's 53,000 troops in Afghanistan, responded that, "If there is the likelihood of even one civilian casualty, we will not strike, not even if we think Osama bin Laden is down there."[80]

According to Dunlap, the former Deputy Judge Advocate General of the Air Force, by creating such "restrictions beyond what the law of armed conflict would require," NATO "encourage[d] the Taliban to shield themselves from air attack by violating the law of armed conflict through embedding themselves among civilians."[81] "This permits a form of lawfare," said Dunlap, "where NATO's adherence to its own rules . . . creates for its adversary a substitute for conventional military weaponry."[82] "For the Taliban to survive," said Dunlap, "it is not necessary for them to build traditional air defenses; rather, just by operating amidst civilians, they enjoy a legal sanctuary created by NATO's own self-imposed restrictions that is as secure as any fortress bristling with anti-aircraft guns."[83]

These actions by the Taliban clearly violated the law of armed conflict. The placement of military assets in or around noncombatant facilities, so as to deter attacks, is a violation of articles 51 and 58 of Additional Protocol I to the Geneva Conventions, both of which are considered to be norms of customary international law.[84] Thus, the Taliban violated these provisions of the law of armed conflict in an effort to draw U.S. forces into taking steps that could be portrayed by the Taliban and others as violating another requirement of the law of armed conflict, namely, to distinguish between the civilian population and combatants and to direct operations only against military objectives. This requirement is principally set forth in article 48 of Additional Protocol I to the Geneva Conventions and is also considered to be a norm of customary international law.[85]

These Taliban lawfare tactics succeeded in causing U.S. armed forces to self-impose restraints that would render them less effective. The tactics also contributed to eroding popular support for the war by making it appear that the United States was waging war in violation of the law of armed conflict. It comes as no surprise, then, that "provoking or exploiting civilian casualties" became a "principal strategic tactic of the Taliban," as Secretary of Defense Gates put it in May 2009.[86]

The Taliban are not the only U.S. adversary to engage heavily in the use of kinetic battlefield tactics designed to gain advantage from the greater leverage that the law of armed conflict and its processes exert over the United States. For example, according to a detailed briefing by the U.S. Defense Department, the Iraqi military under Saddam Hussein engaged in such tactics during both the 1991 and the 2003 Gulf Wars.[87] During the 2003 Gulf War, the Iraqi military "regularly placed air defense missile systems . . . in and around civilian areas, including parks, mosques, hospitals, hotels," and "crowded shopping districts."[88] "This is a well-organized, centrally managed effort," said the Defense Department, "and its objectives are patently clear: preserve Iraq's military capabilities at any price, even though it means placing innocent civilians and Iraq's cultural and religious heritage at risk, all in violation of the fundamental principle that civilians and civilian objects must be protected in wartime."[89]

Most recently, the Islamic State has engaged in such lawfare on the kinetic battlefield. According to a *New York Times* article in May 2015, "Islamic State troops . . . appear[ed] to be taking advantage of the restrictions" the U.S. military had imposed on itself to minimize civilian harm and accusations of war crimes violations, "as the militants increasingly fight from within civilian populations to deter attack."[90]

As an example, the *Times* noted that "American intelligence analysts have identified seven buildings in downtown Raqqa in eastern Syria as the main headquarters of the Islamic State."[91] However, because the Islamic State chose to locate its headquarters in a civilian area, "the buildings have gone untouched during the 10-month allied air campaign."[92] In addition, when "convoys of heavily armed Islamic State fighters paraded triumphantly through the streets of the provincial capital Ramadi in western Iraq after forcing Iraqi troops to flee," their decision to hold the parade in civilian neighborhoods meant that "they rolled on unscathed by coalition fighter-bombers."[93]

As of May 2015, Islamic State "fighters mingle[d] with civilians more than ever," resulting in three out of every four allied air missions returning to "base after failing to find a target they were permitted to hit under strict rules of engagement designed to avoid civilian casualties."[94] While U.S. officials were "not striking significant—and obvious—Islamic State targets out of fear that the attacks will accidentally kill civilians"[95] among whom Islamic State fighters had positioned themselves, the Islamic State was conquering cities and purposefully massacring and raping hundreds of the civilians it captured in them.[96]

2. Compliance-Leverage Disparity Definition

In the phrase "compliance-leverage disparity lawfare," "compliance" refers to compliance with law (and not, for example, "compliance" with the demands of an adversary).[97] "Compliance," as it is meant here, is defined according to Professor Oran Young's suggestion that "compliance can be said to occur when the actual behavior of a given subject conforms to prescribed behavior, and non-compliance or violation occurs when actual behavior departs significantly from prescribed behavior."[98] The term "compliance pull" has been used regularly in the legal and international relations literature on compliance.[99] For example, Thomas Franck equated the compliance pull of a law with its legitimacy,[100] which he defined as "the capacity of a rule to pull those to whom it is addressed toward consensual compliance."[101]

In contrast, the term "compliance-leverage disparity" is not designed to address the phenomenon of some laws exerting more general compliance pull than other laws. Rather, it is designed to address the phenomenon of law and its processes (or particular laws and their processes) having greater leverage over some state or non-state actors (including individuals) rather than over others. This book defines "compliance leverage" as the leverage which law and its processes (or particular laws and their processes) exert, over a particular actor, in the direction of compliance.

3. Compliance-Leverage Disparity: Contributing Factors

There are several factors that can substantially contribute to the different leverage that law and its processes (or particular laws and their processes) exert over some actors as opposed to others. The resultant compliance-leverage disparities can create opportunities for a lawfare practitioner or risks for a potential lawfare target. As a result, potential lawfare practitioners and targets can both benefit from a detailed understanding of these factors and how they contribute to compliance leverage disparities.

This book's analysis, in Chapters 5 and 7, of Hamas engagement with lawfare provides a concrete example of some of these factors at work. As Chapter 7 describes in detail, the compliance-leverage disparity lawfare tactic of positioning fighters and weapons among civilians was used extensively by Hamas in the

2014 Gaza War against Israel. Similar to the Taliban, Hamas deliberately violated the law of armed conflict in a manner that was designed to, and did, elicit alleged Israeli violations of the law of armed conflict.

Chapter 5 provides a detailed analysis of Hamas's late 2014 decision to concur in PA accession to the ICC, despite the fact that Hamas has been more clearly in violation of the ICC statute than is either the PA or Israel. Chapter 5's findings seem applicable to why other actors, including the Taliban, the Islamic State, and Saddam Hussein, have deliberately violated the law of armed conflict in a manner that was designed to, and did elicit alleged violations by Western adversaries of the law of armed conflict. In contrast with U.S. and other NATO or Israeli officials, who may feel ashamed, stigmatized, and placed at risk by accusations of war crimes, the law of armed conflict and its processes currently exert little to no leverage over Hamas. The following subsections, which draw on Hamas and other examples, identify and analyze the specific factors that can contribute to such compliance-leverage disparities.

a. Differing Ideologies Regarding Compliance with Law

Different political and legal cultures and subcultures can vary in their general ideological senses of obligation to comply with law[102] (or a relevant particular type of law). Professor Tom Tyler and others refer to the propensity of a particular society's members to "abide by the laws" as "law abidingness."[103]

Disparities in this regard are illustrated by comparison between the painstakingly law-abiding practices of the U.S. military and the dismissive practices of at least some of its adversaries.

U.S. Defense Department policy requires that all military operations be conducted in strict accordance with applicable international law.[104] According to the relevant Department of Defense directive, "It is DoD policy that . . . members of the DoD Components comply with the law of war during all armed conflicts, however such conflicts are characterized, and in all other military operations."[105]

Similarly, the U.S. Army's Operational Law Handbook states that "Department of Defense (DOD) policy is to comply with the LOAC [law of armed conflict] . . . . [E]very soldier, sailor, airman, marine, and all others accompanying U.S. forces must comply with the LOAC."[106] The Handbook also specifies regarding LOAC that Judge Advocates "must advise commanders and U.S. forces to follow its requirements exactly."[107] In addition, it states that "soldiers not only must avoid committing LOAC violations; they must also attempt to prevent violations of the LOAC by other U.S. soldiers" and "must promptly report any actual or suspected violations of LOAC.[108]

Stewart Baker, an attorney who served from 2005 to 2009 as Assistant Secretary for Policy at the U.S. Department of Homeland Security and earlier as

General Counsel of the National Security Agency, contrasted as follows the difference between the U.S. commitment to law of armed conflict compliance and that of many of its adversaries:

> The rise of JAG authority over every detail of warfighting means that the Pentagon would be exquisitely sensitive to arguable violations of international law in carrying out operations in cyberspace. Our guys would sit with their fingers poised over the "return" button for hours while the JAGs were trying to figure out whether the Belarussian remarks in committee were a consensus or an individual interpretation of article 42bis. And nobody else would give a damn what the treaty said, because they wouldn't expect to get caught and because even implausible deniability can't be rebutted with the certainty needed to make a legal case, let alone send missiles in response.[109]

In contrast with the U.S. Army's Operational Law Handbook and Baker's assessment, the PRC military's *Basics of International Law for Modern Soldiers* states: "We should not feel completely bound by specific articles and stipulations detrimental to the defense of our national interests. We should therefore always apply international laws flexibly in the defense of our national interests and dignity, appealing to those aspects beneficial to our country while evading those detrimental to our interests."[110] The disparities are even more starkly illustrated by the statement of Ayatollah Ali Khamenei, Iran's Supreme Leader, that: "When we want to find out what is right and what is wrong, we do not go to the United Nations; we go to the Holy Koran. For us the Universal Declaration of Human Rights is nothing but a collection of mumbo-jumbo by disciples of Satan."[111] Norms of law-abidingness can, of course, change over time, for example as rules are internalized.

b. Benefits of Compliance

Different state and non-state actors can vary from each other both in the objective benefits they receive from compliance with law (or with a relevant particular law or type of law) and in the weighting they subjectively attribute to those benefits. For example, they can differ in the objective or perceived benefits they receive from contributing to mutual compliance with the law of armed conflict or from having an international or domestic reputation for compliance with it.[112]

c. Risks of Actual or Credibly Alleged Violations

Different state and non-state actors can also vary from each other in the objective and the subjectively perceived risks they face in response to their actual or credibly alleged violations (acts of noncompliance). One of this book's key themes is that calculating these risks is not merely a matter of simply assessing the probability that each particular actor will ultimately receive a punishment for a specified actual or alleged violation. For example, as the book illustrates, the adjudication process itself can be exceptionally costly to some defendants, even if they ultimately emerge victorious. The overall risks to two different actors of the same actual or credibly alleged violation include the following four components, each of which may differ from one actor to another and from one type of violation to another: the probability of being subjected to proceedings, the cost of being subjected to proceedings, the probability of being penalized for violation, and the cost of the penalty for violation. A sophisticated analysis of compliance-leverage disparity lawfare opportunities and vulnerabilities should include each of these components.

i. Disparate Probability of Being Subjected to Proceedings Different state and non-state actors can vary in the objective or subjective (as they perceive it) probability that they will be subject to legal or other proceedings if they violate a particular law or if a credible allegation can be made that they have done so. As discussed in Section IV below, this probability can be higher for potential defendants in more open or litigious legal systems where NGOs or others are likely to bring the alleged violation to light and press for accountability (including by themselves bringing lawsuits or initiating universal jurisdiction criminal proceedings against the accused). The probability can also be higher when a powerful government such as that of the United States decides to prioritize cracking down on particular violators (as Chapter 3 describes the United States doing vis-à-vis banks transacting with Iran).

The probability of being subjected to proceedings will be lower when an actor engages in a particular type of violation that is rarely if ever enforced. For example, as detailed in Chapter 7, international bodies have tended to ignore violations of the obligations not to deploy or disguise fighters and weapons among civilians. The United States also tends to ignore such violations by its adversaries, according to a U.S. Air Force Judge Advocate Officer (JAG) who has worked extensively with detainees in both Afghanistan and Guantanamo.[113] "You would be hard pressed to find a single U.S. military commission case in which an insurgent is charged with not wearing a uniform or otherwise hiding amongst civilians," said the JAG, asserting that "if you are a non-state actor, what is your incentive to wear a uniform, to play by the Marquess of Queensberry rules if nobody is going to hold you to them?"[114]

ii. Disparate Cost of Being Subjected to Proceedings Different state and non-state actors can also vary both in the objective and the relative costs to them of being subjected to legal or other proceedings for a violation or credibly alleged violation. As discussed in Chapter 6, the adjudication process can be extremely costly regardless of the ultimate outcome of the case, a fact that some lawfare practitioners admit is driving initiation of proceedings against their adversaries. The cost of such proceedings can include, for example, attorney fees and the reputational and hassle costs borne by even victorious defendants (as described in Chapter 6).

While some state and non-state actors such as Iran, Al Qaeda, and Hamas have decided not to contest some or all of the legal proceedings against them in U.S. courts, thus not incurring attorney fees, others such as Israel and the Palestinian Authority have incurred large legal bills defending themselves against such proceedings. In addition, while the Israeli government, its officials, and businesses who transact with Israel attribute considerable weight to the reputational and hassle costs of even those trials in Europe which they have ultimately won, Hamas already has such a bad reputation and paucity of overt activities in Europe that it has far less to lose from legal proceedings against it there.

iii. Disparate Probability of an Adverse Judgment Different state and non-state actors can also vary in the objective and subjective (as they perceive it) probability that they will be found guilty or liable (and thus subject to penalties for the actual or credibly alleged particular violation). While factors (i) and (ii) involve the probability and cost of merely being subjected to proceedings (setting aside the issue of the proceedings' outcome), this component involves the probability that the actor will be determined to be guilty or liable.

Such adverse determinations can be rendered in judicial or quasi-judicial proceedings. They can also result from a legislative (e.g., congressional) or administrative rather than a judicial decision-making process. The types of adverse judgments and their associated penalties can thus include (but are not limited to) criminal convictions (resulting in imprisonment or fines), civil judgments (awarding compensatory and punitive damages), and legislative or administrative determinations (imposing, e.g., trade restrictions). In addition to the specific penalties imposed by the adjudicator, adverse judgments typically also create a reputational cost.

To a considerable degree, the probability of state or non-state actors losing a judicial proceeding against them for violation of a particular law is a product of the probability of their being, in the first place, subjected to a proceeding for a violation of that particular law. For example, a higher probability of being sued for recklessly killing a U.S. citizen tends to correlate with a higher probability of losing such suits.

However, the probability of losing proceedings can also depend on the location and type of forum in which the proceedings occur. For example, as illustrated in Chapters 5 and 6, Israel-affiliated defendants are relatively likely to emerge victorious from legal proceedings brought against them in the United States. While it is relatively easy to file a lawsuit in U.S. courts, Israel has widespread popular support and a strong relationship with the U.S. government. In contrast, it is relatively hard to initiate proceedings in the International Court of Justice, but Israel is likely to lose any cases initiated there (many of the judges hail from Israel's adversaries).

Another example of the importance of the forum in which proceedings occur involves Iran. As discussed in Chapter 2, Iran is particularly likely to lose in the United States, where it has been designated a state sponsor of terrorism and is thus one of a handful of governments subject to an exception from sovereign immunity.

Different non-state actors accused of similar acts may also be treated very divergently in a particular forum, depending on whether they are favored or disfavored by the key decisionmaker(s). As discussed vis-à-vis Hamas, a non-state actor may also not understand the law and the legal system well enough to accurately assess the probability of losing the proceedings.

Different forums handle varying types of violations (e.g., U.S. federal courts have jurisdiction over different types of international wrongs than does the ICJ). Thus, two state or non-state adversaries might both find themselves considering violating a law that is subject to proceedings only or largely in forums where one faces a much higher probability of an adverse judgment. The disparate probability of being penalized for noncompliance would contribute to a disparity in compliance leverage and thus, potentially, differing decisions as to whether or not to violate the law.

iv. Disparate Cost of Penalties Different state and non-state actors can also vary in the objective and relative perceived magnitude of penalties or damages or other costs imposed on them if a particular law is determined to have been violated and punishment is imposed. For example, as discussed in Chapter 7, being targeted by the ICC would be perceived as costlier by Israeli officials, who have more to lose in terms of reputation and ability to travel, than by Hamas officials, who are already stigmatized by, and unable to travel to, those Western countries that would likely turn targeted individuals over to the ICC. Similarly, a $1 billion U.S. civil litigation award may have a different deterrent effect on defendants of varying wealth and vulnerability to collection measures. For example, it is typically more difficult to collect from a non-state actor such as Hezbollah than from a nation state such as Iran, which engages in billions of dollars in foreign commercial transactions and has foreign bank accounts and other assets that are readily attributable to it.

4. Compliance Leverage Disparities and Lawfare Outside the Battlefield

Compliance-leverage disparity lawfare is not limited to non-state actors hiding fighters and weapons among civilians. Chapter 4 provides a detailed description and analysis of the Chinese government waging compliance-leverage disparity lawfare in the nonproliferation arena. The Chinese government has done so by entering into legally binding nuclear nonproliferation obligations with which its rivals (including the United States, Japan, and South Korea) tend to comply while China secretly violates those obligations by providing nuclear technology to its allies, often through proxies. The result is the acquisition of nuclear weapons capacity or even arsenals by rogue states allied with China (including Iran, North Korea, and Pakistan) while China's rivals, over which international legal commitments have greater influence, either remain without nuclear weapons (as in the case of Japan and South Korea) or strictly enforce nonproliferation obligations vis-à-vis their own allies (as with aggressive U.S. efforts to discourage South Korea from acquiring nuclear weapons).

In addition, non-state actors have also engaged outside the battlefield in lawfare-leveraging compliance disparities. These often involve the non-state actors making false (and thus illegal) accusations that the United States or a U.S. ally has violated a law (typically a law with which the non-state actor does not itself comply). For example, according to a JAG interviewed for this book who worked extensively with detainees in both Afghanistan and Guantanamo, "almost every detainee in U.S. custody will make false allegations of abuse."[115] "They quickly learn that every allegation will be investigated and will have a significant impact on our operations," he said.[116] "It's hard to blame them, as this is a way for them to keep costing us time and resources even after we have detained them, and there is no cost to them for doing so."[117]

The JAG's assertions are consistent with an Al Qaeda training manual that has surfaced in various locations.[118] The manual directs detainees to "complain of mistreatment while in prison."[119] The assertions are also consistent with the statements of Jack Goldsmith, a political appointee in the George W. Bush administration who is known for his opposition to the "torture memos."[120] In his book *The Terror Presidency*, Goldsmith asserted that "enemies like Al Qaeda who cannot match the United States militarily instead criticize it for purported legal violations, especially violations of human rights or the laws of war."[121] For example, said Goldsmith, "they complain falsely that they were tortured, as we now know al Qaeda training manuals advise them to do."[122]

However, not all detainee allegations have been false. Various detainee accusations of brutal treatment have turned out to be substantiated, including with regard to CIA interrogations and also the Abu Ghraib prison.[123] In releasing a study of the CIA's detention and interrogation program, Senator Dianne Feinstein, the chair of the Senate Select Committee on Intelligence, asserted that the program involved "the use of brutal interrogation techniques in violation of U.S. law, treaty obligations, and our values."[124] Feinstein also asserted that "it is my personal conclusion that, under any common meaning of the term, CIA detainees were tortured."[125] With regard to Abu Ghraib prison, three reservists were convicted of mistreating prisoners, and six others reached plea deals.[126] In addition, the Army reportedly punished more than two hundred other soldiers and officers for detainee abuse in Iraq and Afghanistan.[127] Abuses by U.S. personnel are deplorable in and of themselves. In addition, they lend credibility to, and thus may encourage, false allegations by detainees.

A different noteworthy set of examples of compliance-leverage disparity lawfare involves the Colombian Armed Revolutionary Forces (FARC), a Colombian rebel group designated by the U.S. State Department as a foreign terrorist organization.[128] The FARC reportedly adopted the lawfare tactic of using the "Colombian courts to press false charges . . . against the most capable military leaders" of the Colombian armed forces.[129]

Jose Miguel Vivanco, the director of the Americas division of Human Rights Watch, asserted in 2001 that the FARC regularly violated international rights norms itself while using the principles of the law of armed conflict for its own purposes.[130] According to a Human Rights Watch report, "when the FARC perceives a political advantage, it emphasizes its respect for international humanitarian law . . . however . . when no political advantage is apparent, the FARC makes little if any attempt to abide by international humanitarian law."[131]

"We've come to the conclusion that they're using international humanitarian law as just part of a P.R. operation," said Vivanco.[132] "It's part of their rhetoric," said Vivanco, "but they have shown no will, no intention whatsoever, to enforce those principles in practice."[133] Rebel leaders have reportedly claimed to Human Rights Watch that the law of armed conflict represents "elite interests" and is not applicable to the FARC.[134]

Meanwhile, the Islamic State has reportedly begun to engage in its own compliance-leverage disparity lawfare away from the kinetic battlefield. A *Washington Post* article about the State Department's Center for Strategic Counterterrorism Communications (CSCC), which uses social media to counter Islamic State propaganda, noted that the Islamic State tried to stymie the CSCC both with death threats against CSCC employees and also through "orchestrated campaigns aimed at getting" CSCC "kicked off Twitter and Youtube by bombarding those companies with waves of complaints accusing the CSCC of violating their terms of service."[135]

Notwithstanding the fact that the Islamic State, with its barbarically gruesome videos, extensively violates social media terms of service and the CSCC does not, its initiative against the CSCC reportedly worked "at times," forcing "State Department officials to appeal to the companies to get their accounts restored."[136] Ironically, the Islamic State has thus succeeded in using lawfare to achieve an objective which the U.S. government and its NATO allies had themselves once resorted to kinetic means (bombing) to achieve. The U.S. and its NATO allies had bombed Serb television and radio propaganda outlets to get them off the air during the Kosovo conflict in 1999.[137] Those attacks resulted in a narrowly averted move by the International Criminal Tribunal for Yugoslavia to prosecute NATO officials for alleged war crimes.[138] It will be interesting to see if the Islamic State, emboldened by the successes of both its battlefield lawfare and its risk-free efforts to get the CSCC off the Internet using terms of service complaints, starts waging additional types of lawfare.

As discussed in more detail in Chapter 2 and elsewhere, this book does not recommend that the United States join in making false charges or violating the law of armed conflict, human rights law, or any other law. The U.S. response to compliance-leverage disparity lawfare should be instead to much more creatively and energetically defend against it, including by holding U.S. adversaries accountable for relevant legally binding obligations that they are currently typically flouting with impunity.

Holding U.S. adversaries accountable will, in some cases, be challenging. For the law of armed conflict to be meaningfully enforced against non-state actors such as the Taliban, Islamic State, or Hamas, it may be necessary to devise innovative types of penalties or other forms of leverage over these actors who do not value international approbation and may be happy to die for their cause. In light of the prevalence of compliance-leverage lawfare and its effectiveness against the United States and its allies, developing improved enforcement mechanisms and leverage should be a high priority for U.S. policymakers.

III. AN OVERVIEW OF THE UNITED STATES' APPROACH TO LAWFARE

A. The U.S. Executive Branch's Unsystematic and Largely Defensive Approach to Lawfare

As described in Chapter 2, lawfare has in recent years been waged creatively and impactfully by a number of U.S. private sector and other non-governmental attorneys. Thanks largely to these attorneys' ideas and advocacy, several U.S. states and cities have also been engaged in lawfare against U.S. adversaries. Both the non-governmental lawfare and the state and city lawfare have been supported and facilitated by Congress, through new U.S. laws and other legislative activity. In addition, as described in Chapter 3, one U.S. executive branch agency—the Treasury Department—has waged very sophisticated and aggressive economic lawfare; in particular, financial lawfare against Iran. The U.S. Department of Justice, and especially the U.S. Attorney's Office for the Southern District of New York, has also occasionally waged a form of lawfare, creatively using the expansive jurisdictional hooks provided by U.S. antiterrorism laws to subject some foreign terrorists to U.S. criminal trials and imprisonment when doing so is "a smart alternative to . . . drone strikes."[139] In contrast to these U.S. actors, the rest of the U.S. federal executive branch has taken a remarkably sporadic and unsystematic approach to offensive lawfare in the sixteen years or so since lawfare came to the fore.

The lawfare activity that has been undertaken by the rest of the federal executive branch during those years has been predominantly defensive. In the face of the battlefield tactics of U.S. adversaries, the universal jurisdiction prosecutions of U.S. leaders, the narrowly averted move by the International Criminal Tribunal for Yugoslavia to prosecute NATO officials for alleged war crimes during the 1999 Kosovo campaign,[140] and the sense of urgency created by the September 11 attacks, the George W. Bush administration took a markedly, indeed aggressively defensive approach to lawfare.[141]

Some associated with that administration used the term "lawfare" to derogatorily describe legal work by U.S. human rights NGOs and various American attorneys defending Guantanamo detainees and other defendants in the war on terror.[142] The unfair and unsubstantiated implication was that the NGOs and attorneys were trying to use law to weaken or destroy the United States.[143]

More substantively (and defensibly), the G.W. Bush administration placed considerable weight in its legal policy decisions on protecting the United States from lawfare. For example, the administration opposed U.S. participation in the ICC out of fear that U.S. adversaries might bring about ICC trials of U.S. leaders or soldiers.[144] It reversed President Clinton's signing of the ICC treaty and enacted the American Service-Members' Protection Act, which is sometimes referred to as the "Hague Invasion Act" because it authorizes the President to use "all means necessary and appropriate to bring about the release" of U.S. or allied persons "being detained or imprisoned by, on behalf of, or at the request of the International Criminal Court."[145]

As discussed in more detail in Chapter 5, the United States under the G.W. Bush administration also entered into so-called "Article 98" agreements with over one hundred foreign countries.[146] Countries that enter into "Article 98" agreements with the United States agree not to surrender U.S. persons to the jurisdiction of the ICC.[147] Article 98 is a provision of the ICC Statute that envisions the possibility of such agreements.[148]

That administration also argued for its Guantanamo military tribunals in part on the grounds that standard criminal trials of Al Qaeda operatives could be manipulated by defense counsel to put prosecutors to a choice between revealing sensitive U.S. intelligence sources and methods or letting terrorists go free.[149]

In his indispensable book, *The Terror Presidency: Law and Judgment Inside the Bush Administration*, Jack Goldsmith described how, as a G.W. Bush appointee, he struggled to develop a solution to the challenges posed by lawfare.[150] In one official memo analyzing the challenges, Goldsmith warned that "in the past quarter century, various nations, NGOs, academics, international organizations, and others in the 'international community' have been busily weaving a web of international laws and judicial institutions that today threatens USG interests."[151] "Unless we tackle the problem head-on, it will continue to grow," said Goldsmith, asserting that "the issue is especially urgent because of the unusual challenges we face in the war on terrorism."[152]

In his book, Goldsmith reported that in 2003, then Secretary of Defense Rumsfeld circulated to the National Security Council another Goldsmith memo on lawfare and "demanded action."[153] "Several years of NSC meetings among lawyers and deputies followed," said Goldsmith, "but a concrete plan never emerged."[154] According to Goldsmith, the State Department "argued that any effort by the United States to oppose the increasingly powerful institutions of international justice would seem like a defensive admission of the very war crimes charges it wanted to avoid."[155] The State Department also emphasized that such an effort would "smack of hypocrisy . . . since the United States aggressively used human rights institutions—including universal jurisdiction lawsuits—to check human rights abuses by other nations."[156] The Justice Department "also opposed any anti-universal jurisdiction campaign," recounted Goldsmith, "on the ground that it would jeopardize its ability to bring its own universal jurisdiction prosecutions against foreign leaders and terrorists."[157]

In the end, recounts Goldsmith, the NSC "couldn't figure out what to do about" lawfare.[158] So in March 2005, "Rumsfeld acted alone, setting down a marker in the *National Defense Strategy* that he, at least, understood the threat posed to the United States" by lawfare.[159] The Defense Department's 2005 *National Defense Strategy* infamously declared: "Our strength as a nation state will continue to be challenged by those who employ a strategy of the weak using international fora, judicial processes, and terrorism."[160]

Rumsfeld's statement has been extensively criticized, and rightly so. As Professor David Cole noted, the statement "not only dismisses the rule of law, and especially international law, as a strategy of the weak, of no interest to the 'strong' United States, but likens it to terrorism itself."[161] In critiquing the statement, Professors Gabriella Blum and Philip Heymann pointed out that "by treating national security and international law as inconsistent, the Bush Administration misdiagnosed the American national interest."[162] "International law generally serves, not hampers, American concerns," said Blum and Heymann.[163]

As of summer 2015, the United States' approach to lawfare seems frozen into much the same largely defensive crouch where it was in 2005. Some six years into the Obama administration, the United States still has not joined the ICC, and the Obama administration is using military commissions in certain circumstances,[164] despite various challenges.[165] While both may be unavoidable, the United States' lack of a broader and more sophisticated strategy for defensive lawfare and its continued lack of any strategy and structure for offensive lawfare are clearly and unnecessarily self-defeating.

As this book describes, various developments over the past decade have made lawfare even more powerful than it was in 2005, and many state and non-state actors are taking advantage of the opportunity by waging lawfare more aggressively and systematically than they were before. In the face of this explosion of lawfare, and with the ICC announcing in 2014 that it is conducting a preliminary examination of the possibility that war crimes were committed in Afghanistan by the U.S. military (as discussed in more detail in Chapter 5), the G.W. Bush and Obama administrations' decisions to stay out of the ICC are looking justified.

While the United States' decision to keep in place this particular defensive measure against lawfare is sensible, the United States' failure over the last decade to adopt a broad and systematic lawfare strategy, with a robust offensive component, makes little sense. Chapter 3 details the Treasury Department's sophisticated and impactful financial lawfare strategy against Iran, versions of which have been successfully applied to Iran's energy and insurance sectors. The impact of the campaigns against Iran in these three sectors points to the potential for impactful campaigns against other targets and in other sectors. Some lessons have been applied to U.S. financial lawfare against Russia. But there has been no systematic effort to either develop a whole-of-government U.S. strategy for the broad range of types of lawfare, or to create a focal point for collecting and disseminating lessons learned.

"When it comes to lawfare, the U.S. government's approach is extremely ad hoc and uncoordinated," said Steve Perles, the leading private sector attorney bringing lawsuits against state sponsors of terrorism.[166] "The U.S. government has no overarching strategy for waging lawfare and there is no person or office in the U.S. government that plays a coordinating role,"[167] said Perles, who has interacted on lawfare-related issues for over two decades with officials at the U.S. Departments of Defense, Justice, State, and Treasury.[168] Perles recommended that the National Security Council would be the optimal place for such a focal point, in light of the pivotal importance of coordinating the differing lawfare tools that the various agencies bring to the table.[169]

If the United States is going to wage maximally effective instrumental lawfare against a particular adversary, it needs to deploy a multipronged campaign—going after the adversary itself, its material supporters, and its financial service providers, using criminal and civil legal tools, and, where appropriate, coordinating with any application of kinetic weapons.[170] The campaign should be coordinated both interagency and with civil litigators who may have evidence or claims that could be used to supplement and complement the government's campaign against the adversary.[171] Neither the U.S. government as a whole nor any of the relevant federal agencies individually—including the Departments of Defense, Justice, State, and Treasury—have a point person for coordinating lawfare and collecting best practices. Nor do these agencies systematically engage in coordination on lawfare issues, either with each other or with civil litigators.[172] Such coordination as does occur tends to be ad hoc and limited in scope.

In reviewing the reasons why the G.W. Bush State and Justice Departments opposed "any effort by the United States to oppose the increasingly powerful institutions of international justice," it is ironic to note that one of their principal arguments, as recounted by Goldsmith, is that it would "jeopardize" the United States' "ability to bring its own universal jurisdiction prosecutions against foreign leaders and terrorists." The United States has rarely brought its own universal jurisdiction prosecutions against foreign leaders and terrorists (when the United States has prosecuted such actors, it has, as discussed above, instead done so using U.S. laws that provide jurisdiction pursuant to a connection to the United States, albeit sometimes attenuated). Nor has the U.S. executive branch, outside of the Treasury Department and in discrete instances the Justice Department, energetically and systematically availed itself of the vast array of other types of instrumental lawfare described in this book.

The failure to develop, let alone implement, a U.S. lawfare strategy compares unfavorably with the PRC, which, as detailed in Chapter 4, has, over the last decade or so, systematically adopted and aggressively implemented a lawfare strategy. The failure to create a lawfare focal point within the U.S. government compares unfavorably with a U.S. ally, Israel, which, as detailed in Chapter 6, has developed a special high-powered lawfare office in its Ministry of Justice.

If the G.W. Bush administration, in the wake of the September 11 attacks, was unable to reach consensus on a plan for slowing the global development of lawfare, it seems unlikely that any future administration will be able to do so. Even if some future administration were to come up with such a plan, lawfare seems to be here to stay. Instead of a new plan to push back the tide, the United States needs a plan to ride it.

As mentioned previously, lawfare is both a weapon that can be consistent with the United States' national interests and one that the United States could deploy more effectively than can its adversaries. Instrumental lawfare is a weapon eminently suitable for the U.S. public's aversion to casualties and the current U.S. budgetary situation. In addition, the U.S. advantage in sophisticated legal weapons has the potential to be even greater than its advantage in sophisticated lethal weapons.

As discussed in more detail in Chapter 2, this book's recommended approach to lawfare does not counsel violating either domestic or international law or, as with the torture memos, developing convoluted arguments as to how an unlawful or morally reprehensible course of action can be portrayed as lawful. It simply encourages U.S. and allied lawyers, and the policymakers who seek their counsel, to systematically investigate and inquire (a) whether and how instrumental lawfare can wisely be used to achieve or help achieve policy objectives traditionally achieved by kinetic warfare and (b) how to more effectively deter, constrain, protect, and otherwise defend against adversary lawfare. This book therefore recommends that the United States and its allies enhance their offensive and defensive capacities vis-à-vis instrumental lawfare, and their defensive capacities vis-à-vis compliance-leverage disparity lawfare.

B. Instrumental Lawfare in the Context of the U.S. Legal System and the Rule of Law

Some may object that instrumental lawfare risks contributing to corroding the rule of law. It will be important, both in developing U.S. lawfare strategy and in weighing particular potential deployments of lawfare, to consider how to minimize this risk. However, in doing so, it will be worth considering the extent to which both the U.S. domestic and the international legal system are already so infused by an instrumental view of law that the United States taking a more deliberately and systematically instrumental approach to law in the international arena is unlikely to cause much, if any, harm.

Professor Brian Tamanaha, a renowned scholar of the role of law in society, has written extensively and persuasively that U.S. domestic jurisprudence is already dominated by an instrumental view of law. Tamanaha's views on this subject are particularly noteworthy in light of his being voted the United States' most influential legal educator in a 2013 poll of law deans and professors.[173]

In his celebrated book, LAW AS A MEANS TO AN END: THREAT TO THE RULE OF LAW, and in various articles, Professor Tamanaha asserted that "an instrumental view of law—the idea that law is a means to an end—is taken for granted in the United States, almost part of the air we breathe."[174] "An instrumental view of law," said Tamanaha, "means that law—encompassing legal rules, legal institutions, and legal processes—is consciously viewed by people and groups as a tool or means with which to achieve ends."[175]

"Our contemporary legal culture," said Tamanaha, referring to U.S. legal culture, "pairs a pervasively held instrumental theory of the nature of law with consummately instrumental attitudes towards law."[176] The instrumental view's pervasiveness in the United States is reflected in various ways, said Tamanaha, including "as an account of the nature of law, as an attitude toward law that professors teach students, as a form of constitutional analysis, as a theoretical perspective on law, as an orientation of lawyers in their daily practice, as a strategic approach of organized groups that use litigation to further their agendas, as a view toward judges and judging, as a perception of legislators and administrators when enacting laws or regulations."[177]

For example, said Tamanaha, in U.S. law schools, students are "taught that everything is up for argument, and that legal rules are not binding dictates, but resources to be strategically marshaled and presented with rhetorical agility."[178] In the U.S. public policy arena, "using every available legal channel, beginning in the 1960s and continuing today, a multitude of groups aggressively pursue their agendas: women's groups, immigrant groups, gay rights groups, fundamentalist Christian groups, racial or ethnic groups, environmental groups, labor unions, consumer groups trade associations, merchants associations, professional associations, and more," said Tamanaha.[179]

"In all of these contexts," said Tamanaha, "people see law as an instrument of power to advance their personal interests or the interests or policies of the individuals or groups they support."[180] "Today," he asserted, "law is widely viewed as an empty vessel to be filled as desired, and to be manipulated, invoked, and utilized in the furtherance of ends."[181] U.S. law, he suggested, is therefore "little more than the spoils that go to winners in contests among private interests, who by their victory secure the prize of enlisting the coercive power of the legal apparatus to enforce their agendas."[182]

Many leading scholars have expressed views consistent with Tamanaha's diagnosis. For example, according to Professor Steven D. Smith, "scholars have pointed out that most of the doctrinal formulas articulated by the [Supreme] Court, whether under the First Amendment or the Fourteenth or the commerce clause, are presented in . . . instrumentalist terms," pursuant to which "laws are viewed as means to social ends, and a law's constitutionality is said to depend on how important the law's ends are and how effective and necessary the law is as a means to achieving those ends."[183] Meanwhile, in the practice of law in the United States, said Professor Robert W. Gordon, the "advocacy ideal" provides that while attorneys "should not tell outright lies to judges or fabricate evidence . . . they may, and if it will serve their clients' interest must, exploit any gap, ambiguity, technicality or loophole, any not-obviously-and-totally-implausible interpretation of the law or facts,"[184] even if the result is a failure to "enforce[] the substantive law against its violators."[185]

One of the most explicit proponents of instrumentalism in U.S. jurisprudence is Judge Richard Posner. As discussed in Chapter 2, Posner is both the author of the definitive opinion in the key case (for lawfare) of *Boim v. Holy Land Foundation* and also a prolific writer who has been described as the single most cited legal scholar of the twentieth century.[186] Posner, who advocates what he calls "pragmatic jurisprudence,"[187] has flatly asserted that "legal rules should be viewed in instrumental terms."[188]

Tamanaha contrasted the currently pervasive instrumental view of law with "a few centuries ago" when, "in contrast, law was widely understood to possess a necessary content and integrity that was, in some sense, given or predetermined."[189] Tamanaha provided as examples divine "principles disclosed by revelation" and other "ideas about the nature and content of law" which "have mostly fallen by the wayside in the past century."[190] As Calvin Woodward put it, the triumph of instrumental views of law has "transformed the Law from a 'brooding omnipresence in the sky' into a down-to-earth instrument of social reform and, at the same time, translated . . . the lawyer from a quasi-priestly fig-ure into a social engineer."[191]

According to Tamanaha, the change was accelerated by the turmoil of the 1960s.[192] By 1978, the Dean of Cornell Law School, Roger C. Cramton, was writing that legal instrumentalism had become "the ordinary religion of the law school classroom."[193] "Today, law tends to be viewed in solely instrumen-tal terms," said Cramton, explaining that "the lawyer's task, in an instrumental approach to law, is to facilitate and manipulate legal processes to advance the interest of his client."[194]

Tamanaha expressed concern that "when law is perceived as a powerful instrument . . . combatants will fight to control and use the implements of the law as weapons in social, political, religious, and economic disputes."[195] With his focus on instrumental views of law in the U.S. domestic arena, Tamanaha expressed concern that "these battles will take place in every state and federal arena—legislative, executive, judicial," and "even those groups that might prefer to abstain from these battles over law will nonetheless be forced to engage in the contest, if only defensively to keep their less restrained opponents from using the law as a hammer against them."[196] "Such struggles over and through law are openly visible today," said Tamanaha, "and worsening."[197]

This author tends to agree with Tamanaha that at least some manifestations of the instrumental ethos of U.S. jurisprudence are problematic. For example, this author finds the "advocacy ideal," as characterized by Gordon, to be troublingly widespread within a democratic U.S legal system that might be better served if more attorneys had a stronger sense of ethics and commitment to the public good. However, whether or not Tamanaha is correct in concluding that the pervasively instrumental view of law in the United States is harmful to U.S. citizen inter-ests and in suggesting that it can and should be restrained, his conclusion and proposed antidote should not, in this author's view, be determinative of United States lawfare strategy for the international arena.

C. U.S. Instrumental Lawfare in the Context of the United Nations System

Tamanaha described how hard it is for U.S. society—with its relatively shared values, vibrant democratic institutions, and powerful law enforcement institutions—to agree in principle on what laws were "given or predetermined" and thus should not be subject to instrumental tinkering or manipulation, either in their content or their enforcement. Genuine agreement on core val-ues would be even harder to achieve in the more heterogenous international community. Indeed, in the international community, nation states' ability to instrumentally manipulate the content and enforcement of laws to which they accede is apparently pivotal to their willingness to accede to many, if not most, of those laws.

As discussed in Section IV.B of this chapter, the international community has, notwithstanding its heterogeneity, managed to reach agreement upon many international laws in recent decades. There is a strong argument that numerous nation states have been willing to accede to many international laws primarily because those states understand that these laws, by dint of their ambiguity and the lack of a global enforcement mechanism, are subject to wholesale instrumental manipulation in their interpretation and enforcement. This proposition is supported by data from the field of human rights law, the very subset of international law which it is easiest to hope or imagine might contain rules that are "given or predetermined" or otherwise represent core values.

For example, Professor Oona Hathaway's "large-scale quantitative analysis of the relationship between human rights treaties and countries' human rights practices" found that "countries that ratify human rights treaties often appear less likely, rather than more likely, to conform to the requirements of the treaties."[198] Hathaway explained her findings by noting that countries "are likely to receive" reputational benefits from acceding to human rights treaties "regardless of their actual practices."[199] In other words, because formal international "monitoring and enforcement of human rights treaty obligations are often minimal,"[200] "countries that are parties to the treaties can therefore enjoy the benefits of ratification without actually supplying the human rights protections to which they have committed"[201] and "while suffering little reputational cost from failing to observe the obligations assumed."[202] "Consequently, treaty ratification may become a substitute for, rather than a spur to, real improvement in human rights practices," said Hathaway.[203]

Those who think that Hathaway may be wrong and that the international community of nation states does indeed seriously and uniformly monitor and enforce human rights need look only at the practice of the United Nations Human Rights Council (UNHRC). The UNHRC is the United Nations' principal intergovernmental body "responsible for strengthening the promotion and protection of human rights around the globe and for addressing situations of human rights violations and making recommendations on them."[204]

The UNHRC practice illustrates how U.N. member states predominantly use human rights law instrumentally, as a weapon against states disfavored for other reasons. In March 2015, U.S. Secretary of State John Kerry condemned the UNHRC's "obsession with Israel," providing as an example of its "unbalanced focus on one democratic country" the fact that "no other nation has an entire agenda item set aside to deal with it."[205] "None of the world's worst human rights violators . . . have their own standalone agenda item at this council," said U.S. Ambassador to the UNHRC Keith Harper, noting that "only Israel receives such treatment."[206] U.N. Secretary-General Bank Ki-moon also "voiced disappointment at the Council decision to single out Israel as the only specific regional item on its agenda, 'given the range and scope of allegations of human rights violations throughout the world.'"[207]

Since its creation in 2006, the UNHRC has issued over one hundred resolutions.[208] Over half of these have focused on criticizing Israel.[209] In other words, there have been more resolutions criticizing Israel than criticizing all the other 191 countries in the world combined. For example, the U.N. Human Rights Council, in its session that ended on March 27, 2015, adopted four resolutions condemning Israel, one condemning North Korea, one condemning Syria, one very mild resolution expressing concern about the situation in Iran,[210] and none condemning China, Russia, or Saudi Arabia.[211]

From its founding in 2006 through 2014, the UNHRC, while issuing more than fifty resolutions condemning Israel, had reportedly never issued a single resolution condemning seven of the ten countries that, according to Freedom House, had long had the very worst human rights records in the world—the Central African Republic, Equatorial Guinea, Eritrea, Saudi Arabia, Somalia, Turkmenistan, and Uzbekistan.[212] In addition, the U.N. General Assembly has repeatedly elected egregious human rights violators—including the governments of China, Cuba, Egypt, Kazakhstan, Russia, Saudi Arabia, Venezuela, and Vietnam—to serve among the forty-seven member states on the UNHRC.[213] The failure to condemn the very worst human rights violators, and the election to the UNHRC of other egregious violators, reflects the fact that many of the countries with egregious human rights records are members of voting blocs. For example, the 120 U.N. member states in the Non-Aligned Movement tend to use their U.N. votes to protect and support each other. The fifty-seven U.N. member states in the Organisation of Islamic Cooperation tend to do the same for each other.

"With countries such as China, Cuba, Russia, and Vietnam, among the world's worst human rights abusers, with seats on the council, it should come as no surprise," said Rep. Ileana Ros-Lehtinen, chair of the U.S. House of Representatives Middle East and North Africa Subcommittee, that "the UN Human Rights Council spends more time bashing Israel than on the massive and devastating atrocities and human rights abuses occurring around the world."[214] For such governments, the enforcement of human rights—which the United States' founding fathers deemed self-evidently "unalienable"—is a wholly political, completely disingenuous game.

The disproportionate focus on Israel ensures that the UNHRC spends so much "time focusing on that one state" that governments engaged in gross and systemic abuses are shielded "from scrutiny owing to time constraints."[215] U.N. Secretary-General Kofi Annan took the unusual step of denouncing the UNHRC's focus on Israel as "counterproductive" for "monopoliz[ing] attention at the expense of other situations where there are no less grave violations, or even worse."[216] According to Bill Richardson, who served as U.S. ambassador to the United Nations under President Bill Clinton, "the politics of the UN dominated by the PLO, dominated by the Irans, Cubas, and Syrias" makes the UNHRC "a joke."[217]

It would be a mistake for the United States to completely or largely refrain from instrumental lawfare in the international arena out of concern that to do so would contribute to corroding the rule of law. International laws today are, to a considerable degree, not the product of principled negotiations engaged in by democratically elected representatives of the world's people. According to Freedom House, only 40 percent of the world's population in 2014 lived in the eighty-nine countries rated "Free."[218] Meanwhile, 24 percent of the world's population lived in the fifty-five countries rated "Partly Free," and 36 percent lived in the fifty-one countries rated "Not Free."[219] Freedom House also noted that "the state of freedom in 2014 worsened significantly in nearly every part of the world."[220]

When the PRC Communist party, Vladimir Putin, and various dictators agree to accede to international laws, it is not because they believe that either the laws' content or the rule of law is "given or predetermined" or otherwise reflects core values. Dictators often accede to international laws because they believe that such laws, by dint of their ambiguity and the lack of a global enforcement mechanism, are subject to wholesale instrumental manipulation in their interpretation and enforcement, and thus they can enjoy the benefits of ratification "while suffering little reputational cost from failing to observe the obligations assumed."[221]

In light of the weak or nonexistent legitimacy and commitment to the rule of law of so many of the world's lawmakers, it would make no sense for U.S. policymakers and attorneys to give them more deference than we give to the United States' own domestic lawmaking processes. Why should U.S. lawyers adopt a less instrumental approach to using international law against China, Iran, the Islamic State, or Syria than the advocacy ideal calls for adopting while representing in a U.S. courtroom an alleged murderer the lawyer knows may be guilty? It is surely a peculiarity of U.S. jurisprudence and its practicing attorneys that they, by and large, wield law more aggressively against each other than they do against the United States' foreign adversaries.

D. Questions to Guide U.S. Government Development of a Lawfare Strategy

If the United States abstains from the international instrumental lawfare in which U.S adversaries are already engaging, and fails to develop more effective defenses, it will enable those adversaries to continue and, indeed, increase "using the law as a hammer" against the United States. In contrast, in light of the U.S. expertise in instrumental lawfare that has been honed within the U.S. domestic legal system, and lawfare's relatively lower financial costs to the United States and reduced casualty costs for both lawfare deployers and targets, the U.S. national interest would benefit from the United States increasing its deployment of international instrumental lawfare while improving its defenses against instrumental and compliance-leverage disparity lawfare.

In developing a lawfare strategy, the U.S. government needs to ask itself questions including the following:

1. How can the various relevant U.S. government agencies more effectively coordinate with each other on lawfare, including by waging lawfare synergistically and sharing lessons learned and best practices for more effectively waging and countering lawfare?
2. What types of collateral damage are most likely to be caused by U.S. government lawfare (*see, e.g.,* Chapter 3), and how can U.S. government lawfare be designed to most sensibly minimize such collateral damage?
3. How can U.S. government lawfare be designed to minimize the risks that it will set a problematic precedent that could be used against the U.S. (*see, e.g.,* Chapter 3)? To the extent that such risks cannot be avoided, how much weight should they be given in analyzing the overall advantages and disadvantages of particular lawfare deployments?
4. How can U.S. government lawfare be designed to minimize the risks that it will contribute to corroding the rule of law? To the extent that such risks cannot be avoided, how much weight should they be given in analyzing the overall advantages and disadvantages of particular lawfare deployments?
5. In which additional economic sectors should the United States wage economic lawfare? What are the risks of doing so, and how can they be minimized?
6. To what extent, and how, does it make sense for the U.S. government to wage lawfare through NGO proxies, as the government of Israel did through Shurat HaDin in the Greek flotilla case described in Chapter 8 and as various European governments are doing through Palestinian NGOs as described in Chapter 6?
7. How can the U.S. government improve its ability to draw on the types of non-governmental legal and fact-gathering expertise and creativity that are, as discussed in Chapter 2, increasingly valuable to waging lawfare?
8. In light of this book's illustrations that Congress can wage impactful lawfare even without passing legislation (as described in Chapters 2 and 3), how can Congress and the executive branch work together more effectively to make use of this phenomenon?
9. How can the impact and utility of varying types of lawfare deployments be most effectively measured by the U.S. government?
10. To what extent and how should U.S. law increase or decrease its empowerment of private sector litigators to wage lawfare using civil lawsuits, even if to do so complicates the President's control over foreign policy as discussed in Chapter 2? Assuming that U.S. law continues to do so, how can the executive branch more effectively partner with such litigators?
11. To what extent and how should U.S. law increase or decrease its empowerment of state and local governments to wage lawfare as discussed in

Chapter 2, even if to do so complicates the President's control over foreign policy? Assuming that U.S. law continues to do so, how can the federal executive branch more effectively partner with such state and local lawfare initiatives?

12. How can the U.S. government most effectively maximize coordination and synergies between lawfare and other policy tools, including kinetic military action, so that lawfare can most usefully supplement or, where appropriate, replace such other tools in accomplishing U.S. national security objectives?

13. What can the United States do to more effectively deter, constrain, protect, and otherwise defend against adversary lawfare? For example, how can the U.S. more effectively increase international law's leverage over its adversaries so as to minimize the efficacy against the United States of compliance-leverage disparity lawfare?

14. Which U.S., allied, and international laws should the United States prioritize changing or attempting to change so as to more effectively wage or defend against lawfare?

15. How can the U.S. executive branch train, incentivize, and otherwise facilitate its relevant attorneys to more effectively identify lawfare opportunities and wage lawfare when a policy decision is made to do so?

IV. REASONS FOR LAWFARE'S INCREASING INFLUENCE

The increasing power and prevalence of law as a weapon of war is the result of several factors that began to come to the fore in the mid-1990s and have subsequently continued to grow in importance. Subsection A analyzes a set of such factors that relate to the mutually reinforcing increases in importance of lawfare and other asymmetric warfares. Subsections B through D analyze four key, more lawfare-specific factors that have contributed to lawfare's increasing influence. They are: the increased number and reach of international laws and tribunals (B), the rise of NGOs focused on law of armed conflict and related issues (C), the information technology revolution (D), and the advance of globalization and thus economic interdependence (E).

A. The Mutually Reinforcing Increases in Influence of Lawfare and Other Asymmetric Warfares

The term "asymmetric warfare" came to the fore in 1995,[222] just a few years before Dunlap coined the term "lawfare." As this subsection will illustrate, the two terms have several important conceptual similarities. Most lawfare can be considered a subset of asymmetric warfare. In addition, the increases in influence of lawfare and other forms of asymmetric warfare have, to a considerable degree, been mutually reinforcing.

"Asymmetric warfare" (sometimes referred to as "asymmetrical warfare") is typically defined more or less as follows: attempts to circumvent or undermine an opponent's strengths while exploiting his vulnerabilities using methods that differ significantly from the opponent's usual mode of operations.[223] While some asymmetric warfare definitions use the term "weakness" instead of "vulnerability," this author prefers the latter term. As Professors Robert Pfaltzgraff and Stephen Wright have noted, "it is important to draw a distinction between weakness and vulnerability."[224] While "actors are vulnerable where they are weak," said Pfaltzgraff and Wright, "they may also be vulnerable at points that are indispensable to the maximization of their strengths."[225] Thus, "what is perceived by the superior power to be a strength may in fact become a weakness."[226] Therefore, in the compliance-leverage disparity lawfare context, U.S. adherence to the rule of law, for example, which is an overall source of strength for the United States in so many ways, is much more accurately described as a vulnerability than a weakness.

As was mentioned, both the term "asymmetric warfare" and the term "lawfare" came to the fore between 1995 and 2001. In his book ASYMMETRIC WARFARE, Dr. Rod Thornton includes a thoughtful analysis of that term's genesis and subsequent ascent to the forefront of military thinking. Thornton explains that by the 1990s, "a variety of factors, more than at any time hitherto in the history of human conflict" had begun to create for relatively "small, weak players" both the need and the opportunity "to have great effect on their stronger foes in distinctly new and profound ways."[227] For such relatively weak players, one driver of the need was, and continues to be, the United States' "unrivalled weapons accuracy and unmatched firepower."[228]

As a result of the U.S. technological advantages, "in a symmetrical conflict where tank faces tank" and "aircraft faces aircraft," there is "no contest; the U.S. and its close allies will win every time."[229] Thus, any state or sub-state actor that wishes to achieve warfighting objectives contested by the United States and its allies "must adopt strategies and tactics radically different from those employed by" the United States and its allies.[230]

At the same time that weak players' need to adopt asymmetric approaches has grown, various developments have increased the opportunities for them to have a meaningful impact using asymmetric approaches. Subsections B through E will analyze the reasons lawfare specifically has become increasingly impactful in the last two decades. Over that same time period, other types of asymmetric approaches have been facilitated in various ways by the Internet, which has helped weak players to communicate among themselves and with the wider world, and also has created for strong players a vulnerability to cyberwarfare. The increasing availability of weapons-of-mass-destruction technology recipes (on the Internet) and ingredients (as dual-use equipment becomes more widespread) is also a significant cause for asymmetric concern.

The need and/or the opportunity to engage in asymmetric warfare has led relatively weak adversaries of the United States and its allies to use or explore asymmetric approaches including not only lawfare but also guerrilla warfare, terrorism, cyberwarfare, and weapons of mass destruction. Sometimes, these approaches build upon each other. For example, lawfare can be more usefully deployed, by a weaker foe, against U.S. aircraft bombing its guerrillas hiding among civilians than against advanced U.S. fighter aircraft engaged in aerial combat against whatever inferior fighter aircraft the weaker foe may possess.

In addition, lawfare often builds upon the mismatch between other emergent types of asymmetrical warfare and the international law of armed conflict. As Professor William Banks explained in his book, NEW BATTLEFIELDS/OLD LAWS: CRITICAL DEBATES ON ASYMMETRIC WARFARE, the existing laws of war "do little" to address and "are not well suited" to the newly prominent asymmetric approaches.[231] The laws of war are based, said Banks, on a "Eurocentric conception of war based on symmetric conflicts between state armies of roughly equal military strength and of comparable organizational structures."[232] For example, "the Hague and Geneva Conventions and Protocols do not account adequately for nonstate groups waging transnational attacks or prolonged campaigns of terrorism."[233]

In contrast with today's asymmetrical warfare, "the traditional law on warfare," said Professor Eyal Benvenisti, "was based on two key premises: that it was possible to isolate military and civilian targets with sufficient clarity and that there was a tangible military objective to be attained" from each battle, such as gaining control over territory.[234] According to Benvenisti, "in the asymmetric context there are very few purely military targets."[235] As a result, a regular army determined to comply with the law is "dramatically limit[ed]" in the "arenas where it can legitimately project its power."[236] Benvenisti adds that in the era of asymmetric warfare, it has also "become increasingly unclear what can be considered a military gain, especially since control over enemy . . . territory often proves to be a liability rather than an asset."[237]

According to another analyst, Robert Barnidge, "asymmetrical warfare poses perhaps the greatest challenge to international humanitarian law [the law of armed conflict] since . . . the adoption of the Geneva Conventions in 1949."[238] Certainly, the mismatch between asymmetric warfare and old laws and the law's resulting gaps and ambiguities have contributed greatly to how "legal instruments historically designed to humanize the anarchy of the battlefield have become politicized weapons in contemporary conflicts."[239]

Several factors encourage adversaries (and particularly the current predominantly jihadist adversaries) of the United States and its allies to think that asymmetric warfare might bring victory. First, some adversaries measure victory differently. For example, jihadist suicide bombers measure progress by the harm they have done to their adversary, and can be willing to sacrifice toward that end both their own lives and those of their affiliated civilians. This contrasts with the international law of armed conflict, which is framed on the assumption that "soldiers do not want to die," that they are seeking to achieve traditional battlefield objectives rather than religious "experiences that convey submission to a divine authority . . . by spilling one's (or an infidel's) blood."[240]

In addition to measuring victory based on harm to their adversary, jihadist groups often define their adversary more broadly than does the law of armed conflict. For instance, Al Qaeda "rejects the principles of noncombatant immunity and distinction," maintaining that "it is acceptable to kill noncombatants because they bear responsibility for harms suffered by Muslims" at the hands of the West.[241] Besides rejecting the principles behind the international law of armed conflict, many jihadist groups also reject the law's legitimacy and bindingness (because the treaties comprising the international law of armed conflict are non-Islamic). The jihadists' different victory metrics and legal principles, combined with their disdain for the non-Islamic treaties comprising the international law of armed conflict, help feed the compliance-disparity lawfare waged by Hamas, the Islamic State, the Taliban, and other jihadist groups.

Second, while Westerners have relatively little patience for lengthy wars, some of their adversaries assume that wars will last for decades. In the lawfare context, this may contribute to some adversaries (relatively secular ones such as the PA) placing greater value on incremental lawfare-related victories—such as U.N. votes or I.C.J. investigations or boycotts, or divestment and sanctions measures—which do not immediately change the situation on the ground but can have symbolic propaganda value in the short term and a more significant cumulative impact over time.

A third factor encouraging adversaries to think that asymettric warfare might bring victory is that Western powers have an increasing aversion to casualties.[242] This aversion has been intensified by the increased availability of images of victims—before, during, and after their demise.

For example, U.S. aversion to casualties among its own troops was seen as contributing to its quick defeat in Somalia in 1993. The "Black Hawk Down" incident resulted in eighteen dead U.S. soldiers as well as images, broadcast on U.S. television screens, of some of the dead being dragged through the streets of Somalia's capital city.[243] In the incident's wake, the United States was seen to have abandoned its original mission and left Somalia.[244] According to Osama bin Laden, this incident demonstrated "the weakness, feebleness and cowardliness of the U.S. soldier who fled in the dark of night."[245] In addition, U.S. and allied aversion to casualties among enemy-affiliated and bystander civilians has been pivotal to the successful deployment by their adversaries of much of the compliance-disparity lawfare described in this chapter and in Chapter 7.

B. The Increased Number and Reach of International Laws and Tribunals

Lawfare's increasing prevalence and power is also a result of the web of international law, including the law of armed conflict, becoming both broader and thicker in recent decades. As General James L. Jones, the former commander of NATO and U.S. National Security Adviser, observed: "It used to be a simple thing to fight a battle . . . . [Now] you have to have a lawyer or a dozen. It's become very legalistic and very complex."[246]

International laws and tribunals have increased in both number and reach. As of 2008, national governments worldwide had reportedly entered into "more than 45,000 bilateral treaties and 8,000 multilateral treaties since World War II."[247]

The United States has entered into far fewer treaties during that time period. For example, the United States joined a total of 372 treaties between 1961 and 2009, including 167 new multilateral treaties between 1990 and 2009.[248] However, treaties, which are subject to Senate advice and consent, are far from the only legally binding international agreements into which the United States enters. Indeed, the United States entered into 127 different new legally binding international agreements in 2013 alone.[249]

The typical treaty or international agreement is likely to have a number of different legally binding provisions. While it is likely that most legally binding provisions (and even most entire international agreements) are not useful for lawfare purposes, some are, or could be if they were thoughtfully analyzed and creatively deployed. It would be difficult if not impossible to estimate what percentage of international agreement provisions are susceptible to being deployed in lawfare, and this author has not made an attempt to do so. However, the vast number and reach of international agreements means that even a small percentage of lawfare-useful provisions would add up to a very significant stockpile both quantitatively and, likely, qualitatively.

This book includes several examples of lawfare waged using international agreement provisions. For example, Chapter 5 provides a detailed discussion of lawfare waged by the Palestinian Authority and their allies to first insert and then deploy language that was added by them to the Rome Statute (the ICC Charter—which entered into force in 2002), in order to turn Israeli settlements into war crimes. In addition, Chapter 4 includes a detailed study of lawfare waged by the PRC with regard to the United Nations Convention on the Law of the Sea, which entered into force in 1994.

Recent decades have also seen the creation or significant enhancement of several globally focused tribunals applying international law, including the International Criminal Court (2002), the International Tribunal for the Law of the Sea (1996), and the World Trade Organization dispute settlement provisions (1995). More regionally focused tribunals applying international law that were founded in recent decades include the Special Tribunal for Lebanon (2007), the Extraordinary Chambers in the Courts of Cambodia (2005), the Special Court for Sierra Leone (2002), the International Criminal Tribunal for Rwanda (1994), the North American Free Trade Agreement tribunals (1994), and the International Criminal Tribunal for the former Yugoslavia (1993).[250] The creation and decisions of the six of these tribunals that are focused on issues related to the law of armed conflict and the use of force—ICC, Lebanon, Cambodia, Sierra Leone, Rwanda, and the former Yugoslavia—means that the law of armed conflict has developed more quickly in both scope and complexity than it might have otherwise over the last two decades. One example of lawfare waged using international tribunals is the PA using the ICC to wage lawfare against Israel, as described in Chapter 5.

Another factor contributing to the thickening web of international law has been a more assertive U.N. Security Council. Between the founding of the United Nations in 1945 and the end of the Cold War, the Security Council imposed economic sanctions which were mandatory (legally binding on all U.N. member states) against only two targets: Rhodesia and South Africa. Cold War tensions prevented agreement on sanctions in even exceptionally compelling cases. For example, following the seizure of the U.S. Embassy in Iran in November 1979, the Soviet Union vetoed a Security Council resolution calling for economic sanctions.[251] In 1990, with the Cold War ice broken, the United States and the Soviet Union together voted to impose sanctions on Iraq in response to its occupation of Kuwait.[252] Since then, the Security Council has adopted more than fifty sanctions resolutions against at least twenty different target states and several non-state actors.[253] Chapter 3 includes a detailed analysis of the United States' use of U.N. Security Council resolutions to wage economic lawfare against Iran.

A final factor in the thickening web of international law has been the increased willingness of various national governments to include, and many national and even local courts to apply, international law as part of their jurisprudence. Examples of this include the various "universal jurisdiction" cases described in this chapter and in Chapter 6, as well as cases such as the Riwal/Lima and Raytheon cases discussed in Chapter 6.

C. The Rise of NGOs Focused on Law of Armed Conflict and Related Issues

Another major reason for lawfare's increasing influence and prevalence is the rise of NGOs, in particular those engaged in scrutiny and advocacy regarding the law of armed conflict and other lawfare-relevant issues. As Professor Joseph Nye noted in his classic book, *Soft Power*, "the information age has been marked by an increasingly important role of nonstate actors on the international stage . . . with the number of NGOs . . . increasing from 6,000 to approximately 26,000 during the 1990s alone."[254] "Many nongovernmental organizations claim to act as a 'global conscience' [as] they develop new norms directly by pressing governments and business leaders to change policies, and indirectly by altering public perceptions of what governments and firms should be doing," said Nye.[255]

Global human rights NGOs, including Amnesty International (AI) and Human Rights Watch, have had a particular impact on various issues relating to the law of armed conflict (as well as, of course, human rights law[256]) in recent decades. Such NGOs carry weight because of their large numbers of members (AI reportedly has over 1.8 million worldwide),[257] considerable budgets (AI USA alone had a $39 million budget in 2012),[258] perceived objectivity,[259] prestige (Amnesty International was awarded the Nobel Peace Prize in 1977),[260] and expertise at research, advocacy, and public relations.[261]

AI has contributed to lawfare's increasing influence in several ways. For example, AI has raised awareness of the law of armed conflict and of asserted violations of it, thereby increasing the reputational cost of actual or alleged failures to comply with the law of armed conflict. As Ann Marie Clarke notes in her history of AI, "public criticism of governments' human rights records was not accepted diplomatic practice for states or NGOs at Amnesty's inception."[262]

Sometimes, AI has been the first to bring violations to light. For example, AI was reportedly the first (prior to any media outlet) to publicize the outrageous abuse of prisoners at the Abu Ghraib prison in Iraq by members of the U.S. military.[263] In other cases, AI's contribution has been to systematically collect, package, and disseminate already public alleged violations of the law of armed conflict and other international laws by state actors, for example the United States[264] and Israel (as discussed in Chapter 7),[265] or by non-state actors such as Hamas.[266]

The reports and advocacy of global human rights NGOs such as AI tend to have more influence on target countries or non-state actors to the extent the targets: are responsive to public opinion, care about their international image,[267] are "sensitive to pressure because of gaps between stated commitments and practice,"[268] and contain influential persons who are members of the NGO or otherwise give credence to it. Since these tend to be characteristics of democratic states, the reports and advocacy of global human rights NGOs may, in some cases, contribute to making democracies even more vulnerable to compliance-leverage disparity lawfare than they would be otherwise.

Compilations of data by AI or any other non-governmental (or even governmental)[269] actor can also be used more directly as ammunition for instrumental lawfare by other actors. For example, when the League of Arab States requested an Advisory Opinion from the International Court of Justice on the legality of Israel's security barrier (as discussed in more detail in Chapter 5), they quoted reports by AI in support of their position[270]—this notwithstanding the fact that the Arab League is not otherwise known for its deference to either human rights or human rights NGOs.

Of course, journalists also sometimes compile facts that can be used as lawfare ammunition. AI tends to have more impact on lawfare in this regard because it is more focused and devotes relatively more resources to compiling data on asserted law of armed conflict and other relevant international law violations than does any individual media outlet.

AI's opinions can also be used as ammunition for lawfare by other actors. For example, when a prestigious organization such as AI, with a reputation for objectivity, asserts, as it often does, that a particular action by a state or non-state actor was a violation of international law,[271] that inevitably lends credence to other actors' lawfare deployments based on similar assertions. Given the nature of customary international law—which, as described in Chapter 4, can be influenced by the writings of legal scholars—interpretations of international law by prestigious organizations such as AI can help shape the content of that law. Organizations such as AI can also shape the content of international law more directly, when they campaign in favor of new treaties or provisions. For example, AI played a leading role in advocating for and shaping the International Criminal Court,[272] which, as discussed in Chapter 5, has become a significant lawfare battleground.

The collective influence of NGOs in shaping international law can sometimes rival or exceed that of superpowers, enabling the NGOs to impose additional restrictions on the conduct of armed conflict even over the superpowers' objections. For example, the landmine ban treaty, which entered into force in 1998, was driven forward by NGOs and adopted over the opposition of China, Russia, and the United States.[273] The landmine treaty idea was initiated in 1991 by a handful of activists who founded and built the International Campaign to Ban Landmines (ICBL).[274] The ICBL, in which AI happened not to actively participate,[275] was coordinated in large part via e-mail by Jody Williams from a farmhouse in Vermont.[276] For their efforts, Williams and the ICBL were recognized with the 1997 Nobel Peace Prize.[277]

In addition to its efforts to broadly shape and build awareness of the law of armed conflict, AI has advocated several specific policy positions that would fit the definition of lawfare if the organization's goal was to weaken or destroy the target. These include a report on the 2009 Israel/Hamas conflict in Gaza in which AI called "on the UN, notably the Security Council, to impose an immediate, comprehensive arms embargo on all parties to the conflict, and on all states to take action individually to impose national embargoes on any arms or weapons transfers to the parties to the conflict."[278] In addition, before a planned trip to Switzerland by President George W. Bush in 2011, AI sent to Swiss authorities documents petitioning them to prosecute Bush for torture when he arrived in Geneva.[279] Bush cancelled the trip.[280] Even if AI's goal is not to weaken or destroy the target, such recommendations from such an influential organization can provide significant impetus and ammunition to actors who *are* waging lawfare.

In addition to global NGOs such as AI, numerous smaller NGOs have also played a considerable role in lawfare. Chapters 2 and 6 describe numerous smaller Israeli, Palestinian, U.S., and other NGOs informing, instigating, and sometimes waging lawfare. As Nitsana Darshan-Leitner, the head of a lawfare-waging Israeli NGO, put it, NGOs can sometimes be more aggressive in waging lawfare because while "countries are bound by treaties, national agreements and special relationships," in contrast, "private citizens do not have these limitations."[281]

D. The Information Technology Revolution

The information technology revolution is another major contributor to lawfare's increasing impact and prevalence. As discussed in Chapter 2, the information technology revolution has empowered non-governmental organizations and individuals to inform, instigate, and even wage lawfare. Chapter 2 provides examples of non-governmental lawfare practitioners benefiting from the ready accessibility over the Internet of commercial satellite imagery, ship-tracking websites, corporate annual reports, trade press articles, foreign press articles, international agreements, local laws, and national laws from around the world.

At the same time, personal communications technology and the proliferation of online media outlets have enabled small organizations and even individuals to record and disseminate evidence of war crimes. For example, according to Dunlap, "the U.S. military's most serious setback since 9/11" is perceived to have been the Abu Ghraib detainee abuse scandal, a "strategic military disaster [which] did not involve force of arms, but rather centered on illegalities."[282] Abu Ghraib resonated around the world in considerable part because of the disturbing photos of detainee abuse which were snapped by individual soldiers using personal communications devices and distributed around the world via Internet websites large and small.

E. Globalization and Economic Interdependence

The final major reason for the increasing power and prevalence of lawfare is the advance of globalization, which has vastly increased governments' nonkinetic leverage over other countries and their companies by intensifying international economic interdependence. According to a U.N. analysis, "economic integration and interdependence in the world today have reached an unprecedented level."[283]

In 2012, the world's total cross-border flow of goods, services, and finance equaled an estimated $26 trillion, some 36 percent of global GDP.[284] This reflected a significant increase in total economic integration and interdependence since 1990. For example, the total flow of goods, services, and finance in

2012 was 1.5 times as large relative to GDP as it had been in 1990, when it represented 23 percent of world GDP.[285]

Since 1990, national economies have become much more dependent on trade in goods and services. During that period, "the share of exports and imports of goods and services in GDP (at constant prices) virtually doubled, from around 13% to 27% in developed countries, and from 20% to close to 40% in developing countries."[286] In 2012, 35 percent of goods crossed borders, in comparison with 20 percent in 1990.[287] In 2012 alone, the world's total global flow of goods and services equaled approximately $21.9 trillion.[288]

For much of the period between 1990 and 2010, worldwide cross-border flows of foreign direct investment (FDI) rose even faster than did trade in goods and services.[289] In 2014 alone, global FDI flows totaled $1.3 trillion.[290] Meanwhile, total cross-border capital flows (which include FDI, purchases of foreign bonds and equities, and cross-border loans and deposits), increased from $1 trillion in 1990 to $4.6 trillion in 2012 (in constant 2011 exchange rates).[291]

As a result of the increase in goods and services trade and capital flows, many nations have an increased reliance on international commerce, and many companies are subject to significant leverage in jurisdictions beyond where they are headquartered. Chapter 4 details the increased economic interdependence between the PRC and the United States, and the many potential lawfare targets it has created. For example, as described in Chapter 4, the PRC currently owns some $1.24 trillion in U.S. Treasury securities and also has vast leverage over many major U.S. companies, including those with investments in China and those that are heavily dependent on the Chinese market. At the same time, the U.S. government has regulatory leverage over, for example, the many major Chinese companies that have in the last two decades been listed on U.S. stock exchanges.

While licit international commerce has been multiplying, so has illicit international commerce. Although illicit commerce is relatively hard to quantify, the United Nations estimated that some $1.6 trillion, 2.7 percent of global GDP, was illegally laundered in 2009.[292] Moises Naim, the author of *Illicit*,[293] a book on illicit commerce, estimated in 2009 that money laundering had "grown at least tenfold since 1990."[294] Naim noted that "in the 1990s, revolutionary changes in politics and technology reduced the obstacles that distance, borders, and governments imposed on the international movement of goods, money, and people—legal and illegal."[295]

A number of this book's case studies involve lawfare that leveraged transnational economic interdependence. For instance, in Chapter 2, such examples include: the U.S. law that put foreign companies to a choice between providing gasoline to Iran and exclusion from the U.S. market; members of Congress using an Indian firm's loan guarantees from the U.S. government to pressure it to stop supplying gasoline to Iran; the Marine barracks bombing victims freezing some $2 billion in Iranian government funds that transited a

New York bank account; U.S. state pension funds divesting from foreign companies with investments in Iran; and U.S. prosecutors seizing a Manhattan office tower, which was secretly owned by Iran, to distribute the proceeds to victims of Iranian terrorism.

In Chapter 3, examples of lawfare that leveraged transnational economic interdependence include the U.S. Treasury Department's campaign to use the dollar's primacy to pressure scores of foreign banks to stop laundering money for and otherwise transacting with Iran. In Chapter 4, they include the PRC pressuring Japan by withholding rare earth exports. In Chapter 6, they include antisettlement activists instigating a Dutch criminal investigation of Israel's rental of a construction crane from the Dutch company Riwal. In Chapter 8, they include an Israeli NGO using U.S. law to pressure insurers (who also had business interests in the United States) to drop their coverage of a flotilla in a Greek port.

CHAPTER 2

Lawfare Waged by U.S. Private Sector and Non-Governmental Organization Attorneys

"A moral striking force"

— Raphael Lemkin

A handful of American attorneys outside the U.S. government have waged remarkably impactful lawfare against U.S. adversaries and other foreign targets. In the litigation arena, one team of two attorneys—a father and his daughter—brought a lawsuit that helped shut down an organization raising millions of dollars for Hamas in the United States. A lawsuit brought by a second small team of attorneys resulted in a verdict which established that a bank which knowingly provides financial services to a terrorist group can be held liable for the group's terrorist acts. That verdict will likely help deter banks around the world from continuing to do business with terrorists.

A third small team of attorneys successfully sued Iran for the deaths of 241 U.S. marines killed by Hezbollah's bombing of a Marine barracks in Beirut in 1983. The U.S. executive branch had never retaliated against Iran for the marines' deaths and had done "nothing in response to an attack that killed more service-men in a single day than any other since the Second World War."[1] George Shultz, who was secretary of state at the time, later criticized the lack of a response, stating, "We may never have the kind of evidence that can stand up in an American court of law, but we cannot allow ourselves to become the Hamlet of nations, worrying endlessly over whether and how to respond."[2]

Ironically, it was in an American court of law, on May 30, 2003, almost twenty years after the blast, that Iran was finally held accountable for the Marine barracks bombing. On that day, a U.S. district court judge ruled that Iran was responsible for the Marine barracks bombing and awarded $2.657 billion in compensation to its victims. In 2008, $2 billion in Iranian assets were seized as a result of the verdict. In explaining her motivation for bringing the case, the lead plaintiff, whose brother had been killed in the attack, said: "We don't want to be victims of terror anymore. We want to be soldiers in the war on terrorism; the courtroom is our battlefield."[3]

Private sector litigation lawfare has frequently been criticized as weakening the President's control over U.S. foreign policy. Yet Congress has repeatedly passed laws that enable and facilitate it. As one analyst explained, "who could vote against . . . the belief in the law as the ultimate arbitrator of social justice; the reliance on the rights and energies of the individual; the emotional and moral draw of the common man taking on a dictatorial terrorist state in a courtroom showdown."[4]

U.S. non-governmental attorneys have also impactfully waged lawfare outside the litigation arena. In the late 1940s, the successful campaign to create a U.N. treaty prohibiting genocide was mounted virtually single-handedly by Raphael Lemkin, an American Jewish lawyer who lost forty-nine of his relatives in the Holocaust. Describing his work, he wrote: "I have transformed my personal disaster into a moral striking force."[5]

In the Internet age, information technology has greatly enhanced the ability of individual attorneys to collect and disseminate information at the level of detail necessary to either wage lawfare themselves or spur or assist governments to do so. Corporate annual reports, trade press articles, ship-tracking websites, and commercial satellite imagery have all been used by non-governmental attorneys to identify and act upon illicit activity by foreign terrorist groups and governments, and the companies that do business with them.

This chapter will describe, analyze, and draw lessons from the stories of these and other individual lawfare warriors. Section I focuses on litigation by private sector attorneys in U.S. courts against terrorist groups, their material supporters, and their state sponsors. It concentrates in particular on lawsuits against Middle Eastern terrorist groups and Iran, the targets with regard to which such lawfare has been the most extensive, sophisticated, and effective. The section is organized around the two key U.S. statutes that are currently facilitating such litigation, turning first to examine cases under the Anti-Terrorism Act and then to cases under the state sponsor of terrorism exception to the Foreign Sovereign Immunities Act.

Section II focuses on describing and analyzing other ways, outside the litigation arena, in which U.S. non-governmental attorneys have waged offensive lawfare against U.S. adversaries. This includes developing and advocating changes to international, U.S. federal, state, and local laws; encouraging actions by executive branch policymakers; and collecting and disseminating evidence of adversary violations of laws. Section III assesses the potential future role of

U.S. non-governmental attorneys in lawfare against U.S. adversaries, including the possibility of more extensive cooperation in this regard between the U.S. government and law firm attorneys.

I. PRIVATE CIVIL LITIGATION AGAINST TERRORISTS, THEIR MATERIAL SUPPORTERS, AND THEIR STATE SPONSORS

The handful of private sector U.S. attorneys who sue terrorist groups, their material supporters, and the governments that sponsor terrorism are an exceptional example of lawfare waged by individuals. These lawsuits have been notably effective at times in achieving various objectives, including: (a) seizing assets of and otherwise putting financial pressure on terrorist-supporting states, including Iran; (b) deterring private individuals and NGOs from contributing to terrorist groups; (c) deterring banks from providing financial services to terrorist groups; (d) compensating victims; (e) bringing public and governmental attention to the harm done by terrorists to Americans; and (f) using the American judicial system to find facts and make determinations as to the connections between countries such as Iran and terrorist attacks by groups such as Hezbollah. At the same time, these lawsuits are frequently criticized for interfering with the U.S. government's conduct of foreign policy.

The two principal U.S. laws that are currently facilitating litigation against terrorists, their material supporters, and their state sponsors are the Anti-Terrorism Act (ATA) and the state sponsor of terrorism exception to the Foreign Sovereign Immunity Act (FSIA). While the ATA is typically the legal weapon of choice against terrorists and their non-governmental material supporters, state sponsors of terrorism are typically sued under a special exception to the FSIA. This section will describe and analyze leading cases under the two laws. In doing so, it will analyze the advantages, disadvantages, and future potential of such U.S. private sector litigation lawfare.

A. The Anti-Terrorism Act

Since it became U.S. law in 1990, the ATA has been the vehicle for lawsuits that have won hundreds of millions of dollars on behalf of U.S. victims of terrorism. The ATA provides principally as follows: "Any national of the United States injured in his or her person, property, or business by reason of an act of international terrorism, or his or her estate, survivors, or heirs, may sue therefor in any appropriate district court of the United States and shall recover threefold the damages he or she sustains and the cost of the suit, including attorney's fees."[6] This subsection will describe and analyze the development and implementation of the ATA.

Before analyzing the ATA, it is important to briefly distinguish it from the Alien Tort Statute (ATS), with which it is sometimes confused. The ATS, enacted by the first Congress as part of the Judiciary Act of 1789, states: "The district courts shall have original jurisdiction of any civil action by an alien for a tort only, committed in violation of the law of nations or a treaty of the United States."[7] The ATS remained in obscurity for almost two hundred years, until an attorney named Peter Weiss used it to sue former Paraguayan police inspector Americo Peña-Irala for the torture and killing of Joelito Filartiga. When Weiss initially suggested deploying the obscure 1789 statute, his colleagues at the Center for Constitutional Rights were so skeptical they worried that the "suit would be laughed out of court."[8] Nevertheless, in 1980, the lawsuit resulted in the landmark Second Circuit decision in *Filartiga v. Peña-Irala*, in which the court allowed Dolly Filartiga, a Paraguayan citizen, to sue under the ATS for the torture and murder in Paraguay of her 17-year-old brother Joelito by Americo Peña-Irala, who had subsequently moved to New York City.[9] Dolly Filartiga was awarded a $10 million judgment.[10] Numerous ATS suits followed.[11]

The ATS showed considerable promise as a lawfare tool before it was very significantly narrowed in 2013 by the Supreme Court decision in *Kiobel v. Royal Dutch Petroleum Company*.[12] In *Kiobel*, the Supreme Court held that there is no federal court jurisdiction under the ATS for torts that occur outside the United States.[13] Lower court decisions since *Kiobel* suggest that "*Kiobel* marks the end of the *Filartiga* revolution in the United States."[14]

In contrast to the ATS's eighteenth-century vintage, the ATA was enacted in 1990. The ATA was reportedly inspired in part by a suit filed in federal court by the family of Leon Klinghoffer.[15] Klinghoffer, a wheelchair-bound U.S. passenger on a cruise ship named the *Achille Lauro*, was murdered by PLO-affiliated terrorists after they commandeered the ship.[16] Klinghoffer's wife and daughters sued the PLO. After several years of litigation, the PLO settled the case.[17] Members of Congress viewed the suit favorably and were concerned that the case had only narrowly escaped dismissal.[18] In supporting the ATA, Senator Charles Grassley explained that "the ATA removes the jurisdictional hurdles in the courts confronting victims and it empowers victims with all the weapons available in civil litigation."[19]

As of summer 2015, the three most important ATA cases have been *Boim v. Holy Land Foundation*; *Linde v. Arab Bank*; and *Sokolow v. PLO*. *Boim* was the essential precursor to *Linde* and *Sokolow*.

1. Holding Hamas Funders Liable for Hamas Terrorist Acts: Boim v. Holy Land Foundation

Boim was the first case to clarify that the ATA can impose liability for terrorist acts against persons or entities who provide material support to terrorists. In

Boim v. Holy Land Foundation,[20] the Seventh Circuit Court of Appeals in 2008 affirmed a $156 million award, under 18 U.S.C. § 2333, to the family of David Boim. Boim, a 17-year-old U.S. citizen, had been shot to death in 1996 by two Hamas operatives while waiting for a bus in the West Bank.[21] The $156 million award was against several U.S.-based individuals and organizations found to have provided material support to Hamas, including by raising funds for it.[22]

The *Boim* decision, like most of the other key lawfare court cases featured in this chapter, was years in the making and driven by a very small team of lawyers. The *Boim* litigation had its origin in the creative mind of Nathan Lewin, a law firm partner in Washington, D.C., who teamed up on the case with his daughter Alyza Lewin, also an attorney. A third lawyer, Stephen Landes, an experienced Chicago litigator, eventually joined them and played a leading role, especially in collecting additional facts and presenting the lawsuit to the jury.

Following the murder, David Boim's parents had approached Nathan Lewin and asked whether there was any recourse to be had under U.S. law.[23] Nathan Lewin first tried to get Boim's killers prosecuted under a federal law that criminalizes the killing of "a national of the United States, while such national is outside the United States."[24] Although such prosecutions have been rare, they are not unheard of.[25] Nathan Lewin thought the Boim case presented a particularly good opportunity because one of the two Hamas perpetrators had confessed to the crime in the presence of a U.S. State Department observer.[26] However, the U.S. Justice Department refused to prosecute the case.[27]

Nathan Lewin stated in an interview that in searching for another route to justice, he drew inspiration from the lawsuits of Morris Dees and the Southern Poverty Law Center,[28] who had used civil litigation to bankrupt factions of the Ku Klux Klan.[29] Frustrated by the reluctance of the U.S. government, with its vast resources, to pursue the Hamas foot soldiers who had themselves killed David Boim, attorneys Nathan and Alyza Lewin decided to use civil litigation to "build a case of far greater consequence than nailing a couple of lowly Hamas killers."[30] The father and daughter team decided that they would themselves go after Hamas's leadership and fundraising apparatus.[31]

Nathan Lewin noticed that the ATA's 18 U.S.C. § 2333—which provides that "any national of the United States injured . . . by reason of an act of international terrorism, or his or her estate, survivors, or heirs, may sue therefore"—does not explicitly state who can be the target of such a lawsuit.[32] "It didn't make sense to me," said Nathan Lewin, "that the only person who could be sued would be the gunman."[33] "So I worked up this theory that the statute enabled you to sue anyone who had contributed to Hamas."[34] Alyza Lewin refers to it as "Nat Lewin's Novel Legal Theory."[35]

With the theory in hand, Nathan and Alyza Lewin turned to identifying potential defendants for the litigation.[36] "This was before 9/11," says Alyza Lewin, "and Hamas' funders in the U.S. were very open as to what they were doing."[37] For example, the Lewins discovered that the Holy Land Foundation, which was at the time the United States' largest Muslim charitable organization[38] "collecting funds in most mosques in the United States,"[39] was providing millions of dollars to Hamas under the guise of social welfare.[40]

On May 12, 2000, the Lewins filed a $600 million lawsuit in federal court in Chicago on behalf of David Boim's parents against the Holy Land Foundation and several other Islamic charities and individuals who they alleged had raised money in the United States for Hamas.[41] The novel nature of the suit quickly proved a mismatch for the genteel standard operating procedures of the judge assigned to the case. "Judge Lindberg, who had previously served as a state court judge, had an iron-clad rule: all civil cases before him had to engage in settlement negotiations, with each of the parties present in person themselves," said Nathan Lewin.[42] The Boims were living in Israel at the time.[43] "It was going to be awkward, to say the least, for them to come to the U.S. to sit down with the funders of their son's murder," said Alyza Lewin.[44] But Judge Lindberg insisted, and the settlement conference was held.[45]

"Only one of the defendants was willing to consider any kind of settlement at all," said Nathan Lewin, "and that was the Quranic Literacy Institute, which offered only to publish a book of condolences for all victims of the Middle East conflict, in which they would include David Boim's name and put his photo on the cover along with photos of Palestinian victims."[46] "Mohammed Salah, who we had named as a defendant because he was one of the key Hamas operatives in the U.S., turned to the Boims at the settlement conference," said Nathan Lewin, "and said 'I know where you live.'"[47]

The defendants were represented by Akin Gump, one of the nation's largest firms.[48] The attorneys from Akin Gump were sufficiently confident of victory that they asked the court not only to dismiss the case but also to impose Rule 11 sanctions against the Lewins for bringing a frivolous suit.[49] In December 2000, the Lewins prevailed against that first challenge. However, ultimate victory still seemed far away.

Then came the terrorist attacks of September 11, 2001. "September 11th made all the difference for the case," says Alyza Lewin.[50] All of a sudden, the media, the public, and the federal government saw the battle against terrorism in a very different context. In addition, "after September 11 this became a case not just about the Boims and Hamas funders but also about a potential tool that could be used against the sponsors of the September 11 attacks," says Alyza Lewin.[51] For example, the *Chicago Tribune* reported on September 26, 2001, that "according to lawyers in the case, the court's decision could set a precedent for whether thousands of victims from the Sept. 11 attacks have legal recourse to sue financial backers of Osama bin Laden or others found to be responsible."[52]

After the attacks of September 11, says Alyza Lewin, "I asked myself, 'What could I as an individual do?' But the fact is, we had the Boim case. The fact is, we were able to go to court and make a difference for victims of terrorism. I felt blessed."[53]

One book somewhat breathlessly described Nathan Lewin's role in the post-9/11 era as follows:

> Nathan Lewin was at the forefront of a new warrior force that now began to throw itself into battle. Their theater of war would be the chrome-and-glass towers of Washington and New York, Chicago and Dallas. Most wore smart pinstripes and carried bulging briefcases. Their weapons were computers, dictaphones, and photocopiers. Their smart bomb was the law and their trenches would be the courtrooms of the United States.[54]

In the wake of the September 11, 2001, attacks, the Seventh Circuit requested the executive branch's views on the *Boim* case.[55] On November 14, 2001, the U.S. Department of Justice weighed in to support the *Boim* lawsuit.[56] The Department advised that "neither the First Amendment nor any other part of the Constitution guarantees a right to fund a foreign terrorist organization when it is a natural consequence that the money donated will be used to commit terrorist acts such as murder."[57]

It turned out that the federal government had for several years quietly possessed information definitively linking the Holy Land Foundation to Hamas.[58] For example, the FBI had electronically eavesdropped on a 1993 meeting in Philadelphia at which Holy Land Foundation officials met to discuss what they called "Samah," the backwards spelling of Hamas.[59] According to the FBI, the meeting participants "decided that most or almost all of the funds collected in the future should be directed to" Samah.[60] Also according to the FBI, at a 1994 meeting, two Holy Land Foundation officials stated that "the monies raised by [Holy Land] were strictly for Hamas terrorists."[61]

The U.S. government had designated Hamas as a terrorist organization and had frozen Hamas assets in the United States in January 1995.[62] But the government had not acted on its information linking the Holy Land Foundation to Hamas. Wary of being seen as "bashing Muslims,"[63] the federal government was reportedly reluctant to act against the Holy Land Foundation unless it could directly connect the Foundation "money raised in this country to bombs and bullets unleashed in the Middle East."[64]

Finally, on December 4, 2001, the federal government was spurred to act against the Holy Land Foundation—by a combination of the September 11 attacks, a spate of Hamas suicide bombings in Israel, and the *Boim* litigation, which was advancing without having to demonstrate that Holy Land Foundation funds raised in the United States were used to purchase a particular bomb or bullet. That day, President George W. Bush, Treasury Secretary Paul O'Neill, and Attorney General John Ashcroft held a press conference to announce that the federal government was seizing the Holy Land Foundation's records and assets.[65] Federal agents ultimately seized about $5 million in Holy Land Foundation assets.[66] "Hamas has obtained much of the money that it pays for murder abroad right here in the United States, money originally raised by the Holy Land Foundation," said President Bush.[67] "Money raised by the Holy Land Foundation is . . . used by Hamas to recruit suicide bombers and to support their families," said Bush.[68]

"The Holy Land Foundation masquerades as a charity, while its primary purpose is to fund Hamas," said Treasury Secretary O'Neill.[69] The Holy Land Foundation "exists," said O'Neill, to raise money in the United States to promote terror."[70]

The same assertion that Nathan Lewin and his team had been making in court since May 2000 was suddenly being made by the President and Treasury Secretary of the United States. However, it would not be until 2008 that the *Boim* lawsuit was definitively victorious.

Though it was Nathan Lewin who first identified the ATA's potential, and the Lewins and Stephen Landes who tenaciously pushed the case forward, it was Judge Richard Posner who in 2008 authored the Seventh Circuit's pivotal en banc opinion in the *Boim* case. Posner, a former law professor, is a prolific author who has been described as the single most cited legal scholar of the twentieth century.[71]

During oral argument before Posner and the other Seventh Circuit judges, Matthew Piers, an attorney for one of the defendants (Mohammed Salah), asserted that Boim's family should be required to show a definitive link between the defendants' acts and Boim's death.[72] The comment prompted Judge Posner to inquire as to what that would mean.[73] "Would there have to be a Katyusha rocket with the name Salah engraved on it, something like that? Would his contribution have to be earmarked for a specific weapon or ammunition which is then traced to David Boim—the bullet?," asked Posner.[74] "You can never trace the critical expenditure on the weapon that kills the plaintiff's decedent to a specific donation," Judge Posner said, adding that the ATA would be "completely ineffectual" if such a standard were followed.[75]

In the pivotal en banc opinion, Posner determined that 18 U.S.C. § 2333 was applicable to the *Boim* defendants through a "chain of incorporations by reference."[76] Posner began by noting that the term "act of international terrorism" in 18 U.S.C. § 2333 is defined in 18 U.S.C. § 2331(1) to include not only violent acts but also "acts dangerous to human life that are a violation of the criminal law of the United States."[77] Posner asserted that "giving money to Hamas, like giving a loaded gun to a child (which is also not a violent act), is an act 'dangerous to human life.'"[78] Posner then noted that giving money to Hamas also violated a federal criminal statute, 18 U.S.C. § 2339A(a), which provides that "whoever provides material support or resources . . . , knowing or intending that they are to be used in preparation for, or in carrying out a violation of [18 U.S.C. § 2332]," shall be guilty of a federal crime.[79]

The final link in Posner's chain was when "we go to 18 U.S.C. § 2332 and discover that it criminalizes the killing (whether classified as homicide, voluntary manslaughter, or involuntary manslaughter), conspiring to kill, or inflicting bodily injury on, any American citizen outside the United States."[80] "By this chain of incorporations by reference," said Posner, "we see that a donation to a terrorist group that targets Americans outside the United States may violate section 2333."[81]

Having established this, Posner made the following key additional points as to the scope of 18 U.S.C. § 2333:

- "The fact of contributing to a terrorist organization rather than the amount of the contribution is the keystone of liability."[82]
- "If you give money to an organization that you know to be engaged in terrorism, the fact that you earmark it for the organization's nonterrorist activities does not get you off the liability hook . . . . Anyone who knowingly contributes to the nonviolent wing of an organization that he knows to engage in terrorism is knowingly contributing to the organization's terrorist activities. And that is the only knowledge that can reasonably be required as a premise for liability."[83]
- "Nor should donors to terrorism be able to escape liability because terrorists and their supporters launder donations through a chain of intermediate organizations . . . . As long as A either knows or is reckless in failing to discover that donations to B end up with Hamas, A is liable."[84]

The Boim family ultimately collected only a tiny fraction of the $156 million in damages the court had awarded them.[85] However, collecting damages had never been the lawsuit's primary objective. "We went into this knowing there might be no compensation," said Alyza Lewin, who explained that the motivations for the lawsuit included "shutting down the specific fundraising network" that had contributed to Boim's killers and setting a broad precedent to deter future funding of terrorism.[86] The Boim lawsuit achieved both of those objectives.

When it came to shutting down the specific organizations and individuals that had raised money for Hamas in the United States, the *Boim* lawsuit was victorious itself and also helped the federal government take action. Intensive research and discovery proceedings by Landes and his trial team, including depositions of key Hamas operatives, demonstrated the close links between the domestic defendants and Hamas leadership. According to Alyza Lewin, "we shared with the federal government several key pieces of evidence, acquired as part of our research on the case, that they did not have themselves."[87] Some of this evidence was eventually introduced by the prosecutors in the criminal trial against the Holy Land Foundation and its principals.[88]

In addition, "when Stephen Landes learned before the government did that Holy Land Foundation President Shukri Abu Baker—a defendant which the government was also targeting—was about to leave the country, Landes told DOJ and they immediately arrested Abu Baker before he could depart,"[89] said

Alyza Lewin. Furthermore, when the Justice Department eventually prosecuted Mohammed Salah on various counts, including conspiring to support Hamas, the jury acquitted him of every count except one: a charge of obstruction of justice for lying under oath in written answers he provided in the *Boim* lawsuit.[90] Salah was sentenced to serve twenty-one months in prison for his obstruction of justice in the *Boim* case.[91]

The *Boim* lawsuit has also contributed significantly to more broadly deterring fundraising for terrorist groups. According to Stephen Landes, who joined the Lewins as the chief trial lawyer on the Boim family legal team, a major "purpose [of the suit] was to dry up money going to terrorist organizations."[92] In finding for the Boims, the court "sent a message to every potential contributor to an organization that engages in terrorism that he or she can be sued for millions of dollars," said Nathan Lewin.[93]

The *Boim* case precedent has driven a number of subsequent lawsuits. Posner's vivid analogy between "giving money to Hamas" and "giving a loaded gun to a child," and the legal reasoning that accompanied it, "rippled through the court system."[94] "Upon that single sentence much recent case law has been premised," noted Lanier Saperstein, an attorney defending the Bank of China against terrorism finance allegations in *Wultz v. Bank of China*, a case described at length in Chapter 8.[95]

2. Holding Bankers Liable for Hamas Terrorist Acts: Linde v. Arab Bank

As of summer 2015, the single most important case to build on the *Boim* precedent was the case of *Linde v. Arab Bank*. While the *Boim* case had established that donors to a terrorist group could be held liable for the group's terrorist acts, *Linde v. Arab Bank* took the principle a step further, by establishing that providers of financial services to a terrorist group could be held liable for the group's terrorist acts.

On September 22, 2014, a federal jury in *Linde v. Arab Bank* found Arab Bank PLC liable for damages suffered by victims and family members of victims killed or injured in twenty-four terrorist attacks by Hamas and similar terrorist organizations (Hamas).[96] The *Linde* jury found Arab Bank liable principally on the grounds that the Bank had knowingly provided Hamas with material support in the form of financial services.[97] On April 8, 2015, district court judge Brian Cogan dismissed claims against Arab Bank arising from two of the attacks, but found "ample" evidence to support the rest of the verdict.[98] A separate trial was planned for determining the amount of damages owed by the Bank to the victims and their families as a result of the remaining twenty-two of the twenty-four terror attacks.[99]

The damages trial was scheduled for mid-August 2015.[100] Legal experts surveyed by the *New York Times* in September 2014 suggested that in the damages trial, Arab Bank "may be asked to pay a judgment near or exceeding $1 billion."[101] The September 2014 verdict finding Arab Bank liable is a "message that should be understood and heard by the entire financial community—if you do business with terrorists, you can be held liable" in the United States, said Michael Elsner, an attorney for the plaintiffs.[102]

The attacks for which Arab Bank was found liable had occurred in Israel, Gaza, and the West Bank from 2001 to 2004.[103] Those attacks included the March 27, 2002, suicide attack on a Passover Seder at the Park Hotel in Netanya, Israel, which killed thirty people and wounded one hundred more.[104] They also included the August 9, 2001, suicide bombing of the Sbarro pizzeria in Jerusalem, Israel, which killed or injured 130 people.[105]

Linde v. Arab Bank was the first civil trial of a bank under the ATA, "making the verdict a potential industry landmark."[106] The plaintiffs had specifically alleged that Arab Bank had knowingly provided banking services for Hamas and Hamas operatives, laundered funds for Hamas and its front organizations, and facilitated payments to families of martyred Hamas suicide bombers.[107] The plaintiffs alleged that as of November 2001, Hamas funders had "paid millions of dollars to suicide bombers or their beneficiaries through Arab Bank" and Arab Bank had also "transmitted millions of dollars" to "terrorists or their fronts."[108] Arieh Spitzen, the former head of the Israeli military's Department of Palestinian Affairs, testified before the jury in August 2014 that Arab Bank had from 2000 to 2001 alone transferred about $4 million to Hamas through the Bank's New York Branch.[109]

The *Linde* court relied heavily on Judge Posner's *Boim* decision interpreting the ATA. Judge Cogan quoted Judge Posner's statement that "[g]iving money to Hamas, like giving a loaded gun to a child (which also is not a violent act), is an 'act dangerous to human life.'"[110] Judge Cogan also determined that "Defendant's suggestion that knowingly providing financial services should be treated differently than knowingly donating money is unpersuasive; such financial services increase Hamas' ability to carry out attacks in the same way, and Congress made no distinction between these different forms of material support in criminalizing them."[111]

In Judge Cogan's jury instructions, he required plaintiffs "to prove that Arab Bank 'knowingly' provided banking services to Hamas or Hamas-controlled organizations."[112] The judge instructed the jury that, in deciding whether Arab Bank acted "knowingly," they could consider evidence related to "defendant's policies and procedures, and banking industry standards and practices."[113]

Arab Bank's attorneys had argued that the plaintiffs must prove that the financial services Arab Bank provided to Hamas were used directly to perpetrate the terrorist attacks causing plaintiffs' injuries.[114] But Judge Cogan rejected that test in favor of a less restrictive causation threshold. Judge Cogan instructed the jury that Arab Bank was liable if the plaintiffs could prove that Arab Bank's material support for the terrorists was "a substantial factor in the sequence of events responsible for causing plaintiffs' injuries and that plaintiffs' injuries were reasonably foreseeable or anticipated as a natural consequence of such acts."[115] Judge Cogan added that "plaintiffs are not required to prove that defendant's alleged unlawful acts were the sole cause of their injuries; nor do plaintiffs need to eliminate all other possible causes of injury."[116] "It is enough," instructed Judge Cogan, "if plaintiffs have proved that defendant's acts substantially contributed to their injury, even though other factors may have also significantly contributed as well."[117]

In his *Linde* case Memorandum and Order of April 8, 2015, Judge Cogan further elaborated on the causation threshold and the court's rejection of "defendant's argument that plaintiffs were required to trace specific dollars to specific terrorist attacks."[118] The judge asserted that "requiring 'but for' causation would effectively annul the civil liability provisions of the ATA," which "cannot have been the intent of Congress in enacting them."[119]

Judge Cogan explained that his less restrictive causation threshold was consistent with the Seventh Circuit's opinion in the *Boim* case and the Supreme Court's opinion in an unrelated case, *Holder v. Humanitarian Law Project*. The judge quoted the Supreme Court's statement in the latter case that foreign terrorist organizations "are so tainted by their criminal conduct that any contribution to such an organization facilitates that conduct."[120]

The lead plaintiffs' attorney in *Linde v. Arab Bank* was Gary Osen, head of a six-lawyer firm based in Hackensack, New Jersey. The case grew to encompass the consolidated claims of dozens of victims and family members of victims of the twenty-four terror attacks, represented by a coalition of attorneys from small firms across the United States, including Tab Turner, an Arkansas products liability lawyer; Mark Elsner of South Carolina-based Motley Rice, previously best known for tobacco and asbestos litigation; and Dallas attorney Mark Werbner.[121] "Gary's a blue-collar lawyer after my own heart, not one of these boys in the gleaming corporate offices," said Turner.[122]

Arab Bank was a massive target. As of March 2015, it had over six hundred branches in thirty countries.[123] It also had $35 billion in deposits and reported $577.2 million in profits for 2014.[124] Arab Bank drew on its resources to mount an aggressive defense, hiring public relations consultants,[125] a former senior U.S. diplomat,[126] one of the United States' most-credentialed attorneys, and the world's second largest law firm, to defend itself against the motley coalition of plaintiffs' attorneys.

For example, the Bank hired Paul Clement, who had served as solicitor general in the George W. Bush Administration.[127] The Bank at one point had seventeen attorneys working on the case at the top-tier New York law firm of Dewey & LeBoeuf.[128] In mid-2012, Arab Bank asserted that its legal team had compiled "nearly 1 million pages of documents, expert reports, and exhibits as well as 1,000 hours of depositions" that were, at the time, contained in both electronic files and in hundreds of boxes housed at Dewey & LeBoeuf.[129] As of spring 2015, Arab

Bank's lead law firm on the case was DLA Piper, which—with 1,250 partners, 3,700 lawyers, 80 offices around the globe, and $2.48 billion in revenue—was the world's second largest law firm by revenue and had an average profit per equity partner of $1.49 million.[130]

The first of the several related cases that make up the Arab Bank litigation had been filed in July 2004, more than ten years before the September 2014 jury verdict.[131] During the decade the case took to get to trial, Arab Bank attempted various maneuvers to hinder the case against it. For example, Arab Bank refused to produce banking records which the trial judge ordered it to produce.[132] Then it mounted a large-scale campaign to get the executive branch to intervene and ask the Supreme Court to overturn sanctions which the trial judge imposed in response to the refusal to produce the records.[133] The campaign reportedly resulted in a split, pitting the State Department, which wanted the executive branch to intervene, against the Treasury and Justice Departments, which opposed intervention.[134]

In making its case for intervention, Arab Bank introduced broad policy arguments, warning that the case "threaten[ed] the ruin of the single most important financial institution in the Palestinian territories and Jordan if not the entire Middle East."[135] The Kingdom of Jordan, a key U.S. ally in which the Bank is headquartered, asserted that the trial risked "destabilizing the economies of Jordan and surrounding countries" and posed for Jordan "a very real and grave threat to its economic stability and prosperity."[136]

Edward Gnehm, a former U.S. ambassador to Jordan, wrote an op-ed, identifying himself as "a consultant to Arab Bank," in which he asserted that a verdict against Arab Bank would be "a major diplomatic catastrophe" with an "impact on Jordan's economy" that could be "bigger than that of the 2009 financial crisis on the United States."[137] Gnehm warned that "American trial lawyers and private lawsuits must not be allowed to trump U.S. global interests."[138] "The Supreme Court," said Gnehm, "should not let this disaster develop any further."[139]

However, the executive branch chose not to request the Supreme Court's intervention,[140] and the Supreme Court declined to intervene.[141] Notwithstanding the *Linde* court's September 2014 verdict, Arab Bank reported in February 2015 that its profits had grown by 15 percent during 2014 (to $577.2 million) and its customer deposits had grown by 2 percent (to reach $35 billion).[142]

The *Linde* suit settled in mid-August 2015 (as this book went to press), reportedly for around $1 billion. The plaintiffs had triumphed over a well-funded and sophisticated opponent. As discussed above, the *Linde* litigation benefited in part from the *Boim* precedent, a strong factual case, creative lawyering, and the executive branch's decision to refrain from intervening.

The *Linde* litigation also benefited from the periodic affirmative assistance of the Israeli and U.S. governments. For example, the *Linde* lawsuit was reportedly spurred in part by documents the Israeli military seized during Operation Defensive Shield in 2002.[143] According to Paul McGeough, in his book about

Hamas, "when Operation Defensive Shield was unleashed across the West Bank in 2002, special orders were issued for Israeli troops to raid the paper and electronic archives of the Palestinian Authority's security services and departments, of local charities and of any of the Palestinians' factional offices."[144] At the time, Arab Bank had twenty-two branches in the West Bank and Gaza Strip, making it the leading bank for Palestinian transactions.[145] "The documents showed," says Nitsana Darshan-Leitner, that foreign "charities were raising millions of dollars for Hamas and for the families of the martyrs (that is, suicide bombers), and were transferring the money to the Gaza Strip and the West Bank via the Arab Bank and other banks."[146]

As described in Chapter 8, documents seized by Israel during those 2002 raids were explicitly used as evidence in the United States' criminal prosecution of the Holy Land Foundation and five individuals for providing material support to Hamas.[147] The prosecutions resulted in lengthy jail terms for Foundation leaders, contributed to the Foundation's closure, and helped considerably reduce Hamas fundraising in the United States.[148]

While the decision to bring the *Linde* lawsuit was spurred in part by the seized Israeli documents, the lawsuit benefited directly from the U.S. executive branch's own actions against Arab Bank. In an interesting example of the interplay between public and private lawfare, those U.S. executive branch actions against Arab Bank had themselves been spurred by an earlier stage of the *Linde* litigation. According to Steve Perles, who served as counsel for about half of the U.S. victims and their families whose cases had been folded into the *Linde* litigation, "the filing of these cases led to the U.S. Office of the Comptroller of the Currency (OCC) investigating the Bank in 2004."[149] In addition, Gary Osen shared with U.S. government investigators some of the evidence he had gathered as part of his research for the lawsuit.[150]

The investigation of Arab Bank by the OCC and by the U.S. Treasury Department's Financial Crimes Enforcement Network (FINCEN) led in 2005 to the United States assessing a $24 million penalty against the Bank for failure to implement an adequate anti-money-laundering program and for violating U.S. legal requirements to report suspicious activities.[151] The OCC also ordered Arab Bank's New York branch to shut down its wire transfer operations and restrict itself to very limited banking activities.[152]

The OCC's Acting Comptroller testified before Congress that the OCC took these steps to restrict Arab Bank operations in the United States because an OCC "review disclosed that the branch had handled hundreds of suspicious wire transactions involving individuals and entities with the same or similar names as suspected terrorists and terrorist organizations and that many of these individual and entities were customers of Arab Bank or its affiliates."[153] The *Linde* court allowed the plaintiffs to reference these enforcement actions for the purpose of countering Arab Bank touting the strength of its anti-money-laundering compliance procedures.[154]

Although the *Linde* plaintiffs' argument to the jury included numerous references to banking terminology and legal precedents, it closed on an emotional note. Gary Osen, the lead plaintiffs' attorney, reminded jurors of a witness they had heard at the beginning of the trial, a U.S. man paralyzed in a Hamas bus bombing, whose testimony was shown on video because he had died in 2010 from complications of his injuries.[155] The victim, Steve Averbach, "hoped that this lawsuit would do some good, that it would help stop this process of paying the families of suicide bombers," Osen told jurors.[156] "And all of my colleagues here worked for the last 10 years to hold these people accountable. But in the end, Steve couldn't do the job and we can't do the job. You, and you alone, can finish the job Steve started."[157]

The *Linde* jurors held Arab Bank accountable. Following the case's large settlement in August 2015, it is likely to become a very powerful weapon against terrorists. As discussed in detail in Chapter 3, several of Europe's largest banks, which dwarf the Arab Bank in assets, have already run afoul of U.S. laws restricting business with Iran and other countries designated by the United States as state sponsors of terrorism. These include HSBC, which agreed in December 2012 to pay $1.9 billion in fines to the U.S. government, and Standard Chartered, which that same month agreed to pay $667 million in fines to the U.S. and New York state governments.

As of March 2015, Gary Osen was moving forward with lawsuits that would "piggyback" on these U.S. sanctions actions in a manner analogous to the way the *Linde* case piggybacked on the OCC and FINCEN sanctions against Arab Bank.[158] For example, on November 11, 2014, a few weeks after the *Linde* jury ruled against Arab Bank, Osen filed an ATA suit in federal court against HSBC, Standard Chartered, and three other European banks already sanctioned by the U.S. government, on behalf of relatives of U.S. civilians and soldiers who died in Iraq as a result of attacks linked to Iranian-backed militias and terrorist groups.[159] Osen's filing includes numerous examples of how the defendant banks sought to hide their dealings with Iran, examples drawn from the U.S. government's published reports about the banks' misdeeds.[160]

Osen's filing even includes the infamous statement which the N.Y. State Department of Financial Services reported was made by a Standard Chartered executive in Europe: "You f—ing Americans. Who are you to tell us, the rest of the world, that we're not going to deal with Iranians."[161] According to a reporter who covered the filing, Osen intends to be one of those Americans.[162]

3. Sokolow v. PLO *Holds the PLO Liable for Terrorist Acts (and Poses a Dilemma)*

In February 2015, a federal jury in New York found the PA and the PLO liable under the ATA for six terrorist acts in Israel between January 2001 and January

2004,[163] and awarded $218.5 million in damages to the American victims' families.[164] The ATA automatically tripled the award to $655.5 million.[165] The terrorist attacks at the heart of the *Sokolow v. PLO* case had killed a total of 33 people and injured more than 450.[166] The attacks had occurred at a bus stop, inside a bus, on a crowded street, and in a cafeteria on the campus of Hebrew University.[167]

The *Sokolow* plaintiffs asserted that "many of those involved in the planning and carrying out of the attacks had been employees of the Palestinian Authority, and that the authority had paid salaries to terrorists imprisoned in Israel and had made martyr payments to the families of suicide bombers."[168] Although the Israeli government emphasized that it had no involvement in the case,[169] documents seized by Israel during Operation Defensive Shield in 2002 played a role in informing the *Sokolow* litigation. For example, the *Sokolow* plaintiffs submitted to the court exhibits extensively quoting from Palestinian documents seized by Israel.[170] After the *Sokolow* verdict, PLO executive committee member Hanan Ashrawi complained of the "theft [by Israel] of the Palestinian documents used by the court."[171]

The *Sokolow* case was not the first ATA case involving the PLO and PA. Following enactment of the ATA, several suits pursuant to it moved forward through the U.S. court system against the PLO and PA. For example, the family of Aharon Ellis, a U.S. citizen killed in 2002 by a Palestinian attack on a bat mitzvah reception in Hadera, Israel, sued the PA and PLO under the ATA.[172] The PLO and PA ultimately decided to settle the case by paying an undisclosed sum to the plaintiffs.[173] However, the *Sokolow* case's timing and magnitude make it the most important such case as this book goes to press.

The *Sokolow* case is interesting and significant from a legal perspective. However, it is even more interesting and significant from a policy perspective. As the rest of this subsection will delineate, *Sokolow* provides an exceptional case study of the various, often cross-cutting, and sometimes unintended ways in which a private civil lawfare lawsuit can have policy consequences.

By demonstrating that the PA and PLO under Yasser Arafat had continued to sponsor terrorism, even after signing the Oslo Accords with Israel, the *Sokolow* verdict was "a setback for the Palestinians' image as they seek to rally international support for their independence and to push for war crime charges against Israel."[174] In addition, the *Sokolow* case generated, and put the U.S. court system's stamp of approval on, evidence that could potentially be used against some PA officials in an ICC proceeding.[175] This had particular significance at a time when the PA had joined the ICC and was threatening to take additional lawfare steps against Israel both at the ICC and elsewhere. Yonah Jeremy Bob, the *Jerusalem Post*'s legal affairs correspondent, suggested that by making it clear that "the PA is not coming with clean hands," the *Sokolow* verdict could both discourage the ICC from opening an investigation into the situation in Palestine and discourage the PA from pressing the ICC to do so.[176]

For Shurat HaDin, which says its mission is using "court systems around the world to go on the legal offensive against Israel's enemies,"[177] the *Sokolow* case, in which it played a role, was a useful reminder to those using lawfare against Israel that lawfare is a weapon that can be used by both sides to a conflict.[178]

The same lesson was not, however, lost on leading Palestinians, some of whom asserted that the Palestinian cause's loss in the relatively unfavorable U.S. court system should be responded to with additional and more vigorous litigation in more favorable forums. PLO executive committee member Hanan Ashrawi responded to the *Sokolow* verdict by saying that it highlights the need for the PA to turn to the ICC.[179] Hafez Al-Barghouti, a columnist for the official PA daily, suggested that just as "the Israeli-American Jews played in the American court, which leans in their favor," the Palestinians should "not rely on any American court" but rather "turn to courts in other countries."[180] Issa Karake, Director of the Palestinian Commission of Prisoners' Affairs, similarly responded to the *Sokolow* verdict with a call for escalating the PA's lawfare, stating, "it is fitting that we start suing Israeli officers, soldiers and officials in the courts of countries whose laws allow for it, and that we hurry to turn to the International Criminal Court in order to sue the occupation army and its commanders for the war crimes they perpetrated and continue to perpetrate against our people."[181]

In the kinetic warfare literature, analysts sometimes refer to the concept of "escalation dominance." Herman Kahn defined escalation dominance as "a capacity, other things being equal, to enable the side possessing it to enjoy marked advantages in a given region of the escalation ladder."[182] In Kahn's work, "escalation dominance allows one side to triumph because its rival cannot risk taking the next step on the ladder."[183]

The Palestinian response to the *Sokolow* case reflects that in lawfare, it is also useful to think about which side would be in a better position should escalation occur. Factors affecting the answer at a particular level of escalation can include: which side has the capacity to inflict greater costs on the other at that level, how much it costs each side to inflict costs and defend (to the extent they can) against attacks at that level, what is the impact on domestic support of conflict at that level, and which side would benefit more from escalation to the next level.[184]

However, in lawfare, in contrast with traditional kinetic warfare, there is a very important additional variable in the escalation calculus. Control over lawfare escalation can reside—and in the case of civil litigation lawfare usually does reside—in the hands of non-state organizations or even individuals.

As Yishai Schwartz noted in an article commenting on the *Sokolow* verdict, Palestinian officials have ample reason to believe that lawfare escalation might work in their favor. "In most international fora," as well as in domestic courts in Europe and most other countries, "Palestinians hold a significant set of advantages," said Schwartz.[185] Specifically, "Palestinians are generally seen as victims of a much stronger Israeli state," thereby enjoying "widespread sympathy" with "concrete results—in the kinds of cases prosecutors are tempted to bring, in the verdicts that are likely to be delivered, and for the likelihood that national governments will insert themselves."[186]

"Beyond these structural factors," said Schwartz, "there is growing danger that Israeli *policy itself* . . . faces the prospect of international criminalization."[187] In particular, "in an international legal context where any and all Jewish building beyond the 1948 armistice lines have come to be considered criminal violations (rather than simply contentious or controversial policy), Israel finds itself vulnerable to prosecution for *admitted* activities in a way that Palestinians simply are not."[188]

The risks of harm that Israel might suffer directly as a result of lawfare escalation may be sufficient in and of themselves to give Israel an interest in avoiding such escalation. However, Israel's interest in avoiding lawfare escalation is further increased by the limits placed on Israeli offensive lawfare by Israel's strong interest in not bringing down the PA.

As of summer 2015, Mahmoud Abbas's PA was manifestly better for Israeli interests than Hamas, the likely alternative. As the evidence in the *Sokolow* case demonstrates, the PA and PLO between 2001 and 2004, under Yasser Arafat's leadership, continued to sponsor terrorism, despite signing the Oslo Accords with Israel. However, the PA (and to a considerable degree the PLO) took a different approach after Mahmoud Abbas came to power in 2005—so much so that the head of Israel's Shin Bet general security service said in November 2014 that Abbas "is not interested in terror and is not leading towards terror . . . . He is also not doing that under the table."[189] Jonathan Schanzer, a leading author on Palestinian politics who has been critical of Abbas on other issues, asserted in February 2015 that, "to his full credit, after coming to power in 2005, Palestinian leader Mahmoud Abbas reined in the violent groups responsible for terrorism . . . and he has since upheld this policy of nonviolence, earning him the backing of Israel and the United States as a partner for peace."[190]

With the PA in perilous political and financial straits, it was far from clear, at least in the summer of 2015, that the cause of fighting terrorism would, on balance, be served by removing from the PA's coffers the $655.5 million *Sokolow* award. Israel clearly had qualms about emptying the PA's coffers. On March 27, 2015, Israel announced that it was releasing to the PA the four months' worth of PA tax revenue (about $130 million per month) that Israel had withheld in response to the PA's accession to the ICC.[191] Israel reportedly released the more than $500 million in PA tax revenue at the recommendation of Israel's security establishment, which warned that withholding the revenue was "endangering Israel's own well-being" by undermining the PA.[192] The $655.5 million award is comparable in size to the amount of money that Israel transferred to the PA in order to keep the PA from collapsing. Indeed, it would be the equivalent of some 20 percent of the PA's annual budget.[193] It would also be of a similar magnitude to the $450 million or so per year that the U.S. government was providing to help prop up the PA.[194]

Collection of the *Sokolow* award thus risked facilitating the PA's replacement by the far more radical and violent Hamas. Punishing the PA for terrorism committed prior to its decade of commitment to nonviolence also risked sending a counterproductive message as to the virtue of renouncing violence.

In light of the risks to Israel of lawfare escalation and the PA's collapse, it stands to reason that if the State of Israel had been the *Sokolow* plaintiff in the spring of 2015, it might have chosen to use the verdict's powerful financial leverage over the PA and PLO to extract a PA commitment to not proceed with a State Party referral to the ICC of the situation in Palestine. As discussed in Chapter 5, without such a referral by the PA, the ICC prosecutor would be highly unlikely to open a formal investigation of alleged Israeli war crimes.

The PA and PLO would likely have been open to a settlement, as the PA had assets in the United States and had settled two previous cases.[195] Reuters reporter Alison Frankel noted that "lawyers for victims who have previously obtained default judgments against the Palestinian Authority were successful enough at disrupting" the PA's finances that the PA "quietly settled both cases."[196] Dr. Nasser Abd Al-Karim, a Palestinian economic expert, said that if the PA does not pay, the judgment "will represent a liability for it, and it may encounter difficulties in performing financial transactions and transfers, or in opening bank accounts in the international banking system."[197]

However, the State of Israel was not the *Sokolow* plaintiff, and thus it did not have formal control (and quite possibly not informal control) over the *Sokolow* litigation. Instead, the formal control over this powerful lawfare weapon—so potentially valuable to the State of Israel in its conflict with the PA—resided in the hands of the victims' families and their attorneys. In the *Bank of China* case discussed in Chapter 8, the difference in interests between the government of Israel and plaintiffs which it had explicitly encouraged resulted in considerable acrimony and significant policy problems, including with regard to Israel's strategically important relationship with China.

The U.S. executive branch also retained a degree of influence over the case (in its ability to file with regard to some aspects a statement of interest, to which U.S. federal courts traditionally give considerable but not complete deference).[198] However, in light of the antagonism between President Obama and Prime Minister Netanyahu, it was not clear to what extent the U.S. government would coordinate with Israel or take into account its preferences regarding filing a statement of interest in this case regarding U.S. citizens killed in terrorist attacks on Israeli soil.

The complexity of the United States' and Israel's relationships with the PA requires skillful diplomacy, including the creative deployment and constant recalibration of pressure and encouragement, firmness and concessions, incentives and disincentives.[199] "Private lawsuits, however, are the polar opposite of this kind of diplomacy," said Yishai Schwartz.[200] Civil lawsuits are "initiated in the service of private interests and are adjudicated according to abstract legal principles."[201] "Political exigencies and budgetary realities—for instance, whether the PA is critical for regional stability or whether it is close to broke—are simply irrelevant to the law," said Schwartz, who expressed concern that civil litigation is therefore a "dangerous tool."[202]

B. The Terrorism Exception to the Foreign Sovereign Immunities Act

U.S. courts have long provided that foreign governments are generally immune from being sued in the United States.[203] The Foreign Sovereign Immunities Act of 1976 (FSIA) codified the law of foreign sovereign immunity and provided for exceptions to it. The Antiterrorism and Effective Death Penalty Act of 1996 (AEDPA) then amended the FSIA to create a special exception to sovereign immunity for countries on the State Department's list of state sponsors of terrorism.[204]

Following additional amendment, the terrorism exception to the FSIA currently provides in relevant part that a foreign state designated as a state sponsor of terrorism shall not be immune from the jurisdiction of U.S. courts in cases in which "money damages are sought against a foreign state for personal injury or death that was caused by an act of torture, extrajudicial killing, aircraft sabotage, hostage taking, or the provision of material support or resources for such an act."[205] *Flatow v. Islamic Republic of Iran* was the first U.S. court case to be decided against Iran under the state sponsor of terrorism exception.[206]

1. Holding Iran Liable for Palestinian Terrorism: Flatow v. Islamic Republic of Iran

Alisa Flatow was a 20-year-old American student murdered in the April 9, 1995, bombing of an Israeli bus.[207] The Shaqaqi faction of the Palestinian Islamic Jihad Organization (PIJ) claimed credit for the attack.[208] The PIJ was funded entirely by Iran.[209]

Stephen Flatow, Alisa's father, had been a title insurance attorney in New Jersey.[210] "I decided I would sue Iran out of the terrorism business," said Flatow.[211] Over the course of the coming years, Flatow played a key role in first changing U.S. law to remove Iran's foreign sovereign immunity, then further amending the law to create a cause of action and enable the award of punitive damages. Finally, he successfully sued pursuant to the law he had helped create.

Flatow's principal partner in much of this work was Steven Perles, a D.C.-based attorney. Flatow first reached out to Perles the day after Alisa's funeral.[212] Flatow had read about Perles' successful effort to extract reparations from Germany for Hugo Princz, a Holocaust survivor to whom Germany had denied compensation because Princz was not a German citizen or a refugee but rather a U.S. citizen during his time in Auschwitz.[213] "Stephen Flatow phoned me and said: 'will you do for Alisa to Iran what you did for Hugo Princz to the Germans?'" recounted Perles.[214]

Prior to becoming a litigator, Perles had worked for six years as legal counsel for a U.S. senator. Perles understood both how to sue pursuant to existing federal law and how to amend federal law to facilitate new avenues or types of litigation. By spring 2015, Perles had become the leading private civil litigator against terrorists, their material supporters, and their state sponsors. According to Perles, he had, as of May 2015, collected over $500 million dollars on behalf of the terrorism victim clients and cases on which he had worked.[215]

The first such case for Perles was *Flatow*. Perles and Flatow began by persuading Congress to amend the terrorism exception to create subject matter jurisdiction for lawsuits against state sponsors of terrorism.[216] Then they persuaded Congress to pass another amendment—commonly known as "the Flatow Amendment"[217]—which created a federal cause of action and enabled the award of punitive damages.[218]

The changes to U.S. law facilitated Flatow and Perles bringing a lawsuit for Alisa's death against the Islamic Republic of Iran, the Iranian Ministry of Information and Security (MOIS), and three Iranian leaders.[219] The leaders were Ayatollah Ali Khamenei (who has served as Iran's Supreme Leader since 1989), Ali Akbar Hashemi Rafsanjani (Iran's President at the time of the bombing), and Ali Fallahian-Khuzestani (who served as Iran's Intelligence Minister at the time of the bombing).[220]

Collecting evidence for the case was, at times, a challenge. Alisa Flatow had been killed in Gaza. "The Palestinian security service refused to cooperate with the FBI and provide any information on those who killed Alisa," said Stephen Flatow.[221] According to Perles, President Clinton "sent a team of about a dozen FBI agents to Gaza to collect evidence and do an investigation."[222] Once the team arrived, said Perles, "Yasser Arafat said I'm not letting any American forensic team into my country."[223] "The agents called the State Department for instructions and the Department said 'we have to honor Mr. Arafat's edict so come home'," recalls Perles.[224] "That didn't sit well with me, so I go to the Attorney General of Israel and say I'd like to send a team to Gaza," said Perles.[225] "He said 'that sounds like a great idea to me, I'll be sure you will get escorted in, we have much bigger guns than the Palestinians do, your guys will be fine,'" recalls Perles.[226]

"So I sent people in to take depositions and gather evidence," said Perles.[227] "The single most important piece of evidence we found—as we went door to door—was a guy who had happened to be sitting in a parked car less than one hundred yards from the bombsite, trying out a new camcorder."[228] "The bomb went off, he headed over, and he recorded everything that happened starting about twenty seconds after the bomb went off," said Perles.[229] "That was very important for the U.S. intelligence community and the FBI and the Israeli intelligence community because terrorists like PIJ send intelligence gatherers into the crowd after the bombing to look at how their operation went, to write their after-action reports," said Perles.[230] "If you can do name-face recognitions on the crowd and you see who is there, it will help you figure out who really detonated the bomb."[231] "So in this case PIJ took credit but name-face recognition helped the U.S. intelligence community confirm that PIJ indeed detonated that bomb," said Perles.[232]

In the courtroom, Perles was joined by Thomas Fortune Fay, one of Washington, D.C.'s most effective courtroom advocates.[233] Together, the plaintiffs' attorneys presented evidence that the PIJ had perpetrated the attack and that the PIJ had received from Iran about $2 million annually, which was all of the PIJ's funding.[234]

Royce Lamberth, the U.S. district court judge assigned to the case, concluded that Iran had provided "material support and resources" to PIJ through the MOIS with the approval of the individual defendants.[235] Judge Lamberth held that "Alisa Michelle Flatow's death was caused by a willful and deliberate act of extrajudicial killing" by the PIJ "acting under the direction of Defendants the Islamic Republic of Iran, the Iranian Ministry of Information and Security, Ayatollah Ali Hoseini Khamenei, Ali Akbar Hashemi-Rafsanjani and Ali Fallahian-Khuzestani."[236]

Further, Judge Lamberth determined that "Defendant Ayatollah Ali Hoseini Khamenei performed acts . . . which caused the death of Alisa Michelle Flatow" when he "approved the provision of material support and resources to the Shaqaqi faction of Palestine Islamic Jihad."[237] The court awarded the Flatow family $22.5 million in compensatory damages and $225 million in punitive damages.[238]

Judge Lamberth set the amount of punitive damages at $225 million based on testimony by expert witness Dr. Patrick Clawson that Iran was spending approximately $75 million per year in support of terrorist activities.[239] The judge explained that since the purpose of the terrorism exception to the FSIA "is to deter acts of terrorism which result in the death or personal injury of United States nationals . . . an award of punitive damages in the amount of three times the Islamic Republic of Iran's annual expenditure for terrorist activities is appropriate."[240]

The Flatow family ultimately collected $26 million, as a result of a provision of the Victims of Trafficking and Violence Protection Act of 2000.[241] The provision required the U.S. government to front to Flatow and other victim families $400 million out of U.S. Treasury Department funds, the $400 million amount selected to match the balance of one of the frozen Iranian accounts in the United States.[242] According to *Washington Post* reporter Neely Tucker, the provision was controversial because the $400 million frozen Iranian account does not clearly belong to the United States.[243]

Thus, wrote Tucker, either the United States government or Iran might eventually receive the frozen $400 million.[244] Tucker asserts that if the latter occurs, the result will be that "U.S. taxpayers paid one of the most generous terrorism victim judgments in history—on behalf of Iran, for sponsoring Islamic Jihad."[245] According to Mike Kelly's superb book about the *Flatow* case and a similar subsequent case (*Eisenfeld v. Islamic Republic of Iran*[246]), as of 2014, "the equivalent of a lien had been placed on the Iranian fund—to be negotiated at some point in the future."[247] According to Steve Perles, Flatow received from Jack Lew, who implemented the compensation process in the final days of the Clinton administration, "a personal commitment from Jack Lew that the funds he was being paid were being paid from the Iranian blocked assets and that no taxpayer funds were implicated," and "that is the condition under which he [Flatow] agreed to accept the money."[248]

Notwithstanding the challenges of collecting on the award, the *Flatow* case facts and precedent paved the way for many subsequent cases. For example, according to the *New York Times*, a filing in the *Flatow* case caused the investigation that led to the fines and forfeitures—described in Chapter 2—of $350 million against Lloyds TSB Bank, $536 million against Credit Suisse, and ultimately $8.9 billion against BNP Paribas, for providing financial services to Iran and other state sponsors of terrorism.[249] "The trail that ultimately led to BNP began in 2006," said the *Times*, "when the Manhattan district attorney's office came upon" the civil lawsuit filed by Stephen Flatow against Iran.[250] "Buried in the court filings, prosecutors found a stunning accusation: a charity that owned a gleaming office tower on Fifth Avenue was actually a 'front' for the Iranian government, a claim that the prosecutors later verified."[251]

Following up on Stephen Flatow's accusation, the prosecutors discovered that money was being illicitly transferred between the front, named the Alavi Foundation, and the Iranian government via Lloyds and Credit Suisse, which "stripped out the Iranian clients' names from wire transfers" to and from the Alavi Foundation.[252] The Lloyds and Credit Suisse cases soon triggered the BNP Paribas case.[253] "The fact that our case laid the groundwork for these actions is really a tribute to Alisa," said Stephen Flatow.[254]

The Justice Department ultimately reached a settlement agreement that "forced the Alavi Foundation to forfeit its holdings" in the office tower at 650 Fifth Avenue.[255] "When the government sells the building, the proceeds will flow to the families and estates of victims of terrorism," a nod to the *Flatow* lawsuit's critical role in drawing attention to Iran's ownership of the building just steps from Rockefeller Center.[256] The building is expected to sell for some $800 million.[257] According to Perles, having "already satisfied the Flatow judgment," he is working to channel the office tower proceeds to pay off outstanding judgments held by Marines killed or injured in the Marine Barracks bombing.[258]

In addition to the *Flatow* case's role in spurring the bank investigations, numerous subsequent lawsuits have built on the legal precedent set by the *Flatow* case. In these various cases pursuant to the FSIA terrorism exception, U.S. courts have determined, as they have with ATA cases, that a plaintiff need not establish that the material support or resources provided by a foreign state contributed directly to the terrorist act. Instead, "sponsorship of a terrorist group which causes personal injury or death of a United States national alone is sufficient to invoke jurisdiction."[259]

In addition to victims of Iranian-sponsored terrorism, victims of Cuba, Iraq, Libya, and Syria—all for many years designated as state sponsors of terrorism—have also taken advantage of the exception to the FSIA. Most notably, the families of the victims of the 1988 bombing of Pan Am Flight 103 over Lockerbie, Scotland, and of the 1986 bombing of the La Belle discotheque in Germany ultimately jointly collected $1.5 billion from Libya as a result of their lawsuits against it.[260] Separately, three families of Brothers to the Rescue pilots shot down by the Cuban Air Force won a $187.6 million judgment against Cuba[261]—which they collected on by seizing $96.7 million in Cuban assets in the United States.[262]

In addition, the families of Olin Armstrong and Jack Hensley, two U.S. government contractors who were beheaded by Al Qaeda in Iraq, collected $80 million after winning a judgment against the Syrian government in a case titled *Gates v. Syrian Arab Republic* (Gates was the last name of the lead plaintiff, Armstrong's mother).[263] The Syrian government was found to have provided material support to Al Qaeda in Iraq and to Abu Mus'ab al-Zarqawi, who was videotaped decapitating the victims.[264] Collection of this judgment was facilitated by the Terrorism Risk Insurance Act (TRIA),[265] a U.S. statute that enables judgments for acts of terrorism to be collected against assets of state sponsors of terrorism that have been frozen in the United States.[266]

At the trial stage of *Gates v. Syrian Arab Republic*, the U.S. Department of Defense took the unusual step of providing as expert witnesses, testifying via secure video link, military pathologists who had performed autopsies on the two victims.[267] According to Steve Perles, who represented the plaintiffs, "every federal judge knows that DOD rarely makes expert witnesses available like that; when a judge sees DOD choosing to cooperate like that it sends an implicit but clear message to the judge that DOD wants the terrorist state punished."[268]

Notwithstanding these federal court judgments and the executive branch's occasional assistance to plaintiffs, the state sponsor of terrorism exception to the FSIA has met with considerable criticism. For example, the *Washington Post* editorial board in 1999 opined that "Congress never should have passed, nor President Clinton signed, a law that could only offer Mr. Flatow justice by depriving the administration of control over important instruments of foreign policy."[269] In 2003, during the George W. Bush administration, William H. Taft IV, the State Department Legal Adviser, said in Senate testimony that "the current litigation-based system of compensation is inequitable, unpredictable, occasionally costly to the U.S. taxpayer and damaging to foreign policy and national security goals of this country."[270]

Royce Lamberth, the U.S. district court judge who wrote the *Flatow* opinion and has presided over many of the subsequent state-sponsored terrorism cases against Iran, has himself expressed concern. Judge Lamberth did so in great detail in an unusually wide-ranging opinion in 2009, in which he "respectfully urge[d] the President and Congress to seek meaningful reforms in this area of law in the form of a viable alternative to private litigation as the means of redress for the countless deaths and injuries caused by acts of terrorism."[271]

Judge Lamberth did not call into question the cases' accuracy as a fact-finding mechanism, noting of the cases against Iran that "the plaintiffs in these cases have demonstrated through competent evidence ... that Iran has provided material support to terrorist organizations, like Hezbollah and Hamas, that have orchestrated unconscionable acts of violence that have killed or injured hundreds of Americans."[272] However, Judge Lamberth asserted that "civil litigation against Iran under the FSIA state sponsor of terrorism exception represents a failed policy."[273]

"These cases," said Judge Lamberth, "do not achieve justice for victims, are not sustainable, and threaten to undermine the President's foreign policy initiatives."[274] One major driver of Judge Lamberth's concern expressed in 2009 was his assessment that "the prospects for recovery upon judgments entered in these cases are extremely remote," as "the amount of Iranian assets currently known to exist within the United States is approximately 45 million dollars, which is infinitesimal in comparison to the 10 billion dollars in currently outstanding court judgments."[275] Since then, over $2 billion dollars in additional Iranian assets have been revealed to be within U.S. jurisdiction.[276] In a May 2015 interview, Steve Perles asserted that Judge Lamberth seemed to have ignored the potential for overseas collection of U.S. court judgments.[277] However, according to a July 20, 2015, memorandum by the Congressional Research Service, as of that date, the outstanding terrorism judgments against Iran resulting from lawsuits brought under the FSIA exception for designated state sponsors of terrorism had reached a total of $43.5 billion.[278] $20.5 billion of that amount had been awarded as compensatory damages, and the rest as punitive damages.[279]

While the State Department and Judge Lamberth have been skeptical of civil litigation against state sponsors of terrorism, Congress has tended to be much more sympathetic. As Neely Tucker of the *Washington Post* wrote in a lengthy article about such civil litigation, "there is something in the victims' cause that has proven irresistible to Congress."[280]

According to Steve Perles, congressional support for civil litigation lawfare largely reflects a constituent service mindset.[281] "Members of Congress listen to their constituents," said Perles, "and when they hear again and again that the State Department isn't showing any interest in going to bat for terror victims, Congress is responsive to that."[282]

2. *Holding Iran Liable for the Marine Barracks Bombing:* Peterson v. Islamic Republic of Iran

On October 23, 1983, a truck bomb struck a barracks housing U.S. Marine participants in the multinational peacekeeping force in Beirut, killing 241 marines.[283] It was reportedly the largest nonnuclear bomb blast since World War II.[284]

In *The Twilight War*, David Crist, a senior historian for the Joint Chiefs of Staff, provides a detailed description of how the U.S. executive branch—despite quickly acquiring hard evidence that the attack was orchestrated by Iran—never retaliated against Iran for killing the 241 marines.[285] According to Crist, President Reagan, within twenty-four hours of the Marine barracks bombing, received from the CIA "hard evidence of Iranian culpability," including "a string of communications intercepts from Iran to its embassy in Damascus directing it to 'destroy U.S. targets.'"[286] One NSA-intercepted message from Tehran to Ali Akbar Mohtashemi, Iran's ambassador to Syria, ordered "a spectacular action against the U.S. Marines."[287] Within a few days after the bombing, the CIA had amassed evidence that "clearly linked Iranian agents" at Iran's Sheikh Abdallah barracks in Lebanon "with those who'd attacked the marines."[288]

On October 27, 1983, Reagan told the nation: "Those who directed this atrocity must be dealt justice, and they will be."[289] The next day, Reagan issued a written order to Secretary of Defense Casper Weinberger: "Subject to reasonable confirmation of the locations of suitable targets used by elements responsible for the October 23 bombing; attack those targets decisively, if possible . . . ."[290] However, Weinberger, for the rest of his term as Secretary of Defense, which ended in November 1987, continued to block such a response.[291] In 1994, more than a decade after the blast, Weinberger insisted that "we never had the fidelity on who perpetrated that horrendous act."[292]

The pivotal moment in the executive branch's nonresponse to the Marine barracks bombing occurred about a month after the attack. On November 16, 1983, President Reagan assembled his national security team and planned to target the Sheikh Abdallah barracks.[293] Vice Admiral James Lyons, the Navy's Deputy Chief of Operations, had developed a detailed plan for using Navy aircraft, flying from U.S. aircraft carriers in the Mediterranean, to target the Iranian barracks.[294] After seeing the NSA-intercepted message from Iran that ordered the "spectacular action," Lyons "wanted to clobber" Iran's Sheikh Abdallah barracks.[295] Lyons thought the NSA-intercepted message was as good as intelligence evidence ever got.[296] However, Defense Secretary Weinberger lobbied successfully against the mission, continuing to assert that there was insufficient evidence to take action.[297]

In the end, the Reagan administration did "nothing in response to an attack that killed more servicemen in a single day than any other since the Second World War",[298] prompting Secretary of State George Shultz's earlier quoted remark implicitly criticizing Weinberger's refusal to act while waiting "endlessly" for "the kind of evidence that can stand up in an American court of law."[299]

Ironically, it was in an American court of law, on May 30, 2003, almost twenty years after the blast, that Iran was finally held accountable for the Marine barracks bombing. On that day, Judge Lamberth ruled in *Peterson v. Islamic Republic of Iran* that Iran was responsible for the Marine barracks attack.[300] The vehicle was a lawsuit, brought by attorneys Steven Perles and Thomas Fay, on behalf of 26 marines who had survived the attack, and family members of marines who had died in the bombing.[301] Over nine hundred plaintiffs joined together in the lawsuit.[302]

Peterson was the first case to authorize U.S. military personnel to use the terrorism exception to the FSIA.[303] In authorizing the plaintiffs to do so, Judge Lamberth emphasized that the U.S. military service members at issue were part of a peacekeeping mission, and that they were operating under peacetime rules of engagement.[304]

Judge Lamberth specifically concluded that "MOIS [Iran's Ministry of Information and Security] actively participated in the attack on October 23, 1983, which was carried out by MOIS agents with the assistance of Hezbollah."[305] He based his conclusion on both testimony by witnesses and documentary evidence.

One witness in the *Peterson* case was a Hezbollah member who participated in building the truck bomb and organizing the attack that killed the 241 U.S. Marines.[306] The Hezbollah member, who testified via a pre-recorded videotape deposition—wearing a hood, using a voice modulator, and under the pseudonym "Mahmoud"—described in detail the planning and execution of the attack.[307]

According to Steve Perles, the videotape featuring "Mahmoud" was recorded in a hotel room in the Middle East.[308] "He was one of the senior bombmakers who built the truck bomb which killed the Marines," said Perles.[309] "I hired some specialists who identified and located him," said Perles.[310] We then "got him into a hotel room by trickery—it's not like we put a bag over his head or anything, we tricked him," recalled Perles.[311] "Then we had a long conversation with him and flipped him," persuading him to do the deposition,[312] said Perles. The bombmaker proceeded to describe on camera, in great detail, how the bomb was built, including who designed it and who supplied the explosives, as well as "Iran's role in having the bomb built," said Perles.[313] The bombmaker "even told us that the driver was not Hezbollah, he was IRGC, and identified him by name," said Perles.[314]

Perles asserts that this illustrates one of the benefits of civil litigation lawfare.[315] "The U.S. government had never issued an arrest warrant for this guy, let alone detained him, yet here we were able to track him down and elicit a confession," said Perles, emphasizing that "we passed on to the U.S. government every shred of evidence we collected in the Marine Barracks bombing case—as well as in every other of these lawsuits my office has brought against state sponsors of terrorism."[316] "Congress has effectively tried to unleash the private bar against the bad guys," said Perles, "so if we collect evidence, the United States ought to be the beneficiary of all the evidence we collect."[317]

Another witness in the Marine barracks bombing case was retired Admiral James Lyons, who, as Deputy Chief of Naval Operations, had planned the thwarted mission to retaliate against Iran's Sheikh Abdallah barracks in Lebanon.[318] Also featured at the trial was the declassified NSA intercept of the September 1983 message from Tehran ordering the "spectacular action."[319] In his verdict, Judge Lamberth described the message as having been sent to the Iranian ambassador to Syria, Ali Akbar Mohtashemi, from the Iranian intelligence ministry.[320] According to Judge Lamberth, "the message directed the Iranian ambassador to contact Hussein Musawi, the leader of the terrorist group Islamic Amal, and to instruct him to have his group instigate attacks against the multinational coalition in Lebanon, and 'to take a spectacular action against the United States Marines.'"[321] Part of Admiral Lyons' role at the trial was to testify as to the authenticity and significance of the intercepted message.[322]

After first seeing that message nearly twenty years earlier, Lyons, then Deputy Chief of Naval Operations, had "wanted to clobber" Iran's Sheikh Abdallah barracks but had been ordered to stand down. Now, as a private citizen, Lyons finally got to take action against Iran in response to the NSA intercept.

In 2007, Judge Lamberth ordered Iran to pay $2.657 billion in compensation to the plaintiffs in the *Peterson* case.[323] In doing so, Judge Lamberth noted that the victims' families, "whose hearts and souls were forever broken on October 23, 1983, have waited patiently for nearly a quarter of a century for justice to be done."[324] "The Court hopes," said Judge Lamberth, "that this extremely sizeable judgment will serve to aid in the healing process for these plaintiffs, and simultaneously sound an alarm to the defendants that their unlawful attacks on our citizens will not be tolerated."[325]

Not all of the victims of the Marine barracks bombing had joined or been eligible to join in the landmark *Peterson* litigation. In the wake of the *Peterson* case, Congress passed, and the President signed into law, an amended terrorism exception to the FSIA, which broadened plaintiff eligibility and expanded the types of damages that could be awarded.[326] Over the coming years, Judge Lamberth relied on the findings of fact and conclusions of law in the *Peterson* case to award some $7 billion in additional compensatory and punitive damages against Iran to victims of the Marine barracks bombing case.[327] Among the largest of these subsequent awards were $2.1 billion in *Davis v. Islamic Republic of Iran*,[328] $1.3 billion in *Valore v. Islamic Republic of Iran*,[329] $1.2 billion in *Estate of Bland v. Islamic Republic of Iran*,[330] $813 million in *Brown v. Islamic Republic of Iran*,[331] and $453 million in *Spencer v. Islamic Republic of Iran*.[332]

In 2008, approximately $1.9 billion in Iranian government assets in a Citigroup account was frozen by a federal court in Manhattan on behalf of the *Peterson* plaintiffs.[333] It was the biggest seizure of Iranian assets abroad since the 1979 Islamic revolution.[334] It is unlikely that the Sheikh Abdallah barracks in Lebanon were worth $1.9 billion to Iran. Thus, it is quite possible that the *Peterson* case verdict caused Iran more harm than the Sheikh Abdallah barracks attack would have caused, had it occurred.

Information pointing to the Iranian funds' location in a specific Citigroup account was provided to Perles by the U.S. Treasury Department's Office of Foreign Assets Control (OFAC).[335] At the time, Treasury did not itself have the legal authority to freeze such funds.[336] However, it knew that the Marine barracks victim families had the ability, under New York state law, to freeze the assets pursuant to the *Peterson* judgment.[337] So "OFAC gave Perles the Citi account number."[338] Perles recalls OFAC making it "pretty clear that these assets were subject to flight and we should move right away."[339]

As of April 2015, the $1.9 billion was in a qualified fund under the supervision of a court-appointed trustee, former federal Judge Stanley Sporkin, while awaiting the exhaustion of a petition for certiorari to the U.S. Supreme Court by Bank Markazi, Iran's central bank.[340] It was therefore unavailable for Iran to use for purposes such as state-sponsored terrorism or advancing its nuclear or ballistic missile program.

During the *Peterson* trial, Lt. Col. Larry Gerlach, who was paralyzed in the Marine barracks bombing, said that he hoped his testimony would help achieve "accountability, deterrence, and justice."[341] He said that he was concerned that "the terrorists feel that they can do things with impunity ... ever since [the Marine barracks bombing]," and he wanted to finally bring "accountability" to the perpetrators.[342]

In early May 2015, Steve Perles was working on a new lawsuit against Iran on behalf of the families of a different set of U.S. servicemen. The suit alleges that the Iranian Revolutionary Guard Corps (IRGC) "sponsored, organized, and directed the murder" of three U.S. servicemen—Jacob Fritz, Johnathan Chism, and Shawn Falter—on January 20, 2007, in Karbala, Iraq.[343] At the time, the three Americans were being "held as prisoners" by agents of the IRGC, Hezbollah, and "members of the Khazali Network (an Iraqi Shiite terrorist group operating under the instruction of the Iranian government)."[344]

According to the complaint, Qais Khazali and two other persons involved in the killings were apprehended by U.S. forces in Iraq in March 2007.[345] However, Qais Khazali was released by the United States in December 2009 as part of a prisoner exchange.[346] In filing the lawsuit, Perles asserted that there has been no accountability to date for the deaths of the three Americans.[347] "Hopefully, that will now change," he said.[348]

3. The Iran Judgments and the July 2015 Nuclear Deal

As of early August 2015, tensions over Iran policy between the administration and Congress were headed to a showdown. On July 14, 2015 (after this book was largely completed), the P-5+1 (the U.N. Security Council's five permanent members plus Germany) announced that they had agreed with Iran on a Joint Comprehensive Plan of Action (JCPOA) to address Iran's nuclear program.[349]

The JCPOA provided for the lifting of most nuclear-related sanctions on Iran in exchange for various constraints on Iran's nuclear program. Pursuant to the Iran Nuclear Agreement Review Act, enacted in May 2015, Congress was to have sixty calendar days, following the JCPOA's transmission to Congress, to review the deal and pass a joint resolution of disapproval.[350] The President could then veto the resolution, following which Congress could override the veto, should opponents of the deal muster sufficient votes to do so.

As of early August 2015, the results of the congressional vote on the JCPOA were difficult to predict. Even more difficult to predict was the impact that entry into effect of the JCPOA would have on the existing U.S. lawfare judgments and future litigation against Iran. The JCPOA did not on its face commit the United States to suspend U.S. sanctions on Iran for its involvement with terrorism, or lift Iran's designation as a state sponsor of terrorism.[351] However, in a July 22, 2015, hearing before the House Financial Services Committee, Steven Perles expressed concern that the JCPOA could "interfere" with terrorism victims' ability to collect on existing judgments against Iran.[352] Perles explained that various U.S. "administrative agencies have made recent decisions that raise concerns about their continuing willingness to carry out their legal obligations to enforce antiterrorism sanctions against Iran after nuclear sanctions are removed."[353]

At the same time, some commentators and lawfare practitioners were questioning the propriety of the U.S. government releasing to Iran over $50 billion in Iranian assets pursuant to the JCPOA when U.S. victims of Iranian-sponsored terrorism held over $40 billion in U.S. federal court judgments against Iran.[354] These lawfare practitioners included Shurat HaDin, an Israeli non-governmental organization described in more detail in Chapter 8.

On August 5, 2015, Shurat HaDin, on behalf of several U.S. terrorism victims holding judgments against Iran, filed a lawsuit asking a federal judge to enjoin the unblocking of Iranian funds pursuant to the JCPOA until their judgments against Iran were paid.[355] The complaint cited as authority § 201 of the Terrorism Risk Insurance Act, which plaintiffs asserted provides that federal court judgments against state sponsors of terrorism can be paid using "any asset seized or frozen by the United States" under the authorities used to block the Iranian assets due to be unblocked by the JCPOA.[356] As of the date this book went to press, it was unclear how the judiciary would respond to the lawsuit.

II. U.S. NON-GOVERNMENTAL ATTORNEYS AND LAWFARE OUTSIDE THE LITIGATION ARENA

While the courtroom may be the most spectacular battlefield on which U.S. private sector and other non-governmental attorneys can wage lawfare, it is far from the only one. As a result, litigators are not the only types of non-governmental attorneys who can wage, or contribute to waging, lawfare. This section will discuss how U.S. non-governmental attorneys engage in lawfare outside the litigation arena. In doing so, it will also discuss what motivates U.S. non-governmental attorneys to engage in such lawfare and why the U.S. government might sometimes find it beneficial to partner with them.

As discussed previously, critics of private civil litigation lawfare argue that it does not achieve the plaintiff's objectives and that it threatens "to undermine the President's foreign policy initiatives."[357] The U.S. Supreme Court, in striking down one state-level lawfare initiative (a Massachusetts law targeting Burma), asserted that it was acting to protect the "capacity of the President to speak for the Nation with one voice in dealing with other governments."[358]

As Part A of this section will illustrate, the U.S. Constitution, U.S. Supreme Court jurisprudence, and U.S. practice provide plenty of room for lawfare by actors outside the federal executive branch. Aside from Congress exercising the considerable foreign policy powers provided to it in the Constitution, there is an extensive record of U.S. states, cities, and non-governmental actors undertaking lawfare-type actions to influence U.S. foreign policy. Whether or not it is desirable, the ability of U.S. non-governmental actors to choose to wage lawfare seems unlikely to disappear any time soon.

U.S. citizens who care about foreign policy issues susceptible to lawfare thus have two choices. They can leave the lawfare arena to their adversaries, or they can jump into the fray.

Subsection B of this section includes several case studies of impactful U.S. non-governmental lawfare outside of the litigation arena. In analyzing this phenomenon, Subsection B attempts to shed light on how non-governmental lawfare practitioners have been able to have such an impact, why and how the U.S. government may wish to partner with them in some cases, and how the U.S. government needs to change in order to more effectively wage lawfare itself. In addressing these questions, Subsection B examines the ways in which economic globalization, the information technology revolution, and the continued rigidity of the U.S. government bureaucracy have all in recent decades increased the ease and likelihood of effective ideas emerging from private sector and other non-governmental practitioners of lawfare, rather than from government attorneys.

The U.S. national security agencies' insularity and lack of creativity and nimbleness makes them particularly ill-suited to address this era's increasingly threatening nontraditional national security challenges, let alone deploy the lawfare tools that can play a key role in addressing those challenges. Even for those who agree with all of the executive branch's relevant foreign policy objectives, or believe that they should be dispositive, there is considerable evidence that the executive branch would achieve those objectives more effectively with the assistance of outside legal expertise, creativity, and nimbleness.

A. Non-Governmental Lawfare and the President's Foreign Policy Authorities

While the executive branch has often played the leading role in deciding U.S. foreign policy, the Constitution also provides Congress with considerable foreign policy authorities. According to the Congressional Research Service, "the United States Constitution divides foreign policy powers between the President and the Congress so that both share in the making of foreign policy."[359] For example, the Constitution provides to Congress the power to:

- "provide for the common defence,"[360]
- "regulate Commerce with foreign Nations,"[361]
- "define and punish . . . Offences against the Law of Nations,"[362]
- "declare War,"[363]
- "raise and support Armies,"[364]
- "provide and maintain a Navy,"[365]
- "make Rules for the Government and Regulation of the land and naval Forces,"[366]
- "make all Laws which shall be necessary and proper for carrying into Execution the foregoing Powers, and all other Powers vested by this Constitution in the Government of the United States,"[367] and
- control federal spending (the power of the purse).[368]

The Constitution also provides to the Senate the power to provide "Advice and Consent" to treaties and to the appointment of ambassadors and "all other Officers of the United States."[369]

The two branches' foreign affairs powers clearly were meant to overlap, with each branch having different means for addressing the same policy issues.[370] Edward S. Corwin, a leading presidential scholar, famously described the Constitution's overlap between the foreign policy powers of the President and Congress as "an invitation to struggle for the privilege of directing American foreign policy."[371]

Several of the examples in this chapter of lawfare initiatives by non-governmental attorneys involve their encouraging Congress to take action pursuant to its constitutional authorities. Such initiatives are obviously both lawful and appropriate.

There is also an extensive record of U.S. non-governmental actors affecting U.S. foreign policy through state and local lawfare-type measures that do not directly involve Congress. Much of this has involved action targeting foreign governments, the principal traditional interlocutors of U.S. foreign policy and national security agencies.

A broad range of foreign governments have been targeted by U.S. non-governmental lawfare practitioners. This book analyzes in detail how non-governmental actors have taken lawfare-type action—through litigation and via U.S. state and local legislation—that has been designed to impact foreign governments with regard to issues including the following: the campaign to stop genocide in Darfur; the campaign to halt Iran's nuclear weapons program and state sponsorship of terrorism; and the BDS (Boycott, Divestment and Sanctions) movement against Israel.

In addition to the lawsuits against Iran that are discussed in detail in this book, litigators under the terrorism exception to the Foreign Sovereign Immunity Act have won—and collected as a result of—lawsuits against the governments of Cuba,[372] Iraq,[373] Libya,[374] and Syria.[375] They have also won lawsuits against the government of North Korea.[376] Litigators under the Anti-Terrorism Act have won and collected on lawsuits against various foreign non-state actors.

There has been a remarkably broad range of targets against which non-governmental actors have persuaded U.S. states and local cities to enact lawfare-type legislation:

- at least twenty-seven states and twenty-two cities divested from foreign companies engaged in particular types of business with Sudan;[377]
- at least twenty-four states divested from, and six states prohibited public contracts with, foreign companies with substantial investments in Iran's energy sector;[378]
- numerous states and cities engaged in divestment during the anti-apartheid movement against South Africa;[379]
- one state and several cities—including Berkeley, California; Ann Arbor, Michigan; Cambridge, Massachusetts; and New York City—enacted selective purchasing legislation as part of the Free Burma movement;[380]
- Massachusetts divested from businesses involved in supplying weapons used in Northern Ireland;[381]
- several states enacted laws designed to combat the Arab League boycott of Israel;[382] and
- Florida enacted various laws penalizing companies doing business with Cuba.[383]

State and local lawfare can be impactful because the United States' fifty state governments and numerous local jurisdictions have enormous combined economic power. State and local pension funds control a total of more than $3.3 trillion in total investments (about $2.7 trillion of that is in state pension funds),[384] and state governments oversee more than $1.7 trillion in spending each year.[385] Total annual spending by the fifty U.S. states is about 50 percent larger than total annual spending by the national government of the United Kingdom.[386]

Lawfare-type action has been taken not only by state legislatures but also by governors. For example, in 2007, when Minnesota Governor Tim Pawlenty discovered that an Indian company, Essar, was seeking to both invest some $1.6

billion in Minnesota and over $5 billion in building a refinery in Iran, he put Essar to a choice.[387] Pawlenty threatened to block state infrastructure subsidies and perhaps even construction permits for the Minnesota purchase unless Essar withdrew from the Iranian investment.[388] Essar promptly withdrew from the Iranian investment.[389]

The June 2000 Supreme Court decision striking down a Burma-related Massachusetts law in *Crosby v. National Foreign Trade Council*[390] was expected by many analysts to result in far fewer state and local laws enacting foreign policy sanctions. Frank Kittridge, National Foreign Trade Council president, predicted after the *Crosby* decision that it would "help put an end to state and local efforts to make foreign policy."[391] However, such laws have, for a variety of reasons, continued to be enacted. The foremost reason is that *Crosby* failed to prohibit states and localities from imposing their own sanctions when expressly authorized by federal law. Such federal laws expressly authorizing state sanctions have been enacted with regard to both Iran and Sudan. Another reason is that *Crosby* at least arguably did not prohibit divestment even when not expressly authorized by federal law.[392] In addition, *Crosby* did not affect gubernatorial discretion to take steps such as those taken by Governor Pawlenty.

Although the Supreme Court claimed to be acting in *Crosby* to protect the "capacity of the President to speak for the Nation with one voice in dealing with other governments,"[393] its decision did not have that effect beyond the relatively narrow scope of its holding striking down the Massachusetts Burma law. Nor has the Supreme Court elsewhere prohibited Congress from impacting, or empowering other actors to impact, the international arena in the ways Congress has been doing with regard to lawfare.

In *Zivotofsky v. Kerry*, decided on June 8, 2015, the Supreme Court addressed at length the issue of presidential power to "speak for the Nation with one voice."[394] The Supreme Court's decision in *Zivotofsky* held invalid a statute that required the President to allow U.S. citizens born in Jerusalem to have their birthplace be recorded as Israel in U.S. passports.[395] The executive branch challenged the requirement because of its longstanding position that the United States does not recognize any country as having sovereignty over Jerusalem. [396]

Justice Kennedy's majority opinion in *Zivotofsky* provided several functional arguments in support of the President having the exclusive power to grant formal recognition to a foreign sovereign. Kennedy asserted that "recognition is a topic on which the Nation must 'speak . . . with one voice' [and] that voice must be the President's" because "between the two political branches, only the Executive has the characteristic of unity at all times."[397] "With unity," said Kennedy, "comes the ability to exercise, to a greater degree, '[d]ecision, activity, secrecy, and dispatch.'"[398] As Jack Goldsmith pointed out in his analysis of the decision, "these functional arguments" could in some future case be applied "much more broadly" in support of "presidential exclusivity."[399]

However, Kennedy's majority opinion specified that the holding's scope "is confined solely to the exclusive power of the President to control recognition determinations, including formal statements by the Executive Branch acknowledging the legitimacy of a state or government and its territorial bounds."[400] Thus, while the Supreme Court could conceivably, in some future case, apply some of the majority's reasoning in the *Zivotofsky* opinion to significantly impede lawfare by actors outside the federal executive branch, the *Zivotofsky* case did not do so.[401]

As for Congress, it has chosen to exercise its constitutional authorities, as it interprets them, so as to enable several types of state and local lawfare and several types of litigation lawfare. Thus, non-governmental attorneys have a variety of arenas other than civil litigation in which they can choose to wage lawfare. These can include encouraging or assisting the executive branch, Congress, or U.S. state and local governments.

B. Non-Governmental Lawfare Tools and Executive Branch Shortcomings

While Section I of this chapter describes and analyzes several examples of U.S. private sector attorneys taking lawfare action directly through civil litigation, this section focuses largely on examples of U.S. private sector and other non-governmental attorneys taking lawfare action indirectly: by spurring a government to act or by helping a government to more effectively take action (for example, when a non-state actor's greater expertise or more useful information helps a government take action). When people think of spurring government to act, they may think primarily in terms of binary actions: lobbyists persuading additional legislators to support or oppose a bill that has already been introduced, or advocates pressuring a prosecutor to indict or not indict someone who has been described in the media as violating an existing law.

However, the most sophisticated non-governmental practitioners of lawfare do not limit themselves to such binary actions. Rather than simply supporting or opposing an existing option, they will, when the situation calls for it, create a new option and persuade government(s) to adopt and deploy it. For example, they may write a new draft law or devise a proposed new regulatory step. Or they may collect and share new evidence that will enable and persuade a prosecutor to bring charges or a regulator to add a foreign entity to a list of those on which sanctions are imposed.

In this author's experience speaking about lawfare, he has often been asked: How could someone outside government possibly help wage lawfare other than through a lawsuit or by asking a legislator to support a bill? Don't government officials largely have a monopoly on the relevant expertise, factual information, and sense of what creative new steps would be practical for the government to undertake? The answer is no. A classic example of non-governmental lawfare occurred shortly after World War II: the campaign, led virtually single-handedly by one non-governmental lawyer, to create an international law prohibiting and punishing genocide. Subsection B.1 will describe that classic example. Then, Subsection B.2 will analyze—through other lawfare examples—how economic globalization, the information technology revolution, and the continued rigidity of the U.S. government bureaucracy have all in recent decades increased the ease and likelihood of effective ideas emerging from private sector and other non-governmental practitioners of lawfare, rather than from government attorneys.

1. Raphael Lemkin's Campaign to Create an International Law Prohibiting Genocide

One of the most remarkable campaigns to deter particular acts of war resulted in the UN in 1948 adopting a treaty titled the Convention on the Prevention and Punishment of the Crime of Genocide (Genocide Convention). The Genocide Convention was the first international law prohibiting acts "committed with intent to destroy, in whole or in part, a national, ethnical, racial, or religious group, as such."[402] The Convention specifies that "rulers, public officials," and "private individuals" "shall be punished" for acts including: genocide; conspiracy or attempt to commit genocide; and direct and public incitement to commit genocide.[403]

The Genocide Convention represented an important change from the idea that a nation state's sovereignty was sacrosanct. The Convention contradicted the previous "premises of the international system that how a state behaved toward its own citizens in its own territory was a matter of 'domestic jurisdiction,' i.e., not any one else's business and therefore not any business for international law."[404] It was the very first human rights treaty adopted by the UN and one of the key post-World War II legal instruments stripping rulers of what had been a legal right, with few exceptions, to do whatever they wished with civilians under their control.[405] Instead, rulers could be held accountable and punished for abuses of their own or conquered citizens.

The Convention's prohibitions of genocide and related acts, and provisions for their prevention and suppression, were designed to encourage and legitimize international diplomatic, economic, and other intervention. The prospect of such intervention, plus the requirement that perpetrators be punished, was also designed to deter genocide.

Raphael Lemkin was both the leading conceptual thinker and the chief lobbyist of the campaign which resulted in the Genocide Convention. Lemkin himself coined the word "genocide" as a name for acts committed with intent to destroy national and other groups.[406] He led the call for genocide to be specifically prohibited and punished, and drafted laws designed to do so.[407] In 1945 and 1946,

Lemkin served as an adviser at the Nuremberg Trials, where he persuaded the prosecutors to charge some of the accused with the crime of "genocide, viz., the extermination of racial and national groups."[408] This was the first time that the crime of genocide was referenced in legal proceedings.[409]

Lemkin then shifted his efforts to the UN. There, he acted "purely as a private citizen, without foundational, academic, or institutional support of any kind."[410] Lemkin's successful one-man campaign to build support for General Assembly adoption of the Genocide Convention is memorably described as follows in Samantha Power's book, *A Problem from Hell: America and the Age of Genocide*:

> Lemkin . . . had learned one lesson during the Holocaust, which was that if a UN genocide convention were ever to come to pass, he would have to appeal to the domestic political interests of UN delegates. He obtained lists of the most important organizations in each of the UN member states and assembled a committee that spoke for groups in twenty-eight countries and claimed a remarkable joint membership of more than 240 million people. The committee, which was more of a front for Lemkin, compiled and sent petitions to each UN delegate urging passage of the convention. UN diplomats who hesitated received telegrams—usually drafted by Lemkin—from organizations at home. He used the letters to make delegates feel as if by working for the Genocide Convention, they were representing the wishes of their own people . . . . In Catholic countries he preached to bishops and archbishops. In Scandinavia, where organized labor was active, he penned notes to the large labor groups . . . . A *Times* editorial branded Lemkin "the man who speaks through sixty nations."[411]

All this was done by one man, with a manual typewriter, in the days before the Internet.

2. Government's Shortcomings in Lawfare Expertise, Facts, and Creativity Generate Opportunities for Non-governmental Lawfare

a. Expertise

Law is a broad field with many specialties and subspecialties. Lawfare has thus far been undertaken using the law of at least the following legal specialties and subspecialties: banking law, insurance law, pension law, government contracts law, energy law, maritime law, space law, telecommunications law, aviation law, cyberlaw, law of armed conflict, universal jurisdiction law, counterterrorism law, strategic trade controls law, international organization law, international tribunal law, nuclear nonproliferation law, securities law, criminal law, and corporate law. For many of these substantive types of law, there are variants at the international, national, and subnational levels—for example, international criminal law,

U.S. or Chinese or Belgian national criminal law, and New York criminal law. In addition, lawfare has been undertaken using specialized knowledge of the particular legal procedures of various national and subnational jurisdictions.

The U.S. government has some thirty-five thousand of its own attorneys,[412] and the vast majority are undoubtedly good at what they do. However, what they do lends itself to developing only some of the many types of expertise that are critical for effective lawfare.

As was discussed previously, one of the key factors making lawfare an increasingly powerful weapon is the process of globalization, which is intensifying economic interdependence. Many more companies are subject to numerous jurisdictions. For example, the U.S. and U.K. governments have legal leverage over far more foreign companies than they used to, including the various major Chinese and Russian companies that are readily subject to lawfare because they are listed on the U.S. or U.K. stock exchanges and/or engage in banking, insurance, or other transactions that occur in or transit the United States or United Kingdom. Similarly, of course, many more U.S. companies do business in China and Russia and are thus at greater risk of Chinese or Russian lawfare now than during the Cold War.

Lawfare leveraging this economic interdependence can be a very effective weapon. However, such lawfare does not correlate particularly well with the day-to-day jobs and thus the expertise of U.S. government attorneys. The United States' leading experts in relevant subspecialties of law, such as U.K. maritime insurance law or Belgian or Chinese criminal law, will often be private sector practitioners or academics who focus their work entirely (or almost entirely) in that subspecialty.

Indeed, the United States government has remarkably little foreign law expertise. For example, when this author served during the 1990s as the lead State Department attorney negotiating nonproliferation agreements with Russia, he was faced with numerous questions of Russian law, such as: How can we minimize the risk of U.S. contractors being sued for an accident at a Russian nuclear site they have helped protect? The author was surprised to discover that the U.S. government possessed no expertise in Russian law. He could not find a single federal government attorney who had more than a surface understanding of Russian law. The leading U.S. experts on Russian law were private sector attorneys and professors. From the interviews the author conducted for this book, it is clear that the U.S. government continues to have almost no internal expertise in the laws of many of the most significant foreign countries. In contrast, one U.S.-based law firm, Baker & McKenzie, has 77 offices in 47 countries.[413] Its website lists 39 attorneys in its Russia offices and 203 attorneys in its China offices.[414]

Some or all of the attorneys in a law firm's foreign office may be conflicted out of giving advice to the U.S. government, personally uncomfortable providing advice to the U.S. government, or inappropriate sources of advice from the

U.S. government's perspective (because their loyalties lie with the foreign country and not the United States). The point of the Baker & McKenzie example is not that the United States government can or should hire that or any other firm. The point is to emphasize the vast disparity of particular types of expertise between the U.S. government and the U.S. private sector. If Baker & McKenzie alone has 203 attorneys practicing law in China, the U.S. private bar must include a significant number of U.S.-based active or retired attorneys who have Chinese legal experience, are not conflicted, and would be willing and appropriate sources of expertise on Chinese law.

Once a particular offensive or defensive lawfare idea (for example a particular way of using U.K. maritime insurance law to halt a Gaza-bound flotilla or a particular way of pushing back against a Belgian law targeting U.S. defense contractors or a particular provision of Chinese law that can be creatively used against a nuclear middleman) has been identified, developed, and delineated, the idea will likely be implementable by any good attorney with a solid understanding of the subspecialty (e.g., maritime insurance law) or even the specialty (insurance law or maritime law). However, the initial identification, development, and delineation of the lawfare idea is likely to require deep expertise in the subspecialty. With lawfare at a relatively early stage of its development, many new lawfare ideas have yet to be discovered, and leading private sector experts can play a particularly important role in adding their expertise.

b. Facts

The Internet has greatly enhanced the ability of private sector attorneys and other individuals to collect information at the level of detail necessary to either wage lawfare themselves or spur or assist governments to do so. This subsection will first discuss the concept generally and with a few brief examples. Then the subsection will illustrate the concept in more detail by recounting one of the author's own small forays into non-governmental lawfare.

i. Facts in the Age of Information Technology Several U.S.-based nonprofit organizations have proven exceptionally effective at collecting publicly available information and then using it in lawfare, either themselves directly or as a spur or aid to government action. For example, a reporter has described the Foundation for Defense of Democracies (FDD), a U.S.-based nonprofit organization with which the author is affiliated, as having "carved a niche for itself in the charged debate on Iran with its intensive research" on "the complicated and murky world of Iranian commerce."[415] According to the reporter, FDD's "deep dives into energy markets, global finance and Iran's state-controlled economy have become ammunition for the policymakers using increasingly sophisticated financial sanctions to wage an economic war on Iran."[416]

FDD's executive director, Mark Dubowitz, is an attorney whose previous career was in venture capital. He decided to switch to policy work after his wife witnessed him throwing a shoe in frustration at a television station's coverage of terrorism issues and told him, "Mark, you know, you're throwing shoes at the TV, you either gotta get some therapy or you gotta change careers."[417]

After joining FDD, Dubowitz played a leading role in identifying and explaining the significance of Iran's heavy reliance on the interbank financial messaging services provider called the Society for Worldwide Interbank Financial Telecommunications (SWIFT).[418] The Belgium-based SWIFT provides a secure network used by more than ten thousand financial institutions around the world to exchange financial messages and transactional data.[419] As of February 2012, SWIFT's users included several Iranian banks designated by the U.S. Treasury and the European Union for their involvement in sponsoring terrorism, aiding Iran's nuclear program, or engaging in illicit financial transactions.[420]

Dubowitz and other FDD researchers discovered that Iran depended on SWIFT's network in order to execute financial transactions, especially as other financial avenues were blocked as a result of sanctions. As detailed in SWIFT's annual report,[421] Iran used the SWIFT network to process much of Iran's $35 billion in trade with Europe.[422] While other global financial institutions had already halted their involvement with designated Iranian banks, SWIFT insisted it was not required to implement the sanctions.[423] Instead, SWIFT insisted that its users were responsible for ensuring that their transactions were in compliance with sanctions.[424]

On February 1, 2012, the *Wall Street Journal* published an editorial in which the *Journal's* board called for passage of legislation clarifying that U.S. sanctions targeting transactions with Iranian banks were applicable to SWIFT.[425] In the editorial, the *Journal* described FDD as having "done most of the spadework on the issue."[426] On February 2, 2012, the Senate Banking Committee adopted a bill providing the executive branch with clear authority to impose sanctions on SWIFT for engaging in targeted transactions with Iran.[427] The bill also noted that the EU already had clear authority to take action.[428] Six weeks later, EU regulators ordered SWIFT to expel designated Iranian banks from the SWIFT network.[429] The Senate Banking Committee bill was credited with helping persuade the EU to use its own authorities to crack down on SWIFT.[430]

SWIFT's expulsion of the Iranian banks provided the West with additional leverage over Iran's nuclear program and state sponsorship of terrorism. One reporter described SWIFT sanctions as "cut[ting] off Iran from participating in the global financial and business worlds" by contributing to Iranian banks and businesses having to "schlep cash-stuffed suitcases across borders via couriers to institutions willing to risk doing business with them."[431] Press reports also emphasized the Iranian leadership's eagerness for the SWIFT sanctions to be reversed in exchange for any Iranian nuclear concessions.[432] Not surprisingly,

Iran ensured that the Joint Comprehensive Plan of Action announced by the P-5+1 and Iran on July 14, 2015, specifically provided for the lifting of the EU's SWIFT-related sanctions on Iran.[433]

While Mark Dubowitz's SWIFT lawfare initiative drew on publicly available financial transactions data, other lawfare initiatives have drawn on publicly available maritime data. For example, FDD journalist-in-residence Claudia Rosett has used the Lloyd's List Intelligence shipping database to track vessels linked to Iran and North Korea and draw attention to loopholes and enforcement gaps in U.S. sanctions on Iran's shipping sector.[434] Various free websites can also be used to track ship movements.[435]

United Against Nuclear Iran (UANI), a U.S.-based nonprofit organization led by Mark Wallace, a former commercial and U.S. government attorney,[436] has reportedly used publicly available "satellite transmissions from ship transponders" to expose and halt Iranian schemes for evading sanctions.[437] According to the *New York Times*, UANI has "a reputation for uncovering information about companies that sometimes do business with Iran, in violation of international sanctions."[438] UANI, says the *Times*, "is best known for its 'name and shame' campaigns, which unearth information about Western companies suspected of doing business with Iran."[439] "Using news releases, letters, Facebook, and its website, the group pressures them to stop," says the *Times*, which asserts that "companies frequently respond by cutting ties with Iran."[440]

Other non-governmental organizations have reportedly used commercial satellite imagery to identify, monitor, and document human rights abuses, covert nuclear facilities, and other illicit activity by foreign governments.[441] Until 2000, satellite imagery was available virtually only to national governments.[442] The commercial availability of such imagery has become a powerful tool for non-governmental lawfare. Such imagery can, for example, be used to spot and record destroyed villages, burned houses, large military equipment, mass graves, or the razing of suspected nuclear research workshops.[443] The data can then be used to press for and inform lawfare action by the U.S. and other governments.

Non-governmental organizations have also impactfully waged lawfare by developing and disseminating innovative legal arguments. For example, the Lawfare Project, led by Brooke Goldstein, has developed and disseminated innovative explanations of the inconsistency of anti-Israel boycotts with New York state law.[444]

Other non-governmental organizations have waged lawfare by drafting model legislation, advocating for its passage, and identifying violators. For instance, the Sudan Divestment Task Force developed, and advocated passage of, model legislation for U.S. states to divest their pension funds from companies doing particular types of business with Sudan.[445] The Task Force was co-founded by two college students.[446] Its divestment campaign was designed to help pressure the Sudanese government to stop its genocidal campaign in Darfur.[447] According to the Task Force, sixteen states—including California and New York—passed variants of its model legislation.[448]

The Task Force also systematically researched and published a quarterly "comprehensive listing of companies with problematic business operations linked to Sudan."[449] In addition to its research and legislative drafting and advocacy, the Task Force engaged in "ongoing communication with fiduciaries and asset management firms, foreign policy experts, think tanks, international non-governmental organizations (NGOs), contacts on the ground in Sudan or linked to Sudan, and executives of problematic companies targeted by the Sudan divestment movement."[450]

Interestingly, both the U.S. Congress and the U.S. executive branch seem to have decided that the Task Force and other NGOs could do a better job than could the federal government of developing a list of companies doing targeted business in Sudan. In 2007, Senator Christopher Dodd of Connecticut, the chair of the U.S. Senate Banking Committee, called on the Securities and Exchange Commission (SEC) to make it easier for "shareholders to access reliable information regarding publicly traded companies' business transactions involving Iran and Sudan."[451] The SEC chair concurred, stating that "no investor should ever have to wonder whether his or her investments or retirement savings are indirectly subsidizing a terrorist haven or genocidal state."[452]

In June 2007, the SEC proceeded to include on its website a list and "links to the annual reports of any company doing business in Cuba, Iran, North Korea, Sudan, or Syria."[453] The SEC list and links were criticized as poorly implemented and misleading by influential Democratic and Republican members of Congress, as well as in an op-ed jointly authored by the director of the Sudan Divestment Task Force and the president of a trade association representing companies with international investments.[454]

A month later, the SEC took down the list and links.[455] Later that year, the Senate Banking Committee passed the Sudan Accountability and Divestment Act of 2007, which, after its enactment, explicitly authorized state and local government divestment from companies doing particular types of business with Sudan. The Act specified that state and local governments could identify such companies "using credible information available to the public."[456] The Banking Committee's chair, Senator Dodd, explained that provision as follows in the Committee's report on the bill:

> In its testimony before the Committee, the Department of the Treasury seemed to sanction lists developed by non-governmental organizations (NGOs) produced for purposes of divestment from Sudan, suggesting that the federal government would not be able to add much value given current efforts already under way by NGOs. The Committee therefore discerns that . . . States, local governments, and fund managers may rely on resources provided by internationally-recognized NGOs, and other appropriate sources, to target companies for divestment.[457]

Some lawfare-relevant data is still only accessible to governments or perhaps some criminal organizations—for example, information derived from espionage activities such as telecommunications monitoring or computer hacking. However, this too can provide an opportunity for private sector input. Many governments, including those of the United States and the European Union, may be very reluctant to risk revealing their intelligence "sources and methods" by publicizing information derived using such means. As described in Chapter 3, this was a major problem for the EU in 2013 and 2014.[458] A number of Iranian, Syrian, and other sanctioned entities challenged the evidentiary basis of asset freezes and travel bans imposed on them by the EU.[459] The challenges succeeded for a while because the EU had not yet developed a mechanism for protecting the confidentiality of evidence provided in court, and some member states were "unwilling to share sensitive intelligence information" in order to prove that the complaining entities had engaged in proscribed activities.[460]

While EU and other governments of course have the capacity to collect their own "open source" information, from the Internet or elsewhere, it tends to be a low-priority task at which governments are not necessarily motivated to excel because of the higher quality information they derive through espionage.[461] As a result, governments sometimes welcome non-governmental compilations of reliable information, derived from publicly available sources, that can be offered as public evidence without compromising "source and methods."

ii. Finding Leverage over Iran and its Gasoline Suppliers An example from the author's own experience can help illustrate how data from public sources can be gathered and effectively deployed by private parties in lawfare actions that do not involve litigation.

In 2008, I was a law professor with no relationship with the U.S. government (which I had left when I entered academia four years prior). I was writing a scholarly article about Treasury's financial lawfare, a topic which is described in detail in Chapter 3 of this book. I was struck by one of the financial campaign's most innovative aspects: the way Treasury directly approached foreign banks and persuaded those foreign banks to stop doing business with Iran.[462]

While Treasury's financial sanctions were, at the time, clearly squeezing Iran's economy, they seemed to me insufficient to achieve their goal of coercing Iran to halt its nuclear program. I was curious to know whether there were other economic sectors in which Iran was highly dependent on non-Iranian companies, and in which the go-directly-to-the-company approach, that was working so well in the banking sector, could be replicated.

So I went looking on the Internet for other economic sectors in which Iran was highly dependent on non-Iranian companies, and in which the go-directly-to-the-company approach could be replicated. I quickly discovered that Iran, to my surprise, was remarkably dependent on imports of gasoline. Although

Iranian oil wells were producing far more crude oil than Iran needed, Iran had insufficient capacity to refine that crude oil (turn it into gasoline and diesel fuel). As a result, in 2008, Iran was importing some 40 percent of the gasoline it was consuming.[463]

It didn't take long before I found several articles online in the trade press (e.g., International Oil Daily) that provided the names and supply volumes for Iran's key suppliers. Five foreign companies (four European and one Indian) were supplying the vast majority of Iran's imported gasoline. I then looked online for U.S. leverage over these suppliers and discovered there was plenty. For example, a web search for the Indian supplier, Reliance Industries, revealed articles on the website of the U.S. Export-Import Bank stating that the Bank had provided Reliance with $900 million in loan guarantees, over half of which were for expanding the very refinery in India at which the trade press articles said Reliance was refining 10 percent of Iran's total monthly gasoline consumption.[464] Another web search revealed articles in Florida newspapers stating that the Swiss firm Vitol, which had been providing even more of the gasoline shipped to Iran, was building a $100 million terminal in Port Canaveral, Florida.[465]

I realized that I was onto something that could have a significant policy impact. So I teamed up with a think tank, the Foundation for Defense of Democracies, with which I am still affiliated. They had better media and congressional connections than I had, and I admired the results-oriented approach of Cliff May, Mark Dubowitz, and the rest of their team.

Then I wrote a *Wall Street Journal* op-ed identifying the key foreign companies supplying gasoline to Iran and describing the U.S. leverage over them.[466] I referenced the loan guarantees for Reliance's refinery and the terminal that Vitol was building in Port Canaveral, Florida,[467] and suggested that "Florida officials could consider taking a similar stance with Vitol"[468] to the one taken by Tim Pawlenty with Essar and their planned Iranian investment.

Members of Congress read the op-ed and reached out to me for more information. First, Senators Jon Kyl and Joe Lieberman quietly sent a letter to the Export-Import Bank asking it to review the loan guarantees for Reliance's refinery.[469] Then, eight House members sent a similar letter to the Export-Import Bank, and released the letter to the Indian press.[470] The next trading day, shares in Reliance Industries, which was India's largest company, dropped by 5 percent (over $1 billion) on the Indian stock exchange. Reliance soon stopped supplying gasoline to Iran. *Newsweek* described this development as follows:

> An Arizona State University law professor and former State Department nuclear-nonproliferation official, Orde Kittrie, discovered that Reliance had benefited from two U.S. Export-Import Bank loan guarantees totaling $900 million. Members of Congress—led by Democratic Rep. Brad Sherman of California and Republican Mark Kirk of Illinois—demanded that the Ex-Im Bank cut off U.S. taxpayer assistance. After consulting with its high-priced Washington lobbying firm, BGR,

Reliance quietly passed the word to members of Congress: it was halting all sales to Iran and would insist that its trading partners do the same.[471]

A state senator in Florida, Ted Deutch, also reached out to me. An article in the *Tampa Bay Times* described how "Deutch learned about Vitol from an op-ed article published last month in the *Wall Street Journal* [in which] Kittrie called on Florida leaders to pressure Vitol."[472] Deutch went to work getting the Florida state government to put pressure on Vitol to pull out of Iran.[473]

After Iran's leaders rebuffed the newly elected President Obama's attempts to engage them in 2009, Congress stepped up its efforts to use law to place pressure on foreign energy companies supplying gasoline to Iran. Legislation was introduced, and I was invited to testify in favor. Despite having no gasoline industry expertise when I started my investigation, the op-ed and my subsequent research had made me if not an expert, then at least knowledgeable enough to speak and answer questions on the issue.

In October 2009, Congress passed, and President Obama signed into law, a prohibition on foreign companies selling to the U.S. government's Strategic Petroleum Reserve if they were significantly involved in providing refined petroleum to Iran.[474] Meanwhile, a stronger bill on the topic was moving through Congress. That bill was eventually enacted as the Comprehensive Iran Sanctions, Accountability and Divestment Act of 2010 (CISADA), which in relevant part mandated that the President impose sanctions (up to and including being barred from doing business in the United States) on any foreign company that provided gasoline to Iran.[475]

CISADA had a significant impact on gasoline exports to Iran even before it was signed into law. Different companies stopped their varied forms of involvement in providing gasoline to Iran at different stages in the legislative process. For example, several companies stopped such business once the bill passed both houses of Congress, another company stopped once the conferenced legislation had been passed by both houses of Congress, and another stopped conducting such business with Iran a few days after President Obama signed the bill into law.[476]

President Obama signed CISADA into law on July 1, 2010.[477] Following CISADA's enactment, the Obama administration took, with foreign companies doing business with Iran's energy sector, an analogous approach to the Treasury Department's direct outreach to key foreign private financial institutions. In doing so, the administration applied a "special rule" contained in § 102(g) of CISADA, which allowed the President to, on a case-by-case basis, terminate, or not initiate, an investigation of certain sanctionable activities under the Act if the President certified that the sanctionable entity had stopped the sanctionable activity or had "taken significant verifiable steps toward stopping the activity" and the President had "received reliable assurances" that the sanctionable entity would "not knowingly engage in [such activities] in the future."[478]

As a result, by October 2010, Reliance Industries, Vitol, and each of the other companies that had, two years before, been one of the top five suppliers of gasoline to Iran, had dropped out of supplying gasoline to Iran.[479] The total volume of gasoline imported by Iran in September 2010 was reportedly as much as 90 percent less than what Iran imported in months prior to the July 1, 2010, enactment of CISADA.[480] By using this new kind of trade sanction, the United States and its allies managed to drastically reduce Iran's gasoline supplies without intercepting a single tanker or firing a single shot.

The U.S. government subsequently took an analogous approach to purchasers of crude oil from Iran. As a result of U.S.-led energy and financial lawfare against Iran, Iran's economy declined, and the Iranian regime came to the negotiating table, expressing a willingness to limit its nuclear program and facilitate monitoring of it. In both the Joint Plan of Action (announced in November 2013) and the Joint Comprehensive Plan of Action (announced in July 2015), Iran committed to limit its program and to facilitate the monitoring of it, largely in exchange for the lifting of various economic restrictions imposed on Iran through U.S.-led energy and financial lawfare.

c. Innovation and Nimbleness

Innovative lawfare and other policy ideas from outside the U.S. government are especially important because the U.S. government, and particularly its national security agencies, are remarkably poor at developing and implementing innovative ideas themselves. As noted earlier, U.S. national security agencies are particularly ill-suited to developing maximally effective policies for addressing nontraditional security challenges that increasingly require creativity, flexibility, and non-governmental expertise. This section will provide a brief overview of major current nontraditional security challenges and the U.S. government's difficulties in combating them.

The most recent U.S. National Security Strategy, published in 2015, provides a useful overview of what the U.S. executive branch perceives to be the most important current nontraditional security challenges.[481] During the Cold War, the United States and especially NATO were highly focused on such large-scale military challenges as how to stop Soviet tanks from attacking through the Fulda Gap and how to deter the use of Soviet nuclear weapons. In contrast, the most recent U.S. National Security Strategy has a very different focus.

In the 2015 National Security Strategy, President Obama places high priority on challenges including those posed by: violent extremism; the evolving terrorist threat; cyber threats; climate change; nuclear proliferation; and energy security.[482] In contrast to the major security challenges of the Cold War, these nontraditional security challenges are decentralized, transcend state borders, frequently involve non-state actors, evolve almost continually, and cannot be neutralized using only deterrence or the United States' traditional kinetic toolbox. Instead, combating these nontraditional security challenges tends to require a more comprehensive approach, combining legal, political, diplomatic, economic, military, technological, and scientific initiatives, as well as intensive engagement with the private sector. All in a manner that adapts as necessary to keep up with the rapid evolution of the challenges. In other words, combating these nontraditional security challenges requires nimbler and more creative deployment of different and more numerous policy tools.

The 2015 National Security Strategy, and particularly its introductory letter signed by President Obama, seems to recognize that new tactics and tools are required. A large number of the tools the letter suggests be deployed to combat these challenges are law-related. For example, Obama's letter asserts that "strong and sustained American leadership is essential to a rules-based international order that promotes global security and prosperity as well as the dignity and human rights of all peoples."[483] Indeed, the President's introductory letter mentions not only a "rules-based international order" but also numerous other law-related tools for achieving U.S. policy objectives, including: "tough sanctions," "global standards for cybersecurity," "the advancement of democracy and human rights," "the rule of law," "prohibiting the use of torture," "combat[ing] corruption," "embracing constraints on our use of new technologies like drones," and "upholding our commitment to privacy and civil liberties."[484]

As we know from the news, the U.S. government is currently having a remarkably difficult time combating these nontraditional national security challenges. If law-related tools are going to play a role in more successfully combating these challenges, the law-related tools will need to be much more effectually conceptualized and deployed.

Why are the U.S. government's national security agencies having such a difficult time combating nontraditional security challenges, and how will these obstacles affect the U.S. government's ability to more effectively deploy lawfare and other law-related tools to achieve its objectives? There seem to be at least five major structural hindrances to the U.S. government's national security agencies combating nontraditional security challenges, including with innovative and nimble lawfare:

i. Government Decision-Making Tends to be Slow and Inflexible Except during actual battlefield combat, U.S. national security policy decision-making and resource allocation tend to move very slowly. U.S. policy decisions are largely made by issues rising slowly up through very formal interagency processes that are ponderous and consensus-based and paralyzed by debilitating turf battles. In addition, policy decisions are made in the context of resource allocations that are, to a considerable degree, fixed and inflexible. Funds mostly must be spent, and personnel mostly must be deployed, as required by legislation passed months (or in the case of continuing resolutions) years before.

This puts the U.S. government at a disadvantage vis-à-vis U.S. adversaries who may not have such bureaucratic constraints. Michèle Flournoy, a former U.S. Under Secretary of Defense for Policy, recently questioned whether the United States' national security decision-making processes are "agile enough and responsive enough to . . . keep pace with the speed of the modern world."[485] "Sometimes it feels," said Flournoy, "like our interagency process is horribly slow and clunky compared to the demands being placed on it from the environment."[486]

U.S. non-governmental actors typically do not have such rigid bureaucratic constraints. While they may have far fewer resources than the U.S. government, sometimes time is of the essence, and non-governmental attorneys can take lawfare steps against U.S. adversaries while the U.S. government is still debating what to do.

ii. Innovation by U.S. Government Employees Tends to Be Discouraged The reliance of U.S. national security policymaking on strict hierarchies, its emphasis on failure avoidance, and its general insistence on consensus interagency decision-making tend to limit not only speed but also creativity. For a creative idea to make its way from being thought up by a front-line, expert-level government official to being adopted as U.S. government policy, it must generally first have been thought up or adopted by the particular expert-level government official in whose bailiwick it falls (as opposed to one of the adjacent field experts that Professor Karim Lakhani of Harvard Business School and modern innovation theory tell us are often more likely to come up with fresh ideas).[487] In addition, that official in whose bailiwick the idea falls must decide to take the risk to push the creative idea forward, his or her own hierarchy then needs to take the risk of adopting the idea, and then they need to successfully have it cleared by a long list of other offices and agencies with a real or perceived stake in the issue. Often, at least some of these other offices or agencies will have a concern that the new idea might infringe upon their turf and will seek to trim back or otherwise alter the idea accordingly.

The result is very often the adoption of least-common-denominator, keep-doing-what-we-are-doing policies lacking in creativity and effectiveness. In discussing some of the challenges he faced as the Coordinator for Counterterrorism at the U.S. State Department from 2009 to 2012, Daniel Benjamin described "the difficulty of experimentation in government—there is zero tolerance for risk," noting that it is therefore "easier to do the same stuff over and over and wring your hands."[488] John Hamre, a former Deputy Secretary of Defense who became head of CSIS, a Washington, D.C., think tank, put it simply: "Big bureaucracies do not invent new ideas."[489]

Numerous studies have documented and analyzed the barriers to innovation in the federal government. A recent survey of federal government employees by the Partnership for Public Service revealed that nearly two-thirds believed that there were no rewards for innovation and creativity in their agencies.[490] Another study concluded that "federal employees often find it better to stick to the standard operating procedures than to stick their necks out and try something new."[491] Max Stier, president of the Partnership for Public Service, asserted that many federal employees are risk-averse because they know that "if you do something that doesn't work, there's a very big negative consequence," while "if you do something that does work, there is very little upside."[492]

In light of their smaller size, flatter hierarchies, and more entrepreneurial spirit, creative ideas seem more likely to rise to the top at well-run non-governmental organizations. For example, think tanks "enjoy a different organizational culture from governmental agencies."[493] They "cultivate individual expression, highlight personal achievement, and foster a work environment that supports individual productivity rather than programmatic teamwork and institutional process."[494] At the same time, think tanks often have a sufficient number of former government officials on staff to keep their recommendations attuned to practical realities.[495]

As Margaret Keck and Kathryn Sikkink illustrated in their influential book *Activists Beyond Borders*, advocacy networks are also "among the most important sources of new ideas" and "norms" in the international arena.[496] Keck and Sikkink define such networks as sharing the following characteristics: "the centrality of values or principled ideas, the belief that individuals can make a difference, the creative use of information, and the employment by nongovernmental actors of sophisticated political strategies in targeting their campaigns."[497] "What is novel in these networks," said Keck and Sikkink, "is the ability of nontraditional international actors to mobilize information strategically to help create new issues and categories and to persuade, pressure, and gain leverage over much more powerful organizations and governments."[498] One of the key activities of such advocacy networks is promoting "norm implementation, by pressuring target actors to adopt new policies, and by monitoring compliance with international standards."[499]

The use of lawfare by advocacy networks represents a slight variant on the Keck and Sikkink model. In the lawfare model, a non-governmental actor employs sophisticated legal strategies to gain leverage over more powerful organizations and governments for the purpose of achieving objectives traditionally achieved by kinetic means. The legal strategies are often just one part of the non-governmental actor's arsenal, along with political, economic, and other strategies.

The Boycott, Divestment and Sanctions (BDS) movement, which is discussed elsewhere in this book, is one example of an advocacy network that is engaged in lawfare. Motivated by the strategic goal of "ending the Israeli occupation," it employs sophisticated political and legal strategies to achieve various tactical objectives. For example, it promotes the creation of new EU rules regarding Israel and pressures targeted companies to stop doing business with Israel. Because it is relatively nonhierarchical and what lines of authority it does have are nontransparent, it can move quickly and sharply to take advantage of new opportunities and deploy new tactics. If a new tactic works, it can be adopted and applied elsewhere. If it backfires, retaliation against the network as a whole can be avoided by dismissing the new tactic, whether accurately or inaccurately, as the act of an outsider falsely claiming the movement's mantle.

The even less formal network of non-governmental actors seeking to halt Iran's nuclear weapons program and state sponsorship of terrorism is another example of an advocacy network, albeit a looser one, that is engaged in lawfare. Motivated by the strategic goal of "halting Iran's nuclear program and state sponsorship of terrorism," this network employs sophisticated political and legal strategies to achieve various tactical objectives such as freezing Iranian assets and pressuring target businesses to stop transacting with Iran. In the BDS and Iran examples, the non-governmental actors engaged in the advocacy effort have been able, in many cases, to act more innovatively and quickly than the governments with which they share a common objective.

iii. National Security Lawyers Do Not Prioritize Development of Creative Lawfare Strategies A policymaker at a national security agency traditionally first origi- nates and develops a potential policy step then turns to his or her legal coun- sel and asks whether the policy step would be legal and, if not, how it could be tweaked to make it legal. Policymakers less frequently turn to their lawyers at the start of the policymaking process and ask how law could be used to achieve the policy objective. As Abram Chayes, a former State Department Legal Adviser, put it, international law principally influences foreign policy "first, as a constraint on action; second, as the basis of justification or legitimization for action; and third, as providing organizational structures, procedures and forums" within which political decisions may be reached.[500] Notably, none of the three involves international law being used as a weapon or tool with which to act.

Providing "clearance" on policy decisions is the foremost role of attorneys in the general counsel's offices of the national security agencies. The clearance process often commences only once the policy decision has been sufficiently well developed to be the subject of a draft "decision memorandum" to a senior policy official. In this role of "clearance" provider, attorneys advise policymak- ers whether or not their proposed course of action is consistent with the vari- ous applicable domestic and international laws. If the proposed course of action would be illegal, the attorney will often advise the policymaker on how to adjust the proposed policy step to the minimum extent necessary so as to make it legal. If the proposed course of action would be legal, the attorney may help the policy- maker develop a public statement justifying and legitimizing the course of action by explaining why it is legal.

Illustrative of international law and lawyers being treated as preeminently a constraint on foreign policy action is the leading book on the role of the State

Department Legal Adviser—*Shaping Foreign Policy in Times of Crisis: The Role of International Law and the State Department Legal Adviser.*[501] The book focuses almost entirely on whether and how the ten Legal Advisers profiled had succeeded in persuading policymakers to comply with the constraints of international law, rather than on if and when they had succeeded in creatively harnessing international or domestic law to more effectively achieve U.S. policy objectives.

This compliance-dominated mindset is largely a result of the continuing debate over the extent to which international law, with its general lack of enforcement mechanisms (especially vis-à-vis a superpower), should be complied with by the United States. As Harold Koh, the State Department Legal Adviser during the first Obama administration, notes, there is a school of thought in the United States that "obeying international law should be done only when convenient."[502] The ten former Legal Advisers interviewed in *Shaping Foreign Policy* tended to see their role as more that of a judge of, rather than an advocate for, the aims of the administration they served.[503] The combination of this approach and policymaker skepticism of the importance of international law meant that for these Legal Advisers, "often the most important battle was simply to ensure that [the Legal Adviser's Office] had a proverbial 'seat at the table' at which policy decisions were made."[504]

As a result, the dominant recommendation, emerging from *Shaping Foreign Policy in Times of Crisis*, as to how the Legal Adviser's Office could be more effective going forward, was that it should be more aggressively evangelical in promoting the merits of compliance with international law. "The Legal Adviser's key role is to promote the rule of law . . . [to] urge both our country and others to uphold the rule of international law," concluded Koh in his introduction to the book.[505]

A lawfare approach to international law does not counsel violating international law. Nor does it ignore the considerable value of compliance. Instead, it encourages national security policymakers to recognize, understand, and adapt to law's increasing power as a weapon of war. One part of this adaptation must be at the strategic level, including by investing time and resources in thinking, developing, and enhancing the capacity to systematically and innovatively deploy and counter lawfare.

Another part of this adaptation must be at the tactical level. This includes turning to law and lawyers at the beginning of the policy development process (to ask whether law can be used as a weapon to achieve the policy objective), rather than only at the clearance stage (to ask whether the already-developed policy course of action is legal or can be, if adjusted). So long as the federal government's international lawyers continue to be engaged predominantly as compliance determiners, non-governmental attorneys who see law as not just a constraint but also a potential weapon will continue to provide a fresh and valuable perspective.

iv. The Tyranny of the Inbox Government officials are often so busy responding to the crises at the tops of their inboxes that they can't make sufficient time to systematically brainstorm or otherwise develop creative ideas. Lee Hamilton, the former Chair of the House Committee on Foreign Affairs, referred to it as "the problem that has become known in Washington as 'the tyranny of the inbox,'" in which "the day-to-day problems are so many, and so pressing, that the policymaker cannot free himself to do much thinking about future challenges."[506] The resultant gap can be filled by think tanks and other non-governmental organizations that are able to free their experts to focus on identifying and developing lawfare and other creative approaches to current and future challenges.

v. National Security Agencies Have Difficulty Seeking Outside Assistance As mentioned before, the national security agencies tend to be relatively inexpert at the dual-use commercial sector and other nonkinetic technical and especially legal skills necessary to creatively combat many of the nontraditional security challenges listed by the President. Contracting requirements, the Federal Advisory Committee Act, and restrictions on the acceptance of volunteer services make it complicated for all federal agencies to seek outside assistance from particular experts. For national security agencies, this problem is compounded by the fact that security clearance restrictions limit their ability to reach outside the government, and sometimes even within the government, for expertise. "The application of international law to the formulation of foreign policy nearly always occurs within the closed—and classified—confines of foreign ministries and other government agencies," wrote Michael Scharf and Paul Williams in *Shaping Foreign Policy in Times of Crisis*.[507] Alan Kreczko, then the State Department's Deputy Legal Adviser, stated that even "when we come to a public international law issue like state succession, we are frequently out of our depth, and there ought to be more ways to draw on other resources."[508]

The various services' JAG corps are in a somewhat better position on this issue than is the State Department Legal Adviser's Office because of the large number of reserve JAG officers. For example, while the roughly 200-attorney Legal Adviser's Office does not have a formal relationship with its alumni, the 1,800-attorney Army JAG Corps has approximately 2,000 reservists.[509] According to Col. Guy Roberts, USMC (ret.), a retired U.S. Marine Corps Judge Advocate, when active-duty Judge Advocates are faced with a question on which there is greater expertise among private sector attorneys, they can sometimes get the answers they need by identifying and reaching out to a reserve JAG officer who has developed that expertise in private practice.[510] However, this approach only works when security or other restrictions do not preclude posing the question and is limited by the expertise that JAGs happen to have developed in their private sector careers.

A non-governmental lawfare practitioner who can pick up the phone and call the United States' leading expert on a particular area of Chinese law, even if that expert does not have a security clearance, may therefore be able to act more quickly and effectively than could the U.S. government.

III. THE POTENTIAL FUTURE ROLE IN LAWFARE OF U.S. PRIVATE SECTOR AND OTHER NON-GOVERNMENTAL ATTORNEYS

As of spring 2015, there are remarkably few private sector or other non-governmental attorneys engaged in lawfare. In light of the considerable costs of mounting an ATA or FSIA lawsuit, this is less surprising in the litigation arena than with regard to legislative or executive branch lawfare. Regardless, the number of private sector or other non-governmental attorneys engaged in lawfare of all types seems likely to increase significantly in the coming years. This section will first examine potential new sources of *funding* for non-governmental lawfare. Then it will examine potential new sources of *attorneys* for non-governmental lawfare.

A. New Sources of Funding

In the litigation lawfare arena, the cost of entry can be prohibitively high, especially in light of the particular challenges of collecting on any awards. Most of the cases are brought on a contingency or pro bono basis, and expenses "can easily run to between $2 million and $4 million per lawsuit."[511] In addition to attorney time, bringing a lawfare suit can require hiring translators and expert witnesses, serving subpoenas in distant locations, and collecting evidence in multiple countries.[512] Five years into the decade-long *Boim* case, the Lewins reported that they had already spent more than $1 million in attorney time, before even getting to trial.[513]

As of spring 2015, the funding model for litigation lawfare seemed likely to change. For lawfare litigation that appeared likely to eventually result in a collected award, the prospect emerged of hedge fund investment. For example, with regard to the Marine barracks bombing judgment discussed earlier in this chapter, RD Legal Capital LLC was reported by the *Wall Street Journal* to be "buying rights to some of the payments received by victims' families, as well as fees earned by their attorneys involved in the case, at a discount to face value."[514] The *Journal* noted that "the two lead counsels on the Beirut case, Washington-based Perles Law Firm PC, and Fay Kaplan Law PA, haven't been paid any money from RD Legal in this case."[515] The *Journal* described the RD Legal investments as an example of "litigation finance, a growing industry that bankrolls lawsuits and settlements in the hopes of collecting if damages are paid."[516]

For Steve Perles, the lead attorney in the Marine barracks bombing litigation, the emergence of litigation finance for lawfare litigation is "a very good thing."[517] He noted that the Marine barracks bombing litigation has "a lot of working class family" plaintiffs—military families, mostly not independently wealthy, who are hindered financially by the loss of the victim's earning potential—and had, as of spring 2015, been going on for over thirteen years.[518] "The fact that this litigation is so protracted works an undue hardship on those families and the litigation funder helps bridge that hardship and also takes a huge amount of pressure off of me because in that case I don't have clients that are in financial extremis anymore, so I can take my time and do this case right" rather than settle prematurely, said Perles.[519] Litigation finance "is a tremendous tool for plaintiffs' counsel who are representing people who are not independently wealthy; it helps me expand my capacity to wage lawfare on the bad guys," asserted Perles.[520] Perles predicted that unless these types of cases start lasting far fewer years between initiation and collection, reliance on the litigation finance model is likely to increase.[521]

Perles predicted that the future may also bring more cases involving cooperative arrangements between the Justice Department and civil plaintiffs. He provided as an example the arrangement reached between them regarding the litigation involving the Alavi Foundation and Iran over ownership of the office tower at 650 Fifth Avenue in Manhattan.[522] As discussed earlier in this chapter, Iran's ownership of the office tower came to the Justice Department's attention as a result of the *Flatow* lawsuit. As of spring 2015 (prior to the announcement of the Joint Comprehensive Plan of Action between the P-5+1 and Iran), the office tower appeared to be on its way to being sold by the U.S. government, with the assets going toward compensating victims of Iranian terrorism, including the Marine barracks bombing victims.[523] According to Perles, the arrangement was to be a kind of "sharing agreement" or "joint venture" between the Justice Department and the civil plaintiffs.[524] As discussed in Section II.B.3 of this chapter, it was unclear as of early August 2015, when this book went to press, what impact the Joint Comprehensive Plan of Action might have on the 650 Fifth Avenue case or other U.S. lawfare cases against Iran. It was therefore unknown whether the innovative "joint venture" idea would be implemented with regard to the 650 Fifth Avenue case or simply be on the list of options for future lawfare practitioners to draw from in a future case against another U.S. adversary or a re-targeted Iran.

Perles also predicted that the future may bring more transfers of criminal penalties against state sponsors of terrorism and their material supporters to victims on the basis of the concept of "remission."[525] The Attorney General's "remission authority" enables the Department of Justice to "restore forfeited assets to the victims of any offense that gave rise to the forfeiture."[526] Perles provided as an example the $8.9 billion forfeited to the U.S. Department of Justice by BNP Paribas as a result of the bank's laundering of money for Cuba, Iran, and Sudan (a case discussed in detail in Chapter 3). Perles explained that the remission authority enabled the Justice Department to use the $8.9 billion as compensation for U.S. victims holding U.S court judgments as a result of acts of terrorism that were materially supported by the BNP Paribas money laundering.[527]

According to Perles, such a use of the BNP Paribas funds would be more sensible and consistent with congressional intent and U.S. jurisprudence than the much broader distribution of forfeited BNP Paribas funds which the Department of Justice appeared to be considering.[528] Perles was referring to the Department's launch on May 1, 2015, of a website, titled United States v. BNP Paribas S.A., which invited submissions from all individuals worldwide, "regardless of nationality or citizenship," who claim to have "suffered harm linked to Sudan, Cuba, and Iran from 2004–2012."[529] The website specified that "the information collected will assist the Government in determining use of available forfeited funds,"[530] implying that the U.S. government might distribute some of the funds forfeited to it by BNP Paribas to persons with no nexus to the United States and no U.S. court judgment substantiating their claim.[531]

While public-private joint ventures, litigation finance, and remissions hold promise for helping incentivize and fund some types of litigation lawfare, much litigation lawfare will continue to have only a very small or no prospect of resulting in a collectable award. For such cases, the funding model seemed to be shifting to a donor-driven model.

One example of the donor-driven model is Shurat HaDin, the cutting-edge lawfare NGO based in Israel, which, as of 2015, reportedly had an annual budget of $2.5 million.[532] According to its website, "Shurat HaDin's budget relies entirely on the generosity of donors."[533] "Donations," it explained, "are needed to assist in the funding of the terror victim litigation against the Palestinian terrorist organizations, their leaders and financial patrons," in order to "permit the survivors of the hundreds of killed and injured to seek justice and compensation through the court systems around the world."[534]

Meanwhile, litigation against Israel also seemed to be operating on a donor-driven model. As described in Chapter 6, the Palestinian Centre for Human Rights (PCHR) has been the leading Palestinian NGO promoting universal jurisdiction prosecutions of Israeli officials. Since universal jurisdiction prosecutions are criminal in nature, they do not typically involve any potential compensation for the instigating parties. In addition, as PCHR noted in a report on the topic, after eight years of pursuing them, "thus far none of PCHR's universal jurisdiction cases have resulted in a successful prosecution."[535] The universal jurisdiction prosecution campaign must therefore have been funded by donations of money or attorney time or both. The PCHR website lists the organization's leading donors, which in 2015 included non-governmental organizations such as the Ford Foundation and the Open Society Fund, as well as governments such as the European Commission, Norway, and Denmark.[536] While it was unclear from the PCHR website which donors contributed specifically to the universal jurisdiction litigation, it seemed evident that the litigation did not pay for itself.

NGO Monitor, an Israeli NGO that conducts analyses of foreign funding of Palestinian and left-wing Israeli NGOs engaged in lawfare, has asserted that millions of dollars in pro-Palestinian lawfare has been funded by the EU and by the governments of Norway, Denmark, Sweden, Switzerland, the Netherlands, and the U.K.[537] For example, NGO Monitor pointed to an announcement that

Denmark, the Netherlands, Sweden, and Switzerland provided funding for PCHR and other Palestinian NGOs to collect "documentation of human rights and international humanitarian law violations during the course of Israel's ongoing military offensive on the Gaza Strip."[538] The collection was "for the purposes of supporting national and international mechanisms"[539] (apparently a reference to the ICC and the U.N. Human Rights Commission investigations). The announcement was made by the Human Rights and International Humanitarian Law Secretariat, which describes itself as "a joint donor programme sponsored by Denmark, the Netherlands, Sweden and Switzerland."[540]

As lawfare becomes increasingly widespread, and its power becomes more widely understood, it seems likely that more and more donor funding—both private and governmental—will be directed to supporting lawfare of various types.

B. New Sources of Non-Governmental Attorneys

As of spring 2015, there were only a handful of non-governmental organizations explicitly working on deploying or countering lawfare (as defined by this book). Consistent with the Israeli-Palestinian conflict's cutting-edge role in the lawfare arena, a considerable portion of those organizations were focused on that particular conflict. For example, the Israel-based Shurat HaDin described itself as utilizing "court systems around the world to go on the legal offensive against Israel's enemies,"[541] and the U.S.-based Lawfare Project focused on "identifying, analyzing, and facilitating a response to lawfare"[542] in relation to the Israeli-Palestinian conflict and terrorism.[543] Whether or not they called it "lawfare," Palestinian groups including PCHR and Al-Haq were, in this author's judgment, also clearly working on using law to achieve objectives traditionally achieved by kinetic means, as were law firms such as the ones headed by Steven Perles and Gary Osen.

As lawfare's power continues to increase and become more widely understood, the number of private sector or other non-governmental attorneys engaged in lawfare of various types seems likely to rise significantly. Private philanthropists will likely fund more attorneys to engage in NGO lawfare work on behalf of causes they support. Meanwhile, governments will likely both increase their grant support of NGO lawfare and hire more consultants with lawfare-relevant expertise.

Who will be the most influential players in the new, lawfare era?

As of the spring of 2015, there were relatively few international and national security law experts in residence at some of the leading foreign policy think tanks. For example, in April 2015, the Council on Foreign Relations had two adjunct senior fellows (John Bellinger and Matthew Waxman) focused on international and national security law but no senior fellows in residence who were focused on those topics. In contrast, the Brookings Institution had more international security law expertise and a formal relationship with the Lawfare Blog,[544] which—along with the Just Security[545] and Opinio Juris[546] blogs—featured many of the United

States' leading, most thoughtful, and most practical commentators on international security law issues. It seems likely that as the power of law as a weapon of war increases and becomes better understood, more leading think tanks will take note and add international security law analytical expertise and content.

As of spring 2015, most of the leading international security law commentators in the United States, at the aforementioned blogs and elsewhere, were law professors. While think tanks tend to focus on providing analysis and avoid becoming operational, law schools, at least in the United States, can be sources of both analysis and—through their clinics—action. At least three law school clinics have undertaken lawfare-type work, although not necessarily for lawfare-type reasons.

The Allard K. Lowenstein International Human Rights Law Clinic at Yale Law School was co-counsel for plaintiffs in a federal lawsuit that resulted in a $4.5 billion judgment against Bosnian Serb leader Radovan Karadzic on behalf of victims of abuses during the war in Bosnia.[547] The clinic also represented Eritreans whose property was expropriated when they were expelled from Ethiopia following the outbreak of war between Ethiopia and Eritrea.[548] In addition, the Lowenstein Clinic "worked with counsel who brought" a universal jurisdiction action in Belgium seeking the criminal prosecution of Ariel Sharon, then prime minister of Israel, "on behalf of twenty-three plaintiffs who were injured and lost family members or property in the September 1982 massacre in the Sabra and Shatilla refugee camps in Lebanon."[549]

Separately, the University of Pennsylvania Law School's Criminal Law Research Group, led by Professor Paul Robinson, "undertook a research project in collaboration with the U.S. Military's Special Operations Command-Pacific (SOCPAC) to identify aspects of foreign domestic criminal law that can be used to facilitate the prosecution and detention of foreign terrorist fighters."[550] The project was designed to determine "ways in which fighters may be legally interdicted on their way to join ISIS or coming home from fighting for or supporting ISIS."[551]

In addition, various projects at the Case Western Reserve University School of Law involve lawfare-type work. For example, students in the Terrorism Prosecution Lab "conduct research and prepare legal memos for the Office of the Prosecutor for the Department of Defense Office of Military Commissions."[552]

It seems likely that as the power of law as a weapon of war increases and becomes better understood, more law schools will add lawfare-type clinical projects. Such clinical projects can have an impact in and of themselves. However, their primary influence is likely to be in the training, connections, credentials, and inspiration they provide their students.

As mentioned before, the United States' leading experts on many types of lawfare-relevant legal issues are attorneys at private law firms. Such attorneys are, at present, by far the largest untapped reservoir of lawfare-related legal expertise in the United States.

How could this reservoir be tapped most effectively?

Law firms are businesses. The vast majority of their work is done for paying clients. Most law firms also do some pro bono work.

The national security agencies have large budgets. However, they are not currently well set up either to pay law firm market rates or to quickly contract for one-off analytical products (e.g., an analysis by the United States' leading expert on Greek maritime insurance law of how such law might be deployed to stop a particular vessel due to depart shortly from a Greek harbor). First, federal agencies tend to balk, rightly or wrongly, at paying the rates charged by leading attorneys. The average hourly rate for a partner at a Washington, D.C., law firm was $705 in 2014.[553] With a federal government attorney at the top of the GS scale earning $158,700 in 2015 (around $100 per hour after benefits are factored in), federal agencies tended to be uncomfortable paying several multiples of that to outside legal consultants. Second, federal contracting processes—which tend to be protracted and require competition—do not lend themselves to hiring outside consultants to quickly provide one-off analytical products (e.g., today an analysis of Greek maritime insurance law by attorney *A* at firm *B*, tomorrow an analysis of Chinese criminal law by attorney *C* at firm *D*).

At the same time, the provision of assistance to national security agencies does not fit the traditional conception of pro bono service. The American Bar Association Model Rules of Professional Conduct provision on pro bono service defines it as providing "legal services to those unable to pay."[554] It asserts that "a lawyer should aspire to render at least (50) hours of pro bono publico legal services per year" and "a substantial majority" of those hours should be to either "persons of limited means" or to "charitable, religious, civic, community, governmental and educational organizations in matters which are designed primarily to address the needs of persons of limited means."[555]

As has been widely reported, several leading U.S. law firms each contributed thousands of hours of pro bono work defending Guantanamo detainees against prosecution by the U.S. government.[556] For example, just one firm, WilmerHale, reportedly provided Guantanamo Bay detainees with "35,448 hours of pro bono legal help worth an estimated $17 million."[557] Providing free defense counsel to Guantanamo detainees fits the traditional definition of pro bono service, while providing uncompensated guidance to the Defense Department on how to use Chinese criminal law to stop a supplier of nuclear technology to Iran does not.

However, the fact that providing lawfare-related expertise to the U.S. government does not fit within the traditional definition of pro bono service does not preclude attorneys from providing such expertise. From the author's informal discussions with several law firm partners in Washington, D.C., it appears likely that a number of leading law firm attorneys would be happy to provide lawfare-related expertise to the U.S. government on a pro bono or "low bono" basis ("low bono" is a term used to describe work done at a heavily discounted rate).

One major obstacle to the provision of such work is the potential for client conflicts. In other words, the United States' leading expert on Greek maritime insurance law probably has a lot of clients for whom the expert has or feels an obligation not to set an adverse precedent.

Another obstacle to the provision of such work is the lack of existing mechanisms for linking lawfare-related law firm expertise to lawfare practitioners (whether inside the U.S. government or at NGOs). In light of lawfare's increasing power, and the maxim that necessity is the mother of invention, it seems likely that such mechanisms will be created in the near future.

Barring significant changes to current government contracting rules, the most likely mechanisms for linking lawfare-related law firm expertise to national security agencies may involve the issuance by such agencies of highly flexible large-scale government contracts of the "indefinite delivery, indefinite quantity" variety. Such a contract could enable the contract's holder to hire attorneys on a short-term basis from a variety of law firms to, as needed, quickly provide the agency's lawfare practitioners with expert input (presumably at a "low bono" rate of compensation). Meanwhile, the most effective mechanisms for linking lawfare-related law firm expertise to non-governmental lawfare practitioners may be non-governmental organizations that serve, at least in part, as clearinghouses that provide such connections in various issue areas.

It would also not be surprising to see some sort of a hybrid emerge—a non-governmental organization that regularly engages in lawfare on behalf of the U.S. government and, in doing so, draws extensively on law firm expertise. As this book describes, there are already several models of public-private partnerships to wage lawfare. For example, the chapter on Israeli lawfare describes the Israeli government's past partnership with Shurat HaDin and analyzes why governments may sometimes prefer to wage lawfare through proxies. Although the Israeli government's partnership with Shurat HaDin eventually dissolved in acrimony, it may be that the Israeli, the U.S., or another government could develop a more enduring relationship with a lawfare-waging NGO. The chapter on Palestinian NGO lawfare notes that PCHR and other Palestinian lawfare-waging NGOs are heavily subsidized by European governments. Since these arrangements have continued for several years, the European governments have presumably found them useful.

The U.S. executive branch has generally kept its distance from lawfare-waging firms and other non-governmental organizations. However, it too has occasionally seen fit to partner with them, as exemplified by the U.S. Treasury Department's decision to provide Steve Perles, the attorney for the Marine barracks bombing victims, with the number for a Citibank account containing some $2 billion dollars in Iranian funds.

In light of lawfare's increasing power and its increased deployment by U.S. adversaries, it would not be surprising in the years ahead to see the U.S. executive branch experiment with mechanisms for more closely partnering with lawfare-waging non-governmental organizations.

CHAPTER 3

The U.S. Government's Financial Lawfare Against Iran

The Treasury "has opened up a new battlefield for the United States."
— *U.S. Treasury Secretary Jacob J. Lew*

During the Obama administration's multiyear campaign to halt Iran's nuclear weapons program without bombing it, "Treasury's under secretary for terrorism and financial intelligence [was] sometimes described within the administration as President Obama's favorite combatant commander,"[1] said the *New York Times*. According to Treasury Secretary Jacob J. Lew, Treasury "opened up a new battlefield for the United States."[2] "In a dingy suite of offices, in a Treasury Department annex, the troops . . . blast out advisories ordering banks to block targeted people, then threaten them with consequences—fines that can range into millions of dollars—if they do not," said the *Times*, stating that "today, this is how the Obama Administration goes to war."[3]

At a peak in the campaign, Iranian President Mahmoud Ahmadinejad complained bitterly of how "the enemy has banned Iran's oil sales and banking transactions so Iran is not able to transfer or spend money," referring to it as a "hidden war . . . on a far-reaching global scale . . . a kind of war through which the enemy assumes it can defeat the Iranian nation."[4] "What's increasingly clear," wrote *Washington Post* columnist David Ignatius about U.S. policy toward Iran in 2011, "is that low-key weapons—covert sabotage and economic sanctions—are accomplishing many of the benefits of military action, without the costs."[5]

"Fifteen years ago, the idea that the Treasury Department would be at the center of our national security would have been inconceivable," said Daniel

Glaser, the Treasury Department's Assistant Secretary for Terrorist Financing.[6] "But," explains Glaser, "we have developed a whole new set of tools to put at the President's disposal."[7]

When Russia invaded Ukraine in 2014, it was no surprise that the U.S. response relied heavily on the Treasury Department "using financial weaponry to hit carefully chosen targets" linked to the Russian government.[8] When the Islamic State rose to prominence that same year, the *New York Times* called Treasury the "first line of attack against ISIS" and said Treasury's financial lawfare "may be more important in the fight against the Islamic State than the Tomahawks fired off American warships or the bombs dropped from F-16s."[9] "This is the 21st century version of waging war," said Judith Lee, chair of the international trade group at the law firm of Gibson, Dunn and Crutcher.[10] *Newsweek* asserted that, for the United States at least, "the first salvo in modern warfare is likely to be financial—and the result is increasingly effective."[11]

This chapter will describe and analyze how U.S. financial lawfare works and how it differs from the imposition of traditional economic sanctions. The chapter will also describe and analyze the strengths and weaknesses of U.S. financial lawfare and assess what its future may hold. The chapter will do so largely by focusing on the preeminent and most sophisticated U.S. financial lawfare campaign thus far: U.S. financial lawfare designed to halt Iran's nuclear weapons program and state sponsorship of terrorism.[12]

As of early August 2015, U.S. financial lawfare against Iran was in the midst of a change of unclear dimensions. On July 14, 2015 (after this book was largely completed), the P-5+1 (the U.N. Security Council's five permanent members plus Germany) announced that they had agreed with Iran on a Joint Comprehensive Plan of Action (JCPOA) to address Iran's nuclear program.[13] The JCPOA provided for the lifting of most nuclear-related sanctions on Iran in exchange for various constraints on Iran's nuclear program.

Pursuant to the Iran Nuclear Agreement Review Act, enacted in May 2015, Congress was to have sixty calendar days, following the JCPOA's transmission to Congress, to review the deal and pass a joint resolution of disapproval.[14] The President could then veto the resolution, following which Congress could override the veto, should opponents of the deal muster sufficient votes to do so.

As of early August 2015, the results of the congressional review of the JCPOA were difficult to predict. Also difficult to predict was the precise impact that entry into effect of the JCPOA (or, conversely, its derailment) would have on U.S. financial lawfare against Iran. The JCPOA did not on its face commit the United States to suspend U.S. sanctions on Iran for its involvement with terrorism, or lift Iran's designation as a state sponsor of terrorism.[15] Treasury officials insisted that they planned to continue to vigorously engage in financial lawfare against Iran. For example, Adam Szubin, the Acting Under Secretary of the Treasury for Terrorism and Financial Intelligence, testified before Congress on

August 5, 2015, that notwithstanding the JCPOA, "the United States will maintain and continue to vigorously enforce our powerful sanctions targeting Iran's backing for terrorist groups such as Hizballah."[16]

However, in a July 22, 2015, hearing before the House Financial Services Committee, Steven Perles asserted that various U.S. "administrative agencies have made recent decisions that raise concerns about their continuing willingness to carry out their legal obligations to enforce antiterrorism sanctions against Iran after nuclear sanctions are removed."[17] In addition, even if the U.S. government were to continue to vigorously pursue its financial lawfare designed to halt Iran's state sponsorship of terrorism, it was unclear how the effectiveness of such lawfare would be impacted by factors including the lessening of nuclear-related sanctions on Iran and the resulting release of tens of billions of dollars of Iranian assets from its blocked accounts in Europe and Asia.[18]

As a result, it was unclear, as of early August 2015, to what extent the U.S. financial lawfare described in this chapter would continue to be implemented vis-à-vis Iran. Either way, its various innovations would remain tested options for lawfare practitioners to draw from in a future campaign against another U.S. adversary or a re-targeted Iran.

In describing and analyzing the U.S. financial lawfare campaign against Iran, this chapter will briefly reference other very significant U.S. financial lawfare campaigns, including those against North Korea and Russia. This chapter will also briefly reference some of the U.S. economic lawfare campaigns in other sectors that have been heavily influenced by lessons learned from U.S. financial lawfare. That includes the U.S. energy lawfare campaign against Iran (which is discussed in Chapter 2 as well as this chapter), U.S. insurance lawfare, and the U.S. lawfare campaign against suppliers to Iran's nuclear program (which is discussed in Chapter 4 as well as this chapter). In addition, the role in U.S. financial lawfare of Benjamin Lawsky, the aggressive superintendent of the New York Department of Financial Services, echoes some of the themes raised in Chapter 2's discussion of the pluses and minuses of lawfare waged by U.S. actors other than the federal executive branch.

Section I of this chapter discusses U.S. financial lawfare against Iran in conceptual context. Section II describes and analyzes the key nexus between U.S. financial lawfare and Iran's nuclear weapons program and state sponsorship of terrorism: Iran's use of the international financial system to advance those objectives. Section III provides an overview of key innovative elements of U.S. financial lawfare against Iran. Section IV describes and analyzes the impact that U.S. financial lawfare had against Iran. Section V systematically describes and analyzes how the U.S. government implemented financial lawfare against Iran.

Section VI discusses lessons learned and the future of U.S. financial and other economic lawfare. It concludes that the effects of the various lawfare deployments described in this book indicate that lawfare, deployed in a more coordinated and systematic manner, could likely save U.S. and foreign lives, and U.S. taxpayer dollars, by supplementing or replacing kinetic warfare as a tool for achieving some significant U.S. military objectives. The chapter wraps up with a few thoughts as to how the U.S. government could achieve these benefits by more broadly, systematically, and effectively waging lawfare against U.S. adversaries.

I. U.S. FINANCIAL LAWFARE AGAINST IRAN IN CONCEPTUAL CONTEXT

Each of the four major categories of U.S. governmental economic lawfare against Iran that are discussed in this book—financial, energy, state and local, and WMD-supplier-focused lawfare—differs significantly from traditional economic sanctions. Traditional economic sanctions broadly and bluntly embargo trade between the imposing country (e.g., the United States) and the target country (e.g., Iran). As of spring 2015, nearly all U.S. trade with Iran had been prohibited since 1995.[19] With such embargoes, the focus tends to be relatively straightforward: prohibiting persons in the United States from engaging in all or some trade with an entire foreign country, and then policing U.S. persons and patrolling U.S. borders to ensure compliance.

The focus of U.S. governmental economic lawfare against Iran has instead been on halting some or all commerce between Iran and foreigners located in third countries. While curtailing such international commerce has traditionally been attempted through quarantines imposed by force of arms, economic lawfare principally accomplishes this objective through the creative, dynamic, and aggressive leveraging of U.S. law and jurisdiction to pressure foreign companies that engage in commerce with particular Iranian bad actors. Each of the four referenced types of U.S. governmental economic lawfare against Iran involved an implied or explicit threat of legal action pursuant to U.S. federal, state, or local law, delivered to the foreign company by U.S. federal, state, or local government officials, which persuaded the foreign company to stop doing business with the targets, even though such business may not have been prohibited by the government of the country in which the foreign company is headquartered.

It is in light of these characteristics that this chapter refers to these U.S. economic measures against Iran as economic lawfare. These measures have thus far been more typically referred to in the media as sanctions or "smart sanctions." However, Major General Charles W. Dunlap, Jr., who (as described in Chapter 1) first coined the term "lawfare" to describe the use of law as a weapon of war, included financial warfare within the ambit of lawfare. For example, Dunlap referred to "the use of legal processes to deconstruct terrorist financing" as a type of lawfare[20] and explained that while attacking the funding of terrorist groups "may be called 'financial warfare' rather than 'lawfare'" by some, "it nevertheless depends upon legal instruments and methodologies."[21]

Juan Zarate, a leading architect of these measures during his service as a senior Treasury and White House official, referred to U.S. financial measures against Iran as "financial warfare" in his magisterial book *Treasury's War: The Unleashing of a New Era of Financial Warfare*.[22] It is this book's hypothesis that, consistent with Dunlap's view, these financial measures are also a salient, and indeed paradigmatic, example of lawfare. As this chapter will demonstrate, analyzing Treasury's war from the perspective of lawfare helps in understanding both Treasury's war and the broader power and potential of lawfare.

The pivotal actions undertaken by the officers in Treasury's war involved drafting and enacting innovative laws, innovatively threatening to enforce those laws in scores of meetings directly with foreign private banks, and enforcing those laws with dramatically escalating and eventually unprecedented penalties imposed through settlements or convictions within the U.S. domestic legal system. The law-centered nature of Treasury's war is not surprising, as each of the five Treasury policymakers who were its leading architects and implementers—David Cohen, Daniel Glaser, Stuart Levey, Adam Szubin, and Juan Zarate—were lawyers rather than, for example, bankers.

While Treasury's war reflected a new approach to using U.S. financial muscle to achieve national security objectives, it was equally innovative in its aggressive, impact-focused, yet carefully targeted and calibrated use of law to achieve national security objectives. Many of its legal innovations were not unique to finance but could and would be subsequently applied to the U.S. government's energy, insurance, and WMD-supply lawfare against Iran, and could in the future be applied to lawfare against other targets in other economic sectors. In addition, the financial lawfare measures undertaken by the U.S. government against Iran in several ways provided critical legal underpinnings for private civil litigation and other non-governmental U.S. lawfare against Iran, as described in Chapter 2.

The U.S. Treasury Department's war against Iran took off in 2006 under the George W. Bush administration. It was inspired by various factors including the administration's North Korean Illicit Activities Initiative (NKIAI).[23] The NKIAI, led by David Asher and others, "generated significant diplomatic leverage over North Korea," including especially when the United States imposed financial lawfare measures in September 2005 against Banco Delta Asia, a Chinese bank accused of laundering money for North Korea.[24] However, the NKIAI ultimately did not succeed in curtailing North Korea's nuclear program.[25] Nor did the NKIAI last the entirety of the Bush administration, let alone survive into the Obama administration.[26]

In contrast with the North Korean Illicit Activities Initiative, Treasury's war against Iran lasted until the end of the Bush administration, continued (and indeed increased in firepower) under the Obama administration, and was generally credited with helping convince Iran to negotiate seriously regarding its nuclear program. As discussed earlier in this chapter, the resulting negotiations had, as of early August 2015, resulted in the Joint Comprehensive Plan of Action, pursuant to which most nuclear-related sanctions on Iran were to be lifted in exchange for various constraints on Iran's nuclear program.

In a tribute to the bipartisan appeal of Treasury's war against Iran, the Obama administration had made the extraordinary decision to retain in place Stuart Levey, the Bush-appointed Under Secretary of the Treasury who was principally known as the leading architect of this financial lawfare.[27] Levey served for the first two years of the Obama administration, until he resigned and was replaced by his deputy, David Cohen.[28] After Cohen left to become Deputy Director of the CIA,[29] Obama nominated Adam Szubin to replace him.[30] Szubin had previously served as director of Treasury's Office of Foreign Assets Control, in which capacity he had played a key role in Treasury's war against Iran since its beginning.[31]

During the first six years or so of the Obama administration, the primary objective of U.S. financial lawfare against Iran was halting Iran's nuclear weapons program. The Obama administration's nuclear negotiations with Iran from 2012 to 2015, in which it largely subordinated concerns about Iran's state sponsorship of terrorism in order to focus on Iran's nuclear program, reflect the preeminence which the administration gave to the nuclear issue.

President Obama explained his concerns about Iran's nuclear program in a 2012 speech as follows:

> [The] entire world has an interest in preventing Iran from acquiring a nuclear weapon. A nuclear-armed Iran would thoroughly undermine the non-proliferation regime that we've done so much to build. There are risks that an Iranian nuclear weapon could fall into the hands of a terrorist organization. It is almost certain that others in the region would feel compelled to get their own nuclear weapon, triggering an arms race in one of the world's most volatile regions. It would embolden a regime that has brutalized its own people, and it would embolden Iran's proxies, who have carried out terrorist attacks from the Levant to southwest Asia. And that is why, four years ago, I made a commitment to the American people, and said that we would use all elements of American power to pressure Iran and prevent it from acquiring a nuclear weapon. And that is what we have done.[32]

U.S. economic lawfare, and especially the financial lawfare led by the U.S. Treasury Department, also targeted Iran's state sponsorship of terrorism. Iran was first designated as a state sponsor of terrorism by the U.S. government in 1984 and remained designated as such until at least August 2015.[33] In March 2014, the Treasury Department stated, "Iran remains the world's most active state sponsor of terrorism, planning terrorist attacks, providing lethal aid, and delivering hundreds of millions of dollars per year in support to extremist groups across the globe."[34]

In order to advance its primary objective of halting Iran's nuclear weapons program and secondary objective of halting Iran's state sponsorship of terrorism,

U.S. financial lawfare (as well as energy lawfare) against Iran employed two principal means of leverage: coercion and constraint.[35] Under Secretary of the Treasury Stuart Levey described both aspects of the Obama administration's financial measures against Iran. The coercive aspect was "to sharpen the choice for Iran's leaders between integration with the international community, predicated on fulfilling their international obligations, and the hardship of further isolation."[36] Levey explained that "[b]y dramatically isolating Iran financially and commercially and by capitalizing on Iran's existing vulnerabilities, we can impact Iran's calculations" so as to "create crucial leverage for our diplomacy."[37] The second, constraining aspect was described by Levey, in the nuclear context, as designed to "make it harder for Iran to pursue international procurement for its nuclear and military programs."[38]

Coercing the target (in this case Iran) into halting its illegal behavior succeeds if the costs of the behavior (in this case proceeding with the nuclear weapons program or state sponsorship of terrorism) come to be perceived by the target as outweighing the benefits to the target of proceeding with the behavior.[39] For example, coercion will succeed if all U.S. and allied responses to the nuclear weapons program, including economic lawfare, cost the Iranian regime more than the nuclear program is worth to it. The costs might, for example, include endangering the regime's control over the Iranian people. In contrast, *constraining* the target from engaging in illegal behavior succeeds if all U.S. and allied responses to the nuclear weapons program, including economic lawfare, so materially reduce the target's supply of assets necessary to engage in the illegal behavior that the target is no longer able to engage in some or all of the illegal behavior.

As mentioned previously, Iran is not the only target against which U.S. government entities have waged financial lawfare. Al Qaeda, Hezbollah, North Korea, Russia, Serbia, Syria, and various narcotics traffickers have also been major targets. However, Iran provides the most useful case study, because the financial lawfare against Iran was particularly sustained, systematic, creative, and intensive, and was publicly discussed and explained in extraordinary detail by U.S. officials.

Lawfare was an apt response to Iran in part because in pursuing its nuclear weapons program and state sponsorship of terrorism, the Iranian government egregiously violated international law. For example, Iran for years violated legally binding U.N. Security Council resolutions ordering it to suspend its nuclear enrichment, reprocessing, and heavy water-related activities.[40] In a series of periodic reports, the Director General of the International Atomic Energy Agency determined again and again that "contrary to the relevant resolutions of the Board of Governors and the Security Council, Iran has not suspended all of its enrichment related activities" and "has not suspended work on all heavy water related projects."[41]

Iran also persisted in providing destabilizing support to terrorist groups,[42] including by supplying them with arms in violation of U.N. Security Council

Resolutions 1701 and 1747.[43] In addition, Iran chose to violate numerous other international legal obligations. For example, Iran's brutal response to its opposition Green Movement contravened its human rights obligations under international law, including the International Covenant on Civil and Political Rights.[44]

II. IRAN'S USE OF THE INTERNATIONAL FINANCIAL SYSTEM TO ACCOMPLISH ITS NUCLEAR AND TERRORISM SPONSORSHIP OBJECTIVES

Iran for over a decade utilized the international financial system to accomplish both its nuclear and its terrorism sponsorship objectives.[45] Iran's integration into the international financial system both provided the Iranian government with the global financial capability to support its nuclear and terrorism sponsorship activities and exposed elements of the international financial system to a risk of facilitating these activities.[46]

"Iran uses various techniques to engage in seemingly legitimate commercial transactions that are actually related to its nuclear and missile programs," said Daniel Glaser, Deputy Assistant Secretary of the Treasury for Terrorist Financing and Financial Crimes, in a 2008 Congressional hearing.[47] "This deceptive behavior," said Glaser, "coupled with Iran's access to the global economy, gives the Iranian regime the financial capability to support its activities."[48] "All of this adds up to enormous risks for the international financial system," added Glaser.[49]

One might expect that Iran would have avoided the formal financial system and relied instead on moving money using such methods as *hawala* that can be effectuated without the creation of official financial records. However, Treasury has found that for rogue actors, there is sometimes "no good alternative and, in many cases, no alternative at all" to the formal international financial system.[50]

Proliferation networks, for example, turn out to require letters of credit and other types of financing for many of their purchases.[51] Such networks often depend heavily on generally legitimate businessmen or manufacturers who will supply a proliferation-sensitive item because of profit rather than ideology. Such suppliers may find it harder to turn a blind eye or may be otherwise discomfited by a transaction that avoids the formal financial system. In addition, rogue states, including Iran, themselves depend on the global financial system for such functions as holding reserves and financing both their revenue-earning exports and their imports of such strategic commodities as gasoline.

In order to avoid suspicion and minimize the risk of detection, Iran's state-owned banks and other entities used an array of deceptive practices when employing their global financial ties to advance Iran's nuclear program and sponsorship of terrorism.[52] For example, Iran used front companies and intermediaries to surreptitiously purchase technology and materials for its nuclear and missile programs from countries that would prohibit such exports to Iran.[53]

In addition, Iranian banks asked other financial institutions to remove the Iranian banks' names when processing their transactions through the international financial system.[54] The goal was to allow Iranian banks to remain undetected as they moved money through the international financial system to pay for the Iranian government's nuclear- and missile-related purchases and to fund terrorism.[55] The name-removal tactic was intended to evade the controls put in place by responsible financial institutions further down the line and had the effect of potentially involving those institutions in transactions that were illegal, that placed their reputations at risk, and that they might never have engaged in if they knew who was really involved.[56]

Iran's reliance on deceptive financial transactions to support its nuclear and terrorism sponsorship activities contributed to its persistent unwillingness to meet international standards for the development and implementation of laws and enforcement capabilities that would detect and prevent money laundering or terrorist financing. In February 2015, the Financial Action Task Force (FATF), an intergovernmental body that sets standards for anti-money-laundering (AML) and combating the financing of terrorism (CFT), stated that "[t]he FATF remains particularly and exceptionally concerned about Iran's failure to address the risk of terrorist financing and the serious threat this poses to the integrity of the international financial system . . . . The FATF urges Iran to immediately and meaningfully address its AML/CFT deficiencies."[57]

III. INNOVATIVE ELEMENTS OF U.S. FINANCIAL LAWFARE AGAINST IRAN

The U.S. government's multifaceted financial lawfare campaign against Iran relied heavily on the primacy in international finance of U.S. dollars, the preferred currency of international trade. As of 2012, the U.S. dollar was involved in some 87 percent of the world's foreign-exchange transactions and was the global reserve currency.[58] In leveraging the dollar's primacy, the U.S. financial lawfare strategy deployed several key innovations that will be described in detail in this and subsequent sections. The innovations include: direct outreach to individual foreign private financial institutions, aggressive use of financial regulatory authorities to pursue political goals, effective development and harnessing of intelligence about global financial transactions, a focus on the illicit conduct of lawfare targets, and an eye for deterring transactions beyond what is explicitly prohibited.

In developing and implementing its multifaceted financial lawfare campaign, the United States used the U.N. Security Council or partnered with allies where possible, but also found effective ways to operate outside of such cooperative arrangements. To maximize its effectiveness, the United States worked to convince not only individual foreign governments but also individual non-American companies to join the effort. Identifying ways to persuade such non-American companies was "a particularly daunting challenge given the limits of U.S. jurisdiction over foreign entities."[59]

However, once private sector financial institutions are persuaded to act, they are "able to act much more quickly than governments who often lack the necessary authority or the political will to take action on their own"[60] or who may face cumbersome bureaucratic procedures for exercising whatever relevant authority they do have. The U.S. financial lawfare campaign's focus on directly persuading such non-American companies to curtail financial transactions with Iran, and its success in doing so—both described and analyzed in detail in Section V.C of this chapter—were among the campaign's most significant innovations.

Another of the campaign's most innovative aspects was its use of the U.S. Treasury Department's financial authorities to pursue national security objectives. Treasury had, from time to time, used its financial authorities to pursue criminal justice policy objectives. For example, Al Capone famously received his career-ending jail sentence not for his suspected involvement in dozens of murders (which apparently could not be proven) but for tax evasion—running afoul of the Treasury Department's Internal Revenue Service, which subjected him to a nonrandom audit.[61]

National security policy objectives had, however, long remained off limits. "Years ago," recalled Robert Einhorn, the State Department's former Assistant Secretary for Nonproliferation, "people at State would go to Treasury and say, 'We've got a lot of financial muscle, we should use it to pursue political goals,' but Treasury would always say it didn't want to mess around with the international financial system."[62]

Indicative of the novel approach taken by the architects of U.S. financial lawfare against Iran was G.W. Bush Treasury Secretary Henry Paulson's statement that he and his finance ministry counterparts around the world had a responsibility "to broaden our role beyond economic stewardship and become valuable contributors to help ensure our countries' and our citizens' security."[63] James Wilkinson, chief of staff of the Bush Treasury Department, noted that "[o]ur financial tools are sometimes the most powerful weapons our government has to help change behavior."[64]

Economic sanctions had previously focused largely on transnational trade in goods. Treasury's willingness to use its financial muscle to pursue national security objectives was particularly and increasingly important because "[g]lobal financial flows are growing rapidly and greatly exceed the trade in goods and services."[65]

A third major innovation contributing to the success of U.S. financial lawfare against Iran was Treasury's systematic development and harnessing of intelligence regarding global financial transactions. In 2004, the U.S. Treasury Department became the world's first finance ministry to develop in-house expertise in the collection and analysis of such intelligence.[66] In an era of globalization, such intelligence is increasingly available because "technology and integration have made it more difficult for anyone using the financial system to hide."[67] In order to be useful for purposes of financial lawfare, the financial intelligence must of course be accurate. It also must be shareable, in a way that traditional national security intelligence, which depends heavily on sources and methods that are themselves secret, is often not. Fortuitously, transactions using the international financial system "typically leave a trail of detailed information .... Opening an account or initiating a funds transfer requires a name, an address, a phone number" that is collected and stored by a financial institution.[68] Treasury used such information to identify and target key actors and their networks.[69]

Intelligence about specific financial transactions enabled Treasury to present its financial lawfare as "specifically targeted against those individuals or entities engaging in illicit conduct."[70] In other words, Treasury could assert that the Iranian individuals or entities with whom commerce was being targeted were not targeted simply because they were Iranian but because they had engaged in specific proliferation, terrorism support, deceptive financial, or other illicit activity.

Once sanctions were in place against a particular Iranian entity or individual, efforts by that entity or individual to use deception in an effort to evade the sanctions (for example by fraudulently hiding their engagement in a transaction) could become another reason to sanction that entity or individual. In that case, the illicit "behavior of the actors themselves as they try to access the international financial system" provided a rationale for their isolation.[71]

Deception by the targeted nation's entities and individuals is one of several factors that can result in a chilling effect on transactions beyond what is explicitly prohibited by U.S. law. Although Treasury presented its financial lawfare as targeted against only Iranian bad actors, and U.S. law required foreign financial institutions to halt their transactions only with those bad actors, some foreign financial institutions ultimately halted all business with Iran. In June 2007, within two years of the lawfare campaign's launch, Treasury Secretary Paulson announced that "most of the world's top financial institutions have now dramatically reduced their Iranian business or stopped it altogether."[72] In doing so, Paulson noted that "for the most part, they are not legally required to take these steps but have decided, as a matter of prudence and integrity, that they do not want to be the bankers for such a regime."[73]

It is unclear to what extent the initial goal of U.S. financial lawfare against Iran was in fact to halt Iran's general commercial connectivity with the rest of the world while purporting to be targeting only bad actors. However, this appears to have become the goal by the fall of 2009, after the failure of President Obama's initial outreach to Iran. As Juan Zarate described in his book, *Treasury's War: The Unleashing of a New Era of Financial Lawfare*, a meeting hosted by President Obama in the White House in the fall of 2009 involved then Under Secretary

Levey laying out a plan to "cripple Iran's ability to engage in international commerce."[74] The plan, implemented over the next year, constituted "a financial pressure campaign premised on attacking the enablers of Iran's connectivity to the rest of the world."[75]

In addition to the risk of unwitting engagement in a transaction with a bad actor, the sheer complexity of Treasury's financial sanctions, combined with the aggressiveness with which they were enforced, also had a chilling effect on transactions beyond the scope of what was explicitly prohibited. A detailed examination of financial sanctions by *Newsweek* reported that "a number of lawyers and executives from big banks and multinationals privately told *Newsweek* that their confusion over how to apply the sanctions is only exceeded by their fear of violating them."[76] *Newsweek* asserted that "Treasury does not provide exact guidance on how to apply sanctions to third parties and leaves much up to the guesswork of banks while also 'reserving the right to fine the banks if they happen to guess wrong.'"[77]

In an article published in October 2012, Sean Thornton, who had served from 2005 to early 2012 as chief counsel for Treasury's Office of Foreign Assets Control (OFAC), acknowledged widespread "confusion about what U.S. secondary sanctions actually target," resulting in part from the existence of "so many different legal authorities, which overlap and occasionally contradict themselves."[78] In the article, Thornton discussed one of the key terms in U.S. sanctions laws, "control," and noted that "control is not defined, and U.S. authorities seem likely to keep the concept vague."[79] "Because these lines seem almost purposefully confusing," said Thornton, "many non-U.S. financial institutions . . . steer well clear of the line."[80]

Whether or not Treasury intentionally left their sanctions more confusing than necessary,[81] they were exceptionally complex, leading to the already-mentioned chilling effect on transactions beyond the scope of what was explicitly prohibited. Such a chilling effect is heightened when the fines imposed for violations are of the magnitude of the fines, in the hundreds of millions and even billions of dollars, that are described later in this chapter.

IV. IMPACT OF U.S. FINANCIAL LAWFARE AGAINST IRAN

As a result of these innovations, Treasury's financial lawfare differed not only in design but also, ultimately, in result from traditional economic sanctions, which have the reputation of being ineffective in pressuring rogue actors, disproportionately harmful to innocent persons, and riddled with unaddressed cheating by private businesses that evade sanctions while their governments turn a blind eye.[82] In sharp contrast with the reputation of traditional economic sanctions, many key foreign banks, in an abundance of caution, reportedly eventually went even beyond the letter of the law in implementing financial measures against Iranian individuals and entities.[83]

In part because so many banks were so responsive, the financial lawfare had an impact on the Iranian economy that was both significant and relatively quick in getting started. The retreat of major global banks from the Iranian market soon disrupted key Iranian trading relationships, including in its vital energy sector.[84] As a result of the financial lawfare, by January 2008, it had reportedly become almost impossible in Europe to arrange for transactions involving Iranian companies using a letter of credit, the standard payment guarantee used in international trade.[85]

Even India's second largest company, Reliance Industries,[86] high atop the Global Fortune 500,[87] was forced to halt its gasoline sales to Iran for several months in 2007 because it could no longer arrange from its European banks the letters of credit on which the transactions had depended[88] (as described in Chapter 2, Reliance ultimately withdrew entirely from the Iranian market for other reasons). By October 2008, the *New York Times* was reporting that "ordinary businesses" had also been "hard hit" by Treasury's "financial squeeze on Iran," with both "big companies and small *bazaaris*—as traditional merchants are called in Iran . . . increasingly forced to pay for imports in advance, in cash."[89]

The financial measures also affected Iran's ability to finance petroleum development projects, with Iran's oil minister admitting in March 2007 that "overseas banks and financiers have decreased their cooperation" on such projects.[90] Within just two years, U.S. financial lawfare reportedly increased the cost of imports to Iran by some 20 to 30 percent.[91]

In November 2008, sixty leading Iranian economists called in an open letter for the regime to drastically change course, saying that Iran's "'tension-creating' foreign policy has 'scared off foreign investment and inflicted heavy damage' on the economy."[92] The economists said that the U.S. measures had cost Iran "many billions of dollars" by forcing a "large part" of its imports and exports to be "carried out through middlemen."[93]

It seems evident that by 2008, U.S. financial lawfare was already costing the Iranian regime funds that might otherwise have gone toward furthering its nuclear ambitions or supporting terrorism. This constraining effect was significant.[94] However, it took several more years before the financial lawfare—sustained over several years and combined with U.S. energy sector lawfare—contributed to a coercive effect on Iranian decision-making, and then only with regard to Iran's nuclear program.

In November 2011, Iran's President Mahmoud Ahmadinejad, who had previously been dismissive of the sanctions, admitted that: "Our banks cannot make international transactions anymore."[95] By 2012 and 2013, the financial lawfare had "cut off Iran's access to most of its hard currency held outside the country,"[96] with estimates that as much as $80 billion out of Iran's total $100 billion in hard currency reserves could not be repatriated due to compliance with U.S. measures by foreign financial institutions.[97]

The contemporaneous implementation of U.S., U.N., and EU financial and nonfinancial measures during the period from 2010 to early 2013 makes it difficult to attribute a specific outcome to a particular measure, unless, as with the transactions hindrances and asset repatriation difficulties, a particular measure is the major one that would be likely to have had that outcome.[98] In addition to financial lawfare, energy lawfare also clearly contributed to a 60 percent reduction in Iranian crude oil sales from 2011 to 2013; the combination reduced Iran's revenue from crude oil sales from $100 billion in 2011 to about $35 billion in 2013.[99] Iran's revenue from crude oil sales fell even further after the worldwide price of crude oil started to slump in June 2014 after remaining stable for nearly five years.[100]

By July 2012, the combination of financial and economic lawfare had reduced Iran's total foreign currency reserves by as much as $110 billion,[101] and the value of Iran's currency, the rial, had dropped by 80 percent.[102] In 2013, Iran's gross domestic product dropped about 5 percent (its first drop in two decades).[103] Under Secretary of the Treasury David Cohen testified before the Senate in January 2015 that Iran's economy was at that point 15 to 20 percent "smaller than it would have been had sanctions not been imposed."[104]

Particularly hard hit was Iran's manufacturing sector, which relied heavily on foreign parts.[105] Many Iranian manufacturers were unable to obtain credit and had to pay in advance, often through complex and costly mechanisms, to obtain parts from abroad.[106] Iran's production of cars fell by about 40 percent from 2011 to 2013.[107]

In the June 2013 Iranian presidential election, Hassan Rouhani ran on a platform of ending Iran's international isolation and easing sanctions.[108] Economic pressure was widely regarded as the major reason Iran, in the wake of Rouhani's election, came to the negotiating table in 2013 and 2014 to discuss and, at least for an interim period, limit its nuclear program.[109] In April 2015, CIA Director John Brennan stated in public remarks at Harvard's Kennedy School of Government that Iran's Supreme Leader, Ayatollah Khamenei, had become more flexible in negotiations with the West because Rouhani had persuaded Khamenei that "six years of sanctions had really hit," and Iran's economy was "destined to go down" unless a deal was reached with the West and sanctions were lifted.[110]

On July 14, 2015 (after this book was largely completed), the P-5+1 (the U.N. Security Council's five permanent members plus Germany) announced that they had agreed with Iran on a Joint Comprehensive Plan of Action (JCPOA) to address Iran's nuclear program.[111] The JCPOA provided for the lifting of most nuclear-related sanctions on Iran in exchange for various constraints on Iran's nuclear program. In his July 14, 2015, and August 5, 2015, statements praising the JCPOA, President Obama attributed the Iranian concessions to "the sanctions that have proven so effective,"[112] that "were put in place precisely to get Iran to agree to constraints on its program."[113]

As of early August 2015, many commentators, and many members of Congress from both parties, were criticizing the JCPOA's curtailments of Iran's nuclear program for being insufficiently long-term and verifiable.[114] Some commentators suggested that the deal could have been more favorable to the United States if the economic pressure had been stronger. For example, in announcing in early August that he would "vote to disapprove the agreement," Senator Charles Schumer (D-NY) said that it would be "better to keep U.S. sanctions in place, strengthen them, enforce secondary sanctions on other nations, and pursue the hard-trodden path of diplomacy once more, difficult as it may be."[115] Other commentators suggested that the U.S. negotiating position could also have been strengthened if economic pressure had been supplemented with a more credible threat to halt Iran's nuclear weapons program by force of arms if all other options failed.[116]

Although they were divided on the sufficiency of the JCPOA, most, if not all, key supporters and opponents of the JCPOA seemed to agree that the U.S. economic lawfare campaign had proven a valuable weapon against Iran's nuclear weapons program. They all seemed to credit the economic lawfare campaign with achieving significant (albeit to some, insufficient) curtailment of an Iranian nuclear program that otherwise might only have been curtailed by kinetic means.

V. IMPLEMENTATION OF U.S. FINANCIAL LAWFARE AGAINST IRAN

The U.S. government implemented its financial lawfare campaign against Iran through the following three interrelated initiatives: (1) imposition by the United States of unilateral financial restrictions targeting Iran's nuclear and terrorism sponsorship activities; (2) promoting financial measures against Iran by key international organizations and foreign governments; and (3) direct outreach to key foreign financial institutions.

A. U.S. Imposition of Unilateral Financial Restrictions Targeting Iran's Nuclear and Terrorism Sponsorship Activities

1. U.S. Executive Orders and Designations

U.S. financial lawfare against Iran relied heavily on two Executive Orders: Executive Order 13224 and Executive Order 13382. The key statutory authority for both executive orders was the International Emergency Economic Powers Act (IEEPA), a little-known statute that provides the President with extraordinarily powerful authority "to deal with any unusual and extraordinary threat, which has its source in whole or substantial part outside the United States, to the national security, foreign policy, or economy of the United States, if the President declares a national emergency with respect to such threat."[117]

Once the President has declared such a national emergency, he has the authority, pursuant to IEEPA, to prohibit the following with respect to "any person, or with respect to any property, subject to the jurisdiction of the United States": "transfers of credit or payments between, by, through, or to any banking institution, to the extent that such transfers or payments involve any interest of any foreign country or a national thereof."[118] Once such a national emergency has been declared, the President may also, pursuant to IEEPA, block, "nullify, void, prevent or prohibit, any acquisition, holding, withholding, use, transfer, withdrawal, transportation, importation or exportation of, or dealing in, or exercising any right, power, or privilege with respect to, or transactions involving, any property in which any foreign country or a national thereof has any interest by any person, or with respect to any property, subject to the jurisdiction of the United States."[119]

Executive Order 13224, issued pursuant to IEEPA by President Bush on September 23, 2001 (and still in effect as of summer 2015), authorized the Treasury Department to designate, and block the assets of, foreign persons determined "to have committed, or to pose a significant risk of committing, acts of terrorism that threaten the security of U.S. nationals or the national security, foreign policy, or economy of the United States."[120] In addition, the Executive Order authorized Treasury to block the assets of persons that provide support, services, or assistance to, or are "otherwise associated with" terrorists and terrorist organizations designated under the Order.[121]

Blocking (sometimes also referred to as "freezing") assets is a principal tool deployed by Treasury in its financial lawfare against Iran and other targets. When an asset is blocked, the title to it remains with the targeted person or entity. However, the exercise of the powers and privileges normally associated with ownership, including transfers or transactions of any kind, is prohibited without authorization from Treasury's Office of Foreign Assets Control.[122]

The entities designated under Executive Order 13224 included, for example, Iran's state-owned Bank Saderat.[123] Bank Saderat was designated in October 2007 for being "used by the Government of Iran to channel funds to terrorist organizations, including Hizballah and EU-designated terrorist groups Hamas, PFLP-GC, and Palestinian Islamic Jihad."[124] In designating Bank Saderat, Treasury noted that "from 2001 to 2006, Bank Saderat transferred $50 million from the Central Bank of Iran through its subsidiary in London to its branch in Beirut for the benefit of Hizballah fronts in Lebanon that support acts of violence," that Hamas has "had substantial assets deposited in Bank Saderat," and that "in the past year, Bank Saderat has transferred several million dollars to Hamas."[125]

Executive Order 13382,[126] issued pursuant to IEEPA by President Bush in June 2005 (and still in effect as of summer 2015), provided for blocking the assets of designated persons engaged in proliferation of weapons of mass destruction, as well as the support networks of such persons. Designations under Executive Order 13382 prohibited all transactions between the designees and any U.S. person, and froze any assets the designees might have under U.S. jurisdiction. The Executive Order delegated to the Treasury and State Departments the authority to designate WMD proliferators and their supporters, and they designated scores of Iran-related individuals and entities under this authority.

Iranian entities designated for their direct involvement in production of weapons of mass destruction and their delivery systems included the Atomic Energy Organization of Iran, Iran's Aerospace Industries Organization, Iran's Islamic Revolutionary Guard Corps (IRGC), and Iran's Ministry of Defense and Armed Forces Logistics.[127] The designation of the IRGC, which explicitly included a list of companies owned or controlled by the IRGC and its leaders, had a particularly strong impact on the Iranian economy because, as Treasury noted, the "IRGC has significant political and economic power in Iran, with ties to companies controlling billions of dollars in business and construction and a growing presence in Iran's financial and commercial sectors."[128] "The IRGC," Treasury noted, "is involved in a diverse array of activities, including petroleum production and major construction projects across the country."[129]

Multinationals seeking to do business with Iran would have found it particularly difficult to avoid Khatam ol-Anbia, an engineering contractor wholly owned by the IRGC.[130] Khatam ol-Anbia was one of Iran's largest conglomerates.[131] As of 2014, it reportedly had up to forty thousand employees and more than $50 billion in contracts with the Iranian government to build port, highway, oil and gas field, refinery, and other infrastructure across the country.[132] Set up in 1989 to provide employment for members of the Revolutionary Guards following Iran's war with Iraq, Khatam ol-Anbia grew rapidly under former President Mahmoud Ahmadinejad, who directed contracts to companies controlled by the Guards in order to solidify their support for him.[133]

The designees under Executive Order 13382 also included some two dozen Iranian banks.[134] For example, Bank Melli, Iran's largest bank, was designated in October 2007 for providing a range of "banking services to entities involved in Iran's nuclear and ballistic missile programs, including entities listed by the U.N. for their involvement in those programs."[135] Bank Melli "facilitated numerous purchases of sensitive materials for Iran's nuclear and missile programs."[136] In the process of "handling financial transactions on behalf of the IRGC, Bank Melli . . . employed deceptive banking practices," such as requesting that its name be removed from financial transactions, to hide its involvement from the international banking system.[137]

Several other executive orders played a narrower role in U.S. financial lawfare against Iran. For example, Executive Order 13622, issued by President Obama on July 30, 2012, was designed to help constrict Iranian oil export revenues by deterring foreign financial institutions from conducting business with Iran's energy sector.[138] The Executive Order principally authorized sanctions against foreign banks found to have knowingly conducted or facilitated significant transactions for the purchase of petroleum from Iran.[139] The sanctions included being prohibited from opening or maintaining correspondent or payable-through accounts in the United States.[140]

As of January 2013, Treasury had—under the various Iran-related executive orders—designated more than 360 individuals and entities linked to Iran's WMD programs and support for terrorism.[141]

In addition to executive orders, and the designations pursuant to them, several other executive branch steps played key roles in the campaign of financial lawfare against Iran. For example, in November 2008, the United States revoked authorization for so-called "u-turn" transactions with Iran.[142] The "u-turn" authorization had allowed foreign transactions with Iran, which originated and terminated outside the United States, to transit the U.S. financial system just long enough to be converted into dollars, and then be sent back out of the country.[143] Revocation of the authorization meant that foreign banks and institutions facilitating the financing for Iranian oil and other transactions were no longer permitted to "use their American correspondent relationships" to dollarize their transactions.[144]

Another key executive branch step in its campaign of financial lawfare against Iran was the November 2011 finding that the entire Islamic Republic of Iran was a jurisdiction of "primary money laundering concern" under § 311 of the USA PATRIOT Act.[145] In issuing the finding, the U.S. government stated that it was thereby identifying "the entire Iranian financial sector, including Iran's Central Bank . . . as posing illicit risks for the global financial system."[146] According to Juan Zarate, this step made it clear that the goal of Treasury's financial lawfare against Iran was "intended as a full financial strangulation."[147]

The U.S. executive orders restricting foreign banks in the U.S. financial system from engaging in particular transactions with Iran were supplemented with several statutory measures, which are described in the following Subsection 2. Violations of these restrictions by various foreign banks were then aggressively enforced, as described in Section C, below.

2. Statutory Measures

Between 2010 and 2013, Congress passed, and the President signed, several new laws enhancing U.S. financial lawfare against Iran. These laws typically reflected compromises between Congress and the Administration. While key members of Congress tended to want "more pressure, faster" against Iran, the administration took a more gradualist approach, for fear of harming the overall international financial system or causing "allies in Europe and Asia to resist further cooperation because of perceived American threats or overreach."[148] The following are the key provisions of these laws.

a. Section 104 of the Comprehensive Iran Sanctions, Accountability, and Divestment Act

Section 104 of the Comprehensive Iran Sanctions, Accountability, and Divestment Act of 2010 (CISADA), signed into law in July 2010, required the Secretary of the Treasury to "prohibit, or impose strict conditions on, the opening or maintaining in the United States of a correspondent account or a payable-through account by a foreign financial institution" that knowingly engaged in activities including one or more of the following: facilitating the WMD program or terrorism support efforts of the Iranian government, or "facilitat[ing] a significant transaction or transactions or provid[ing] significant financial services for" the IRCG or any of its agents or affiliates, or any financial institution designated pursuant to Executive Order 13224 or 13382.[149]

The reference to engagement with any financial institution designated pursuant to the two executive orders "gave the Secretary of the Treasury the authority for the first time to require U.S. banks to terminate correspondent banking relationships with foreign banks that knowingly engaged in significant transactions with designated Iranian banks."[150] According to then Under Secretary of the Treasury David Cohen, this was a "particularly powerful provision."[151]

Foreign financial institutions that do not have their own operations in the United States typically access the U.S. financial system by establishing correspondent accounts or payable-through accounts with U.S. banks.[152] Such access to U.S.-based banks is "critically important" to the ability of these foreign banks to offer dollar-denominated services to their clients.[153] "This is new in the sense that it puts at risk something that's very important to every financial institution, namely their access to the United States," said then Under Secretary of the Treasury Stuart Levey in discussing the provision shortly after its enactment.[154]

Cohen said that after the provision's enactment, he and his colleagues "fanned out around the globe to explain the new law, visiting or talking to government counterparts in over 50 countries and representatives from more than 150 foreign financial institutions."[155] The Treasury officials explained that "CISADA offered foreign banks a choice: they could do business with banks in the U.S., or they could do business with designated Iranian banks."[156] "But," emphasized Cohen, "they could not do both."[157]

Treasury reemphasized the choice in July 2012 when it imposed sanctions under CISADA § 104 against a Chinese bank (the Bank of Kunlun) and an Iraqi bank (Elaf Islamic Bank) for knowingly facilitating significant transactions and providing significant financial services for designated Iranian banks.[158] Any banks in the United States that had correspondent or payable-through accounts for either the Bank of Kunlun or Elaf Islamic Bank were required to close them, thus effectively barring the two banks from accessing the U.S. financial system.[159] In May 2013, Treasury lifted sanctions on Elaf Islamic Bank on the grounds that it had verifiably changed its behavior.[160] After the designation, Elaf had, according to Treasury, "immediately engaged the Treasury Department and began an intensive course of action to stop the conduct" that led to the designation.[161]

While § 104 was CISADA's most important provision from a financial perspective, the new law also contained several other key measures, particularly in relation to Iran's energy sector. One such measure—related to Iran's gasoline imports—is described in more detail in Chapter 2. Several of CISADA's key measures had an impact on Iran even while the legislation was making its way through Congress. Seeing the writing on the wall, some foreign banks and energy companies halted business with Iran as soon as they saw it would be proscribed, without waiting for CISADA to be passed and signed into law.[162]

b. Section 1245 of the Fiscal Year 2012 National Defense Authorization Act

Section 1245 of the Fiscal Year 2012 National Defense Authorization Act (NDAA), signed into law in December 2011, targeted the involvement of the Central Bank of Iran (CBI) in the international financial system. It did so by requiring the President to prevent a foreign financial institution from opening a correspondent or payable-through account in the United States, and to impose strict limitations on a foreign financial institution's existing such accounts, if that financial institution knowingly conducted or facilitated any significant transaction with the CBI or any other designated Iranian financial institution.[163]

Foreign financial institutions could be granted an exemption from these restrictions if the President determined that the parent country of the financial institution had "significantly reduced" its crude oil purchases from Iran during a specified period.[164] In other words, under this provision, "foreign banks involved in significant transactions with the CBI—including making payments for Iranian oil—can be cut off from the United States banking system unless their home jurisdiction has significantly reduced its oil imports from Iran."[165]

Section 1245 used financial lawfare to reduce Iran's oil exports by, to an extent, holding foreign banks hostage to the level of Iranian oil imports of their home jurisdictions.[166] Then Under Secretary Cohen explained that the provision "leverages foreign banks' desire to have access to the U.S. financial system to drive down Iran's oil revenues."[167] Countries that import oil from Iran were provided a "powerful incentive" to reduce those imports, said Cohen, "namely, if they significantly reduce their Iranian oil imports, their banks will be protected, for a period of time, against the possibility of sanctions for transactions with the CBI."[168]

Following enactment of § 1245, Cohen and his colleagues embarked on a campaign to explain the provision to foreign governments and businesses and "encourage importers of Iranian oil to protect their banks from sanctions by significantly reducing their imports."[169] According to Cohen, the response was "quite positive," with "every country that imported oil from Iran taking "steps to significantly reduce the volume of their Iranian oil imports—driving down Iran's oil revenues."[170]

In June 2015, the Congressional Research Service published a chart showing major reductions in various countries' crude oil imports from Iran between 2011 (at the end of which § 1245 went into effect) and implementation in January 2014 of the Joint Plan of Action (JPA) between Iran and the P-5+1.[171] For example, China reduced its purchases from 550,000 to 410,000 barrels per day; Japan reduced its purchases from 325,000 to 190,000 barrels per day; and India reduced its purchases from 320,000 to 190,000 barrels per day.[172] Pursuant to the JPA, the President waived § 1245 in January 2014, meaning that Iran's oil customers would not be required to further reduce oil purchases from Iran while the JPA remained in effect.[173]

c. Sections 302 and 504 of the Iran Threat Reduction and Syria Human Rights Act

Section 302 of the Iran Threat Reduction and Syria Human Rights Act of 2012, signed into law in August 2012, required imposition of at least five out of a menu of twelve listed sanctions on entities that knowingly materially assisted or provided financing or other support for the IRGC.[174] The sanctions menu included a prohibition on U.S. government procurement from the entity, a prohibition on transactions in foreign exchange by the entity, exclusion from the United States of corporate officers, blocking of the sanctioned entity's U.S.-based assets, and a prohibition on any credit or payments between the entity and any U.S. financial institution.[175]

Section 504 of the Iran Threat Reduction and Syria Human Rights Act of 2012 amended § 1245 of the Fiscal Year 2012 NDAA by requiring that any funds owed to Iran as a result of exempted transactions (e.g., purchases of Iranian oil) be credited to an account located in the country with primary jurisdiction over the foreign bank making the transaction.[176] This had the effect of preventing Iran from bringing earned hard currency back to Iran, leading it to instead either use the funds to buy products from the customer countries[177] or have the funds remain in those countries. According to then Under Secretary Cohen, "because almost all of the countries that purchase oil from Iran run a significant trade deficit—that is, they import more from Iran than they sell to Iran—this provision should 'lock up' a significant portion of Iran's earnings in each of these countries."[178] Pursuant to the JPA, the President issued a waiver applicable to § 504 in January 2014 "to allow Iran to receive some hard currency from ongoing oil sales" in installments while the JPA remained in effect.[179]

B. Promoting Financial Measures Against Iran by Key International Organizations and Foreign Countries

Recognizing that economic restrictions, including those in the financial arena, are almost always more effective when they are multilateral, the U.S. government's financial lawfare campaign against Iran placed considerable emphasis on, where possible, promoting financial measures against Iran by key international organizations and foreign countries. These efforts focused on: (1) including financial components in U.N. Security Council resolutions addressing Iran, (2) working through the Financial Action Task Force, and (3) direct outreach to key foreign governments.

1. Including Financial Components in Security Council Resolutions

Prior to the JCPOA, the four principal U.N. Security Council resolutions imposing sanctions on Iran were Resolution 1737 of December 23, 2006; Resolution 1747 of March 24, 2007; Resolution 1803 of March 3, 2008; and Resolution 1929 of June 9, 2010 (the Iran sanctions resolutions). On July 20, 2015, six days after the P-5+1 and Iran announced the JCPOA, the Security Council passed Resolution 2231.[180]

Resolution 2231 provided that the Iran sanctions resolutions were to terminate upon receipt by the Security Council of a report from the IAEA confirming that Iran had taken various actions specified in the JCPOA.[181] However, Resolution 2231 also included a procedure pursuant to which the Iran sanctions resolutions could be reimplemented if a JCPOA participant state were to notify the Council of "an issue that the JCPOA participant State believes constitutes significant non-performance of commitments under the JCPOA."[182]

As of early August 2015, the U.S. Congress had yet to vote on the JCPOA (a vote which held the possibility of derailing the JCPOA). In addition, the IAEA had yet to confirm that Iran had taken the various specified actions necessary for the sanctions resolutions to terminate.

As a result, it was unclear, as of early August 2015, how much longer the sanctions resolutions would continue to be implemented vis a vis Iran. Regardless, the various innovations contained within the resolutions would remain tested options for lawfare practitioners to draw from in a future campaign against either another target or a re-targeted Iran.

The Iran sanctions resolutions contained the following principal provisions related to financial measures:

a. legally binding requirements that member states freeze the assets of, and block commerce with their jurisdiction by, specified persons or entities associated with Iranian nuclear and missile programs, as well as persons or entities owned or controlled by them or acting on their behalf or at their direction;[183]

b. legally binding requirements that member states prohibit resource transfers and other financial activities relating to Iran's nuclear and missile programs;[184]

c. a legally binding requirement that all states require persons or firms subject to their jurisdiction "to exercise vigilance when doing business with entities incorporated in Iran or subject to Iran's jurisdiction" and any individuals or entities acting on their behalf or at their direction "if they have information that provides reasonable grounds to believe that such business could contribute to Iran's proliferation-sensitive nuclear activities or the development of nuclear weapon delivery systems";[185]

d. a nonbinding call upon member states to "exercise vigilance over the activities of financial institutions in their territories with all banks domiciled in Iran";[186]

e. a nonbinding preambular reference to "the potential connection between Iran's revenues derived from its energy sector and the funding of Iran's proliferation-sensitive nuclear activities";[187] and

f. in Resolution 1929, nonbinding calls upon member states to prevent or prohibit various activities "if they have information that provides reasonable grounds to believe that such [activities] could contribute to Iran's proliferation-sensitive nuclear activities or the development of nuclear weapon delivery systems," including:

– to prevent the provision of financial services or assets or other resources if they have such information;[188]

– to prohibit in their territories the opening of "new offices of Iranian banks," or other activities by Iranian banks including "establishing or maintaining correspondent relationships," if they have such information;[189] and

– to prohibit financial institutions within their jurisdiction from opening offices or subsidiaries or "banking accounts in Iran," if they have such information.[190]

Key Iranian entities specifically targeted by these resolutions included the Atomic Energy Organization of Iran, the Islamic Revolutionary Guard Corps, the Islamic Republic of Iran Shipping Lines, and three Iranian banks: Bank Sepah, Bank Melli, and First East Export Bank. Since each of these targets had previously been designated by the U.S. government under Executive Order 13382, the Security Council resolution listings had the effect of multilateralizing aspects of Treasury's unilateral actions against Iran's proliferation infrastructure.

While the resolutions' legally binding requirements most directly contributed to this multilateralization, the nonbinding "calls-upon" and even preambular provisions also contributed, including by providing multilateral reinforcement of Treasury's warnings to foreign governments and banks. For example, the U.S. Department of the Treasury deemed the "all-banks-domiciled-in-Iran" provision of Security Council Resolution 1803 to be of "critical importance" as it "signifi-cantly reinforces the concerns Treasury has expressed for many months."[191] The nonbinding "calls-upon" provisions also contributed by providing "hooks" for action by individual states, as described in Subsection 3 below.

2. Working Through the Financial Action Task Force

The Financial Action Task Force (FATF) is an intergovernmental body that, as of summer 2015, had thirty-six members including the five permanent members of the United Nations Security Council, the European Commission, India, Japan, South Korea, and Turkey.[192] The FATF's stated objectives were "to set standards and promote effective implementation of legal, regulatory and operational mea-sures for combating money laundering, terrorist financing and other related threats to the integrity of the international financial system."[193]

The FATF promulgated a series of "Recommendations," recognized as "the international standard for combating of money laundering and the financing of terrorism and proliferation of weapons of mass destruction."[194] The FATF's stan-dards were endorsed by the World Bank, the International Monetary Fund, and the United Nations and recognized by more than 175 countries.[195]

While the FATF focused for many years on anti-money laundering and com-bating the financing of terrorism (which it sometimes referred to as AML/CFT), in February 2012, the FATF formally agreed that "the proliferation of weapons of mass destruction is a significant security concern, and financial measures can be an effective way to combat this threat," and adopted a new recommendation aimed at ensuring consistent and effective implementation of targeted finan-cial sanctions related to proliferation when the U.N. Security Council calls for them.[196] The proliferation recommendation was adopted as part of the FATF's newly renamed International Standards on Combating Money Laundering and the Financing of Terrorism & Proliferation.[197]

In addition to setting standards for countering money laundering and terrorist and proliferation finance, the FATF also singles out jurisdictions with serious vul-nerabilities in their relevant legal frameworks. In October 2007, the FATF issued a public statement expressing its concern that Iran's "lack of a comprehensive anti-money laundering/combating the financing of terrorism (AML/CFT) regime represents a significant vulnerability within the international financial system."[198] FATF noted that its "members are advising their financial institutions to take the risk arising from the deficiencies in Iran's AML/CFT regime into account for enhanced due diligence."[199] Iran thereafter adopted an AML law.[200] However, the FATF concluded that Iran's AML/CFT regime remained deficient and issued statements of concern about Iran in both February 2008 and October 2008.[201]

The October 2008 FATF statement noted Iran's steps toward remedying its AML deficiencies and urged Iran to "address the remaining weaknesses."[202] In this October 2008 statement, the FATF expressed particular concern that Iran's "lack . . . of effort" to "address the risk of terrorist financing continues to pose a serious threat to the integrity of the international financial system" and declared that "urgent action to address this vulnerability is necessary."[203] The FATF called on its members, and urged all jurisdictions, to "strengthen preventive measures to protect their financial sectors from this risk."[204] In response to these warnings, the governments of several major economic powers warned their financial institutions that choosing to do business with Iran would entail significant risks.[205]

As of February 2015, the FATF remained dissatisfied with Iran's financial system and continued to warn its members about the risks posed by transactions with Iran. "The FATF remains particularly and exceptionally concerned about Iran's failure to address the risk of terrorist financing and the serious threat this poses to the integrity of the international financial system . . . . The FATF urges Iran to immediately and meaningfully address its AML/CFT deficiencies," said the FATF.[206] The FATF also said that it "reaffirms its call on members, and urges all jurisdictions, to advise their financial institutions to give special attention to business relationships and transactions with Iran, including Iranian companies and financial institutions."[207] The FATF also urged "all jurisdictions to apply effective counter-measures to protect their financial sectors from money laundering and financing of terrorism (ML/FT) risks emanating from Iran."[208]

In addition to its broader warnings about Iran's financial system, the FATF also played a significant role in promoting effective implementation by its members of the specific financial measures contained in the Security Council resolutions targeting Iran. For example, the FATF issued guidance in June 2007,[209] September 2007,[210] and October 2007[211] on implementation of these measures. This FATF work was recognized in Security Council Resolution 1803, which explicitly welcomed the guidance issued by FATF to assist states in implementing their Security Council obligations. Then, once the FATF formally adopted a proliferation finance recommendation, it issued a document containing guidance addressing all of the relevant financial provisions of Security Council resolutions countering the proliferation of weapons of mass destruction.[212] Such detailed guidance is particularly important in light of the typically brief and ambiguous phrasing of requirements as they are set forth in Security Council resolutions.

3. Direct Outreach to Key Foreign Governments

Treasury Department officials built upon the Security Council resolution financial provisions and FATF guidance with intensive outreach to foreign governments. Such outreach was essential because many national governments have a poor record of implementing even the mandatory requirements of Security Council resolutions. The outreach was also vital because the resolutions, including especially Resolution 1929, additionally contained very significant nonbinding "calls-upon" recommendations that the U.S. government hoped foreign governments would choose to implement.

In order to take financial measures against Iran of the type Treasury was requesting, many foreign governments needed or preferred, for domestic legal or political reasons, an international law requirement or "hook."[213] A legally binding requirement contained in a treaty or U.N. Security Council resolution can, of course, serve as a basis for action; indeed, it obligates the government to take the specified action. However, in many countries, a "calls-upon" provision of a U.N. Security Council resolution can be a sufficient "hook" for action,[214] if the government chooses to use it.

The nonbinding "calls-upon" provisions in Security Council resolutions provided "hooks" for many U.N. member states to impose their own legally binding restrictions on transactions with Iran.[215] According to David Cohen, then Treasury's Under Secretary for Terrorism and Financial Intelligence, the "hooks" in Resolution 1929 were particularly useful to such governments because their evidentiary standard—"reasonable grounds to believe" that these activities "could contribute" to Iran's nuclear or missile programs—was relatively easy to meet, and Treasury "had a wealth of information" demonstrating how Iranian banks used deceptive practices to facilitate Iran's proliferation activities.[216] According to Cohen, these "hooks" in Resolution 1929 contributed in the summer and fall of 2010 to the EU, U.K., Japan, South Korea, Canada, Australia, Norway, and Switzerland taking "robust action to restrict Iran's banking activities."[217]

In 2012, the EU took further steps to restrict Iran's banking activities. These included financial sanctions against the Central Bank of Iran[218] and a prohibition, described in more detail in Chapter 2, restricting the provision of specialized financial messaging services to persons and entities designated by the UN or EU or otherwise associated with Iran's nuclear weapons and missile programs.[219]

C. Direct Outreach to Key Foreign Financial Institutions

1. Warning Meetings with Key Foreign Banks

From early in its financial lawfare initiative against Iran, senior Treasury Department officials engaged in an unprecedented campaign of outreach to the international financial private sector. Following Secretary Paulson's initiation of this outreach in the fall of 2006, Treasury met, over the next eighteen months, "with more than 40 banks worldwide to discuss the threat Iran poses to the international financial system."[220]

According to then Secretary Paulson, within the first nine months of the campaign, "most of the world's top financial institutions" either committed to

Treasury officials that they would halt or scale back their business with Iran, or simply did halt or scale back their transactions.[221] By fall 2008, Stuart Levey, the Under Secretary of the Treasury for Terrorism and Financial Intelligence, had made more than eighty foreign visits of his own to talk to more than sixty banks.[222] By then, more than eighty banks had curtailed their business with Iran.[223] While some committed to Treasury that they would do so, others simply curtailed their business. "We haven't had Chinese banks tell me that they won't do deals with Iran . . . they just stop," said Levey in October 2008.[224]

While some of the commitments could, of course, have been less than genuine, there is open-source evidence that many of the banks kept their word. One indication is the campaign's swift impact on Iran's trading relationships, which is described in Section IV of this chapter.

Another window into banks' actual behavior during this time period is provided by the U.S. government's forfeiture agreements, for illicit transactions with Iran, with several of the world's largest non-U.S. banks. The major such forfeiture agreements are summarized later in this section. It is interesting to note that only two of these banks appear to have engaged in illicit transactions with Iran after 2008, and only one of those appears to have engaged in illicit transactions with Iran after 2009. Based on the agreements, several of the other banks appear to have stopped by 2008. For example, in June 2012, ING, a Dutch bank, agreed to forfeit $619 million to the United States and New York State for illicit transactions, on behalf of Iranian and other clients, that continued until 2007.[225] In December 2012, HSBC, a U.K. bank which was the largest in Europe,[226] forfeited $1.256 billion and agreed to pay an additional $665 million in penalties for various violations of sanctions laws,[227] including illicit transactions with Iran that lasted until the end of 2006.[228]

The one bank that continued to engage in illicit transactions with Iran after 2009 was BNP Paribas, which ultimately admitted that from 2004 to 2012, it "knowingly and willfully moved more than $8.8 billion through the U.S. financial system on behalf of Sudanese, Iranian, and Cuban sanctioned entities," according to a Department of Justice press release.[229] At least in part because of the dates on which it was continuing to engage in illicit transactions, BNP Paribas's penalty was by far the largest of any of the banks—$8.9736 billion (including an $8.8336 billion forfeiture and a $140 million fine).[230] Thus, it appears that BNP Paribas was an outlier, and at least several of the world's largest non-U.S. banks largely or entirely halted their illicit transactions with Iran in response to Treasury's outreach campaign between fall 2006 and the end of 2008.

The momentum of Treasury's campaign to persuade foreign banks to curtail their business with Iran slowed somewhat during 2009, while the newly inaugurated President Obama focused on diplomatic outreach to Iran.[231] However, during the subsequent three years, Treasury officials "conducted outreach to more than 145 foreign financial institutions in more than 60 countries,"[232] including many banks outside the ranks of the world's largest.

As described in detail in Section IV of this chapter, Treasury's financial lawfare against Iran had an impact that was more powerful and quicker than that typically caused by traditional economic sanctions. The strength and speed of Treasury's financial lawfare stemmed largely from its direct outreach to foreign banks. Rather than relying, for example, on asking the Swiss government to halt Swiss banks from conducting proliferation- or terrorism-related business with Iran, Treasury officials went directly to the Swiss banks. Treasury officials found that their unprecedented direct outreach to a country's key private financial institutions could yield results much more quickly than could outreach to that same country's government.[233]

Once a foreign private bank decides to halt business with entities or individuals of concern, the bank's competitors have an increased risk of harming their reputations if they continue doing such business. After all, the last Swiss bank still transacting with designated Iranian banks will look shady to upstanding customers.

In addition, those banks that halted some or all business with Iran often preferred to see their competitors also lose out on that market, and certainly did not want to see their competitors pick up the Iranian business they lost. Thus, foreign banks that exited the Iranian market would often quietly cooperate with the United States in putting pressure on those who had not yet done so,[234] including by providing U.S. officials with evidence of their competitors' continued transactions. In light of the quality of competitive intelligence banks are able to collect, this cooperation was often very valuable. As a result of the reputational and competitor cooperation factors, the exit of one bank from a country often soon led to the exit of others.[235]

Such private sector decisions could, in turn, make it more politically feasible for foreign governments to impose restrictions, because some or all of the major relevant companies in their jurisdiction had already forgone the business.[236] Treasury's financial measures were also seen as more palatable because, unlike sanctions of the past that targeted entire countries and were criticized as harming innocent people, Treasury's measures were perceived as more targeted.[237]

What specifically did Treasury officials say to the foreign banks to get them to curtail business with Iran? As Daniel Glaser, who served beginning in 2004 as Deputy Assistant Secretary and then Assistant Secretary of the Treasury for Terrorist Financing, described it, in their meetings with foreign bankers, Treasury officials largely "shared information about Iran's deceptive financial behavior and raised awareness about the high financial and reputational risk associated with doing business with Iran."[238] Treasury officials attributed the success of their outreach efforts to their emphasis on Iran being "demonstrably engaged" in illicit financial conduct and to the sensitivity of the international financial private sector to reputational and business risk.[239] In their outreach to both foreign governments and international private financial institutions, Treasury officials emphasized that the issue is not just "conduct that the U.S. doesn't like politically, but conduct that's contrary to international law or international standards and norms."[240]

Treasury officials also raised the prospect that doing even prima facie licit business with Iran posed a significant risk of inadvertently doing business with proscribed Iranian entities. For example, Treasury Secretary Paulson cautioned business executives that in light of Iran's deceptive financial practices, including its use of front companies, and since "[t]he IRGC is so deeply entrenched in Iran's economy and commercial enterprises, it is increasingly likely that if you are doing business with Iran, you are somehow doing business with the IRGC."[241] Similarly, Under Secretary of the Treasury Stuart Levey said he told foreign firms that "if they're dealing with Iran it's nearly impossible to protect themselves from being entangled in that country's illicit conduct."[242]

For international private financial institutions, this was reputationally daunting given the IRGC's leading role in Iran's terrorism and proliferation activities.[243] It was also legally daunting for them in light of the Treasury Department's designation of the IRGC under Executive Order 13382 and the Security Council's requirement that member states freeze the assets of, and block commerce with their jurisdictions by, the IRGC and "any individuals or entities acting on their behalf or at their direction," as well as "entities owned or controlled by them."[244]

Such warnings had an impact. As Stuart Levey noted, "[f]inancial institutions want to identify and avoid dangerous or risky customers who could harm their reputations and business."[245] Accordingly, "[r]ather than comply with just the letter of the law, we have seen many in the banking industry voluntarily go beyond their legal requirements because they do not want to handle illicit business," said Daniel Glaser.[246]

Consistent with Glaser's assessment, many banks around the world decided to screen their customers against Treasury's list of designees, even when they were not required to do so by the laws of the country in which the bank was domiciled.[247] Major U.S. and foreign banks became so cognizant of the risks posed to them by the infiltration of illicit money that many of them hired large numbers of staff dedicated to protecting against such infiltration. For example, HSBC reportedly had seven thousand people, about 10 percent of its employees worldwide, working on risk and compliance issues at the end of 2014 (a fourfold increase from before its $1.9 billion settlement with Treasury in 2012 for illicit transactions with Iranian and other proscribed entities).[248] Citigroup, which had also been penalized for illicit transactions with Iran, had nearly 30,000 employees working on regulatory and compliance issues at the end of 2014, 13 percent of the bank's total 244,000 employees.[249] Meanwhile, J.P. Morgan Chase & Co. said that it would hire 13,000 new staff in compliance, audit, and other areas during 2014, after being the subject of fines for various non-Iran-related compliance problems. Treasury's designations helped advise such compliance officers as to "who they need to protect against."[250]

At least while they were in office, Treasury officials tended to characterize their Iran-related financial outreach as educating rather than threatening banks. For example, in describing Treasury's outreach campaign, G.W. Bush administration Treasury Secretary Paulson said: "We never threaten . . . . We talk about how important it is not to violate the rules and engage in illicit transactions."[251]

Despite Treasury officials' tendency to downplay it, foreign banks clearly curtailed Iran-related business in response to Treasury's outreach principally because those banks were concerned that continued transactions with Iran could result in U.S. regulatory penalties, such as fines or even loss of access to the U.S. market. According to Juan Zarate, bank executives often understood individualized briefings by Treasury officials to be "not-so-subtle threats of sanctions and enforcement to come" if they didn't halt business with the target country.[252]

The following subsection describes the major enforcement actions taken by Treasury and other U.S. government agencies between 2004 and 2014 against foreign banks that engaged in illicit transactions with Iran. The fines were remarkably large. In addition, the size of the U.S. market and the primacy of the dollar and of U.S. banks in the international financial system naturally made many banks leery of putting their access to the U.S. banking system at risk for the sake of maintaining financial ties to terrorists, proliferators, or even benign actors in Iran.

2. Prosecuting Banks

The evidence described in the following enforcement case studies demonstrates, sometimes colorfully, the remarkable disregard that several major foreign banks had for U.S. sanctions on Iran prior to 2007. The evidence illustrates banks deliberately and systematically flouting U.S. legal requirements prior to Treasury's crackdown.

Also notable in these case studies is the growing magnitude of the fines and other punishments imposed on the various penalized banks, especially for violations that occurred after 2007 and 2008, the years when the banks were first put on notice by visits from Treasury officials. The fines and other punishments were typically (but not always) imposed as part of deferred prosecution agreements, described in this context as agreements pursuant to which "corporate defendants pay fines, don't dispute they've done wrong, and promise to reform—all with the threat looming of a potential future criminal indictment" if they don't follow through on their promise to reform.[253] The growing penalties demonstrate the increasing determination, even ferocity, with which Treasury and, after a time, the New York Department of Financial Services waged their financial lawfare campaign against Iran as the campaign approached and reached its peak.

a. Tens of Millions of Dollars Each in Penalties Against UBS and ABN Amro

In May 2004, the U.S. Federal Reserve fined UBS, a Swiss bank that was at that time Europe's largest, $100 million.[254] Between 1996 and 2003, UBS employees had illicitly transferred over $4 billion to Cuba, Iran, Libya, and Yugoslavia, and intentionally hidden the transactions by filing false monthly reports with the Federal Reserve.[255]

In December 2005, ABN Amro NV, a large Dutch bank, was fined $80 million by U.S. federal and state financial regulators. The Chicago and New York branches of the bank had, from 1997 to 2004, participated in wire and other transactions that violated sanctions on Libya and Iran.[256] ABN's Dubai branch had modified payment instructions on wire transfers, letters of credit, and checks issued by Iran's Bank Melli and a Libyan bank in order to hide their involvement in the transactions and enable access to the U.S. banking system.[257] In 2008, one former Treasury official attributed the Department's 2007 successes in persuading foreign banks to curtail transactions with Iran in part to other banks' eagerness "to avoid being the 'next ABN AMRO.'"[258]

b. Hundreds of Millions of Dollars Each in Penalties Against Lloyds TSB, Credit Suisse, Barclays PLC, ING, and Standard Chartered

In January 2009, Lloyds TSB Bank forfeited $350 million to the United States and the New York County District Attorney's Office.[259] From 1995 to January 2007, Lloyds had altered or "stripped" wire-transfer information to hide the identities of Iranian and Sudanese clients in order to deceive American financial institutions and enable the clients to access the U.S. banking system.[260] The stripping of wire-transfer information "made it appear that the transactions originated at Lloyds TSB Bank" in the United Kingdom rather than in the sanctioned countries.[261]

In December 2009, Credit Suisse agreed to pay $536 million to the United States and New York for illegally concealing the involvement of sanctioned parties in the routing of thousands of wire transfers and securities transactions to and through the United States.[262] The U.S. government determined that Credit Suisse had deliberately removed customer names and addresses from payment messages, and sometimes inserted false names, so that the wire transfers would pass undetected through filters at U.S. banks.[263] Credit Suisse had done so from 1995 (or earlier) to 2006,[264] in over $1.6 billion worth of transactions.[265] The majority of the transactions involved Iran.[266]

U.S. prosecutors emphasized that the illicit Credit Suisse transactions reflected company policy rather than the work of rogue employees.[267] For example, U.S. Assistant Attorney General Lanny Breuer asserted: "In essence, Credit Suisse said to sanctioned entities, 'We've got a service, and that service is helping you evade U.S. banking regulations.'"[268] A Department of Justice press release stated that Credit Suisse "trained its Iranian clients to falsify wire transfers so that such messages would pass undetected through the U.S. financial system" and "promised" its Iranian clients that "no message would leave the bank without being hand-checked by a Credit Suisse employee to ensure" that it had been formatted to pass U.S. filters.[269]

In 1998, Credit Suisse even "provided its Iranian clients with a pamphlet" that provided detailed instructions on "how to avoid triggering U.S. OFAC filters or sanctions."[270] Somewhat surprisingly, no individual at Credit Suisse was charged with a crime in connection with these transactions.[271]

In August 2010, Barclays PLC agreed to a $298 million settlement with U.S. and New York prosecutors in connection with transactions Barclays had conducted on behalf of customers from Iran and other sanctioned countries.[272] According to the Department of Justice, "from as early as the mid-1990s until September 2006, Barclays knowingly and willfully moved or permitted to be moved hundreds of millions of dollars" in violation of U.S. economic sanctions.[273] Barclays "followed instructions," from banks in Iran and other sanctioned countries, "not to mention their names in U.S. dollar payment messages" sent to financial institutions located in the United States.[274] It did so by methods including amending and reformatting the messages to remove information identifying the sanctioned entities.[275]

The factual statement to which Barclays agreed as part of the August 2010 settlement stated that "Barclays' standard operating procedures allowed and even educated its employees how to bypass . . . the U.S. financial institution's OFAC filters to permit illegal payments."[276] For example, Barclays occasionally sent payment messages back to the senders with a fax coversheet stating: "Payments to U.S. must NOT contain the word listed below."[277] The senders would then resend the same payment messages "without the offending language," for example, the name of a sanctioned entity or country.[278]

OFAC Director Adam Szubin emphasized that the Barclays fine could have been much higher, however "all of the apparent violations were voluntarily self-disclosed by the bank."[279] In approving the settlement, U.S. District Court Judge Emmet Sullivan criticized the agreement as a "sweetheart deal," expressing concern that the settlement would be paid by shareholders, not corporate executives, and that no individuals were being prosecuted.[280] In defending the agreement, U.S. Justice Department attorney Kevin Gerrity asserted that the four-year internal investigation undertaken by Barclays in connection with the case had cost it an additional $250 million.[281] The *Wall Street Journal*, in reporting the agreement, noted that "the penalty isn't a painful financial blow for Barclays, which had about $4.6 billion in profits for the first six months."[282]

In June 2012, ING, a Dutch bank, agreed to forfeit $619 million to the United States and New York State.[283] ING had moved more than twenty thousand transactions, totaling more than $2 billion, through the U.S. financial system on behalf of Cuban, Iranian, and other clients subject to sanctions, whose identifying information was intentionally removed from the transactions by bank staff.[284] The transactions began in the early 1990s and continued until 2007.[285]

According to the U.S. Department of Justice, this conduct occurred in ING "locations around the world with the knowledge, approval, and encouragement of senior corporate managers and legal and compliance departments" at ING, which even "threatened to punish certain employees if they failed to take specified steps to remove references to sanctioned entities in payment messages."[286] The bank at one point posted on the company intranet a how-to guide to the practice of stripping identifying information out of such transactions.[287]

In announcing the settlement with ING, OFAC Director Adam Szubin noted its expected deterrent effect, stating: "Today's historic settlement should serve as a clear warning to anyone who would consider profiting by evading U.S. sanctions."[288] Cyrus Vance, Jr., the Manhattan district attorney, whose office participated in the case, emphasized that such cases "ensure that rogue regimes and human-rights abusers are isolated and feel economic pressure from sanctions."[289]

In August 2012, Standard Chartered Bank, based in London, reached a $340 million settlement with the New York Department of Financial Services (NYDFS), headed by Benjamin Lawsky.[290] As part of the agreement, the Bank also agreed to "install a monitor for a term of two years who will report directly to DFS and who will evaluate the money-laundering risk controls in the New York branch and implementation of appropriate corrective measures."[291]

The Standard Chartered settlement was announced the day before a hearing at which Lawsky had said he was planning to revoke the bank's license to operate in New York.[292] The U.S. dollar clearing operations of Standard Chartered reportedly made up an estimated 15 percent to 20 percent of the bank's total revenues.[293] As a result, the bank's stock market value reportedly dropped 23 percent ($17 billion) the day after the threat to revoke its license was announced.[294] In the agreement with Lawsky's office, the bank stipulated that from 2001 through 2007, it had "removed or omitted Iranian information from U.S. dollar wire payment messages" with respect to "approximately 59,000 transactions totaling approximately $250 billion."[295]

A NYDFS report about Standard Chartered contained several remarkable details. According to the report, the bank's CEO for the Americas had warned a bank senior official in London in 2006 that the bank's business with Iran risked "catastrophic reputational damage" to the bank and "serious criminal liability" for its officers.[296] The senior official in London reportedly replied: "You fucking Americans. Who are you to tell us, the rest of the world, that we're not going to deal with Iranians."[297]

The $340 million settlement between Standard Chartered and NYDFS was controversial because Lawsky had acted without coordinating with federal law enforcement agencies that were working on the same case.[298] Standard Chartered subsequently agreed to pay an additional $327 million to the U.S. government.[299] In announcing the federal settlement, Ronald C. Machen, Jr., U.S. Attorney for the District of Columbia, said the agreement "holds Standard Chartered Bank accountable for intentionally manipulating transactions to remove references to Iran, Sudan, and other sanctioned entities, and then further concealing these transactions through misrepresentations to U.S. regulators."[300] According to a U.S. Department of Justice press release announcing the settlement, this conduct occurred in "locations around the world" and "with the knowledge and approval of senior corporate managers and the legal and compliance departments of SCB."[301]

In August 2014, Standard Chartered was ordered to pay another $300 million penalty to the NYDFS "because of its failure to remediate anti-money laundering compliance problems as required" by the bank's 2012 settlement with NYDFS.[302] The bank's "compliance remediation failures were uncovered" by the monitor that NYDFS had "installed at Standard Chartered as part of the 2012 agreement."[303] In addition to the fine, SCB was ordered to suspend dollar clearing through its New York Branch for high-risk retail business clients at its SCB Hong Kong subsidiary"; "exit" high-risk small and medium business clients at its branches in the United Arab Emirates; and "not accept new dollar-clearing clients or accounts across its operations without prior approval from DFS."[304] The *New York Times* called the 2014 settlement "a rare regulatory strike against corporate recidivism" and noted that it may reflect a new trend, with Lawsky "considering an effort to routinely double-check banks' transactions for signs of money-laundering."[305]

c. Billions of Dollars Each in Penalties—and Individual Accountability—Against HSBC and BNP Paribas

In December 2012, HSBC, a U.K. bank which was at that time the largest in Europe,[306] forfeited $1.256 billion and agreed to pay an additional $665 million in penalties for various violations of sanctions laws.[307] A U.S. Senate committee report alleged that from 2001 to 2007, "two HSBC affiliates sent nearly 25,000 transactions involving $19.4 billion through their HBUS [HSBC's US bank] accounts over seven years without disclosing the transactions' links to Iran."[308] According to the U.S. Department of Justice, violations included the processing, from the mid-1990s through 2006, of approximately $660 million in OFAC-prohibited transactions from which HSBC "followed instructions from sanctioned entities such as Iran" and removed or obscured identifying information that would have revealed the involvement of Iranian and other sanctioned entities.[309] HSBC had also failed to adequately monitor suspicious transactions with Mexico from 2006 to 2010, leading it to be "the preferred financial institution for drug cartels and money launderers."[310]

In addition to the settlement, HSBC reportedly spent at least $990 million to strengthen its compliance regime.[311] In announcing the settlement, the Department of Justice also noted that "HSBC has replaced almost all of its senior management."[312]

The HSBC settlement was followed by several smaller-scale settlements. In December 2013, the Royal Bank of Scotland (RBS), which was majority owned by the U.K. government,[313] agreed to pay $100 million in penalties for transactions involving Iran, Sudan, Burma, and Cuba.[314] From 2005 to 2009, RBS had removed "references to U.S.-sanctioned locations or persons from payment messages sent to U.S. financial institutions."[315] RBS was credited with uncovering and reporting the violations itself.[316] In addition to the financial penalties, the bank also fired four employees as part of the settlement.[317] Benjamin Lawsky, superintendent of the New York Department of Financial Services, applauded the employment moves.[318] Sounding a theme he would reiterate with regard to subsequent cases, Lawsky said, "If we truly want to deter future wrongdoing, we should move increasingly toward exposing individual misconduct and holding individuals accountable."[319]

In January 2014, Clearstream Banking, based in Luxembourg, agreed to pay $152 million for permitting Iran to evade restrictions on dealing with U.S. banks.[320] From December 2007 to June 2008, Clearstream used an account at a U.S. financial institution in New York to hold $2.8 billion in securities on behalf of the Central Bank of Iran.[321] "Clearstream provided the Government of Iran with substantial and unauthorized access to the U.S. financial system," said OFAC Director Adam Szubin.[322] "Today's action should serve as a clear alert to firms operating in the securities industry that they need to be vigilant with respect to dealings with sanctioned parties," said Szubin.[323]

The Clearstream settlement was announced only three days after the P-5+1 and Iran began implementing the Joint Plan of Action, an interim agreement with a six-month duration, which was later extended by mutual consent.[324] The *New York Times* characterized the January 23, 2014, settlement announcement as part of "intensified efforts" by the Obama administration "to counter what officials called a misimpression that the six-month nuclear agreement with Iran had opened the door to new economic opportunities with the country."[325]

On June 30, 2014, BNP Paribas, the largest French bank and the world's fourth largest, agreed to plead guilty and pay $8.9736 billion in fines for helping Iran, Sudan, and Cuba gain illegal access to the U.S. financial system.[326] This was reportedly the largest criminal fine ever imposed by the U.S. government. It was more than twice the size of the second largest criminal fine (the penalties assessed on BP as part of the Deepwater Horizon spill), but less than the $13 billion in civil penalties paid by JP Morgan Chase in

2003 in connection with its mortgage business.[327] From 2004 to 2012, BNP Paribas had "knowingly and willfully moved more than $8.8 billion through the U.S. financial system on behalf of Sudanese, Iranian, and Cuban sanctioned entities," said a Department of Justice press release.[328] The bank did so "through various sophisticated schemes designed to conceal from U.S. regulators the true nature of the illicit transactions."[329]

"Sanctions are a key tool in protecting U.S. national security interests, but they only work if they are strictly enforced . . . . If sanctions are to have teeth, violations must be punished," said Attorney General Eric Holder in announcing the settlement.[330] During the lead-up to the settlement announcement, French Foreign Minister Laurent Fabius complained publicly that BNP's alleged actions did not violate European law and that the fine was excessive.[331] Deputy Attorney General James Cole, in his remarks during the settlement announcement, said the extraordinary magnitude of the penalty was attributable to BNP Paribas's "failure to cooperate" with the U.S. investigation of it as well as the "prolonged" nature of the bank's misconduct.[332] Some observers speculated that the criminal charges and fine also reflected an effort by Attorney General Eric Holder to walk back a comment he had made in 2013 that it was "difficult for us to prosecute" institutions when they are "so large" that a prosecution would "have a negative impact on the national economy, perhaps even the world economy."[333]

In addition to the financial penalty, BNP Paribas agreed with the New York State Department of Financial Services to "terminate or separate from the bank" thirteen senior employees and "suspend U.S. dollar clearing operations . . . for one year for business lines on which the misconduct centered."[334] Benjamin Lawsky, the Department's Superintendent, reportedly achieved these steps by threatening to revoke BNP Paribas's license to do business in New York, the center of the international financial system.[335] The employee consequences originally suggested by BNP Paribas had merely included three particular senior executives being docked their annual bonuses for the year.[336]

Lawsky successfully insisted the employees be fired.[337] In doing so, Lawsky was apparently implementing principles he had spelled out in a March 2014 speech to the Exchequer Club in Washington, D.C.[338] In that speech, Lawsky suggested that bad conduct is not adequately deterred "if we're just getting large fines from the corporations," fines that are typically paid by "shareholders who usually had nothing to do with the violations."[339] He asserted that "to get real deterrence, we need to have individuals who are personally held to account," who "face real, serious penalties and sanctions when they break the rules."[340] Lawsky also suggested that in some cases, corporate fines should be supplemented by "new and creative corporate penalties" that may boost deterrence, such as by prohibiting "a company from conducting the type of business that was at the heart of its misconduct."[341]

VI. LESSONS LEARNED AND THE FUTURE OF U.S. FINANCIAL LAWFARE

A. Incomplete Success

U.S. financial lawfare against Iran was clearly very successful in hindering Iranian financial transactions. The significant impact on Iranian transactions that was seen as early as 2007 and 2008 had reached a new, even higher level of impact by 2014. By 2014, major international banks were taking quick action in response to changes to Treasury's list of designated entities, and designated entities were finding it harder and harder to find any bank with which to do business. "The biggest, most sophisticated banks have it built into their filters and start screening out potential transactions within minutes," said then OFAC Director Adam Szubin in April 2014.[342] "Once you're on an OFAC list, no bank anywhere will deal with you," said Judith Lee, chair of the international trade group at the law firm of Gibson, Dunn and Crutcher.[343]

This impact on Iranian transactions in turn greatly weakened the Iranian economy. In August 5, 2015, congressional testimony, Szubin, then serving as Acting Under Secretary of the Treasury for Terrorism and Financial Intelligence, detailed the effect on the Iranian economy of the U.S. financial lawfare against Iran in the years preceding the July 14, 2015 JCPOA announcement.[344] "The powerful set of U.S. and international sanctions on Iran . . . effectively isolated Iran from the world economy," said Szubin.[345]

Szubin provided several metrics of "the impact of the sanctions campaign."[346] He said that "today, the Iranian economy is estimated to be only 80 percent the size that it would have been . . . absent our sanctions."[347] In addition, "Iran has foregone approximately $160 billion in oil revenue alone since 2012, after our sanctions reduced Iran's oil exports by 60 percent."[348] Szubin added that the Iranian currency had also "declined by more than 50 percent."[349]

Assessing the extent to which U.S. financial lawfare had succeeded by 2015 in achieving its ultimate objectives of halting Iran's nuclear weapons program and state sponsorship of terrorism was more complicated. With regard to the secondary objective, Iran's state sponsorship of terrorism, the bottom line was that Iran's sponsorship continued unabated. For example, the State Department asserted in its report on state sponsorship of terrorism during 2012 that Iran's sponsorship of terrorism underwent "a marked resurgence" that year, reaching levels not seen in twenty years.[350] The State Department's reports on state sponsorship of terrorism during 2013 and 2014 asserted that "Iran continued its terrorist-related activity" during those years and provided extensive descriptions of such activity.[351] The report covering 2014 was released in June 2015. In a June 19, 2015, news article about the report's release, the *New York Times* stated: "Although the report covers 2014, American officials said the Iranian policies described in it had continued this year."[352]

As of summer 2015, U.S. financial lawfare had clearly failed to coerce Iran into halting its state sponsorship of terrorism. In addition, while U.S. financial lawfare had undoubtedly increased the cost to Iran of its sponsorship of terrorism, the constraining effect of the U.S. campaign was apparently insufficient to cause Iran to reduce its support for its terrorist allies.

In contrast, U.S. financial lawfare (combined with U.S. energy and insurance lawfare) was generally credited with helping coerce Iran to negotiate more seriously about its nuclear weapons program. For example, as mentioned above, in April 2015, CIA Director John Brennan stated that Iran's Supreme Leader, Ayatollah Khamenei, had become more flexible in negotiations with the West because Rouhani had persuaded Khamenei that "six years of sanctions had really hit," and Iran's economy was "destined to go down" unless a deal was reached with the West and sanctions were lifted.[353]

On July 14, 2015 (after this book was largely completed), the P-5+1 (the U.N. Security Council's five permanent members plus Germany) and Iran announced that they had agreed on a Joint Comprehensive Plan of Action (JCPOA) to address Iran's nuclear program.[354] The JCPOA provided for most nuclear-related sanctions on Iran to be lifted in exchange for various constraints on Iran's nuclear program.

In his August 5, 2015, congressional testimony, Adam Szubin, then Acting Under Secretary of the Treasury for Terrorism and Financial Intelligence, attributed the newly agreed constraints on Iran's nuclear program to "the global sanctions coalition built and led by the United States that gave us the leverage necessary to secure unprecedented nuclear concessions from Iran."[355] "The point of these efforts was clear: to change Iran's nuclear behavior, while holding out the prospect of relief if Iran addressed the world's concerns about its nuclear program," said Szubin.[356] "This campaign yielded results," asserted Szubin, explaining that "after years of intransigence, Iran came to the table prepared to negotiate seriously over its nuclear program."[357]

Former Senator Joseph Lieberman, chair of United Against Nuclear Iran, a non-governmental organization critical of the JCPOA for containing insufficient constraints on Iran's nuclear program,[358] put it very similarly. "It was only because of the sanctions adopted by Congress, and ultimately signed by President Obama," said Lieberman, "that sufficient economic pressure was put on the Iranian government that its leaders came to the negotiating table."[359]

In early August 2015, with congressional votes over the JCPOA looming, commentators and members of Congress were divided over whether the JCPOA's curtailments of Iran's nuclear program were sufficiently long-term and verifiable.[360] Some suggested that the deal could have been more favorable to the U.S. if the economic pressure had been stronger. For example, in announcing in early August that he would "vote to disapprove the agreement," Senator Charles Schumer (D-NY) said that it would be "better to keep U.S. sanctions in place, strengthen them, enforce secondary sanctions on other nations, and pursue the hard-trodden path of diplomacy once more, difficult as it may be."[361] Other commentators suggested that the U.S. negotiating position could also have been strengthened if economic pressure had been supplemented with a more credible threat to halt Iran's nuclear weapons program by force of arms if all other options failed.[362]

Although they were divided on the sufficiency of the JCPOA, most, if not all, key supporters and opponents of the JCPOA seemed to agree that the U.S. economic lawfare campaign had proven a valuable weapon against Iran's nuclear weapons program. They all seemed to credit the economic lawfare campaign with achieving significant (albeit to some, insufficient) curtailment of an Iranian nuclear program that otherwise might only have been curtailed by kinetic means.

B. Iranian Countermeasures

Not surprisingly, Iran had, from the start, worked assiduously to counter the U.S. economic lawfare against it. "Yes, of course, we bypass the sanctions,"[363] said Iranian President Hassan Rouhani in a news conference on August 30, 2014. "We believe they are illegal and crimes against humanity," explained Rouhani.[364]

As discussed previously in this chapter, Iranian entities and individuals often requested that banks hide their involvement in transactions so as to facilitate access to the U.S. financial system. Similar tactics were used by the Iranian shipping industry, which regularly changed ship names, flags, owners, operators, and managers, and also obscured the ownership of its vessels using shell companies, in order to stay one step ahead of designations.[365] When Iranian deception involved conventional transaction channels over which the United States had leverage, it proved to a considerable degree counterproductive. Iran's efforts to cloak its worst actors' involvement in particular business activities fed the U.S. argument that foreign companies subject to U.S. authority had to be careful when trading with any Iranian partners. As former Under Secretary Stuart Levey put it: Treasury has "told governments and the private sector . . . that the Iranian government engages in deception, so they need to look beyond lists of sanctioned entities to protect themselves from potential illicit transactions."[366]

Some Iranian entities and individuals turned to *hawala* as an alternative to banks. According to the U.S. Treasury, "*hawala* works by transferring money without actually moving it."[367] In a *hawala* transaction, the sender transfers money to a *hawaladar* (hawala agent) who then instructs an associated *hawaladar*, usually one located near the final recipient, to deliver the equivalent funds (minus a small commission) to the final recipient. *Hawala* transactions are based on trust and usually involve no promissory instrument or other written record identifying the specific transaction.[368] Settlement between the *hawaladars* is usually done over several transactions, for example through import of goods or *hawala* transactions in the reverse direction.[369] While *hawala* can work well for relatively small transactions, for very large transactions it can be risky or infeasible (e.g., if there is no prospect of a similarly sized flow in the other direction). It was thus of limited value to Iranian efforts to evade U.S. financial lawfare.

Iran also sought to circumvent U.S. financial lawfare by turning to barter transactions, which can be conducted without banks.[370] However, barter transactions require each party to have something they wish to acquire from the other party, and such arrangements can result in "considerable inconvenience and cost."[371]

One notable evasion scheme involved Iran buying gold in Turkey with Turkish payments for gas imported from Iran.[372] The Iran Freedom and Counter-Proliferation Act of 2012, a U.S. law enacted in January 2013, closed the so-called "golden loophole" that enabled this scheme to evade U.S. lawfare.[373] The Act did so by subjecting to U.S. sanctions any persons determined to have knowingly engaged after July 1, 2013, in selling, supplying, or transferring, directly or indirectly, to or from Iran any precious metal.[374]

Iran mounted a more frontal counterattack on U.S. lawfare by initiating its own lawfare challenges to the legal validity of designations. Iran's challenges followed in the wake of precedents set by the European Court of Justice (E.C.J.) in the case of Yassin Abdullah Kadi, a Saudi national who had been designated by the EU in 2001 for association with Al Qaeda.[375] The E.C.J. upheld the EU General Court's annulment of Kadi's EU designation, notwithstanding that, pursuant to Security Council Resolution 1267, the U.N. Security Council had included Kadi on its list of individuals and entities associated with Al Qaeda.[376]

In annulling Kadi's designation by the EU, the E.C.J. held that "the Courts of the European Union must ensure the review, in principle the full review, of the lawfulness of all European Union acts in the light of fundamental rights, including where such acts are designed to implement Security Council resolutions."[377] The E.C.J also held, in a 2013 decision addressing an appeal of the Kadi case, that the procedures for delisting at the UN do not provide to the person whose name is listed a "guarantee of effective judicial protection," as required for a listing by the EU.[378] The E.C.J. then set out various procedural and substantive obligations that must be met by an EU designation decision.[379]

Following in the wake of the E.C.J.'s *Kadi* decisions, some Iranian challenges to EU designations were successful, but typically only temporarily. For example, in September 2013, the EU's second highest court annulled twenty-six of the EU Council's sanctions designations, including those of various banks and that of the Islamic Republic of Iran Shipping Lines (IRISL), insisting that the EU Council had failed to provide sufficient evidence that specific entities belonged on the sanctions list.[380] However, the EU court maintained the designations in effect for two months to enable the EU Council to respond, and the EU Council relisted all but two of the designees in November 2013, with new evidence to buttress the designations.[381]

Iranian entities and individuals nevertheless continued to challenge EU designations. For example, EU courts in July 2014 annulled the designations of several Iranian entities including the Sharif University of Technology, located in Tehran,[382] only to see Sharif University relisted a few months later.[383]

The challenges had been successful largely because while the EU Council had often relied initially on classified information in determining its designation targets, the EU court system, unlike the U.S. court system, had been unable to review classified information without declassifying it,[384] and some member states were "unwilling to share sensitive intelligence information" in order to prove that the complaining entities had engaged in proscribed activities.[385] That problem was addressed in February 2015 with new EU rules that created a mechanism for EU member states to offer confidential evidence to judges.[386] It was expected that lawfare challenges to EU designations would be hindered by the new rules, but not necessarily stopped.

In addition, as of early August 2015, the JCPOA was (assuming it was not derailed by a congressional vote of disapproval) expected to greatly reduce, although not entirely eliminate, EU designations of Iranian entities.[387] Regardless of the JCPOA's fate, the U.S. and EU economic lawfare tools employed against Iran in the years prior to 2015, and the Iranian efforts to blunt them, would continue to provide valuable lessons for lawfare practitioners to draw from in a future campaign against another adversary or a re-targeted Iran.

C. Concerns About Collateral Damage

Aside from the question of whether and how U.S. lawfare could generate sufficient leverage to achieve particular U.S. objectives vis-à-vis Iran's nuclear weapons program, the deployment of U.S. financial lawfare against Iran also raised concerns as to possible collateral damage. For example, the Iranian government and others blamed Western sanctions for making it difficult to import medicine and other humanitarian goods.[388]

However, the humanitarian impact of U.S. economic lawfare against Iran appeared to be minimal, especially when compared with the reportedly grave humanitarian impact of the broader U.S. sanctions on Iraq during the 1990s. This was due to the fact that U.S. lawfare against Iran was specifically designed not to hinder Iranian acquisition of food and medicine, and was repeatedly adjusted to ensure that it did not have that effect.[389] Indeed, even U.S. legal restrictions on exports from the United States to Iran (let alone U.S. measures against third country companies) excluded food, medicine, and medical devices,[390] and such exports from the United States to Iran remained substantial even at the height of U.S. lawfare against Iran.[391]

Concerns were also raised as to the potential impact of U.S. financial lawfare on the dollar's primacy in the international financial system. The dollar's primacy in the international financial system has long served various U.S. interests. For example, it allows the United States to borrow and spend more than it might otherwise. In addition, U.S. financial lawfare depends largely on the dollar's primacy in the international financial system. As Treasury Secretary Paulson stated: "Treasury can effectively use these tools largely because the U.S. is the key hub of the global financial system."[392]

Should the dollar's primacy wane, either because financial lawfare deters dollar usage or because the U.S. economy declines in relative influence, the United States' ability to wage financial lawfare will likely wane along with it. U.S. rivals, including China and Russia, have, for a variety of reasons, periodically tried to bypass the U.S. dollar.[393] This is a significant concern for the United States, which should give strong consideration as to how to design future financial lawfare so as to minimize its risk to the dollar's primacy. One way of minimizing the risk to the dollar's primacy is, to the extent possible, to implement financial lawfare jointly with the issuers of key alternative currencies. One of the numerous benefits of partnering with the European Union on many of the financial measures against Iran was that waging financial lawfare against Iran with the dollar, euro, and pound sterling left the dollar less exposed.

D. The Risk of Setting a Precedent Useful Against the United States

U.S. financial and other economic lawfare risks setting precedents that could be used against the United States by its adversaries and even by allies that disagree strongly with some aspects of its policies. Chapter 4 discusses and analyzes the particular risk that economic lawfare could be used against the United States by the PRC.

Economic lawfare style measures have already been impactfully deployed against the United States in Europe by Europeans. For example, Belgian laws prohibit the financing of companies producing cluster munitions,[394] landmines,[395] and depleted uranium ammunition or armor.[396] Belgian financial institutions are thus potentially subject to punishment for providing credits or bank guarantees or acquiring any financial instruments issued by leading suppliers of weapons to the U.S. government which allegedly produce such munitions,[397] including, allegedly, General Dynamics (depleted uranium ammunition)[398] and Textron (cluster munitions).[399] The Belgian prohibition on financing General Dynamics is ironic because Belgium is a member of NATO and deploys various weapons manufactured by General Dynamics, including armored personnel carriers[400] and the F-16A aircraft.[401]

These Belgian laws are among the sharpest tools of the broader international movement to prohibit disfavored munitions and divest from companies producing them. However, they are far from the only ones. France, Ireland,

Italy, Luxembourg, Switzerland, and the Netherlands all have laws more narrowly focused on banning financing of or investment in producers of cluster munitions.[402]

In addition, many leading European asset managers, including government pension funds, have divested from U.S and other manufacturers of a variety of disfavored weapons. For example, the Norwegian government pension fund as of May 2015 excluded investments in numerous companies that it stated were involved in "production of weapons that through their normal use may violate fundamental humanitarian principles."[403] This included three major U.S. companies that it listed as being involved in production of cluster munitions (Textron, Raytheon, and General Dynamics) and five major U.S. companies that it listed as being involved in production of nuclear arms (Alliant Techsystems, Lockheed Martin, Babcock & Wilcox, Northrop Grumman, Honeywell, and Boeing).[404]

The Norwegian government pension fund's divestment from U.S. companies involved in production of nuclear arms was ironic because Norway is a member of NATO, and the most recent NATO Deterrence and Defense Posture Review states that "nuclear weapons are a core component of NATO's overall capabilities for deterrence and defence," and "the supreme guarantee of the security of the Allies is provided by the strategic nuclear forces of the Alliance, particularly those of the United States."[405] The Norwegian government pension fund's divestment from Lockheed Martin since June 2013 was particularly ironic because the Norwegian defense ministry was at the same time engaged in purchasing from Lockheed Martin the F-35 fighter plane. As Norwegian Defense Minister Ine Eriksen Soreide announced in January 2014, "We have concluded that these planes are the best ones for us."[406]

Meanwhile, Danske Bank, a commercial enterprise that is the largest Danish bank, has also divested from Lockheed Martin and several other listed major U.S. companies because of their involvement in production of antipersonnel mines, cluster munitions, and nuclear weapons.[407] As Chapter 6 notes, Danske Bank is apparently subject to divestment by Illinois state pension funds, pursuant to a new Illinois state law, because of Danske Bank's divestment from Israeli companies. Perhaps Illinois, which contains several Lockheed Martin facilities, will also subject Danske Bank to divestment because of its divestment from Lockheed Martin. Lawfare-style interactions between Illinois and Danske Bank alone could become increasingly complex.

The Belgian government, Norwegian government pension fund, Danske Bank, and many other advocates of banning these disfavored weapons almost certainly do not see the U.S. military as an adversary that they wish to weaken or destroy. Thus the Belgian and other European laws and Scandinavian divestment policies do not meet this book's definition of lawfare.

However, these examples are worth noting (and are characterized as "lawfare-style") because they so strikingly implicate the first of this book's two tests for lawfare, including by impacting the key armed force decision-making and capabilities of the target. The movement to ban cluster munitions has reportedly led the U.S. government to phase out its use of cluster weapons even though the United States refused to accede to the treaty banning cluster munitions.[408] In addition, the U.S. Navy is reportedly phasing out depleted uranium ammunition,[409] and the U.S. Air Force has announced that it will not fire depleted uranium ammunition in combat against the Islamic State, even though it used such rounds in Iraq in 1991 and 2003.[410] The United States has also stopped producing and acquiring antipersonnel mines, and has announced that it hopes to eventually accede to the treaty banning antipersonnel mines.[411] These lawfare-style activities targeting U.S. companies are also important because they could provide a template for more nefariously motivated activities by U.S. adversaries.

The risk of setting adverse precedents must be factored into U.S. economic lawfare decision-making. To the extent possible, each U.S. lawfare deployment should be designed to minimize the risk that it will set a problematic precedent that could be used against the United States by current or future adversaries. If such a risk cannot be avoided, it should be included in policymakers' analysis of the overall advantages and disadvantages of the particular lawfare deployment.

The U.S. government should also develop a strategy to discourage U.S. allies from adopting such financing prohibitions and divestment campaigns against companies for manufacturing weapons at the U.S. government's behest. The strategy could start by pushing back against lawfare-style activities by allied foreign governments such as those of Belgium and especially Norway whose kinetic defenses depend on the very weapons against which they are waging lawfare-style activities. U.S. laxity in confronting its allies over such tactics may encourage its adversaries to adopt similar ones with more malign motivations.

In addition, such tactics may already be costly to the U.S. economy and the U.S. taxpayer. According to survey results published in 2012 by the European Social Investment Forum (EUROSIF),[412] "almost half of Europe's total assets under management have policies in place which specify the exclusion of companies involved in the manufacture certain types of weapons, the most common being those subject to the international Conventions on Cluster Munitions and Anti-Personnel Mines."[413] EUROSIF estimated that the total assets under management by European asset managers at the end of 2011 was 13.8 trillion euros, meaning that some 6.5 trillion total European assets under management excluded investment in manufacturers of at least some disfavored weapons.[414] According to EUROSIF, "this remarkable result shows that international conventions and treaties can have a real impact on the financing decisions of the industry."[415]

Analyzing trends in European investment exclusions, EUROSIF noted that "experience shows that a few large pioneers can have strong influence on the market and lead to a proliferation of certain strategies."[416] "One example of this," explained EUROSIF, "is the Norwegian Government Pension Fund—Global, often called the 'Gold standard' in institutional responsible investing."[417]

The U.S. companies from which such divestment has occurred include major employers of U.S workers. To take just a few of the major U.S companies on the Norwegian government pension divestment list, as of 2015, General Dynamics had 99,500 employees,[418] Northrup Grumman had 64,300 employees,[419] and Lockheed Martin had 112,000 employees.[420] The U.S. government also purchases billions of dollars in products from these U.S. companies each year. To the extent the companies are being penalized for producing and selling for the U.S. government, including by finding it harder to borrow money, they may need to charge the U.S. government, and thus the U.S. taxpayer, more for their products.

E. The Challenges of Waging Lawfare Amid Negotiations with the Target

In addition to these concerns, the U.S. deployment of financial lawfare against Iran also raised questions as to the most effective way of waging economic lawfare amid negotiations with the target. During 2009, while the newly inaugurated President Obama reached out to the Iranian government, Under Secretary Levey "was instructed to hold his powder dry while the administration attempted to reach out to the regime in Tehran," wrote Juan Zarate. "Meetings with bankers, designations of Iranian entities, and enlistment of partners to isolate Iranian financial activity stopped."[421] This pause inevitably meant a gradual weakening of the pressure on Iran, with the United States failing to respond as Iranian entities changed their names and found other ways to evade sanctions. Especially when a lawfare campaign is aimed at pressuring foreign actors to restrict commerce with designated target state actors, the designations must be kept up to date if they are to be effective.

During the 2012–2015 negotiations with Iran (which concluded with the JCPOA), the Obama administration took a somewhat different approach than it did in 2009. While strongly opposing the imposition of new types of sanctions on Iran, and lifting some sanctions in exchange for Iranian concessions on the nuclear front, the administration continued to implement some existing sanctions.[422] Although Iranian officials expressed displeasure with the continued implementation, they did not step away from the negotiating table. However, their interest in making concessions on the nuclear front also seemed to wane, apparently in part because of the decreased pressure on their economy. As discussed earlier in this chapter, many commentators and members of Congress criticized the JCPOA as containing insufficient Iranian concessions, and suggested that the deal could have been more favorable to the United States if the economic pressure had been stronger. Striking the most effective balance while negotiating with the target will continue to be a challenge for practitioners of economic lawfare.

The "diplomatic respite" in 2009 "also undermined the credibility of the stated reason for the financial isolation—to protect the international financial system against Iran's illicit financial activities," asserted Juan Zarate.[423] "Suspension of financial pressure appeared to be an admission by the US government that the financial measures against Iran were really just driven by geopolitics," said Zarate.[424]

Just as with traditional warfare, economic lawfare is constantly evolving. To be maximally effective, designations must be constantly revised because a particular adversary such as Iran will rename designated entities. New tactics and strategies must also be constantly devised because the international financial system (the "financial battlespace," as Zarate puts it) is constantly evolving, and illicit actors are constantly looking for new ways to route assets.[425] The challenges of making such constant adjustments can be increased by the inevitable pressure to take into account the fluctuations of negotiations with the targeted adversary.

F. The Challenges of Unwinding Financial Lawfare

Somewhat analogous to the difficulty of adjusting financial lawfare amid negotiations with the target is the challenge of unwinding financial lawfare if the objective is met (or a decision is otherwise made by the U.S. federal government to curtail the lawfare, for example as part of a deal with the adversary that addresses some but not all of the objectives). The potential challenges of unwinding U.S. and allied economic lawfare against Iran were the subject of considerable discussion as the nuclear negotiations proceeded.[426] One set of challenges had to do with the complex and intertwined provisions, and varying suspension and termination criteria, of the relevant U.S. laws. For example, some provisions could be waived, but not terminated, by the administration without new congressional legislation.[427] This reduced the magnitude of the incentives that U.S. executive branch negotiators could guarantee Iran in exchange for Iranian nuclear concessions.

Another challenge posed by curtailing financial lawfare against Iran in implementation of the JCPOA was similar to that posed by the "diplomatic respite" in 2009. This was the risk that curtailing financial measures against Iran solely in exchange for nuclear concessions by Iran could undermine the credibility of the stated reason for Iran's financial isolation—to protect the international financial system against Iran's illicit financial activities. Such harm to the credibility of financial measures could undercut their future use against both other adversaries and Iran (for example, in response to Iranian noncompliance with the JCPOA or continued Iranian sponsorship of terrorism).

Juan Zarate and others raised such concerns in response to the planned lifting of financial and other economic measures in exchange for Iran's nuclear concessions in the JCPOA (which included no financial integrity concessions by Iran).[428] For example, in congressional testimony on July 30, 2015, Zarate said that "the

JCPOA sanctions unwinding framework does damage to the conduct-based sanctions and measures that have been so effective and driven most of the listings and designations by the United States and the international community."[429] Zarate provided as an example the JCPOA "allowing most of the Iranian banks back into the international financial order without dealing with their underlying conduct or controls."[430]

Similarly, in congressional testimony on August 5, 2015, Matthew Levitt, a former Treasury official, noted that several "entities to be delisted under this deal have engaged in the kind of deceptive banking practices that threaten the integrity of the international financial system."[431] Levitt expressed concern that these entities were being delisted although the JCPOA did "nothing to stop them" from continuing to engage in such practices and to "represent a hazard to the international financial community."[432]

Another set of challenges posed by curtailing financial lawfare against Iran in implementation of the JCPOA had to do both with financial lawfare's dependence on market sentiment and also its variety of practioners. Much as extralegal factors, including reputational risk, contributed to some banks voluntarily forgoing licit business with Iran at the height of U.S. financial lawfare against Tehran, there was no guarantee that all banks would choose to re-enter the Iranian market once U.S. federal legal restrictions were withdrawn. In addition, as demonstrated by the separate punishments of some banks by NYDFS head Benjamin Lawsky, as well as the material support lawsuits Gary Osen was planning against the banks that had done business with Iran (as described in Chapter 2), the U.S. federal government did not even necessarily control all of the relevant U.S. legal levers over financial transactions with Iran. Both the dependence on market sentiment and the variety of practitioners posed the potential risk that Iran might not receive some of the economic relief it was expecting even if it complied with its commitments under the JCPOA and the U.S. federal government wanted it to receive that relief.

This is one way in which ending financial lawfare can be more complicated than ending kinetic warfare. In this era of modern telecommunications, when a President orders troops to stop bombing an adversary and orders U.S. diplomats to return to the adversary's capital, the bombing stops and the diplomats return. In contrast, when a President orders the executive branch to stop waging financial lawfare against an adversary, state officials and private sector litigators may find ways of continuing the war, and private sector banks may for that or their own reasons not choose to resume business with the adversary.

As discussed in more detail in Chapter 2, the ability of U.S. non-federal actors to continue waging lawfare against an adversary with which the federal government has made peace poses difficult issues. Congress should—as discussed in that chapter—retain and vigorously exercise its constitutional authorities to wage, enable, and halt lawfare. Consistent with this, continued consideration should be given as to in which circumstances, and with regard to what types of lawfare, it is beneficial for U.S. laws to restrict or prevent U.S. non-federal actors from continuing to wage lawfare against adversaries with which the U.S. federal government has made peace.

G. Financial Lawfare's Role in Future U.S. Strategy

The impact of the U.S. government's financial lawfare on Iran—which cost the Iranian regime tens of billions of dollars without causing disproportionate humanitarian damage—calls into question the accuracy of the dominant paradigm in the scholarly literature regarding sanctions, which derides unilateral sanctions as inevitably ineffective in a globalized economy. To the extent U.S. economic lawfare failed to achieve its ultimate objectives with regard to Iran's nuclear weapons program and state sponsorship of terrorism, the result might well have been different if the lawfare had been more vigorous and combined with a more credible threat to halt Iran's nuclear weapons program by force of arms if all other options failed.[433] The considerable economic impact of the U.S. government's financial lawfare against Iran, in addition to the considerable impacts of several of the other lawfare deployments described in this book, provide support for the proposition that lawfare, deployed systematically and effectively, may be able to save U.S. and foreign lives by supplementing or replacing kinetic warfare as a tool for achieving some significant U.S. military objectives.

The relative success of U.S. government financial lawfare against Iran has already inspired imitation. As mentioned earlier, the United States applied a similar approach with regard to Iran's energy trade and insurance sector. The United States also drew from the Iran model in waging vigorous financial lawfare against Russia[434] and the Islamic State.[435]

Treasury seems certain to continue to wage financial lawfare against U.S. adversaries. It will do so not only against new targets but also in new ways. Treasury officials' experience and creativity, new evasive maneuvers by U.S. adversaries, the differing economies of U.S. adversaries, and changes in the financial markets and regulatory regimes will lead Treasury to enhance and refine the financial lawfare tools described in this chapter.

Meanwhile, the innovative components of Treasury's financial lawfare against Iran seem highly likely to continue to influence the design of U.S. economic lawfare against other targets. These innovations include the previously referenced direct outreach to individual foreign private companies, aggressive use of U.S. regulatory authorities to pursue traditionally military objectives, and effective development and harnessing of intelligence about global private sector business transactions.

Globalization has inevitably increased the business interests in the United States of many leading foreign companies, leaving them subject to

U.S. government regulation and leverage and reliant on the goodwill of the U.S. government and consumers. As a result, major foreign companies in sectors beyond finance, energy, and insurance may also be susceptible to U.S. government economic lawfare. Foreign companies in exceptionally globalized, strategic, regulated, and information-rich sectors such as mobile telecommunications, the Internet, aviation, and shipping could be next in line.

Before the U.S. government expands its economic lawfare into additional sectors, it will want to analyze and weigh both the risk posed by such U.S. lawfare to U.S. economic and regulatory preeminence in those sectors and the risk that such lawfare might set problematic precedents that could be used against the U.S. by current or future adversaries. However, given U.S. economic lawfare's proven efficacy (against target economies if not target policies), the lack in many situations of usable kinetic or other alternative weapons, and policymakers' tendency to discount future risks, the expansion of U.S. government economic lawfare into additional sectors seems highly likely.

One set of key issues going forward will involve what magnitude and type of U.S. penalties to impose on recalcitrant companies and their employees. A second set will involve the extent and type of U.S. government cooperation with U.S. nongovernmental lawfare practitioners. A third set will involve the extent and type of interagency cooperation on U.S. lawfare initiatives.

As discussed above, the type of U.S. penalties was raised by Benjamin Lawsky, head of the NYDFS, who asserted that "to get real deterrence, we need to have individuals who are personally held to account," who "face real, serious penalties and sanctions when they break the rules."[436] U.S. Senator Elizabeth Warren has made similar comments. For example, at a Senate committee hearing in March 2013, Warren noted of the money laundering activity for which HSBC was fined $1.9 billion: "HSBC didn't do it just one time . . . . They did it over and over and over again . . . . They were caught doing it, warned not to do it, and kept right on doing it."[437] "Now, HSBC paid a fine, but no individual went to trial," said Warren, noting that "no individual was banned from banking and there was no hearing to consider shutting down HSBC's activities in the US."[438] "If you're caught with an ounce of cocaine, you're going to jail," said Warren, "but if you launder nearly a billion dollars . . . and violate sanctions you pay a fine and you go home and sleep in your own bed at night."[439]

At least one bank, BNP Paribas, has, as described in a previous section, had to shut down some activities in the United States since Warren's comments (interestingly, the requirement was imposed by the NYDFS, not Treasury). Whether or not individuals are jailed for refusing to comply with U.S. economic lawfare requirements will likely depend on several factors. One is recidivism—whether companies or individuals persist in violations even after signing on to settlement agreements. Another factor is likely to be the nature of the economic sector. As the U.S. government expands economic lawfare into additional sectors, most if not all of which will be less cash-intensive than banking and some of which will involve companies with relatively less presence in or reliance on the U.S. market, it may need to adjust the type and magnitude of its penalties.

The extent to which U.S. government lawfare practitioners should and will cooperate with U.S. nongovernmental lawfare practitioners is another key question going forward. Chapter 2 contains extensive discussion of that question, including examples of past such cooperation and options for the future.

The extent of interagency cooperation on U.S. lawfare initiatives will be another important issue going forward. As of summer 2015, a few models for such interagency cooperation already existed. For example, the U.S. government's lawfare campaign to stop Karl Lee (Li Fangwei) from continuing to ship missile-related materials from China to Iran culminated in a series of steps announced together on April 29, 2014.[440] Those steps, discussed in detail in Chapter 4, included the coordinated deployment of lawfare tools by federal agencies including the Departments of Commerce, Justice, State, and Treasury.[441] "These charges are an important part of the 'all tools' approach our government is taking against Li Fangwei to shut down . . . his proliferation activities," said Assistant Attorney General John Carlin, asserting that "this case is an outstanding example of multiple agencies working together to focus various enforcement efforts on the significant threat to our national security posed by such proliferation networks."[442]

However, interagency cooperation on U.S. lawfare initiatives is nowhere near as systematic as it could or should be. As discussed in Chapter 1, the U.S. government's approach to lawfare remains ad hoc and uncoordinated, with no overarching strategy and no person or office in the U.S. government serving as a point person for coordinating lawfare and collecting best practices. Indeed, as Chapter 4 describes, it took eight years from the time a Karl Lee front company was first designated by the U.S. government (and six years since he was first designated) before the U.S. government imposed against Karl Lee its coordinated, creative, and impactful lawfare measures of April 29, 2014. In the meantime, Lee shipped over thirty-five tons of material to Iran's missile program.

As this chapter has demonstrated, lawfare waged by the U.S. government has tremendous potential for achieving U.S. objectives with less loss of life and at reduced expenditure of taxpayer dollars. Without systematic coordination, U.S. government lawfare will not be as effective as it could be—as lessons of prior lawfare efforts are left unlearned, lawfare deployment opportunities are not systematically identified, limited lawfare resources are deployed inefficiently, interagency synergies are not realized, and lawfare innovation is not methodically pursued.

CHAPTER 4

The Chinese Government Adopts and Implements a Lawfare Strategy

"Defeating the enemy without fighting is the pinnacle of excellence."
—Sun Tzu

I. LAWFARE IN CHINESE STRATEGY AND CULTURE

Sun Tzu, the preeminent Chinese military strategist, asserted in the sixth century BC that "[t]o win one hundred victories in one hundred battles is not the pinnacle of excellence; defeating the enemy without fighting is the pinnacle of excellence."[1] Consistent with this maxim, the People's Republic of China (PRC) is one of the most explicit and active practitioners of lawfare, the use of law as a tool to achieve traditional military objectives absent the clash of arms. As PRC President Jiang Zemin told a group of Chinese international law experts in 1996, "we must be adept at using international law as a weapon."[2] This chapter will describe and analyze how the PRC, in the two decades since, has adopted lawfare as a strategy and systematically waged it against the United States and other adversaries and potential adversaries.

The PRC's embrace of lawfare is notable in part because the PRC seems likely to be the United States' leading rival for global dominance during the balance of the twenty-first century. Although the United States is a far more law-oriented society, with a much higher percentage of its best minds going into the legal field, the PRC is currently waging lawfare much more diligently and systematically than is the United States. While the United States seems far better suited to be a lawfare superpower, it is currently leaving the field disproportionately to the PRC.

In contrast with the U.S. government, the PRC has explicitly adopted lawfare (the synonymous term in Chinese is *falu zhan* or "legal warfare") as a major component of its strategic doctrine. In 2003, the Chinese Communist Party Central Committee and the Chinese Central Military Commission approved the concept of "Three Warfares," asserting the prominent place in their warfare doctrine of the following non-kinetic tools:

> 1) *Psychological Warfare:* the use of propaganda, deception, threats, and coercion to affect the enemy's ability to understand and make decisions; 2) *Media Warfare:* the dissemination of information to influence public opinion and gain support from domestic and international audiences for China's military actions; and 3) *Legal Warfare:* the use of international and domestic laws to gain international support and manage possible political repercussions of China's military actions.[3]

Since this decision, several PRC military texts have been dedicated entirely to *falu zhan.*[4] For example, the People's Liberation Army (PLA) in 2004 published a book titled *Analysis of 100 Cases of Legal Warfare,* coauthored by leading Chinese jurist Cong Wensheng. The book describes and analyzes case studies of other countries, including the United States, using lawfare. It discusses "controlling the enemy through the law, or using the law to constrain the enemy."[5] The book concludes that "users can find a lot of room for manipulation in the respects of the content, timing, and extent of application [of the law of war]" and that "in the future military struggles, our army should . . . enhance the art and level in the application of the law of war so as to attain the best effect."[6]

In 2005, the PLA published a book titled *Legal Warfare in Modern War,* by Xun Hengdong, an attorney who is a high-ranking military officer.[7] Xun writes that no country involved in armed conflict complies fully with the law of armed conflict, since the pressures of war do not allow such restraint.[8] He concludes that the law of armed conflict should therefore be seen not as an inviolable set of boundaries but rather as a weapon to achieve such objectives as manipulating the perceptions of the international community.[9]

In 2007, the PLA published a text titled *Under Informatized Conditions: Legal Warfare,* which defines "legal warfare" to include "activities conducted by using the law as the weapon and through measures and methods such as legal deterrence, legal attack, legal counterattack, legal restraint, legal sanctions, and legal protections."[10]

In addition, several important PRC military texts with a broader ambit have discussed legal warfare. For example, the PLA Academy of Military Science text, *The Science of Military Strategy,* notes that "war is not only a military struggle, but also a comprehensive contest on fronts of politics, economy, diplomacy, and law."[11]

Additional conceptual context for the PRC's use of legal warfare is provided by a treatise titled *Unrestricted Warfare,* which was written by two PLA colonels, Qiao Liang and Wang Xiangsui, and published by the PLA in 1999.[12] The treatise suggests various tactics—including legal warfare—that developing countries, in particular China, could use to compensate for their military inferiority vis-à-vis the United States.[13] Liang was subsequently promoted to major general and, as of 2014, served as deputy secretary of the PRC's National Security Policy Committee.[14]

At least one PRC defense think tank has closely followed the U.S. literature on lawfare, in particular the key articles on lawfare written by retired U.S. Major General Charles Dunlap, Jr., who coined the term in English.[15] The Knowfar Strategy and Defense Institute, a PRC defense think tank, translated and published Dunlap's article *Lawfare: A Decisive Element of 21st Century Conflicts?*[16] Dunlap's article defines lawfare, as he does elsewhere, as "the strategy of using—or misusing—law as a substitute for traditional military means to achieve an operational objective."[17] Each time Dunlap's article uses the term "lawfare," the Knowfar translation into Chinese uses *falu zhan*, implying that—at least for those at Knowfar—the term *falu zhan* means what Dunlap means by the term lawfare.[18] In addition, the meaning of the term *falu zhan* in the rest of the Chinese literature described above seems very similar if not identical to the English term "lawfare" as defined by Dunlap and this book. This chapter will thus use the term lawfare as generally interchangeable with the term *falu zhan*.

In 2008, the U.S. State Department's International Security Advisory Board noted that China was engaged in the nonkinetic "Three Warfares" even in the absence of kinetic warfare between China and the United States:

> It is essential that the United States better understand and effectively respond to China's comprehensive approach to strategic rivalry, as reflected in its official concept of "Three Warfares." If not actively countered, Beijing's ongoing combination of Psychological Warfare (propaganda, deception, and coercion), Media Warfare (manipulation of public opinion domestically and internationally), and Legal Warfare (use of 'legal regimes' to handicap the opponent in fields favorable to him) can precondition key areas of strategic competition in its favor.[19]

The PRC's use of lawfare seems consistent with the doctrines of the Chinese Communist Party Chairman Mao Zedong, as well as those of Sun Tzu. Unlike many Western strategists, Mao also tended to think of the clash of arms as just one element, and not necessarily the most important element, of conflict.[20]

China's vigorous use of lawfare is rooted in the exceptionally instrumental role of law in historical and contemporary Chinese culture. In pre-Communist imperial China, law served as a tool of authority, not a constraint upon it.[21] Following the Communist revolution of 1949, China adopted the Marxist view that law serves as an instrument of politics (rather than, for example, a check on politics and an autonomous, objective arbiter of justice).[22]

Then, during the Cultural Revolution of 1966 to 1976, China dismantled its legal system, including by closing down its Ministry of Justice, abolishing its law schools, and re-educating lawyers by ordering them to work as farmers and factory workers.[23] China became practically a "lawless nation."[24] Mao Zedong reportedly "abhorred the notions of law and of a legal system" because he believed they "would dam up the free flow of the revolution."[25]

China's legal system was substantially rebuilt in the three decades following the Cultural Revolution and Mao's death in 1976. By 2008, China had "sophisticated legal institutions," hundreds of laws, thousands of regulations, and "the third largest number of lawyers in the world."[26] As it was before the Cultural Revolution, Chinese law was largely an instrument of (rather than a constraint upon) state power.[27] As a result of these and other factors, including a perception that the legal system was significantly corrupt, popular confidence in the Chinese legal system remained low.[28] However, there was a perception, at least among many observers, that progress was being made.[29]

The years following 2008 saw a significant deterioration of the progress toward rule of law that had been made between 1976 and 2008. The Chinese legal system began to experience greater party control and increasingly harsh punishments for attorneys taking on sensitive cases defending people's rights against the government.[30] The new state of affairs was characterized as "the Chinese government's new dual strategy of outward lip service to a 'rule of law,' coupled with an inward retrenchment of . . . authoritarian rule."[31] The result, warned Jiang Ping, who served as the President of the China University of Political Science and Law in the 1980s and was one of the key drafters of China's current civil and administrative codes, was that "China's rule of law is in full retreat."[32]

Indicative of the combination of lip service and retrenchment were the rhetoric and policies of Xi Jinping, who became General Secretary of China's Communist Party in 2012 and President of China in 2013. After coming to power, Xi repeatedly used in his speeches a term that has been translated into English by the Chinese government as "rule of law," reportedly for Western consumption, but is reportedly more accurately translated as "law and order."[33] Xi at the same time resuscitated Mao's metaphor of the state's judicial and police functions as a knife, while also asserting that the party must ensure "the handle of the knife is firmly in the hands of the party and the people."[34]

By 2015, political repression in China was reportedly at its most severe point in twenty-five years.[35] In July 2015, the Chinese government conducted what one commentator called "a judicial blitzkrieg across the country, arresting over 190 prominent human rights lawyers" and several high-profile law professors.[36] The attorneys were accused of "running a criminal syndicate to smear the Communist Party and 'create social chaos' through their litigation."[37] According to the New York Times, experts and rights advocates said the Chinese government appeared to be using its legal system, through these arrests and charges, in "an aggressive attempt to discredit all rights lawyers and activists as greedy schemers who menace social order."[38]

Consistent with the PRC's sharply instrumental use of law domestically, China was, as of 2015, engaged in lawfare in several international arenas. Section II of this chapter addresses PRC lawfare involving the instrumental use of laws and legal fora to achieve military objectives. Section III addresses PRC lawfare tactics designed to gain advantage from the greater influence that law and its processes exert over the United States and other PRC adversaries. Section IV addresses the future of PRC lawfare and potential U.S. and allied responses to it.

II. PRC INSTRUMENTAL LAWFARE

In the conception of PRC strategists, legal warfare should begin, and can be exceptionally valuable, "before the outbreak of physical hostilities."[39] In each of the following arenas—maritime, aviation, space, and cyber—the PRC is waging lawfare today in an effort to tilt to its advantage future kinetic battlegrounds.

In the first three arenas—maritime, aviation, and space—China is using lawfare in relatively analogous ways to advance the same basic objective. That objective is to create and promote international legitimacy for expanding China's sovereignty rights as part of its access control strategy. The most troubling lawfare tool the PRC is deploying in these three arenas is military operations, openly undertaken, which Beijing asserts are consistent with its own interpretations of international law (yet are inconsistent with international law as understood by most others). President Obama made a veiled reference to these and other instances of Chinese strategic lawbreaking in November 2011, when he said the United States welcomes "a rising, peaceful China" but asserted that "with their rise comes increased responsibilities."[40] "It's important for them to play by the rules of the road," said President Obama, noting that "there are going to be times when they're not, and we will send a clear message to them that we think that they need to be on track in terms of accepting the rules and responsibilities that come with being a world power."[41]

In addition to military operations consistent with the PRC's own interpretations (but inconsistent with international law as generally understood), China's lawfare tools in the maritime, aviation, and space arenas include: advocacy, in international legal fora, designed to shape international law in favor of its preferred interpretations; the production of scholarly articles and symposia designed to shape international opinion in favor of China's preferred interpretations;[42] and domestic laws and official statements reflecting the PRC's preferred interpretations of international law.

A. Maritime and Aviation Lawfare

Maritime and aviation lawfare are the two areas of PRC lawfare that have been most studied in the West. In the maritime realm, according to James Kraska and Brian Wilson, two senior U.S. Navy attorneys, "China has begun to engage in a resourceful legal warfare, or 'lawfare' strategy to deny access to its coastal seas to warships and aircraft of the United States, Japan, and other countries in the region."[43] Kraska and Wilson noted that "Chinese strategists have taken an increasing interest in international law as an instrument to deter adversaries prior to combat . . . [including by shifting the law of the sea] away from long-accepted norms of freedom of navigation and toward interpretations of increased coastal state sovereign authority."[44]

Kraska and Wilson warned that "China continues to advance on the battle-field of international law."[45] By changing international law today, so as to push U.S. and other ships and aircraft farther away from China's coastline, China is providing its military more breathing room tomorrow.

Specifically, China has asserted that it can regulate passage on the seas, and also overflight within the airspace, in an Exclusive Economic Zone (EEZ) that extends two hundred miles from its coastal baseline. In the view of the United States and a majority of other states, this is "clearly inconsistent with international law," which provides in the U.N. Convention on the Law of the Sea (UNCLOS) that a state cannot regulate passage in, or overflight over, its EEZ.[46] Raul Pedrozo, a profes-sor of military law at the U.S. Naval War College, referred to China's "untenable position that foreign military activities in the EEZ are subject to coastal notice and consent"[47] as part of "China's ongoing lawfare strategy to misstate or misapply international legal norms to accommodate its anti-access strategy."[48]

China has used its inaccurate interpretation of EEZ law to justify the inter-ception and harassment of U.S. and other nations' ships operating within its EEZ, and of U.S. and other nations' aircraft flying above its EEZ. According to Pedrozo, "unlawful Chinese interference with U.S. military activities in the EEZ has become a matter of routine."[49] Sometimes, Chinese military ships and aircraft "aggressively interfere with U.S. military ships and aircraft in violation of interna-tional law."[50] From time to time, ostensibly private Chinese "cargo ships and fish-ing vessels are used as government proxies to interfere with U.S. ships."[51] Using fishing vessels in this manner "provides the Chinese government with some level of plausible deniability" from a legal perspective, although from a practical per-spective "the pattern of behavior is easily ascribable to the Chinese government."[52]

China's continued actions pursuant to its inaccurate interpretation of EEZ law appear to be aimed at changing customary international law. Customary interna-tional law can be nullified or even changed through state practice undertaken in con-junction with an assertion that such practice is consistent with international law.[53]

In the law of the sea context, customary international law can, over time, be affected by maritime operations, diplomatic statements, domestic implementing legislation, and the writings of legal scholars, as well as statements from, for exam-ple, the UNCLOS International Law of the Sea Tribunal, International Seabed Authority, and Commission on the Limits of the Continental Shelf.[54] In addition to its maritime operations, China's EEZ lawfare strategy includes "declaratory state-ments incorporated into China's UNCLOS ratification depositary instrument," domestic legislation formally claiming security interests in its EEZ, development of supportive legal scholarship, and a strategic communications campaign.[55]

One set of particularly aggressive PRC lawfare steps has involved its dissemination of its so-called nine-dash map. In May 2009, the PRC government circulated to all U.N. member states two formal notes stating, "China has indisputable sovereignty over the islands in the South China Sea and the adjacent waters, and enjoys sovereign rights and jurisdiction over the relevant waters as well as the seabed and subsoil thereof (see attached map)."[56] The notes added that "the above position is consistently held by the Chinese government, and is widely known by the international community."[57] The ambiguously marked map referred to in the notes depicted nine line segments (dashes) encircling waters, islands, and other features of the South China Sea.[58] The nine-dash map appears to represent an extremely expansive assertion of Chinese sovereignty, an assertion that, according to the U.S. government, "does not accord with the international law of the sea."[59] "Vindication of China's nine-dashed line," said Professor Jerome Cohen, "would, at a minimum, vastly expand the area subject to a Chinese EEZ."[60] This is particularly significant, said Cohen, because "China, as illustrated by its clashes with American reconnaissance ships and planes, claims broad powers over its EEZ."[61]

Some of China's maritime operations also appear to be designed to establish title to specific islands and bodies of water. Under international law, sovereignty over an island can be used to claim control over a sea zone around it. UNCLOS article 121 defines an island as "a naturally formed area of land, surrounded by water, which is above water at high tide."[62] It also specifies that mere "rocks which cannot sustain human habitation or economic life of their own" do not create some types of sea zone.[63] The PRC is engaged in construction designed to turn submerged reefs into inhabited islands.[64] For example, the PRC recently built on Johnson South Reef, a previously submerged reef, an "island with an area of 100,000 square meters."[65] "As time goes on," said Professor Ingrid Wuerth, "it may become harder and harder to document which features were 'rocks,' which were 'islands' and which were neither prior to construction—and these determinations may be essential to resolving contested maritime claims in the region."[66]

However, for the PRC, such lawfare activities as turning reefs into islands are not necessarily designed to create an argument that would win before the International Court of Justice next year. Sometimes, the activity is apparently designed in part to create a legal or legal-sounding argument that can create a narrative today that will "persuade the Chinese people that their government's actions are justified."[67] The activity may also, or instead, be designed to plant the seed of arguments that will grow in strength as the PRC causes customary international law to evolve and/or as neighbors, intimidated by the PRC's military might, acquiesce to its claims.

Demonstrating continuing control over a specific body of water or island is "vitally important to claims of sovereignty" over it under theories of historic title, customary international law, and UNCLOS.[68] The extent to which other states accept or contest a historic claim is a key criteria for establishing the claim.[69] Since inaction may be viewed as acquiescence to the claim, China benefits legally from creating or bolstering a claim by creating a new island or other facts, and then militarily dissuading other states from contesting the claim.[70]

Despite the opposition of the United States and several of China's neighbors to the PRC's EEZ maritime and aviation lawfare, this strategy for obtaining sovereignty over South China sea islands and waters is, as one U.S. Navy legal expert put it, "slowly proving effective . . . if successful, China will have achieved through the use of lawfare what it traditionally would have had to achieve almost solely through military force."[71] In March 2015, the Chairmen and Ranking Members of the Senate Armed Services Committee and the Senate Foreign Relations Committee sent a letter to the Secretary of State and the Secretary of Defense expressing concern that China's "land-reclamation and construction activities on multiple islands" in the South China Sea were designed in part to "enhance" the PRC's "sovereignty claims."[72] The senators expressed concern that the executive branch lacked "a formal policy and clearly articulated strategy" to address these developments and urged "the development and implementation of a comprehensive strategy."[73]

B. Outer Space Lawfare

Much as China is using lawfare to prepare to its advantage the maritime and aviation battlefields, it is also using lawfare to prepare to its advantage the outer space battlefield.[74] For example, there are an "increasing number of scholarly articles published by Chinese authors claiming that China's terrestrial borders extend indefinitely upward through outer space and that all the space within those perimeters is China's sovereign territory."[75] In this regard, Bin Cheng, the author of *Studies in International Space Law*, warned that "States which object to certain types of satellites, such as those that engage in remote sensing, [may] claim sovereignty over national space above the usual heights at which such satellites orbit so as to subject them to the consent and control of the States overflown."[76]

This idea is not without precedent. For example, the prominent eighteenth-century English jurist William Blackstone wrote, *cujus est solum, ejus est usque ad coelom* ("whoever's is the soil, it is theirs all the way to Heaven").[77]

However, the assertion of sovereignty over outer space above national territory is contrary to current international law, including the Outer Space Treaty and the Convention on International Civil Aviation (both of which China is a party to) as they are generally understood.[78] The difference could set the stage for conflict with the United States, which asserts that all countries "have the rights of passage through and operations in space without interference."[79] In the "U.S. National Space Policy," the United States also "rejects any claims to sovereignty by any nation over outer space . . . or any portion thereof, and rejects any limitations on the fundamental right of the United States to operate in and acquire data from outer space."[80]

According to Major John W. Bellflower, a U.S. Air Force expert on space law, China's "legal argument, if ultimately successful, would have the strategic effect of rendering American military satellites useless and could establish a lawful predicate for Chinese military action against those satellites."[81] "International acquiescence or acceptance of Chinese assertions of vertical sovereignty" would also, he said, "effectively vitiate national means of verification of compliance regarding any existing or new arms reduction treaties."[82] Bellflower urged that the United States undertake "strategic lawfare to combat such efforts," including by "swiftly and cogently oppos[ing] any claim of vertical sovereignty and shap[ing] international law to eliminate attempts at curbing American freedom of action in space."[83]

In addition, some PRC experts have asserted that in time of war, China would have the legal right to attack the surveillance satellites of belligerents wherever in the common areas of outer space they might be located (e.g., not just over national territory but also over the common high seas).[84] This is inconsistent with the U.S. view of international law and what constitutes a satellite engaged in peaceful and thus protected uses. The U.S. position is that peaceful uses that are protected in common areas need be only nonaggressive and thus may include surveillance satellites.[85] In contrast, Chinese experts assert that protected peaceful uses need be nonmilitary (and thus do not include surveillance satellites).[86]

PLA strategists have observed the high value of communications and remote sensing satellites to the information age warfare waged by the United States.[87] The PRC interpretations of outer space law appear to represent a PRC response to its current technological inferiority in space as compared to the United States. The PRC seems to be deploying an asymmetric strategy to deny U.S. use of space as much as possible,[88] including through lawfare justifying the development and deployment of capabilities to damage and interfere with American satellite systems so as to blind the U.S. military in the event of conflict.[89] "China is beginning to use international law as a means of countering American space power," said Major Bellflower, because it is "aware that military options are not a viable choice at this time given the financial, military, and technological gap between it and America."[90]

C. Insisting That the Law of Armed Conflict Does Not Apply in Cyberspace

The PRC has repeatedly refused to recognize that international law, including the law of armed conflict (LOAC), applies in cyberspace.[91] While the PRC joined in a 2013 U.N. Group of Governmental Experts report which stated that international law is applicable to the cyber arena, that step appears to be an outlier,[92] as the PRC in 2015 returned to its pre-2013 position that international law does not apply in cyberspace. For example, in January 2015, the PRC (and five other members of the Shanghai Cooperation Organization) submitted to the U.N. Secretary General a draft voluntary "code of conduct for information security," which suggested that "China continues to resist applying existing international law to cyberspace."[93] At an April 2015 meeting of a U.N. Group of Governmental Experts on cyberspace security, the PRC reportedly aggressively asserted that international law does not apply in cyberspace, with PRC delegates going so far as to propose to "delete all the sections having to do with international law."[94]

In contrast, the U.S. government insists that cyberspace activities *are* governed by international law including LOAC.[95] NATO[96] and the European Union[97] take the same position.

There are reportedly several different sets of reasons why the PRC is disinclined to have cyberspace activities governed by international law (including LOAC). Some of these sets of reasons have to do with the PRC's desire to control the flow of information to its people.

Another set of reasons the PRC would prefer that LOAC, in particular, not apply to cyberspace provides a preeminent example of how lawfare could tilt to China's advantage a future kinetic battleground between it and the United States. Cyberspace plays a central role in Chinese military thinking. Lieutenant-General Qi Jianguo, Deputy Chief of the General Staff of the Chinese military, said, "in the information era, seizing and maintaining superiority in cyberspace is more important than seizing command of the sea and command of the air were in World War II."[98] In light of cyberspace's key role in Chinese military strategy, continued Chinese insistence that LOAC does not apply in cyberspace would provide China with a considerable advantage, especially if the United States continues to insist that its own cyberspace activities are constrained by LOAC. Given the centrality of LOAC to U.S. warfighting today, and U.S. domestic pressures promoting increasingly strict interpretations of LOAC, it would be nearly impossible for the United States to reverse its current position and decide that its cyberspace activities would not be governed by LOAC.

The advantages to the PRC of LOAC not applying to cyberspace are illustrated by the potential role of cyberwar with regard to one of China's avowed top priorities—reuniting Taiwan with the mainland. PLA military strategy suggests that in an attack on Taiwan, the PLA would aim to delay or degrade U.S. reinforcements sufficiently to allow the PLA to conquer some or all of the island, thereby presenting the United States with "a *fait accompli* upon arrival in the combat operations area."[99] PLA military strategy suggests that it would seek to achieve this objective by attacking the United States with cyber weapons in the opening phases of such a conflict. These Chinese cyberattacks would be designed to slow and corrupt U.S. information and support systems sufficiently for the PLA to achieve its campaign objectives without facing direct combat with superior U.S. forces.[100]

For the PLA, "using cyberwarfare against U.S. information systems to degrade or even delay a deployment of forces to Taiwan offers an attractive asymmetric strategy," wrote James Mulvenon in THE PEOPLE'S LIBERATION ARMY IN

THE INFORMATION AGE.[101] "If PLA information operators using PCs were able to hack or crash these systems, thereby delaying the arrival of a U.S. carrier battle group to the theater . . . Taipei might be quickly brought to its knees and forced to capitulate to Beijing."[102]

Such large-scale and inevitably wide-ranging cyberattacks on U.S. information and support systems would be severely constrained by two major requirements of LOAC, if LOAC applies. One constraint would be the proportionality requirement, reflected in article 57 of Additional Protocol I to the Geneva Conventions, that the civilian harm expected to be caused by an attack not be "excessive in relation to the concrete and direct military advantage anticipated."[103] This rule is a norm of customary international law applicable in both international and non-international armed conflicts.[104]

While the proportionately requirement is notoriously vague, it seems likely that it would be violated by a large-scale Chinese cyberattack designed to slow the Navy's departure from West Coast ports. Such a cyberattack could cause, for example, hundreds of deaths of U.S. civilians through collateral malfunctions or shutdowns of critical infrastructure, hospitals, and the like in the United States. Indeed, Shi Haiming, a researcher at China's National University of Defense Technology, has asserted that one reason LOAC should not apply to cyberspace is because "the proportionality requirement is much more difficult in cyberspace because of the expanse and penetration of the Internet and the difficulty in containing unintended effects of attacks."[105]

A second LOAC constraint on a wide-ranging PRC cyberattack on U.S. information and support systems would be the principle of distinction, which is set forth in article 48 of Additional Protocol I to the Geneva Conventions. Article 48 states as follows: "In order to ensure respect for and protection of the civilian population and civilian objects, the Parties to the conflict shall at all times distinguish between the civilian population and combatants and between civilian objects and military objectives and accordingly shall direct their operations only against military objectives."[106] The basic rule of distinction set forth in article 48 is considered to be a norm of customary international law applicable in both international and noninternational armed conflicts.[107]

The principle of distinction specifically requires that combatants both restrict attacks to military objectives and employ weapons the effects of which can be limited to military objectives. For example, article 51(4) of Additional Protocol I to the Geneva Conventions states:

Indiscriminate attacks are prohibited. Indiscriminate attacks are:
   (a) those which are not directed at a specific military objective;
   (b) those which employ a method or means of combat which cannot be directed at a specific military objective; or

(c) those which employ a method or means of combat the effects of which cannot be limited as required by this Protocol; and consequently, in each such case, are of a nature to strike military objectives and civilians or civilian objects without distinction.[108]

The prohibition of indiscriminate attacks, which is set forth in article 51(4), is considered to be a norm of customary international law applicable in both international and noninternational armed conflicts.[109] In light of this prohibition, Shi Haiming has asserted that LOAC should not apply to cyberspace because "it is impossible to distinguish between civilian and military assets."[110]

Given Chinese press reports that more than 95 percent of the U.S. military's cyber communications network is connected to the Internet,[111] it could be very tempting for the PLA to try to attack it by broadly targeting the Internet. The LOAC requirements of proportionality and distinction could severely constrain PLA cyberattacks against key U.S. transportation hubs and civilian communications networks used by the military, including with cyber viruses, which do not discriminate between military and civilian objectives and thus may threaten computer-controlled hospitals, dams, civilian airliners, and other forbidden targets.

Because PLA cyberattacks could be pivotal to the success of a PRC campaign to conquer Taiwan, Chinese success in insisting that LOAC does not apply in cyberspace could be a decisive element of such a conflict, one decided in legal fora long before the traditional warfare begins. As such, this PRC initiative to render LOAC inapplicable to cyberspace seems a preeminent example of Sun Tzu's maxim that "defeating the enemy without fighting is the pinnacle of excellence."[112]

III. THE PRC AND COMPLIANCE-LEVERAGE DISPARITY LAWFARE

A. The PRC, the United States, and Compliance-Leverage Disparity Lawfare

The effectiveness of PRC lawfare designed to gain advantage from the greater influence that law and its processes exert over the United States is driven by the starkly disparate attitudes toward international law and compliance with it of the U.S. and PRC governments. The PLA handbook on international law instructs PLA officers that they "should not feel completely bound" by international laws that are detrimental to the defense of China's "national interests" but rather should focus on those international laws beneficial to China "while evading those detrimental to our interests."[113] According to Wang Xiangsui, a colonel in the PLA who coauthored the prominent book titled *Unrestricted Warfare*, "war has rules, but those rules are set by the West."[114] "We are a weak country," said Wang, "so do we need to fight according to your rules? No."[115] This contrasts sharply with a U.S. military that is scrupulous about obeying international laws, as detailed in Chapter 1.

The PRC is in at least one arena—nonproliferation—clearly waging compliance-leverage disparity lawfare designed to gain advantage from the greater influence that law and its processes exert over the United States and its allies. As described in Section II of this chapter, the PRC is aggressively and mostly openly pushing to change international law in the maritime, aviation, space, and cyber arenas so as to improve its position in a future kinetic conflict. In contrast, the PRC's actions in the nonproliferation arena involve the PRC publicly binding itself to international laws and agreed interpretations of them but then quietly using proxies to violate them while the PRC asserts it is acting in good faith. The PRC's successful exploitation of its compliance-leverage disparity in the nonproliferation arena is a source of concern to U.S. policymakers both in and of itself and because of the risk that the PRC might apply its successful template to other arenas.

It is worth noting that some of the practical results of PRC instrumental lawfare and PRC compliance-leverage disparity lawfare can be identical—a failure of the PRC to comply with international laws with which its adversaries are complying. For example, PRC non-compliance while the United States and its allies comply can be a practical result of PRC behavior in the cyber arena if it violates the law of armed conflict (LOAC) while openly proclaiming LOAC does not apply to cyber warfare. PRC non-compliance while the United States and its allies comply can also be a practical result of PRC behavior in the nonproliferation arena when it violates its nonproliferation law obligations while either claiming a lack of capacity to implement its obligations or denying that the violation is occurring.

However, as discussed in Section III.B below, the PRC's compliance-leverage disparity lawfare can provide it with an additional set of benefits. For example, in the nonproliferation arena, its compliance-leverage disparity lawfare results in it receiving both the benefits of violating its nonproliferation obligations and also the benefits of formal adherence to those obligations.

B. PRC Compliance-Leverage Disparity Lawfare in the Nonproliferation Arena

1. Overview

The PRC has a long history of gaming the international legal system by entering into legally binding nuclear nonproliferation obligations with which its rivals (including the United States, Japan, and South Korea) tend to comply while the PRC secretly violates those obligations by providing nuclear technology to its allies, often through proxies.[116] The result is the acquisition of nuclear weapons capacity or even arsenals by rogue states allied with China (including Iran, North Korea, and Pakistan) while China's rivals, over which international legal commitments have greater influence, either remain without nuclear weapons (as in the case of Japan and South Korea) or strictly enforce nonproliferation obligations vis-à-vis their own allies (as with aggressive U.S. efforts to discourage South Korea from acquiring nuclear weapons).[117]

The PRC's compliance-leverage disparity lawfare, as exemplified by its nonproliferation actions, can be summarized as follows:

- The PRC formally adheres to a binding legal obligation and thus receives the various benefits of that formal adherence.
- While receiving the benefits of formal adherence, the PRC uses proxies to violate the obligation.
- The PRC thus receives both the benefits of formal adherence and the benefits of violating the obligation, to the considerable disadvantage of those parties that comply with the obligation because law has greater influence over them.

The following subsection will describe and analyze two case studies of why and how the PRC has for years engaged in such lawfare with regard to Iran's nuclear program.[118]

2. PRC Compliance-Leverage Disparity Lawfare Regarding Iran in the Nonproliferation Arena

a. Why the PRC Wages Compliance-Leverage Disparity Lawfare Regarding Iran in the Nonproliferation Arena

As this subsection will describe, the PRC has, in recent decades, chosen to enter into several key nuclear nonproliferation obligations that are binding under international law. The PRC benefits in several ways from formally entering into those obligations. For example, it is able to portray itself as a responsible member of the international community. In addition, its economy has benefited from the ability to import high-technology dual-use goods that the United States and its allies typically export only to adherents to the Nuclear Nonproliferation Treaty (NPT) and other nonproliferation regimes. Furthermore, by contributing to the universality of treaties such as the NPT, the PRC fortifies the treaties' compliance-leverage on law-sensitive members such as Japan and South Korea.

At the same time, the PRC has, as this subsection will illustrate, allowed or enabled purportedly private sector brokers in China to supply Iran with pivotal dual-use technologies and materials for both Iran's uranium enrichment program (key to creating a nuclear warhead) and its missile program (key to delivering a nuclear warhead). By using private sector proxies, the PRC is able to claim that it is fully committed to its nuclear nonproliferation obligations but simply lacks the capacity to enforce them. The PRC also sometimes flatly denies that the violations are occurring, an ignorance that is more plausible with regard to private sector brokers in China than it would be were the PRC's own officials or state-owned companies shipping proscribed items to Iran. The PRC can thus continue to receive the various benefits of acceding to its nuclear nonproliferation obligations, while also receiving the international security benefits of violating those obligations.

The international security benefits to the PRC of such compliance-leverage disparity lawfare in the case of Iran were significant. For example, by remaining on relatively good terms with Iran and letting Chinese companies do business with Iran that others declined, the PRC vastly increased its share of the Iranian market for licit as well as illicit trade. For example, PRC support for Tehran helped persuade Iran that China was "a reliable partner in developing Iran's energy resources"[119] and gave to Beijing "leverage to access Iran's oil riches."[120] Thus, "by 2010, China had become the major foreign investor in Iran's energy sector, far exceeding any other country."[121] Energy-starved China, for which oil imports are a strategic necessity, also became Iran's largest oil customer.[122]

In addition, according to Professor John Garver, evidence suggests that "at least some of China's leaders believe a strong, nuclear-armed or nuclear-armed-capable Iran would be a valuable check on U.S. influence in the Persian Gulf and move the world in the direction of multipolarity."[123] For example, "a strong Iran resistant to U.S. dictates" would "force Washington to keep large military forces" in the Middle East, thereby "limiting the ability of the United States to concentrate forces in East Asia, where China's core interests lie."[124] A United States distracted by a nuclear-armed or nuclear-weapons threshold Iran would mean "the chances for China's successful rise without having to confront the United States would increase."[125]

"China sees Iran as a potential partner in countering U.S. power," according to Michael Singh, former senior director for Middle East affairs at the National Security Council.[126] Thus, said Singh, "rather than using its clout as one of Iran's largest energy customers and vendors-of-last-resort to secure Iranian compliance with U.N. Security Council and nonproliferation norms, Beijing appears to fuel the very behavior that is most provocative to the United States and its allies—behavior that could destabilize the Middle East."

The rest of this subsection describes and analyzes how the PRC engages in compliance-leverage disparity lawfare regarding Iran in the nonproliferation arena, and how the United States might respond. Subsection *b* identifies the PRC's major nuclear nonproliferation obligations with regard to Iran between 2010 and 2015. Subsection *c* details and analyzes the PRC's record of noncompliance with regard to Iran's nuclear program. Subsection *d* considers U.S. options for responding to this particular type of impactful PRC lawfare.

b. The PRC's Binding Nonproliferation Obligations Regarding Iran

The major nuclear nonproliferation commitments with regard to which the PRC was waging compliance-leverage disparity lawfare vis-à-vis Iran in the years prior to 2015 were the NPT, to which China adhered in 1992, and the several United Nations Security Council resolutions that imposed sanctions in response to Iran's nuclear program. The resolutions principally included United Nations Security Council Resolution 1737, regarding Iran's nuclear program, for which China voted in 2006,[127] and United Nations Security Council Resolution 1929, for which China voted in 2010.[128]

The PRC's principal substantive nuclear nonproliferation obligations regarding Iran are the following:

i. Article I of the Nuclear Nonproliferation Treaty specifies as follows: "Each nuclear-weapon State Party to the Treaty undertakes not to transfer to any recipient whatsoever nuclear weapons or other nuclear explosive devices or control over such weapons or explosive devices directly, or indirectly; and *not in any way to assist, encourage, or induce any non-nuclear-weapon State to manufacture or otherwise acquire nuclear weapons or other nuclear explosive devices,* or control over such weapons or explosive devices." (emphasis added)

ii. In Paragraph 3 of U.N. Security Council Resolution 1737, the Council: "Decides that all States shall take the necessary measures to prevent the supply, sale or transfer directly or indirectly from their territories, or by their nationals or using their flag vessels or aircraft to, or for the use in or benefit of, Iran, and whether or not originating in their territories, of all items, materials, equipment, goods and technology which could contribute to Iran's enrichment-related, reprocessing or heavy water-related activities, or to the development of nuclear weapon delivery systems . . . ."

iii. In Paragraph 9 of U.N. Security Council Resolution 1929, the Council: "Decides that Iran shall not undertake any activity related to ballistic missiles capable of delivering nuclear weapons, including launches using ballistic missile technology, and that States shall take all necessary measures to prevent the transfer of technology or technical assistance to Iran related to such activities."

c. The PRC's Record of Noncompliance Vis-à-Vis Iran's Nuclear Program

As this author and his coauthors described in their book, *U.S. Nonproliferation Strategy for the Changing Middle East,* published in January 2013,[129] China was in 2010 through 2012 reportedly the leading procurement and transshipment point used by Iran to illicitly procure the additional parts and components it needs for its advancing nuclear and missile programs. The PRC remained noncompliant in the years between 2012 and July 2015, when the P-5+1 (including the PRC) and Iran announced agreement on the Joint Comprehensive Plan of Action. For example, three leading U.K. experts wrote in October 2013 that "China continues to be *the* key source of goods and technology for the prohibited nuclear and missile programs of Iran and North Korea, with some officials estimating that China is used as a transit route for up to 90% of goods destined for those programs."[130]

In April 2014, David Albright, Ian Stewart, and Andrea Stricker, leading experts on proliferation procurement, wrote that, "a major cause for Iran's success in evading trade controls and sanctions lies with the lack of Chinese implementation and enforcement of . . . both its own trade control laws and UN Security Council sanctions on Iran."[131] The authors warned that "China's poor record in this regard should be recognized as an international problem requiring urgent action."[132]

The PRC failed to crack down on violations of its nonproliferation obligations vis-à-vis Iran despite numerous requests that it do so. For example, in October 2010, the *Washington Post* reported that "[t]he Obama administration has concluded that Chinese firms are helping Iran to improve its missile technology and develop nuclear weapons, and has asked China to stop such activity, a senior U.S. official said."[133] The *Post* quoted a senior U.S. official explaining that "China so far has not devoted resources to crack down on violators."[134] "It's one thing to have a system that looks good on the books," he said, "and it's another thing to have a system that they enforce conscientiously. . . . Where China's system is deficient is on the enforcement side."[135]

Some two years later, the PRC remained unresponsive both to its legal obligations and to U.S. requests that the PRC implement them. In August 2012, the *Post* reported that "[a]lthough Iran has used Chinese go-betweens in the past, U.S. officials said sanctions have forced the isolated and besieged Iranian government to rely increasingly on China for economic help and access to restricted goods."[136] The article quoted a senior Justice Department official stating, "As some countries have retreated from the Iranian market with the imposition of increased sanctions, many Chinese companies appear to have moved into the void."[137]

The August 2012 *Post* article provided as an example maraging steel, which "is a critical material in a new, highly efficient centrifuge that Iran has struggled for years to build."[138] "Barred by sanctions from buying the alloy legally, Iranian nuclear officials have sought," said the article, "to secretly acquire it from Western companies."[139] According to the article, "in recent years, U.S. officials say, an increasing number of Chinese merchants have volunteered to help, serving as middlemen in elaborate schemes to obtain the steel and other forbidden material for Iran's uranium enrichment plants as well as its missiles factories."[140]

"The flow of Western technology to Tehran is so persistent," said the *Post* in August 2012, "that it has emerged as an irritant in relations between Beijing and

Washington, prompting the Obama administration to dispatch two delegations to Beijing since 2010 to complain."[141] "Yet, despite repeated protests," according to the August 2012 article, "Chinese businessmen continue to offer crucial assistance to Iran's procurement efforts without fear of punishment or censure, U.S. officials and nuclear experts say."[142]

Several recent U.S. court cases provide specific, publicly available evidence that Iran has used brokers in China to illicitly divert to Iran even exceptionally sensitive high-tech goods manufactured by U.S. companies. For example, Sihai Cheng, a Chinese citizen, arrived in Boston in December 2014 after being extradited from the U.K.[143] Cheng was captured at London's Heathrow airport in February 2014 when he entered the U.K. from China to attend a soccer tournament.[144] Cheng faced U.S. charges for exporting from China to Iran various sensitive U.S.-origin items that were barred from being retransferred to Iran.[145] The indictment alleged that beginning in 2005, Cheng sold "thousands of parts that have nuclear applications, including U.S. origin goods, to Eyvaz, an Iranian company involved in the development and procurement of parts for Iran's nuclear weapons program."[146]

Beginning in 2009, Cheng shipped from China to Iran "more than 1,000 MKS pressure transducers" manufactured in the United States.[147] MKS is a company headquartered in Massachusetts.[148] Pressure transducers are crucial to operation of a gas centrifuge plant.[149] Since Iran has been unable to manufacture pressure transducers itself, it has had to acquire them overseas for its enrichment plants.[150] Because pressure transducers have a lifespan of only about three years, Iran needs to continue acquiring them.[151] Publicly available photographs of then President Mahmoud Ahmadinejad at Natanz, an Iranian uranium nuclear enrichment facility, show numerous MKS transducers attached to Iran's gas centrifuge cascades.[152] The transfer of such pressure transducers from China to Iran violated U.S. export control laws.[153]

According to Albright, Stewart, and Stricker, "it appears that Chinese authorities took no enforcement action in this case or against illicit exporters of pressure transducers more generally that have been operating from its territory in recent years."[154] "It seems unlikely that the Chinese authorities were not aware" of Cheng's activities, said Albright, Stewart, and Stricker.[155] They noted that "this case is similar to another involving the now infamous serial proliferator Karl Lee of the Chinese company Limmt."[156] "For years, international partners asked China to take action to halt Lee's shipments of missile components and materials to Iran, but Chinese authorities appear to have taken no enforcement action," said Albright, Stewart, and Stricker.[157]

The PRC's purposeful failure to comply with its nonproliferation obligations under international law is exemplified by the multiyear saga of LIMMT, a Chinese company, and its manager Karl Lee (also known as Li Fangwei). According to a *Reuters* report in March 2013, Lee was still "making millions of dollars" from sales of missile parts to Iran.[158] At a May 12, 2015, Senate hearing on U.S. nuclear cooperation with China, Thomas Countryman, the U.S. Assistant Secretary of State for International Security and Nonproliferation, said the United States and China were engaged in "a longstanding dialogue about Karl Lee" and told the senators "I will be happy to come back when it produces some meaningful results."[159]

The U.S. dialogue with China regarding Lee had, as of May 2015, been going on, without meaningful results, for some eleven years. Over those eleven years, the U.S. government had taken steps including the following against LIMMT and Lee:

- In 2004, LIMMT was publicly sanctioned by the U.S. State Department pursuant to § 3 of the Iran Nonproliferation Act for having "engaged in . . . the transfer to Iran . . . of equipment and technology controlled under multilateral export control lists . . . or otherwise having the potential to make a material contribution to the development of weapons of mass destruction (WMD) or cruise or ballistic missile systems."[160]

- In 2006, LIMMT was publicly sanctioned by the U.S. Treasury Department under Executive Order 13382 for providing material support to Iran's missile program.[161] Executive Order No. 13382 is an authority aimed at freezing the assets of weapons of mass destruction proliferators and those who support them.

- In April 2009, the U.S. Treasury Department publicly sanctioned Karl Lee under Executive Order 13382 for his connection to Iran's missile proliferation network and identified eight aliases used by previously designated LIMMT to circumvent sanctions.[162]

- Also in April 2009, Lee was indicted by the Manhattan district attorney in New York state court on 118 counts of falsifying business records in violation of New York Penal Law section 175.10, for including false information on bank transactions that went through New York City.[163] The indictment referenced Lee's sales to an Iranian military agency of specialized metals, with uses in long-range missiles and nuclear weapons production, that were specifically banned by the United Nations for sale to Iran.[164] According to an analysis by the Center for Science and Security Studies at King's College London, the specialized exports by Lee to Iran which were referenced in the New York State indictment included: 30,000 kilograms of tungsten-copper alloy plates suitable for producing jet vanes for missiles; 17,000 kilograms of tungsten powder suitable for producing nose cones for missiles; 24,500 kilograms of maraging steel rods suitable for producing gas centrifuge components and missile fuselages; 15,000 kilograms of high strength aluminium alloys suitable for producing gas centrifuge components and missile propellant tanks; and 200 metric tonnes of high power graphite electrodes and 450 metric tonnes of furnace electrodes, both suitable for refining furnaces useful for nuclear purposes.[165] In announcing the 2009 indictment, Manhattan District

Attorney Robert M. Morgenthau referred to Lee's company, LIMMT, as "perhaps the largest supplier of weapons of mass destruction to the Iranian government."[166] Adam Kaufmann, an assistant district attorney who oversaw the investigation, told the *New York Times* that Lee also violated Chinese law by filing fraudulent shipping documents and said: "We will see what the impact of this indictment and announcement will be on his [Lee's] operations. One of the goals is to hopefully seek the assistance of the Chinese government in making sure he is shut down."[167]

- The U.S. government unsuccessfully asked the PRC several times in 2009 to halt specific transactions involving Lee and his company, LIMMT, transferring technology to Iran.[168]

- In February 2013, the U.S. State Department publicly sanctioned Karl Lee for having "engaged in missile technology proliferation activities."[169] A State Department official explained that Lee had been sanctioned because of his "proliferation to Iran" since his 2009 indictment.[170]

- In April 2014, the U.S. Justice Department unsealed new charges against Lee, the Treasury Department sanctioned eight Chinese companies for serving as front companies for Lee, the State Department offered a $5 million reward for information leading to Lee's arrest, and the Commerce Department announced regulatory actions against several companies linked to Lee.[171] In addition, the U.S. Department of Justice announced the seizure of some $6.9 million in funds from accounts at U.S. banks held in the names of foreign banks that hold money for Lee.[172] In its indictment, the U.S. Justice Department stated that Lee has sold "to Iranian entities various metallurgical goods and related components that are banned for transfer to Iran by, among others, the United Nations because the items are controlled by the Nuclear Suppliers Group (a multinational group that maintains 'control lists,' which identify nuclear-related dual-use equipment, material and technology.)"[173] In its description of Lee in conjunction with the reward announcement, the State Department stated that "it is alleged that from 2006 through the present time he illicitly and routinely has used front companies based in Eastern China to defraud United States banks, regulators, and customers, and frequently arranges for the procurement of United States and other dual-use products in violation of United States law and international sanctions against Iran."[174] It also stated that "he is allegedly a prolific supplier to the ballistic missile program of the Government of Iran."[175]

- In December 2014, the State Department published a designation of Lee and LIMMT pursuant to § 3 of the Iran, North Korea, and Syria Nonproliferation Act, the successor to the Iran Nonproliferation Act pursuant to which Lee was first designated by the State Department in 2004.[176] The notice made it clear that Lee was still engaged in the transfer of goods, services, or technology "having the potential to make a material contribution to the development of weapons of mass destruction (WMD) or cruise or ballistic missile systems."

Despite these U.S. efforts, Lee had, since the 2009 indictment, allegedly traveled often to Iran and supplied to firms that make Iranian missiles "15 metric tons of high-grade aluminum alloy, more than 20 metric tons of ultra-high strength steel, and 1,700 kg of graphite cylinders."[177] Lee also allegedly supplied fiber-optic gyroscopes that can be used in missiles.[178] In other words, Lee's "activity was allowed to continue despite U.S. requests for Chinese intervention."[179] Indeed, "there is little evidence that the Chinese government undertook substantial investigative action with any consequence in this case."[180]

Remarkably, the PRC's response to the extraordinary U.S. measures undertaken against Lee in April 2014 was to condemn them. "China resolutely opposes the United States citing domestic law to unilaterally impose sanctions on Chinese companies or individuals. We believe that what the United States has done will not help resolve the issue and will harm bilateral cooperation on counter proliferation," said China's Foreign Ministry spokesman Qin Gang.[181] "China urges the United States to stop these wrong acts of putting sanctions on Chinese companies and individuals and return to the correct path of anti-proliferation cooperation," said Qin.[182]

It is hard to see the PRC's continued failure to halt Karl Lee's exports to Iran's missile program, in the face of repeated U.S. requests to do so, as other than a purposeful evasion of China's legal responsibilities. This looks like an example of the type of behavior advised by the PLA's handbook on international law, which instructs PLA officers that they "should not feel completely bound" by international laws that are detrimental to the defense of China's "national interests" but rather should focus on those international laws beneficial to China "while evading those detrimental to our interests."[183]

China's nonproliferation policies have evolved over time. During the 1980s and 1990s, several of China's largest state-owned enterprises sold missiles and complete nuclear and missile production facilities to various countries.[184] A number of these state-owned enterprises were sanctioned by the United States.[185] Their large size and broad activities made them relatively vulnerable to economic pressure, and their state ownership made it hard for the PRC government to claim it was unable to control their exports.

China agreed to abide by the Missile Technology Control Regime guidelines in 1991, adhered to the Nuclear Nonproliferation Treaty in 1992, became a member of the Zangger Nuclear Exporters Committee in 1997, and joined the Nuclear Suppliers Group in 2004.[186] China has also voted for all of the U.N. Security Council Resolutions imposing sanctions on Iran's nuclear and missile programs. On paper, China became a member of the nonproliferation regime.

In recent years, Chinese state-owned enterprises have reportedly largely ceased their involvement in proliferation.[187] Instead, China's private sector is now the primary Chinese source of goods for prohibited programs.[188]

In the May 2015 Senate hearing on U.S. nuclear cooperation with China, Assistant Secretary Countryman asserted that continued private sector illicit exports from China to Iran's nuclear program are "a separate question from direct Chinese government assistance to a nuclear program in Iran," which he said "China terminated."[189] "Over the last 15 or 20 years," said Countryman, "what we've seen is that Chinese state-owned enterprises are out of the business of proliferating technology to North Korea and Iran."[190]

Countryman added that "the Chinese government simply does not have currently the bureaucratic enforcement capability, and does not yet have all the legislation it ought to have in order to adequately control dual-use exports."[191] When asked why the Chinese government did not have this in place, Countryman stated "they need a higher level of political commitment to meet the standards" and said "they have not yet committed the resources that would be necessary."[192]

Senator Edward Markey (D-MA), a longtime leading congressional advocate for nonproliferation, responded that "it's preposterous to conclude that the Chinese government is incapable of shutting this down."[193] "The Chinese government says they . . . can't figure out how to shut [Karl Lee] down or guys like him," said Markey, noting that at the same time, "they figured out how to jail 44 journalists last year" and "they figured out how to put 27,000 Muslim minorities in the Uighur region in prison last year."[194] "Maybe China has just subcontracted this out to the private sector," said Markey, "maybe China has done this in order to protect the guilty—you know, the Chinese government . . . so their fingers aren't on it, but yet they can do the favors for Iran, Pakistan, other countries."[195] "That's what I think is going on," said Markey, stating that "the reason it's too hard is that they've subcontracted this out to Karl Lee."[196]

In a July 2015 Newsweek article, Jeff Stein reported that "starting with the Clinton administration over a decade ago, China's response to behind-the-scenes protests from the U.S. over Lee's activities has ranged from 'never heard of him' to 'go fish,' according to present and former officials."[197] "Many Lee-watchers," said Stein, "think he's Beijing's man in Tehran, a very useful cutout for arms sales, a 'private businessman' they can pretend is freelancing."[198]

The scale and persistence of Karl Lee's activities do appear to indicate that he acted as a proxy for the PRC government. Lee's role in supporting Iran's missile program appears analogous to the role of private sector Chinese cyberattackers in hacking the computers of Western governments and businesses. The PRC government reportedly sponsors vast numbers of such illicit cyber intrusions by ostensibly private actors in China in such a manner as to make it very difficult for the U.S. government to hold the PRC government accountable.[199]

Because Lee is ostensibly a private actor, the U.S. government has been unsuccessful in holding any element of the Chinese government accountable for his activities. The large size and broad activities of the Chinese state-owned entities engaged in proliferation during the 1980s and 1990s made them relatively vulnerable to economic lawfare, and their state ownership made it hard for the PRC government to claim it was unable to control their exports. In contrast, with Karl

Lee, the PRC government has been able to gain the policy benefits of aiding Iran's missile program without paying any economic penalties and while still claiming to be a member in good standing of the nonproliferation regime.

So long as it is ostensibly private Chinese companies that are involved, the PRC apparently can argue, with enough plausibility to get away with it, that it is not in violation of its international legal obligations. The PRC can assert—vis-à-vis its Resolution 1737 and 1929 obligations to prevent the supply to Iran of items and technology that could contribute to Iran's nuclear weapon delivery systems—that it took the necessary measures as best it could, but had insufficient capacity to police private transactions.[200]

d. U.S. Lawfare Options for Responding

What options do the United States and other concerned states have in these circumstances? Is there a way for the United States and other concerned states to attribute proliferation by Karl Lee and other ostensibly private persons on Chinese territory to the PRC government and hold the PRC directly accountable under international law?

The threshold under international law for such attribution is remarkably high. Many scholarly articles have been written on the topic of state responsibility under international law, a detailed discussion of which is outside the scope of this book. The preeminent "state responsibility" test is the ICJ's judgment in the *Nicaragua* case.[201] In that case, the ICJ held that for an act of a non-state armed group to be attributable to a state requires "effective control" by the state, such that even "financing, organizing, training, supplying and equipping" as well as "the selection of its military or paramilitary targets and the planning of the whole of its operation" is not enough to meet the exacting threshold.[202]

This would make it very difficult for the United States to attribute Lee's activities to the PRC government. It certainly seems unlikely that the United States could bring a successful ICJ case against the PRC for failure to implement its U.N. Security Council resolution and other nonproliferation obligations. Nor, in light of the United States' own challenges controlling the activities of private U.S. persons, would such an action, setting such a precedent, be advisable.

So, what are the United States' options? In *U.S. Nonproliferation Strategy for the Changing Middle East*,[203] this author and his coauthors recommended that the U.S. government formally designate the PRC as a "destination of diversion concern" under U.S. law. Title III, "Prevention of Diversion of Certain Good, Services, and Technologies to Iran," was enacted on July 1, 2010, as part of the Comprehensive Iran Sanctions, Accountability, and Divestment Act (CISADA).[204] Title III provides that "the President shall designate a country as a Destination of Diversion Concern if the President determines that the government of the country allows substantial diversion of goods, services, or technologies described in section 302(b) through the country to Iranian end-users or Iranian intermediaries."[205]

Title III defines the term "allow" to mean "the government of the country knows or has reason to know that the territory of the country is being used for such diversion."[206] Such a designation would require enhanced licensing requirements, including a presumption of denial, for exports from the United States to China of the types of proliferation-sensitive goods, services, and technologies that the President determines have been diverted through China to Iran.[207]

Publicly available information—including the PRC's failure to crack down on Sihai Cheng and especially Karl Lee—indicates that the Chinese government has acted in a manner inconsistent with CISADA Title III, in that the Chinese government "allows substantial diversion of goods, services, or technologies described in subsection 302(b) through the country to Iranian end-users or Iranian intermediaries,"[208] and that the Chinese government "knows or has reason to know that the territory of the country is being used for such diversion."[209] China thus fits CISADA's definition of a "Destination of Diversion Concern." The Joint Comprehensive Plan of Action, which was announced by the P-5+1 and Iran on July 14, 2015, and the related U.N. Security Council Resolution 2231 of July 20, 2015, provide for continued restrictions on the supply to Iran of various proliferation-sensitive goods, services, and technologies that fall within the ambit of CISADA Title III.

Designating China as a "Destination of Diversion Concern" could reduce the dangerous supply to Iran of proliferation-sensitive goods, services, or technologies by (1) requiring enhanced scrutiny by U.S. government licensing agencies of specific proliferation-sensitive exports from the United States to China; (2) increasing pressure on the Chinese government to crack down on diversion through China to Iranian end users and Iranian intermediaries; and (3) helping secure support from other countries that likewise face challenges in ensuring that their exports to China do not end up in Iran.

This provision would seem on its face to be a clever, albeit mild example of lawfare. It is a legal tool carefully calibrated to match China's ostensibly permissive rather than directive proliferation to Iran. However, the executive branch has refrained from making such a designation, reportedly in part because the PRC tends to retaliate against U.S. executive branch naming and shaming (and especially of China as a nation rather than particular Chinese entities). The U.S. executive branch is particularly vulnerable to such retaliation, including because its diplomats, unlike members of Congress, regularly seek meetings and engage in negotiations with Chinese officials on a variety of issues. As an example of how such retaliation works, "after U.S. arms sales to Taiwan, Chinese government officials have previously become unavailable to meet with U.S. officials connected with arms and non-proliferation controls."[210]

So the U.S. government in summer 2015, after at least ten years of trying, had apparently not found a way to successfully pressure the PRC government to crack down on Karl Lee. While the United States is obviously not averse to using kinetic warfare, including especially drone strikes, against adversaries of other nationalities, that does not seem to be an option with regard to a Chinese national, especially one located in China. In light of PRC drone capabilities, such a kinetic attack by the United States would set a very dangerous precedent.

What lawfare options does the United States have for taking direct action against individual Chinese brokers such as Karl Lee? Karl Lee has already been designated and indicted several times, to no evident effect, and avoids traveling to countries where the United States could seize him.[211]

As of summer 2015, the most impactful lawfare tool the U.S. government had deployed against Karl Lee (also known as Li Fangwei) was likely the U.S. Justice Department's April 2014 seizure of some $6.9 million in funds from accounts at U.S. banks held in the names of foreign banks that were holding money for Lee.[212] This unusual move appeared to be a deployment against Lee personally of the type of lawfare that Chapters 2 and 3 describe the United States undertaking against third-country banks and energy companies doing business with the government of Iran. The move against Lee was a particularly aggressive variant of such pursuit of businesses transacting with a target. It was arguably a kind of lawfare version of the incident described in Chapter 8 of Israeli special forces forcibly seizing from an Arab Bank branch the precise numbers of dollars that were held there in various terrorist-related bank accounts. Similar to in the Arab Bank raid, in this Lee case "the onus is placed on Li's bank to make itself whole again, by deducting assets from Li's personal accounts."[213]

According to the Department of Justice, the $6.9 million in "seized funds are substitutes for money held by Li Fangwei's front companies at banks in China and were seized from accounts at U.S. banks held in the name of foreign banks used by these front companies to conduct U.S. currency transactions."[214] The $6.9 million "represents funds used by the Li Fangwei front companies to engage in transactions that violate the U.S. sanctions laws and thus are subject to forfeiture."[215] The Justice Department emphasized that "there are no allegations of wrongdoing by the U.S. or foreign banks that maintain these accounts."[216] "Because the funds used in those transactions are held in banks overseas, the United States is unable to seize the funds directly," said the Justice Department.[217] However, pursuant to U.S. law, the United States can "seize funds located in a bank's correspondent accounts in the United States if there is probable cause to believe that funds subject to forfeiture are on deposit with that bank overseas," and did so in this case.[218]

The fund seizure likely will help deter banks from doing business with Karl Lee. It will likely also be a cost borne by him personally, and may impact his ability to pay for goods he has ordered.[219]

In light of the relatively little direct leverage the United States has over individual Chinese brokers like Karl Lee, it would not be surprising to see the U.S. government begin to engage more frequently in identifying and pressuring the larger businesses that provide key services to such brokers and similar targets.

Chapters 2 and 3 describe and analyze the effectiveness of U.S. lawfare in dissuading third-country banking and energy companies from doing business with Iran. Chapter 8 describes and analyzes the effectiveness with which an Israeli NGO, Shurat HaDin, prevented a Gaza-bound flotilla from leaving Greece by using lawfare to dissuade maritime insurance and telecommunications companies from providing services to the flotilla.

Drawing a lesson from these successes, as well as the bank seizures in the Karl Lee case, the United States might be able to significantly hinder or stop Karl Lee by identifying and pressuring several of the larger Chinese businesses that provide him with services—including Internet, telephone, airline, shipping, and other services. As one business in a sector stops providing him with service, others might be deterred from jumping in (potentially, as in the energy sector, by the United States deploying information gathered by the business that has already stopped and does not want to see its rivals fill the gap). If multisector third-party sanctions can, in this globalized era, be imposed effectively on an entire nation such as Iran and a Gaza-bound flotilla, perhaps they can also be imposed effectively on particular bad actor individuals and proxies such as Karl Lee.

IV. FUTURE PRC LAWFARE AND POTENTIAL U.S. AND ALLIED RESPONSES

A. The Future of PRC Lawfare

The PRC will likely become far more adept at waging lawfare over the coming decades. While the PRC's engagement with international law has grown significantly over the last decade, the PRC's engagement was starting from a low baseline and still has considerable room to grow.

Until the last decade or so, China's engagement with international law was relatively minimal. The PRC was admitted as a member of the U.N. system only in 1971, when it replaced Taiwan. Thus, the PRC did not have a seat at the table when the rules were written for the major post-World War II international institutions, including the United Nations, the World Bank, and the International Monetary Fund. The PRC's engagement with international law was also minimized by internal factors, including the Cultural Revolution of 1966 to 1976, when China abolished its law schools and diverted lawyers to other fields.[220] Even as late as the 1990s, the PRC had, in the recollection of this author, a very low profile and very little influence in the several U.N. treaty negotiations at which he represented the United States. The PRC was, at that time, severely hampered in international legal fora by its diplomats' poor English and unsophisticated understanding of international law.

In contrast, the PRC now has "sophisticated legal institutions" and "the third largest number of lawyers in the world."[221] Within the last decade, the

PRC has taken an "increasingly assertive and proactive stance" within international organizations and has "evolved into a highly effective player."[222] "Both in terms of its ability to advance its own agenda, as well as its ability to deflect objectionable proposals from other quarters," the PRC has become "a shrewd, savvy, and successful operator."[223] In contrast with the past, the PRC has in recent years sent "extremely smart, capable, articulate and frequently Western-educated individuals to represent its interests" before international organizations.[224]

One reflection of China's growing emphasis on developing world-class international lawyers is the expanding, and increasingly successful, involvement of Chinese teams in the Philip C. Jessup International Law Moot Court Competition. Jessup is the world's largest moot court competition, with participants from over 550 law schools in more than eighty countries.[225] Carol Kalinoski, an American lawyer, helped introduce the Jessup competition to China in 2002 and has served since as a judge for the Jessup competition international rounds.[226] According to Kalinoski, the Chinese teams have, over the past decade, improved more than any other country's teams.[227] "While the U.S. teams seem to be getting weaker in recent years," says Kalinoski, "the Chinese teams keep improving."[228] For example, in 2014, the team from China's Wuhan University submitted the sixth-highest ranked written presentation, scoring higher than all but two participating U.S. law schools.[229]

For the United States and its allies, it is critical to attempt to identify and prepare for the additional lawfare arenas and types of lawfare in which the PRC seems most likely to engage in the future. Such an analysis is best organized in terms of (a) which specific additional lawfare arenas and types the PRC might engage in whether or not armed conflict breaks out between the PRC and the United States or its allies and (b) which specific additional lawfare arenas and types the PRC might engage in if, but only if, armed conflict breaks out between the PRC and the United States or its allies.

If U.S.-PRC tensions increase significantly, even in the absence of armed conflict between the two, the PRC seems likely to strongly consider using its economic leverage over the United States and its allies to wage economic lawfare. As illustrated in Chapter 3, U.S. economic lawfare has relied in significant part on Washington's regulatory jurisdiction over individual private companies, including many that are based outside the United States. It is important to note that many U.S. companies now have significant assets located in, or otherwise subject to the regulatory jurisdiction of, the PRC. For example, as of 2013, U.S. foreign direct investment in China totaled $61 billion, and China was estimated to be a $350 billion annual market for U.S. firms, the third-largest U.S. export market.[230]

Many major U.S. firms are heavily dependent on the Chinese market. For example, General Motors reportedly sold more motor vehicles in China than in the United States each year from 2010 to 2014, and Boeing predicted in 2014 that over the next twenty years, China will be its largest commercial airplane customer outside the United States.[231] China was also estimated to be the largest source of U.S. imports, with the United States importing $67 billion in computer equipment alone from China in 2014.[232]

It would not be surprising to see the PRC explore ways of using that leverage to influence U.S. policy toward the PRC. Indeed, following the U.S. sale of new military equipment to Taiwan in 2009, PRC officials threatened to impose sanctions on U.S. companies conducting business in China.[233] Although no such sanctions were imposed, it was made clear that the PRC was willing to at least strongly consider leveraging U.S. access to Chinese markets to achieve foreign policy objectives.[234]

Another arena in which the PRC has considerable leverage over the United States is the financial arena. By December 2014, Chinese investment in U.S. Treasury securities had reached $1.24 trillion, some 20 percent of the total foreign investment in U.S. Treasury securities.[235] According to Juan Zarate, a former assistant secretary of the U.S. Treasury, "China's deep investment in U.S. Treasuries gives it enormous potential leverage in a confrontation with the United States, yet it has restrained itself from doing anything to undermine the value of the dollar or confidence in the U.S. economic system."[236] It has been said that "if you owe the bank $10,000 the bank owns you, if you owe the bank $10 million you own the bank." The size of the PRC's investment may be so great as to make the PRC feel that, in the absence of extreme circumstances, it has a stake in maintaining the health of the U.S. financial system.[237] The PRC may nevertheless find a creative way of using its investment in U.S. Treasuries as lawfare leverage against the United States.

The PRC has already engaged in at least one instance of economic lawfare against Japan. In September 2010, a Chinese fishing boat collided with two Japanese coast guard ships about forty minutes apart as the boat tried to fish in waters controlled by Japan but long claimed by the PRC.[238] Japan detained the Chinese boat's captain and refused at first to release him, saying his case was being handled by Japan's court system.[239] The PRC government then quietly blocked exports to Japan of rare earth elements, a category of minerals that play a critical role in Japan's manufacturing sector.[240] The PRC reportedly did so by quietly advising Chinese companies to halt rare earth exports and quietly ordering PRC customs officials to discretely block any such exports.[241] Publicly, PRC officials denied having imposed an embargo,[242] while asserting that all of China's rare earth exporters "simultaneously decided to halt shipments because of their personal feelings towards Japan."[243] Had there been a public announcement of a government-mandated export ban, Japan could have filed an immediate complaint with the World Trade Organization, alleging a violation of free trade laws.[244] However, the PRC's quiet blocking of such exports, combined with a public denial that it was taking such a step, sent a message to Japan without incurring legal consequences. A few days later, Japan released the Chinese captain.[245] When China lost a WTO ruling in 2014 in relation to its formal restrictions on rare earth exports, the ruling did not address the PRC's informal embargo on Japan, nor prevent a future such informal embargo.[246]

Since China mines some 70 to 90 percent of the world's rare earth minerals,[247] it would not be surprising to see the PRC continue to leverage this trade for foreign policy purposes. The U.S. military could be particularly vulnerable to rare earth lawfare, as rare earths are used in equipment including U.S. tanks, naval vessels, and missile guidance systems.[248] In a July 2014 report, the Inspector General at the U.S. Department of Defense expressed concern about the risk that rare earth "shortfalls will adversely affect critical weapons systems production . . . and overall DOD readiness."[249]

Should armed conflict break out between the PRC and the United States or an East Asian country such as Japan that is relatively heavily influenced by law and public opinion, it would not come as a shock to see the PLA engage, as have the Taliban and Hamas, in placing military assets in or around schools and hospitals, in the hopes of either deterring attacks or, if attacks do take place, accusing China's adversary of harming innocent civilians. Such battlefield lawfare tactics would be consistent with both China's legal warfare doctrine and also its psychological warfare doctrine and media warfare doctrine. For example, the PLA's text *The Science of Military Strategy* discusses the need to "reveal a lot of the war crimes committed by the opponent in violation of law so as to win over universal sympathy and support from the international community . . . to compel [the] opponent to bog down in isolation and passivity."[250]

In his superb article titled *Winning Without Fighting: Chinese Legal Warfare*, Dean Cheng, an expert on China's military doctrine, asserts that the PLA sees lawfare as "an offensive weapon capable of hamstringing political opponents and seizing the political initiative in wartime," including by raising "doubts . . . about the legality of adversary actions, thereby diminishing political will and support."[251] Such legal warfare dovetails with PLA psychological warfare, which is designed to disrupt "the enemy's decision-making capacity by sapping their will, arousing anti-war sentiments . . . and causing an opponent to second-guess himself—all while defending against an opponent's attempts to conduct similar operations."[252]

Should armed conflict break out between the PRC and the United States or any other adversary, the PRC would likely engage in various types of offensive instrumental lawfare. Because the PRC is better prepared than are its potential adversaries for offensive instrumental lawfare during armed conflict, especially at the tactical level, it is likely to see it as an advantage and engage in it quite vigorously.

The PRC is better prepared in two major ways. First, the PRC's formal adoption of lawfare as a major component of its strategic doctrine, and the fact that its published lawfare literature is far more developed than that of its potential adversaries (including the United States), almost certainly indicates that it has spent far more time developing specific plans and tactics for engaging in lawfare during armed conflict.

Second, in comparison with the United States, decision-making for PRC offensive lawfare operations is more closely integrated with PRC kinetic warfare operations. Because the primary responsibility for PRC lawfare is assigned to the PLA, and PRC discussions of lawfare "emphasize the importance of coordinating military and legal operations," PRC "legal warfare operations may be integrated into military operations more smoothly than in Western military operations."[253] In the U.S. government, in contrast, the Treasury and State Departments, rather than the Defense Department, currently play the leading role in the United States' relatively limited "offensive" lawfare activities. Cheng notes that not only are these U.S. actions "not necessarily coordinated with military actions; they are not even necessarily considered (by the implementing bodies) to be offensive legal warfare."[254]

PRC offensive instrumental use of lawfare during wartime could occur in a variety of arenas. Noting that the success of U.S. military operations in the Far East may hinge on access to foreign bases, Cheng suggests that the PRC in wartime could, presumably via local lawyer proxies, file a variety of legal motions—in U.S., Japanese, Philippine, Australian, or other courts—designed to complicate and delay any U.S. intervention.[255] For example, Japan's pacifist constitution and other laws could conceivably provide grounds for raising legal issues about any wartime "support provided by Tokyo to the United States."[256] Even if such challenges are ultimately unsuccessful, they could both help undercut Japanese political will to assist the United States and force the U.S. military to invest resources in alternative plans and bases.

Alternatively, the PRC might wage lawfare directly against particular U.S. or allied commanders. PRC analyses of the second Iraq War have noted with great interest that the U.S.-led coalition contacted Iraqi generals directly to warn them that they would be prosecuted if they followed any orders by Saddam Hussein to use weapons of mass destruction.[257] Given Chinese cyber prowess, it would not be surprising if the PLA during wartime were to find a way to reach out to U.S. officers via the Internet and seek to dissuade them from engaging in some or all military activities by asserting that such activities would violate international law.

Such assertions might be particularly effective if combined with PRC use of local proxy lawyers deploying universal jurisdiction provisions to persuade third-party nation courts to issue warrants for the arrest of U.S. and allied military and political leaders.[258] As described in Chapters 1 and 6, universal jurisdiction complaints alleging war crimes in Afghanistan and Iraq were brought in Europe against former President George W. Bush,[259] then Secretary of Defense Rumsfeld,[260] and then Secretary of State Colin Powell,[261] in most cases by nongovernmental organizations. A campaign secretly organized and funded by the vast resources of the PLA could take such universal jurisdiction complaints against U.S. officials to a whole new level.

B. Potential U.S. and Allied Responses to Future PRC Lawfare

What steps might the United States and its allies take now to protect themselves against such future PRC lawfare?[262] Dean Cheng provides several excellent suggestions.[263] The following options include several of Cheng's suggestions plus several more from this author.

1. Weigh New Obligations in Light of Lawfare Risks

The United States and its allies should weigh any relevant new international legal obligations in light of the possibility that the PRC might try to use those obligations to hamstring the United States in the event of a Sino-American armed conflict while not itself complying with the rules it invokes.[264] This is particularly the case for international legal obligations in arenas—such as maritime, aviation, space, cyberlaw, and nonproliferation—where the PRC is already waging lawfare.

2. Prepare for PRC Battlefield Lawfare

The United States and its allies should prepare in advance for the possibility that the PLA will engage, as have the Taliban and Hamas, in placing military assets in or around schools and hospitals, in the hopes of either deterring attacks or, if attacks do take place, accusing China's adversary of harming innocent civilians. As described in Chapter 7, Israel has developed relatively sophisticated countermeasures to such lawfare, including by providing Israel's combat units with equipment and specialists that acquire real-time videos of military activities. The United States and its allies should prepare to use such methods to counteract the PLA.[265]

3. Prepare to Systematically Identify and Publicize PRC Violations

The United States and its allies should be prepared to, in case of a Sino-American armed conflict, systematically identify and publicize PRC violations of international laws.[266] The capacity to do so will be particularly important if the PRC vigorously accuses the United States and its allies of violating international laws while the PRC itself has a far worse record of compliance.

4. Consider Options for Increasing PRC Compliance

The United States and its allies should consider now whether there are ways to start encouraging increased PRC compliance with international law, and especially the law of armed conflict. This is particularly important since some types of PRC lawfare are rendered more effective by the current greater U.S. emphasis on compliance with international law, including the law of armed conflict. A study of how and why relevant other countries have increased their compliance with international law, and especially the law of armed conflict, could help identify ideas applicable to fostering PRC compliance.

5. Emulate PRC Seriousness About Lawfare

The United States and its allies should immediately consider adopting lawfare as a major component of their strategic doctrines, as the PRC has done. The United States and its allies should also strongly consider closely integrating their lawfare operations with their kinetic military activities, as the PRC has done.[267]

6. Identify Potential U.S. and Allied Points of Lawfare Leverage over the PRC

As described in the previous section, the PRC has several points of considerable economic leverage over the United States and its allies that China could relatively quickly use to wage economic lawfare. The United States and its allies should identify points of "low-hanging" economic and other leverage over the PRC and assess in which circumstances, if any, and how they could wisely be used to wage lawfare against the PRC or to deter or counter lawfare by the PRC.

For example, the U.S. government has regulatory leverage over many major Chinese companies because they are listed on U.S. stock exchanges. The first Chinese company was listed on the New York Stock Exchange in 1992,[268] and the first was listed on the NASDAQ in 2000.[269] As of September 2014, 106 Chinese companies were listed on the New York Stock Exchange and the NASDAQ, including giant state-owned companies such as PetroChina and Chinamobile.[270]

In addition, China (excluding Hong Kong) had FDI (foreign direct investments) in the United States totaling some $8.1 billion as of 2013.[271] Some Chinese investments in the United States could have both lawfare and other national security significance if tensions increase between the United States and PRC. For example, Lenovo, a Chinese-owned company, acquired Motorola Mobility, a U.S.-based cellphone manufacturer, in October 2014.[272] In February 2013, CNOOC, a Chinese state-owned entity, acquired Nexen, a Canadian oil and gas company with production assets within U.S. jurisdiction in the Gulf of Mexico.[273] The U.S. government should analyze whether there are circumstances in which it would make sense to use such leverage, for example to deter or respond to PRC deployment of some or all of its economic lawfare leverage against the United States.

7. Assess Advantages and Disadvantages of Various Types of Offensive U.S. Lawfare Against the PRC

In addition to identifying points of leverage for deterring or responding to PRC lawfare, the United States and its allies should carefully assess the advantages and disadvantages of adopting a strategy of using offensive lawfare against the PRC as systematically and actively as the PRC is using lawfare against the United States and its allies. Are there specific objectives that could be usefully achieved by a U.S. lawfare campaign against PRC targets? Would such a campaign be, on balance, beneficial to U.S. interests? For example, how useful would creative new lawfare strategies be for going after PRC cyber hackers and nuclear traffickers that currently seem to be operating largely with impunity? In making such an assessment, the United States and its allies should carefully weigh how, and to what extent, their employment of such lawfare against the PRC might set a precedent that the PRC could use against them.

8. Prepare for PRC-Instigated Civil Litigation and Universal Jurisdiction Lawfare

The United States and its allies should start analyzing, and prepare to defend against, how PRC-funded attorneys could use various laws in countries where the United States has bases to complicate or delay U.S. military activities.[274] The United States and its allies should also familiarize themselves with, and be prepared to defend against, universal jurisdiction provisions in third-party national laws that could be used to bring war crimes charges against U.S. and allied officials in the event of a Sino-American armed conflict.[275]

9. Identify and Prepare for PRC Next Steps in Current Lawfare Arenas

The United States and its allies should carefully assess what the PRC's next and future steps, including in the event of a Sino-American armed conflict, might be in the maritime, aviation, space, cyber, and other arenas in which the PRC is currently waging lawfare. As part of this assessment, the United States and its allies should consider what steps should be taken now to deter, constrain, and protect against future PRC attacks in those arenas.

10. Identify and Prepare for PRC Waging Lawfare in New Arenas

The United States and its allies should systematically seek to identify and analyze other, new arenas in which the PRC might effectively wage lawfare, including in the absence of armed conflict, and consider what steps should be taken now to deter, constrain, and protect against future PRC attacks in those new arenas. Several such arenas were discussed earlier in this chapter. One of those arenas is potential PRC use of its regulatory leverage over the many U.S. companies that now have significant assets located in, or which otherwise are subject to the regulatory jurisdiction of, the PRC. The PRC seems likely to explore replicating the United States' willingness to use civilian regulatory muscle to pursue national security goals through the tactic of direct threats to take legal action against individual foreign private companies. A second arena includes natural resources (such as rare earth) or manufactured items with regard to which the PRC has a monopoly or near monopoly. A third arena is China's vast holdings of U.S. Treasury securities.

11. Minimize Exploitable Differences Between Allies

The United States and its allies in East Asia should quickly take steps to identify and address any differences between their legal systems and legal advisers that could create points of vulnerability in a Sino-American armed conflict.[276] NATO operations have at times been hampered by differences between NATO members over what qualified as a legitimate military target.[277] Such problems are likely to be considerably worse in a conflict waged in partnership with major but non-NATO allies such as Australia, Japan, New Zealand, South Korea, and the Philippines, and against the PRC, which is exceptionally prepared to wage legal warfare, including by exploiting differences between allies.

12. Consider Whether Useful Options Exist for Agreements to Limit Lawfare

The United States should consider whether a bilateral or multilateral agreement limiting in some ways the waging of lawfare between the United States and PRC would be feasible and useful. Any such consideration should include an assessment of the likelihood of the PRC complying in different circumstances and the potential for effectively monitoring such compliance.

13. Maximize Current U.S. Preeminence in Shaping International Law

The United States should systematically analyze how best to take advantage of, and if possible lengthen, its current window of preeminence in shaping international law. As Professor Philip Bobbitt put it, crafting enduring legal rules is one way "the U.S. can extend its influence beyond its temporary preeminence."[278] In light of the rapid increase in quality of the PRC's international lawyers, the United States should consider how to (a) take advantage of or lock in its preeminence while it still exists and (b) enhance its expertise in key areas in which the PRC improvement could tip the balance of future lawfare between the two countries.

CHAPTER 5

The Palestinian Authority's Lawfare Against Israel

"Internationalization of the conflict as a legal matter."
—Mahmoud Abbas

I. INTRODUCTION

The Israeli-Palestinian conflict is the closest thing the world has to a lawfare laboratory. Hamas, Israel, the Palestinian Authority (PA), and their allies are each vigorously waging lawfare, albeit in different ways. Much as the Spanish Civil War served as a testing ground for weapons and tactics subsequently used in World War II,[1] the Israeli-Palestinian conflict is foreshadowing lawfare strategies and tactics that will soon be replicated in other conflicts. In light of the cutting-edge sophistication, intensity, and variety of lawfare in the Israeli-Palestinian conflict, this book includes four chapters on lawfare in that conflict.

This first of the chapters focuses on the PA's use of law as a weapon against Israel and on Israel's and Israel's allies' responses to that lawfare. PA President Mahmoud Abbas explained the PA's lawfare strategy in a 2011 *New York Times* op-ed, in which he wrote that United Nations recognition of Palestine as a member state "would pave the way for the internationalization of the conflict as a legal matter, not only a political one."[2] "It would also pave the way for us to pursue claims against Israel at the United Nations, human rights treaty bodies and the International Court of Justice," wrote Abbas.[3] What the PA cannot seem to win from Israel through the negotiations process, or militarily, it is thus trying to win through "internationalization of the conflict as a legal matter."

As this chapter will describe, the PA's lawfare campaign against Israel has been remarkably impactful. For example, in 2013, in exchange for a nine-month hiatus from the PA's lawfare campaign, Israel agreed to release from its prisons dozens of terrorists, many of whom had brutally murdered Israeli civilians. The PA's accession to the International Criminal Court in early 2015, following the conclusion of that hiatus, was poised to have a particularly significant impact on numerous aspects of the Israeli-Palestinian conflict, including conventional Israeli military tactics, Israeli settlements, and lawfare in other forums.

Chapter 6 focuses on the somewhat different type of lawfare being waged against Israel by the PA's non-governmental allies—including both Palestinian and non-Palestinian non-governmental organizations. It also discusses the responses of Israel and its allies to that NGO lawfare. While the PA is waging lawfare against Israel on the battleground of international organizations and treaties, the PA's non-governmental allies are principally waging lawfare on the battleground of national courts of third countries (i.e., neither Israel nor Palestine).

The lawfare being waged against Israel by Palestinian and allied NGOs has been remarkably impactful. Although Israel and its allies have won almost every court case, the process has typically been very costly. Several foreign companies doing business with Israel have been subjected to multiyear litigation, police raids, and the like. The cost of the process has deterred a number of the companies, including some who have won in court, from continuing to do business with Israel. In addition, while not a single one of several "universal jurisdiction" lawsuits has resulted in the conviction of an Israeli official, several high-ranking Israeli officials have had their freedom of movement curtailed. Almost all of the national court litigation relating to Israel has been based on accusations that the defendants are complicit in Israeli violations of international law. If the PA's lawfare in the international arena continues to gain ground on Israel, the number of national court actions may increase significantly, and their dispositions could become far less favorable to Israel and its allies.

Chapter 7 focuses on the very different lawfare being waged against Israel by Hamas. While the PA and its allies have used law as a weapon against Israel in international forums and national courts, Hamas has proven to be one of the world's most persistent wagers of compliance-leverage disparity lawfare. Hamas deploys battlefield tactics designed to gain advantage from the far greater leverage which international law and its processes exert over Israel than over Hamas. According to a study published by the U.S. Army, Hamas "prefers to hide and fight among the civilian population, using civilians as protection."[4] By hiding behind civilians, Hamas forces Israel to either forgo attack or attack and risk being accused of war crimes. Hamas thus manages to accomplish several objectives, including causing Israeli armed forces to fight with one hand tied behind their back and eroding support for Israel by making it appear that Israel is to blame for civilian casualties and waging war in violation of international law.

Hamas hiding behind the civilian population of Gaza appears to have reached new heights during the 2014 war between Israel and Hamas, during which the *New York Times* reported that Hamas stored weapons in mosques and schools, launched rockets from near homes and schools, and encouraged residents not to flee their homes when alerted by Israel to pending strikes.[5] The government of Israel has developed a number of exceptionally sophisticated mechanisms and strategies for defending against Hamas's battlefield lawfare, including the establishment of a special counterlawfare office in its Ministry of Justice.

The fourth and final chapter on lawfare in the Palestinian-Israeli conflict (Chapter 8) will focus on Israeli offensive lawfare. Unlike the PA, the government of Israel has rarely, if ever, played a front and center role in the conduct of offensive lawfare, reportedly in order to avoid setting precedents that could be used against Israel by its adversaries. However, Israeli government officials have on several occasions quietly and effectively provided pivotal information to private sector litigators engaged in offensive lawfare activities against Israel's adversaries. For example, Israel's use of lawfare in 2011 to successfully stop a Gaza-bound flotilla from leaving port in Greece is a classic case study in tactical offensive lawfare.

II. LAWFARE, THE RIVAL PALESTINIAN GOVERNMENTS, AND A FEW WORDS ABOUT TERMINOLOGY

As of this writing, the Palestinian territories of the West Bank and Gaza are ruled by two rival Palestinian organizations—the Palestine Liberation Organization (PLO) and Hamas. The two Palestinian governments have different international status and are engaged in different types of lawfare against Israel. This book will thus address the two rival Palestinian organizations in separate chapters. In order to avoid confusion, a few words about chronology and terminology are in order before we turn to the details of each Palestinian government's engagement in lawfare.

The Palestinian Authority was formed in 1994 to serve as the governing body of the Palestinian autonomous regions of the West Bank and Gaza Strip that were established as part of interim peace agreements between Israel and the PLO (known in Arabic as Fatah).[6] The West Bank and Gaza were jointly ruled by a PLO-led PA government until 2006. Following Hamas's victory in Palestinian Legislative Council elections in January 2006, tensions escalated between the two Palestinian factions.[7] In June 2007, Hamas militants seized control of the Gaza Strip.[8] The PA President, the PLO-affiliated Mahmoud Abbas, appointed a "technocratic" government to rule the West Bank under his leadership.[9]

From 2007 until this book was completed in summer 2015, the Palestinian territories continued to be ruled by two rival governments. The West Bank continued to be ruled by the PLO, a secular nationalist movement led, since Yasser

Arafat's death in 2004, by the comparatively moderate Mahmoud Abbas. The Gaza Strip continued to be ruled by Hamas, a Sunni Muslim Brotherhood militant movement that refused to recognize the State of Israel and was designated by the U.S. government as a Foreign Terrorist Organization, a Specially Designated Terrorist, and a Specially Designated Global Terrorist.[10]

From 2007 to 2013, the PLO-controlled government of the West Bank referred to itself (and was generally referred to) as the Palestinian Authority. Since January 2013, the PLO-controlled government has referred to itself as the State of Palestine,[11] in light of U.N. General Assembly Resolution 67/19, which decided "to accord to Palestine non-member observer State status in the United Nations."[12]

In order to clearly distinguish between the Hamas-controlled Palestinian government of Gaza and the PLO-controlled Palestinian government of the West Bank, and because much of this chapter's analysis relates to activities prior to January 2013, this book will generally refer to the PLO-controlled government of the West Bank as the Palestinian Authority (PA) and the Hamas-controlled government of Gaza as the Hamas government. While the two rival governments have occasionally joined together in a "unity government," these have generally lasted only briefly and have not interrupted the basic pattern of a Hamas-controlled government of Gaza and a PLO-controlled government of the West Bank.

III. SEEKING FULL STATEHOOD AND U.N. MEMBERSHIP OUTSIDE THE NEGOTIATIONS PROCESS

The goals of the PA's offensive lawfare initiative against Israel were succinctly described by PA President Abbas in his 2011 *New York Times* op-ed in which he wrote that the Palestinian campaign to be recognized as a state by the United Nations "would pave the way for the internationalization of the conflict as a legal matter," and "also pave the way for us to pursue claims against Israel at the United Nations, human rights treaty bodies and the International Court of Justice."[13] "If we don't obtain our rights through negotiations, we have the right to go to international institutions," said Abbas.[14]

PA lawfare against Israel can be divided into three major elements, each of which will be addressed in a separate section of this chapter. The first major element of PA lawfare against Israel—to be discussed here in Section III of this chapter—is the campaign to gain recognition of Palestine, as a full sovereign member state of the international community, outside the negotiations process with Israel and thus without any Palestinian concessions that such negotiations might require. This includes the campaign for designation of Palestine as a U.N. member state, which, as of summer 2015, had resulted in non-member state status at the UN. The recognition campaign also includes the PA drive to join various relatively noncontroversial international organizations and treaties in an effort to incrementally bolster its diplomatic status. The second major element of PA lawfare against Israel—to be discussed in Section IV of this chapter—is the PA's January 2015 decision to use its lawfare "nuclear option" and join the International Criminal Court. The third and final major element of PA lawfare against Israel—to be discussed below in Section V—is the PA's efforts to use the processes of international organizations and treaties, including those to which it is not a party, to advance its claims against Israel.

A. The Campaign for Recognition of Palestine as a U.N. Member State

In a speech to the U.N. General Assembly on September 23, 2011, PA President Abbas stated that he had just submitted to the Secretary General of the United Nations "an application for the admission of Palestine on the basis of the 4 June 1967 borders, with Al-Kuds Al-Sharif as its capital, as a full member of the United Nations."[15] The PA's application was controversial.

The United States and several of its allies opposed the application on the grounds that a lasting peace can only result from the parameters of Palestinian statehood being set in the context of Palestinian negotiations with Israel.[16] A former legal adviser to Israel's Foreign Ministry stated[17] that the Palestinian application violated Article XXXI(7) of the Israeli-Palestinian Interim Agreement on the West Bank and Gaza Strip, which specifies that "Neither side shall initiate or take any step that will change the status of the West Bank and the Gaza Strip pending the outcome of the permanent status negotiations."[18] In addition, some commentators argued that Palestine did not meet the international legal standards for independent statehood.[19]

To become a member of the United Nations requires an affirmative vote of the Security Council, in which the United States holds a veto. In 2011 and 2012, the U.S. government made clear it would use its veto to prevent the Security Council from granting member state status to Palestine.[20] The PA therefore sought a vote in the U.N. General Assembly, which, on November 29, 2012, passed U.N. General Assembly Resolution 67/19, which "accord[s] to Palestine non-member observer State status in the United Nations."[21] The resolution passed by a margin of 138 countries in favor, 9 opposed, and 41 abstaining.[22]

In addition to granting Palestine non-member state status, Resolution 67/19 included language that could be seen as fortifying the PA's positions on other issues subject to negotiation between Israel and the PA. For example, the resolution referenced a "contiguous . . . State of Palestine" (which is not a given in light of the lack of contiguity of the West Bank and Gaza under even Israel's pre-1967 borders) and asserted "the right of the Palestinian people" to independence "on the Palestinian territory occupied since 1967" (language more favorable to the Palestinians than the language of the canonical U.N. Security Council Resolution 242, which omits the word "the" before the word "territories").[23]

B. The U.S. and Israeli Response and the PA's Two-Year Pause in Efforts to Use Lawfare to Achieve Statehood without Negotiation

During the two years between the November 2012 U.N. General Assembly vote granting Palestine non-member state status in the UN and the PA's January 2015 ICC application, the PA very carefully wielded the threat of applying to join additional international treaties and organizations. The PA's caution appears to have been driven by several factors, including U.S. threats to defund U.N. agencies that admitted the PA, the PA's own dependence on U.S. bilateral assistance, and the PA's fear of Israeli responses. In addition, during this period, the PA extracted substantial concessions from Israel in exchange for the PA temporarily holding off on joining international treaties and organizations.

The interplay of PA lawfare threats and U.S and Israeli responses provides considerable insight into options for deploying offensive lawfare. It also suggests the strengths and weaknesses of various options for waging defensive lawfare in this context.

1. UNESCO and the Threat by the United States to Defund U.N. Agencies Admitting the PA

The PA had long held "observer" status at various specialized U.N. agencies, many of which have their own admissions procedures.[24] The PA's first success in joining a specialized U.N. agency as a full member predated by a year the U.N. General Assembly vote granting to Palestine non-member state status in the UN as a whole. On October 31, 2011, the United Nations Educational, Scientific, and Cultural Organization (UNESCO) voted to admit Palestine as a full member.[25] The UNESCO General Conference vote on Palestinian membership was 107 votes in favor and 14 votes against, with 52 abstentions.[26]

This UNESCO vote triggered a provision of U.S. law that mandates that no U.S. funds "shall be available for the United Nations or any specialized agency thereof which accords the Palestine Liberation Organization the same standing as member states."[27] As a result, the United States government, which had been providing $80 million per year to UNESCO, 22 percent of the agency's funding, stopped providing funding to UNESCO.[28]

This lawfare step by the United States did not come without a cost to U.S. interests. In 2013, two years after the United States stopped funding UNESCO, a provision of the UNESCO constitution required UNESCO to suspend U.S. voting rights in the organization. This made it harder for the United States to advance UNESCO-related causes that it supported and to influence the selection of UNESCO's director general, and impossible for the United States to vote against UNESCO proposals that it opposed.[29] U.S. Ambassador to the UN Samantha Power asked Congress (unsuccessfully) for authority to waive the prohibition, stating that, "In the event that the Palestinians seek and obtain membership in a UN agency . . . it would be a double win for them to secure a win in an agency on the one hand, and then the exclusion of the United States from that very agency, leaving the agency at the mercy of the leadership from Russia, China, Cuba, Venezuela—the countries that tend to fill the space when we depart."[30]

Notwithstanding its costs to other U.S. interests, the defunding of UNESCO—combined with U.S. leveraging of aid to the PA, as discussed in the next subsection—reportedly had a significant deterrent effect on PA applications to join other international organizations. As of April 1, 2014, the PA had developed a list of sixty-three international organizations and treaties to which it was poised to submit letters requesting membership.[31] The list reportedly included several major specialized U.N. agencies with large budgets dependent on U.S. contributions.[32] These included the World Bank, the International Monetary Fund, the International Civil Aviation Organization, and the International Maritime Organization.[33]

The United States is the single largest contributor to the regular U.N. budget, paying 22 percent per year. Because there is no waiver provision in the U.S. law mandating that U.S. funds shall not be available for any U.N. agency "which accords the Palestine Liberation Organization the same standing as member states," any U.N. agency that admits the PA as a member runs a high risk of losing the U.S.-contributed 22 percent of its budget. Reportedly, officials of at least some of the U.N. agencies at risk of defunding sought to discourage the PA from seeking to join their organizations.[34]

When the PA announced on April 1, 2014, that it would apply to join fifteen of the international instruments on its list, the fifteen it selected were all treaties, not organizations.[35] The U.S. funding prohibitions were irrelevant for seven of the selected treaties, which either did not have associated organizations or had associated organizations that were not U.N. entities.[36] Eight of the selected treaties had associated organizations that were U.N. entities.[37] However, they were not budget-intensive organizations, and thus the annual U.S. withholding for all eight would have reportedly totaled no more than $6 million.[38]

The list of eighteen international instruments the PA applied to join in its second tranche of applications, on December 31, 2014,[39] also seemed designed in considerable part to avoid U.S. funding prohibitions. All but two of the eighteen were treaties with either no associated U.N. organization or an associated organization with a minimal budget.[40] One of the two exceptions was the International Criminal Court, to which the United States is not a party and thus does not contribute.

The other was the Treaty on the Non-Proliferation of Nuclear Weapons (NPT).[41] The NPT is closely associated with the International Atomic Energy Agency (IAEA), a UN-related organization[42] that has a relatively large budget to which the U.S. contributes significantly. However, IAEA membership does not automatically accrue to NPT parties.[43] IAEA membership requires a separate application, which must be approved by the IAEA's General Conference (which meets once a year normally in September and is composed of the representatives of all of the Agency's member states) on the recommendation of the IAEA Board of Governors (which comprises the representatives of thirty-five member states).[44] It is presumably no accident that as of April 2015, the PA had not applied to join either the IAEA or other of the budget-intensive international organizations that would risk U.S. defunding if the PA were accepted.

2. The United States Leverages Its Aid to the PA to Deter PA Applications

In addition to pressuring U.N. agencies not to admit the PA, the U.S. Congress has also leveraged the PA's own dependence on U.S. bilateral assistance to deter the PA from joining additional treaties and, especially, international organizations. From fiscal year 2012 to 2015, U.S. bilateral assistance to the West Bank and to eligible entities in the Gaza Strip (U.S. law prohibits aid for Hamas or Hamas-controlled entities) averaged around $450 million per year.[45] The PA budget for 2014 was $4.2 billion.[46] Because the United States was providing approximately 10 percent of the PA's annual budget, it had significant but not overwhelming leverage.

Congress took several different types of steps to deter PA applications by leveraging U.S. aid to the PA. For example, in August 2011, Rep. Ileana Ros-Lehtinen (R-Fla.), then Chair of the House Committee on Foreign Affairs, joined with Rep. Kay Granger (R-Tex.), Chair of the State and Foreign Operations Subcommittee of the House, to put a hold on $147 million in fiscal year 2011 U.S. economic support fund assistance to the Palestinians because they objected to the Palestinian push for recognition at the UN.[47] Although the U.S. executive branch generally does not disburse funding over the objections of members of Congress on key committees,[48] Secretary of State Hillary Clinton decided in April 2012 to move forward with the $147 million despite Ros-Lehtinen's hold (Granger had earlier lifted hers).[49] Ros-Lehtinen said she was disappointed that "the Administration would employ hard-ball tactics against Congress and threaten to send, over Congressional objections, U.S. taxpayer dollars to the Palestinian Authority."[50]

Then, in December 2011, Congress moved to enact into U.S. law the leveraging of U.S. aid to deter PA applications. Section 7086 of the Department of State, Foreign Operations, and Related Programs Appropriations Act for Fiscal Year 2012 (2012 Appropriations Act) prohibited economic support funds from being made available to the Palestinian Authority "if the Palestinians obtain, after the date of enactment of this Act, the same standing as member states or full membership as a state in the United Nations or any specialized agency thereof outside an agreement negotiated between Israel and the Palestinians."[51] The vast majority of U.S. bilateral aid to the Palestinians in fiscal year 2012 was economic support funds ($395.7 million of the total $495.7 million).[52] Because the 2012 Appropriations Act was enacted on December 23, 2011, the restriction did not apply to Palestinian membership in UNESCO, which had occurred on October 31, 2011. In addition, because U.N. General Assembly Resolution 67/19 of November 2012 conferred only non-member state status, it did not trigger the aid restriction.

However, the 2012 Appropriations Act restriction appears to have had a significant deterrent effect, especially when combined with the U.S. threat to defund U.N. agencies that grant membership to the PA. As discussed in the previous subsection, each of the two tranches of PA accessions between the Act's enactment and April 2015 seemed designed to avoid U.S. funding prohibitions—by focusing on joining treaties rather than budget-intensive U.N. specialized agencies. Thus, the U.S. financial lawfare threats appear to have helped deter the PA from undertaking those particular lawfare actions to which the U.S. threats were applicable.

3. Israel Uses Its Financial Leverage to Deter PA Applications

Israel has also used financial leverage to attempt to deter Palestinian applications to international organizations and treaties. Pursuant to the Oslo Accords, Israel collects over $100 million a month in tax revenues on behalf of the PA, and then transfers them to the PA.[53] Declaring that the PA had violated the Oslo Accords when it unilaterally sought an upgrade of its status at the UN, Israel responded to the U.N. General Assembly's passage of Resolution 67/19 by announcing that it would halt the tax transfers to the PA for four months.[54] Israel explained that it would instead use the funds to pay off debts the PA owed to the Israel Electric Corporation.[55] However, Israel reversed the decision the following month, amid speculation that it had no interest in seeing the PA collapse.[56]

Similarly, after the PA applied to join eighteen international instruments, including the ICC, on December 31, 2014, Israel responded by withholding some $127 million of monthly tax revenue that it had been collecting on behalf of the PA.[57] This tax revenue was estimated to provide as much as 80 percent of the PA's $160 million per month operating budget at the time.[58] The withholding reportedly prompted the PA to institute various budget cuts, including reducing most of its employees' salaries by 40 percent.[59] However, on March 27, 2015, Israel announced that it would release the withheld payments, amid warnings that the financial pressure risked the PA's collapse.[60]

In order to buy nine months of peace-process negotiating time, U.S. Secretary of State John Kerry engineered a July 2013 deal in which Israel promised to release 104 Palestinian prisoners, in several tranches, in exchange for the PA refraining from joining international organizations and treaties for nine months.[61] Saeb Erekat, the lead Palestinian negotiator, described the deal as follows: "I made the deal personally with John Kerry that if Netanyahu gives me the 104 prisoners . . . we will refrain from going to these agencies for nine months."[62] When the prisoner release deal was announced, a Palestinian official told the *New York Times*, "This is the biggest achievement we will have had this year."[63]

The deal lasted for eight months. During those eight months, the PA refrained from joining additional organizations and treaties, and Israel released, in three tranches, seventy-eight Palestinian prisoners who had been convicted of terrorist activities prior to the entry into force of the Oslo Accords.[64] Many of the prisoners had been convicted of murdering Israeli civilians. The prisoners who were released in exchange for the PA's lawfare hiatus included the following:

- Muammar Ata Mahmoud Mahmoud and Salah Khalil Ahmad Ibrahim, convicted of stabbing to death Menahem Stern, a history professor at Hebrew University, as he walked to the university's library in June 1989.[65]
- Yakoub Muhammad Ouda Ramadan, Afana Mustafa Ahmad Muhammad, and Da'agna Nufal Mahmad Mahmoud, convicted of stabbing to death in a Tel Aviv suburb in January 1993 Sara Sharon, age thirty-seven, a mother of seven.[66]
- Damara Ibrahim Mustafa Bilal, convicted of murdering forty-eight-year-old Steven Friedrich Rosenfeld, a U.S.-born immigrant to Israel, while Rosenfeld was hiking outside the West Bank settlement of Ariel in June 1989.[67]
- Abu Mohsin Khaled Ibrahim Jamal, convicted in 1991 of murdering Shloma Yahya, a seventy-six-year-old gardener, in a public park in Israel's Moshav Kadima.[68]
- Sawafta Sudqi Abdel Razeq Mouhlas, who stabbed Yosef Malka to death in Malka's home in Haifa, Israel, in December 1990.[69]
- Abu Hadir Muhammad Yassin Yassin, who shot Yigal Shahaf in the head while Shahaf and his wife were walking through Jerusalem's Old City toward the Western Wall.[70]

The International Criminal Court (ICC) was the primary international institution that Israel paid, with these prisoner releases, for the PA to refrain from joining. "The ICC is supposed to be an instrument of justice, not a bargaining chip," said Professor Eugene Kontorovich.[71] The PA nevertheless "consistently used the ICC as a very explicit cudgel to demand concessions from Israel," said Kontorovich.[72]

Kontorovich noted the irony that "a Court whose mission is to punish mass atrocity is being used as a tool for the mass *release* of convicted murderers."[73]

C. PA Statehood Lawfare Resumes: The April 2014 Tranche of Accessions

On April 1, 2014, PA President Abbas signed on live television documents of application for fifteen international treaties.[74] Abbas said that he was doing so because Israel had failed to release a fourth tranche of Palestinian prisoners by the end of March 2014 as promised.[75] Israeli officials said they were not bound by the pledge because no meaningful negotiations had occurred since November 2013.[76]

Saeb Erekat, the chief PA negotiator, had, on several occasions prior to April 2014, stated that the PA had a list of sixty-three international organizations and treaties to which it was poised to submit letters requesting membership.[77] However, on April 1, 2014, Abbas signed application documents for only fifteen, all of them treaties.

The fifteen treaties contain various mechanisms for deciding whether an applicant may join. For example, Switzerland is the depositary for the four Geneva Conventions of 1949 and Additional Protocol I; the Netherlands is the depositary for the Hague Convention Respecting the Laws and Customs of War; and the U.N. Secretary-General is the depositary for the other treaties, which most notably include the Vienna Convention on Diplomatic Relations, the Convention on the Rights of the Child, the Convention Against Corruption, the Convention Against Torture, the International Covenant on Civil and Political Rights, and the International Covenant on Economic, Social, and Cultural Rights.[78]

Within a few days, the UN and Swiss decision-makers had approved Palestinian membership.[79] The U.S. response to the PA applications was strikingly low key. Despite a statement to Congress that week by Samantha Power, the U.S. Ambassador to the UN, that "we will oppose attempts at upgrades in status anywhere,"[80] the United States reportedly made no effort to dissuade the depositaries from accepting the PA applications. Several commentators noted that eight of the treaties have bodies that are funded through the U.N. regular budget, and the U.S. law prohibiting U.S. funding of any U.N. organization that "accords the Palestine Liberation Organization the same standing as member states" would appear to require a cutoff of aid to these bodies.[81] However, the U.S. government did not take this step.

The United States did, however, subsequently submit brief letters to the depositaries "regarding the purported accession of the 'State of Palestine'" to the various treaties.[82] In the letters, the U.S. government states that it "does not believe the 'State of Palestine' qualifies as a sovereign State and does not recognize it as such," notes that accession to the treaty is "limited to sovereign States," declares that the U.S. government "believes that the 'State of Palestine' is not qualified to accede" to the treaty, and "affirms" that the U.S. government will not consider itself to be in a treaty relationship with the 'State of Palestine'" under the treaty.[83] Canada submitted similar letters.[84]

When the PA applied in April 2014 to join those fifteen treaties, it notably did not apply to join any of the international organizations in the top two tiers of concern for the government of Israel. The international organization reportedly at the very top of Israel's list of concern was the International Criminal Court.[85] Next down from the top on Israel's list of particular concern was a group of organizations reportedly including the International Civil Aviation Organization (ICAO), the International Maritime Organization (IMO), the International Telecommunications Union (ITU), and the World Trade Organization WTO).[86] This second group of organizations are distinguished by their exceptional importance for Israeli security and trade,[87] as well as by the previously discussed applicability to them of U.S. funding prohibitions that would be triggered by PA accession.

As of July 2015, the PA had still not applied to join ICAO, the IMO, the ITU, or the WTO. However, at the end of 2014, the PA did apply to join the ICC.

IV. THE PA DEPLOYS ITS MOST POWERFUL LAWFARE WEAPON: JOINING THE INTERNATIONAL CRIMINAL COURT

On December 31, 2014, in a ceremony broadcast live on Palestine TV, PA President Abbas signed applications for Palestinian membership in the International Criminal Court (ICC) and nineteen other international organizations and treaties.[88] One week later, the PA's application was accepted by the ICC.[89] Palestine's accession to the ICC entered into force on April 1, 2015 (following a waiting period prescribed for all new parties by the Rome Statute, the ICC's charter).[90]

On January 16, 2015, the prosecutor of the ICC, Mrs. Fatou Bensouda, "opened a preliminary examination into the situation in Palestine."[91] The ICC explained: "A preliminary examination is not an investigation but a process of examining the information available in order to reach a fully informed determination on whether there is a reasonable basis to proceed with an investigation pursuant to the criteria established by the Rome Statute."[92]

Israel and the United States had for years warned the PA against joining the ICC. For example, the Military Advocate General of the Israeli Defense Forces, Avichai Mandelblit, "warned that PA pursuit of Israel through the ICC would be viewed as war" by the Government of Israel.[93] In April 2014 testimony before Congress, U.S. Ambassador to the UN Samantha Power had stated:

> The ICC is of course something that we have been absolutely adamant about. Secretary Kerry has made it very, very clear to the Palestinians, as has the president. I mean, this is something that really poses a profound threat to Israel, is not something—is not a unilateral action that will be anything other than devastating to the peace process.[94]

The PA had reportedly also been pressured by other Western governments—including Australia, Canada, France, Germany, Italy, and the U.K.—to refrain from applying to join the ICC.[95]

In addition, as discussed earlier in this chapter, Israel provided the PA with substantial concessions in exchange for the PA holding off on joining the ICC. When Israel in July 2013 agreed to release 104 Palestinians convicted of terrorist activities in exchange for the PA refraining for nine months from joining international organizations and treaties, the International Criminal Court (ICC) was at the top of the list of bodies Israel wanted to stop the PA from joining. "The International Criminal Court has become perhaps the most important weapon in the lawfare campaign against Israel," wrote Professor Eugene Kontorovich, a leading expert on the topic, prior to the PA's accession.[96] "It is difficult to overestimate the impact that a threat of an ICC investigation has on Israel," says Kontorovich, who stated that "the ICC hangs over Israeli decision-making from the tactical to the strategic level."[97]

The PA's accession to the ICC provides a fascinating case study in lawfare decision-making. This section will first analyze the PA's motivations for acceding to the ICC, despite the pressure not to do so, and Hamas' motivations for concurring in that accession despite the risks posed to Hamas. Then it will analyze the PA's and ICC's potential next steps with regard to allegations of Israeli and Palestinian war crimes. The analysis of the ICC's options will include discussion of relevant ICC precedents and equities. Finally, the section will discuss the potential risks to, and responses by, Israel, the United States, and their allies.

A. The Palestinian Decision to Join the ICC

1. Why Did the PA Choose to Join the ICC?

For the PA, the decision to join the ICC involved several key factors. Weighing in favor of accession were the perceived domestic political and international lawfare benefits. Weighing against accession were the concessions to be gained from holding off and the potential costs of joining—including the cost of Israeli and U.S. sanctions and the risk that PA or Hamas officials would end up in the dock.

Several analysts have opined that Abbas's decision to join the ICC was driven largely by domestic Palestinian politics. The day before the application signing ceremony, the *New York Times* reported "intense domestic political pressure" on Abbas to "regain credibility among an increasingly critical" Palestinian public.[98] Abbas was on the defensive because Hamas, during the 2014 Gaza War, had worked to contrast their combatant attitude toward Israel with Abbas's more peaceful approach (which Hamas characterized as too accommodating). A December 2014 poll showed that only 35 percent of Palestinians approved of Abbas's performance, down from 50 percent before the 2014 Gaza War.[99] Abbas, having cancelled elections in 2010, was in the tenth year of a five-year term as President.[100] The poll showed that if elections had been held in December 2014, Abbas and the PLO party he leads would have been defeated by Hamas.[101]

An Israeli official who works closely with the PA assessed that the ICC accession decision was motivated principally by Abbas's desire to increase his legitimacy and burnish his legacy.[102] Mostafa Elostaz, a Palestinian lawyer focused on the peace process, assessed that, "Abbas' motivations included empowering the PA, increasing his own popular approval within Palestinian society, and, with an eye to his legacy, doing something significant which Arafat had not done—take this major legal action against Israel."[103]

For Abbas, the ICC accession offered an opportunity to be seen by his people as striking a painful blow against the enemy, yet without abandoning his professed opposition to violence. Some Israeli leaders, including Prime Minister Netanyahu, have charged that Abbas has incited or quietly encouraged terrorism against Israel.[104] However, in November 2014, the head of Israel's Shin Bet general security service (Israel's equivalent of the FBI) said that Abbas "is not interested in terror and is not leading towards terror. . . . He also is not doing that under the table."[105] Writing in February 2015, Jonathan Schanzer, a leading analyst of Palestinian politics who has been critical of Abbas on other issues, stated that, "to his full credit, after coming to power in 2005, Palestinian leader Mahmoud Abbas reined in the violent groups responsible for terrorism . . . and he has since upheld this policy of nonviolence, earning him the backing of Israel and the United States as a partner for peace."[106]

Whether or not Abbas has incited or quietly encouraged terrorism against Israel, the PA under Abbas' leadership has clearly made a point of avoiding large-scale violent warfare against Israel (despite several wars between Hamas and Israel during this period). Ratcheting up the PA's lawfare against Israel is a way for Abbas to be seen by the Palestinian people as openly attacking Israel with more than rhetoric, while at the same time not risking all-out violent warfare.

The PA described its December 31, 2014, application to join the ICC as a response to the U.S. and Israeli success, the day before, in preventing passage of a Security Council resolution demanding an end to Israel's occupation.[107] "There is aggression practiced against our land and our country, and the Security Council has let us down—where shall we go?," said Abbas during the December 31, 2014, meeting in which he signed the ICC application papers.[108] "We want to complain to this organization," he said, referring to the ICC.[109]

However, there is evidence that the PA's goal in pushing for the December 30, 2014 resolution may not have been victory for that resolution but rather a defeat designed to provide a pretext for the turn to the ICC. The Security Council resolution fell one vote short of the nine necessary for passage, which could then have been stopped only by a permanent member of the Council (such as the United States) deploying its veto power. The Security Council's composition was scheduled to change on January 1, 2015, two days later, to a membership more likely to provide the PA with nine votes (thus enabling the PA to force the United States to wield its veto power).[110] "Abbas moved forward at the UN Security Council that day, rather than wait for a new, more supportive set of Council members, because he wanted an excuse to go to the ICC," Mkhaimar Abusada, a professor of political science at Al-Azhar University in Gaza, told this author in an interview.[111]

In addition, unlike most draft Security Council resolutions, which become more accommodating as the drafters bargain for additional support, the draft of this resolution became more hardline over time.[112] The combination of the PA's decision to push for a vote on December 30, which surprised Western diplomats,[113] and the increasingly hardline draft seemed intended to result in defeat.

What, then, did the PA perceive as the value—from an international law rather than domestic politics perspective—of acceding to the ICC?

One value of the ICC application was that, unlike a Security Council nine-vote "victory" destined to be vetoed by the United States and thus remain purely symbolic, the PA was confident that it would be accepted as an ICC party. The previous round of PA applications to join international organizations and treaties had been accepted without a hitch.[114] In addition, the ICC's chief prosecutor, Fatou Bensouda, had written in a remarkably forward-leaning August 2014 op-ed that her office had examined the implications of the November 2012 U.N. General Assembly vote upgrading Palestine's status to non-member observer state and had "concluded that . . . Palestine could now join the Rome statute" (the ICC's charter).[115] It was surprising, and perhaps inappropriate, for the ICC prosecutor to pronounce on such an issue prior to being formally presented with it. Regardless, Bensouda's op-ed made clear to the PA that their application would be accepted.

The PA had reportedly concluded that ICC accession could also help advance the Palestinian cause in other, more substantive ways. For example, an eventual ICC conviction of an Israeli officer or official was seen by the Palestinians as holding the possibility of bringing some measure of justice to their victims, vindicating the Palestinian narrative, tarnishing Israel, and deterring future Israeli military and settlement actions adverse to the Palestinian cause. Even a mere open ICC investigation of alleged Israeli war crimes was seen by the Palestinians as holding the possibility of vindicating the Palestinian narrative, tarnishing Israel, and deterring future Israeli actions adverse to the Palestinian cause. In addition, the Palestinian leadership reportedly believed that it would retain at least some measure of control over ICC proceedings against Israel, thus helping tilt the balance of negotiating power between the PA and Israel.

The "advancement of justice" and deterrence rationales for PA accession to the ICC were encouraged by various Palestinian and international non-governmental organizations. For example, in May 2014, a group of seventeen Palestinian and international human rights groups, including Amnesty International and Human Rights Watch, wrote a joint letter to PA President Abbas urging him to "ensure that Palestine pursues the jurisdiction of the International Criminal Court

(ICC) by promptly acceding to the Rome Statute and/or filing a further decla-ration accepting the Court's jurisdiction over crimes committed on Palestinian territory from 1 July 2002" (the date the Rome Statute, which governs the ICC, entered into force).[116] "Taking such steps," said the letter, "could ensure access to international justice for victims of war crimes and crimes against humanity com-mitted on Palestinian territories, and would send an important message that such crimes cannot be committed with impunity."[117]

More specifically, according to Palestinian legal expert Mostafa Elostaz, the Palestinian accession to the ICC could be "a defense mechanism with regard to any future war against Gaza."[118] As a result of the ICC accession, Elostaz says "the Palestinians may see a deterrent effect on future Israeli action . . . . Israel may start to think twice regarding both settlements and wars."[119] Similarly, Daoud Kuttab, a leading Palestinian journalist, wrote that "success at the ICC is likely to not only hold Israel responsible and accountable for its actions, but immediately produce the kind of deterrence that has been missing in the Palestinian arsenal of nonviolent weapons."[120]

Both Israeli and Palestinian analysts told me in early 2015 that Abbas had been convinced that the PA would retain sufficient control over the ICC proceedings against Israel to enable the PA to use it as a bargaining chip—for example, trad-ing PA-initiated pauses in the ICC proceedings for Israeli releases of prisoners or settlement freezes or tax revenues. Consistent with this, a senior Palestinian official told an Israeli journalist in January 2015 that a PA complaint to the ICC regarding Israeli settlement activity "would be withdrawn if Israel were to freeze settlement construction, and added that the Palestinian Authority had conveyed to Israel an official message to that effect, through Jordan and Egypt."[121]

"Abbas believes he is holding as a card the control over moving a case forward against Israel at the ICC," Mkhaimar Abusada, a professor of political science at Al-Azhar University in Gaza and leading Palestinian analyst, told me in an interview.[122] "Abbas wants to return to negotiations with Israel—the ICC move is designed to provide Abbas with more leverage in such negotiations," said Abusada.[123] "The PA intends to hold off on pursuing cases at the ICC as long as Israel is negotiating seriously with them—each time the Israelis don't negotiate seriously, the Palestinians will move forward at the ICC," explained Abusada.[124]

In the months following the PA's accession to the ICC, there appeared to be confusion among leading experts as to the extent, if any, that the PA leadership in fact retained control over ICC proceedings against Israel. One leading Israeli expert suggested that Abbas might have been misled by his advisers on this mat-ter, as the Israeli assessment was that the ICC arrow had left the PA's bow at the moment the PA acceded to the Court.[125]

Other ICC experts also asserted that the Palestinian leadership was in error if it believed that it would retain much control over ICC proceedings against Israel. For example, Professor Kevin Jon Heller wrote that the Rome Statute does not allow Palestine to pursue "a kind of bargaining strategy" with regard to its complaints to the ICC.[126] Heller suggested that now that Palestine has ratified the Rome Statute and submitted a jurisdiction declaration, the PA "has no say in what, if anything the OTP [ICC Office of The Prosecutor] decides to investigate. . . . [T]he fate of the investigation into the situation in Palestine lies solely in the hands of the OTP."[127] The ICC prosecutor could, says Heller, "investigate and prosecute settlement-related activity even if the PA was completely opposed to it doing so."[128]

However, a different view was expressed by Alex Whiting, a Harvard University professor who served from 2010 to 2012 as the Investigation Coordinator for the ICC Prosecutor's Office (responsible for managing all investigations by the Office) and from 2012 to 2013 as the Prosecution Coordinator (responsible for managing all prosecutions by the Office).[129] Whiting noted that pursuant to articles 14 and 15 of the Rome Statute, the prosecutor could move from a preliminary examination to a formal investigation only: (a) if there is a state party referral pursuant to article 14; (b) if the prosecutor acts on her own authority (which would require authorization from the Pre-Trial Chamber); or (c) if there is a Security Council referral (which seemed highly unlikely).[130]

Whiting emphasized the difference between a state party conferring jurisdiction on the ICC, as the PA did in January 2015, and a state party formally referring a matter to the ICC.[131] Per article 14 of the Rome Statute, "a State Party may refer to the Prosecutor a situation in which one or more crimes within the jurisdiction of the Court appear to have been committed requesting the Prosecutor to investigate the situation . . . ."[132] Whiting also emphasized the significance of the fact that on April 1, 2015, the date that Palestine's accession to the ICC entered into force, the PA said that it would "hold off for now" on a state party referral of the situation in Palestine.[133] As of early summer 2015, when this chapter was completed, the PA had not yet made a state party referral of the situation in Palestine.

"Without an Article 14 referral," said Whiting, "it is hard to imagine the Prosecutor ever opening a formal investigation in Palestine."[134] According to Whiting, the prosecutor would be highly unlikely to open a formal investigation on her own authority.[135] "Israel plainly will not cooperate" with the prosecutor's investigation, said Whiting, "and if Palestine does not even ask for an investigation under article 14, then that would be a important signal to the Prosecutor that perhaps it is also not so eager to have an investigation."[136]

"Since the ICC requires cooperation from states to conduct its investigations," said Whiting, "the Prosecutor will want a clear indication from Palestine that it is fully committed to an investigation before she commits precious resources to one."[137] Thus, according to Whiting, the PA would, at least until such time as the PA were to issue an article 14 referral (and quite possibly beyond), retain significant control over the ICC transitioning from the "preliminary examination" which Bensouda opened in January 2015 to a "formal investigation" of a particular crime alleged to have occurred within Palestine. Thus, Palestine could "use the article 14 referral as a bargaining chip in ongoing negotiations with Israel or other international actors."[138] This could arguably be done for an article 14 referral of the 2014 Gaza conflict and, separately, for an article 14 referral of the West Bank settlements. As of early April 2014, there were reports that such a bifurcation was in fact what the PA had in mind.[139]

The PA leadership was aware that ICC action—particularly with regard to the 2014 Gaza conflict—could pose a risk to Palestinians as well as Israelis. Several months before the decision to join the ICC, a senior Israeli official told *Reuters* that an ICC legal action against Israel would prompt an Israeli legal action at the ICC against the Palestinians, including against the administration of President Abbas.[140] "We are talking about terrorism involving officials, security personnel and others, from his administration, and emanating from areas under his control," said the Israeli official.[141] On April 1, 2015, PA Foreign Minister Riyad al-Malki conceded that it was "probable" that Palestinians as well as Israelis would be charged if the ICC proceeded with regard to the 2014 Gaza conflict.[142]

2. Why Did Hamas Concur in Joining the ICC?

In light of the risks to Palestinians, PA President Abbas insisted that the ICC accession not proceed without the written assent of all Palestinian factions including Hamas.[143] Because of the tactics Hamas has used in its several recent wars with Israel, Hamas is far more vulnerable to war crimes prosecution than is either Abbas or Israel. Nevertheless, Hamas announced in August 2014 that it had "signed the document" of support for joining the ICC.[144]

After the ICC prosecutor announced she was opening a preliminary investigation into "the situation in Palestine," Fawzi Barhoum, a Hamas spokesman, welcomed potential ICC involvement as follows: "We are ready to provide (the court) with thousands of reports and documents that confirm the Zionist enemy has committed horrible crimes against Gaza and against our people."[145] The same day, Israeli Prime Minister Netanyahu said: "Here's the ultimate folly of this decision—it is the democracy of Israel, a world leader in fighting terrorism, which is to be hauled to the dock in The Hague, while the terrorist war criminals of Hamas are the ones who are going to be pressing the charges."[146] The U.S. State Department, referencing the rockets fired by Hamas at Israel, said that it was "a tragic irony that Israel, which has withstood thousands of terrorist rockets fired at its civilians and its neighborhoods, is now being scrutinized by the ICC."[147]

Hamas was initially opposed to Palestine joining the ICC.[148] Hamas's opposition was likely influenced by the fact that its record of firing thousands of rockets at Israel in a manner that did not discriminate between military and civilian targets would make Hamas a relatively easy target for ICC prosecution.[149] According to Professor Kevin Jon Heller, "Hamas's deliberate rocket attacks on civilians would be by far the easiest of all the crimes" for the ICC to prosecute, much easier, for example, than Israel's alleged war crimes vis-à-vis the 2014 Gaza conflict or settlements.[150]

The requirement that a warring party distinguish between military and civilian persons and objects, and not direct their attacks at civilian persons or objects, is a fundamental principle of the law of armed conflict. It is customary international law applicable in both international and noninternational armed conflicts[151] and codified in articles 48, 51, and 52 of Additional Protocol I to the Geneva Conventions.[152] Article 13 of Additional Protocol II also contains the requirement as it pertains to civilian persons.[153] In addition, article 8 of the Statute of the International Criminal Court specifies that "intentionally directing attacks against the civilian population as such or against individual civilians not taking direct part in hostilities" constitutes a war crime in both international and noninternational armed conflicts.[154]

Ibrahim Khreisheh, the PA's representative to the U.N. Human Rights Council, warned of this in a July 2014 interview on Palestinian Authority TV, in which he said, "The missiles that are being launched against Israel—each and every missile constitutes a crime against humanity whether it hits or misses, because it is directed at civilian targets . . . targeting civilians—be it one civilian or a thousand—is considered a crime against humanity."[155] "Therefore," cautioned Khreisheh, "people should know more before they talk emotionally about appealing to the ICC."[156]

In light of Hamas's particular vulnerability to war crimes prosecution, its decision to concur in PA accession to the ICC seems surprising. A close examination of how Hamas balanced the opportunities and risks of this key lawfare decision provides interesting insight into how lawfare looks from the perspective of Hamas and perhaps other entities engaged in compliance-leverage disparity lawfare.

Several factors reportedly influenced Hamas's decision. First, at least some in the Hamas leadership reportedly believed that its battlefield tactics either did not make it vulnerable to ICC prosecution or made it less vulnerable than Israel was to ICC prosecution. For example, in explaining Hamas's decision to concur, Hamas official Mushir al-Masri told *Reuters*: "There is nothing to fear, the Palestinian factions are leading legitimate resistance in keeping with all international laws and standards. We are in a state of self-defence."[157]

The law of armed conflict is both exceptionally complex and nonintuitive. Yet in contrast with the PA—which had numerous attorneys serving in its Negotiations Support Unit, several law schools within its territory, and several leading international legal experts willing to provide it with advice—Hamas had access to very little legal expertise. According to Mkhaimar Abusada, a professor of political science at Al-Azhar University in Gaza, "whatever international law might say on the matter, Hamas feels the smaller number of Israelis killed, most of them soldiers, compared to the larger number of Palestinians killed, most of them civilians, means that any price Hamas will pay at the ICC will be smaller than the price Israel will pay at the ICC."[158] "Hamas also does not feel it will or should be held to the same standard as Israel," said Abusada, noting that, unlike Israel, Hamas did not possess precision-guided weapons.[159]

Second, Hamas leaders reportedly took into consideration that ICC enforcement had proven to be relatively toothless, especially with regard to Arab leaders. Because the ICC does not have its own police force, it must rely on state parties to arrest and surrender suspects. The ICC first issued an indictment and arrest warrant for Sudanese President Omar al-Bashir in 2009.[160] As of summer 2015, he had yet to be arrested. "Everyone is aware of how Omar al-Bashir continues to travel all over Africa and the Arab world," said Professor Abusada.[161] "If the price of ICC action is not being able to travel to Europe or America, that might be a significant cost to Israeli leaders but not to Hamas leaders," said Professor Abusada.[162]

According to Professor Eugene Kontorovich, the Palestinians (including their particularly vulnerable Hamas faction) may also have "turned to the ICC" in part because "the ICC has proven itself completely incapable of prosecuting a case against" an uncooperative authoritarian regime.[163] On December 12, 2014, nineteen days before the PA application, ICC prosecutor Bensouda announced that she felt compelled to "hibernate" the genocide case against al-Bashir due to the lack of Security Council and state party cooperation in securing his arrest.[164]

In addition, Kontorovich noted that the case against Kenyan President Uhuru Kenyatta, which was withdrawn by the ICC in May 2014 because of Kenya's lack of cooperation, "has created a playbook" for authoritarian regimes "wanting to frustrate ICC proceedings."[165] As ICC prosecutor Bensouda withdrew the ICC's charges against Kenyatta, she stated that "despite my persistent efforts and those of my committed Team . . . those who have sought to obstruct the path of justice have, for now, deprived the people of Kenya of the accountability they deserve."[166]

Since the ICC does not have its own enforcement power, it cannot: compel witnesses to testify, visit crime scenes, or collect such evidence as phone and bank records without the permission of national governments.[167] "The Kenyan government's non-compliance compromised the Prosecution's ability to thoroughly investigate the charges," said Bensouda.[168] She explained that despite the Kenyan government's "assurances of its willingness to cooperate with the Court . . . the hurdles we have encountered in attempting to secure the cooperation required for this investigation have in large part, collectively and cumulatively, delayed and frustrated the course of justice."[169]

The Kenyatta playbook seems particularly likely to be useful to countries like Palestine, which combine authoritarian governance with large numbers of allied countries. Tactics used by the Kenyan government for "beating the ICC" reportedly included the intimidation, bribery, and killing of witnesses; the falsification of records; organizing pressure on the ICC by the African Union group of African countries; and convincing the annual gathering of ICC member states to change the ICC rules.[170] ICC prosecutor Bensouda specifically confirmed the effectiveness of several of these tactics when she withdrew the case against Kenyatta. In doing so, she noted, for example, that "several people who may have provided important evidence regarding Mr. Kenyatta's actions have died, while others were too terrified to testify for the Prosecution."[171] "This has been about as comprehensive a process of undermining as you can imagine," said Dr. Phil Clark, an ICC specialist at London's School of Oriental and African Studies, in describing Kenyatta's battle against the ICC.[172]

Kontorovich suggested that the ICC's withdrawal of its case against the uncooperative Kenyatta, seven months before the PA decided to accede, could have encouraged Hamas and other Palestinians to calculate "that they can nominally accept legal exposure while maintaining de facto impunity."[173] "Noncooperation with ICC investigations is easy in a place like Gaza, where the killing of 'collaborators' is institutionalized," says Kontorovich.[174]

Third, even if Hamas leaders were to be incarcerated, "it is important to keep in mind," said Mostafa Elostaz, "that this is a group which has carried out suicide bombings, for which self-sacrifice for the cause" is expected and honored.[175] In contrast to Israeli officials, who would be embarrassed to be dragged before the ICC, "Hamas officials," said Elostaz, "would see being taken to the ICC as a heroic act, saying look they are prosecuting us for fighting for our freedom."[176] Similarly, Professor Aeyal Gross, a leading Israeli expert on the ICC, noted that in cases of Hamas or other "Palestinians attacking Israelis, they are already at risk of assassination by Israel or long prison terms if caught."[177] "In contrast," said Gross, "Israelis have enjoyed de facto immunity from prosecution for Israel's actions."[178] Palestinian accession to the ICC, said Gross, "is designed to lift this immunity."[179]

B. Potential Next Steps by the PA and ICC

The PA and ICC steps in January through April 2015 provided important, but not dispositive, signals of the direction in which each was inclined to take Palestinian accession to the ICC.

1. Next Steps for the PA

For ICC state parties, acceptance of the ICC's retroactive jurisdiction is a separate step from acceding to the Rome Statute and thereby granting prospective jurisdiction to the ICC.[180] On January 1, 2015, the Palestinian government, having applied to join the ICC, took that separate step of submitting to the ICC a document declaring Palestine's acceptance of the jurisdiction of the ICC back to June 13, 2014.[181] Specifically, the document, signed by PA President Abbas, stated that "the Government of the State of Palestine hereby recognizes the jurisdiction of the Court for the purpose of identifying, prosecuting and judging authors and accomplices of crimes within the jurisdiction of the Court committed in the occupied Palestinian territory, including East Jerusalem, since June 13, 2014."[182]

It is important to note that the PA had some flexibility in determining the date on which ICC jurisdiction would begin. The ICC determined that the PA was "able to accept the jurisdiction of the Court from 29 November 2012 onward," that being the date of the U.N. General Assembly vote granting Palestine "non-member observer State" status in the UN.[183]

The June 13, 2014 date, eighteen months later, appears to have been selected because June 12, 2014, the previous day, was the date on which Hamas-affiliated Palestinians[184] kidnapped and murdered three Israeli teenagers—Naftali Fraenkel, Gilad Shaar, and Eyal Yifrach.[185] Saleh Arouri, a senior leader of Hamas, had boasted that Hamas's military wing was behind the abductions, which he described as a "heroic action" designed to use the three teens as bargaining chips to be traded for Palestinian prisoners held in Israeli jails.[186] By selecting June 13, 2014, the PA arranged for ICC jurisdiction to apply to Israel's response to the kidnapping, but not to the kidnapping itself.

Shawan Jabarin, director of Al Haq, a Ramallah-based rights group, noted that the same date had previously been selected by the U.N. Human Rights Commission (UNHRC) when it created the investigatory commission originally to be led by William Schabas.[187] The commission's mandate was to "investigate all violations of international humanitarian law and international human rights law in the Occupied Palestinian Territory . . . in the context of the military operations conducted since 13 June 2014, whether before, during, or after."[188] However, unlike the UNHRC investigatory commission's mandate, the PA grant of jurisdiction to the ICC did not encompass any activities "before" June 13, 2014.

Saeb Erekat, the PA official most closely associated with the ICC accession, announced in January 2015 that the PA was preparing two dossiers to submit to the ICC.[189] One would be a dossier urging ICC prosecutions in response to Israel's attacks on Gaza during July and August 2014.[190] Al Haq's Jabarin reportedly suggested to the Palestinian leadership that the Palestinian position on this issue was likely to be strengthened by the report to be published by the UNHRC's commission of inquiry into the 2014 Gaza War.[191]

The other PA dossier was to address Israel's building of settlements in the West Bank.[192] Hassan al-Aouri, a legal adviser to PA President Abbas, said the PA would submit to the ICC a "file regarding settlements" because they "affect the core of the conflict and are considered a war crime."[193]

On January 21, 2015, the PLO announced the formation of a special national council, headed by Erekat, to oversee and coordinate Palestinian activity vis-à-vis the ICC.[194] Wasil Abu Yousef, a member of the PLO's executive committee, stated that the council would comprise "all" Palestinian "factions, including Hamas, Islamic Jihad, and human rights and civil society organizations—in order to go ahead with two primary issues: settlements and the aggression on Gaza."[195]

However, as discussed earlier in this chapter, the PA, contrary to expectations, did not, on April 1, 2015—the date that Palestine's accession to the ICC entered into force—submit to the ICC any article 14 state party referrals. Since the ICC prosecutor would be hesitant to open a formal investigation of the situation in Palestine without a state party referral, it appeared that the PA may have been trying to use the article 14 referral or referrals as a bargaining chip in negotiations with Israel or the United States.

2. Next Steps for the ICC

The ICC prosecutor, Fatou Bensouda, had moved quickly to open a "preliminary examination into the situation in Palestine." She opened the preliminary examination on January 16, 2015, after receipt of the PA's accession and jurisdiction submissions but before the PA accession's entry into force on April 1, 2015.

A preliminary examination is only the first of several stages prior to an ICC trial. During a preliminary examination, the prosecutor determines "whether there is a reasonable basis to proceed with an investigation," which would be the next stage. An investigation could be followed by a "prosecutor's summonses," then a "pre-trial phase," and then a full trial.

A preliminary examination may never result in an investigation. As the ICC explained: "Depending on the facts and circumstances of each situation, the Office will decide whether to continue to collect information to establish a sufficient factual and legal basis to render a determination; initiate an investigation, subject to judicial review as appropriate; or decline to initiate an investigation."[196]

In addition, as the ICC stated in announcing the preliminary examination, "there are no timelines provided in the Rome Statute for a decision on a preliminary examination."[197] Emeric Rogier, the head of the analysis unit at the ICC prosecutor's office, confirmed that "the office will look into allegations against all sides," including "alleged crimes committed by Israeli forces" and by "Palestinian groups."[198] He estimated that the preliminary examination "could take a few months but sometimes it has taken a few years," noting that "it depends on cooperation we receive and access to the field, also it depends on the existence of national proceedings in the relevant countries."[199]

As discussed above, Alex Whiting emphasized that in the absence of an article 14 referral by the PA, the prosecutor would be highly unlikely to move from a preliminary examination to a formal investigation of alleged war crimes in Palestine. "In that scenario," said Whiting, "the Prosecutor could quite justifiably say that given limited resources and the demands of other situations and cases, she is not going to expend resources on a situation where neither side has demonstrated a clear commitment to the ICC investigating and prosecuting."[200] "The principal lesson to be drawn from the ICC's first decade of work," said Whiting, "is that international criminal investigations and prosecutions will succeed only if there is sustained support either within the country where the cases arose or from the international community at large."[201]

Even if the PA makes such an article 14 referral, "the challenges of the cases arising out of the Israeli-Palestinian will cause the OTP to move slowly and cautiously," said Whiting, "and the Office will likely stay at the preliminary examination phase for a number of years."[202] Professor Kevin Jon Heller asserted that the ICC prosecutor "knows full-well how to slow-walk a preliminary examination" until such time, if any, that the prosecutor sees an "upside for the ICC in opening a formal investigation."[203]

The report by the U.N. Human Rights Council's commission of inquiry into the 2014 Gaza War[204] was published after this chapter was largely completed. A full analysis of the report, which Benjamin Wittes and Yishai Schwartz of the Brooking Institution attacked as "a bad piece of work,"[205] is thus outside the scope of this book.

However, it is important to briefly note that Alex Whiting, the former Investigation Coordinator and Prosecution Coordinator for the ICC Prosecutor's Office, opined that the report's analyses of "rockets and mortars fired by Palestinian armed groups" and of "15 air strikes on residential buildings in Gaza" by Israel contained evidence that "will push the ICC Prosecutor a long way toward opening a formal investigation" of both Palestinian and Israeli actors.[206]

Addressing the report's evidence relating to the Israeli air strikes, Whiting explained that, "taken on its face," the evidence "discloses that the war crimes of intentionally targeting civilians or civilian objects, or using disproportionate or indiscriminate force, may have occurred," thus meeting the "reasonable basis to believe" part of the test for the ICC opening a formal investigation.[207] However, Whiting explained that "there is a long way between" such "information sufficient to open an investigation and evidence that will support bringing (and sustaining) individual criminal charges."[208] Whiting assessed that "it is a closer question with regard to the mortar and rocket attacks by Palestinian armed groups, but certainly with respect to the Israeli attacks, the Report falls well short of establishing crimes beyond a reasonable doubt" (the standard necessary for conviction).[209]

a. The Palestine Situation in the Context of Other ICC Cases

The status of other ICC cases provides some context for the Palestine preliminary examination. As of March 13, 2015, the ICC had convicted a total of two people since it opened in 2002. In May 2014, the ICC had convicted Germain Katanga, a Congolese militia leader, to twelve years in prison for aiding and abetting murder and looting in a village where more than two hundred civilians were shot or hacked to death.[210] In July 2012, the ICC convicted Thomas Lubanga, also a Congolese militia leader, to fourteen years in prison for using child soldiers in his rebel army.[211] In addition to these two convicted persons, the ICC also had six suspects in custody as of March 13, 2015.[212]

Since 2002, the ICC, as of March 13, 2015, had issued a total of twenty-seven arrest warrants.[213] Thirteen of the warrants had been implemented, twelve suspects remained at large, and two warrants had been withdrawn following the deaths of the suspects.[214]

For reasons including the fact that the first two convicted persons were African, the ICC had received considerable criticism for disproportionately focusing on African wrongdoers.[215] Such criticism had clearly struck a nerve with Fatou Bensouda, a Gambian citizen who became the ICC prosecutor in 2012.[216] Some analysts speculated that this criticism might encourage the ICC to aggressively pursue the Palestine situation.[217] However, the Palestine situation was far from the ICC's only option for aggressively pursuing non-Africans.

As of March 13, 2015, the ICC was conducting preliminary examinations regarding nine situations: Afghanistan, Colombia, Georgia, Guinea, Honduras, Iraq, Nigeria, Palestine, and Ukraine.[218] It was conducting "investigations" of crimes allegedly committed in nine other situations.[219] In addition, seven cases were at the trial stage.[220]

Israel was not the first Western democracy to be subject to an ICC preliminary examination. The ICC's 2014 "Report on Preliminary Examination Activities" stated that both the United Kingdom and the United States were the subjects of active ICC preliminary examinations.[221]

The ICC's 2014 "Report on Preliminary Examination Activities" stated that its preliminary examination of the situation in Iraq, previously concluded in 2006, had been reopened following the ICC's receipt in January 2014 of information "alleging the responsibility of United Kingdom (UK) officials for war crimes involving systematic detainee abuse in Iraq from 2003 until 2008."[222] The information was received from two non-governmental organizations: the European Center for Constitutional and Human Rights and a group called Public Interest Lawyers.[223] While Iraq is not a party to the ICC, the U.K. acceded to the ICC in October 2001. The ICC therefore "has jurisdiction over war crimes, crimes against humanity and genocide committed on UK territory or by UK nationals as of 1 July 2002."[224]

The ICC's 2014 Report on Preliminary Examination Activities (2014 Report) also stated that "the alleged torture or ill-treatment of conflict-related detainees by U.S. armed forces in Afghanistan in the period 2003–2008 forms another potential case identified by the Office" of the ICC prosecutor.[225] While the United States is not a party to the ICC, Afghanistan acceded to the ICC in 2003, and the ICC "has jurisdiction over Rome Statute crimes committed on the territory of Afghanistan or by its nationals from 1 May 2003 onwards."[226]

The 2014 Report also stated that "certain of the enhanced interrogation techniques apparently approved by US senior commanders in Afghanistan in the period from February 2003 through June 2004 could, depending on the severity and duration of their use, amount to cruel treatment, torture or outrages upon personal dignity as defined under international jurisprudence."[227] The 2014 Report noted that "the development and implementation of such techniques is documented inter alia in declassified US Government documents released to the public, including Department of Defense reports as well as the US Senate Armed Services Committee's inquiry."[228] The 2014 Report concluded that the Prosecutor's Office would continue "to assess the admissibility of the potential cases identified above in order to reach a decision on whether to seek authorization from the Pre-Trial Chamber to open an investigation of the situation in Afghanistan."[229]

The "preliminary examination of the situation in Afghanistan" has been ongoing since at least 2007, when it was made public.[230] However, it was not until the 2014 Report that the ICC explicitly stated in a public document that the prosecutor was examining the possibility that war crimes had been committed in Afghanistan by the U.S. military.[231]

The U.S. government did have some advance notice. In early 2013, Bensouda reportedly sent a letter to U.S. officials describing evidence that U.S. forces had mistreated more than two dozen detainees held in Afghanistan.[232] Bensouda invited the U.S. government to provide her office with information about those cases and related matters. According to Professor David Bosco, a leading ICC scholar, the letter resulted in a U.S. delegation flying to The Hague to urge the ICC "not to publish the allegations, even in preliminary form."[233] The delegation "warned that the world would see any ICC mention of possible American war crimes as evidence of guilt, even if the court never brought a formal case."[234]

The 2014 ICC decision to publicly state that it is examining torture or ill treatment by U.S. forces in Afghanistan, as well as to open an examination of possible U.K. war crimes in Iraq, appears to represent a change from the ICC's first decade of operation. During those first ten years, according to Bosco, the Court "mostly steered clear of investigations that would entangle it directly with the most powerful states."[235]

Stephen Rapp, the Obama administration's Ambassador-at-Large for War Crimes Issues, responded to the 2014 Report by reiterating the longstanding U.S. policy that "the ICC should not have jurisdiction over non-parties."[236] However, in the wake of Israeli Prime Minister Netanyahu's re-election, the United States in March 2015 was reportedly considering "altering current U.S. policy that opposes Palestinian efforts to take complaints against Israel to the International Criminal Court."[237]

b. Israel/Palestine Alleged Crimes Most Likely to be Pursued by the ICC

Although ICC prosecutor Bensouda had not, as of March 2015, specified which potential crimes would be the focus of her "preliminary examination into the situation in Palestine," the most likely candidates include: Israeli tactics during the 2014 Gaza War, Israeli settlements, and Palestinian rocket and mortar launches from Gaza. It is important to note that the Rome Statute provides the ICC with jurisdiction over a relatively limited set of crimes: currently, the crime of genocide; crimes against humanity; and war crimes (with the crime of aggression due to be added after January 1, 2017). Each of the crimes within the ICC's jurisdiction is defined in detail by the Rome Statute. The ICC can only convict persons for acts that fall within the Rome Statute's definition of those crimes. It is also important to understand that the ICC can only try individual persons. In contrast, disputes between states are addressed by the International Court of Justice.

Israel's accusers have portrayed Israeli troops during the 2014 Gaza War as having committed various war crimes subject to the Rome Statute, including the Statute's prohibitions on "attacks directed at civilian objects or at civilians, or disproportionate and indiscriminate attacks that kill or injure civilians."[238] Israel's accusers have described Israeli settlements as having violated the Rome Statute war crime of "the transfer, directly or indirectly, by the Occupying Power of parts of its own civilian population into the territory it occupies."[239] Hamas's accusers have portrayed Hamas rocket attacks against Israel as having committed various war crimes subject to the Rome Statute, including prohibitions on "indiscriminate or deliberate attacks on civilians."[240]

c. Prosecutorial Discretion and the ICC's "Sword of Damocles"

This book assesses in more detail elsewhere the accuracy of each of these sets of charges of potential war crimes. For purposes of understanding the ICC's next steps, it is important to understand that, regardless of the merits of any of these charges, the ICC's preliminary investigation analysis, and any further steps, regarding Israel's battle tactics in Gaza in 2014 is likely to differ substantially from the ICC's preliminary investigation analysis, and any further steps, regarding settlements in the West Bank and Hamas rocket attacks against Israel. The difference will be driven by the principle of complementarity, which is at the heart of ICC jurisprudence.

Pursuant to the principle of complementarity, the "primary responsibility for trying" perpetrators is said to remain with member states.[241] The ICC "can investigate and, where warranted, prosecute and try individuals only if the State concerned does not, cannot or is unwilling genuinely to do so."[242] The Rome Statute and other ICC documents suggest several manifestations of a state being unwilling genuinely to prosecute and try individuals. These include "where proceedings are unduly delayed or are intended to shield individuals from their criminal responsibility."[243]

Article 17 is the key Rome Statute provision setting forth the principle of complementarity. With regard to complementarity, article 17 specifies that "the

Court shall determine that a case is inadmissible where . . . the case is being investigated or prosecuted by a State which has jurisdiction over it, unless the State is unwilling or unable genuinely to carry out the investigation or prosecution."[244] Article 17 also specifies that "the Court shall determine that a case is inadmissible where . . . the case is not of sufficient gravity to justify further action by the Court."[245]

Consistent with article 17's complementarity provision, article 20 crucially specifies as follows:

> No person who has been tried by another court for conduct also proscribed by [the Rome Statute] shall be tried by the Court with respect to the same conduct unless the proceedings in the other court:
>
> (a) Were for the purpose of shielding the person concerned from criminal responsibility for crimes within the jurisdiction of the Court; or
>
> (b) Otherwise were not conducted independently or impartially in accordance with the norms of due process recognized by international law and were conducted in a manner which, in the circumstances, was inconsistent with an intent to bring the person concerned to justice.[246]

These, then, are the two key bars to admissibility of a case involving a crime within the ICC's jurisdiction: the case is inadmissible on complementarity grounds because the state is handling it (or has handled it) satisfactorily; or the case is not of sufficient gravity to warrant the Court's expenditure of resources.

Assessing the genuineness of a nation state's investigations, prosecutions, and trials, or the gravity of a particular crime, is inherently a subjective enterprise. It vests considerable discretion in the ICC and thus its prosecutor. Bensouda has repeatedly emphasized the prosecutor's independence and thus discretion, noting, for example, that "it is the Prosecutor who, with complete independence and on the basis of the criteria laid down by the Rome Statute, initiates preliminary examinations, selects situations and cases, and decides whether or not to open an investigation into a situation" that has been referred to it.[247]

Bensouda is clearly determined to make maximal use of the ICC's ability to encourage "positive complementarity." She has defined "positive complementarity" in the ICC context as "a proactive policy of cooperation and consultation, aimed at promoting national proceedings and at positioning itself as a sword of Damocles, ready to intervene in the event of unwillingness or inability by national authorities."[248]

Bensouda has repeatedly referred to the ICC's use of law in instrumental terms, referring to it not only, or even primarily, as an arbiter of justice but also as having "introduced a new paradigm in international relations: utilizing law as a global tool to promote peace and international security."[249] Rather than a body like the U.S. Supreme Court, which focuses on relatively passively determining what the law is and applying that law to the facts of the cases before it, Bensouda has expressed hope that the ICC would have a "role to play in managing mass violence in real time."[250]

Bensouda has also repeatedly spoken of how ICC cases not only can bring justice to a particular perpetrator but also can have a broader impact. She has referred to having a broader impact not only on the particular conflict in which a perpetrator has engaged but also, through "the shadow of the Court," on other conflicts and potential crimes. For example, referring to the ICC trial of Jean-Pierre Bemba, a Congolese rebel group leader, Bensouda said: "[U]nlike any other court, the ICC's decision will influence the behavior of thousands of military commanders from at least 121 states parties."[251] Thus, Bensouda appears to see her role not so much as a determiner of justice in discrete cases but as a supranational wager of lawfare.

Bensouda has written that a major objective of the prosecutor's preliminary examination activities is to "stimulate genuine national proceedings against those who appear to bear the greatest responsibility for the most serious crimes."[252] She has said that the use of positive complementarity during the preliminary examination phase "is one of the most remarkable efficiency tools we have at our disposal as it encourages national prosecutions and prevents or puts an end to abuses," while allowing the Court "to avoid opening investigations and prosecutions" and thus conserve its resources.[253]

The ICC's limited resources have also, according to Bensouda, contributed to a policy of focusing on the most senior officials responsible for Rome Statute crimes. "Given the Court's limited resources," said Bensouda, the Office of the Prosecutor has determined that it "ought to focus the efforts and resources employed in investigation and prosecution on persons bearing the greatest responsibility, like heads of States or other organizations presumed to be responsible for these crimes."[254]

Much of the interaction between the ICC and Israel—especially during the preliminary examination stage (and assuming an article 14 referral by Palestine)—will likely turn on the degree to which Israel and its allies can persuade Bensouda of one or more of the following:

- Israel has satisfactorily engaged in positive complementarity as a result of Bensouda's "sword of Damocles"—by, for example, the Israeli legal system holding Israeli persons responsible for any Rome Statute crimes they have committed;
- Any Rome Statute crimes by Israeli persons which the Israeli legal system has not satisfactorily addressed are "not of sufficient gravity to justify further action by the Court;" or
- It is not, overall, in the interest of Bensouda and the ICC to get further entangled in the Israeli-Palestinian conflict and/or take on a particular aspect or issue which would result in the U.S. or other major powers imposing serious repercussions on the ICC.

C. Potential Responses by Israel

For Israel, the ICC preliminary examination is a major national security challenge. Israeli Foreign Minister Avigdor Lieberman described the preliminary examination as an attempt to "harm Israel's right to defend itself against terror."[255]

Israel quickly responded to the PA's ICC accession by freezing the transfer of more than $100 million a month in taxes and customs receipts that Israel was collecting for the PA.[256] This put significant financial pressure on the PA, as these transfers reportedly accounted for as much as 80 percent of the PA's budget.[257] The Israeli government, with a strong interest in not seeing the PA collapse, restored the tax revenue transfers soon after the Israeli election of March 2015.[258] It did so amid rumors that the PA had agreed in exchange to hold off on an article 14 referral or referrals.[259]

After the ICC's announcement of a preliminary examination, Israel again quickly responded, this time with a campaign by Foreign Minister Lieberman to persuade key countries that fund the ICC to cut their contributions to it.[260] More than half of the ICC's $158 million annual budget comes from its top seven donor countries—Japan, Germany, France, Britain, Italy, Spain, and Canada.[261] Since the ICC is reportedly already financially stretched, a threatened withdrawal of funds by some or all of the Court's key donors could have had a significant impact.[262] However, those countries reportedly rebuffed Lieberman's request.[263]

While Israel's first public substantive responses to the PA accession and ICC preliminary examination announcement involved the tax transfer cutoff and ICC defunding campaign, Israel will likely also feel the need to respond to the ICC preliminary examination, and any further steps by the ICC, more squarely. While Kenya and Sudan have, as discussed above, managed to thwart ICC action through lack of cooperation, this may be harder for Israel. While Kenyan noncooperation was able to prevent the ICC from gathering sufficient evidence to move forward, Israel is not an authoritarian state, and, as Professor Kontorovich notes, "a bevy of Israeli NGOs will be lined up to supply the prosecutor with the dirt on alleged Israeli misdeeds."[264] In addition, much information pertaining to relevant Israeli activity is available in the public domain. It does seem highly unlikely that Israel will turn its personnel over to the ICC for trial. Thus, an Israeli government policy of noncooperation might succeed in protecting Israeli personnel against imprisonment, but not against indictments or arrest warrants.

From a legal perspective, a cooperative Israeli response to the ICC's preliminary examination, and any further ICC steps, regarding Israel's battle tactics in Gaza in 2014 is likely to differ substantially from Israel's response to the ICC's preliminary investigation, and any further steps, regarding settlements in the West Bank.

With regard to Israel's battle tactics in Gaza in 2014, Israel will undoubtedly make a detailed argument that it has a policy of complying with the law of armed conflict and punishing any personnel who deviate from that policy in the heat of battle. Israel's efforts to demonstrate "positive complementarity" with regard to the 2014 Gaza conflict will likely continue to be heavily influenced by a February 2013 report of Israel's Turkel Commission (named for its lead member, former Israeli Supreme Court Justice Jacob Turkel).[265] The 474-page February 2013 report assessed whether Israel's system for investigating alleged war crimes by its troops was up to international law standards.[266]

The Turkel report asserted that Israel's investigative system does meet international law standards.[267] However, the report also included eighteen recommendations for systemic improvement.[268] According to Yonah Jeremy Bob, the legal affairs correspondent for the *Jerusalem Post*, "how Israel has implemented" the eighteen recommendations "made by its own quasi-government Turkel Commission . . . may be decisive in whether the ICC views Israel's investigative apparatus as 'reasonable.'"[269]

As of January 2015, the Israeli military had reportedly implemented many, but not all, of the Turkel Commission's most important recommendations for systemic improvement.[270] For example, in response to what has been viewed as the most important of the Turkel recommendations,[271] the Israeli military established a permanent Fact-Finding Assessment Mechanism in order to provide its Military Advocate General (MAG) "with as much factual information as possible in order to enable the MAG to reach decisions regarding whether or not to open a criminal investigation" with regard to combat "incidents where the MAG has decided that additional information is required in order to determine whether there exists reasonable grounds for suspicion of a violation of the law."[272] The Israeli military announced that the MAG's decisions—as to whether to close a case, recommend disciplinary measures, or order the opening of a criminal investigation into the combat incident—will be "publicized" and may be challenged before the Attorney General of Israel and subject to judicial review by the Supreme Court of Israel.[273]

With regard to the Gaza 2014 conflict in particular, Israel quickly began working to demonstrate that it was genuinely investigating potential violations of the Rome Statute that may have occurred during that conflict. For example, on March 20, 2015, the Israeli military released its third major report on Israel's investigation of potential war crimes in the 2014 Gaza conflict.[274] The report stated that Israel was reviewing 120 incidents, and had opened 19 criminal investigations into the conduct of its own soldiers.[275] If allegations such as those in a 240-page report[276] by an Israeli NGO called "Breaking the Silence" were true, Israel may end up convicting some of its soldiers, including the tank gunner whose testimony was included in the report and who subsequently told the *Washington Post*, "war crime is a big word . . . . I didn't rape and kill anybody, but yeah, I shot at random civilian targets sometimes, just for fun, so yeah."[277]

With regard to settlements, however, Israel will likely find it far harder to demonstrate "positive complementarity." According to Ido Rosenzweig, the chairman of Israel's Association for the Promotion of International Humanitarian Law, there is "one issue which complementarity won't resolve, and that's the settlements."[278] Professor Aeyal Gross noted that "the establishment of the settlements was based on cabinet decisions and with Israeli government funding."[279] "A finding that the court does not have jurisdiction if the relevant state has investigated a matter itself" would not be relevant here, said Gross, because the settlements involve "government policy."[280]

On the settlements issue, Israel can thus be expected to focus not on complementarity but rather on other types of responses to an ICC preliminary investigation or further steps. For example, Israel might, in the absence of complementarity, be particularly eager to coerce or induce the PA to hold off on an article 14 referral regarding the settlements. In addition, there are several legal theories Israel may consider pursuing. For example, Rosenzweig suggested that Israel might argue that the settlements issue should be declared inadmissible via article 17's requirement that the Court shall determine a case to be inadmissible where "the case is not of sufficient gravity to justify further action by the Court."[281]

Professor Aeyal Gross suggested that Israel might claim, as it has in the past, that "the settlements were not banned by international law because the Geneva Convention does not apply to territory in which there was no previous sovereign."[282] However, Gross asserted that "this claim was rejected" by the International Court of Justice in its case regarding Israel's separation fence.[283]

Israel likely will also rely on the fact that the vast majority of settlement activity occurred, and almost all of the settlements were established, before the date on which ICC jurisdiction commenced over "the situation in Palestine."[284] Such prior settlement activity is likely "grandfathered" into being exempt from ICC action.[285]

In analyzing the possibility of an ICC case about Israeli settlements, Professor Eugene Kontorovich concluded that such a case, by an ICC that has thus far never pursued crimes that do not involve large-scale murder, would be "unprecedented along several dimensions."[286] However, asserted Kontorovich, ICC bias against Israel is "baked into the Court's statute" because the Rome Statute's definition of war crimes "borrows its definitions word-for-word from the Geneva Convention" with the exception of new language, inserted by the Arab League, which "succeeded in inventing an entirely new offense previously unknown to international criminal tribunals," an offense "designed to make a war crime out of" Israeli settlements.[287]

Kontorovich referred to the Rome Statute's addition of the words "directly or indirectly" to the Geneva Convention language potentially addressing settlements. The Rome Statute thus prohibits "[t]he transfer, directly or indirectly, by the Occupying Power of parts of its own civilian population into the territory it occupies . . . ."[288] According to Kontorovich, the change was intended to "go beyond the Geneva Conventions to encompass the self-motivated migration of Israelis into the West Bank."[289]

Kontorovich asserted that neither the Geneva Convention language on transferring population into occupied territory nor the Rome Statute provision has seen prosecutions in any international or national courts.[290] Thus, an ICC prosecution of Israelis for violating this provision would be a first.

Kontorovich also suggested that the situation in occupied Northern Cyprus, in which Turkish settlers have reached a "major demographic tipping point, constituting roughly half the population," is a far stronger candidate to be a violation of international law than are the Israeli settlements in the West Bank.[291] Kontorovich provided several reasons, including because the Geneva provision was "designed to protect against fundamental demographic changes in the occupied territory," and the Israeli settler population remains "a small fraction (less than 10%) of the total population of the territories the Palestinians claim are occupied."[292] Kontorovich concluded that for the ICC to "investigate Israeli settlements" while ignoring the Turkish ones in Cyprus would "deprive the proceedings of any legitimacy."[293]

While seeking to fend off potential ICC steps against Israeli personnel involved in settlements or the 2014 Gaza conflict, Israel will also face the question of what to do about potential ICC action against Palestinian war crimes. In August 2014, prior to the PA acceding to the ICC, a senior Israeli official told *Reuters* that an ICC legal action against Israel would prompt an Israeli legal action at the ICC against the Palestinians, including against the administration of President Abbas.[294] "We are talking about terrorism involving officials, security personnel and others, from his administration, and emanating from areas under his control," said the Israeli official.[295]

Palestinian analysts have noted that Abbas may be vulnerable to ICC action because of his "signing an agreement with Hamas to form a national reconciliation government" and that Hamas and perhaps PLO officials are vulnerable due to the firing of rockets at Israeli territory.[296] Professor Kevin Jon Heller, a leading commentator on the ICC, has said, "it is highly likely that, if the OTP investigated the situation in Gaza, Palestinians would end up in the dock long before Israelis."[297] "From a legal perspective," says Heller, "Fatou Bensouda would find it much easier to prosecute Hamas's deliberate attacks on Israeli civilians than Israel's disproportionate attacks, collective punishment of Palestinians, and transfer of its civilians into occupied territory, [which] are fraught with ambiguity and difficult to prove."[298]

However, the Israeli government would undoubtedly be happier for the ICC to stay entirely out of the Israeli-Palestinian conflict. It would not wish to encourage ICC action against Palestinians if to do so would increase the likelihood of ICC action against Israelis. Thus, until such time as Israel determines that Israelis will be placed in the ICC dock, it seems likely that the Israeli government will tread carefully when it comes to encouraging potential ICC action against the Palestinians. At the same time, Israel may wish to ensure that if Israelis are placed in the dock, Palestinians will be as well. Thus, it seems likely that the Israeli government might already have begun preparing itself for a time when it will, either itself—or, more likely through proxies—decide to present the strongest possible ICC case against the Palestinians.

D. Potential Responses by Israel's Allies

As discussed above, the ICC's top seven donor countries have considerable potential financial leverage over the Court. While they were reportedly unwilling to use that leverage in response to the ICC's opening of a preliminary examination of "the situation in Palestine," it is possible they might reconsider using that leverage, quietly if not publicly, if the ICC takes further steps that are seen as either fundamentally unfair to Israel or setting a problematic precedent for the United States or for those donors themselves.

Of the top seven donor countries, the one with its own relevant interests that are most similar to those of Israel is likely the U.K., which also regularly has troops involved in combat. The ICC's recent opening of a preliminary examination into war crimes by U.K. troops in Iraq may be a sign that the U.K. is hesitant to strong-arm the ICC even when the U.K.'s own interests are directly implicated. However, the preliminary examination of U.K. war crimes may also mean that should it appear, further down the line, that substantive precedents are about to be set against Israel that could be used against U.K. troops in a more advanced (and thus more dangerous) stage of ICC proceedings, the U.K. would have incentive to discourage the ICC from setting that precedent.

The U.S. government's initial response to the PA joining the ICC was sharp. "Today's action is entirely counter-productive and does nothing to further the aspirations of the Palestinian people for a sovereign and independent state," State Department spokesman Jeff Rathke said in a statement.[299] "It badly damages the atmosphere with the very people with whom they ultimately need to make peace."[300]

Because the United States is not a party to the ICC, it has relatively little direct leverage over it. In particular, the United States is not a donor to the ICC and thus has no direct financial leverage over it. The United States' relative lack of leverage over the ICC was demonstrated by the ICC's decision, discussed above, to publicly state that it is examining torture or ill treatment by U.S. forces in Afghanistan, despite U.S. efforts to dissuade the ICC from doing so.

In testimony before Congress following the adoption of the Rome Statute, the lead U.S. negotiator, Ambassador David Scheffer, described as follows key U.S. concerns about the ICC's potential jurisdiction over the troops of countries that had not joined the ICC:

> Multinational peacekeeping forces operating in a country that has joined the treaty can be exposed to the Court's jurisdiction even if the country of the individual peacekeeper has not joined the treaty. Thus, the treaty purports to establish an arrangement

whereby United States armed forces operating overseas could be conceivably prosecuted by the international court even if the United States has not agreed to be bound by the treaty. Not only is this contrary to the most fundamental principles of treaty law, it could inhibit the ability of the United States to use its military to meet alliance obligations and participate in multinational operations, including humanitarian interventions to save civilian lives.[301]

During the Bush administration, the United States—concerned about scenarios such as that laid out by Scheffer—took several steps to insulate its own troops from ICC jurisdiction. The United States might consider taking similar steps to protect Israeli troops. However, with the growing tensions between the Obama administration and Israeli Prime Minister Netanyahu that were manifest in spring 2015, it seems possible that the United States would only take such steps if it became clear that substantive precedents were about to be set against Israel that could be used against U.S. troops in a more advanced (and thus more dangerous) stage of ICC proceedings than the current preliminary examination regarding U.S. troops in Afghanistan.

Professor Eugene Kontorovich has presented a detailed analysis of how ICC proceedings against Israel, which has not joined the ICC, could "set dangerous precedents" for U.S. efforts to prevent ICC jurisdiction over U.S. troops.[302] Kontorovich explained that "for the ICC to act against Israeli nationals, it would have to establish a number of novel precedents and rulings, which could then serve as precedents for proceedings against the U.S."[303]

In January 2015, a bipartisan group of U.S. senators declared: "If the ICC makes the egregious mistake of accepting the Palestinian Authority as a member, given that it is not a state, Congress will seek ways to protect Israeli citizens from politically abusive ICC actions."[304] The U.S. government may quietly use U.S. aid to the PA as leverage to deter the PA from issuing an article 14 referral or referrals (or to pressure the PA to discourage ICC action against Israel even following referral). The United States will likely balance such a leveraging of aid against its desire to avoid bringing down the PA. In addition, U.S. efforts to urge Israel to undertake a settlement freeze are likely to add the new argument that such a freeze would help protect Israel against the ICC.

However, should the United States decide to take vigorous action to directly protect Israeli personnel from ICC prosecution, it has several options. For example, one step the U.S government has taken to help protect U.S. officials from the reach of the ICC is to enter into so-called "Article 98" agreements with numerous foreign governments.[305] Article 98 of the Rome Statute states in relevant part as follows:

> Article 98 *Cooperation with respect to waiver of immunity and consent to surrender*:
> 2. The Court may not proceed with a request for surrender which would require the requested State to act inconsistently with its obligations under international

agreements pursuant to which the consent of a sending State is required to surrender a person of that State to the Court, unless the Court can first obtain the cooperation of the sending State for the giving of consent for the surrender.[306]

Countries that enter into Article 98 agreements with the United States agree not to surrender U.S. persons to the jurisdiction of the ICC.[307] The United States has concluded such agreements with at least one hundred countries.[308] Obviously, the United States has more leverage over foreign governments than does Israel. Indeed, Congress conditioned U.S. military aid to some countries on their agreeing to enter into such Article 98 agreements with the United States.[309]

With respect to close allies such as Israel, the United States could conceivably either help those allies enter into their own Article 98 agreements with key foreign countries or, possibly, bring those close allies within the umbrella of the United States' Article 98 agreements with key foreign countries. An inability to get access to the accused has already caused the ICC prosecutor to suspend investigation of the Sudanese President's involvement in atrocities in Darfur.[310] Knowing that it would face severe difficulties getting access to accused Israeli officials could deter the ICC from opening formal investigations into the lesser crimes of which they have been accused.

The American Service-Members' Protection Act, which conditioned U.S. military aid to some countries on their agreeing to enter into such Article 98 agreements with the United States, already includes language protective of close U.S. allies. Section 2008 of the Act specifies that "the President is authorized to use all means necessary and appropriate to bring about the release of any person described in subsection (b) who is being detained or imprisoned by, on behalf of, or at the request of the International Criminal Court."[311] The persons described in subsection (b) include "covered United States persons" and "covered allied persons."[312]

The term "covered allied persons" is defined by the Act to mean "military personnel, elected or appointed officials, and other persons employed by or working on behalf of the government of a NATO member country, a major non-NATO ally (including Australia, Egypt, Israel, Japan, Jordan, Argentina, the Republic of Korea, and New Zealand), or Taiwan, for so long as that government is not a party to the International Criminal Court and wishes its officials and other persons working on its behalf to be exempted from the jurisdiction of the International Criminal Court."[313] Thus, as Professor Kontorovich notes, "if a country were to fulfill a potential ICC arrest warrant for Israelis, the President would automatically be empowered to effect their release by any" means he saw fit.[314]

Consistent with this, it is important to note that although the United States is not a party to the ICC and thus not a donor to it, the top seven donor countries that provide over half of the ICC's annual budget are all close U.S. allies. All of these allies are either NATO partners or depend heavily on a U.S. defensive umbrella. At some point, the United States might decide that a particular pending ICC move against Israel threatens core U.S. national security interests, either because Israel is a close ally or because the ICC is about to set against Israel a precedent that is dangerous for U.S. efforts to prevent ICC jurisdiction over U.S. troops. While the top seven donor countries reportedly rebuffed Israeli Foreign Minister Lieberman's request for intervention with regard to the ICC's preliminary examination into the situation in Palestine, some or all of them might feel differently if the United States were to approach them on an issue that the United States asserted was a threat to a core U.S. national security interest.

V. PA USE OF INTERNATIONAL ORGANIZATION AND TREATY PROCESSES TO ATTACK ISRAEL

In addition to its campaign to gain recognition of Palestine as a full sovereign member of the international community, PA lawfare has also included efforts to use the internal processes of international organizations and treaties—including those to which it is not a party—to attack Israel and otherwise advance Palestinian claims against Israel. The previous section, on the PA and the ICC, discussed the relatively small number of levers that the post-accession PA will reportedly have to influence ICC processes.

This section will focus on two examples of the PA having already used the internal processes of an international organization or treaty to wage lawfare against Israel. The first example is the PA's use of its UNESCO membership. The second is its use of the International Court of Justice (where it is not a member). In addition, the first section of the next chapter discusses the somewhat analogous phenomenon of a Palestinian NGO's effort to use the Organization for Economic Cooperation and Development (where the PA is not a member) to attack Israel.

As noted by previous sections of this chapter, by spring 2015, the PA had joined over two dozen international treaties and seemed very likely to thereafter accede to additional international treaties (and possibly various international organizations). The PA's use of UNESCO and ICJ processes in its lawfare campaign against Israel may thus be replicated in years to come with regard to many additional international organizations and treaties.

A. PA Efforts to Use Its UNESCO Membership Against Israel

The Palestinians have used their UNESCO membership to advance claims of Palestinian self-determination.[315] They have also sought to use their membership to encourage international intervention into their conflict with Israel and to drive a wedge between Israel and its Christian allies in the West.

In June 2012, UNESCO, at the PA's request, voted to designate the Church of the Nativity as both a World Heritage Site and a World Heritage Site in Danger.[316]

The Church of the Nativity is located in Bethlehem, which is administered by the PA. The Church is identified by Christian tradition as the birthplace of Jesus.[317] According to UNESCO, "the list of World Heritage in Danger is designed to inform the international community of conditions for which a property was inscribed on the World Heritage List, and to encourage corrective action."[318] Inclusion on the list "alerts the international community . . . in the hope that it can join efforts to save these endangered sites."[319]

Prior to the vote, UNESCO's own advisory panel determined that although the Church did need renovation and conservation, it "did not appear to be in imminent danger."[320] The United States and Israel opposed the move to list the Church as endangered, viewing it as politically motivated.[321]

Since the PA emphasized the potential harm from Israel's "occupation," security barrier, and settlements in claiming that the Church was in danger,[322] the PA was able to portray UNESCO's decision to list the Church as a World Heritage Site in Danger as ratifying its allegations that these Israeli policies endangered one of Christianity's holiest sites, and that the PA was saving Jesus's birthplace from Israeli-caused harm. For example, Hanan Ashrawi, who led the Palestine Liberation Organization's Department of Culture and Information, said that the UNESCO decision "emphasizes that Israel [is] a major threat to the safety and the responsible preservation of that important segment of human civilization in Palestine."[323] Ashrawi made this statement despite the fact that UNESCO technical experts, prior to the vote, determined that the major risk to the Church, which is located in a Palestinian-administered area and maintained by Christian clerics, comes from water leaks attributable to lack of maintenance and repair of the roof and to pollution due to the number of vehicles and small industries within the Palestinian-controlled town of Bethlehem.[324]

B. PA Efforts to Use the International Court of Justice Against Israel

Although the Palestinian Authority was not a party to the International Court of Justice (ICJ) in 2004, the PA and its allies won a considerable lawfare victory against Israel in a July 2004 I.C.J. Advisory Opinion titled "Legal Consequences of the Construction of a Wall in the Occupied Palestinian Territory."[325] The *Wall* Advisory Opinion stemmed from an Israeli government decision in 2002 to construct a "security fence" separating Israel from much of the West Bank territory it had conquered from Jordan in 1967. The fence's route differs from the "Green Line"—the armistice line that served as Israel's border with the West Bank from 1949 to 1967,[326] placing some 8 to 10 percent of the West Bank on the Israeli side of the fence.[327]

The declared purpose of the fence was to "save Israeli lives by preventing Palestinian terrorists" from infiltrating Israel and killing Israeli civilians.[328]

According to the Israeli Ministry of Defense, in the three years prior to beginning the fence construction, "117 Palestinian terrorists" crossed into Israel and "in the act of blowing themselves up murdered 477 people."[329] Israel's ambassador to the UN, Daniel Gillerman, stated that "a security fence is one of the most effective non-violent methods of preventing the passage of terrorists and their armaments . . . to the heart of civilian areas."[330] Senior figures of both Palestinian Islamic Jihad and Hamas have reportedly admitted that the security fence hinders suicide bombing attacks against Israel.[331] The Military Advocate General of the Israel Defense Forces asserted that "the fence has proven to be an extremely effective means for combating terrorism," resulting in a "decline of approximately 90%" of the number of terrorist attacks within Israel by Palestinian terrorists from fenced-off areas.[332]

The Palestinian Authority, the Arab League, and others criticized the fence's construction as a violation of international law and described it as a de facto annexation having deleterious effects on the life of the Palestinian population.[333] In a December 2003 resolution, the General Assembly requested the ICJ to render an advisory opinion on the following question: "What are the legal consequences arising from the construction of the wall being built by Israel, the occupying Power, in the Occupied Palestinian Territory, including in and around East Jerusalem, as described in the report of the Secretary-General, considering the rules and principles of international law, including the Fourth Geneva Convention of 1949, and relevant Security Council and General Assembly resolutions?"[334] The General Assembly resolution requesting the opinion had been introduced on the PA's behalf by a group of Arab states.[335]

The General Assembly request took note of article 65 of the I.C.J. Statute, which provides that the ICJ "may give an advisory opinion on any legal question at the request of whatever body may be authorized by or in accordance with the Charter of the United Nations to make such a request."[336] Article 96 of the U.N. Charter provides that "[t]he General Assembly or the Security Council may request the International Court of Justice to give an advisory opinion on any legal question."[337]

Both Israel and the United States urged the ICJ to exercise its discretion and decline to issue an advisory opinion.[338] Neither addressed the merits of the question.[339]

The I.C.J. Advisory Opinion, issued on July 9, 2004, included the following statements:

- "The Court concludes that the Israeli settlements in the Occupied Palestinian Territory (including East Jerusalem) have been established in breach of international law."[340]
- The construction of the wall "constitutes breaches by Israel of various of its obligations under the applicable international humanitarian law and human rights instruments."[341]

- "The construction of the wall being built by Israel, the occupying Power, in the Occupied Palestinian territory, including in and around East Jerusalem, and its associated regime, are contrary to international law."[342]
- Israel "is under an obligation to cease forthwith the works of construction of the wall being built in the Occupied Palestinian Territory, including in and around East Jerusalem, to dismantle forthwith the structure therein situated, and to repeal or render ineffective forthwith all legislative and regulatory acts relating thereto."[343]
- Israel is "under an obligation to return" any immovable property "seized from any natural or legal person for purposes of construction of the wall" and "has an obligation to compensate, in accordance with the applicable rules of international law, all natural or legal persons having suffered any form of material damage as a result of the wall's construction."[344]

On most of the ICJ's findings, the only one of the fifteen judges who voted against was Judge Thomas Buergenthal, the U.S.-national judge. Buergenthal criticized the majority opinion on various grounds, including that it adopted the "legally dubious conclusion that the right of legitimate or inherent self-defence is not applicable in the present case."[345]

In the wake of the I.C.J. Opinion, which was advisory and thus nonbinding, the government of Israel continued to build the fence. On two occasions, the Supreme Court of Israel ordered the government to adjust the route of the fence so as to reduce its negative impact on Palestinians.[346] While some international law experts welcomed the I.C.J. Opinion,[347] others, including several leading U.S. experts, criticized it, including for too narrowly interpreting the scope of the right to self-defense.[348]

In May 2014, nearly ten years after the I.C.J. Advisory Opinion, the Prime Minister of Israel stated that "the security barrier has saved thousands of lives."[349] A few weeks later, at a U.N. meeting held to mark the exact date of the tenth anniversary of the I.C.J. Advisory Opinion, U.N. Secretary-General Ban Ki-moon called for "adhering to the Advisory Opinion," and called on "all Member States" to comply with their "obligation not to recognize the illegal situation resulting from the construction of the wall" and their "obligation to ensure compliance by Israel with international humanitarian law."[350] He also noted that he had established an office to register the damage caused by the wall and said the office had "collected 42,600 claims and over 1.1 million supporting documents."[351]

Ban's statement made no reference to, or acknowledgment of, claims that the security barrier had hindered terrorist attacks against civilians. For the Secretary-General, the I.C.J. Advisory Opinion had discredited the security fence as illegal and worthy only of dismantlement.

Thus, in this example, Palestinian lawfare achieved an I.C.J. advisory opinion declaring both that Israeli settlements are illegal and that Israel is "under an obligation" to "dismantle forthwith" a security barrier that Israel and terrorist groups had all described as an exceptionally effective means of protecting Israeli civilians against suicide bombing attacks. This particular deployment of Palestinian lawfare did not have the same effect as traditional kinetic warfare. In other words, it did not make the wall or the settlements go away. However, it did mobilize the U.N. Secretary General to use the prestige and leverage of his office to pressure Israel to dismantle the wall and the settlements.

In addition, and perhaps more impactfully, the I.C.J. Advisory Opinion served as the basis for at least one criminal prosecution in a national court (and perhaps more to come). As Chapter 6 will describe, the I.C.J. Opinion served as the basis for a three-year Dutch criminal investigation of a Dutch company for allegedly committing war crimes. The Dutch company's offense was that it had rented out construction equipment used by the Israeli government in construction of the wall and settlements for a total of sixteen days.

CHAPTER 6

Palestinian NGOs and Their Allies Wage Lawfare Against Israel

"Companies which are complicit must pay a heavy price."
— Omar Barghouti, *BDS movement co-founder*

While the Palestinian Authority (PA) is waging lawfare against Israel on the battleground of international organizations and treaties, Palestinian NGOs and their allies are waging lawfare against Israel principally on the battleground of national courts. This chapter describes and analyzes the lawfare being waged against Israel by Palestinian NGOs and their allies.

Section I of this chapter focuses on the growing and multifaceted Boycott, Divestment, and Sanctions (BDS) movement against Israel. Many BDS activities involve the deployment of laws and law-related forums as tools to achieve boycotts of, divestment from, and sanctions against entities or persons that either are Israeli or do business with Israel. This section begins by analyzing two examples of the use of multilateral or regional forums: the use of OECD guidelines to pressure a U.K. company to stop doing business with Israel and the creation of EU guidelines restricting grants to Israel. The section then analyzes the phenomenon of the BDS movement citing Israeli "war crimes" as legal justification in defense of BDS disruption and physical damage to Israeli-affiliated businesses. After that, the BDS section addresses the deployment of lawfare by Israel supporters seeking to combat BDS targeting of Israeli products.

The following two sections of this chapter address two types of offensive lawfare against Israel that do not seem to fit neatly within the boycott, divestment, and sanctions framework. Section II focuses on the attempt by Palestinian NGOs and their allies to use "universal jurisdiction" statutes to generate third-country (neither Israel nor Palestine) prosecutions of Israeli officials and former officials for alleged war crimes. Section III analyzes how various Palestinian NGOs and their allies have instigated legal action in third-country national courts against third-country companies for allegedly "aiding and abetting" Israeli "war crimes."

Section IV of this chapter discusses Israeli responses thus far to Palestinian NGOs and their allies. Section V analyzes how and why the Palestinians' sophisticated and extensive waging of lawfare against Israel contrasts strikingly with the poor records of compliance with international law and the rule of law of both the PA and Hamas. The chapter's final section, Section VI, analyzes lessons learned and assesses the future of lawfare by the PA and by Palestinian NGOs and their allies, as well as the future of Israeli responses to such lawfare.

I. THE BOYCOTT, DIVESTMENT, AND SANCTIONS MOVEMENT AGAINST ISRAEL

A. Overview of the BDS Movement

The BDS movement is an international campaign—launched in July 2005 by a coalition of Palestinian non-governmental organizations—that deploys legal, economic, and political pressure on Israel in an effort to achieve Israeli compliance with the following stated goals of the movement:

1. Ending its occupation and colonization of all Arab lands and dismantling the Wall;
2. Recognizing the fundamental rights of the Arab-Palestinian citizens of Israel to full equality; and
3. Respecting, protecting, and promoting the rights of Palestinian refugees to return to their homes and properties as stipulated in UN resolution 194.[1]

In its founding document, the BDS organizers declared that they were "inspired by the struggle of South Africans against apartheid."[2] They also called upon civil society "all over the world to impose broad boycotts and implement divestment initiatives against Israel similar to those applied to South Africa in the apartheid era" and to pressure governments "to impose embargoes and sanctions against Israel."[3]

The justifications for BDS activities of all types are typically presented in highly legalistic terms, which tend to characterize the BDS activities as lawful responses to allegedly illegal Israeli activities. For example, the BDS movement's founding document justifies its boycott, divestment, and sanctions campaign as an effort to respond to Israel's "persistent violations of international law."[4]

The BDS movement is at least nominally led by the Palestinian BDS National Committee (BNC), which asserts that it is "the Palestinian coordinating body for the BDS campaign worldwide."[5] However, both Palestinian and non-Palestinian activists can and do take action "in the name of BDS" without seeking explicit approval from the BNC. In light of the many different organizations involved in advancing the Palestinian agenda against Israel in many different forums, it can be very difficult to attribute a particular development to a particular organization or leader. Thus, it is difficult if not impossible to neatly divide BDS activities from other activities intended to advance the Palestinian agenda against Israel.

This book will use the term "BDS movement" to describe the somewhat amorphous numbers of non-governmental persons around the world who are seeking to advance the following "BDS activities" in furtherance of the Palestinian cause: (a) imposition of consumer boycotts and implementation of divestment initiatives against some or all persons that either are Israeli or do business with Israel and (b) pressuring their governments to impose embargos and sanctions against Israel.

Given the disparate and evolving nature of BDS activities, it is difficult to estimate their potential costs to the Israeli economy (which in 2014 had a gross domestic product of $295 billion).[6] There have nevertheless been at least two studies that have attempted to develop such an estimate. A 2015 study by the RAND Corporation, a U.S. think tank, estimated that a successful BDS campaign against Israel could cost the Israeli economy a cumulative $47 billion over a decade.[7] A leaked Israeli government report contained a lower estimate, that BDS of all types could cost Israel's economy $1.4 billion per year.[8]

Especially since BDS activists choose their targets for maximal impact, it is possible that some opportunities of which Israel is deprived by BDS may have strategic value for Israel that is greater than their nominal economic costs. In addition, BDS can also have important, even harder to quantify delegitimization, scientific and professional isolation, and other impacts on Israel and its citizens.

As mentioned previously, the book will address in separate sections of this chapter two types of litigation-oriented offensive lawfare against Israel that do not fit neatly within the BDS framework: the attempt to use "universal jurisdiction" statutes to generate third-country prosecutions of Israeli officials and former officials for alleged war crimes, and attempts to instigate legal action in third-country national courts against third-country companies for allegedly "aiding and abetting" Israeli "war crimes."

Some BDS activities involve the deployment of multilateral regional, national, or local legal mechanisms or forums (such as the OECD and EU guidelines described below) against some or all entities or persons that either are Israeli or do business with Israel. Other BDS activities simply seek to persuade third parties (including musicians and academics) to stop doing business with some or all Israeli entities and persons. Such persuasion campaigns are largely outside the scope of this book on lawfare as they do not seek to change or apply law.

With regard to such persuasion campaigns, it is important simply to note that their rhetoric—as with the BDS movement's rhetoric more broadly—is typically framed in highly legalistic terms. For example, some of the most publicized BDS activities have been campaigns to persuade musicians to boycott Israel.[9] The BDS activists often justify their calls for boycotting Israel by referring to allegedly illegal Israeli activities. For instance, in a March 3, 2015, statement urging jazz vocalist Gregory Porter to cancel a scheduled performance in Tel Aviv, the Palestinian Campaign for the Academic and Cultural Boycott of Israel (PACBI) called on Porter not to "commit musical genocide."[10] PACBI stated that "playing in a country with such a horrific record of human rights violations and persistent breaches of international law cannot but be seen as a whitewash of these crimes committed by Israel against the Palestinian people."[11]

Similarly, in seeking to encourage voluntary divestment from particular companies doing business with Israel, the BDS movement often accuses such companies of being complicit in Israeli violations of international law. For example, on July 25, 2014, the Palestinian BDS National Committee urged divestment from Hewlett Packard and a boycott of its laptops, printers, and ink on the grounds that "Hewlett Packard is involved in various Israeli violations of international law through providing the Israeli occupation forces with a vast range of IT services and infrastructure solutions."[12] The Palestinian BDS National Committee has also asserted that the "many international companies that are complicit in Israeli violations of international law . . . include HP, Caterpillar, Volvo, Hyundai, among many others."[13] The BDS movement focuses heavily on foreign companies doing business in Israel in part because there are relatively few Israeli products for overseas consumers to boycott—some 95 percent of Israeli exports are sold in business-to-business transactions rather than directly to individual consumers.[14]

In February 2014, the Birzeit University Institute of Law issued a publication, titled *Advocating for Palestinian Rights in Conformity with International Law*, that provided a detailed strategy for using international law claims and language to condemn Israel and its policies towards the Palestinians.[15] According to Anne Herzberg, one of Israel's leading opponents of the BDS movement and its NGO organizers, "the adoption of legal rhetoric is almost universal" in publications by NGOs that are advocating BDS or otherwise hostile to Israel.[16] "By couching political attacks in legal terms," said Herzberg, "NGOs seek to create a veneer of credibility and expertise, thereby increasing international pressure against Israel and further delegitimizing counter-terror measures."[17]

Interestingly, the Palestinian Authority seems to have a mixed relationship with the BDS movement. In December 2013, PA President Abbas said, "No, we do not support the boycott of Israel."[18] He added that "we ask everyone to boycott the products of the settlements . . . but we don't ask anyone to boycott Israel itself. We have relations with Israel, we have mutual recognition of Israel."[19] Several BDS movement leaders excoriated Abbas for this statement. For example, Omar Barghouti, one of the most prominent Palestinian BDS activists, stated: "Any Palestinian official who today explicitly speaks against boycotting Israel . . . only shows how aloof he is from his own people's aspirations for freedom, justice and equality, and how oblivious he is to our struggle for their inalienable rights."[20]

Then, in April 2014, Palestinian police arrested four Palestinian protestors for disrupting an Indian dance troupe's performance in Ramallah.[21] The protestors were BDS movement activists who said they were disrupting the performance—which was attended by senior PA officials[22]—because the dance troupe had previously performed in Tel Aviv.[23] In May 2014, the PA formally charged the protestors with "provoking riots and the breach of public tranquility."[24] According to Khaled Abu Toameh, a Palestinian reporter for the *Jerusalem Post*, the PA sees BDS activists as "trouble-makers" who "make the Palestinians appear as if they are not interested in peace and coexistence with Israel."[25]

However, in February 2015, the PLO movement announced a campaign to boycott, within the Palestinian market, products made by six major Israeli food companies.[26] The PA, led by President Abbas, reportedly asked the PLO movement, which he also heads, to lead the boycott campaign because the PA wanted to itself avoid violating past agreements with Israel.[27]

The campaign to boycott the six companies' products was described as a response to Israel's decision to halt the transfer of tax revenues to the PA.[28] Abdullah Kmail, the boycott leader, said the boycott would end if Israel resumed the tax revenue transfer.[29] Israel had halted the transfer in response to the Palestinian decision to join the International Criminal Court. The PLO's boycott of the six food companies was criticized by the BDS movement because it was narrow in scope and temporary.[30] As of late March 2015, the official policy of the PA was reportedly still to boycott products made in Israeli settlements in the West Bank but not to boycott products made within Israel's pre-1967 borders.[31]

B. Palestinian NGO Lawfare Uses Organization for Economic Cooperation and Development Against Israel

The Palestinian BDS National Committee (BNC) has, for several years, identified G4S, a British security company, as one of its top targets. G4S is a provider of security and screening equipment reportedly used in Israeli prisons, military checkpoints, and a police station in the West Bank.[32] The BNC stated that G4S "provides systems" for prisons in Israel "which hold Palestinian political prisoners" in violation of "Article 76 of the Fourth Geneva Convention."[33] The BNC said that G4S also "provides services and equipment to Israeli checkpoints in the West Bank that form part of the route of Israel's illegal Wall" and to "military bases and police stations and businesses in illegal Israeli settlements."[34]

The PA is not a member of the Organization for Economic Cooperation and Development (OECD), which Israel joined in 2010. Nevertheless, an NGO called Lawyers for Palestinian Human Rights impactfully used the OECD Guidelines for Multinational Enterprises to pressure G4S to stop doing business with Israel.

In 2011, the OECD, an international organization consisting of many of the world's wealthiest countries, expanded its Guidelines for Multinational

Enterprises to include compliance with human rights. The Guidelines state that multinational enterprises "should . . . [r]espect human rights, which means they should avoid infringing on the human rights of others and should address adverse human rights impacts with which they are involved."[35]

The Guidelines have long occupied a unique position as corporate social responsibility guidelines that are formally endorsed by a group of governments.[36] Adhering countries are required to set up National Contact Points (NCPs) that are tasked with "providing a mediation and conciliation platform for resolving issues that arise from the alleged non-observance of the *Guidelines*."[37]

The OECD states that "observance of the Guidelines by enterprises is voluntary and not legally enforceable."[38] It explains that "NCPs are not judicial bodies" and the grievances they handle "are not legal cases."[39] However, "the countries adhering to the *Guidelines* make a *binding* commitment to implement them."[40] Once an interested party has submitted to the NCP a complaint (a "specific instance" of "alleged non-observance of the *Guidelines*"), NCP consideration is composed of three phases.[41] The first phase is an "initial assessment" in order "to determine if the issues raised merit further examination."[42] If further examination is considered warranted, the NCP embarks on a second phase, in which it is to "facilitate access to consensual and non-adversarial means to resolve the issues."[43] In the third phase, the NCP issues a statement or report indicating whether or not an agreement has been reached and if a party has been unwilling to participate in the procedures.[44]

The addition of the human rights compliance provision was led by Harvard professor John G. Ruggie, the U.N. Secretary-General's Special Representative for Business and Human Rights. "What's unique about the OECD Guidelines," explained Ruggie, "is that they come with a complaints mechanism, so that people who feel that their human rights have been harmed can actually bring a complaint against a company."[45]

A few days after the U.K. government's National Contact Point for the OECD launched an investigation[46]—at the behest of Lawyers for Palestinian Human Rights—into G4S's activities in Israel and the West Bank, G4S announced at its annual meeting that it would not renew security and screening contracts to provide services to Israeli prisons and to checkpoints in the Palestinian territories.[47] The complaint was submitted on behalf of Lawyers for Palestinian Human Rights by Leigh Day, a British law firm. It was part of a multipronged campaign against GS4 involvement with Israeli security operations, which also included pressure on investors to divest from GS4.[48]

Tareq Shrourou, director of Lawyers for Palestinian Human Rights, described the complaint against G4S as a "considered utilization of the OECD evidence-based mediation, investigation, and accountability process."[49] He hailed the U.K. government's decision as setting an important precedent for successfully using the implementation mechanism for the OECD guidelines to combat Israeli actions against Palestinians.[50]

The U.K. government's National Contact Point for the OECD ultimately found largely in favor of G4S.[51] G4S was cleared of causing "adverse human rights impacts" in Israel.[52] The National Contact Point found no evidence of any "broad failure by G4S to respect the human rights of people on whose behalf the complaint is made."[53] It did not recommend that G4S cease doing business with the Israeli government.[54] But it did recommend that G4S consider "how it may be able to work with business partners in Israel to support action to address adverse impacts referred to in the complaint."[55]

Despite the largely favorable finding, the G4S precedent was quite worrisome for Israel. Israel's embassy in the U.K. stated: "Israel views with concern the fact that political groups with a clear anti-Israel agenda have tried to abuse a professional complaint mechanism in order to advance their political agenda."[56] As discussed above, G4S had felt pressured to announce, days after the investigation commenced, that it would not renew security and screening contracts to provide services to Israeli prisons and to checkpoints in the Palestinian territories. Even after that announcement, G4S had been subjected to a seventeen-month investigation.[57]

The OECD Guidelines for Multinational Enterprises are adhered to by all thirty-four OECD countries and by twelve non-OECD countries.[58] Eight of the top ten nations from which Israel imports are adherents to the Guidelines—the United States, Germany, Switzerland, Belgium, Italy, the Netherlands, the United Kingdom, and Turkey.[59] While observance of the Guidelines by business enterprises is "voluntary and not legally enforceable,"[60] the "countries adhering to the Guidelines make a binding commitment to implement them."[61] As discussed elsewhere in this book, with lawfare, the process itself can be sufficiently onerous to dissuade companies from doing business with Israel, even if they emerge from the process victorious. Should the U.K. government's National Contact Point for the OECD launch additional "investigations" of U.K. companies doing business with Israel, and especially if additional OECD member states follow suit, the OECD Guidelines for Multinational Enterprises could become a very impactful tool for lawfare against Israel.

C. The EU Guidelines Restricting Grants to Israel

The BDS movement's single largest success as of spring 2015 was likely the EU guidelines, issued in 2013, which restrict "the award of EU support to Israeli entities or to their activities in the territories occupied by Israel since June 1967."[62] The guidelines are binding on EU institutions. "Support" is defined to include "grants, prizes, or financial instruments."[63] At stake for Israel was hundreds of millions of euros in funding.[64] As a result, in the end, Israel largely backed down from its initial refusal to accept the conditions.[65]

Michael Deas, the Palestinian BDS National Committee's Coordinator in Europe, said: "These guidelines show that grassroots civil society pressure is forcing the European Union to acknowledge its legal responsibility to not recognize Israel's regime of occupation, colonization and apartheid against the Palestinian people and to end some aspects of its deep complicity in maintaining this illegal and criminal system."[66] Zaid Shuaibi, the Committee's spokesperson, welcomed the guidelines as helping implement "the 'S' in BDS."[67]

PLO executive committee member Hanan Ashrawi hailed the EU guidelines and threatened further lawfare targeting Israeli settlements.[68] Ashrawi stated that "the EU guidelines are just the beginning of holding Israel accountable (for settlement building)," and said that if settlement-building continued the PLO was poised to have "recourse to international judicial processes through international institutions."[69]

The EU stated that the "aim" of the restrictions was to "ensure the respect of EU positions and commitments in conformity with international law on the non-recognition by the EU of Israel's sovereignty over the territories occupied by Israel since June 1967."[70] EU foreign policy chief Catherine Ashton said that the guidelines were not meant to "prejudge the outcome of peace negotiations between Israel and the Palestinians."[71] However, Israeli government officials complained that the binding guidelines supported Palestinian demands that Israel relinquish the territories it conquered in 1967.[72]

Meanwhile, two U.S. law professors asserted that the EU guidelines were "singularly discriminatory against Israel," including because the EU did not impose similar limitations on its grants to "numerous countries that maintain settlements in what Europe considers occupied territory, such as Morocco, Turkey, and Russia."[73] Noting that "the EU has a grant program specifically aimed at funding Turkish 'settlers of Northern Cyprus,'" Professors Avi Bell and Eugene Kontorovich said that "if the EU is serious about the legal theory it is using to promote the Guidelines, it means that the EU violates international law with its grant programs in Northern Cyprus."[74] The professors predict that "future challengers to EU policy in Northern Cyprus, as well as other occupied territories like Western Sahara, will use EU arguments regarding the Guidelines to convince courts to rule that EU policy violates international law."[75]

D. BDS Activists Cite Israeli "War Crimes" as Legal Justification for Disrupting and Physically Damaging Israeli-Affiliated Businesses

Ahava, an Israeli company that creates beauty products from Dead Sea minerals, opened a shop in the Covent Garden area of London, England.[76] Some of the products were reportedly processed by an Israeli settlement in the West Bank.[77] Two protesters entered the shop on October 2, 2010, and refused to leave.[78] The protesters were arrested for "aggravated trespass" in violation of section 68 of the UK's Criminal Justice and Public Order Act of 1994.[79] The protestors argued that they should be acquitted on the grounds that Ahava was aiding and abetting an Israeli war crime and was otherwise engaged in unlawful activities.[80]

According to the U.K. Supreme Court, the "aggravated trespass" offense "criminalises the conduct of a person A who (i) trespasses on land, (ii) where there is a person or persons B lawfully on the land *who is engaged in or about to engage in a lawful activity*, (iii) and A does an act on the land, (iv) intended by A to intimidate all or some Bs from engaging in that activity, or to obstruct or disrupt that activity."[81] The defendants contested the charge that they had engaged in "aggravated trespass," arguing that Ahava's activities were not "lawful" since they involved the commission of one or more of the following four criminal offenses:

(1) The defendants argued that Ahava was guilty of the alleged war crime of "aiding and abetting the transfer by Israeli authorities of Israeli citizens" to the occupied territories.
(2) The defendants argued that since the items sold in the shop were the products of the alleged war crime, Ahava was "guilty of the offence of using or possessing criminal property."
(3) The defendants argued that the products had been imported into the U.K. under an EC-Israel agreement that conferred tax advantages, but since the products had originated in the occupied territories, not Israel, Ahava was guilty of the offense of cheating the tax collector.
(4) The defendants argued that although the products were labeled as made in "Dead Sea, Israel" they were in fact made in the occupied territories, and thus Ahava was guilty of violating laws requiring accurate labels.[82]

The defendants' conviction in the U.K. magistrates court was upheld by the divisional court and then ended up before the U.K. Supreme Court, the U.K.'s final court of appeal.[83] In February 2014, five U.K. Supreme Court judges unanimously upheld the conviction for trespass.[84] The court held that an activity is "unlawful" for purposes of the aggravated trespass statute only if "the criminal offence is integral to the core activity carried on" and not "when there is some incidental or collateral offence, which is remote from the activity."[85]

Applying that conclusion to the facts of the case, the U.K. Supreme Court found that "of the postulated offences all were either not demonstrated to have been committed by the occupants of the shop at the time of the defendants' trespass or were at most collateral to the core activity of selling rather than integral to that activity."[86] "The occupants of the shop were, accordingly, engaged in the lawful activity of retail selling at the time," said the court, and the defendants' claims that Ahava was engaged in unlawful activity "provided no defence to the defendants."[87]

Although the protesters lost in court, they appear to have achieved the objective of hindering Ahava sales in the U.K. Ahava had closed the targeted shop in September 2011, "after four years of protests and counter-protests outside its premises."[88] The U.K. Supreme Court victory, two and a half years after the closure, must have served as cold comfort.

The U.K. Supreme Court's Ahava decision had been preceded by at least three separate U.K. lower court decisions in which defendants who had relied on similar defenses were acquitted. In each of those lower court decisions, the targeted facility's alleged contribution to Israeli "war crimes" had been treated as justifying protesters breaking into and damaging the facility.

For example, in 2010, a U.K. jury acquitted several activists who admitted breaking into and damaging an EDO MBM Technology company weapons factory because they believed it manufactured F-16 parts for Israel.[89] The activists had mounted a "lawful excuse" defense, arguing that they had committed the break-in and £89,000 worth of damage in order to prevent the more serious "war crimes being committed by Israel against the Palestinians."[90] The protesters' defense team used the opportunity to present testimony by an academic who presented a litany of alleged war crimes by Israel "since its creation in 1948."[91] The EDO managing director was reportedly cross-examined "for over five days."[92]

During his summing up of the EDO case, Judge George Bathurst-Norman expressed strong sympathy for the defendants, asserted that the academic's testimony had provided evidence of "war crimes being committed by Israel in Gaza," compared scenes in Gaza to the destruction caused by the Nazis, and suggested that one of the defendants be awarded a medal for his actions.[93] Judge Bathurst-Norman instructed the jury that under U.K. law, "a person has a lawful excuse if he destroys or damages property in order to protect property belonging to another and at the time of the act alleged he honestly believed that the property was in immediate need of protection and that the means of protection which he adopted were reasonable, having regard to all the circumstances."[94]

Applying this law to the specific facts of the EDO case, Judge Bathurst-Norman further instructed the jury that the defendants would have had a "lawful excuse" for breaking into and damaging the factory if one of their purposes in doing so was "to prevent the destruction by the Israeli Air Force of property in Gaza."[95]

After the trial, the U.K. Office for Judicial Complaints investigated Judge Bathurst-Norman's handling of the proceedings and formally reprimanded him on the grounds that a number of his "observations" during the trial and summing up "did not arise directly from the evidence at trial and could be seen as an expression of the judge's personal views on a political question."[96] However, in spite of this, the defendants' acquittal was not overturned.

In Northern Ireland, two separate groups of protestors were on similar grounds acquitted of damaging a Raytheon facility in Londonderry. In 2008, the first group of protestors said that they had forced their way into the facility and damaged it in 2006 in order to "protect the lives and property" of people in Lebanon from being attacked by Israeli forces who bought weapons from Raytheon.[97] They were acquitted.[98] In 2010, the second group of protesters stated that they had forced their way into the facility and damaged it in 2009 in order to "prevent crime, a crime against humanity which continues to be inflicted on the people of Gaza by the Israeli defence forces."[99] They were also acquitted.[100]

In contrast with the EDO case, this author could find no record of a judicial reprimand in either Raytheon case. Raytheon's Londonderry facility had previously been occupied by demonstrators protesting the use of Raytheon weapons by the United States and its allies in Iraq.[101] There is no record of a prosecution in that instance. Indeed, the Londonderry City Council in 2009 asked the City Solicitor to inform Raytheon of the Council's opposition to any manufacture of military equipment in the city, "putting this in the context of existing Council policies opposing rendition flights, the conflict in Palestine and the arms trade generally."[102]

Raytheon eventually decided to close its Londonderry facility.[103] Press coverage of the closure decision referenced the City Council's action, the protests, and also a document from Invest Northern Ireland (part of Northern Ireland's Department of Enterprise, Trade, and Investment) that reported frustration among Raytheon's senior management at the acquittals of the protestors.[104]

The U.K. Supreme Court's decision in the Ahava case made it harder for BDS activists to cite Israeli "war crimes" as legal justification for at least some types of physical interference with Israeli-affiliated businesses in the United Kingdom. However, the scope of the decision's impact may be tested. An analyst sympathetic to the BDS movement asserted that the Ahava case ruling "only actually adjudicated on the application of the defence in [an] aggravated trespass case" and "does not rule out the use of similar defences in criminal damage cases like those" of the Raytheon and EDO defendants "who were found not guilty after breaking into arms factories linked to the supply of arms to Israel and destroyed machinery and computers in order to stop war crimes."[105]

Whatever the legal disposition of any future efforts by BDS activists in the U.K. to cite Israeli "war crimes" as justification for physically interfering with Israeli-affiliated businesses, the phenomenon may not be limited to the U.K. Depending on the content of trespassing and similar laws in other countries, the phenomenon could surface elsewhere.

E. Pro-Israel Activists Use Lawfare Against BDS Targeting of Israeli Products

Pro-Israel activists and their allies have themselves, on occasion, used law as a weapon to counter BDS efforts to halt commerce and other interchange between Israel and the rest of the world. The most important example of this phenomenon is the series of strikingly effective lawfare actions against BDS in France. Also important in this regard is the potential deployment of U.S. law to counter BDS in a manner similar to how U.S. law was deployed to counter the Arab League boycott of Israel.

1. Lawfare Against BDS in France

In at least one arena—France—lawfare has been remarkably effective against BDS activities. For example, several BDS activists have been convicted in response to complaints filed by pro-Israel NGOs pursuant to France's so-called Lellouche law. The Lellouche law, article 132-76 of the French Penal Code, specifies as follows:

> Where provided for by law, the penalties for a felony or misdemeanour are increased when the offense is committed because of the victim's actual or supposed member-ship or non-membership of a given ethnic group, nation, race or religion. The aggravating circumstances defined in the first paragraph are established when the offence is preceded, accompanied or followed by written or spoken words, images, objects or actions of whatever nature which damage the honour or the reputation of the victim, or a group of persons to which the victim belongs, on account of their actual or supposed membership or non-membership of a given ethnic group, nation, race or religion.[106]

Those felonies or misdemeanors to which increased penalties apply under French law in cases of hate crimes reportedly include murder, acts of violence, extortion, threats, theft, "obstructing the normal exercise of any given economic activity," and the destruction, defacement, or damage of property belonging to other persons.[107] French law also prohibits the publication of material that is defamatory or insulting, or that incites discrimination, hatred, or violence against a person or a group of persons on account of place of origin, ethnicity or lack thereof, nationality, race, or specific religion.[108]

The law was named for Pierre Lellouche, the French parliamentarian (and Harvard-trained law professor) who introduced it in 2003.[109] Under the French legal system, the responsibility to present evidence that a felony or misdemeanor was motivated by hate (and thus subject to the Lellouche law) does not rest with the government, but rather depends on the filing of a complaint.[110] Complaints can be filed either by the individual victim or by various non-governmental organizations.[111]

Various French organizations, including the National Bureau of Vigilance Against Anti-Semitism, have lodged complaints against the BDS movement in courts all over France. As of early 2014, the Lellouche law had reportedly been used in at least ten trials against BDS activists, which had resulted in only one acquittal.[112] For example, in February 2010, a court in Bordeaux convicted

Saquina Arnaud-Khimoun for labeling Israeli products with a sticker stating "Boycott Apartheid Israel."[113] The court ruled that she had "hindered the normal exercise of economic activities by making a distinction on the basis of nationality."[114] The ruling was eventually upheld by France's highest court, the Cour de Cassation.[115]

The Lellouche law has been described as "among the world's most potent tools to fight the growing Boycott, Divestment, and Sanctions movement" and as having "catapulted France to the forefront of efforts to counter the movement through legal means."[116] Pascal Markowicz, the head of the BDS legal task force of the umbrella group of French Jewish communities, claimed that the law appears to have resulted in France seeing less divestment from Israel than has occurred in other European countries, such as the Netherlands.[117]

Prior to the Lellouche law's entry into force, during a 2002 session of his town's council, Jean-Claude Willem, mayor of the French town of Seclin, had called for a boycott of Israeli products.[118] Willem was convicted of provoking discrimination.[119] His conviction was also upheld by France's highest court.[120] The European Court of Human Rights (ECHR) held in 2009 that Willem's conviction had not violated the freedom of expression article (article 10) of the European Convention on Human Rights.[121] The ECHR determined that Mr. Willem "had not been convicted for his political opinions but for inciting the commission of a discriminatory, and therefore punishable, act."[122]

In another case, also in France, the French distributor of SodaStream, an Israeli company, used a somewhat different legal tool—a civil lawsuit—to successfully combat boycott calls by BDS activists.[123] The French Palestine Solidarity Association (FPSA) had targeted SodaStream by lobbying French retailers to remove SodaStream products from their shelves and encouraging consumer boycotts of the product.[124] SodaStream's French distributor filed a civil lawsuit against the FPSA in 2010 for activities that included "falsely claiming that the products are 'illegally sold' as a result of being manufactured in 'occupied territories' while bearing the 'Made in Israel' label" and advising French stores that "selling SodaStream products constitutes a fraud, and that store managers could be prosecuted for doing so."[125]

In January 2014, a French court ruled that the FPSA could not use the words "illegal" or "fraudulent" to describe the "Made in Israel" labeling of SodaStream products manufactured in the West Bank.[126] The court held that the FPSA's campaign violated French law, including because it falsely claimed that SodaStream was guilty of fraud.[127] The FPSA was ordered to pay SodaStream's distributor 4,000 euros in compensatory damages and 2,500 euros to cover the distributor's legal fees.[128] The FPSA was also ordered to remove from its website all descriptions of SodaStream products as "illegal," "illicit," or "fraudulent."[129]

In the meantime, SodaStream had become the target of a global boycott campaign.[130] Notwithstanding the courtroom victory in France, SodaStream announced that it would move its main factory from a West Bank settlement to a location within Israel's pre-1967 borders.[131] Rafeef Ziadah, a spokeswoman for the BDS movement, said that the closure shows that the movement "is increasingly capable of holding corporate criminals to account for their participation in Israeli apartheid and colonialism."[132] SodaStream CEO Daniel Birnbaum had previously stated that the West Bank factory, which employed 500 Palestinians, was a successful example of Arab-Jewish coexistence.[133] When Birnbaum announced that the factory would be moving to Lehavim, a town near Beersheba in southern Israel, the Palestinian BDS National Committee announced that they would continue to boycott SodaStream on the grounds that its new location, in an existing industrial park, abets dispossession of Bedouin land in Israel.[134]

2. Potential Deployment of U.S. Law to Counter BDS

The BDS movement has manifested in the United States as primarily an effort to persuade academics and artists to boycott Israel. The freedom of speech protections contained in the First Amendment to the U.S. Constitution would undoubtedly complicate or preclude any efforts to enact U.S. federal or state legislation barring such persuasion campaigns.

However, to the extent that some BDS activities affect interstate or foreign commerce, they may be vulnerable to prohibitory U.S. legislation. Many of the BDS movement's calls to boycott Israel are reminiscent of those of the Arab League boycott, compliance with which is deterred by two existing U.S. laws. The two U.S. laws targeting the Arab League boycott may, either as currently written or in amended form, be used to counter the BDS movement. In 2015, the U.S. Congress passed, and the President signed into law, legislation specifically designed to address the BDS movement's calls to boycott Israel. While the new law seemed likely to be relatively ineffectual, it may be a sign of more to come.

a. U.S. Laws Countering the Arab League Boycott of Israel

The Arab League is a regional organization of twenty-two Arab countries (including Palestine, which the League treats as independent). The organization's charter specifies that each member state has one vote, that decisions taken by a unanimous vote shall be binding on all member states, and that decisions reached by a majority vote "shall bind only those that accept them."[135]

The Arab League began in 1945 to boycott Zionist goods and services in the British-controlled territory of Palestine.[136] With Israel's independence in 1948, the League established a boycott targeting the State of Israel and its citizens.[137] The boycott has long included the following tiers:

(a) a primary boycott prohibits doing business with the Israeli government or citizens
(b) a secondary boycott prohibits doing business with any entity in the world that does business with Israel—a blacklist of such entities is maintained by the League's Central Boycott Office
(c) a tertiary boycott prohibits doing business with an entity that itself does business with companies blacklisted by the Arab League[138]

Implementation of the boycott has waned in recent years,[139] with the U.S. government playing a leading role in the boycott's erosion.[140] Two U.S. laws have weakened the boycott by deterring U.S. persons from cooperating with it: Section 8 of the Export Administration Act (as reflected in the Export Administration Regulations) and the Ribicoff Amendment to the 1976 Tax Reform Act. The former is implemented by the Commerce Department and the latter by the Treasury Department.

The Commerce Department antiboycott provisions principally prohibit U.S. persons from engaging in the following conduct with the intent to comply with, further, or support an unsanctioned foreign boycott:

• refusing to do business with or in a boycotted country, or with a national of a boycotted country[141]
• refusing to employ or otherwise discriminating against a U.S. person on the basis of race, religion, sex, or national origin[142]
• furnishing information about the race, religion, sex, or national origin of any U.S. person or any owner, officer, director, or employee of any corporation that is a U.S. person[143]
• furnishing information concerning any person's past, present, or proposed business relationships with or in a boycotted country or with a business or national of that country[144]
• furnishing information about any person's membership in, contributions to, or other involvement with the activities of any charitable or fraternal organization that supports a boycotted country[145]
• paying, honoring, confirming, or otherwise implementing a letter of credit that contains any prohibited boycott condition or requirement[146]

Civil penalties per violation of the Commerce Department antiboycott provisions are up to $250,000 or twice the value of the transaction, whichever is greater.[147] Criminal penalties are a maximum of $1 million per violation or twenty years in prison.[148]

The Treasury Department's antiboycott provisions do not carry criminal or civil penalties. Instead, they deny tax benefits for certain types of boycott-related activities.[149]

It is important to note that while these two antiboycott laws were designed to combat the Arab League boycott of Israel, they "apply," according to the U.S. Commerce Department, "to all boycotts imposed by foreign countries that are unsanctioned by the United States."[150] The Commerce Department website explains that the antiboycott laws "have the effect of preventing U.S. firms from being used to implement foreign policies of other nations which run counter to U.S. policy," including other nations' policies that encourage, and in some cases require, "U.S. firms to participate in foreign boycotts that the United States does not sanction."[151]

The Commerce Department antiboycott law, which is the more impactful of the two provisions, has an unusual status. This status complicates implementation and interpretation of the law and significantly affects the process by which the law would be amended. The Commerce Department antiboycott law was originally passed by Congress and enacted as part of § 8 of the Export Administration Act (EAA). The law is reflected in the Export Administration Regulations (EAR) that implement the EAA. The EAA has expired and is no longer U.S. law. However, the EAR is kept in force by an executive order issued by the President pursuant to the International Emergency Economic Powers Act (IEEPA).[152]

The principal chapeau of EAA § 8 specifies that

> the President shall issue regulations prohibiting any United States person, with respect to his activities in the interstate or foreign commerce of the United States, from taking or knowingly agreeing to take any of the following actions with intent to comply with, further, or support any boycott *fostered or imposed by a foreign country* against a country which is friendly to the United States and which is not itself the object of any form of boycott pursuant to United States law or regulation.[153]

However, as mentioned previously, the EAA has expired. The IEEPA statute, under which the EAR is being kept in force, has broad authorities in no way limited by the "fostered or imposed by a foreign country" limitation. It is thus at least arguable that the EAR need not be limited by the parameters of the EAA but only by the broader parameters of IEEPA.

The EAR prohibitions each specify that they apply "only with respect to a United States person's activities in the interstate or foreign commerce of the United States and only when such activities are undertaken to comply with, further, or support an unsanctioned foreign boycott."[154] The EAR does not explicitly define "unsanctioned foreign boycott." However, several of the EAR prohibitions reference a "boycotting country," for example, in prohibiting refusals to do business "when such refusal is pursuant to an agreement with the boycotting country, or a requirement of the boycotting country, or a request from or on behalf of the boycotting country."[155]

The question has arisen as to the applicability of the Commerce Department's antiboycott law to boycott activities promoted by the BDS movement. A definitive assessment of this complex issue is beyond the scope of this book. However, it is worth highlighting the key arguments on either side. Opponents of using the Commerce Department's antiboycott law to counter boycott activities promoted by the BDS movement will raise the following objections:

• The antiboycott law is framed in terms of refusing to do *any* business with or in a boycotted country or with a national of such a country. The BDS movement typically claims to be targeting businesses and persons not because they are Israeli but because they are involved with West Bank settlements.

• The antiboycott law is, to at least some degree, framed in terms of prohibiting U.S. persons from complying with, furthering, or supporting any boycott "fostered or imposed by a foreign country." For example, according to the National Lawyers Guild, "BDS campaigns that are conceived independently, rather than as support for or in response to pressure by a hostile foreign government or in concert with the Arab League's boycott of Israel, do not violate the anti-boycott laws."[156] "A boycott against the State of Israel or an Israeli company or concern," says the NLG, "would be prohibited under the EAA only if the boycott is specifically intended to support or comply with boycotts initiated by foreign countries."[157]

Advocates of using the Commerce Department's antiboycott law to counter boycott activities promoted by the BDS movement will presumably make one or more of the following assertions:

• BDS boycotts are an extension of the Arab League boycott, which is clearly covered by the antiboycott law.[158] The argument is that although the BDS boycotts may not be "imposed" by the members of the Arab League, they are "fostered" by them.[159]

• BDS boycotts are on behalf of the "boycotting country" of Palestine. This would require arguing that Palestine falls within the meaning of "country," even if it is not recognized by the United States as an independent state. Proponents of this argument note that the Commerce Department antiboycott law does not define the term "foreign country."[160]

• Since the EAR, and not the EAA, is being kept in force pursuant to IEEPA, the scope of the EAR need not be limited by the "fostered-or-imposed-by-a-foreign-country" language of the EAA. BDS boycotts can therefore fall within the meaning of "unsanctioned foreign boycott," even in the absence of a "boycotting country."

• Since the EAR is kept in force via executive order, it should be possible to amend it either with new congressional legislation or executive action to clarify that an "unsanctioned foreign boycott" need not be the product of a "boycotting country."

b. U.S. Legislation Addressing BDS Activities

By summer 2015, both the U.S federal government and at least one state (Illinois) had enacted legislation specifically designed to combat the BDS movement's calls to boycott Israel. On June 29, 2015, President Obama signed into law Public Law 114-26,[161] trade promotion authority legislation, which included an anti-BDS provision inspired by two bills: S. 619 (The United States-Israel Trade Enhancement Act of 2015[162]) and H.R. 825 (The U.S.-Israel Trade & Commercial Enhancement Act[163]).

Section 102(b)(20) of Public Law 114-26 asserts, using hortatory "Sense of the Senate"-type language, various specific "principal negotiating objectives of the United States" with respect to "an agreement that is proposed to be entered into with the Transatlantic Trade and Investment Partnership countries."[164] This is a reference to a trade and investment agreement that was being negotiated between the United States and the European Union.[165] The provision asserts that the United States' "principal negotiating objectives" with regard to the agreement with the EU include the following:

(i) To discourage actions by potential trading partners that directly or indirectly prejudice or otherwise discourage commercial activity solely between the United States and Israel.

(ii) To discourage politically motivated actions to boycott, divest from, or sanction Israel and to seek the elimination of politically motivated nontariff barriers on Israeli goods, services, or other commerce imposed on the State of Israel.

(iii) To seek the elimination of state-sponsored unsanctioned foreign boycotts against Israel or compliance with the Arab League Boycott of Israel by prospective trading partners.[166]

The provision defines the term "actions to boycott, divest from, or sanction Israel" to mean "actions by states, non-member states of the United Nations, international organizations, or affiliated agencies of international organizations that are politically motivated and are intended to penalize or otherwise limit commercial relations specifically with Israel or persons doing business in Israel or in Israeli-controlled territories."[167]

The day after the bill was signed into law, a State Department spokesman issued a statement asserting that "by conflating Israel and 'Israeli-controlled territories,' [this] provision of the Trade Promotion Authority legislation runs counter to longstanding U.S. policy towards the occupied territories, including with regard to settlement activity."[168] In light of this statement, it was far from clear that the executive branch's negotiators with the European Union would heed the provision's nonbinding assertion that its implementation be made one of their principal negotiating objectives.

It is worth considering Section 102(b)(20) of Public Law 114-26 in the context of other legislation, including the two bills that inspired it and also the existing Commerce Department antiboycott law. S. 619, The United States-Israel Trade Enhancement Act of 2015, contained hortatory "Sense of the Senate"-type language similar to what ended up as Section 102(b)(20) of Public Law 114-26.[169]

In contrast, H.R. 825, The U.S.-Israel Trade & Commercial Enhancement Act, had contained several other, more substantive provisions that did not make it into the final law. First, the bill would have required the President to submit to Congress an annual "report on politically motivated acts of boycott, divestment from, and sanctions against Israel."[170] The report was to include "description of specific steps being taken by the United States" to encourage foreign countries and international organizations to "cease creating" and to "dismantle" "barriers to trade" against "United States persons operating or doing business in Israel, with Israeli entities, or in Israeli-controlled territories."[171]

Second, the bill would have amended § 13 of the Securities Exchange Act of 1934 to require foreign issuers to disclose, inter alia, whether and, if so, how "the issuer has discriminated against doing business with Israel in the last calendar year."[172] Third, the bill would have provided that no court in the United States "may recognize or enforce any judgment which is entered by a foreign court against a United States person carrying out business operations" that is based on a "determination by the foreign court that the location in Israel, or in any territory controlled by Israel, of the facilities at which the business operations are carried out is sufficient to constitute a violation of law."[173]

In urging support for H.R. 825, the American Israel Public Affairs Committee (AIPAC) said that the bill "takes on perhaps the most dangerous element of the international BDS campaign—deliberate efforts by European nations and international institutions to target Israel economically for political reasons."[174] AIPAC stated that the bill "seeks to leverage the United States' economic weight to counter this element of BDS."[175]

Section 102(b)(20) of Public Law 114-26, S. 619, and even H.R. 825 were far weaker than the existing Commerce Department antiboycott law. Even if H.R. 825 had been enacted into law, it was hard to imagine it making more than a marginal contribution to combatting BDS lawfare.

Given the U.S. federal government's past history of using lawfare, in the form of the antiboycott laws, to combat the Arab League's attempted economic isolation of Israel, it seems likely that in the coming years, the antiboycott laws will be either supplemented with new statutes or amended to address the growing attempted isolation of Israel by the BDS movement. Section 102(b)(20) of Public Law 114-26 is almost certainly not the last word on this issue from the U.S. federal government.

The Illinois anti-BDS law, signed by Governor Bruce Rauner in July 2015, was more substantive. It required that Illinois' state-funded retirement systems divest from "companies that boycott Israel."[176]

The Illinois law was particularly impactful because of its relatively broad definitions of "boycott Israel" and "company." "Boycott Israel" was defined to include "engaging in actions that are politically motivated and are intended to penalize, inflict economic harm on, or otherwise limit commercial relations with the State of Israel or companies based in the State of Israel or in territories controlled by the State of Israel."[177] "Company" was defined to include "any sole proprietorship, organization, association, corporation, partnership, joint venture, limited partnership, limited liability partnership, limited liability company, or other entity or business association . . . that exist for the purpose of making profit."[178]

The Illinois law's impact was reduced somewhat by its provision stating that "it is not the intent of the General Assembly . . . to cause divestiture from any company based in the United States of America."[179] Its effect was also reduced, to an unclear degree, by an ambiguous de minimis provision stating that "a retirement system may cease divesting from . . . companies . . . if clear and convincing evidence shows that the value of investments in such companies becomes equal to or less than 0.5% of the market value of all assets under management by the retirement system" (at least on its face, the bill did not seem to make clear whether the 0.5 percent was meant to be cumulative of all divestment target companies or was applicable to each separate divestment target company).[180]

The Illinois legislation would at least arguably make the following entities subject to divestment (assuming the de minimis threshold was met):

- The several Dutch supermarket chains that reportedly removed from their shelves all products manufactured in Israeli settlements.[181]
- Danske Bank, Denmark's largest bank, which reportedly stopped investing in three Israeli companies due to their involvement in settlement construction.[182]
- The scores of foreign rock bands that have, for political reasons, announced that they would boycott Israel.[183]

As discussed elsewhere in this chapter, European governments have for several years been noting[184] or creating[185] legal and economic risks for European companies doing business with Israel companies, and especially Israeli companies with a West Bank presence. In the wake of the Illinois law, "the EU will—if it is honest—have to warn businesses of the legal and economic risks of consciously refusing to do business with such Israeli companies," according to Eugene Kontorovich.[186]

If the Illinois law is replicated in other U.S. states, as seems likely, there could be an even greater deterrent effect on foreign companies boycotting Israel. Illinois state pension funds controlled about $95 billion in assets as of 2013.[187] All U.S. state pension funds collectively controlled about $2.7 trillion in total investments in 2013.[188] As noted in Chapter 2, at least twenty-four states (including most of the largest ones) have in recent years adopted policies of divestment from foreign companies with substantial investments in Iran's energy sector.[189]

It would not be surprising to soon see many of the same states adopt legislation similar to the Illinois law.

It would also not be surprising to see U.S. activists opposed to European divestment from Israeli-affiliated companies form a legislative alliance with the several major U.S. companies which have themselves, for reasons unconnected to Israel, been subjected to divestment by major European asset managers. As described in Chapter 3, this includes major U.S. employers such as Lockheed Martin, Northrup Grumman, and General Dynamics that have been subjected to divestment in Europe because of their involvement in manufacturing nuclear and other disfavored weapons. It also includes the United States' single largest private employer—Wal-Mart Stores, which employs some 1.3 million American workers.[190]

The Norwegian government pension fund that, as described in Chapter 3 is considered the divestment "gold standard" which other asset managers tend to follow, states that it has divested from Wal-Mart because investing in the American retail chain "constitute[s] an unacceptable risk of the Fund contributing to . . . serious or systematic human rights violations."[191] Between Walmart, the various U.S. manufacturers of disfavored weapons, and a few other categories, the Norwegian government pension fund's divestment list includes over a dozen major U.S. companies. The Norwegian government pension fund's divestment list also includes a total of three Israeli companies. The three are construction companies—Africa Israel Investments, Danya Cebus, and Shikun & Binui—from which the pension fund states that it has divested "due to an unacceptable risk of the companies, through their construction activity in East Jerusalem, contributing to serious violations of the rights of individuals in situations of war or conflict."[192] It would not be surprising to see the Norwegian government pension fund and similarly aggressive asset managers, including especially those controlled by allied governments, be the subject of legislative pushback from the U.S. Congress.

II. USE BY PALESTINIAN NGOS AND THEIR ALLIES OF THIRD-COUNTRY "UNIVERSAL JURISDICTION" STATUTES AGAINST ISRAELI OFFICIALS AND FORMER OFFICIALS

Hamas, Hezbollah, and especially several Palestinian NGOs have all openly worked to have senior Israeli leaders arrested when they visit European countries. They have done so principally by deploying the concept of "universal jurisdiction." "Universal jurisdiction" lawsuits have also been brought against various sitting and former U.S. officials, as described in Chapter 1 of this book.

Traditionally, a nation's courts exercise jurisdiction over crimes to which the nation has a particular nexus, for example, crimes committed in its territory or "committed abroad by its nationals, or against its nationals, or against its national interests."[193] "Universal jurisdiction" is based in the notion that "certain crimes are so harmful to international interests that states are entitled—and even obliged—to bring proceedings against the perpetrator," even if there is no traditional nexus and the crime is totally foreign—in other words "regardless of the location of the crime or the nationality of the perpetrator or the victim."[194]

According to Anne Herzberg, one of Israel's leading advocates opposing NGO lawfare against Israel, "universal jurisdiction" lawsuits against Israeli officials and former officials "regularly ignore Palestinian responsibility and culpability under international law, and seek judicial declarations that Israel's defensive policies are illegal and amount to 'war crimes.'"[195] These suits, says Herzberg, "attempt to minimize or erase the context of terror and terrorists' use of human shields, base themselves primarily on unreliable eyewitness testimony, and seek to impose distorted interpretations of the laws of armed conflict, in particular, 'proportionality' and 'distinction.'"[196]

In 2009, Diya al-Din Madhoun, a Hamas leader, described the group's "policy," which he was coordinating, of seeking to have senior Israeli leaders arrested when they visit European countries.[197] The *Times of London* reported that "Hamas says that it initiated" a British arrest warrant issued against Tzipi Livni, who served as Foreign Minister of Israel during the 2008 war in Gaza.[198] According to the *Times*, in the United Kingdom, "the campaign by Hamas" took "advantage of an aspect of law in England and Wales that allows anyone to apply for an arrest warrant for alleged war crimes without the need for a prosecuting lawyer."[199] As a result of the warrant, Livni, who had been scheduled to address a meeting in London in December 2009, was forced to cancel her visit.[200]

In 2010, Hezbollah Secretary-General Hassan Nasrallah described his organization's lawfare against Israel as follows: "We have to sue the Israeli leaders anywhere possible in the world. Suing Israel for its crimes will render Israeli leaders beleaguered and perplexed."[201]

The leading Palestinian NGO promoting universal jurisdiction prosecutions of Israeli officials is the Palestinian Centre for Human Rights (PCHR), which describes this work in documents including a 184-page report titled *The Principle and Practice of Universal Jurisdiction: PCHR's Work in the Occupied Palestinian Territory.*[202] The report stated that "universal jurisdiction is the only viable legal option available to Palestinian victims of Israeli war crimes"[203] and detailed the PCHR's instigation of various universal jurisdiction and related cases. For example:

- In 2002, the PCHR "instructed British human rights solicitor Imran Khan" to lodge various complaints, with the U.K.'s Crown Prosecution Service, against Israeli Defense Minister Shaul Mofaz for alleged war crimes undertaken in the West Bank and Gaza by the Israeli Defense Forces while Mofaz served as its chief of staff from 1998 to 2002.[204] The U.K. government responded that it would pursue no action because Mofaz, as Defense Minister, was entitled to diplomatic immunity.[205]

- On September 10, 2005, one day before retired Israeli Major General Doron Almog was to arrive in the U.K. for a visit, the PCHR persuaded London magistrate Timothy Workman to issue a warrant for Almog's arrest.[206] The warrant was issued on the grounds that Almog was suspected of committing breaches of the Geneva Conventions while he was commander of Israeli military operations in Gaza.[207] It did so in reliance on a fifty-year-old act of Parliament, the Geneva Conventions Act, which incorporated the Geneva Conventions into British law.[208] Reportedly, no warrant had ever before been issued under the Act, and no one had ever been prosecuted pursuant to it.[209] The principal charge against Almog involved the destruction of fifty-nine houses in the Rafah refugee camp.[210]

When Almog's El Al Israel Airlines flight landed on September 11, 2005, British police were waiting at the immigration desk to arrest him.[211] However, the Israeli embassy got word to him before he deplaned, and El Al denied police permission to board the plane.[212] Almog stayed on the plane and returned on it to Israel.[213] The U.K.'s Foreign Secretary at the time, Jack Straw, subsequently apologized to his Israeli counterpart over the incident.[214] However, a number of former Israeli commanders reportedly stayed away from the U.K. in the years following the Almog incident.[215]

In a voluminous 2010 report, the PCHR admitted that, after eight years of pursuing them, "thus far none of PCHR's universal jurisdiction cases have resulted in a successful prosecution."[216] As of 2013, there was still not a single universal jurisdiction case that had resulted in the conviction of an Israeli official.[217] "However," emphasized the PCHR, "the cases have received high profile media coverage, and additionally, several high ranking Israeli officials have had their freedom of movement curtailed in certain countries."[218] In other words, "the process can often be the punishment."[219]

A somewhat analogous case was brought against Israel in Germany by two members of the German parliament who were on board the Mavi Marmara flotilla to Gaza when Israel stormed the flotilla in 2010.[220] The parliamentarians filed criminal complaints for "numerous potential offences, including war crimes against individuals and command responsibility . . . as well as false imprisonment" during the Mavi Marmara seizure, against "unknown responsible parties of Israel's armed forces."[221] Shortly after the case was filed, a German expert on international criminal law stated, in an interview about the case with Germany's Der Spiegel newspaper, that "there is cause to believe that false imprisonment was perpetrated as understood by German law," and that German criminal law would have jurisdiction "irrespective of the fact that the act was perpetrated on the high seas."[222] Four years later, the German prosecutor dismissed the criminal complaints, reportedly on the grounds that the flotilla ships were themselves engaged in military action, and Israel's response to them was not criminal.[223]

The Mavi Marmara flotilla to Gaza contained numerous non-Palestinian nationals, including these two German parliamentarians and also a Swedish cabinet minister.[224] It is worth noting that foreign nationals, and perhaps especially foreign officials, engaging in such acts of "solidarity" may be useful to the Palestinian cause not only from a public relations perspective but also from a lawfare perspective. A third-country court reluctant or unable to exercise "universal jurisdiction" over a case involving solely Israeli defendants and Palestinian victims might rule differently if some of the victims were that third country's own nationals or officials, even if the incident in question occurred far from that third-country's territory.

Lawfare such as that waged by the PCHR and the German parliamentarians can achieve significant goals even if the complaints fail, in fact even if the complaints fall far short of the standard for conviction.[225] In addition to media coverage, "universal jurisdiction" prosecutions, including those that are unjustified, can potentially influence the decision-making calculus of Israeli commanders; contribute to Israel's delegitimization and demoralization; and reduce Israel's ability to conduct diplomatic relations and communicate effectively with foreign audiences.

For unsuccessful prosecutions, the damage to the targeted defendant and country is particularly strong while the case is pending, during the typically several years between the case's initiation and dismissal. In cases where unjustified universal jurisdiction prosecutions influence the decision-making calculus of commanders, it may lead them to excessive risk aversion and to placing their military objectives or even troops in jeopardy by reducing the risk to civilians even beyond what is required by international law.[226]

Several of the European countries that were the most significant "universal jurisdiction" venues in the decade after 2001 have subsequently reduced the reach of their laws. For example, Belgium repealed its "universal jurisdiction" law in 2003 when then Secretary of Defense Donald Rumsfeld threatened to move NATO headquarters out of Belgium after cases were filed—for alleged war crimes in Iraq—against Rumsfeld, General Norman Schwarzkopf, former President George H.W. Bush, and then Secretary of State Colin Powell.[227]

Spain amended its "universal jurisdiction" laws in 2009 and then again in 2014 to limit investigation of cases that do not involve Spanish victims or perpetrators.[228] The change was reportedly due in part to pressure from China after a Spanish judge issued arrest orders for a former Chinese President and a former Chinese Prime Minister as part of a case regarding alleged human rights violations in Tibet.[229] Another factor was reportedly Spanish discomfort with what could be termed "a taste of its own medicine": an Argentine judge's investigation of war crimes committed in Spain during the era of the Spanish dictator Francisco Franco.[230]

The U.K.'s "universal jurisdiction law" was changed in 2011 to require the consent of the U.K. government's Director of Public Prosecutions, a civil servant, "before an arrest warrant is issued in universal jurisdiction cases brought by individuals."[231] The U.K. Ministry of Justice explained that "this change to the law will ensure that the system is no longer open to abuse by people seeking warrants for grave crimes on the basis of scant evidence to make a political statement or to cause embarrassment."[232] Shortly after the new law entered into force, former Israeli Foreign Minister Tzipi Livni, for whom a U.K. arrest warrant had been issued in 2009, paid an official visit to the United Kingdom.[233] However, former Israeli Major General Almog decided to cancel an unofficial visit in 2012 on the advice of the Israeli government, which advised him that even under the new law, it could not fully guarantee an arrest warrant would not be issued again.[234]

It is important to note that the trimming back of "universal jurisdiction" statutes by Belgium, Spain, and the U.K.—the European countries that had been the most significant "universal jurisdiction" venues in the decade after 2001—does not mean that the international community has seen the last of "universal jurisdiction" actions. It seems likely that "universal jurisdiction" actions will shift to new jurisdictions rather than disappear. According to a study by Amnesty International, as of 2011, at least 163 out of 193 states had laws providing for "universal jurisdiction" over one or more of the following international law crimes—war crimes, crimes against humanity, genocide, and torture.[235] In February 2011, former President George W. Bush cancelled a visit to one of those states, Switzerland, amid threats of legal action against him there for alleged mistreatment of suspected militants at Guantanamo.[236] Former Israeli officials would presumably be equally vulnerable, if not more so.

III. PALESTINIAN AND ALLIED NGO LEGAL ACTIONS AGAINST FOREIGN COMPANIES FOR "AIDING AND ABETTING ISRAELI WAR CRIMES"

Various Palestinian and allied NGOs have instigated legal action in the national courts of third countries (countries other than Palestine and Israel) against companies from those third countries for allegedly "aiding and abetting" Israeli "war crimes." The legal actions have taken the form of both civil lawsuits and criminal proceedings. For Israel, these legal actions are of significant concern. Since both the Israeli security establishment and the Israeli economy as a whole depend heavily on foreign procurements, and foreign companies have discretion as to where they choose to do business, such legal actions pose a risk of significantly undermining both Israeli security and the Israeli economy by deterring exports to Israel.

Once such legal actions enter the courtroom, they typically become public, and the impact on the targeted company can be traced in the public domain, as has been done with the examples detailed below. However, there are reports that the mere threat of adversarial action has caused other companies to stop doing some or all business with Israel. Daniel Reisner, an attorney in private practice who previously served as head of the Israel Defense Forces' International Law Department, is known as the go-to attorney in Israel for companies faced with pressure to stop doing business with Israel. According to Reisner, most of the companies targeted by such pressures "don't want anyone to know."[237] He says that they turn to him for advice "quietly, in the evening, where no one can hear them," and sometimes exit Israel in the same quiet way.[238]

A. Lawsuit in the United States Against Caterpillar Incorporated

In 2005, the Palestinian Centre for Human Rights (PCHR) and several other NGOs brought a lawsuit in U.S. federal court against Caterpillar Incorporated on behalf of American activist Rachel Corrie, who was allegedly killed by an Israeli-operated Caterpillar bulldozer in Gaza, and four Palestinian families whose homes were allegedly destroyed and members killed by Israeli-operated Caterpillar bulldozers.[239] The plaintiffs claimed that by providing the Israel Defense Forces with the bulldozers, Caterpillar had aided and abetted: (1) war crimes (breach of Geneva Convention); (2) extrajudicial killing under the Torture Victim Protection Act (a U.S. law); (3) cruel, inhuman, or degrading treatment or punishment; (4) violations of the Racketeer Influenced and Corrupt Organizations Act (a U.S. law); (5) wrongful death; (6) public nuisance; and (7) negligent entrustment.[240] Jurisdiction over the plaintiffs' claims was alleged on the basis of the Alien Tort Statute,[241] which is described in more detail in Chapter 2.

From the PCHR's perspective, Caterpillar was supplying equipment used by the Israeli military to solidify Israeli control over Palestinian territory by destroying Palestinian lives and property.[242] Rather than destroy the Israeli-owned equipment with bombs or use superior armed force to stop its deployment, the PCHR used lawfare to try to deter the supply of additional such equipment.

The federal district court dismissed the action on the basis that the act of state and political question doctrines precluded the court from reaching the merits of the claims and also, alternatively, held that all of plaintiffs' claims failed on the merits.[243] The court's reasoning included that "[s]elling products to a foreign government does not make the seller a participant in that government's alleged international law violations."[244] The court stated that the case "must also be dismissed because it interferes with the foreign policy of the United States of America. . . . For this court to preclude sales of Caterpillar products to Israel would be to make a foreign policy decision and to impinge directly upon the prerogatives of the executive branch of government."[245] The U.S. Court of Appeals for the Ninth Circuit then upheld the dismissal.[246]

While Caterpillar won the legal case, the two years of legal proceedings and publicity surrounding the case meant that Caterpillar incurred significant costs in attorney fees and reputation. From an Israeli perspective, the PCHR, in bringing a case with no realistic chance of success, had used law as a weapon to achieve the aim of weakening Israel's defenses by deterring manufacturers of equipment Israel uses to protect itself against terrorists.

B. Lawsuit in France Against Veolia Transport, Alstom, and Alstom Transport

In 2007, the PLO and the Association France Palestine Solidarité (AFPS) filed a complaint in French court against three French multinational companies: Veolia Transport, Alstom Transport, and Alstom.[247] The complaint alleged that the three companies' involvement in building the Jerusalem light rail system, which serves both the western and eastern parts of the city, made them complicit in Israeli violations of international law, including the Fourth Geneva Convention's articles 49 and 53 and also the Hague Convention Respecting the Laws and Customs of War on Land.[248] Alstom was providing the rail cars and laying the track, while Veolia was due to operate the system.[249] The complaint sought: annulment on grounds of unlawfulness of the contract signed by the companies with the State of Israel; prohibition to proceed with the contract; and compensation.[250]

From the perspective of the PLO and the AFPS, the French companies were helping build a rail system that solidified Israeli control over Palestinian territory.[251] Rather than destroy the rail system with bombs, the PLO and AFPS used lawfare to try to deter or hinder its construction.

After six years of maneuvering within the French court system, the case ended in 2013 with a French appeals court dismissing the case and ordering the Palestinian groups to pay a total of 90,000 euros in damages to the French firms.[252] The court noted that "there has been no international condemnation to date of the construction of the light rail" and that under the Hague Convention, "the introduction of a public means of transport was one of the activities that could be conducted by an occupying power's administration . . . so that the construction of a light rail by the State of Israel was not prohibited."[253] The court also held that the companies "cannot be held accountable for violations of international norms that refer only to obligations incurred by the occupying power," as "the legal instruments [treaties] that were allegedly violated create obligations only vis a vis states."[254]

The companies did not stop doing business in Israel,[255] and the Jerusalem light rail system opened in 2011, five years after construction began.[256] However, even

though the French companies ultimately won the case, the six years of legal proceedings and publicity surrounding the case meant that they incurred significant
costs in attorneys' fees and reputation. The companies complained to the court
that the legal proceedings were "a mere pretext for conducting a media-based
political trial aimed at their public defamation."[257]

Imposing those costs appears to have been part of the purpose of the litigation. Omar Barghouti, a leading Palestinian activist in the BDS movement, said
the French companies' costs should serve as a "big lesson" to other companies
that "there is a price tag associated with complicity with Israel's violations of
international law."[258] "Companies which are complicit must pay a heavy price,"
said Barghouti.[259]

C. Dutch Criminal Investigation of Riwal/Lima

This case provides a notable example of how one lawfare step can build upon
another. In this instance, the ICJ's *Wall* advisory opinion was used to instigate a three-year-long criminal investigation by the Dutch police of a Dutch
company that rented out construction equipment which was relatively briefly
used by the Israeli government during construction of settlements and the
security fence.

The case began in March 2010, when Liesbeth Zegveld, a Dutch attorney
acting on behalf of Al-Haq, a Palestinian NGO, filed a criminal complaint in
the Netherlands against Riwal, a Dutch company also known as Lima Holding
B.V.[260] In this complaint, Al-Haq alleged that there had been "war crimes and
crimes against humanity committed in the Netherlands and/or the Occupied
Palestinian territories during the period of 2004 to present by the company Lima
Holding B.V. and other companies of the Riwal Group," in particular "contributions by these Riwal companies to the construction of the Wall and settlements
by Israel in the West Bank."[261]

Al-Haq's complaint referenced the ICJ's Wall Advisory Opinion of 2004 as
supporting the proposition that Israel's construction of the separation fence and
settlements in the West Bank violate the Fourth Geneva Convention.[262] Pointing
to statements and photos, Al-Haq alleged that "it is an established fact that Riwal
machines were used in the construction of the Wall near Al-Khader and Hizma
and the settlement near Bruqin," and that "there are good reasons to assume that
Riwal knew that the company's machines were used for the contested work."[263]
The statements referenced by Al-Haq included one by a Riwal spokesperson saying: "Riwal Israel rents out cranes to a big client for the Israeli separation wall
along the West Bank. To Riwal, this is a commercial assignment which has only
been accepted and is being executed as such."[264]

Al-Haq's complaint also alleged that the fence and settlement construction "to which Riwal culpably contributed, constitute war crimes and crimes

against humanity within the meaning of the International Crime Act," a Dutch law.[265] The complaint concluded that crimes under the International Crime Act, which the Dutch government were "obliged" to prosecute, "were committed in the Netherlands and/or the Occupied Palestinian Territories," for which Riwal "made a contribution . . . that is culpable under criminal law" because Riwal was "involved in the punishable construction of the Wall and the settlements near the villages of Al-Khader, Hizma and Bruqin."[266] "Renting out machines for the punishable construction of the Wall and settlements," said Al-Haq, "indicates complicity, a form of participation in an offence of which . . . persons could be guilty under Dutch law."[267]

Even before the complaint was filed, the Dutch government had several times criticized Riwal in response to press reports alleging its involvement in the construction. For example, after photos were published in 2006 of Riwal cranes being used in such construction, the Dutch Ministry of Foreign Affairs had contacted Riwal to complain.[268]

After the complaint was filed in March 2010, the Dutch police proceeded to investigate Al-Haq's allegations. In October 2010, as part of the investigation, Riwal's headquarters was reportedly raided by more than forty Dutch police officers who ordered the staff to stay in the cafeteria as they searched the building and seized documents.[269] The Dutch police also raided the homes of officials of the corporation.[270]

In May 2013, the Dutch National Prosecutions Office announced that it would not prosecute Riwal/Lima in connection with the crane rentals.[271] However, in doing so, it issued a warning making it clear that it was not letting Riwal/Lima entirely off the hook. The Prosecutions Office stated that its investigation found that Riwal/Lima had rented out cranes and aerial platforms that were used for construction work in the West Bank over the course of a total of sixteen days.[272] The Prosecutions Office said that "the construction of the barrier and/or a settlement may be considered to be a violation of International Humanitarian Law, among which the Geneva Conventions of 1949," an assertion the Office said was "supported by inter alia," the ICJ's Wall advisory opinion.[273]

The Prosecutions Office warned that "participation in a violation of International Humanitarian Law by Dutch persons and legal entities is a crime proscribed by" the Dutch International Crimes Act.[274] It emphasized that under that Act, "persons and legal entities within the Dutch jurisdiction are required not in any way to be involved in, or contribute to, possible violations of the Geneva Conventions or other rules of International Humanitarian Law."[275]

The Prosecutions Office provided several reasons for its decision "to not further investigate or prosecute" Riwal/Lima and its managing directors and to "dismiss their criminal cases."[276] First, the investigation had revealed that Riwal/Lima's involvement in the construction was "relatively minor," as the investigation had shown that its equipment was used over the course of only sixteen days and that on some of those occasions, the equipment had been rented out to "third parties."[277] Second, "the danger of repetition" was deemed "minor" because Riwal/Lima had taken "far-reaching steps to halt its activities in Israel and the occupied territories."[278] Third, "it was also considered that" Riwal/Lima and "its managing directors have been affected by the consequences" of their actions, including "by the searches of homes and company premises and by the (media) attention which ensues from an investigation such as the present one."[279]

Fourth, "the question whether the conduct of" Riwal/Lima and its managing directors "with regard to the abovementioned activities results in a violation as described, is complex and cannot, without further investigations, be answered with certainty."[280] Such further investigations, noted the Prosecutions Office, would "consume a significant amount of resources of the police and/or the judiciary" and would be hampered "due to lack of cooperation from the Israeli authorities."[281] The Prosecutions Office nevertheless retained the possibility of reopening the case, noting that its decision to dismiss "may be reconsidered on the basis of new facts and/or circumstances."[282]

Although Riwal/Lima avoided a conviction, the raids and three years of legal proceedings and publicity surrounding the case meant that the company incurred significant costs in attorneys' fees, reputation, and distress to its employees. Imposing those costs appears to have been part of the purpose of the litigation. According to the *Associated Press*, Liesbeth Zegveld, the Dutch attorney who filed the criminal complaint on behalf of Al-Haq, said that while she and Al-Haq were disappointed by the Dutch government's decision not to prosecute, "the three-year investigation should serve as a warning to companies involved in Israeli construction work in occupied territories."[283]

In addition, Riwal/Lima apparently either decided on its own, or as part of an informal settlement with the Dutch government, to halt not only all involvement with West Bank separation barrier and settlement construction but also apparently all activities anywhere in Israel.[284] From an Israeli perspective, Al-Haq succeeded in using law as a weapon to both deprive Israel of equipment it was using to build a fence to protect itself against suicide bombers and drive a major equipment rental company out of doing any business anywhere in Israel.[285]

Al-Haq succeeded in doing so on the basis of evidence that the Dutch company had rented out construction equipment that was then used by the Israeli government during construction of settlements and the security fence over the course of a total of a mere sixteen days. In light of the relatively common and banal commercial activity in which Riwal/Lima engaged (renting out construction equipment) and the dismissal's rationale, other Dutch companies, or companies with a Dutch presence, that do business in Israel have ample reason to be nervous that they could be the next target of a costly criminal complaint for aiding and abetting Geneva Convention violations.

IV. ISRAEL'S SYSTEMIC RESPONSES TO PA AND ALLIED NGO LAWFARE

This chapter and the previous one have described and analyzed how the PA and its NGO allies have used law as a weapon against Israel in fora including international organizations, treaties, and national courts. Along the way, the book has discussed how Israel and its allies have defended themselves using various tactics on a case-by-case basis.

For example, in various specific cases Israel has:

- released terrorists in exchange for a hiatus in PA lawfare;
- withheld tax revenues it collects on behalf of the PA;
- warned the PA and Hamas that they are also vulnerable for having violated war crimes;
- sought to persuade key countries that fund the ICC to cut their contributions to it;
- advised its officials and former officials to avoid particular "universal jurisdiction" destinations; and
- begun working to demonstrate "positive complementarity."

In addition, the U.S. government has, in various cases, defunded a U.N. agency that admitted the PA and threatened to defund others, threatened to cut funding to the PA, and voted in support of Israel in lawfare situations where it has had a vote. Israel's allies in the U.S. Congress and state governments have introduced legislation that is designed to leverage the United States' economic weight to counter BDS in Europe. Finally, in France, Israel's NGO allies have successfully lodged complaints against the BDS movement in courts all over the country, and an Israeli company successfully used a lawsuit to combat boycott calls by BDS activists.

In addition to deploying this "grab bag" of case-by-case responses, the government of Israel has developed a sophisticated mechanism and strategy for systematically defending against lawfare by the PA and its NGO allies. At the heart of the systematic response mechanism is the establishment in 2009, by decision of Israel's Security Cabinet, of a special office within Israel's Ministry of Justice for "handling all international legal proceedings against Israel, Israeli soldiers or officials."[286] According to Yuval Shany, an international law expert and the dean of Israel's Hebrew University law school, establishment of the office is "evidence that the Israeli Government has come to terms with the new state of 'law fare' in which it finds itself."[287]

The counterlawfare office's initial principal purpose was to address universal jurisdiction cases and potential ICC cases against Israeli officials and former officials.[288] However, the office's mandate has reportedly expanded to include participation in civilian oversight of the legal advice and policy units of Israel's

Military Advocate General.[289] The Turkel Commission report of February 2013, which assessed Israel's apparatus for investigating alleged violations by its troops of the law of armed conflict, specifically recommended such an expansion of the office's mandate.[290]

As discussed in Chapter 5, the Turkel Commission report was an important assessment of how to improve Israel's system for investigating alleged war crimes by its troops. Many of its recommendations have reportedly been implemented.[291] Their implementation will make it easier for Israel to argue the sufficiency of its system for investigating such alleged crimes. As a result, Israel will find it easier to defend against some types of lawfare, including especially the generation by its adversaries of ICC investigations. The Justice Ministry's counterlawfare office will be the unit taking the lead in mounting such defenses.

In recent years, the Justice Ministry's counterlawfare office has been in the center of responses to most if not all of the various major international law controversies in which Israel has been involved, including those relating to the Goldstone Report and the Mavi Marmara flotilla raid, as well as universal jurisdiction cases against Israeli officials and former officials.[292] In addition to defending Israel and its officials in these specific cases, the office has also engaged in proactive legal public diplomacy. For example, the office has played a leading role in developing explanations of the consistency with international law of various Israeli government policies and actions. It has also sought to systematically and proactively shape international law and its processes in ways that are conducive to Israel's interests.[293]

The first head of the office was Dr. Roy Schondorf, who in 2013 was promoted to the position of Deputy Attorney General for International Affairs.[294] Under Schondorf's leadership, the office became known as an elite division of the Justice Ministry, attracting many of the ministry's most talented attorneys, including experts in both international law and the laws of key foreign jurisdictions.[295]

One of the most interesting, and in retrospect significant, elements of the office's initial mandate was the authority to "establish throughout the world a legal network of law firms that have relevant legal expertise in international law in order to provide immediate legal advice and representation when needed."[296] The network is especially important because several of the "universal jurisdiction" actions brought against Israeli officials and ex-officials have involved arrest warrants that have materialized either just before or during the individual's visit to a foreign country.

There is very little information publicly available about the office's legal network. However, it is not hard to imagine that in order to be maximally effective, network attorneys would be identified and vetted in advance of an emergency. Prior to an emergency, they could be employed to identify laws, precedents, and mechanisms, as well as attorneys sympathetic to the other side, which could be used for a "universal jurisdiction" proceeding. With that information in hand, they could seek to amend those laws or develop ways of defending against them, and identify and cultivate potential allies within the mechanisms. The network could even watch for and seek to influence cases that do not directly involve the client but could set a problematic precedent (e.g., a "universal jurisdiction" case against someone of another nationality).

Because "universal jurisdiction" and other lawfare actions in foreign countries can achieve some of their goals (e.g., media coverage and deterring travel and trade) even if the complaints fail, it is, from the Israeli perspective, particularly important to detect and stop them in their very early stages. Members of a country's transnational legal network could potentially not only lay the groundwork for combating the complaints but also serve as detection sensors for such complaints, able to learn about them in time to potentially stop them before they achieve their objectives.

In addition to the initiatives led by the counterlawfare office in the Ministry of Justice, Israel has also sought to combat the phenomenon, discussed in more detail in Section V below, of European governments and NGOs providing funding to PA offices and Palestinian NGOs that engage in lawfare. Israel's systemic responses to that phenomenon are set forth in more detail in Section VI below.

V. PALESTINIAN LAWFARE AND THE ROLE OF LAW IN PALESTINIAN SOCIETY

The Palestinians' sophisticated and extensive waging of lawfare against Israel contrasts strikingly with the poor records of compliance with international human rights law and the rule of law of both Hamas and the PA. Analysis of this phenomenon sheds important light on the development of Palestinian lawfare, the future of Palestinian lawfare, and the potential future of lawfare deployment by other state and non-state actors in the developing world.

This section will first contrast the parties' records of compliance with human rights law and the rule of law. Then it will analyze the somewhat surprising impact of the international community's extensive investment in improving Palestinian legal institutions and training since the first Palestinian law school was founded in 1992. Finally, it will take a step back and assess the differing reasons each of the two main Palestinian factions—the PA and Hamas—are choosing to so heavily invest their limited legal resources in waging lawfare against Israel.

According to Freedom House, the Hamas-ruled Gaza Strip in 2014 scored at or near the bottom on both political rights (with a "freedom" rating of 7 on a scale where 1 represents the most free and 7 represents the least free) and civil liberties (with a "freedom" rating of 6), to score an overall "freedom rating" of 6.5 (on the scale where 1 represents the most free and 7 represents the least free).[297] A particular irony, in light of Hamas efforts to take advantage of Israel's allegiance to international law and its processes, is that Gaza received the worst possible subscore for rule of law.[298]

The Freedom House rankings for 2014 provided moderately higher numerical scores for the other Palestinian jurisdiction, the PA-ruled West Bank. West Bank political rights received a "freedom rating" of 6, and West Bank civil liberties received a "freedom rating" of 5.[299] The PA-run West Bank's regular judicial system is characterized as "partly independent," while the PA-run "military court system . . . lacks almost all due process."[300] As a result, the West Bank is scored an overall "freedom rating" of 5.5.[301]

Israel, the target of Hamas and PA lawfare, received from Freedom House for 2014 a "freedom rating" of 2 for civil liberties and a "freedom rating" of 1 for political rights, with an overall "freedom rating" of 1.5 (on the scale with 1 representing the most free and 7 representing the least free).[302] For comparison, the United States received from Freedom House for 2014 a "freedom rating" for civil liberties of 1 and a "freedom rating" of 1 for political rights, with an overall "freedom rating" of 1.[303]

According to Freedom House, corruption is a particular "major problem" in the West Bank.[304] Prime Minister Salam Fayyad, appointed by Abbas in 2007, was "credited with significantly reducing corruption at the higher levels of the PA."[305] However, Fayyad resigned in 2013. The Hamas-led government of Gaza "campaigned on an anticorruption platform" in 2006.[306] However, according to Freedom House, "humanitarian organizations and donor countries allege that Hamas exerts almost total control over the distribution of funds and goods in Gaza, and allocates resources according to political criteria with little or no transparency, creating ample opportunity for corruption."[307]

The first Palestinian law school was founded in 1992.[308] There are now several major law schools in the Palestinian territories. USAID's project on Supporting Rule of Law Reform in the West Bank and Gaza funded work on legal education reform with one Palestinian faculty of law in Gaza and four in the West Bank.[309] USAID's Palestinian Justice Enhancement Program worked with law schools and other Palestinian institutions to improve the capacity of Palestinian legal professionals.[310] In addition, within the last two decades, many Palestinians have received their first or second law degrees at foreign law schools, often funded by initiatives such as the Open Society Institute's Palestinian Rule of Law Program.[311]

The extensive efforts to improve Palestinian legal institutions and training do not appear to correlate with a significant improvement in adherence to the rule of law by Palestinian governmental institutions. For example, the PA-administered territories received from Freedom House an overall "freedom rating" of 5.5 in 1998, the first year they were rated.[312] For 2014, the West Bank received the same poor overall score of 5.5, and the Gaza Strip received a dismal overall score of 6.5.

However, the extensive efforts to improve Palestinian legal institutions and training does correlate with a vast increase in the sophistication and efficacy of Palestinian legal engagement with Israel, including its waging of lawfare against Israel.

Part of the reason for this may be that much of the foreign assistance to improve Palestinian legal institutions and training, including especially the assistance from Europe, has reportedly been either intended or used to enhance Palestinian legal engagement with Israel, including anti-Israel lawfare, rather than improve adherence to the rule of law by Palestinian governmental institutions. For example, the Palestinian Centre for Human Rights, the leading Palestinian NGO waging lawfare against Israel, lists as funders the European Commission, Irish Aid ("the Irish government's programme for overseas development"[313]), the Norwegian Refugee Council, the Government of Finland, the Government of Norway, the Spanish Agency for International Cooperation ("an institution of Spain's Ministry of Foreign Affairs and Cooperation"[314]), and Trocaire ("the official overseas development agency of the Catholic Church in Ireland"[315]).[316]

At least some of these European funds have been used specifically to wage lawfare against Israel. For example, in November 2008, the PCHR held a conference, titled "Impunity and Prosecution of Israeli War Criminals," the banner for which acknowledged EU funding of the conference.[317] Al-Haq, another leading Palestinian NGO waging lawfare against Israel, lists as funders the government of Belgium, Irish Aid, the Norwegian Ministry of Foreign Affairs, and the Spanish Agency for International Cooperation.[318]

The current Palestinian interest in, and sophistication about, international law represents a remarkable change over the last two decades. The lack of legal sophistication of the Palestinian team in the initial Oslo negotiations with Israel during the early 1990s is exemplified by the fact that the Palestinian delegation chose not to have a legal adviser on their negotiating team. Joel Singer, an experienced international lawyer, arrived in Oslo partway through the negotiations to join the Israeli delegation as their legal adviser.[319] It was in Oslo that the two sides negotiated the Declaration of Principles on Interim Self-Government Arrangements (DOP), which was signed on the White House lawn in September 1993. In his book, *Through Secret Channels*, Mahmoud Abbas, the senior PLO leader (and subsequently President) who signed the DOP for the Palestinians on the White House lawn in September 1993, wrote as follows:

> I must admit that throughout the Oslo negotiations we did not review the texts with a legal consultant for fear of leaks.... I tried to make use of the remnants of the legal knowledge I had acquired while studying law at Damascus University, but I could not draw much comfort from them.[320]

Only "when all the outstanding points of difference had been resolved and it had been agreed to meet in Oslo to initial the DOP" did Abbas summon the PLO's legal consultant, Taher Shash, from Cairo.[321] Shash arrived in Oslo and was handed the text to review. "A few hours later," Shash advised that "it was a good text with no shortcomings."[322] The next day, the DOP was initialed in Oslo.[323]

"The Palestinians have always had international law on their side," stated Mostafa Elostaz, a leading Palestinian expert on international law, "but at the end of the day that does you no good if you don't have good lawyers representing you."[324] "As with the OJ trial," said Elostaz, "he who has the best lawyers often wins, regardless of the laws and facts."[325]

In the last two decades, the PLO, and the PA which it leads, have greatly bolstered their international law expertise. For example, in recent years, numerous skilled Palestinian attorneys have served in, advised negotiators from, and waged lawfare from, the Legal & Policy Department of the PLO Negotiations Affairs Department.[326] This department, founded in 1998, is funded by the governments of Denmark, the Netherlands, Norway, Sweden, and the United Kingdom.[327]

In April 2014, Saeb Erekat, the chief Palestinian negotiator, described his legal team as follows: "I have 22 lawyers on my team. They're Palestinians from all over Earth. From Chile, from Argentina, from London, from Paris, from Harvard, from Italy, from Canada. The top of the top. Palestinians who left their offices in New York, in Harvard, in London, and came, and they're living in Ramallah, paying their own rates to serve their country."[328] When Erekat negotiated with Israel for nine months in 2013 and 2014, he had an attorney sit in on all sessions, as did the Israelis.[329]

In addition, several non-Palestinian experts in international law have reportedly been instrumental in Palestinian lawfare strategy. According to Elostaz, "the key architects of the Palestinian lawfare strategy have been international advisers" to the Palestinians.[330]

Based on the Palestinian experience, it seems that impactful lawfare can be waged by governments that themselves have poor records of compliance with international law and the rule of law. It also appears that U.S. and European assistance to improve legal institutions and training in a foreign jurisdiction may help improve that jurisdiction's ability to wage lawfare, even without contributing to an improvement in the rule of law in that jurisdiction.

Why are the PA and Hamas engaging in lawfare? The PA and Hamas appear to be engaging in lawfare for different reasons. For the first several decades after its founding by Yasir Arafat, the PLO (the PA's dominant faction) was openly dedicated to the destruction of Israel, and its militants regularly engaged in airplane hijackings, terrorist attacks against civilians, and other egregious violent transgressions of international law.[331] The PA under Mahmoud Abbas appears to have set aside the goal of destroying Israel militarily.[332] Thus, it has in recent years (and especially since the second intifada ended in 2005) generally avoided military conflict with Israel.

However, while Israel is far stronger than the PA militarily, the PA has support from more U.N. member states, especially amongst the Islamic states (the 57 member states of the Organisation of Islamic Cooperation) and the Nonaligned Movement (with its 120 member states). PA lawyers also believe that they have a strong legal case to make (especially on refugee and border issues)[333] and international tribunals, dominated as they are by Islamic and Nonaligned Movement justices, seem likely to find the Palestinian case compelling. However, many international fora, such as the International Court of Justice and International Criminal Court, are only or largely open to independent states. Thus, the PA has sought recognition as an independent state at least in part to facilitate lawfare against Israel in these various fora.

As discussed in Chapter 5's analysis of the PA's decision to join the ICC, this particularly important and indicative lawfare step appears to have been motivated by several factors. For PA President Abbas, the ICC accession offered an opportunity to be seen by the Palestinian people as striking a painful blow against the enemy, yet without abandoning his professed opposition to violence. In addition, given the PA's belief that it has a strong legal case to make, and its understanding that international organizations view it with favor, ICC accession was seen as having the potential to bring some measure of justice to Palestinian victims, vindicate the Palestinian narrative, tarnish Israel, and deter future Israeli military and settlement actions adverse to the Palestinian cause.

In light of Abbas's record of nonviolence since coming to power in 2005, he must have assessed that ICC accession was highly unlikely to result in proceedings against him. He may well have believed that subjecting the Palestine situation to ICC scrutiny was more likely to cause problems for Israeli officials than for himself, as he could withstand the scrutiny better than they could.

Hamas, in contrast, seems to have considerable vulnerability to ICC scrutiny, as evidenced by its persistent rocket attacks on Israeli civilians. Hamas also has an exceptionally poor record of compliance with international political and civil rights norms. For Hamas, lawfare is apparently just another way to promote Israel's destruction.

As discussed in Chapter 5's analysis of Hamas's decision to concur in the PA joining the ICC, this particularly important and indicative offensive lawfare step by Hamas appears to have been motivated by several factors. The foremost and in many ways overarching factor is Hamas's assessment that international laws and its processes exert far more leverage over Israel than they do over Hamas. As Chapter 5 discusses, the ICC has thus far proven incapable of prosecuting cases against uncooperative authoritarian regimes that have large numbers of allied countries. In addition, in contrast with Israeli officials, who like to travel to Europe and would be embarrassed to be dragged before the ICC, Hamas officials are already unwelcome in Europe and would see being taken to the ICC as a heroic act.

In addition, this book's next chapter (Chapter 7) discusses how, for somewhat similar reasons, Hamas has made itself one of the world's most persistent wagers of compliance-leverage disparity lawfare on the kinetic battlefield. As the chapter describes, Hamas systematically deploys battlefield tactics which, while themselves in clear violation of the law of war, are designed to gain advantage from the far greater leverage that international law and its processes exert over Israel than over Hamas. In doing so, Hamas manages to accomplish several objectives, including causing Israeli armed forces to fight with one hand tied behind their back and eroding support for Israel by making it appear that Israel is to blame for civilian casualties and waging war in violation of international law.

Thus, for the PA (and especially Abbas), lawfare is an arena in which much can be gained while maintaining a nonviolent high ground, and with little risk of suffering legal consequences. In contrast, lawfare helps Hamas wage violence more effectively while posing a significant risk of accruing legal consequences that Hamas would find relatively bearable.

VI. LESSONS LEARNED AND THE FUTURE OF PALESTINIAN INSTRUMENTAL LAWFARE AND ISRAELI RESPONSES

For the PA, Palestinian NGOs, and their allies, lawfare against Israel in international organizations and treaties and in national courts has proven to be an exceptionally useful tool, one that holds the promise of even greater utility in the future. As a result, the PA, Palestinian NGOs, and their allies seem likely to expand their use of such offensive lawfare.

A. Lessons Learned and the Future of PA Lawfare Against Israel

As of spring 2015, the PA's own use of offensive lawfare against Israel could claim achievements including the following:

- The PA's campaign to join international organizations and treaties and use them against Israel helped the PA's dominant faction, the PLO, to rebrand itself to a considerable degree. The international-law-violating PLO of airline hijackings and the Munich Olympic Village massacre could now portray itself as peacefully seeking to (a) subject itself to international law and (b) maximize its adversary's compliance with international law.
- The PA had successfully deployed lawfare to gain negotiating leverage over Israel without risking Israel recapturing the West Bank. Since large-scale anti-Israel violence explicitly sponsored by the PA could lead to Israel reconquering the West Bank, it would be counterproductive. Yet the PA still sought leverage over Israel in the on-and-off peace negotiations. Lawfare provided such leverage.
- Israel had been willing to pay an extraordinarily high price for the PA refraining from lawfare. In 2013, U.S. Secretary of State John Kerry engineered a deal in which Israel promised to release 104 Palestinians convicted of terrorist activities in exchange for the PA refraining for nine months from joining international organizations and treaties. A PA official deemed the release the

PA's biggest achievement of the year. The deal lasted for eight months, during which Israel released 78 Palestinian prisoners, many of whom had been convicted of murdering Israeli civilians, in exchange for eight months of the PA refraining from joining international organizations and treaties.

- The July 2004 I.C.J. Advisory Opinion titled "Legal Consequences of the Construction of a Wall in the Occupied Palestinian Territory" was significantly damaging to Israel. Notwithstanding the U.S. judge's view that the Advisory Opinion misinterpreted international law, and the security barrier having significantly reduced terrorist killings of Israelis, the I.C.J. Advisory Opinion discredited the fence as illegal. Although the opinion-instigating question posed to the ICJ by the General Assembly focused on the legality of the security barrier, the ICJ took the opportunity to assert the illegality of all Israeli settlements in Gaza and the West Bank (including East Jerusalem). Even though the opinion was merely advisory and thus nonbinding, its assertions have been treated as dispositive in some fora, including the Dutch court system. For example, the ICJ's Wall Advisory Opinion was used to instigate the three-year-long criminal investigation by the Dutch police of Riwal/Lima. Future, more damaging cases could similarly build on the Wall Advisory Opinion.
- The language contained in the U.N. General Assembly's resolution recognizing Palestine as a non-member observer state helped fortify the PA's position on several issues subject to negotiation between Israel and the PA.
- The PA used its UNESCO membership to advance claims of Palestinian self-determination and to try to encourage international intervention against Israel and drive a wedge between Israel and its Christian allies. While PA lawfare using its UNESCO membership had thus far not had a major impact on the status of the conflict with Israel, this lawfare deployment's precedent and template could have a significant cumulative impact if replicated over various other international organizations (including ones with greater importance for Israeli security and trade).
- The PA's accession to the ICC had, as of spring 2015, created a new deterrent to future Israeli military and settlement actions adverse to the Palestinian cause. Depending on how ICC Prosecutor Bensouda decided to proceed, the PA accession held the possibility of creating significant future problems for some key officials of both Israel and the PA's rival Hamas movement.

When the PA has in recent years applied for status upgrades subject to vote by international organization members, it has triumphed by large margins. When the PA has, since the UNGA vote, applied to join international treaties, it has been quickly accepted.

As a result of the impact and ease of such lawfare, the PA is likely to continue to threaten to join international organizations and treaties and to use them against Israel. If Israel is willing to pay a high enough price, the PA will refrain from joining and/or using some or all for limited periods of time. If Israel is not willing to pay a high enough price for the PA refraining from joining and/or using, the PA will join international organizations and treaties and/or use them against Israel. Particular deployments against Israel of these organizations and treaties may also be either traded to Israel for limited periods, where possible, or undertaken. Lawfare will become, for the PA, a major new arsenal of weapons in its conflict with Israel.

B. Lessons Learned and the Future of Lawfare Against Israel by Palestinian NGOs and their Allies

As of spring 2015, lawfare against Israel by Palestinian NGOs and their allies could claim achievements including the following:

- The BDS movement had deployed a number of lawfare tactics that, while causing relatively minor damage to Israel in their initial iterations, set potentially dangerous precedents. These tactics could cause considerable cumulative damage if they are able to be replicated against other targets or otherwise expanded. This included the use of OECD guidelines to pressure a U.K. company to stop doing business with Israel and the creation of EU guidelines restricting grants to Israel. It also included the phenomenon of the BDS movement citing Israeli "war crimes" as legal justification for disrupting and physically damaging Israeli-affiliated businesses.
- While none of the universal jurisdiction cases brought against Israeli current or former officials had resulted in a successful prosecution, several such Israelis had to significantly curtail their travels to key countries in Europe. Such cases contributed to Israel's delegitimization and reduced Israel's ability to conduct diplomatic relations and communicate with foreign audiences. Although several of the most significant "universal jurisdiction" venues in Europe reduced the reach of their laws, Israel was reportedly still warning some former officials against travel to these countries.
- Although none of the legal actions in foreign jurisdictions against foreign companies for allegedly "aiding and abetting" Israeli violations of the law of armed conflict had resulted in civil liability or a successful prosecution, the targeted companies nevertheless incurred significant costs in legal fees and reputation over multiple years of proceedings. As a result, these legal actions reportedly had a chilling effect on some foreign companies' plans to do business in Israel.

As a result of the relative ease of such lawfare, the significant impact it has, even when cases are eventually dismissed, and the potential for legal victory, Palestinian NGOs and their allies are likely to continue pursuing offensive lawfare against Israel. The G4S precedent may indicate that the OECD Guidelines for Multinational Enterprises could become a very impactful tool for lawfare against Israel.

In addition, although several European countries have reduced the reach of their universal jurisdiction laws, at least 163 out of 193 countries worldwide have universal jurisdiction laws. So the Palestinian NGOs and their allies seem likely to shift such actions to new jurisdictions.

An even greater priority for the Palestinian NGOs and their allies is likely to be the bringing of legal actions in foreign courts against foreign companies for allegedly "aiding and abetting" Israeli "war crimes." In contrast to Israeli officials, whose service to their country is unlikely to be deterred by foreign litigation, reputational and litigation risk is known to significantly impact where international companies choose to do business. The cases thus far indicate that even when Israel's suppliers win cases brought by Palestinian NGOs and their allies, the targeted companies may incur significant costs in attorneys' fees and reputation. In light of the heavy dependence on foreign trade of both the Israeli security establishment and the Israeli economy as a whole, such legal actions pose a risk of significantly undermining both Israeli security and the Israeli economy.

From a Palestinian perspective, the most encouraging such case of those discussed in this chapter is likely to be Riwal/Lima. Although the Dutch Prosecutions Office ultimately decided to drop the case, the reasons it gave for doing so left open the possibility of future prosecutions of Riwal/Lima or other companies conducting analogous business in Israel. These reasons include the finding that Riwal/Lima's involvement was "relatively minor" since its equipment had been used over the course of only sixteen days and the reference to the company's decision to halt its activities in both the occupied territories and Israel. A future case, against a company with less minor involvement and that refuses to leave Israel, could result in a conviction.

For Israel, lawfare by the PA, Palestinian NGOs, and their allies has thus far proven to be damaging but not disastrous. However, such lawfare appears to hold the potential to become significantly more damaging to Israel. The extraordinarily high price Israel paid for an eight-month hiatus in PA lawfare seems to reflect that this risk assessment is shared by the Israeli government.

C. Lessons Learned and the Future of Israeli Responses to Palestinian Instrumental Lawfare Challenges

Israel seems likely to take a variety of future steps to address the challenge of Palestinian instrumental offensive lawfare. For example, Israel will likely continue to expand the size, scope, and expertise of its counterlawfare office. In light of the receding threat of universal jurisdiction prosecutions against Israelis in the countries they are typically most interested in visiting (e.g., in Western Europe), and the PA's important recent moves to join and utilize international organizations and treaties, the counterlawfare office will likely focus increasingly on defending against the latter. In addition, Israel is likely, at least for contingency purposes, to seek to develop (if not publicize or implement) strategies for deploying lawfare offensively against the Palestinians in such international bodies.

With regard to the ICC in particular, Israel seems likely to continue to ramp up its efforts to demonstrate "positive complementarity." It will do so both on a case-by-case basis and by implementing as many as possible of the Turkel Commission's recommendations for improving Israel's system for investigating alleged violations by its troops of the law of armed conflict.

There are at least five specific areas where Israel and its supporters seem likely to turn to the U.S. government for assistance against Palestinian lawfare. First, Israel and its supporters will continue to urge the U.S. government to vote in support of Israel (including wielding a veto when it has one) in lawfare situations where the United States has a vote. Second, Israel and its supporters seem likely to press the United States to aggressively implement its laws linking U.S. funding of the PA and UN to Palestinian moves to upgrade its U.N. status by joining additional U.N. organizations. Third, Israel and its supporters may also seek new U.S. legislation leveraging U.S. funding of the PA and UN to deter PA use against Israel of international organizations and treaties, whether or not the PA has joined them.

Fourth, Israel and its supporters seem almost certain to continue to urge that U.S. antiboycott laws be either supplemented with new statutes or amended to directly and vigorously address the growing attempted isolation of Israel by the BDS movement. Fifth, Israel and its supporters may also seek U.S action to protect Israeli personnel from ICC prosecution, either using the United States' "Article 98" agreements with foreign countries or otherwise in implementation of § 2008 of the American Service-Members' Protection Act.

Israel also seems likely to continue to press foreign governments and NGOs to either halt or place conditions on their funding of PA offices and Palestinian NGOs that engage in lawfare against Israel. The Israeli law, enacted in 2011, which requires NGOs in Israel to publicly report funding by foreign governments seems likely in the future to be followed by additional, more stringent and direct legislation.[334] Israel will also likely continue to target Israeli NGOs that participate in lawfare. In April 2015, the Israeli Supreme Court upheld a law that empowers the finance minister to fine, or remove tax breaks from, Israeli NGOs calling for boycotts of businesses in pre-1967 Israel or in West Bank settlements, and enables individuals to sue boycott-advocating individuals or organizations for damages directly caused by such boycotts.[335] More such legislation seems probable.

Israel will reportedly also seek to decrease its exposure to lawfare by shifting its trade toward countries where it is less likely to be attacked. In January 2015, amid fears of anti-Israel lawfare ramping up in Europe, Israeli Prime Minister

Netanyahu told his cabinet: "We definitely want to reduce our dependence on certain markets in Western Europe."[336]

Israel will also likely seek new partners in its battle against lawfare. In light of the PRC's success in pressuring Spain to trim back its universal jurisdiction law, the Chinese government's sophistication and aggressiveness in combating lawfare, and the Chinese government's far greater clout on the world stage, Israel may seek to quietly partner with China in combating lawfare. For these and other reasons, Israel is unlikely to again engage in lawfare against China as it did in the Bank of China case described in Chapter 8 of this book.

Israel also seems likely to enhance its efforts to reach out to sympathetic private sector lawyers, especially in the United States, for ideas and assistance. As discussed in Chapter 2, effective lawfare often requires specialized expertise in particular fields and subfields, such as maritime insurance law and the law of a particular state; there is far more such expertise among U.S. private sector attorneys than among the lawyers of any individual government or NGO. U.S. private sector attorneys have a long tradition of supplementing their regular client work with interesting work even for clients whose policies they do not favor (for example, representation of Guantanamo detainees). It may be relatively easy for Israel or any other foreign country to which a significant number of U.S. lawyers are sympathetic (e.g., Canada, India, Ireland, Italy, or the U.K.) to more effectively draw on the skills and expertise of some among the vast number of U.S. private sector attorneys.

CHAPTER 7

Hamas Battlefield Lawfare Against Israel

"That is the fate of democracy, in whose eyes not all means are permitted, and to whom not all the methods used by her enemies are open. At times democracy fights with one hand tied behind her back."

— Aharon Barak, *President of the Supreme Court of Israel (1995–2006)*

In contrast to the PA and its dominant PLO faction, Hamas has in recent years regularly engaged Israel in armed conflict. In the course of these armed conflicts, Hamas has frequently engaged in compliance-leverage disparity lawfare on the kinetic battlefield. In other words, Hamas has deliberately used battlefield tactics designed to gain advantage from the greater leverage which the law of armed conflict and its processes exert over Israel than Hamas. This chapter will refer to such tactics as "battlefield lawfare."

Before focusing on Hamas's battlefield lawfare, it is important to note that battlefield lawfare is far from the only type of lawfare in the Israeli-Palestinian struggle that deploys the law of armed conflict. This book's other chapters on lawfare and the Israeli-Palestinian struggle provide case studies of how the law of armed conflict and its processes have been used—by a variety of actors, with a variety of motivations—to exert pressure over Israel in a number of international and third-country legal forums. For example:

- Alleged violations of the law of armed conflict by particular Israeli officials have formed the basis for "universal jurisdiction" prosecutions of those officials in European courts, as described in Chapter 6.
- Alleged violations of the law of armed conflict by Israel were offered as justifications for activists breaking into, disrupting, and physically damaging European companies doing business with Israel, as described in Chapter 6.

- Alleged violations of the law of armed conflict by Israel formed the basis for civil lawsuits and criminal proceedings in European courts against European companies doing business with Israel, as described in Chapter 6.
- Alleged violations of the law of armed conflict by Israel and Hamas during the 2014 Gaza War were, as of spring 2015, reportedly being preliminarily examined by the International Criminal Court prosecutor following the PA's accession to the ICC, as described in Chapter 5.

Alleged Israeli violations of the law of armed conflict are also frequently deployed against Israel in nonlegal forums. For example, they form the basis of frequent condemnations of Israel in nonbinding resolutions of U.N. bodies including the U.N. General Assembly and the U.N. Human Rights Council. They also serve as ammunition in BDS campaigns to persuade academics, artists, and companies to boycott and/or divest from Israel.

Having noted the other chapters' analyses of how alleged Israeli violations of the law of armed conflict are deployed against Israel and its officials in particular legal forums, this chapter will focus on the kinetic battlefield itself. Section I of this chapter describes and analyzes Hamas's engagement in battlefield lawfare, including its violating the law of armed conflict in a manner designed to elicit alleged Israeli violations of the law of armed conflict. Section II of this chapter describes and analyzes key claims that Israel itself has, usually in response to Hamas battlefield lawfare, violated the law of armed conflict.

Section III of this chapter describes several types of responses that the Israeli military has thus far undertaken in order to protect itself against Hamas battlefield lawfare. This includes: (1) changes to Israeli battlefield tactics—including combating Hamas using airstrikes rather than Israeli ground troops and trying to minimize Palestinian civilian casualties by providing extensive warning prior to airstrikes; (2) enhancing Israel's legal public diplomacy—including efforts to build support for its preferred interpretations of international law; (3) expanding the role of military lawyers in Israel's combat decision-making; (4) enhancing Israel's own investigations into alleged war crimes by its troops; and (5) providing the press and public with extensive data, including videos, illustrating Israeli targeting decision-making.

Section IV of this chapter takes a step back and identifies broad lessons learned. It also attempts to forecast the future of Hamas battlefield lawfare and Israeli responses.

I. HOW HAMAS WAGES BATTLEFIELD LAWFARE AGAINST ISRAEL

Chapter 1 of this book introduced the concept of compliance-leverage disparity lawfare, which the book defines as lawfare designed to gain advantage from the greater influence that law and its processes exert over an adversary. Battlefield lawfare is a subset of compliance-leverage disparity lawfare. It is the use of tactics on the kinetic battlefield which are designed to gain advantage from the greater leverage that international law, and especially the law of armed conflict, and its processes exert over an adversary.

As Chapter 1 describes, battlefield lawfare has been deployed by various non-state actors against more militarily powerful and law-sensitive adversaries. For example, Major General Charles Dunlap, Jr., the U.S. Air Force Deputy Judge Advocate General who coined the term lawfare, provided as an example of it various tactics designed by the Taliban to leverage the United States' greater sensitivity to alleged violations of the law of armed conflict.[1]

Battlefield lawfare tactics are typically designed to achieve two main objectives: (1) causing the more law-sensitive adversary to self-impose restraints that render its armed forces less effective and (2) eroding public and international support for the more law-sensitive adversary by causing it to actually or arguably violate the law of armed conflict. Hamas has successfully used battlefield lawfare to achieve both objectives against Israel.

Hamas engaged in battlefield lawfare during both the 2009 and the 2014 Gaza conflicts with Israel. According to a study published by the U.S. Army in 2009, "Hamas . . . prefers to hide and fight among the civilian population, using civilians as protection against overwhelming Israeli firepower and intelligence, surveillance, and reconnaissance (ISR) assets."[2] "Mosques, schools, hospitals and private homes have all been used as weapon storage sites, fighting positions and communication centers," said the report.[3] "Indeed, such facilities are often used as bait for Israeli kinetic action, and the resulting carnage documented and broadcasted for Hamas . . . [information operations] benefit."[4] In addition, during the Gaza War in 2009, the prime minister of Hamas and other senior Hamas commanders reportedly operated out of a wing of the Shifa Hospital, Gaza's largest and most important hospital, on the assumption that "Israel would not target the hospital."[5]

Hamas used similar tactics during the 2014 Gaza War, both using civilian locations for military purposes and openly encouraging civilians to stand in front of targets to deter Israeli attacks. Hamas's use of civilian locations for military purposes was exemplified by a *Washington Post* report that Hamas leaders again used the Shifa Hospital in Gaza City as a "de facto headquarters" during the conflict.[6] Also during the 2014 Gaza War, the UN found Hamas rockets hidden in three of the schools it runs in Gaza.[7] The *New York Times* reported that Hamas "stored weapons in mosques and schools" and launched rockets from "near apartment buildings, schools and hotels."[8] The *New York Times* also reported that during the 2014 Gaza War, virtually all Hamas fighters (who do wear uniforms during peacetime parades)[9] wore civilian clothes so as to blend in among civilians.[10]

During the 2014 Gaza conflict, French television aired footage of Hamas rocket launchers just outside homes, a U.N. building, and the main Gaza hotel in which journalists were staying.[11] A reporter from the *Toronto Globe and Mail* witnessed two rockets being launched from near a school used to house refugees and concluded that "Hamas, or some militant group, clearly is hoping the Israelis won't strike at the launchers . . . because they're so close to the school and so many refugees."[12]

Hamas also launched rockets from church property in Gaza. Gaza's most prominent Christian leader, Archbishop Alexios, took a reporter "to the roof terrace outside his office to show how Islamists used the church compound to launch rockets into Israel."[13]

Hamas also specifically encouraged civilians to stand in front of targets to deter Israeli attacks. In a July 8, 2014, interview, Hamas spokesman Sami Abu Zuhri described a Hamas policy of encouraging civilians to stand on the roof of a targeted building "in order to prevent the Zionist occupation's warplanes from targeting it."[14] "The policy of people confronting the Israeli warplanes with their bare chests in order to protect their homes has proven effective . . . . We in Hamas call upon our people to adopt this policy,"[15] said Zuri. Hamas had advance notice that particular buildings were being targeted because the Israeli military, in an effort to minimize civilian casualties, provided notice prior to attacking those buildings. This Israeli policy is discussed in the section below on airstrikes and warnings.[16]

In addition, Hamas urged residents to ignore Israeli army urgings to depart specific areas. For example, Hamas on July 13, 2014, announced: "We call on our Palestinian people, particularly the residents of northwest Gaza . . . to remain in their homes and disregard the demands to leave, however serious the threat may be."[17]

These actions by Hamas clearly violated several provisions of the law of armed conflict. For example, both the placement of military assets in or around non-combatant facilities so as to deter attacks and encouraging civilians to stand in front of targets to deter attacks are a violation of articles 51 and 58 of Additional Protocol I to the Geneva Conventions. The rule set forth in article 51 is considered to be a norm of customary international law applicable in both international and noninternational armed conflicts.[18] Article 51(7) states:

> The presence or movements of the civilian population or individual civilians shall not be used to render certain points or areas immune from military operations, in particular in attempts to shield military objectives from attacks or to shield, favour or impede military operations. The Parties to the Conflict shall not direct the movement of the civilian population or individual civilians in order to attempt to shield military objectives from attacks or to shield military operations.[19]

The official commentary on Article 51(7) specifies that its prohibition applies both to cases where civilians are given no choice in the matter by their government and also where the government encourages civilians to shield military objectives from attack.[20]

In addition, article 58, which is also considered customary international law,[21] requires the parties to the conflict to:

(a) ... endeavour to remove the civilian population, individual civilians and civilian objects under their control from the vicinity of military objectives;

(b) avoid locating military objectives within or near densely populated areas;

(c) take the other necessary precautions to protect the civilian population, individual civilians and civilian objects under their control against the dangers resulting from military operations.[22]

Hamas's battlefield lawfare tactics of using civilian locations for military purposes and encouraging civilians to stand in front of targets received considerable international attention during the 2014 Gaza War. President Obama said, "Hamas acts extraordinarily irresponsibly when it is deliberately siting rocket launchers in population centers, putting populations at risk because of that particular military strategy."[23] The EU announced that it "strongly condemns calls on the population of Gaza to provide themselves as human shields."[24] U.N. Secretary-General Ban Ki-moon said, "We condemn the use of civilian sites—schools, hospitals, and other civilian facilities—for military purposes."[25]

According to Bassem Eid, executive director of the Palestinian Human Rights Monitoring Group, "Hamas needs these deaths .... Death of its own people empowers Hamas ...."[26] The *New York Times* noted that Hamas "on some level benefit in the diplomatic arena from the rising casualties."[27] According to Nathan Thrall, coauthor of an International Crisis Group report on Gaza, "Hamas knows that . . . as the civilian death toll mounts, there is increasing pressure to end the war immediately, and what that typically entails, if past is precedent, is making some concessions to Hamas."[28]

This willingness or perhaps eagerness to incur Palestinian civilian casualties helps explain why Hamas "at times encouraged residents not to flee their homes when alerted by Israel to a pending strike."[29] It also helps explain why, in the years prior to the conflict, Hamas "did not build civilian bomb shelters" while at the same time it constructed scores of underground tunnels designed to sneak militants across the border into Israel.[30]

Remarkably, the report of the U.N. Human Rights Council's Independent Commission of Inquiry on the 2014 Gaza Conflict (UNHRC Commission) largely disregarded Hamas's use of civilian locations for military purposes and of civilian persons as human shields.[31] The report addressed these issues neither in its overview description of the laws of armed conflict applicable to the Gaza Conflict nor in its recommendations for corrective and future action by the parties.

The UNHRC Commission report was issued on June 22, 2015, after the drafting of this chapter was largely completed. The Commission reported that it "was able to gather substantial information pointing to serious violations of international humanitarian law and international human rights law by Israel and by

Palestinian armed groups."[32] "In some cases," said the report, "these violations may amount to war crimes."[33]

Unsurprisingly, commentators' views on the report were mixed. Amnesty International praised the report as "a key step towards justice for victims on both sides,"[34] the *New York Times* reported that it included "efforts at evenhandedness,"[35] and Benjamin Wittes and Yishai Schwartz at the Lawfare blog characterized it as "better" than previous similar U.N. investigations but still "a bad piece of work."[36] Daniel Reisner, a former head of the Israel Defense Forces' International Law Department noted that the report "appears to many to be much more balanced than previous similar UN interventions," including especially the 2009 report of the Goldstone Commission, but called into question whether that assessment was correct.[37] A complete analysis of the report is outside the scope of this book. However, it is critical, in this book about lawfare, to note how the report largely failed to address, and thus had the effect of encouraging, Hamas's battlefield lawfare.

As Professor Laurie Blank pointed out, the UNHRC Commission report's overview of the legal principle of distinction as it applies to the Gaza conflict "omits" the prohibitions on "using protected objects, such as hospitals or religious buildings, for military purposes" and on "using civilians as human shields."[38] "In the context of Gaza, where Hamas and other armed groups deliberately—as they themselves proclaim—comingle with the civilian population and turn the failure to distinguish into an art form, this omission is remarkable in its shortsightedness," said Blank, a leading expert on the law of armed conflict.[39] Professor Geoffrey Corn, a retired lieutenant colonel who previously served as the U.S. Army's senior law of war expert adviser, similarly stated that the UNHRC Commission report "fails to emphasize, or even identify" the law of armed conflict's "obligation on belligerents to distinguish themselves from civilians and civilian property."[40]

Blank noted that the report's overview of applicable legal principles also ignored the customary international law responsibilities of defending parties which are reflected in article 58 of Additional Protocol I to the Geneva Conventions, including the requirements to: remove civilians from the vicinity of military objectives; avoid locating military objectives within or near densely populated areas; and take other precautions to protect civilians from the dangers of military operations.[41] According to Blank, "violations of these precautions are the mainstay of the Hamas playbook," yet the UNHRC Commission report "does not even mention these fundamental obligations in its statement of the principles of precautions."[42]

There is a brief section, in the middle of the Commission report, that discussed "patterns of behavior of Palestinian armed groups which may have had a negative impact on the protection of the civilian population and of civilian objects in Gaza."[43] In that section, the report delicately stated that "given the number of cases in which Palestinian armed groups are alleged to have carried out military operations within or in the immediate vicinity of civilian objects and specifically protected objects, it does not appear that this behavior was simply a consequence of the normal course of military operations."[44] "Therefore," said the report, "the obligation to avoid to the maximum extent possible locating military objectives within densely populated areas was not always complied with."[45] "If it is confirmed," said the report, "that in using the aforementioned locations to conduct military operations, armed groups did so with the intent to use the presence of civilians or persons *hors de combat* in locations such as shelters or hospitals to prevent their military assets from being attacked, this would constitute a violation of the customary law prohibition to use human shields, reflected in article 51(7) of Additional Protocol I [and] would amount to a war crime."[46]

This section of the report also briefly addressed various statements by the Gaza authorities requesting Gaza residents not to heed the various warnings to evacuate which were issued by the Israeli military. The report stated that "[w]hile the commission cannot conclude that in making these declarations the authorities in Gaza had the specific intent to use the presence of civilians to protect Palestinian armed groups from attack, the declarations are a clear indication that the authorities in Gaza did not take all the necessary precautions to protect the civilian population under its control as required by international humanitarian law."[47]

The final section of the report, titled "Recommendations," contained a number of specific calls for corrective and future action by each of the parties.[48] In its recommendations directed at "the authorities in Gaza and Palestinian armed groups," the section remarkably included, as Blank noted, "no recommendations at all with regard to the use of civilians as human shields, comingling with the civilian population and using civilian objects and infrastructure for military purposes (such as launching rockets from hospitals, mosques or United Nations schools), or fighting while disguised as civilians."[49]

As a result, said Blank, "the report hands Hamas and other Palestinian armed groups a free pass to continue their *modus operandi*."[50] Blank concluded that "the report's glaring omissions of foundational legal principles emasculate the law, weakening the essential tools for the protection of civilians and emboldening those who use civilians as pawns for their own strategic gain."[51]

In their analysis of the UNHRC Commission report, Benjamin Wittes and Yishai Schwartz expressed a related concern: that the Commission "lets [Hamas] practices shift the responsibility for civilian death from Hamas's own behavior to Israeli targeting decisions."[52] Wittes and Schwartz said that while Hamas's tactics should have been "the fundamental lens through which Israeli conduct got analyzed," in fact, "the conduct of Hamas does not in any way shape the report's evaluation of Israeli targeting."[53] "When one side systematically violates the rules designed to protect civilians, after all, and a lot of civilians then get killed, those systematic violations have to be central to the inquiry into the reasons for those civilian deaths," wrote Wittes and Schwartz.[54] "In this report, those systematic violations are an afterthought," said Wittes and Schwartz, noting that "somewhat shockingly—and very tellingly—they are also entirely absent from the report's 'conclusions and recommendations.'"[55]

In addition to violating the principles of distinction and precaution with regard to Palestinian civilians, Hamas also violated the law of armed conflict with its targeting of Israeli civilians. Many of the rockets and mortars Hamas fired from Palestinian civilian facilities, in violation of the law of armed conflict, targeted Israeli civilian persons and objects. Hamas's targeting of Israeli civilian persons and objects violated various provisions of the law of armed conflict. While these rocket and mortar attacks are not themselves a manifestation of lawfare, they are important to note because their violation of the law of armed conflict creates for Hamas a vulnerability to international judicial processes, whether or not generated by Israeli lawfare. This vulnerability was (as described in Chapter 5 of this book) an important factor in PA decision-making as to whether its lawfare-motivated accession to the International Criminal Court would, on balance, advance the Palestinian cause.

In the decade after Israel withdrew from the Gaza Strip in 2005, more than 11,000 rockets and mortars were reportedly fired from there at Israel.[56] As many as 9,000 rockets and mortars reportedly hit just one Israeli town, Sderot, which is located within Israel's pre-1967 borders, about one mile from Gaza.[57] Mahmoud al-Zahar, a senior Hamas official who has served as the organization's foreign minister, explained the attacks against Sderot as follows: "Rockets against Sderot will cause mass migration, greatly disrupt daily lives and government administration and can make a much huger impact on the government. We are using the methods that convince the Israelis that their occupation is costing them too much."[58]

Amnesty International assessed that during the Gaza conflict of July and August 2014, "Palestinian armed groups fired thousands of unguided rockets and mortars towards Israel, in many cases directing them towards Israeli civilians and civilian objects, in violation of international law."[59] Similarly, Human Rights Watch concluded of rocket attacks from Gaza during the November 2012 fighting that "[t]he absence of Israeli military forces in the areas where rockets hit, as well as statements by leaders of Palestinian armed groups that population centers were being targeted, indicate that the armed groups deliberately attacked Israeli civilians and civilian objects."[60] Human Rights Watch used nearly identical language to describe rocket fire from Gaza during the 2008–2009 Gaza War.[61]

The law of armed conflict clearly prohibits each of the following: targeting civilian persons and objects, acts the primary purpose of which is to terrorize civilians, and indiscriminate attacks. For example, the requirement that a warring party distinguish between military and civilian persons and objects and not direct its attacks at civilian persons or objects is a fundamental principle of the law of armed conflict. This fundamental principle is customary international law applicable in both international and noninternational armed conflicts[62] and is codified in articles 48, 51, and 52 of Additional Protocol I to the Geneva

Conventions.[63] Article 13 of Additional Protocol II also contains the requirement as it pertains to civilian persons.[64]

Article 48 of Additional Protocol I to the Geneva Conventions sets forth the basic rule of distinction: "In order to ensure respect for and protection of the civilian population and civilian objects, the Parties to the conflict shall at all times distinguish between the civilian population and combatants and between civilian objects and military objectives and accordingly shall direct their operations only against military objectives."[65] The basic rule of distinction set forth in article 48 is considered to be a norm of customary international law applicable in both international and noninternational armed conflicts.[66]

More particularly, article 51(2) of Additional Protocol I to the Geneva Conventions states: "The civilian population as such, as well as individual civilians, shall not be the object of attack. Acts or threats of violence the primary purpose of which is to spread terror among the civilian population are prohibited."[67] The rule set forth in article 51 is also considered to be a norm of customary international law applicable in both international and noninternational armed conflicts.[68] In addition, article 8 of the Statute of the International Criminal Court specifies that "intentionally directing attacks against the civilian population as such or against individual civilians not taking direct part in hostilities" constitutes a war crime in both international and noninternational armed conflicts.[69]

Hamas has claimed, for example in its official response to the Goldstone Report, that it "does not deliberately aim at civilian targets" and has instead "often called upon the Palestinian armed groups to refrain from harming civilians."[70] "The armed Palestinian groups have indeed," said Hamas, "affirmed their commitment to the directives of the international humanitarian law in their media announcements, and they have also announced on several websites that they attack only military targets and avoid attacking civilian ones."[71]

Hamas asserted that the inaccuracy of Hamas's weapons is to blame for any harm to Israeli civilians, asserting that "during firing, [projectiles] can steer off course, resulting in harm to civilian targets, despite the considerable efforts to avoid causing casualties among civilians."[72] However, international law does not excuse the use of weapons that are incapable of being directed at a specific military objective. For example, article 51(4) states:

Indiscriminate attacks are prohibited. Indiscriminate attacks are:

(a) those which are not directed at a specific military objective;
(b) those which employ a method or means of combat which cannot be directed at a specific military objective; or
(c) those which employ a method or means of combat the effects of which cannot be limited as required by this Protocol; and consequently, in each such case, are of a nature to strike military objectives and civilians or civilian objects without distinction.[73]

The prohibition of indiscriminate attacks set forth in article 51(4) is considered to be a norm of customary international law applicable in both international and noninternational armed conflicts.[74]

Article 85 includes among its list of "grave breaches" of the Protocol willfully "making the civilian population or individual civilians the object of attack."[75] Also included in this list of grave breaches is willfully "launching an indiscriminate attack affecting the civilian population or civilian objects in the knowledge that such attack will cause excessive loss of life, injury to civilians or damage to civilian objects."[76]

Ibrahim Khreisheh, the PA's representative to the U.N. Human Rights Council, in a remarkable July 2014 interview on Palestinian Authority TV, described these Hamas violations as follows: "The missiles that are being launched against Israel—each and every missile constitutes a crime against humanity whether it hits or misses, because it is directed at civilian targets . . . targeting civilians—be it one civilian or a thousand—is considered a crime against humanity."[77]

II. ALLEGATIONS ISRAEL VIOLATED THE LAW OF ARMED CONFLICT DURING THE 2014 GAZA WAR

The Israeli military continues to grapple with the challenges posed by Hamas battlefield lawfare, much as the U.S. military has grappled with similar challenges posed by the Taliban, Islamic State, and other adversaries. The Israeli government is avowedly committed to abiding by the law of armed conflict, is determined to avoid having its commanders or soldiers prosecuted by the ICC or national courts, and is aware that Palestinian civilian casualties are a key source of criticism of Israel in the international community. "Obtaining the support of world public opinion is a major political objective" whenever "tiny Israel" is involved in an armed conflict, asserts Robbie Sabel, former Legal Adviser to Israel's Foreign Ministry, noting that, "if a state action is seen to be illegal, the state involved will invariably lose public support in the democratic world."[78]

Leading international human rights groups have asserted that the Israeli military violated the law of armed conflict during the 2014 Gaza conflict, including by committing "attacks directed at civilian objects or at civilians, or disproportionate and indiscriminate attacks that kill or injure civilians."[79] For example, Amnesty International declared in February 2015 that during the fifty days of the Gaza conflict during the summer of 2014, "Israeli forces committed war crimes, including disproportionate and indiscriminate attacks on Gaza's densely populated civilian areas as well as targeted attacks on schools sheltering civilians and other civilian buildings that the Israeli forces claimed were used by Hamas as command centres or to store or fire rockets."[80]

More specifically, Amnesty International, having studied eight cases in which "Israeli aircraft dropped aerial bombs on or launched missiles at homes they knew or should have known had civilians inside," concluded that "the mass casualties and extensive destruction of civilian objects that could have been foreseen were in excess of the military advantage anticipated by these attacks."[81] Amnesty International assessed that "the fighters who were the apparent targets could have been targeted at a different time or in a different manner that was less likely to cause excessive harm to civilians and destruction of civilian objects."[82]

In these and many other such cases, the accusations by human rights groups that Israeli troops violated the law of armed conflict during the 2014 Gaza War are not accusations that Israeli troops violated a bright-line rule. Rather, they are accusations that Israeli troops applied a complex balancing test differently than the accuser would have, had the accuser been in the same situation. This is also the case with much of the report of the U.N. Human Rights Council's Independent Commission of Inquiry on the 2014 Gaza Conflict.

Remarkably, practically all of these alleged war crimes involved Israeli attempts to target Hamas fighters, command centers, and weapons that Hamas had deployed among civilians in violation of the law of armed conflict. In other words, Hamas deliberately violated the law of armed conflict in a manner that was designed to, and did, elicit alleged Israeli violations of the law of armed conflict. Chapter 5 analyzed Hamas's decision to concur in PA accession to the ICC, despite the fact that Hamas is more vulnerable to ICC prosecution than either the PA or Israel. Hamas's strategy of deliberately violating the law of armed conflict in a manner designed to elicit alleged Israeli violations is presumably motivated by some of the same factors.

In contrast to Israeli officials, who would be embarrassed to be subjected to an ICC or "universal jurisdiction" prosecution, and upset to be unable to travel to a European country that might extradite them in response to an ICC warrant, international law enforcement has little to no leverage over Hamas officials who are already condemned in, and unable to travel to, Europe.[83] As a result, the Israeli military is more fearful of taking steps that could possibly be condemned as law of armed conflict violations than is Hamas of taking steps that are clear violations.

"Israel is sensitive to international criticism that it has used its firepower indiscriminately, resulting in a disproportionate number of civilian casualties," wrote a *Washington Post* reporter in August 2014.[84] As Amnesty International implied, and the *New York Times* stated, "the ratio of civilians to combatants killed" was, with regard to the 2014 Gaza conflict, "widely viewed . . . as a measure of whether the commanders in the field acted proportionately to the threat posed by militants—or, in the eyes of Israel's critics, committed war crimes."[85]

However, the ratio of civilians to combatants killed is in fact not a reasonable measure of whether the commanders in the field acted proportionately or instead committed war crimes. This is particularly true in the Gaza conflict, where the Hamas tactics described in Section I of this chapter—such as hiding among civilians and discouraging them from fleeing the combat arena—appear to be designed to knowingly, and in some cases purposefully, sacrifice Palestinian civilians. Despite this, it is worth noting that the ratio of Palestinian civilians to combatants killed during the 2014 Gaza War[86] was far better than the ratio of Iraqi civilians to combatants killed by U.S. airstrikes during the Iraq War.[87]

In addition, the ratio of civilians to combatants killed is not the legally specified measure of whether the commanders in the field acted proportionately. The proportionality restriction applicable under the law of armed conflict involves a complicated, vague, and highly disputed balancing test. According to Hays Parks, who served as the lead U.S. Army specialist on law of war issues, "[b]y American domestic law standards, the concept of proportionality . . . would be constitutionally void for vagueness."[88] Articles 51.5(b) and 57.2(b) of Additional Protocol I of the Geneva Conventions contain the preeminent version of the proportionality test.

Article 57.2(b) requires that "an attack shall be cancelled or suspended if it becomes apparent that the objective is not a military one or . . . that the attack may be expected to cause incidental loss of civilian life, injury to civilians, damage to civilian objects, or a combination thereof, which would be excessive in relation to the concrete and direct military advantage anticipated."[89] According to a study by the International Committee of the Red Cross, "state practice establishes this rule as a norm of customary international law applicable in both international and non-international armed conflicts."[90]

The proportionality requirement turns in large part on the meaning of the phrase "excessive in relation to the concrete and direct military advantage anticipated," which was left unclear.[91] The official commentary on article 57 states that "this rule . . . is by no means as clear as it might have been, but in the circumstances it seems a reasonable compromise between conflicting interests."[92] As one commentator notes, "it is, of course, impossible to measure human lives against a military advantage to be gained."[93]

The official commentaries on articles 57, 51 (Protection of the Civilian Population), and 52 (General Protection of Civilian Objects) provide some guidance particularly relevant to combat such as that which occurred during the Gaza War. The commentary on article 51 states: "In combat areas it often happens that purely civilian buildings or installations are occupied or used by the armed forces and such objectives may be attacked, provided that this does not result in excessive losses among the civilian population."[94]

The commentary on article 52 states that "a school or a hotel is a civilian object, but if they are used to accommodate troops or headquarters staff, they become military objectives."[95] The commentary on article 57 states that "in general, the presence of enemy troops in buildings, structures or installations will make an attack against them legitimate."[96] Thus, according to the commentary on article 57, "it is clear that a belligerent who accommodates troops in purely civilian buildings, for example, in dwellings or schools, or who uses such buildings as a base for combat, exposes them and the civilians present there to serious danger: even if attacks are directed only against members of the armed forces, it is probable that they will result in significant damage to the buildings." [97]

In all cases, the proportionality test does not hinge on the relative number of casualties. Proportionality prohibits attacks expected to cause incidental death or injury to civilians, or damage to civilian objects, if this harm would, on balance, be excessive in relation to the overall legitimate military accomplishment anticipated. The law of war thus recognizes that mistakes are inevitable and does not criminalize soldiers who seek in good faith to avoid them.

Professor Laurie Blank emphasizes that "proportionality is a prospective analysis," as indicated by the requirement's reference to "expected" civilian casualties and "anticipated" military advantage gained.[98] "Commanders," says Blank, "must assess whether the risk of civilian harm is excessive given the anticipated military advantage" based on what is known to the commanders at the time.[99] "Hindsight has no role here," states Blank.[100] Thus, "an effects-based analysis—that is, using the numbers of casualties and extent of destruction to make legal claims—is simply incorrect."[101] In addition, emphasizes Blank, "a focus on effects incentivizes the enemy to simply surround himself with civilians in every conceivable location and circumstance, effectively guaranteeing greater civilian casualties."[102]

In light of the law of armed conflict principles of proportionality and distinction, the emergence of the ICC, and other factors, one of the most important issues faced by regular armies, such as those of the United States and Israel, while fighting adversaries hiding among civilians is "the extent to which armies should sacrifice military gains to reduce the risk of harming civilians, and in particular risk the lives of their soldiers in the process."[103] This question is particularly important in light of the increased aversion to their own soldiers' casualties of both the U.S. and the Israeli publics.

Israel appears to have settled on an approach that significantly sacrifices its military gains to reduce the risk of harming Palestinian civilians, while posing a relatively low risk to Israeli soldiers. The next section of this chapter (Section III) will describe and analyze that approach. It will then describe several other major steps the Israeli military has thus far undertaken in order to protect itself against Hamas battlefield lawfare.

III. ISRAEL'S RESPONSES TO HAMAS BATTLEFIELD LAWFARE

A. Changes to Israeli Battlefield Tactics—Airstrikes and Warnings

Israel's policy of relying on airstrikes and the pre-attack warnings they facilitate was extensively implemented and received substantial publicity during the 2014 Gaza War. For example, the U.N. Office for the Coordination of Humanitarian

Affairs reported on July 16, 2014, that "the Israeli military delivered text messages to virtually all the residents of Ash Shuja'iyya and Az Zaitun neighborhoods in eastern Gaza city, approximately 100,000 people, warning them to leave their homes by 8 am today (16 July), ahead of attacks to be launched in the area."[104]

The *Washington Post* reported that in attacking the house of a Hamas operative on a different occasion, "Israel telephoned the man, dropped two non-lethal warning rockets on the roof, and then leveled the whole building five minutes later," with "no injuries."[105] The *New York Times* reported that "the Israelis have used such telephone calls and leaflets . . . in a stated effort to reduce civilian casualties and avoid charges of indiscriminate killings or even of crimes against the rules of war."[106]

Ibrahim Khreisheh, the PA's representative to the U.N. Human Rights Council, described this phenomenon in a July 2014 interview on Palestinian Authority TV, in which he said, "many of our people in Gaza appeared on TV and said that the Israeli army warned them to evacuate their homes before the bombardment."[107] "In such a case," said Khreisheh, "if someone is killed, the law considers it a mistake rather than an intentional killing, because [the Israelis] followed the legal procedures."[108]

Lieutenant Colonel (res.) Tal Keinan, an Israeli pilot, described as follows the warnings and their cost to Israeli military objectives:

> I have friends in foreign air forces who think that the efforts we take to avoid civilian casualties are outrageous, bordering on irresponsible for a military tasked, first and foremost, with defending its own citizens. Let's be clear: calling and sending text messages to civilians warning them to evacuate a structure, and instructing them on exactly where to go for safety, demands tremendous resources. How do you get the telephone numbers? How do you plot a route to safety for civilians in each individual circumstance? How do you communicate it clearly, in Arabic, so that the specific warning is actionable? Of course, you are also providing the enemy with actionable intelligence. The 'Knock on the roof' policy is not just a warning to civilians. It is also a statement to the enemy saying 'This is what we plan to do in five minutes, and this is exactly where we plan to do it.' This is obviously a questionable military tactic. It allows Hamas forces to remove rocket launchers from target structures, prepare ambushes for IDF forces, or as has been a deeply cynical modus operandi, send civilians into these structures, forcing us to abort important missions, or incur terrible consequences.[109]

A turning point for Israel in its decision to focus on using air strikes while warning Palestinian civilians was the Israeli military's assault on the West Bank city of Jenin in early April 2002, during the Second Intifada. A bombing campaign by Hamas, the Al-Aqsa Martyrs Brigade, and Palestinian Islamic Jihad had resulted in thirteen separate terrorist attacks against Israeli civilians during March 2002 alone, including the bombing of a Passover seder at Netanya's Park Hotel, which left 30 dead and 140 wounded, and an attack at a restaurant in Haifa that killed 16.[110] Of the one hundred terrorists who carried out suicide bombing attacks against Israel between October 2000 and early April 2002, twenty-three, including the Haifa restaurant bomber,[111] were reportedly from the West Bank city of Jenin (with seven more suicide bombers from Jenin intercepted before attacks took place).[112] Israel decided to raid terrorist bases in various West Bank cities, including Jenin, in order to prevent further attacks.

Israel could have destroyed the main terrorist base in Jenin while minimizing casualties among its own troops had it bombed from the air. But that would have risked considerable Palestinian civilian casualties. So Israel sent in ground troops. Faced with Palestinian militants hiding in booby-trapped civilian homes, Israeli troops fought house by house at great risk to both themselves and civilians.[113] "In the battle of Jenin," says Professor Asa Kasher, who authored the Israeli Defense Forces' (IDF) Code of Ethics, "the IDF knew that the refugee camp was booby-trapped [but] they still insisted on not bombing from the air in order to keep from harming civilians, and they suffered terrible losses."[114] According to Kasher, the decision to send in Israeli ground troops was "a mistake."[115] Rather, Israel "should have made an effort to get the civilian population out of the terrorist environment, and then there would have been no need to send in the infantry."[116]

Despite Israel's efforts to minimize civilian casualties, at the cost of the lives of its own troops, Israel was, during and immediately after the fighting, widely accused of a massacre in Jenin. Palestinian leaders and media reports claimed that hundreds of Palestinian civilians were killed by Israeli soldiers in Jenin.[117] The charge was disproved by a U.N. report, issued several months after the fact, which found that the overall number of Palestinians killed was in fact fifty-two—around half of whom may have been civilians—while Israel lost twenty-three soldiers.[118]

By the time of the Gaza War in late 2008 and early 2009, Israel had turned to a different method for minimizing Palestinian civilian casualties, one that was significantly less costly in Israeli soldiers' lives.[119] The IDF gave extensive warnings to the citizens of Gaza during the 2008–2009 war, including distributing leaflets urging civilians to leave the conflict zone; making recorded warning calls to 160,000 Gaza phone numbers; and adopting the new "knock on the roof" tactic of firing nonexplosive but noisy ammunition before launching an explosive attack.[120]

As noted above, the IDF continued during the 2014 Gaza War to use these tactics designed to minimize Palestinian casualties. According to Martin Dempsey, a U.S. Army four-star general and the Chairman of the U.S. Joint Chiefs of Staff, "Israel went to extraordinary lengths to limit collateral damage and civilian casualties" during the 2014 Gaza conflict.[121] Dempsey said the civilian casualties during the conflict were "tragic, but I think the IDF did what they could" to avoid them.[122] Dempsey also said the Pentagon sent a "lessons-learned team" of senior officers and noncommissioned officers to work with the Israeli military and learn from the Gaza operation, "to include the measures they took to prevent civilian casualties."[123]

Richard Kemp, a retired colonel in the U.K. infantry who served as commander of U.K. Forces in Afghanistan in 2003, also asserted that the Israeli military went to exceptional lengths to limit civilian casualties during the 2014 Gaza conflict. "No other army that I have served in or alongside or that I have studied and researched has yet taken such extensive precautions . . . to minimize harm to civilians in a combat zone," said Colonel Kemp in a submission to the United Nations Independent Commission of Inquiry on the 2014 Gaza Conflict.[124] "This includes British and US forces," said Kemp.[125]

In contrast, U.S. State Department spokesperson Jen Psaki said that it was the "position of the Administration" that "Israel could have done more to prevent civilian casualties" during the 2014 Gaza conflict.[126] In addition, Amnesty International, in its study of eight cases of Israeli air strikes described in this chapter's Section II, concluded that "there was a failure to take necessary precautions to avoid excessive harm to civilians and civilian property, as required by international humanitarian law."[127]

B. Combating Lawfare by Enhancing Israel's Legal Public Diplomacy

Depending on how the duty of discrimination is interpreted, the IDF's warnings are "seen either as a very real attempt to meet the requirements of discrimination and protect enemy civilians from harm or as a poor alternative to risking ground troops."[128] In his interesting and extensively researched book titled *International Legitimacy and the Politics of Security: The Strategic Deployment of Lawyers in the Israeli Military*, Alan Craig argues that international humanitarian law (IHL) (the law of armed conflict) has so many gray areas, especially with regard to the key principles of proportionality and distinction, that "the legal advisor should accept the troubling notion that in many situations there is not IHL but IHLs and advise the military accordingly."[129] In other words, the legal adviser must exercise "choice among competing constructions of IHL"[130] and work to promote at the international level their state's preferred constructions of IHL on key issues.

Cognizant of this, part of Israel's response to Hamas's battlefield lawfare involves building support for Israel's preferred interpretations of international law. Much of Israel's campaign in this regard has been led by Roy Schondorf, who became Israel's deputy attorney general for international affairs after serving as head of its office focused on countering lawfare.[131] The legal public diplomacy work of Schondorf and the Justice Ministry's counterlawfare office is discussed in further detail in Chapter 6 of this book.

The magnitude and significance of the gaps between competing constructions of the law of armed conflict was highlighted by the United Nations Fact Finding Mission on the Gaza Conflict, which issued in September 2009 what is commonly referred to as the Goldstone Report (after the mission's chair,

Richard Goldstone). The Goldstone Report was established by the President of the U.N. Human Rights Council and given the mandate "to investigate all violations of international human rights law and international humanitarian law that might have been committed at any time in the context of the military operations that were conducted in Gaza during the period from 27 December 2008 and 18 January 2009, whether before, during, or after."[132]

The Goldstone Report was highly critical of Israeli military actions during the war.[133] Following the report's release, Israeli Prime Minister Netanyahu was so concerned that he said: "We face three major strategic challenges: The Iranian nuclear program, rockets aimed at our civilians and Goldstone."[134]

Some of the Report's strongest charges, including that Israeli forces intentionally targeted civilians as a matter of policy, were rescinded by Goldstone himself in an op-ed published in April 2011.[135] Even more interesting than their differences regarding the facts, the Goldstone Report and the Israeli report issued in response to it contained significantly different interpretations of the international law principles of proportionality and distinction.

The Israeli position was much closer to the view of Hays Parks, the U.S. Army's longtime lead specialist in the law of armed conflict, who has stated: "[un]intentional injury is not a violation of the principle of non-combatant immunity unless, through willful and wanton neglect, a commander's actions result in excessive civilian casualties that are tantamount to an intentional attack."[136] Several U.S. government officials expressed concern about the Goldstone Report and its potentially problematic precedent for U.S. military operations. For example, Michael Posner, the U.S. Assistant Secretary of State for Democracy, Human Rights and Labor, expressed concern at the Goldstone Report's "failure to deal adequately with the asymmetrical nature of this conflict or assign appropriate responsibility to Hamas for its decision to base itself and its military operations in heavily civilian-populated urban areas."[137]

One reason the Goldstone Report was so antithetical to the Israeli position was apparently that Israel refused to cooperate with the Goldstone Mission, while the PA provided its cooperation.[138] As a result, the Goldstone Mission heard largely from Israel's adversaries. According to the Report, "by refusing to cooperate with the Mission, the Government of Israel prevented it from meeting Israeli Government officials, but also from travelling to Israel to meet Israeli victims."[139] Goldstone himself, in his April 2011 op-ed, regretted that the record before his mission "unfortunately did not include any evidence provided by the Israeli government."[140] Referencing particular such evidence, Goldstone stated: "I regret that our fact-finding mission did not have such evidence explaining the circumstances in which we said civilians in Gaza were targeted, because it probably would have influenced our findings about intentionality and war crimes."[141]

The Goldstone Report debacle reportedly contributed to Israel's decision to cooperate with the Palmer Commission, which was established by the U.N. Secretary-General in August 2010 to investigate the deaths aboard a flotilla stopped by Israel from running the Gaza blockade in May 2010.[142] From the Israeli perspective, the Palmer Report, issued in September 2011, was considerably more balanced than the Goldstone Report had been.[143] The Palmer Report concluded that Israel's blockade of Gaza was a "legitimate security measure" that "complied with the requirements of international law,"[144] while criticizing Israel for what the Report said was "excessive and unreasonable" use of force while boarding the ships.[145] According to Professor Gerald Steinberg, a leading Israeli critic of the Goldstone Report, other factors contributing to the Palmer Report's greater balance included its more even-handed mandate and participants, as well as the fact that it was conducted under the auspices of the U.N. Secretary-General rather than the U.N. Human Rights Council (which has a reputation for exceptional bias against Israel).[146]

The Palmer Report also repeatedly cited, and appears to have been significantly influenced by the legal reasoning of, a 300-page report issued by a public commission known as the Turkel Commission, which was appointed by the Israeli government to examine the flotilla incident. The commission was headed by a former justice of Israel's Supreme Court, Jacob Turkel, and included two international observers (Lord David Trimble of the United Kingdom and Retired Brigadier General Kenneth Watkin of Canada) and two special consultants (leading law of armed conflict experts Dr. Wolff Heintschel von Heinegg of Germany and Professor Michael Schmitt of the United States).[147] The Turkel Commission issued two influential reports. The first report examined the flotilla incident, and the second report, which is discussed in Chapters 5 and 6 of this book, focused on assessing the Israeli government's system for investigating alleged violations by its troops of the law of armed conflict.[148]

However, despite the successful cooperation with the Palmer Commission, the Israeli government decided not to formally cooperate with the commission of inquiry established by the U.N. Human Rights Council (UNHRC) in July 2014 to investigate the 2014 Gaza conflict.[149] Israel's Foreign Ministry announced that the decision not to cooperate took into account the UNHRC's "obsessive hostility towards Israel," the commission of inquiry's "one sided mandate," and "the publicly expressed anti-Israel positions" of the commission's chair.[150] The UNHRC had selected as commission chair William Schabas, a law professor who had publicly suggested that Israel's prime minister, Benjamin Netanyahu, should face trial at the ICC.[151]

While neither the commission of inquiry nor the UNHRC has the ability to issue legally binding decisions, Israeli officials and their allies expressed concern that Schabas was determined to write the commission report so as to help lay the groundwork for ICC prosecution of Israeli troops for their actions during the 2014 Gaza conflict. One Israeli official told me he was convinced that "Schabas aimed for the commission to be a springboard for the ICC, to advance universal jurisdiction against Israelis, and to fuel the BDS movement."[152]

Schabas resigned from the commission in the face of questions over his impartiality.[153] Schabas was replaced as chair by Mary McGowan Davis, a former New York State judge, and the commission's report was issued on June 24, 2015.[154] As discussed in Section I of this chapter, the UNHRC Commission report was issued after the drafting of this chapter was largely completed.

A complete analysis of the UNHRC Commission report is outside the scope of this book. However, it is worth noting that Israeli officials and their allies were apparently correct in predicting that the report would help lay the groundwork for ICC prosecution of Israeli officials and troops for their actions during the 2014 Gaza conflict.

One expert outside of the ICC Prosecutor's Office who is exceptionally familiar with that Office's thinking is Alex Whiting, a Harvard law professor who served in the Office from 2010 to 2013, first as the Investigations Coordinator, overseeing all of the Office's investigations, and then as Prosecutions Coordinator overseeing all of the Office's prosecutions.[155] In a commentary on the UNHRC Commission report and its implications for the ICC, Whiting wrote, as mentioned in Chapter 5, that the report's analyses of "rockets and mortars fired by Palestinian armed groups" and of "15 air strikes on residential buildings in Gaza" by Israel contained evidence that "will push the ICC Prosecutor a long way toward opening a formal investigation" of both Palestinian and Israeli actors.[156] Whiting assessed that "an ICC investigation seems inevitable," explaining that from the prosecutor's perspective, "given the evidence that is now available to her, it is difficult to see how she avoids, at the end of the day, opening an investigation."[157]

Commenting on Israel's decision not to cooperate with the UNHRC inquiry into the 2014 Gaza conflict, an Israeli official told me that "Israel had a difficult decision to make regarding how to proceed."[158] "We have a case and want to present it, yet on the other hand," he said, "this is a biased mandate and if you cooperate, it limits your ability to condemn the report afterwards."[159]

"Israel has nevertheless improved its efforts to advance its narrative," said the Israeli official.[160] Thus, although the Israeli government did not formally cooperate with the commission of inquiry into the 2014 Gaza conflict, it did not discourage a group of Israelis living near the Gaza border from testifying before the commission about their experience of being attacked by Hamas rockets.[161] In addition, Israel's publicly reported self-investigations of alleged war crimes by its troops during the 2014 Gaza conflict—undertaken more quickly than after the previous Gaza conflict—were expected by the Israeli government to help undercut and perhaps soften any commission recommendation that the ICC move toward prosecuting Israelis for actions during that conflict.[162]

The debate over whether or not Israel should have cooperated with the UNHRC Commission continued after the report's release. In an interview with an Israeli newspaper, the Commission's chairperson, Mary McGowan Davis, said: "I certainly think it would have been different if Israel had cooperated . . . . We could have met with Israeli victims and seen where rockets landed, talked with commanders, watched videos and visited Gaza."[163] "We talked to a lot of witnesses," said McGowan Davis, "but of course an investigation needs to be as close to the scene as possible and it would have looked different."[164]

C. Expanding the Role of Lawyers in Israel's Combat Decision-making

In addition to altering Israel's battlefield tactics and enhancing Israel's legal public diplomacy, the Israeli government responded to the battlefield lawfare engaged in by Hamas (and also Hezbollah) by expanding the role of military lawyers in Israel's targeting decisions.

The role of the International Law Department of the IDF in operational decision-making expanded rapidly over the fifteen years or so prior to 2015.[165]

During the 2006 Lebanon War against Hezbollah, every Israeli Air Force target was reportedly vetted by military lawyers, who, if they determined an operation was not legal, had the authority to call it off no matter how late in the day.[166] After the war, the Winograd Commission was appointed to investigate the IDF's relatively ineffectual operational conduct during the conflict. The Commission was critical of the extensive involvement of IDF lawyers in combat operations.[167] While it reported no evidence that lawyers' involvement had caused adverse military outcomes,[168] the Commission did recommend that the growth of legal involvement be curtailed:

> We fear that the increasing leaning on legal advisers during military action can divert responsibility from the elected figures or commanders to the advisers, and can disrupt both the essential nature of the decisions and the military activity. It seems to us that it is appropriate that fighting forces, certainly at field ranks, concentrate on fighting and not consulting with legal advisers.[169]

Notwithstanding the Winograd Commission, the role in combat decision-making of the IDF's International Law Department reportedly increased significantly in the decade following the 2006 Lebanon War.[170] International law and enemy lawfare continued to heavily influence Israeli military decision-making, through both the IDF's International Law Department and the other primary institution through which Israeli lawyers influence Israeli military operations: the Israeli Supreme Court.

Israeli courts enforce customary international law as part of the "law of the land," and, in a long series of decisions, the Israeli Supreme Court has ordered the Israeli government, army, and security services to change policies that, in the court's view, were in violation of customary international law.[171] For example, in one case, the Israeli Supreme Court prohibited Israeli government interrogators from employing forcible interrogation against terrorists even in a "ticking bomb"

situation. In his decision, Justice Aharon Barak described the challenging security situation in which Israel found itself and stated:

> We are aware that this judgment of ours does not make confronting that reality any
> easier. That is the fate of democracy, in whose eyes not all means are permitted, and to
> whom not all the methods used by her enemies are open. At times democracy fights
> with one hand tied behind her back. Despite that, democracy has the upper hand,
> since preserving the rule of law and recognition of individual liberties constitute an
> important component of her security stance. At the end of the day, they strengthen
> her and her spirit, and allow her to overcome her difficulties.[172]

Perhaps uniquely among national court systems, the Israeli Supreme Court has
even intervened in actual combat situations.[173] For example, during one particular hostage-taking episode, "the Supreme Court effectively ran the negotiations
over the release of Palestinian fighters."[174] According to leading experts, "the
Israeli Supreme Court is engaged in an almost daily application of international
law to IDF military operations,"[175] and the Israeli military has a strong record of
complying with such court orders.[176]

D. Enhancing Israel's Investigations into Alleged War Crimes by Its Troops

As discussed in detail in Chapter 5, enhanced Israeli investigations of alleged war
crimes by its own troops are another means by which Israel has been working to
address the risk posed by Hamas battlefield lawfare. Consistent with the Turkel
Commission's recommendations, such investigations involve senior officers, are
allocated significant resources that might otherwise be deployed in combat, and
begin while conflict is still occurring.[177] For instance, the Turkel Commission
recommended that in cases where a war crime may have been committed, traditional operational debriefings (in which troops who are not lawyers discuss what
went right or wrong militarily during a mission) be quickly supplemented with
separate "fact-finding assessments"—to include experts in military operations,
investigations, and international law.[178]

The fact-finding assessments were reportedly recommended "as a way to inject
lawyers into the earliest stages of reviewing an incident in which IDF personnel
may have committed a war crime."[179] They were motivated in part by concern
that traditional operational debriefings could "skew later criminal investigations,
by allowing IDF personnel to coordinate their stories in a way which promotes
cover-ups of war crimes."[180] Critics of the proposed changes expressed concern
that "pushing aside or even setting up a parallel process to operational debriefings will over-legalize the IDF's culture, to a point where soldiers will hesitate in

battle and no longer own up honestly to mistakes for fear of legal prosecution."[181] Despite these concerns that changes to the debriefing process would reduce military effectiveness, the Israel military adopted the fact-finding assessment recommendations.[182]

E. Media Campaign Explaining Targeting Decision-making

While some lawfare combat occurs through international and domestic courts and the contents of U.N. fact-finding reports, much of it takes place in the court of public opinion. The combination of Israel's decision to rely heavily on air strikes and the worldwide dissemination of advanced information and communications technology has made it both easier to maximize compliance with international law and easier to publicly demonstrate such compliance.

The use of air strikes rather than ground forces makes it much easier for the attacking force to halt an attack if, at the last minute, it appears that civilians will be unnecessarily endangered. Israel's former Air Force chief, Eliezer Shkedy, stated in an interview that "[t]here are at least 10 operations we don't carry out for every one that we do. . . . If we know that [the terrorist] is holding his son's hand, we do not fire. Even if the terrorist is in the midst of firing a Kassam . . . ."[183]

The use of air strikes also makes it easier to photograph or videotape the attack. During both the 2008–2009 and the 2014 Gaza conflicts, Israel used targeting videos and other recordings as part of extensive media campaigns designed to explain its targeting decision-making and push back against accusations that its uses of force violated the laws of war. For example, as the 2014 Gaza conflict launched, Israeli defense minister Moshe Yaalon reportedly issued a special written directive that units take photos and document all events in real time.[184] Each unit of the Israel Defense Forces had a dedicated photographer assigned to the task, and each aircraft—including F-16 fighters, helicopter gunships, and unmanned aerial vehicles—was set up to "take high-resolution photos of everything that moves on the ground."[185]

A specific example of this tactic was the Israeli military's decision during the 2014 Gaza War to post online a multimedia presentation illustrating its decision to attack Gaza's Wafa Hospital building, which Israel asserted had been turned into a "command center, rocket-launching site, observation point, sniper's post, weapons storage facility, [and] cover for tunnel infrastructure."[186] The presentation included a video recording of shooting from the hospital and a tunnel access point, audio recordings of phone calls by the Israeli military to the hospital to ascertain it had been evacuated of civilians, and a video recording of the air strike and several subsequent secondary explosions which visibly confirmed that ammunition was present at the hospital site.[187]

The Israeli military also posted online a forty-page multimedia document titled "Hamas War Tactics: Attacks from Civilian Centers," which contains a compilation of "evidence of Hamas' violations of international law through use of civilian facilities and densely populated areas for terror."[188] One American commentator said the document "resembles an unsealed indictment against Hamas."[189] The document contains sections with titles such as "Launches from Educational Facilities," "Launches from UN and Red Cross Facilities," "Launches from Mosques," "Launches from Power Plants," "Launches from Hospitals," and "Launches from Media Hotels." Each section contains still and video images illustrating particular Hamas launches from the specified types of facilities. The presentation concludes that "Hamas' tactics flagrantly violate international law . . . given these tactics, the ultimate responsibility for the damage done to civilians as well as the civilian infrastructure of Gaza lies with Hamas."[190]

Since this collection of evidence of Hamas firing from civilian facilities was aimed in part at defending Israeli damage to such facilities, it has been described as a "defense dossier."[191] Israel reportedly also considered, but rejected, publicizing an "offense dossier," which would be designed primarily to demonstrate Hamas targeting of Israeli civilians.[192] According to a senior Israeli defense establishment official, such an "offense dossier" would have "featured every rocket launch from Gaza at Israel," showing "the type of rocket, where exactly it was going to hit and how many casualties it would have inflicted had it not been intercepted by the Iron Dome missile defense system."[193] The official also asserted that international law should judge such rocket launches based on the damage they would have caused had they not been intercepted.[194]

IV. LESSONS LEARNED AND THE FUTURE OF HAMAS BATTLEFIELD LAWFARE AND ISRAELI RESPONSES

A. Lessons Learned and the Future of Hamas Battlefield Lawfare Against Israel

For Hamas, battlefield lawfare against Israel has proven to be one of the most valuable tools in its arsenal, one that holds the promise of even greater utility in the future. As a result, Hamas seems likely to continue and, where possible, expand its use of battlefield lawfare.

Hamas would seem to be an extraordinarily unsympathetic combatant. It is an avowedly genocidal movement that remains dedicated to Israel's destruction.[195] The respected Freedom House rankings deem Hamas to have one of the world's worst records for respecting political and civil rights and the rule of law.[196]

Hamas or its military wing is designated a terrorist organization by the United States,[197] the United Kingdom,[198] Canada,[199] the European Union,[200] Australia,[201] and Japan.[202] When Hamas, in a relatively rare deployment of PA-style instrumental lawfare,[203] succeeded in persuading an EU court to annul the EU listing of Hamas as a terrorist organization on procedural grounds, the EU Council appealed the judgment and moved quickly to reimpose the listing.[204]

Hamas is also banned in Egypt.[205] In the 2014 Gaza War between Hamas and Israel, it was Israel that reportedly received the backing of Egypt, Saudi Arabia, and the United Arab Emirates.[206]

Since 2007, when Hamas took control of the Gaza Strip,[207] more than 10,000 rockets have been fired from Gaza into Israel,[208] which had evacuated all of its settlers and troops from Gaza in 2005.[209] Hamas's strategy of intentionally launching rockets at Israeli civilians is in clear violation of the law of armed conflict, as described in detail earlier in this chapter.[210]

Yet when Hamas fought Israel in 2008–2009 and again in 2014, Hamas's use of battlefield lawfare resulted in Israel, more prominently than Hamas, being vilified by much of the international community. Hamas's choice to hide and fight among Gaza's civilian population—including by wearing civilian clothing, storing weapons in mosques and schools, using the Shifa Hospital as its headquarters, and encouraging civilians to stand in front of targets—achieved the following:

- Protected Hamas's headquarters against all Israeli attacks and its fighters and weapons elsewhere against some Israeli attacks.
- Required Israel to expend resources on calling, and sending text messages to, civilians warning them to evacuate, and on nonexploding "knock on the roof" munitions.
- Required Israel to, in providing such advance notice, sacrifice the benefit of surprise, thereby enabling Hamas forces to remove fighters, weapons, and other assets from targeted locations and to deploy civilians in or around those locations.
- Heightened international condemnation of Israel, and pressure on Israel to make concessions to Hamas, by increasing Palestinian civilian casualties when Israel did attack.
- Contributed to Israel being subjected to one-sided, reputation-harming, and time-consuming investigations established by the U.N. Human Rights Council.
- Required Israel to expend considerable resources on media campaigns that illustrate and explain targeting decision-making by declassifying imagery and revealing intelligence sources and methods.

B. Lessons Learned and the Future of Israeli Responses to Hamas Battlefield Lawfare

The harm caused to Israel by Hamas battlefield lawfare has been somewhat mitigated by various Israeli measures, including trying to minimize Palestinian civilian casualties by providing warning prior to attacks, expanding the role of military lawyers in targeting decisions, enhancing Israel's investigations of alleged war crimes, and providing the press and public with multimedia presentations illustrating and explaining Israeli targeting. Israel will undoubtedly continue to take such measures.

While extensive warnings and expanding the role of military attorneys may be sufficient to maximize Israel's compliance with the law of armed conflict, they are clearly insufficient to quiet the intense international diplomatic and public relations harm caused to Israel by Hamas battlefield lawfare. In order to quiet the furor that erupts every time Israel engages in battle against Hamas, Israel may have two options. Ideally, Israel would, if it were able to (and this seems unlikely to be possible), devise new tactics and/or weapons that reduce Palestinian civilian casualties to much closer to zero while still achieving the Israeli military objectives of protecting its citizens against Hamas rockets and tunnels.

In addition, or alternatively, Israel must find a way of much more effectively waging legal public diplomacy. In short, Israel must do a much better job of promoting at the international level its preferred constructions of the law of armed conflict, especially with regard to combatants hiding themselves and their weapons among civilians.

Israel's key asset in this regard is likely to be the fact that influential Western governments, other world powers such as China and Russia, and especially their militaries have similar constructions of the law of armed conflict and are, to varying degrees, concerned that the interpretations and processes being applied to Israel may someday be applied to them. Tony Blair, the former British Prime Minister, commented on this issue in a 2010 speech:

> A constant conversation I have with some, by no means all, of my European colleagues is to argue to them: don't apply rules to the Government of Israel that you would never dream of applying to your own country. In any of our nations, if there were people firing rockets, committing acts of terrorism and living next door to us, our public opinion would go crazy. And any political leader who took the line that we shouldn't get too excited about it, wouldn't last long as a political leader. . . . I remember the bomb attacks from Republican terrorism in the 1970s. There weren't many arguing for a policy of phlegmatic calm.[211]

During the 2014 Gaza war, Israeli leaders made some efforts to explain the risk to other Western democracies of a failure to stand with Israel against Hamas battlefield lawfare. For example, Prime Minister Netanyahu asserted that allowing Hamas to "attack with impunity" from schools or mosques or hospitals "would validate and legitimize Hamas's use of human shields, and it would hand an enormous victory to terrorists everywhere and a devastating effect to the free societies that are fighting terrorism."[212] Netanyahu continued:

> If this were to happen, more and more civilians will die around the world, because this is a testing period now. Can a terrorist organization fire thousands of rockets at cities of a democracy? Can a terrorist organization embed itself in civilian areas? Can

it dig terror tunnels from civilian areas? Can it do so with impunity because it counts on the victimized country to respond as it must, as any country would, and then be blamed for it? Can we accept a situation in which the terrorists would be exonerated and the victims accused?

This is the issue that stands not only before the international community today regarding Israel; it stands before the international community with a wave of radical terrorists that are now seizing vast cities, civilian populations and doing exactly the same tactic that Hamas is doing. That's exactly what ISIL is doing, what Hezbollah is doing, what Boko Haram is doing. . . . And the test now is not merely the test for the international community's attitude towards Israel—an embattled democracy using legitimate means against these double war crimes of targeting civilians and hiding behind civilians. The test is for the civilized world itself, how it is able to defend itself.[213]

As illustrated in Chapter 1, Hamas efforts to hide among civilians are indeed very similar to tactics engaged in by other militants against other Western militaries, including by the Taliban against U.S. and NATO forces in Afghanistan.

In a similar vein, Natan Sharansky, chairman of the Jewish Agency for Israel and a former deputy prime minister of Israel, called for leading military experts from Israel, the United States, the U.K., and other countries, along with international lawyers, to "develop and uphold" new common standards for how "the free world can defend itself . . . against armies of terror . . . in view of the developing global war between the free world and terror."[214]

Israel seems likely to continue to attempt to mobilize other governments and militaries that share similar constructions of the law of armed conflict and may be concerned that the interpretations and processes being applied to Israel could someday be applied to them. It is likely to do so not only through the media but also through diplomatic, military, and legal channels. Specific objectives it might attempt to accomplish in this regard include:

- Persuading European governments to reduce funding of NGOs that promote constructions of the law of armed conflict that are more congenial to terrorists hiding amongst civilians. European governments might be more open to taking such a step if they are persuaded that their own interests are at risk.
- Persuading key Western governments and other world powers such as China and Russia, which currently do or may face combat against terrorists hiding among civilians, that they should use their international influence to bolster shared constructions of the law of armed conflict and derail or mitigate the new trend of subjecting Israel, after every conflict, to one-sided investigations established by the U.N. Human Rights Council.
- Persuading international bodies to much more assertively "hold non-state actors and others accountable for the failure to distinguish themselves from innocent civilians."[215]

According to Laurie Blank, far more international jurisprudence has focused on the obligations not to deliberately or indiscriminately target civilians than on the obligations not to hide fighters and weapons amongst civilians.[216] Blank noted that various international bodies—including a U.N. Panel of Experts on Accountability in Sri Lanka and the Goldstone Report—have, for example, ignored the illegality of "the practice of militants attacking while disguised as civilians," thereby in practice encouraging "militants to embed themselves within the civilian population."[217] Blank said that there has been a similar failure by international bodies, including the UNHRC Commission on the 2014 Gaza conflict, to hold militants accountable for violating the law of armed conflict by hiding and firing rockets, missiles, and other weapons in or near schools, mosques, homes, and other civilian buildings.[218]

When the law of armed conflict has as much leverage over genocidal terrorist groups as it does over the democracies they target, the terrorist groups will stop violating the law of armed conflict in a manner designed to elicit alleged violations of the law of armed conflict by the targeted democracies. As a result, casualties on both sides will drop dramatically.

CHAPTER 8

Israeli Offensive Lawfare

"Countries are bound by treaties, national agreements and special relationships. Private citizens do not have these limitations."
                    — Nitsana Darshan-Leitner

The government of Israel has rarely, if ever, played a front and center role in the conduct of offensive lawfare, partly in order to avoid setting precedents that could be used against it by its adversaries. However, Israeli government officials have, on several occasions, quietly (but on the public record) provided pivotal information to private sector litigators and to U.S. prosecutors engaged in offensive lawfare activities against Israel's adversaries.

This chapter will focus on three case studies involving such low-key sharing of information. The first two involve a private sector litigator, Nitsana Darshan-Leitner, who leads the Israel-based Shurat HaDin Law Center.[1] As the two case studies will describe, Darshan-Leitner and the Israeli government have a volatile relationship. Israeli officials have occasionally provided Darshan-Leitner with pivotal information. However, Darshan-Leitner's Shurat HaDin Law Center, an Israeli NGO, has also sometimes engaged in innovative lawfare against Israel's adversaries without cooperation from the Israeli government. Shurat HaDin has also at times taken aggressive legal action against the Israeli government itself.

Shurat HaDin provides, in some ways, an interesting point of comparison with the Palestinian Centre for Human Rights and other Palestinian NGOs described in the chapters on Palestinian lawfare against Israel. While the Palestinian NGOs seek to use lawfare to advance what they consider to be

Palestinian interests, sometimes at the behest of the Palestinian governments and sometimes not, Shurat HaDin seeks to use lawfare to advance what it considers to be Israeli interests, sometimes at the behest of the Israeli government and sometimes not.

As the case studies will make clear, the first case of offensive lawfare cooperation with Shurat HaDin (which is described in Section I) was, from the Israeli government perspective, a tremendous success. The second case (described in Section II) was, from the Israeli government perspective, a disaster. Together, they illustrate the potential and pitfalls of public-private sector collaboration on lawfare.

The third case study (described in Section III) focuses less on the nature of public-private sector collaboration on lawfare. Instead, it describes the surprising source of some of the financial evidence that has fueled a number of the cases against Israel's adversaries which are described in this book. As discussed in Chapter 1, lawfare is defined as "the strategy of using—or misusing—law as a substitute for traditional military means to achieve a warfighting objective."[2] The third case study provides an example of the lawfare paradigm turned on its head—Israel's use of kinetic warfare (traditional military means) to seize documents which are then turned over to public and private attorneys for deployment in criminal and civil lawfare litigation in the United States.

This chapter's conclusion (Section IV) derives lessons learned from Israel's offensive lawfare experiences thus far. It then discusses the future of Israeli offensive lawfare.

I. USING OFFENSIVE LAWFARE TO PREVENT A GAZA-BOUND FLOTILLA FROM LEAVING GREECE

The Shurat HaDin Law Center has undertaken numerous offensive lawfare activities, several of them remarkably impactful. "Shurat HaDin" is a Hebrew term roughly translatable to "path of justice." The Shurat HaDin website describes its methods as follows: "By using legal action and civil lawsuits, Shurat HaDin assists in bankrupting terror groups and grinding their activity to a halt."[3] "We have modeled ourselves on the Southern Poverty Law Center, a non-profit organization that for decades has effectively confronted and shut down racist groups across the United States,"[4] says the website.

Shurat HaDin, which has a staff of ten attorneys[5] and an annual budget of $2.5 million,[6] has reportedly won more than one billion dollars in judgments.[7] It has also reportedly frozen more than $600 million in terrorist assets[8] and collected $150 million on behalf of its clients.[9]

Some of Shurat HaDin's activities have reportedly been undertaken with pivotal information provided by Israeli government officials.[10] In such cases, the information has reportedly sometimes been provided pursuant to high-level policy decisions of the Israeli government[11] and on other occasions by Israeli officials acting on their own initiative. According to Darshan-Leitner, private citizens like herself have more flexibility in pursuing lawfare than do governments. "Countries are bound by treaties, national agreements and special relationships," said Darshan-Leitner.[12] "Private citizens do not have these limitations."[13]

Other Shurat HaDin litigation activities have been undertaken in opposition to the Israeli government. These include a lawsuit to prevent the Israeli government from proceeding with the release of Palestinian prisoners[14] and a lawsuit to compel the Israeli government to rescue Palestinians facing execution in the Gaza Strip for alleged collaboration with Israel.[15] Shurat HaDin has also threatened to sue the Israeli government to compel it to stop concurring in Egypt's increasing of troop levels in the Sinai Desert beyond the levels Darshan-Leitner believes are authorized by the Egypt-Israel Peace Treaty.[16] As described in detail in Section II of this chapter, Shurat HaDin has also battled with the Israeli government regarding the Bank of China litigation.

Some of Shurat HaDin's litigation has also put it directly at odds with the U.S. government.[17] Both Shurat HaDin's periodic cooperation with the Israeli government and its periodic insistence on undertaking litigation in opposition to the Israeli government have made it very controversial in Israel and elsewhere. Whether or not one endorses any of Shurat HaDin's lawfare activities, several of them provide fascinating case studies in the use of lawfare.

Shurat HaDin's most interesting and impactful success was its use of lawfare, in cooperation with Israeli government officials, to prevent a Gaza-bound flotilla from leaving Greece. The decision to block the 2011 flotilla's departure from Greece was taken in the context of the widely publicized controversy that erupted after armed Israeli forces in May 2010 stormed a similar flotilla that sailed from Turkey with the goal of violating Israel's coastal blockade of the Hamas-controlled Gaza Strip.[18] The mid-sea confrontation in May 2010 resulted in the deaths of nine armed militants aboard the *MV Mavi Marmara* and injury to several Israeli soldiers.[19]

Israel was widely criticized for its handling of the 2010 flotilla. For example, the U.N. Human Rights Council (UNHRC) appointed a fact-finding mission which issued a scathing report,[20] which the UNHRC then endorsed.[21]

A separate commission of inquiry into the 2010 flotilla incident, appointed by U.N. Secretary-General Ban Ki-moon, was led by former New Zealand Prime Minister Geoffrey Palmer. The Palmer Commission determined that Israel's blockade of the Gaza Strip was legal but stated that the "decision to board the vessels with such substantial force at a great distance from the blockade zone and with no final warning immediately prior to the boarding was excessive and unreasonable."[22] The Palmer Commission recognized that the Israel Defense Forces (IDF) were met with "organized and violent resistance from a group of passengers" upon boarding the vessel and therefore force was necessary for purposes of self-defense, but concluded that "the loss of life and injuries resulting from the use of force by Israeli forces during the take-over of the *Mavi Marmara* was unacceptable."[23]

As a result, when the 2010 flotilla organizers announced a plan to try again in June 2011 to breach the Gaza blockade, with a flotilla leaving from Greece, Israel was determined to find a way of stopping it before it got underway. Shurat HaDin suggested that offensive lawfare might be a more effective alternative than force. "There is no need for Israeli soldiers to rappel down ropes in order to stop the next flotilla—all that's needed is some courage and original thinking," said Nitsana Darshan-Leitner, the Shurat HaDin director, in an interview at the time with the Jerusalem Post.[24] "The flotilla should not be left for the Special Forces to fight alone," said Darshan-Leitner, explaining that "there are various ways to prevent, postpone, limit and avert the danger—and force isn't always the best way."[25]

With assistance from Israeli government officials,[26] Shurat HaDin took the following key steps to stop the flotilla:

A. Warnings to Maritime Insurance Companies

Shurat HaDin learned that ships are generally prohibited from departing Greek harbors without having maritime insurance.[27] Darshan-Leitner said that Shurat HaDin did not at first know the identities of the flotilla ships' insurers.[28] However, it determined that almost all maritime insurance in the relevant region is provided by a known set of several dozen companies, including Lloyd's of London.[29]

Shurat HaDin sent letters to each of the several dozen relevant maritime insurance companies.[30] The letters placed the companies "on notice"[31] concerning the Gaza flotilla. Specifically, the letters warned that if the companies knowingly insured boats being used to breach the Gaza blockade and conduct smuggling into Gaza, the companies would find themselves open to charges of materially supporting terrorism and legally liable for any future terrorist or rocket attacks perpetrated by Hamas, on the grounds that the boats provided material support to Hamas.[32]

Darshan-Leitner said that in her letters, she referenced or included copies of the U.S. Supreme Court decision in *Holder v. Humanitarian Law Project*[33] in support of her assertion that the flotilla's breach of Israel's blockade and its transportation of goods to Gaza was tantamount to providing material support or resources to Hamas and thus inconsistent with U.S. law. The *Humanitarian Law Project* case centered on 18 U.S.C. § 2339B, which makes it a federal crime to "knowingly provid[e] material support or resources to a foreign terrorist organization."[34] "Material support or resources" is defined to include "any property, tangible or intangible, or service."[35]

The *Humanitarian Law Project* case had been brought by plaintiffs who wished to support the "lawful, nonviolent activities" of two organizations which, like Hamas, had been designated by the U.S. State Department as "foreign terrorist organizations."[36] The Court held that the material support prohibition is constitutional as applied to the particular forms of nonviolent support that plaintiffs sought to provide to the two foreign terrorist organizations—the Partiya Karkeran Kurdistan (PKK) and the Liberation Tigers of Tamil Eelam (LTTE).[37] In doing so, the Court specifically rejected plaintiffs' argument that the material support statute should be interpreted to require proof that a defendant intended to further the terrorist organization's illegal activities.[38] In coming to this conclusion, the Court relied in part on "the considered judgment of Congress and the Executive that providing material support to a designated foreign terrorist organization—even seemingly benign support—bolsters the terrorist activities of that organization."[39]

Several of the maritime insurance firms, including Lloyd's of London, wrote back to Shurat HaDin saying they would not insure the flotilla boats in light of the information provided in the Shurat HaDin letters.[40] For example, Lloyd's wrote as follows in a letter to Shurat HaDin:

> As you correctly point out in your letter, Hamas is subject to UK and EU terrorist-financing sanctions. As such, any vessel identified as being owned or controlled by that organization would not be permitted to be insured by underwriters at Lloyd's, or any other EU insurer. The Lloyd's Market has robust systems in place to ensure international sanctions are followed, and therefore any underwriter identifying an insured or prospective insured acting on behalf of, or for the benefit of Hamas, would not insure such a risk.[41]

Meanwhile, the *Times of London* reported as follows:

> Lloyd's said that it would refuse to underwrite a vessel backed by terrorist or related organizations on any trip that would be in breach of sanctions . . . . Any ship owner planning to send vessels into Gaza would have to notify the Lloyd's of London market in advance, providing details of the cargo . . . . Lloyd's indicated that if its members had been deceived about the true purpose of a trip the insurance cover would instantly be invalid.[42]

B. Warnings to the Inmarsat Global Satellite Company

Shurat HaDin determined that under Greek law, no ship the size of those in the flotilla could depart from that country's harbors without having a functioning satellite communications system. It discovered that Inmarsat, which is based in the United States and the U.K., was the sole commercial provider of maritime communications services in the region and was providing satellite communications services to the *Mavi Marmara* vessel, which had been part of the 2010 flotilla and was poised to participate in the new flotilla.[43]

Shurat HaDin sent warning letters to both Inmarsat and its senior corporate officers in the United States and the U.K., stating that under U.S. law, Inmarsat and its officers would be open to both criminal charges and civil liability if it were to provide satellite communication services to the Gaza flotilla ships.[44] The letters said that Inmarsat's failure to terminate satellite services to the ships would be a violation of U.S. criminal statutes prohibiting the provision of material support to terrorism (18 U.S.C. §§ 2339A and 2339B) and noted that "as officers and senior employees of Inmarsat, you might also be criminally liable for such conduct."[45]

The letters also claimed that if Inmarsat continued to provide the flotilla with such services, Inmarsat would be civilly liable, pursuant to 18 U.S.C. § 2333, "for all physical or economic harm caused by the flotilla to any U.S. citizens."[46] In addition, the letters stated that "if the flotilla succeeds in conveying its cargo to Gaza, Inmarsat will also be liable for all attacks carried out in the future by Hamas," and that "as officers and senior employees of Inmarsat, you would share Inmarsat's civil liability."[47]

In asserting the potential liability of Inmarsat and its officers and senior employees for future Hamas attacks, Shurat HaDin cited to the case of *Boim v. Holy Land Foundation*, 549 F.3d 685 (2008), in which the Seventh Circuit Court of Appeals affirmed a $156 million award by the district court, under 18 U.S.C. § 2333, to the family of David Boim, a U.S. citizen killed in a Hamas terrorist attack in the West Bank.[48] As described in detail in Chapter 2 of this book, the *Boim* verdict was against several U.S.-based individuals and organizations found to have provided material support to Hamas, including by raising funds for it.[49] In an en banc opinion authored by Judge Richard Posner, the Seventh Circuit decided that "if you give money to an organization that you know to be engaged in terrorism, the fact that you earmark it for the organization's nonterrorist activities does not get you off the liability hook .... Anyone who knowingly contributes to the nonviolent wing of an organization that he knows to engage in terrorism is knowingly contributing to the organization's terrorist activities."[50]

When Inmarsat did not respond, Shurat HaDin filed a civil suit in Florida state court against Inmarsat (which had an office in Brickell, Florida) and its CEO (who was a resident of and owned property in Florida).[51] The suit was filed on behalf of Michelle Fendel, a U.S. citizen living in Sderot, Israel.[52] The complaint stated that "Hamas' rocket and missile attacks against civilian targets in Sderot continue until today, and constitute a present and on-going danger to the life, person and property of Plaintiff Michelle Fendel and other residents of Sderot."[53]

The suit alleged that "the provision of satellite communications services by Inmarsat to the Flotilla Ships constitutes a violation of" 18 U.S.C. §§ 2339A and 2339B, which prohibit material support for terrorism.[54] In support of that assertion, the complaint referenced the case of Javed Iqbal,[55] who was indicted and pleaded guilty to having provided material support to Hizballah, a foreign terrorist organization, by providing satellite transmission services to Al Manar, Hizballah's television station.[56]

The complaint also alleged that "Inmarsat's provision of satellite communication services to the Flotilla Ships directly enables and facilitates the Flotilla Ships' effort to provide material support to Hamas, which enhances Hamas' ability to carry out attacks against Sderot."[57] "Inmarsat's conduct," alleged the complaint, "therefore constitutes a present and on-going danger to the life, person, and property of Plaintiff Michelle Fendel and other residents of Sderot."[58]

On the basis that "Inmarsat's provision of satellite communication services to the Flotilla Ships is illegal and endangers the life, person and property of Plaintiff, Michelle Fendel," the suit requested remedies including a permanent injunction directing the defendants to "immediately and permanently cease the provision of any services, including without limitation communication services, to any of the Flotilla Ships."[59]

The requested injunction was not issued. According to Darshan-Leitner, Inmarsat nevertheless ceased providing service to the flotilla.[60] After the flotilla disbanded, the plaintiff voluntarily dismissed the action.[61]

C. Lawsuit to Seize the Boats

Shurat HaDin also filed a lawsuit in federal court to seize the ships in the flotilla on behalf of Dr. Alan Bauer, an American who had been seriously injured in a March 2002 suicide bombing by Palestinian terrorists.[62] The suit sought to confiscate the ships on the grounds that they were outfitted with funds unlawfully raised in the United States by anti-Israel groups including the Free Gaza Movement.[63]

The lawsuit contended that furnishing and outfitting ships that are to be used for hostilities against a country with which the United States is at peace triggers a rarely invoked statute, the Neutrality Act (18 U.S.C. § 962), which allows a plaintiff ("informer") to seize such property and retain one half of the proceeds.[64] The lawsuit was dismissed in April 2013 on the grounds that § 962 of the Neutrality Act "lacks an express private cause of action," and the executive branch had not instituted forfeiture proceedings.[65] The dismissal was subsequently affirmed by the Court of Appeals for the District of Columbia Circuit on the grounds that Dr. Bauer lacked standing to pursue the claim.[66]

D. Prodding the Greek Government

Following its warning letters to insurance companies and Inmarsat, Shurat HaDin formally notified the Ministry of Civil Protection in Greece that boats in the flotilla may have lacked insurance or been improperly registered.[67] Greek authorities were reportedly obligated to inspect the ships after receiving such a complaint.[68] Shurat HaDin also demanded that the Greek Coast Guard undertake thorough regulatory inspections of all boats involved in the flotilla.[69]

Several of the ships were reportedly unable to sail because of insurance problems.[70] Then Greek officials, who were said to be relatively sympathetic to Israel's concerns about the flotilla,[71] proceeded to prohibit ships destined for Gaza from leaving Greek ports.[72] The Greek government enforced the ban by intercepting several of the flotilla's ships as they tried to leave port.[73] At least one ship's captain was arrested and detained on charges of setting sail without permission and endangering passengers.[74] The flotilla's organizers said the Greeks had blocked the boats' departure as a result of actions taken by Shurat HaDin.[75]

In the end, some fourteen flotilla ships were prevented from leaving Greece. Their passengers eventually gave up and went home. The *New York Times* reported that the flotilla was halted "largely because of the efforts of an Israeli advocacy group"—Shurat HaDin.[76] One small boat managed to set sail for Gaza after falsely informing the Greek Coast Guard that its destination was Alexandria, Egypt.[77] However, the Israeli Navy managed to peacefully intercept the lone small boat.[78]

Through Shurat HaDin, the Israeli military objective of stopping the flotilla from breaching the Gaza blockade was accomplished without bloodshed, at relatively little cost, and largely without putting the government of Israel's own assets and reputation at risk.

II. SUING BANK OF CHINA FOR FINANCIAL TRANSFERS TO TERRORISTS

A second major collaboration between Shurat HaDin and the Israeli government illustrates the perils for both sides of public-private sector collaboration on lawfare. This collaboration involved a set of interrelated lawsuits brought against Bank of China in U.S. federal court by families of victims of Islamic Jihad and Hamas terrorist attacks that occurred in 2006, 2007, and 2008. Shurat HaDin represented the families of most of the victims, while the family of one victim, Daniel Wultz, was represented by other attorneys, including David Boies and Lee Wolosky.[79]

The suits allege that Bank of China facilitated the attacks by knowingly allowing and facilitating transfers of funds to the two terrorist groups through accounts held by a Palestinian named Said al-Shurafa, and also that the Bank was "negligent in failing to employ proper safeguards to prevent its wire transfer services from being used for such illicit means."[80] Bank of China, which is China's fourth-largest bank,[81] is owned by the Chinese government.[82]

A. "They Asked Us to Do the Lawsuit"

The Israeli government reportedly requested that the plaintiffs undertake the litigation. "They asked us to do the lawsuit, and they said they'll fully cooperate with us and give us anything we need to win," said Tully Wultz, the father of Daniel Wultz (a U.S. citizen who was killed by a suicide bomber near the Tel Aviv bus station in 2006).[83] In a court filing, Wultz's attorneys stated that the Israeli government "asked Daniel's family and its representatives to bring to justice those responsible for financing the attack that caused his death: Iran, Syria, and BOC."[84] "Israel promised," said the filing, "that if the Wultzes would agree to bring a lawsuit in a U.S. court, Israel would provide the evidence they would need to prove their claims."[85] According to Lee Wolosky, one of the Wultz family's lawyers, those commitments were pivotal in persuading the family to proceed with the case.[86]

According to a report by Alison Frankel of *Reuters*, filings in the litigation "detail Israel's novel tactic of using litigation to advance its national security objectives: After Israeli diplomacy couldn't convince the Chinese to shut down suspicious accounts, Israeli operatives, according to the plaintiffs' briefs, fed hard-won intelligence about alleged Bank of China terrorist accounts to private lawyers, with the express intention of prompting American victims to sue the bank."[87] In addition, "high-ranking Israeli officials personally assured some of the victims' families that private U.S. litigation was in Israel's national security interest."[88]

The suits appeared to hinge on whether Bank of China knew, at the time of the terrorist attacks, that it was involved in terrorist financing. Uzi Shaya, a former Israeli intelligence official, was expected to testify in 2013 before the U.S. federal court hearing the case that Bank of China had known it was involved in terror financing at the time of the 2006 and subsequent attacks.[89] Shaya was reportedly prepared to testify that he knew this because as an Israeli official, he had met with Bank of China officials in 2005 and provided them with evidence, after which bank accounts referenced during the meeting, including those of al-Shurafa, remained open.[90] "Shaya's testimony will bury the Chinese," said Darshan-Leitner, "but without it, success in the case is far from certain."[91]

B. Priorities Shift

According to Tully Wultz, the Israeli government offered Shaya as a witness.[92] Then, in early 2013, reports surfaced that the Israeli government would not only not facilitate Shaya's testimony but would instead prevent him from testifying. In November 2013, the Israeli government indeed filed a motion in U.S. federal court to block Shaya from testifying.[93]

Darshan-Leitner asserted that the Israeli government turned its back on the plaintiffs out of concern that Shaya's testimony would hurt relations with the Chinese government.[94] Trade with China is worth more than $8 billion a year to the Israeli economy.[95] In addition, Israel needs China to help pressure Iran over its nuclear program. Israeli press reports stated that Beijing had threatened to cancel Netanyahu's visit to China in May 2013 if he did not prevent Shaya from testifying.[96] One article quoted a letter from Chinese officials to Netanyahu as stating: "You have committed that no current or former employee shall testify. This commitment made it possible for you to visit China. The Chinese expect you to honor your commitment."[97]

In contrast, former Israeli National Security Council head Yaakov Amidror suggested that since the suit had already changed the bank's behavior, it had already achieved its principal goal.[98] Prime Minister Netanyahu's office has said it blocked Shaya from testifying in the interests of protecting classified information and international cooperation in fighting terrorist financing.[99]

C. An "Embarrassing Situation"

In response to the Israeli government's steps to block Shaya's testimony, David Boies, an attorney for the Wultzes, filed a brief stating that "the State of Israel should not be allowed to sabotage a case, which it set in motion in the courts of the United States to advance its own national agenda, by using the expansive pretext of national security—an interest that it has never previously raised during the five-year pendency of this lawsuit."[100] In addition, lawyers for Wultz filed a brief in federal court detailing alleged Israeli government encouragement of, and assistance to, the lawsuit in its earlier stages.[101]

The Wultz lawyers' briefs included detailed assertions that the Israeli government's instigation of the Wultz litigation reflected a national policy of waging offensive lawfare against terrorists and their financiers through encouraging and assisting private civil litigation in foreign courts. One filing by lawyers for the victims' families stated, for example, that "from 2002 to 2010, the Mossad and the Office of the Prime Minister implemented a national policy of combating terrorist financing by providing information to victims of terrorist attacks or their representatives to enable them to bring civil litigations against entities that supported terrorism."[102]

Another filing by lawyers for the victims' families stated that "the Israeli Prime Minister's office established a special unit charged with tracking and obstructing the terrorists' financial operations.... [T]his unit was called in Hebrew *Tziltzal* (Hebrew for "Harpoon").... [T]he agents of the Harpoon unit recognized that civil lawsuits litigated in foreign court systems against banking and financial institutions could serve as a powerful means of deterring and obstructing terrorist financing and deterring banks from involvement with the terrorist organizations."[103] Similar assertions have also been made in the Israeli press[104] and in a book by Ronen Bergman, a leading Israeli investigative journalist, as described in more detail in Section III of this chapter.[105]

Also in the wake of the Israeli government's decision to block Shaya's testimony, Shurat HaDin went to Israel's Supreme Court to demand that the Israeli government provide the U.S. court with particular documents relating to the case.[106] Shurat HaDin said the documents would play "a critical role in the case, following the government of Israel's maneuvering to prevent key Israeli intelligence officials from testifying in the case."[107] At the Israeli Supreme Court hearing, Justice Elyakim Rubinstein said the government "has fallen into one or another kind of embarrassing situation," having made promises to the terror victim's families but then "deciding to shift its stance toward the direction" favored by China.[108]

Separately, Israel's decision to block Shaya from testifying reportedly angered U.S. Congresswoman Ileana Ros-Lehtinen (R-Fla.), who wrote to Netanyahu to urge him to allow the testimony to proceed and "reaffirm Israel's solemn commitment to the victims of terror to ensure that justice be done."[109] The *Wall Street Journal* reported that "if Israel prevents the deposition, Mr. Netanyahu would risk being accused of betraying the commitment to battling terrorism on which he built his political career" and "would also risk alienating two of Israel's most powerful congressional allies, Ms. Ros-Lehtinen and House majority leader Eric Cantor."[110] Eric Cantor happened to be the first cousin of Sheryl Cantor Wultz, the mother of Daniel Wultz, the terror victim at the heart of the litigation.[111]

Shurat HaDin and the Wultz family lawyers reportedly never expected the litigation to get this far. They reportedly "initially believed that the Chinese Bank would seek . . . a face-saving settlement" out of court.[112] Instead, Bank of China aggressively sought to defeat or otherwise halt the cases against it.

In addition to deploying Chinese government pressure on Netanyahu, Bank of China reportedly threatened Darshan-Leitner with "defamation lawsuits seeking millions."[113] While employing these lawfare hardball tactics, Bank of China also demonstrated its lawfare finesse, or that of the lawyers it hired, by successfully (and embarrassingly) forcing Israel's Bank Hapoalim, not a party to the Wultz and related suits, to disclose records showing sixteen wire transfers to al-Shurafa's Bank of China account that originated from Bank Hapoalim between 2004 and 2007.[114]

Bank of China successfully justified its demand for such Bank Hapoalim records (and for related testimony by Bank Hapoalim officials) by noting that "the fact that Shurafa was the beneficiary was clearly indicated on the wire transfer orders that Hapoalim originated."[115] "The Israeli government had the jurisdiction, the authority, and the ability to halt any of those Shurafa transfers originated by Hapoalim," said Bank of China.[116] It said it sought "Hapoalim's testimony to determine whether the Israeli government made such efforts," because "testimony confirming the absence of Israeli government efforts, at home in Israel, to block Hapoalim's origination of transfers to Shurafa would make it unreasonable to infer that the Israeli government at the same time traveled thousands of miles to China in an effort to block Shurafa's receipt of such transfers."[117] U.S. District Court judge Shira Scheindlin found this argument persuasive and granted Bank of China's motions forcing Bank Hapoalim's disclosures and testimony.[118]

In July 2014, a federal court judge in New York "delivered a major blow to the case," by granting Israel's request to block Shaya from testifying on behalf of the families."[119] Bank of China "has continued to provide banking services to Hamas and aid in financing Hamas, possibly to this day, and certainly until 2012," said Darshan-Leitner in July 2014.[120]

Whether or not Bank of China is still providing services to Hamas, the public-private lawfare partnership between the Israeli government and Shurat HaDin on this case led to serious problems for both the public and the private side of the partnership. For the Israeli government, the case led to tensions between Israel and China, frustration among some of Israel's biggest supporters in Congress, harm to Prime Minister Netanyahu's reputation for being tough on terrorism, and the undermining of one of Israel's key lawfare stratagems.

On the private side of the partnership, the case led to a feeling of betrayal on the part of the Wultz family and other victims of terrorism, embarrassment and costly legal fees for one of Israel's largest private banks (despite the fact it was not a party to the suits), and, for Shurat HaDin, worrisome litigation threats from Bank of China and a potentially vast loss of time and resources invested in the case.

III. DEPLOYING KINETIC WARFARE IN SUPPORT OF LAWFARE

In March 2001, Prime Minister Ariel Sharon "set up a new counterterror body within the Prime Minister's office, reporting directly to him, to concentrate on gathering information on the finances of terror," wrote renowned Israeli investigative journalist Ronen Bergman in his book THE SECRET WAR WITH IRAN.[121] "The new department," says Bergman, was code-named 'Harpoon.'"[122] This is the same "Harpoon" unit that was described in plaintiffs' filings in the Bank of China case analyzed in Section II of this chapter.

Following the unit's creation, the Israeli military seized paper records of terror finance transactions in a series of "raids on charities, businesses and other locations in the West Bank and Gaza" in 2002.[123] The seized documents indicated that "Arab Bank provided financial services for Hamas and at least 41 organizations and individuals allegedly related to it or to Islamic Jihad."[124] "To get more evidence on terror funding," the Israeli military "conducted a series of raids beginning in mid-2003 targeting alleged terrorist charities and offices of Arab Bank."[125] The next step was to deploy the documents.

On February 25, 2004, Israeli "special forces raided the premises of the Arab Bank and the Cairo-Amman Bank in the West Bank city of Ramallah, and ordered the astonished staff to help them locate certain accounts and to determine the balance in each account," wrote Bergman.[126] "Armed with the figures, the Israelis then ordered the clerks to open the vaults, and took out cash equaling the total amount of the accounts," said Bergman.[127] An Arab Bank vice president told the *Christian Science Monitor* that Israeli soldiers "forced us to print out the balances for the accounts" and then "forced us to open the safe."[128] "Our teller went in and counted the money and gave it to the soldiers," said the Bank vice president.[129] "The soldiers gave us a receipt and took the money out of the bank."[130] According to Bergman, "this entirely novel method of confiscating" terrorist funds yielded "some $9 million in various currencies" from several hundred accounts that "belonged to various societies connected to Hamas and the Islamic Jihad."[131]

This kinetic warfare operation to seize terrorist funds turned out to be a public relations disaster. As an operative who helped plan the operation told Bergman, "it was seen in the world as a bank robbery in broad daylight carried out by the State of Israel."[132] From a counterterrorism perspective, the operation also was flawed because the seizures depended on which terrorist accounts happened to have money in them that day. "How do you confiscate an overdraft?," questioned the operative. "After all, some of the accounts were in the red."[133] "In the wake of devastating criticism," said Bergman, "Israel decided against any repeat operations" seizing terrorist cash from banks.[134]

Israel's efforts to stop terror finance shifted back from using seized documents to confiscate actual dollars from terror financiers to turning seized documents over to public and private attorneys for deployment in criminal and civil lawfare litigation in the United States. For example, documents seized by Israel were explicitly used as evidence in the United States' criminal prosecution of the Holy Land Foundation and five individuals for providing material support to Hamas.[135] The prosecutions resulted in lengthy jail terms for Foundation leaders, contributed to the Foundation's closure, and helped to considerably reduce Hamas fundraising in the United States.[136]

The Fifth Circuit noted in *United States v. El-Mezain*, a principal case against Hamas's material supporters, that the U.S. "[g]overnment's evidence ... included evidence seized by the Israeli military from the zakat committees and the PA's headquarters in Ramallah"[137] and that "the Israeli military operation ... was the source of much of the evidence introduced at trial."[138] In denying a defense challenge to the introduction of some of the seized documents, the Fifth Circuit said, "we agree with the Government that evidence seized from HLF and the zakat committees, including images of violence and videos glorifying Hamas and depicting Hamas leaders, was probative of the motive or intent of the committees and HLF to support Hamas."[139] The court proceeded to cite in support of the prosecution several "documents seized from the zakat committees by the Israelis."[140]

In addition, as described in Chapter 2 of this book, bank and other documents seized in Israeli raids played a pivotal role in informing a precedent-setting civil lawsuit against Arab Bank. On September 22, 2014, a federal jury in that case, *Linde v. Arab Bank*, found Arab Bank PLC liable for damages suffered by victims and family members of victims killed or injured in twenty-four terrorist attacks by Hamas and similar terrorist organizations (Hamas).[141] The *Linde* jury found Arab Bank liable principally on the grounds that the Bank had knowingly provided Hamas with material support in the form of financial services.[142]

One illustration of Arab Bank's role in providing material support for terrorist groups was "in a table the Israelis say they seized from the Elehssan Charitable Society of Tulkarm."[143] The table "lists 13 families, their Arab Bank account numbers, and the payments they allegedly received in connection with their participation in the fight against Israel."[144] For example, "the table states that the father of Rami Ghanem received $21,000 in his Arab Bank account after the young man blew himself up outside the London Cafe in Netanya—$14,000 in compensation for the loss of his house and $7,000 for the loss of his son."[145] In contrast with the $9 million in cash that Israeli troops confiscated in their February 25, 2004, raids on Arab Bank and Cairo-Amman Bank branches in Ramallah, the settlement against Arab Bank in the *Linde* case was anticipated to be about $1 billion.[146]

Bank and other documents seized in Israeli raids also played a key role in an investigation of Arab Bank by the U.S. Office of the Comptroller of the Currency and by the U.S. Treasury Department's Financial Crimes Enforcement Network. As described in Chapter 2 of this book, that investigation led in 2005 to the United States assessing a $24 million penalty against the Arab Bank for failure to implement an adequate anti-money-laundering program and for violating U.S. legal requirements to report suspicious activities.[147]

Israel disseminated many of the terror finance documents it had seized by simply posting images and translations of them on the Internet.[148] In a July 26, 2005, hearing of the U.S. Senate Banking Committee, Senator Richard Shelby, the committee chair, expressed concern about the investigative capacities of U.S. banking regulators.[149] Shelby said that "in the case of the New York branch of the Arab Bank ... we have an institution that had repeatedly received the highest grades, only to precipitously become the recipient of a consent order that effectively shut it down."[150] "Equally troubling," noted Shelby, "is the fact that most of what became known about Arab Bank's New York branch was due to civil suits against the bank and the publication on the Internet of documents seized by the Israeli Army when it raided West Bank branches of the bank, not by the supervisor's regulators."[151]

Despite these successes, the special Israeli intelligence unit called "Harpoon," which used "lawsuits and the threat of lawsuits" to fight terror financing, was reportedly "mothballed."[152] The unit's closure apparently occurred in the wake of the Bank of China debacle described in Section II of this chapter.[153]

IV. LESSONS LEARNED AND THE FUTURE OF ISRAELI OFFENSIVE LAWFARE

This chapter has thus far focused on three sets of prominent and illustrative examples of the offensive lawfare in which Israel has so far engaged. As is typical of Israel's offensive lawfare to date, all three sets of examples have involved partnerships in which either private attorneys or foreign (i.e., U.S.) prosecutors have taken the lead in the courtroom.

This concluding section will first derive lessons learned from these public-private lawfare partnerships and discuss the future of such partnerships. This section will then assess Israel's offensive lawfare options should the Palestinian government continue to join international organizations and treaties and seek to use them against Israel (as described in Chapter 5).

A. Public/Private Partnerships

The first two case studies (stopping the flotilla and suing Bank of China) illustrate both the potential and pitfalls of public-private sector collaboration on offensive lawfare. In light of the resounding success, from Israel's perspective, of the lawfare campaign to halt the flotilla, Israel seems likely to look for similar opportunities in the future, while seeking to avoid the problems that marked the disastrous Bank of China case.

The rancor between the government of Israel and Shurat HaDin in the Bank of China case (and other cases in which Shurat HaDin has acted contrary to the Israeli government's wishes) may mean that there will be few if any future lawfare partnerships between the two. However, as lawfare increases in potency, it seems highly likely that both Israel and other Western governments will partner with other non-governmental attorneys in waging lawfare against the governments' international adversaries. Such partnerships are likely to occur both with regard to achieving real-time operational objectives, akin to halting the flotilla, and with regard to longer-term litigation designed to seize assets, halt financial flows, or otherwise hinder and deter adversaries.

It is worth noting that while the flotilla and Bank of China cases involved interactive partnerships, in which back-and-forth collaboration occurred (or was to occur), the third case study involves a different model. According to sources including the *Wall Street Journal* and U.S. Senate Banking Committee Chair Richard Shelby, the terror finance documents that were seized by Israel in its kinetic warfare raids and which then fueled the *Linde* lawsuit and U.S. Treasury investigations were largely or entirely disseminated by Israel simply posting images and translations on the Internet.[154] By posting the documents on the Internet, Israel provided advance notice to its adversaries as to what to expect in the courtroom. On the other hand, Israel freed itself of the risk of being subject to the sort of pressure the PRC exerted on Prime Minister Netanyahu to prevent Uzi Shaya's testimony in the Bank of China case.

Based on Israel's experience with these three sets of cases, Israel—or indeed any Western government waging lawfare—may consider the following when weighing future engagement in offensive lawfare:

- Public-private partnerships on lawfare have the potential to be exceptionally powerful, as the flotilla example demonstrates, in peacefully and inexpensively achieving real-time military objectives traditionally achieved by force of arms.
- The U.S. statutes banning, and imposing liability in response to providing, material support to terrorists can be a very effective lawfare tool not only in protracted litigation but also in real-time action lawfare against service providers to terrorist groups.
- Public-private lawfare partnerships can be powerful in part because, as Darshan-Leitner has noted, private citizens have more flexibility in pursuing lawfare than do governments, because while countries are bound by treaties, national agreements, special relationships, and fear of setting adverse precedents, private citizens are less affected, if at all, by such limitations.
- Public-private lawfare partnerships may be at their most effective, from the perspective of the government, when the instigating government's hand is relatively hidden (as in the flotilla example) or when the instigating government clearly no longer controls the key evidence (as in the seized documents posted on the Internet) rather than as in the Bank of China case (where it became clear that the case might hinge on whether the Israeli government permitted the testimony of a witness it continued to control).
- Because a government's hidden instigating role (and the details of it) can in some circumstances contain the potential for embarrassment—if revealed or perhaps especially if the government publicly changes its mind about facilitating the lawfare—the government might consider carefully vetting, and reaching a kind of prenuptial agreement with, the private partner to ensure that the partner does not turn against the government.
- Parties might wish to avoid instigating lawfare against adversaries that can, as did Bank of China, mobilize allies as powerful as the PRC government. When push came to shove, the PRC government seemed either to have more leverage over Israel than Israel had over it or to care more about the litigation, or some combination thereof. As a result, it forced Israel to sabotage the litigation that Israel had itself initiated. Since the PRC government's ownership of Bank of China was no secret, the ultimately costly decision to deploy lawfare against them in this circumstance appears to have been a self-inflicted wound.

- The PRC government and the enterprises it owns may be particularly poor targets for offensive lawfare. Rather than settle, they are evidently willing and able to fight back, with a combination of hardball tactics and skillful litigation (waged by them and by the top-flight attorneys they are willing and able to invest in hiring).
- Targets of public-private lawfare partnerships may seek to identify and exploit any differences of interest between the public and private partners. The public and private partners may themselves wish to identify any such differences at the outset, consider how they might be exploited by the targets, and take prophylactic measures.

Based on these illustrative cases (and particularly the Bank of China case), private attorneys considering entering into a lawfare partnership with a government may take into account the following:

- The government partner might, at any point, withdraw from a public-private lawfare partnership. Governments have a variety of interests, which both differ from those of their private partner and can change over time.
- In weighing whether to enter into a lawfare partnership with a government, the private attorney will likely weigh:
  - the extent to which government withdrawal at various stages would reduce the chances of victory;
  - whether the government can be prevailed upon to make as many as possible of its pivotal contributions (e.g., provide witnesses or documents) either at the beginning or relatively early in the case (i.e., before the target is able to gear up); and
  - what the private attorney's exposure might be (e.g., a defamation lawsuit by the other side) if the partner government withdraws.

B. Offensive Lawfare by Israel Directly Against Palestinian Governments

As discussed in Chapter 5, the PA is increasingly joining international organizations and treaties and seeking to use them against Israel. International organizations and treaties typically only provide standing to national governments, and usually only to national governments that are a party to that particular organization or treaty. This is unlike, for example, a U.S. federal court, where an individual can have standing to bring legal action.

Israel is a party to most of the international organizations and treaties that the PA has either already joined or is reported to be planning to join. If Israel is going to bring legal action against the PA in these organizations and treaties, it typically will not be able to rely on private attorneys or organizations to take the lead, as occurred in this chapter's three sets of case studies. In international forums, Israel is either going to have to bring lawfare action itself or persuade an allied government to do so.

Israel's strong supporters in international forums usually number in the single digits. For example, the U.N. General Assembly resolution—vociferously opposed by Israel—which in November 2012 accorded Palestine "non-member State status in the United Nations," passed by a margin of 138 countries in favor, 9 opposed, and 41 abstaining.[155] Thus, unless Israel is able to persuade the United States (or perhaps a friendly country such as Canada) to wage offensive lawfare on its behalf in such an international forum, it will have to do so itself. Either way, Israel will likely be on the losing end of almost any vote. Even in the U.N. Security Council, where the United States is at its most powerful, the United States is able to veto any adverse resolution but can have considerable difficulty advancing its own proactive resolutions (in light of the Chinese and Russian vetoes).

As described in detail in Chapter 5, the PA is clearly susceptible to both incentives and pressure to refrain from lawfare in international forums. In light of the voting margins against Israel in international forums, it seems unlikely that Israel will, except in rare cases, succeed in deterring PA lawfare with threats of Israeli offensive lawfare against the PA within those same international forums. If Israel is going to prevent PA lawfare in international forums, it will typically have to do so with outside incentives and pressures. These may include U.S. incentives or pressures targeting the PA or international forum, or Israeli incentives or pressures targeting the PA.

High on the list of potential Israeli tools for pressuring the PA is likely to be lawfare waged against the PA in those forums (i.e., U.S. courts) that are more favorable to Israel. However, as reflected in the three sets of case studies in this chapter, as well as in the *Sokolow v. PLO* case study in Chapter 2 of this book, Israel's use of private sector proxies to wage lawfare means that control over this powerful weapon—so potentially valuable to the State of Israel—resides in the hands of individuals (typically victims' families) and their attorneys. It will be interesting to see how the cross-cutting interests and resultant complications shape the future strategies and tactics of Israeli offensive lawfare. Other Western governments that are using, or are considering using, lawfare proxies will want to pay careful attention to this and other future developments in the lawfare laboratory that is the Israeli-Palestinian conflict.

Conclusion

The number, variety, and impact of lawfare deployments—by actors of all types—are virtually certain to increase in the coming years. This book has sought to provide both a systematic overview of lawfare and a call to action.

The call to action is directed to legal and national security practitioners and also to scholars. As a former attorney and policy official in the U.S. government, the author has sought with this book to draw the attention of the U.S. legal and national security community to the missed opportunities and increasing vulnerabilities created by the U.S. government's failure to engage with lawfare in a systematic and coordinated manner. As a scholar, the author has sought with this book to encourage further lawfare scholarship by illustrating the practical and theoretical significance of lawfare, providing a more detailed conceptual analysis of lawfare, and identifying some of the most important remaining gaps in the literature regarding this relatively new concept.

With an eye to both practitioners and scholars, the author has undertaken in this book to describe and analyze key lawfare case studies, to identify significant commonalities and themes, and to suggest preliminary answers to a number of important questions raised by lawfare. Over the course of the book, the author has suggested preliminary answers to key questions including:

- Why is law becoming an increasingly powerful weapon of war?
- How can lawfare be most usefully defined and divided into categories?

- What is the state of the literature on lawfare?
- What is the relationship between economic lawfare and economic sanctions?
- What is the relationship between lawfare and compliance with international law, including especially the law of armed conflict?
- How has lawfare thus far been deployed? For example, by what types of actors, against what types of actors, using what types of laws, and in which types of forums?
- What types of relationships have existed between governmental deployers of lawfare and non-governmental allies or proxies? What have been the advantages and disadvantages of such cooperation for either side, and what types of complications have ensued?
- What are the advantages and disadvantages, for different types of actors, of waging lawfare?
- What has motivated key actors to engage in lawfare?
- How have key actors responded to the emergence of lawfare? For example, how have key actors organized themselves to address lawfare?
- What have been the specific types and magnitudes of the impacts that lawfare has had on targets (e.g., U.S. lawfare imposing financial penalties on Iran or Hamas lawfare forcing Israel to change its battlefield tactics)?
- How and why can the same lawfare tactic have widely disparate impacts on differing targets?
- In what ways does lawfare build on itself? For example, in what way can lawfare deployments using one type of law or forum lay the groundwork for lawfare using other types of law or forums?
- What measures have thus far been undertaken to defend against lawfare, and what has been their efficacy?
- What are the potential benefits and costs of the U.S. government enhancing and expanding its efforts to wage and defend against lawfare?
- How could the U.S. government more effectively wage and defend against lawfare?

It is inevitable in scholarly publications, and particularly initial books on complex topics, to have to leave some questions and more definitive answers to future scholarly work by the author or others. Although this author has attempted to place lawfare in historical and theoretical context while also conducting this initial mapping of the field of lawfare, there is more work that could be done, particularly in the theoretical arena.

For example, there is a broad range of legal and international relations scholarship that could inform, and be informed by, the study of lawfare. Though detailed work in this arena will be left to future scholarship by this or other authors, it seems worth highlighting here, in the concluding pages of this introductory volume, some key opportunities for next steps in the study of lawfare. The following are some interesting, somewhat overlapping questions about lawfare that could inform legal and international relations scholarship and vice versa.

I. WHAT CAN LAWFARE LEARN FROM SCHOLARSHIP ON THE EFFICACY OF ECONOMIC SANCTIONS, AND VICE VERSA?

As discussed in Chapters 1 and 3, both this book and the seminal lawfare scholarship of Charles Dunlap define lawfare to include several types of law-intensive economic sanctions. At the same time, many other manifestations of lawfare (e.g., PA efforts to leverage the ICC or Hamas efforts to employ battlefield lawfare) do not obviously overlap with economic sanctions. In addition, as discussed in Chapter 3, economic lawfare differs in some respects from the traditional economic embargoes that have supplied many of the case studies used in the economic sanctions literature. As Gary Hufbauer, one of the leading analysts of traditional economic sanctions, has commented, U.S. financial lawfare is very different and "really quite novel" in comparison and has created "a huge inconvenience and risk for the authorities in Tehran."[1]

Despite the differences, many of the analytical concepts in the relatively developed economic sanctions efficacy literature are clearly applicable to both economic lawfare and some types of non-economic lawfare. Thus, Chapter 3 of this book analyzes U.S. financial lawfare against Iran using coercion and constraint language borrowed from economic sanctions specialists including David Cortright, Kimberly Elliott, Gary Hufbauer, and George Lopez.

The economic sanctions literature will also be useful as a starting point for identifying how to rigorously and systematically measure how effective a lawfare deployment has been or is likely to be "with respect to which goals and targets, at what cost, and in comparison with what other policy instruments."[2] It should be a particular priority, for both scholarly and policy purposes, to develop maximally accurate methods of making such comparisons. It is important for policy analysts in particular to be able to reliably compare relative rates of efficacy both within tool types and across tool types. For example, policymakers would benefit from being able to reliably compare the efficacy of different types of lawfare with each other and with traditional economic sanctions.[3]

The economic sanctions literature will also likely help with understanding lawfare efficacy issues including:

- the link between first order lawfare impact on the target (e.g., economic deprivation or criminal indictment) and ultimate policy objective (e.g., policy changes by the target);
- how lawfare can most effectively be used to contribute to desired outcomes by supplementing other types of measures including incentives, covert action, quasi-military measures, or regular military operations;[4]

- anticipating and minimizing the potential unintended costs and consequences of particular types of lawfare;
- how to tailor lawfare to the desired objective; and
- how to unwind or adjust lawfare deployments as objectives are met or other circumstances change.

II. WHAT KINDS OF DATA SETS CAN AND SHOULD BE COLLECTED TO INFORM THE STUDY OF LAWFARE?

Achieving an accurate understanding of all aspects of lawfare, including with regard to efficacy, depends to a considerable degree, of course, on the availability and careful selection and collection of data. Fortuitously for scholars, lawfare often involves tangible and measurable results (e.g., courtroom victories, laws enacted, or battlefield targets left untouched). The relative transparency that surrounds much of lawfare and its processes is also useful to scholars. Litigation and legislation both tend to generate long and detailed paper trails. In addition, the intersection between lawfare and kinetic warfare against non-state actors by the United States and its democratic allies tends to be heavily documented by NGOs, the media, and, in Israel's case, by the Israeli government itself. For example, as detailed in Chapter 7, it is relatively easy to trace a detailed lawfare dialogue between the numerous media reports of Hamas firing from among civilians, Israel's extensive multimedia presentations explaining and illustrating its decisions to target Hamas gunmen hidden among civilians, and the lengthy U.N. Human Rights Council reports accusing Hamas and Israel of noncompliance with international law.

In light of the analytical similarities between economic sanctions and, at a minimum, economic lawfare, the economic sanctions literature will be a valuable starting point for identifying what specific types of quantitative and qualitative data should be collected about lawfare, and the potential weaknesses in their explanatory power. Given that lawfare is a relatively nascent field of study, it is important to be deliberate and explicit in choosing what types of data should be collected and explaining why that data is best suited for making valid inferences about this novel subject matter.

As tempting as it may be to immediately jump to quantitative methods to make broad inferences about lawfare, for instance on the global level, it may make more sense for scholars to first develop additional in-depth case studies such as those in this book. Acquiring a richer conceptual, empirical, and grounded understanding of what lawfare is and how it functions in different contexts, before embarking on large-N studies, will help ensure that researchers focus on the optimal data and variables, selecting and weighting them in analytically equivalent and context-appropriate ways, rather than risk unknowingly comparing apples to oranges and therefore reaching misleading conclusions about the subject matter.[5]

One example of the challenge and how it can be clarified by in-depth case studies is provided by this book's analysis in Chapter 5 of the different costs that Israeli and Hamas officials ascribe to prosecution by the International Criminal Court (ICC). An analyst with no understanding of Hamas's particular ideology might predict that Hamas officials would not be willing to engage in a clear violation of the law of armed conflict in order to elicit a less definite Israeli violation, since the Hamas violation would be more likely to result in an International Criminal Court prosecution.

However, this book's in-depth case study reveals that it would be misleading to make such a prediction based on the clarity or severity of the violations and commensurate risks of prosecution, because Hamas officials typically find the prospect of ICC prosecution to be far less daunting than do Israeli officials. For example, one analyst noted that while Israeli officials would be ashamed to be dragged before the ICC, "Hamas officials would see being taken to the ICC as a heroic act, saying look they are prosecuting us for fighting for our freedom."[6]

A second example is provided by this book's analysis of the considerable reputational, attorney fee, and other costs imposed on Israel-affiliated lawfare targets by judicial proceedings even when the targets ultimately were victorious in the courtroom. The first example cautions against placing undue emphasis, in measuring lawfare efficacy, on the percentage risk of being prosecuted, because the perceived cost of such a scenario may differ across different types of actors. The second example cautions against placing undue emphasis, in measuring lawfare efficacy, on the target having been acquitted (in a criminal prosecution) or found not liable (in a lawsuit).

III. WHAT ARE THE KEY SOURCES OF LAWFARE POWER?
HOW CAN THE LAWFARE POWER OF DIFFERENT ACTORS
BE COMPARED?

Another arena in which lawfare scholarship may be able to learn from international relations scholarship, and vice versa, has to do with identifying and comparing sources of lawfare power. As David Baldwin has noted, "power has been prominent in discussions of international interaction from Thucydides to the present day."[7]

Robert Dahl suggested that power can be understood fundamentally as follows: "A has power over B to the extent that he can get B to do something that B would not otherwise do."[8] Joseph Nye defined power as "the ability to influence the behavior of others to get the outcomes one wants."[9] Both the economic sanctions literature and Nye's book, *Soft Power*, reflect the continued search by scholars and policymakers for new types and sources of nonkinetic power.

Questions I and II above have to do with how to measure and maximize the power of particular deployments and types of lawfare. In contrast, this question focuses on how to measure and maximize a particular actor's capacity to wage impactful lawfare. As this book has illustrated, actors can draw lawfare power from a variety of sources. For example, the U.S. government draws its lawfare power in part from the primacy of the dollar, the PRC has a lawfare advantage because it has developed and implemented a more deliberate and systematic lawfare strategy than has the United States, Israel draws its lawfare power in part from its alliance with an economic superpower (the United States), and the Palestinian Authority draws its lawfare power in part from the number of votes it can attract in international organizations from Arab and Muslim governments.

Among sub-state actors, U.S. state and local governments have lawfare power in part because their pension funds collectively control more than $3.3 trillion in investments. Among non-governmental organizations, several possess lawfare power because of their expertise in legislative advocacy, media relations, or extracting and deploying information from commercial satellite imagery, ship-tracking websites, corporate annual reports, trade press articles, foreign press articles, international agreements, local laws, and national laws from around the world. Among individuals, civil litigator Steven Perles has sufficient power to win and collect hundreds of millions of dollars from state sponsors of terrorism in part because he understands both how to sue pursuant to existing U.S. federal law and how to amend federal law to facilitate new avenues or types of litigation and collection.

Analysis of these types of lawfare power would undoubtedly benefit from a systematic application of international relations and other scholarly theories of power. Perhaps data on power in the lawfare arena could also inform and help advance those existing scholarly theories of how to understand, measure, or maximize power.

IV. WHAT CAN COMPLIANCE THEORY LEARN FROM LAWFARE SCHOLARSHIP, AND VICE VERSA?

The question of to what extent and why states comply with international law is one of the most important and hotly debated topics in international legal scholarship. José Alvarez has explained that "compliance scholars" in the field of international law "are hoping to identify which characteristics of the actors involved in an activity, the international environment, or the instrument involved (such as a treaty) have an impact on the likelihood that any international norm will be given effect."[10]

International relations scholars also periodically address these issues, although they tend to be more wary of claims that international law significantly impacts how states behave. Beth Simmons observed that while "most legal scholars and practitioners believe that" international laws "matter to the design of foreign policy and the conduct of international relations," scholars of international relations "have been far more skeptical."[11]

As this book has illustrated, lawfare case studies can provide interesting data and raise interesting questions regarding compliance with international law. The data are most applicable to questions relating to compliance with the law of armed conflict and its sibling, human rights law (with regard to which there is a richer compliance literature).

A. Increasing Costs of Noncompliance?

For example, international law has frequently been denigrated because of its lack of enforcement mechanisms. It is worth considering to what extent lawfare does or could represent the beginning of a change to that paradigm, at least for some actors.

The book includes several examples of significant costs incurred for actual or alleged violations of international law. These costs have, in most cases, been incurred as a result of one or more of the same four factors that this book asserts are making lawfare an increasingly powerful and prevalent weapon of war. For example, the increased reach of international law—as reflected in the willingness of many national courts to apply it as part of their jurisprudence—has resulted in universal jurisdiction cases threatening various Israeli and U.S. officials and former officials, as described in Chapters 1 and 6. The increased reach of international tribunals has subjected the U.S., U.K., Israeli, and other militaries to preliminary examination, and possible prosecution of their officials, by the ICC for alleged war crimes, as described in Chapter 5.

The rise of NGOs focused on promoting general compliance with human rights and the law of armed conflict has, as described in Chapter 1, increased awareness of the law of armed conflict and of asserted violations of it, thereby increasing the reputational cost—especially to democracies—of lawfare-instigated actual or alleged failures to comply with the law of armed conflict. For example, Israel has been heavily criticized by international human rights NGOs for its alleged violations of international law during the Gaza wars, as described in Chapter 7. The information technology revolution has empowered NGOs and even individuals to record and publicize various types of evidence of actual or alleged war crimes, as described in Chapter 2.

Finally, and perhaps most important, globalization and economic interdependence has made it much easier for relative outsiders—including foreign governments, sub-national jurisdictions, and even individual civil litigators—to impose costs for actual or alleged violations of international law. The numerous examples in this book include the hundreds of millions of dollars in costs imposed directly on Iran for its illegal acts of terrorism and killings of U.S. servicemen, as described in Chapter 2, and the billions of dollars in costs imposed on foreign banks for facilitating Iran's illicit activities, as described in Chapter 3. Examples also include the various companies including Riwal and G4S that incurred costs for their alleged involvement in purported Israeli violations of international law, as described in Chapter 6.

The increased costs of noncompliance associated with the rise of NGOs are consistent with various theories long-referenced in the compliance literature, including the transnational legal process model (with its focus on the role of NGOs in internalizing international norms, such as through the formation of epistemic communities);[12] liberal international relations theory (with its focus on domestic NGOs and other actors pressuring their own governments);[13] and the theory of transnational advocacy networks (with its focus on such networks generating outside pressure on governments).[14] However, such effects are largely lacking with regard to authoritarian governments and non-state actors such as Hamas, the Islamic State, and the Taliban, which are far less susceptible and subject to these influences.

As Eric Neumayer concluded from a detailed cross-national empirical study, a country more likely will comply with its human rights treaty obligations "the more democratic the country is" and "the stronger a country's civil society, that is, the more its citizens participate in international NGOs."[15] This is consistent with liberal international relations theory, pursuant to which it has been widely observed that "governments based on the rule of law and, especially, the independence of the judicial branch are . . . much more likely to comply with international obligations than those that are not."[16] Oona Hathaway put it as follows: "as liberalists note, liberal democracies contain powerful domestic interest groups that mobilize to pressure their governments to comply with their international legal obligations."[17]

Conversely, "in the absence of democracy and a strong civil society, treaty ratification has no effect and is possibly even associated with more human rights violations," said Neumayer.[18] This book's analysis of lawfare indicates that the increased reach of international law and tribunals and the rise of NGOs focused on promoting general compliance with human rights and the law of armed conflict has, unsurprisingly, intensified the compliance pressure on governments that are based on the rule of law.

However, this book also documents how the rise of another significant factor—the dramatic increase in economic interdependence—can be used to enforce compliance with international law. It appears as if this factor provides at least some compliance leverage over state actors, such as the PRC and Iran, that do not have governments based on the rule of law but are heavily dependent on international commerce.

For example, Treasury's use of economic lawfare to pressure Iran to comply with its nonproliferation law obligations had a significant impact despite the lack of rule of law in Iran. The impact occurred because Iran's heavy dependence on international trade in goods—including crude oil export sales and gasoline import purchases, and on the international financial and insurance transactions necessary to facilitate that trade—left Iran vulnerable to curtailment of each of those types of commerce (and especially all of them together).

Treasury's use of economic lawfare to pressure Iran benefited not only from Iran's heavy dependence on international commerce but also from the general economic interdependence of third countries. The rise of economic interdependence has made nearly every country in the world heavily and increasingly dependent on the integrity of the international financial system and other underpinnings of international commerce. Many third countries may be unwilling to help hinder, or impose costs for, foreign human rights or state sponsorship of terrorism or even nonproliferation violations because they see such violations as political or as not implicating their core interests. In contrast, Treasury's financial lawfare against Iran cleverly made the issue not just Iran's desired ends but also Iran's means to achieve those ends: Iran's deceptive and other abuses of the international financial system, on which nearly every country is heavily and increasingly dependent. As far back as 1997, Professor Harold Koh noted that "in areas such as international commercial law ... states tend to abide fastidiously by international rules without regard to whether they are representative democracies."[19] That fastidiousness is presumably even more pronounced today, with the vast increase in economic interdependence as described in Chapter 1.

To the extent that the imposition of costs for human rights, state sponsorship of terrorism, law of armed conflict, or nonproliferation violations can directly leverage the increasing economic interdependence of target states (as with the seizure of Iran's office building in Manhattan on behalf of victims of Iranian terrorism), that could help increase target state compliance. To the extent that human rights and other such violations can, as in the Iran case, be identified as integrally connected to violations of international commercial law, that could help engage third countries in imposing noncompliance costs on the target state.

Writing in 2002, Oona Hathaway asserted that "direct sanctions in the form of economic or military reprisal for human rights treaty violations are so rare ... that states are unlikely to conform their actions to a treaty solely on that basis."[20] Future compliance scholarship might profitably give consideration to whether and how the rise in economic interdependence over the last fifteen years—combined with escalating outside pressure from NGOs and the IT revolution— might help increase compliance leverage and counter the phenomenon, identified by Hathaway and discussed in Chapter 1, of countries enjoying the benefits of treaty ratification without actually observing the obligations assumed.

Such an analysis of whether and how the rise in economic interdependence could help increase compliance leverage might make an interesting contribution to the scholarship on how commercial linkages between states influence the likelihood of armed conflict between them. As Stephen Brooks has noted, "scholars and statesmen have debated the influence of international commerce on war and peace for thousands of years."[21] Brooks asserted that scholars' arguments for how the international economy can influence security "can be boiled down to three general mechanisms: the global economy can influence security by changing capabilities, incentives and the nature of the actors."[22]

John Stuart Mill famously predicted in the nineteenth century: "It is commerce which is rapidly rendering war obsolete, by strengthening and multiplying the personal interests which are in natural opposition to it . . . the great extent and rapid increase of international trade [is] the principal guarantee of the peace of the world."[23] If Mill's prediction is finally to be reflected in an actual diminution of armed conflict in the twenty-first century, at least between nation states, perhaps lawfare can help by leveraging globalization to deter states from violating international laws and by providing states with a robust nonkinetic alternative for achieving some of their lawful objectives.

B. Widening Compliance-Leverage Gap Between State and Non-State Actors?

While the increased reach of international law and the rise of NGOs, information technology, and economic interdependence have imposed on some state actors—including the United States, the U.K., Israel, and even Iran—new costs for purported or actual noncompliance with international law, violent non-state actors—including Hamas, Islamic State, and the Taliban—seem to be escaping these same costs even for clear-cut violations of international law. Future compliance scholarship, informed by lawfare, might usefully address questions such as the following: Is this a sign of a widening compliance-leverage gap between state actors and violent non-state actors? If so, what does it mean for international law, and how can it be addressed? How can the United States and its allies develop and implement new ways of holding violent non-state actors accountable, including for their law of armed conflict violations (as suggested in Chapter 7)?

V. WHAT CAN SCHOLARSHIP ON THE ROLE OF NON-STATE ACTORS LEARN FROM LAWFARE SCHOLARSHIP, AND VICE VERSA?

The role of non-state actors—including international organizations,[24] sub-state actors,[25] terrorist groups and other violent non-state actors,[26] non-governmental organizations,[27] multinational corporations,[28] and individuals—has received considerable scholarly attention in recent decades. Liberal international relations theory, the transnational legal process model, the theory of transnational advocacy networks, and the debates on asymmetric warfare have all examined the role of non-state actors of various types. This has been an important departure from the traditionally state-centric focus of international relations theory.

As this book has demonstrated, all of these types of non-state actors can and do play significant roles in lawfare. Their engagement in lawfare has been not only frequent but in many cases also very impactful.

The study of lawfare and of particular lawfare case studies can help further inform and sharpen scholars' understanding of non-state actors' roles in the international arena. Future international relations scholarship might benefit from examining and integrating the following types of lawfare case studies and the referenced questions they raise. Conversely, future lawfare scholarship would benefit by systematically drawing from and applying the literature regarding the role in international relations of each of these types of non-state actors.

A. International Organizations

As described in Chapters 1, 5, and 6, the PA and its allies have turned numerous international organizations into lawfare battlegrounds. As a result, one international organization (UNESCO) has been weakened by having its budget slashed, and another (the U.N. Human Rights Council) has been largely diverted from accomplishing its original mandate. If such lawfare continues or becomes more prevalent (with other actors using other international organizations as lawfare battlegrounds), it could have a significant impact on the efficacy and legitimacy of a broad range of international organizations. The relationship between lawfare and international organizations might therefore be a fruitful area of investigation for scholars interested in such organizations.

B. Sub-State Actors

Sub-state actors have been usefully defined as "semi-autonomous territorial entities that are legally dependent upon, or associated with, independent sovereign states."[29] They include sub-national components of federal states (which, in the United States, would include such sub-national components as states, counties, and cities) as well as overseas "and other dependent territories of existing states."[30]

Chapters 2, 3, and 6 provide examples of U.S. sub-state actors (including both states and cities) waging impactful lawfare. These include states divesting their hundreds of billions of dollars in pension funds from companies transacting with

Iran or Sudan, New York State imposing a $640 million penalty on a foreign bank laundering money for Iran, and Governor Pawlenty threatening to block a foreign company from receiving Minnesota infrastructure subsidies and construction permits until it withdrew from investing $5 billion in an Iranian refinery. Lawfare against America's adversaries by U.S. states and cities will almost certainly continue to be a source of conflict between those sub-state actors and the U.S. federal executive branch, which prefers to maximize its control over foreign policy. As discussed particularly in Chapter 2, the role in lawfare of such sub-state actors can inform future scholarly inquiry into the benefits, detriments, and practice of decentralized control over U.S. foreign policy.

C. Terrorist Groups and Other Violent Non-State Actors

As discussed earlier in this chapter, lawfare raises broadly important questions regarding the compliance-leverage gap between state actors and violent non-state actors with regard to the law of armed conflict. Chapters 1 and 7 describe and analyze in detail the successful waging of compliance-leverage battlefield lawfare by the Islamic State, Hamas, the Taliban, and Colombian rebel groups against the United States and its allies.

For example, Chapter 7 discusses how Hamas's battlefield lawfare against Israel has proven to be one of the most valuable weapons in its arsenal, heavily influencing the behavior of Israel, other state actors, and the international community as a whole. It has led to Israel being condemned by much of the international community (including traditionally allied states) and being pressured to make concessions to Hamas. On the battlefield, it has required Israel to sacrifice the benefit of surprise and otherwise fight Hamas with one hand tied behind its back, including by deterring Israeli attacks against Hamas's headquarters in Shifa Hospital and, on many occasions, against Hamas fighters and weapons elsewhere.

This raises broad questions for future scholarship such as: the extent to which such non-state actors are currently empowered by the disparity; how state actors should adjust their wartime tactics in light of this phenomenon; whether continuing to allow Hamas, Islamic State, and other leaders to hide among civilians actually saves fewer civilian lives than it costs (by extending the conflict in general and enabling them in particular to keep on purposefully killing civilians); and how such non-state actors can more effectively be held accountable or otherwise encouraged to comply with international law.

D. Non-Governmental Organizations

Chapters 1, 2, 6, and 8 provide examples of non-governmental organizations (NGOs) such as United Against Nuclear Iran (UANI), Shurat HaDin, and the

Palestinian Centre for Human Rights (PCHR) waging significantly impactful lawfare, including by developing and advocating legislation, bringing lawsuits, instigating prosecutions, and using information technology to collect and disseminate evidence of violations. Among the questions within the scope of Section IV of this chapter is what compliance theory can learn from the role of awareness-raising by human rights NGOs in increasing the cost of actual or alleged failures to comply with the law of armed conflict. Future international relations scholarship could also be informed by analyzing the direct engagement in lawfare of NGOs such as UANI, Shurat HaDin, and PCHR.

In light of the scholarly literature on public-private partnerships,[31] another interesting subject for future scholarship to either draw upon or focus on could be the potential synergies and pitfalls of public-private partnerships to wage lawfare. Relevant case studies in this book include: Congress passing laws repeatedly enhancing the ability of private civil litigators to wage lawfare using U.S. courts, as described in Chapter 2; the U.S. executive branch's occasional provision of bank account numbers, expert witnesses, and other assistance to private civil litigators suing Iran and terrorist groups, as described in Chapter 2; the EU's funding of NGOs waging lawfare against Israel, as described in Chapter 6; and the mixed results of the Israeli government's use of Shurat HaDin as a lawfare proxy, as described in Chapter 8. Future scholarship on public-private partnerships could also be informed by lawfare's interesting illustrations, as described in Chapter 2, of how and why the most effective U.S. non-governmental lawfare practitioners are benefiting from being more creative and nimble and less insular than their government counterparts.

E. Multinational Corporations

In several of this book's case studies, multinational corporations have served as targets or vehicles for lawfare. Some of the reasons multinational corporations have been a focus of attention are addressed in Chapter 1's discussion of the relationship between the rise of lawfare and the rise of economic interdependence. The phenomenon of lawfare focusing on multinational corporations is epitomized by Treasury's financial lawfare against Iran, which, as discussed in Chapter 3, innovatively and effectively emphasized directly pressuring third-country banks doing business with Iran rather than pressuring the governments of the countries in which the banks were located.

This appears to be a significant development in the international relations role played by multinational corporations. Treasury's innovative direct approach to banks has already been replicated with insurance and energy companies doing business with Iran, and it seems likely to be replicated with regard to future economic lawfare against other targets. It has already cost several foreign banks hundreds of millions of dollars each (in the case of BNP Paribas, $8.9 billion). Furthermore, its politicization of U.S. financial regulatory authorities threatens the primacy of the dollar and perhaps the legitimacy of some types of international commercial law.

In addition to its significant alteration of the international relations role played by at least some multinational corporations, Treasury's financial lawfare campaign against Iran has also resulted in the release, during the proceedings, of banking records that have provided fascinating documentation of and insights into the disdainful attitudes and circumventing practices previously adopted by several multinational banks toward U.S. regulations.

The book also includes several case studies of multinational corporations that were held liable for, or nearly held liable for, actual or alleged crimes by actors to which they provided services. This includes the lawsuit in U.S. court (*Linde v. Arab Bank*), which, as described in Chapter 2, resulted in Arab Bank being held liable for damages suffered by victims and family members of victims killed or injured in terrorist attacks by Hamas. The amount of damages, which was scheduled to be set in a separate trial scheduled to begin on August 17, 2015, was estimated to be around $1 billion.[32]

However, on August 14, 2015 (as this book was in its final copyediting stages), Arab Bank reportedly reached a framework settlement agreement with the plaintiffs.[33] The amount of the agreement was not publicly announced before this book went to press. The *American Lawyer* reported the settlement was for "slightly more than $1 billion," but an Arab Bank spokesman called that statement inaccurate.[34] Jimmy Gurule, a former Under Secretary of the Treasury for Enforcement, said the settlement would send "shock waves across the global financial services community," with other banks "concerned that they could be next."[35]

Another example of a multinational corporation serving as a lawfare target was the Dutch company Riwal. As described in Chapter 6, Riwal was investigated at length by Dutch police for war crimes allegedly committed by its rental of construction equipment to Israel for sixteen days. Israel allegedly used the equipment during those days for work on construction of the separation fence and settlements in the West Bank.

In light of these various examples, the relationship between lawfare and multinational corporations might be a fertile area of investigation for scholars interested in the international relations role played by multinational corporations.

F. Individuals

The vast majority of scholarship about the impact of individuals on international relations is, of course, about kings, presidents, foreign ministers, and other political figures who directed vast bureaucracies, movements, or other large organizations. There is also a considerable amount of scholarship about the impact on international relations of various theorists and other scholars. For a variety of reasons discussed in Chapters 1 and 2, there have until recently been relatively few Raphael Lemkin-type private citizen practitioners of international relations who singlehandedly, without institutional support, affected international relations in a sustained and sophisticated way (as opposed to, for example, a lone assassin who takes a single blunt action).

As Chapters 2 and 8 illustrate, the rise of lawfare litigation, economic interdependence, and information technology enables solo attorneys (or a very small team of attorneys) to have a significant impact on international relations. While such attorneys typically work through courts (which limits their discretion to some degree), they nevertheless retain a significantly different type of independent maneuvering ability than do most or all political leaders or even non-governmental organizations. In addition, as illustrated by the United Against Nuclear Iran name-and-shame tactic described in Chapter 2 and the Gaza-bound flotilla case study described in Chapter 8, individual lawfare practitioners could sometimes have a significant impact by directly communicating threats and other information to other non-state actors—in other words, without working through any governmental entity at all.

It is possible that the international relations roles and motivations of the solo practitioners (and very small teams of attorneys) described in this book do not meaningfully differ from the roles and motivations of much larger private sector non-profit or for-profit organizations. However, in light of the growing influence of such individual lawfare practitioners, it seems like it might be worth further analysis.

* * * * *

Lawfare is a weapon that can be used for good or for ill. This first wide-ranging English language book on lawfare has been written in full awareness that there is a long history of weapons inventors and developers who came to regret their role in creating, enhancing, or popularizing the weapons on which they worked.[36]

However, as this book has explained in great detail, the United States—of which this author is a former official and grateful citizen—has the potential to be the dominant lawfare superpower. As Philip Bobbitt eloquently put it, the United States is not doomed to a binary "stark choice" between "supporting law to the exclusion of strategic concerns ... or ignoring law altogether on allegedly strategic grounds."[37] This book advocates and illuminates a third way: more effectively using (but not abusing) law to achieve strategic objectives. The United States leads the world in the quality of its attorneys, many of whom are already experienced in aggressively leveraging its domestic legal system. All the United States government has to do is develop and implement a strategy for waging and defending against lawfare in a more sophisticated, systematic, and coordinated manner. Recommendations for how the United States could do so are included throughout this book, and particularly in its first four chapters.

The U.S. government's current approach to lawfare represents tremendous missed opportunities and poses increasingly important vulnerabilities, but could be rectified quickly and at relatively little cost. The benefits would include achieving some U.S. national security objectives with less or no kinetic warfare, thereby saving U.S. taxpayer dollars and some U.S. and foreign lives.

NOTES

FOREWORD

1. Carleton W. Kenyon, *Legal Lore of the Wild West: A Bibliographical Essay*, 56 CALIF. L. REV. 681, 683, 685, 687, 694–95 (1968), http://scholarship.law.berkeley.edu/cgi/viewcontent.cgi?article=2809&context=californialawreview.
2. *Id.* at 697–98.
3. I made similar points twelve years ago in my Introduction to *The National Interest on Law & Order* (2003). Sadly, the international arena remains at least as Hobbesian today as it was then.
4. Robert W. Gordon, *The Independence of Lawyers*, 68 B.U. L. REV. 1, 20 (1988).
5. *Id.* at 10.
6. DAVID CRIST, THE TWILIGHT WAR: THE SECRET HISTORY OF AMERICA'S THIRTY-YEAR CONFLICT WITH IRAN 148 (2012).
7. *Id.* at 152–53.
8. CSIS ANNUAL REPORT 2012, at 5, http://csis.org/files/publication/130305_annualreport_finalPDF-sm4.pdf.
9. *Thinking Over the Horizon: Michele Flournoy on Prudential Foreign Policy in the World Today*, YALE J. INT'L AFF., Mar. 19, 2015, http://yalejournal.org/interview_post/thinking-over-the-horizon-michele-flournoy-on-prudential-foreign-policy-in-the-world-today/.
10. *Id.*
11. Neely Tucker, *Pain and Suffering; Relatives of Terrorist Victims Race Each Other to Court, but Justice and Money are Both Hard to Find*, WASH. POST, Apr. 6, 2003.

CHAPTER 1

1. Charles J. Dunlap, Jr., *Lawfare Today . . . and Tomorrow, in* INTERNATIONAL LAW AND THE CHANGING CHARACTER OF WAR 315 (Raul A. "Pete" Pedrozo & Daria P. Wollschlaeger eds., 2011).
2. Mahmoud Abbas, *The Long Overdue Palestinian State*, N.Y. TIMES, May 16, 2011, http://www.nytimes.com/2011/05/17/opinion/17abbas.html.
3. *See, e.g.*, Richard Spencer, Adrian Blomfield & David Millward, *Britain Stops Russian Ship Carrying Attack Helicopters for Syria*, THE TELEGRAPH, June 19, 2012, http://www.telegraph.co.uk/news/worldnews/middleeast/syria/9339933/Britain-stops-Russian-ship-carrying-attack-helicopters-for-Syria.html.
4. *See, e.g.*, Stephen Stewart, *Cargo Ship MV Alaed Carrying Attack Helicopters Bound for Syria Is Halted off Scottish Coast*, DAILY RECORD, June 20, 2012, http://www.dailyrecord.co.uk/news/politics/cargo-ship-mv-alaed-carrying-1129794.
5. James Kraska & Brian Wilson, *China Wages Maritime "Lawfare,"* FOREIGN POLICY, Mar. 12, 2009, http://foreignpolicy.com/2009/03/12/china-wages-maritime-lawfare/.

6. Raul Pedrozo, *The Building of China's Great Wall at Sea*, 17 OCEAN & COASTAL L.J. 253 (2012).

7. Lieutenant Commander Robert T. Kline, *The Pen and the Sword: The People's Republic of China's Effort to Redefine the Exclusive Economic Zone Through Maritime Lawfare and Military Enforcement*, 216 MIL. L. REV. 122 (Summer 2013).

8. *See, e.g.*, Orde F. Kittrie, *Lawfare and U.S. National Security*, 43 CASE W. RES. J. INT'L L. 393, 396 (2011).

9. Charles J. Dunlap, Jr., *Does Lawfare Need an Apologia?*, 43 CASE W. RES. J. INT'L L. 121, 134 (2011) ("By creating restrictions beyond what the law of armed conflict would require, NATO's pronouncements encourage the Taliban to shield themselves from air attack by violating the law of armed conflict through embedding themselves among civilians.").

10. *Id.* at 134.

11. Charles J. Dunlap, Jr., Colonel, USAF, *Law and Military Interventions: Preserving Humanitarian Values in 21st Conflicts* (paper prepared for the Humanitarian Challenges in Military Intervention Conference, Carr Ctr. for Human Rights Policy, Kennedy Sch. of Gov't, Harvard Univ., Washington, D.C., Nov. 29, 2001), http://people.duke.edu/~pfeaver/dunlap.pdf.

12. Charles J. Dunlap, Jr., *Lawfare Today: A Perspective*, 3 YALE J. INT'L AFF. 146, 146 (2008).

13. *See, e.g.*, Ruth Walker, *Other Ways Than by (Kinetic) Warfare*, CHRISTIAN SCI. MONITOR, Jan. 23, 2009, http://www.csmonitor.com/The-Culture/The-Home-Forum/2009/0123/p18s01-hfes.html.

14. Phillip Carter, *Legal Combat*, SLATE, Apr. 4, 2005, http://www.slate.com/articles/news_and_politics/jurisprudence/2005/04/legal_combat.single.html.

15. *Id.*

16. Author interview of Steven Perles (May 2, 2015).

17. Kittrie, *supra* note 8, at 394.

18. Charles J. Dunlap, Jr., *Lawfare Today ... and Tomorrow*, in INTERNATIONAL LAW AND THE CHANGING CHARACTER OF WAR 315–25 (2011), *available at* http://scholarship.law.duke.edu/faculty_scholarship/2465/.

19. HUGO GROTIUS, THE FREEDOM OF THE SEA vii (1608) (introductory note by James Brown Scott, 1916).

20. R.P. Anand, *Maritime Practice in South-East Asia Until 1600 A.D. and the Modern Law of the Sea*, 30 INT'L & COMP. L.Q. 440, 442 (1981).

21. *Id.* at 442.

22. GROTIUS, *supra* note 19, at 28.

23. Glenn M. Sulmasy & Chris Tribolet, *The United Nations Convention on the Law of the Sea*, in NATIONAL SECURITY LAW IN THE NEWS (2012) (Sulmasy is professor of law at the U.S. Coast Guard Academy).

24. John W. Bellflower, *The Influence of Law on Command of Space*, 65 AIR FORCE L. REV. 107, 112 n.27 (2010), http://www.afjag.af.mil/shared/media/document/AFD-100510-068.pdf.

25. DONG WANG, CHINA'S UNEQUAL TREATIES: NARRATING NATIONAL HISTORY 128 (2005) (quoted in Jonathan G. Odom, *A China in the Bull Shop? Comparing the Rhetoric of a Rising China with the Reality of the International Law of the Sea*, 17 OCEAN & COASTAL L.J. 201, 223 (2012)).

26. *See, e.g.*, PLA SENIOR COLONELS ON GLOBALISM AND NEW TACTICS: "UNRESTRICTED WARFARE": PART III (2000) (translation of book by U.S. Embassy Beijing), http://fas.org/nuke/guide/china/doctrine/WEBRES3.htm.

27. *Id.* at Part II.

28. Qiao Liang & Wang Xiangsui, Unrestricted Warfare (1999) (translation of book by CIA's Foreign Broadcast Information Service), http://www.cryptome.org/cuw.htm.

29. David B. Rivkin, Jr. & Lee A. Casey, *The Rocky Shoals of International Law*, Nat'l Interest 35, 35 (Winter 2000/2001).

30. *Id.* at 38

31. *Id.* at 36.

32. *Id.* at 36.

33. *Id.* at 41.

34. *Id.* at 36.

35. *Id.* at 36, 41.

36. John Carlson & Neville Yeomans, *Whither Goeth the Law—Humanity or Barbarity*, in The Way Out—Radical Alternatives in Australia (1975), http://www.lace-web.org.au/whi.htm (last visited Apr. 25, 2015).

37. *Id.*

38. Charles J. Dunlap, Jr., Colonel, USAF, *Law and Military Interventions: Preserving Humanitarian Values in 21st Conflicts* (paper prepared for the Humanitarian Challenges in Military Intervention Conference, Carr Ctr. for Human Rights Policy, Kennedy Sch. of Gov't, Harvard Univ., Washington, D.C., Nov. 29, 2001), http://people.duke.edu/~pfeaver/dunlap.pdf.

39. *Id.*

40. *Id.*

41. Dunlap, *supra* note 18.

42. Dunlap, *supra* note 18.

43. Dunlap, *supra* note 9 at 122.

44. Dunlap, *supra* note 9 at 122.

45. Dunlap, *supra* note 9 at 122.

46. Dunlap, *supra* note 38.

47. Dunlap, *supra* note 38.

48. Dunlap, *supra* note 17.

49. Dunlap, *supra* note 9 at 124.

50. Dunlap, *supra* note 18.

51. Dunlap, *supra* note 9 at 125.

52. Dunlap, *supra* note 9 at 124 n.16.

53. Dunlap, *supra* note 9 at 123.

54. *Id.*

55. *Id.* at 123–24.

56. *About Lawfare: A Brief History of the Term and the Site*, Lawfare: Hard National Security Choices Blog, http://www.lawfareblog.com/about-lawfare-brief-history-term-and-site.

57. *Id.*

58. *Id.*

59. *What Is Lawfare?*, The Lawfare Project, http://www.thelawfareproject.org/what-is-lawfare.html (last visited April 27, 2015).

60. *Warfare*, Merriam-Webster Dictionary, http://www.merriam-webster.com/dictionary/warfare (last visited April 27, 2015) (one definition is "an activity undertaken by a political unit (as a nation) to weaken or destroy another <economic *warfare*>").

61. Michael P. Scharf & Shannon Pagano, *Foreword: Lawfare!*, 43 Case W. Res. J. Int'l L. 1, 10 (2011).

62. The issue is available at http://law.case.edu/journals/jil/PastIssues.aspx.

63. Most of these key Dunlap articles are included in these endnotes.

64. *See, e.g.*, Jonathan G. Odom, *A China in the Bull Shop? Comparing the Rhetoric of a Rising China with the Reality of the International Law of the Sea*, 17 OCEAN & COASTAL L.J. 224 (2012); Pedrozo, *supra* note 6; Commander Robert C. De Tolve, JAGC, USN, *At What Cost? America's UNCLOS Allergy in the Time of "Lawfare,"* 61 NAVAL L. REV. 1 (2012); Lieutenant Commander Robert T. Kline, *The Pen and the Sword: The People's Republic of China's Effort to Redefine the Exclusive Economic Zone Through Maritime Lawfare and Military Enforcement*, 216 MIL. L. REV. 122 (Summer 2013); James Kraska & Brian Wilson, *China Wages Maritime "Lawfare,"* Mar. 12, 2009, http://foreignpolicy.com/2009/03/12/china-wages-maritime-lawfare/.

65. This document, listed on Amazon as a sixty-six-page monograph published by BiblioScholar in 2012, is apparently very similar, if not identical, to the fifty-seven-page monograph by Juan Manuel Padilla, U.S. Army Command & General Staff College, *Lawfare: The Colombian Case* (May 20, 2010), *available at* http://www.dtic.mil/dtic/tr/fulltext/u2/a523182.pdf.

66. Paul A. Stempel, Capt., USAF, *Reading Lawfare in Chinese: The Meaning of the Term "Falu Zhan" ("Lawfare") in Chinese Military Literature* (July 2011), unpublished article. Stempel notes that when the Chinese government printed a translated version of an article titled *Lawfare: A Decisive Element of 21st-Century Conflicts?* by Major General Charles Dunlap, the former U.S. Deputy Judge Advocate General who coined the term "lawfare," the PRC's translators used the term *falu zhan* where Dunlap used the term "lawfare."

67. Stempel, *supra* note 66.

68. UNDER INFORMATIZED CONDITIONS: LEGAL WARFARE 7 (Song Yunxia ed., 2007) (quoted in Jonathan G. Odom, *A China in the Bull Shop? Comparing the Rhetoric of a Rising China with the Reality of the International Law of the Sea*, 17 OCEAN & COASTAL L.J. 224 (2012)). Another leading Chinese book on lawfare, which has not been translated into English, is XUN HENGDONG, LAWFARE IN MODERN WAR (2005).

69. *See, e.g.*, CLAUDE BOWERS, MY MISSION TO SPAIN: WATCHING THE REHEARSAL FOR WORLD WAR II (1954) (Bowers was U.S. ambassador to Spain from 1933 to 1939; the Spanish Civil War was fought from 1936 to 1939).

70. *See, e.g.*, U.S. DEP'T OF STATE, GROUND RULES FOR INTERVIEWING STATE DEPARTMENT OFFICIALS, *available at* http://www.state.gov/r/pa/prs/17191.htm (last visited Apr. 27, 2015).

71. David E. Sanger, *Global Crises Put Obama's Strategy of Caution to the Test*, N.Y. TIMES, Mar. 16, 2014, http://www.nytimes.com/2014/03/17/world/obamas-policy-is-put-to-the-test-as-crises-challenge-caution.html?_r=0.

72. Matt Apuzzo, *Justice Dept. Moves to Shield Anti-Iran Group's Files*, N.Y. TIMES, July 27, 2014, http://www.nytimes.com/2014/07/28/us/politics/us-justice-dept-moves-to-shield-anti-iran-groups-files-united-against-nuclear-iran.html?_r=0.

73. Dunlap, *supra* note 38.

74. *Id.*

75. Noor Khan, *Afghan Civilians Said Killed in Clash*, WASH. POST, June 30, 2007, http://www.washingtonpost.com/wp-dyn/content/article/2007/06/30/AR2007063000028.html.

76. *Id.*

77. *Id.*

78. *Id.*

79. Pamela Constable, *NATO Hopes to Undercut Taliban with "Surge" of Projects*, WASH. POST, Sept. 27, 2008, http://www.washingtonpost.com/wp-dyn/content/article/2008/09/26/AR2008092603452.html.

80. *Id.*

81. Dunlap, *supra* note 9 at 134.

82. *Id.*

83. *Id.*

84. JEAN-MARIE HENCKAERTS & LOUISE DOSWALD-BECK, CUSTOMARY INTERNATIONAL HUMANITARIAN LAW, vol. 1, at 68–74, 337 (Rules 22–23, 97) (2005), *available at* http://www.icrc.org/eng/assets/files/other/customary-international-humanitarian-law-i-icrc-eng.pdf.

85. *Id.* at 3–8 (Rules 1, 2).

86. Robert Gates, Sec'y of Defense & Adm. Michael Mullen, Chairman, Joint Chiefs of Staff, Press Conference with Secretary Gates and Adm. Mullen on Leadership Changes in Afghanistan from the Pentagon (May 11, 2009), transcript *available at* http://www.defense.gov/transcripts/transcript.aspx?transcriptid=4424.

87. Senior Defense Official, U.S. Dep't of Defense, Briefing on Human Shields in Iraq (Feb. 26, 2003), transcript *available at* http://www.defense.gov/Transcripts/Transcript.aspx?TranscriptID=1948.

88. *Id.*

89. *Id.*

90. Eric Schmitt, *U.S. Caution in Strikes Gives ISIS an Edge, Many Iraqis Say*, N.Y. TIMES, May 26, 2015, http://www.nytimes.com/2015/05/27/world/middleeast/with-isis-in-crosshairs-us-holds-back-to-protect-civilians.html.

91. *Id.*

92. *Id.*

93. *Id.*

94. Id.

95. *Id.*

96. *See, e.g.,* Kate Pickles, *ISIS Slaughters 400 Mostly Women and Children in Ancient Syria City of Palmyra Where Hundreds of Bodies Line the Street*, DAILY MAIL, May 24, 2015, http://www.dailymail.co.uk/news/article-3094956/ISIS-slaughters-400-women-children-ancient-Syria-city-Palmyra-hundreds-bodies-line-street.html; Michael E. Miller, *Islamic State's "War Crimes" Against Yazidi Women Documented*, WASH. POST, Apr. 16, 2015, http://www.washingtonpost.com/news/morning-mix/wp/2015/04/16/islamic-states-war-crimes-against-yazidi-women-documented/; Nick Cumming-Bruce, *United Nations Investigators Accuse ISIS of Genocide Over Attacks on Yazidis*, N.Y. TIMES, Mar. 19, 2015, http://www.nytimes.com/2015/03/20/world/middleeast/isis-genocide-yazidis-iraq-un-panel.html.

97. Beth A. Simmons, *Compliance with International Agreements*, 1 ANN. REV. POL. SCI. 75, 78 (1998).

98. ORAN YOUNG, COMPLIANCE AND PUBLIC AUTHORITY (1979).

99. *See, e.g.,* THOMAS M. FRANCK, THE POWER OF LEGITIMACY AMONG NATIONS (1990); Simmons, *supra* note 97, at 78 (1998); Andrew T. Guzman, *A Compliance-Based Theory of International Law*, 90 CAL. L. REV. 1823 (2002); Kal Raustiala & Anne-Marie Slaughter, *International Law, International Relations, and Compliance*, in HANDBOOK OF INTERNATIONAL RELATIONS 538 (Walter Carlsnaes, Thomas Risse & Beth A. Simmons eds., 2013).

100. Thomas M. Franck, *International Law in an Age of Power Disequilibrium*, 100 AM. J. INT'L L. 88, 95 (2006).

101. *Id.* at 93 (2006).

102. *See, e.g.,* TOM TYLER, WHY PEOPLE OBEY THE LAW (1990).

103. Tom R. Tyler, *Trust and Law Abidingness: A Proactive Model of Social Regulation*, 81 B.U. L. REV. 361, 394 (2001), *available at* http://digitalcommons.law.yale.edu/cgi/

viewcontent.cgi?article=4033&context=fss_papers. According to Tyler, "Americans are typically law-abiding people." TOM TYLER, WHY PEOPLE OBEY THE LAW 3 (1990).

104. Commander Robert C. De Tolve, JAGC, USN, *At What Cost? America's UNCLOS Allergy in the Time of "Lawfare,"* 61 NAVAL L. REV. 1, 8 (2012) (citing U.S. Dep't of Defense Directive 2311.01E, Law of War Program para. 4.1 (May 9, 2006) (change 1 of Nov 15, 2010)).

105. U.S. Dep't of Defense Directive 2311.01E, Law of War Program (May 9, 2006) (change 1 of Nov. 15, 2010; certified current as of Feb. 22, 2011), *available at* http://www.dtic. mil/whs/directives/corres/pdf/231101e.pdf.

106. INT'L & OPERATIONAL LAW DEP'T, JUDGE ADVOCATE GENERAL'S LEGAL CTR. & SCH., U.S. ARMY, OPERATIONAL LAW HANDBOOK 2014, at 11, *available at* http:// www.loc.gov/rr/frd/Military_Law/pdf/operational-law-handbook_2014.pdf.

107. *Id.* at 15.

108. *Id.* at 42.

109. Stewart Baker, *Going Wobbly on Russia's Cybersecurity Disarmament Proposal?*, WASH. POST., THE VOLOKH CONSPIRACY (June 6, 2010, 10:18 PM), http://volokh. com/2010/06/06/going-wobbly-on-russias-cybersecurity-disarmament-proposal/.

110. BASICS OF INTERNATIONAL LAW FOR MODERN SOLDIERS 3 (Zhao Peiying ed., 1996) (quoted in Jonathan G. Odom, *A China in the Bull Shop? Comparing the Rhetoric of a Rising China with the Reality of the International Law of the Sea*, 17 OCEAN & COASTAL L.J. 201, 222 (2012)).

111. ANN ELIZABETH MAYER, ISLAM AND HUMAN RIGHTS: TRADITION AND POLITICS 36 (5th ed. 2012); Abdulmumini A. Oba, *New Muslim Perspectives in the Human Right Debate*, *in* ISLAM AND INTERNATIONAL LAW 234 (Marie-Luisa Frick & Andreas Muller eds., 2013).

112. *See, e.g.*, Andrew T. Guzman, *A Compliance-Based Theory of International Law*, 90 CAL. L. REV. 1823, 1849 (2002).

113. Author interview of member of the U.S. Air Force JAG Corps (Apr. 26, 2015).

114. *Id.*

115. *Id.*

116. *Id.*

117. *Id.*

118. U.S. DEP'T OF JUSTICE, THE AL QAEDA MANUAL, http://www.justice.gov/sites/ default/files/ag/legacy/2002/10/08/manualpart1_1.pdf (last visited Apr. 30, 2015); Donna Miles, Am. Forces Press Servs., *Al Qaeda Manual Drives Detainee Behavior at Guantanamo Bay* (June 9, 2005), http://www.defense.gov/news/newsarticle. aspx?id=16270.

119. *Id.*

120. *See, e.g.*, Jeffrey Rosen, *Conscience of a Conservative*, N.Y. TIMES, Sept. 9, 2007, http:// www.nytimes.com/2007/09/09/magazine/09rosen.html?pagewanted=all.

121. JACK GOLDSMITH, THE TERROR PRESIDENCY: LAW AND JUDGMENT INSIDE THE BUSH ADMINISTRATION 58 (2009).

122. *Id.* at 58.

123. *See, e.g.*, Mark Mazzetti, *Panel Faults C.I.A. Over Brutality and Deceit in Terrorism Investigations*, N.Y. TIMES, Dec. 9, 2014, http://www.nytimes.com/2014/12/10/ world/senate-intelligence-committee-cia-torture-report.html; S. SELECT COMM. ON INTELLIGENCE, COMMITTEE STUDY OF THE CENTRAL INTELLIGENCE AGENCY'S DETENTION AND INTERROGATION PROGRAM (Dec. 3, 2014), http://www.intel-ligence.senate.gov/sites/default/files/press/findings-and-conclusions.pdf; David S. Cloud, *Private Found Guilty in Abu Ghraib Abuse*, N.Y. TIMES, Sept. 27, 2005, http:// www.nytimes.com/2005/09/27/national/27england.html.

124. Foreword by Senate Select Committee on Intelligence Chairman Dianne Feinstein, S. Select Comm. on Intelligence, *supra* note 123.

125. *Id.*

126. David S. Cloud, *Private Found Guilty in Abu Ghraib Abuse*, N.Y. Times, Sept. 27, 2005, http://www.nytimes.com/2005/09/27/national/27england.html.

127. *Id.*

128. U.S. Dep't of State, Foreign Terrorist Organizations, http://www.state.gov/j/ct/rls/other/des/123085.htm (last visited May 1, 2015).

129. Mary Anastasia O'Grady, *What About Colombia's Terrorists?*, Wall St. J., Oct. 5, 2001, http://www.wsj.com/articles/SB1002237197885029400; Mary Anastasia O'Grady, *Seeking the Truth About a Massacre in a Colombia Hamlet*, Wall St. J., Sept. 23, 2005, http://www.wsj.com/articles/SB112743867847049494. However, it is worth noting that in the entirety of his fifty-seven-page monograph titled *Lawfare: The Colombian Case*, Juan Manuel Padilla, a colonel in the Colombian Army, Padilla provides no evidence for this specific tactic. Juan Manuel Padilla, U.S. Army Command & General Staff College, *Lawfare: The Colombian Case* (May 20, 2010), *available at* http://www.dtic.mil/dtic/tr/fulltext/u2/a523182.pdf.

130. Juan Forero, *Rights Group Lists Abuses by Guerrillas in Colombia*, N.Y. Times, July 10, 2001, http://www.nytimes.com/2001/07/10/world/10COLO.html.

131. Human Rights Watch, *Guerrilla Violations of International Humanitarian Law: FARC* (May 5, 1997), http://www.hrw.org/legacy/reports/reports98/colombia/Colom989-05.htm (last visited May 1, 2015).

132. Forero, *supra* note 130.

133. *Id.*

134. *Id.*; Human Rights Watch, *Colombia: Beyond Negotiation: International Humanitarian Law and its Application to the Conduct of the FARC-EP* (Aug. 2001), http://www.hrw.org/reports/2001/farc/index.htm#TopOfPage.

135. Greg Miller & Scott Higham, *In a Propaganda War Against ISIS, the U.S. Tried to Play by the Enemy's Rules*, Wash. Post, May 8, 2015, http://www.washingtonpost.com/world/national-security/in-a-propaganda-war-us-tried-to-play-by-the-enemys-rules/2015/05/08/6eb6b732-e52f-11e4-81ea-0649268f729e_story.html.

136. *Id.*

137. *See, e.g.*, Steven Erlanger, *NATO Missiles Strike a Center of State-Linked TV and Radio*, N.Y. Times, Apr. 21, 1999, http://www.nytimes.com/1999/04/21/world/crisis-balkans-belgrade-nato-missiles-strike-center-state-linked-tv-radio.html.

138. Goldsmith, *supra* note 121, at 61.

139. *See, e.g.*, Stephanie Clifford, *Growing Body of Law Allows Prosecution of Foreign Citizens on U.S. Soil*, N.Y. Times, June 9, 2015, http://www.nytimes.com/2015/06/10/nyregion/growing-body-of-law-allows-prosecution-of-foreign-citizens-on-us-soil.html?_r=0; United States v. Al Kassar, 660 F.3d 108 (2d Cir. 2011), *cert denied sub nom.* Al Kassar v. United States, 132 S. Ct. 2374 (2012); United States v. Yousef, 2010 U.S. Dist. LEXIS 86281 (S.D.N.Y. Aug. 23, 2010), *aff'd*, 2014 U.S. App. LEXIS 8107 (2d Cir. N.Y. Apr. 29, 2014).

140. Goldsmith, *supra* note 121 at 61.

141. This and the subsequent several paragraphs derive heavily from Orde F. Kittrie, *Lawfare and U.S. National Security*, 43 Case W. Res. J. Int'l L. 398–401 (2010).

142. *See, e.g.*, Jeff Breinholt, *Is Lawfare Being Abused by American Lawyers?*, Findlaw, Mar. 9, 2007, http://writ.news.findlaw.com/commentary/20070309_breinholt.html.

143. It is worth nothing that the implication may not be far off the mark in the specific case of American attorney Lynne Stewart, who was convicted in 2005 by a U.S. federal

district court of smuggling information from an imprisoned client, Sheik Omar Abdel Rahman, to violent followers in Egypt. For example, Stewart conveyed messages from Abdel Rahman in which he advised his followers that he was withdrawing his support for a ceasefire with the Egyptian government. United States v. Stewart, 686 F.3d 156 (2d Cir. 2012), http://law.justia.com/cases/federal/appellate-courts/ca2/10-3185/10-3185-2012-06-28.html; Lorenzo Ferrigno & Ray Sanchez, *Dying Defense Lawyer Lynne Stewart Released from Jail*, CNN, Jan. 1, 2014, http://www.cnn.com/2013/12/31/justice/lynne-stewart-compassionate-release/.

144. GOLDSMITH, *supra* note 121, at 61–63.
145. American Service-Members' Protection Act of 2002, § 2008, 22 U.S.C. § 7427 (2002).
146. *See, e.g.,* International Criminal Court—Article 98 Agreements Research Guide, Georgetown University Law Library, http://www.law.georgetown.edu/library/research/guides/article_98.cfm.
147. *See, e.g., id.*
148. Rome Statute of the International Criminal Court, http://www.icc-cpi.int/NR/rdonlyres/ADD16852-AEE9-4757-ABE7-9CDC7CF02886/283503/RomeStatutEng1.pdf.
149. GOLDSMITH, *supra* note 121, at 109; Colonel Frederic L. Borch, III, *Why Military Commissions Are the Proper Forum and Why Terrorists Will Have "Full and Fair" Trials*, THE ARMY LAWYER 10, Nov. 2003, http://www.loc.gov/rr/frd/Military_Law/pdf/11-2003.pdf. At the time this article was published, Borch, a colonel in the U.S. Army JAG Corps, was Chief Prosecutor (acting) in the Office of Military Commissions at the U.S. Department of Defense. *Id.*
150. GOLDSMITH, *supra* note 121.
151. *Id.* at 59.
152. *Id.*
153. *Id.* at 62–63.
154. *Id.* at 63.
155. *Id.*
156. *Id.*
157. *Id.*
158. *Id.*
159. *Id.*
160. U.S. DEP'T OF DEFENSE, THE NATIONAL DEFENSE STRATEGY OF THE UNITED STATES OF AMERICA, p. 5, Mar. 2005, http://www.defense.gov/news/Mar2005/d20050318nds2.pdf.
161. David Cole, *"Strategies of the Weak,"* in THE CONSTITUTION IN 2020, at 297 (2009).
162. GABRIELLA BLUM & PHILIP B. HEYMANN, LAWS, OUTLAWS, AND TERRORISTS: LESSONS FROM THE WAR ON TERRORISM 27–28 (2010).
163. *Id.*
164. Charlie Savage, *Judge Delays Resumption of Guantanamo Trial*, N.Y. TIMES, Oct. 15, 2010, http://www.nytimes.com/2010/10/15/us/15gitmo.html# ("Mr. Obama had been a critic during the presidential campaign of Mr. Bush's use of military commissions. But his administration eventually decided that the tribunals were necessary if certain detainees were to receive trials, because they offered greater flexibility than civilian courts in the admission of certain kinds of evidence, like hearsay and materials gathered under battlefield conditions.")
165. *See, e.g.,* Steve Vladeck, *The Shrinking Military Commissions, Redux*, JUST SECURITY, Feb. 18, 2015, http://justsecurity.org/20190/shrinking-military-commissions-redux/.
166. Author interview of Steven Perles (May 2, 2015).

167. *Id.*

168. *Id.*

169. *Id.*

170. *Id.*

171. *Id.*

172. *Id.*

173. Washington Univ. Law, Faculty Profiles, Brian Z. Tamanaha, https://law. wustl.edu/faculty_profiles/profiles.aspx?id=7287

174. Brian Z. Tamanaha, Law as a Means to an End: Threat to the Rule of Law 1 (2006).

175. *Id.* at 6.

176. *Id.* at 7.

177. *Id.* at 1.

178. Brian Z. Tamanaha, *How an Instrumental View of Law Corrodes the Rule of Law,* 56 DePaul L. Rev. 469, 472 (2007).

179. *Id.* at 482.

180. Tamanaha, *supra* note 174, at 1.

181. *Id.*

182. Tamanaha, *supra* note 178, at 483.

183. Steven D. Smith, *The Academy, the Court, and the Culture of Rationalism, in* That Eminent Tribunal: Judicial Supremacy and the Constitution (C. Wolfe ed., 2004).

184. Robert W. Gordon, *The Independence of Lawyers,* 68 B.U. L. Rev. 1, 20 (1988).

185. *Id.* at 10.

186. Noah Charney, *How I Write: Richard Posner,* The Daily Beast, Nov. 7, 2013, http:// www.thedailybeast.com/articles/2013/11/07/how-i-write-richard-posner.html.

187. *See, e.g.,* Richard A. Posner, Overcoming Law 405 (1995).

188. *Id.* at 391.

189. Tamanaha, *supra* note 174, at 1.

190. *Id.*

191. Calvin Woodward, *The Limits of Legal Realism: An Historical Perspective,* 54 Va. L. Rev. 689, 732 (1968).

192. Tamanaha, *supra* note 174, at 110–12, 116, 127, 143, 160, 192.

193. Roger C. Cramton, *The Ordinary Religion of the Law School Classroom,* 29 J. Legal Educ. 247 (1978).

194. *Id.* at 257.

195. Tamanaha, *supra* note 174, at 2.

196. *Id.*

197. *Id.*

198. Oona A. Hathaway, *Do Human Rights Treaties Make a Difference?,* 111 Yale L.J. 1935, 1989 (2002).

199. *Id.* at 2011.

200. *Id.* at 2007.

201. *Id.* at 2009.

202. *Id.* at 2011.

203. *Id.* at 2009.

204. Office of the High Commissioner for Human Rights, *Welcome to the Human Rights Council,* http://www.ohchr.org/EN/HRBodies/HRC/Pages/AboutCouncil.aspx.

205. Sec'y of State John Kerry, U.S. Dep't of State, Remarks at the 28th Session of the Human Rights Council (Mar. 2, 2015), http://www.state.gov/secretary/ remarks/2015/03/238065.htm.

206. Tovah Lazaroff, US "Disappointed UN Rights Council Continues to Single Out Israel," Jerusalem Post, Mar. 27, 2015, http://www.jpost.com/Israel-News/Politics-And-Diplomacy/US-disappointed-UN-rights-council-continues-to-single-out-Israel-395354.

207. Secretary-General Welcomes Agreement on Details of UN Human Rights Review, U.N. News Centre, June 20, 2007, http://www.un.org/apps/news/story.asp?NewsID=2 2984&Cr=rights&Cr1=council&tr=y&auid=3018115#.VWym82BXmKy.

208. Ido Aharoni, How the United Nations Human Rights Council Unfairly Targets Israel, Time, July 30, 2014, http://time.com/3060203/united-nations-human-rights-council-israel/.

209. Id.; Ron Prosor, The U.N.'s War on Israel, N.Y. Times, Mar. 31, 2015, http://www.nytimes.com/2015/04/01/opinion/united-in-ignominy.html.

210. U.N. Human Rights Council, Situation of Human Rights in the Islamic Republic of Iran, A/HRC/28/L.17, Mar. 20, 2015, http://ap.ohchr.org/documents/dpage_e.aspx?si=A/HRC/28/L.17.

211. Anne Bayefsky, UN Says Israel, Not Iran, North Korea or Syria Worst Violator of Human Rights, FoxNews.com, Mar. 29, 2015, http://www.foxnews.com/opinion/2015/03/29/un-says-israel-not-iran-north-korea-or-syria-worst-violator-human-rights.html.

212. Denis MacEoin, The United Nations "Human Rights" Council, Gatestone Inst., Aug. 9, 2014, http://www.gatestoneinstitute.org/4573/united-nations-human-rights-council.

213. Office of the High Commissioner for Human Rights, Current Membership of the Human Rights Council, 1 January–31 December 2015, http://www.ohchr.org/EN/HRBodies/HRC/Pages/CurrentMembers.aspx; Office of the High Commissioner for Human Rights, List of Past Members of the Human Rights Council, http://www.ohchr.org/EN/HRBodies/HRC/Pages/PastMembers.aspx.

214. Congresswoman Ileana Ros-Lehtinen, UN's Annual "Bash Israel Day" Disgusting Reminder of Organization's Bias, Destructive Effect on Human Rights, Mar. 26, 2015, http://ros-lehtinen.house.gov/press-release/un's-annual-"bash-israel-day"-disgusting-reminder-organization's-bias-destructive.

215. Rosa Freedman, The United Nations Human Rights Council: More of the Same?, 31 Wis. Int'l L.J. 208, 223 (2015).

216. Press Release, U.N. Sec'y-Gen., Secretary-General Tells Security Council Middle East in Profound Crisis, Calls for "New and Urgent Push for Peace" (Dec. 12, 2006), http://www.un.org/press/en/2006/sgsm10796.doc.htm.

217. Bill Hoffmann, Bill Richardson: UN Human Rights Panel a "Joke" for Israel Slam, Newsmax, Apr. 2, 2015, http://www.newsmax.com/Newsmax-Tv/Bill-Richardson-Israel-United-Nations-UN/2015/04/02/id/636113/.

218. Arch Puddington, Freedom in the World 2015: Discarding Democracy: A Return to the Iron Fist, Freedom House, https://freedomhouse.org/report/freedom-world-2015/discarding-democracy-return-iron-fist#.VVpk4s5XmKw.

219. Id.

220. Id.

221. Hathaway, supra note 198, at 2011.

222. Rod Thornton, Asymmetric Warfare 19 (2007).

223. See, e.g., Roger W. Barnett, Asymmetrical Warfare 15 (2008).

224. Robert L. Pfaltzgraff, Jr. & Stephen E. Wright, The Spectrum of Conflict: Symmetrical or Asymmetrical Challenge?, in The Role of Naval Forces in 21st Century Operations 13 (2000).

225. Id.

226. Id.

227. Thornton, *supra* note 222, at 5.

228. *Id.*

229. *Id.* at 6.

230. *Id.*

231. William C. Banks, *Toward an Adaptive International Humanitarian Law: New Norms for New Battlefields*, in New Battlefields/Old Laws: Critical Debates on Asymmetric Warfare 2, 6 (2011).

232. *Id.* at 5.

233. *Id.* at 3.

234. Eyal Benvenisti, *The Legal Battle to Define the Law on Transnational Asymmetric Warfare*, 20 Duke J. Comp. & Int'l L. 339, 343 (2010), http://scholarship.law.duke.edu/cgi/viewcontent.cgi?article=1043&context=djcil.

235. *Id.*

236. *Id.* at 343–44.

237. *Id.* at 344.

238. Robert P. Barnidge, Jr., *The Principle of Proportionality Under International Humanitarian Law and Operation Cast Lead*, in New Battlefields/Old Laws: Critical Debates on Asymmetric Warfare 188 (2011).

239. Banks, *supra* note 231, at 3.

240. *Id.* at 2.

241. *Id.* at 11.

242. Thornton, *supra* note 222, at 9–12.

243. *Id.* at 10, 12.

244. *Id.* at 10.

245. *Id.*

246. Lyric Wallwork Winik, *A Marine's Toughest Mission*, Parade Magazine (Jan. 19, 2003).

247. Thomas J. Miles & Eric A. Posner, *Which States Enter Into Treaties, and Why?* 2 (Univ. of Chicago Law Sch., Working Paper in Law & Econ. No. 420, 2d series, Aug. 2008), http://www.law.uchicago.edu/files/files/420.pdf.

248. Cindy Galway Buys, *An Empirical Look at U.S. Treaty Practice*, AJIL Unbound, May 7, 2014, http://www.asil.org/blogs/empirical-look-us- treaty-practice-some-preliminary-conclusions-agora-end-treaties.

249. U.S. Dep't of State, Treaties in Force 2014 — Supplement: A List of Treaties and Other International Agreements of the United States Which Have Entered into Force During the Year 1/1/2013–12/31/2013, http://www.state.gov/documents/organization/235185.pdf (last visited May 14, 2015).

250. *See, e.g.*, Leitner Ctr. for Int'l Law & Justice, Fordham Law Sch., International Criminal Tribunals: A Visual Overview, http://www.leitner-center.org/files/News/International%20Criminal%20Tribunals.pdf.

251. *See* Andreas F. Lowenfeld, *Unilateral Versus Collective Sanctions: An American's Perception*, in United Nations Sanctions and International Law 95 (2002).

252. S.C. Res. 661 (Aug. 6, 1990).

253. *See, e.g.*, Rep. of the S.C., Special Research Report, UN Sanctions, at 17 (Nov. 2013), http://www.securitycouncilreport.org/atf/cf/%7B65BFCF9B-6D27-4E9C-8CD3-CF6E4FF96FF9%7D/special_research_report_sanctions_2013.pdf.

254. Joseph Nye, Jr., Soft Power 90 (2004).

255. *Id.*

256. The law of armed conflict (sometimes referred to as international humanitarian law) applies in situations of armed conflict. The "principal goal of human rights," which

typically protect the individual in both war and peace, "is to protect individuals from arbitrary behavior by their own governments." INT'L COMM. OF THE RED CROSS, WHAT IS THE DIFFERENCE BETWEEN HUMANITARIAN LAW AND HUMAN RIGHTS LAW? (Jan. 1, 2004), https://www.icrc.org/eng/resources/documents/misc/5kzmuy. htm.

257. *Amnesty International USA*, CHARITY NAVIGATOR, http://www.charitynavigator. org/index.cfm?bay=search.summary&orgid=3294#.VVVIEc5XkmY (last visited May 14, 2015).

258. *Id.*

259. ANN MARIE CLARK, DIPLOMACY OF CONSCIENCE: AMNESTY INTERNATIONAL AND CHANGING HUMAN RIGHTS NORMS 11 (2001) (asserting that AI's "ability to influence human rights norms rests on three unique attributes: it bases its actions on loyalty to the moral principles of human rights; it cultivates a position as a disinterested and autonomous 'third party' actor in the international system; and it deploys expertise and large amounts of specific information in the service of general assertions about the need for norms.")

260. *The Nobel Peace Prize: 1977*, NOBELPRIZE.ORG, http://www.nobelprize.org/ nobel_prizes/peace/laureates/1977/.

261. NYE, *supra* note 254, at 91.

262. CLARK, *supra* note 259, at 13.

263. *See, e.g., Chronology of Abu Ghraib*, WASH. POST, http://www.washingtonpost.com/ wp-srv/world/iraq/abughraib/timeline.html (updated Feb. 17, 2006).

264. AMNESTY INT'L, USA: CRIMES AND IMPUNITY (Apr. 2015), http://www.amnesty-usa.org/sites/default/files/usa_crimes_and_impunity_report.pdf.

265. *See, e.g.,* AMNESTY INT'L, ISRAEL AND THE OCCUPIED PALESTINIAN TERRITORIES: FAMILIES UNDER THE RUBBLE: ISRAELI ATTACKS ON INHABITED HOMES (Nov. 5, 2014), https://www.amnesty.org/en/documents/MDE15/032/2014/en/.

266. *See, e.g.,* AMNESTY INT'L, UNLAWFUL AND DEADLY: ROCKET AND MORTAR ATTACKS BY PALESTINIAN ARMED GROUPS DURING THE 2014 GAZA/ISRAEL CONFLICT (Mar. 26, 2015), https://www.amnesty.org/en/documents/mde21/1178/2015/en/.

267. MARGARET E. KECK & KATHRYN SIKKINK, ACTIVISTS BEYOND BORDERS 29 (1998).

268. *Id.*

269. S. SELECT COMM. ON INTELLIGENCE, *supra* note 123.

270. *See, e.g.,* Legal Consequences of the Construction of a Wall in the Occupied Palestinian Territory (Request for Advisory Opinion), Written Statement by the League of Arab States, Jan. 2004, pp. 53, 56, http://www.icj-cij.org/docket/files/131/1545.pdf.

271. *See, e.g.,* AMNESTY INT'L, STATE OF THE WORLD 2014/2015 (Feb. 26, 2015), http:// www.amnestyusa.org/research/reports/state-of-the-world-20142015-0.

272. *See, e.g.,* Yvonne Terlingen, *Amnesty International's Work on Intergovernmental Organizations: A New York Perspective, in* 50 YEARS OF AMNESTY INTERNATIONAL: REFLECTIONS AND PERSPECTIVES, AMNESTY INTERNATIONAL 127, 166–67 (2011), http://sim.rebo.uu.nl/wp-content/uploads/2013/10/simspecial36.pdf.

273. Raymond Bonner, *How a Group of Outsiders Moved Nations to Ban Landmines*, N.Y. TIMES, Sept. 20, 1997, http://www.nytimes.com/1997/09/20/world/how-a-group-of-outsiders-moved-nations-to-ban-land-mines.html.

274. *Id.*

275. CLARK, *supra* note 259, at 9.

276. *See, e.g.,* Scott Baldauf, *Nobel Laureate's Long Trip from Vermont Farm to Fame*, CHRISTIAN SCI. MONITOR, Oct. 14, 1997, http://www.csmonitor.com/1997/1014/ 101497.us.us.4.html.

277. Carey Goldberg, *Peace Prize Goes to Land-Mine Opponents*, N.Y. Times, Oct. 11, 1997, http://www.nytimes.com/1997/10/11/world/peace-prize-goes-to-land-mine-opponents.html.

278. Amnesty Int'l, Fueling Conflict: Foreign Arms Supplies to Israel/Gaza (Feb. 2009), https://www.es.amnesty.org/uploads/tx_useraitypdb/Fuelling_conflict_Israel_Gaza_08.pdf.

279. James Risen, *Protest Threats Derail Bush Speech in Switzerland*, N.Y. Times, Feb. 5, 2011, http://www.nytimes.com/2011/02/06/world/europe/06bush.html?_r=0.

280. *Id.*

281. Sarah Hershenson, *A New Type of Warfare*, Jerusalem Post, Sept. 21, 2012.

282. Charles J. Dunlap, Jr., *Lawfare: A Decisive Element of 21st-Century Conflicts?*, Joint Forces Q. (3d quarter 2009).

283. U.N. Conference on Trade & Development, *Trade and Development Report 2011*, p. I, http://unctad.org/en/Docs/tdr2011_en.pdf.

284. Global Flows in a Digital Age, McKinsey Global Inst. (Apr. 2014), http://www.mckinsey.com/insights/globalization/global_flows_in_a_digital_age.

285. *Id.*

286. U.N. Conference on Trade & Development, *Trade and Development Report 2014*, p. III, http://unctad.org/en/PublicationsLibrary/tdr2014_en.pdf.

287. Global Flows, *supra* note 284.

288. *Id.*

289. *See, e.g.*, David M. Marchick & Matthew J. Slaughter, *Global FDI Policy*, Council on Foreign Relations, June 2008.

290. *FDI in Figures*, OECD, Apr. 2015, http://www.oecd.org/daf/inv/investment-policy/FDI-in-Figures-April-2015.pdf.

291. Financial Globalization: Retreat or Reset?, McKinsey Global Inst. (Mar. 2013), http://www.mckinsey.com/insights/global_capital_markets/financial_globalization.

292. U.N. Office on Drugs & Crime, Estimating Illicit Financial Flows Resulting from Drug Trafficking and Other Transnational Organized Crimes 7 (Oct. 2011), http://www.unodc.org/documents/data-and-analysis/Studies/Illicit_financial_flows_2011_web.pdf (noting that $580 billion of the total $1.6 trillion estimate for laundering consisted of flows relating to drug trafficking and other transnational organized crime activities).

293. Moises Naim, Illicit (2005).

294. Moises Naim, *It's the Illicit Economy, Stupid*, Foreign Policy, Oct. 21, 2009, http://foreignpolicy.com/2009/10/21/its-the-illicit-economy-stupid/.

295. *Id.*

CHAPTER 2

1. David Crist, The Twilight War: The Secret History of America's Thirty-Year Conflict with Iran 148 (2012).

2. *Id.* at 152–53.

3. *"We Want to Hurt Iran,"* Newsweek, Mar. 18, 2003, http://www.newsweek.com/we-want-hurt-iran-132447.

4. Neely Tucker, *Pain and Suffering; Relatives of Terrorist Victims Race Each Other to Court, but Justice and Money are Both Hard to Find*, Wash. Post, Apr. 6, 2003.

5. Payam Akhavan, Reducing Genocide to Law: Definition, Meaning, and the Ultimate Crime 97 (2012).

6. 18 U.S.C. § 2333.

7. 28 U.S.C. § 1350.

8. Jeffrey Davis, Justice Across Borders: The Struggle for Human Rights in U.S. Courts 19 (2008).

9. Filartiga v. Peña-Irala, 630 F.2d 876 (2d Cir. 1980).

10. Davis, *supra* note 8, at 21.

11. *See, e.g.*, Arlene Levinson, *Foreign Torture Victims Seek Justice in U.S. Courts*, L.A. Times, Feb. 28, 1999, http://articles.latimes.com/1999/feb/28/local/me-12505.

12. Kiobel v. Royal Dutch Petroleum Co., 133 S. Ct. 1659 (2013).

13. *Id.*

14. Roger Alford, *Lower Courts Narrowly Interpret Kiobel*, Opinio Juris, Sept. 23, 2013, http://opiniojuris.org/2013/09/23/lower-courts-narrowly-interpret-kiobel/.

15. Benjamin Weiser, *A Settlement with P.L.O. over Terror on a Cruise*, N.Y. Times, Aug. 12, 1997, at A6.

16. Esther Schrader, *Hijacking Plotter Dies in U.S. Custody*, L.A. Times, Mar. 10, 2004, http://articles.latimes.com/2004/mar/10/world/fg-lauro10.

17. Weiser, *supra* note 15, at A6.

18. Adam N. Schupack, *The Arab-Israeli Conflict and Civil Litigation Against Terrorism*, 60 Duke L.J. 207, 213 (2010), http://scholarship.law.duke.edu/cgi/viewcontent.cgi?article=1475&context=dlj; Boim v. Quranic Literacy Inst., 291 F.3d 1000 (2002).

19. 137 Cong. Rec. S8143 (1991) (statement of Sen. Grassley).

20. 549 F.3d 685 (7th Cir. 2008).

21. Boim v. Quranic Literacy Inst., 2012 U.S. Dist. LEXIS 126063 (2012).

22. *Id.*; Matt O'Connor, *$156 Million Award in Terrorist Killing*, Chicago Tribune, Dec. 9, 2004, http://articles.chicagotribune.com/2004-12-09/news/0412090101_1_anti-terrorism-texas-based-holy-land-foundation-david-boim.

23. Author interview of Nathan and Alyza Lewin (Apr. 8, 2015).

24. 18 U.S.C. § 2332.

25. Nathan Lewin, *A Promise the U.S. Makes, but Does Not Keep*, Jewish World Rev., Aug. 27, 2002, http://www.jewishworldreview.com/0802/lewin_inaction.asp.

26. *Id.*

27. *Id.*

28. Author interview of Nathan and Alyza Lewin, *supra* note 23.

29. Regarding the Dees lawsuit, see, e.g., Bruce Smith, *Klan Must Pay $37.8 Million Over Arson*, AP, July 24, 1998, http://www.apnewsarchive.com/1998/Klan-Must-Pay-$37-8M-Over-Arson/id-f8b9aa6dbb829c0284491d7f3b3f7e38.

30. Paul McGeough, Kill Khalid: The Failed Mossad Assassination of Khalid Mishal and the Rise of Hamas 298 (Kindle ebook).

31. *Id.*

32. Author interview of Nathan and Alyza Lewin, *supra* note 23.

33. *Id.*

34. *Id.*

35. *Id.*

36. *Id.*

37. *Id.*

38. *No Cash for Terror: Convictions Returned in Holy Land Case*, Fed. Bureau of Investigation, Nov. 25, 2008, http://www.fbi.gov/news/stories/2008/november/hlf112508.

39. Author interview of Nathan and Alyza Lewin, *supra* note 23.

40. *No Cash for Terror, supra* note 38.

41. Judith Miller, *Suit Accuses Islamic Charities of Fund-Raising for Terrorism*, N.Y. TIMES, May 13, 2000, http://www.nytimes.com/2000/05/13/us/suit-accuses-islamic-charities-of-fund-raising-for-terrorism.html.

42. Author interview of Nathan and Alyza Lewin, *supra* note 23.

43. *Id.*

44. *Id.*

45. *Id.*

46. *Id.*

47. *Id.*

48. *Id.*

49. *Id.*

50. *Id.*

51. *Id.*

52. Matt O'Connor, *U.S. Appeals Court Debates a Lawsuit Over Israel Slaying*, CHICAGO TRIBUNE, Sept. 26, 2001.

53. Barbara Sofer, *Profile: Nathan and Alyza Lewin*, HADASSAH, Feb./Mar. 2014, http://www.hadassahmagazine.org/2014/03/17/profile-nathan-alyza-lewin/.

54. McGEOUGH, *supra* note 30, at 295–96.

55. *Id.* at 308–09.

56. James V. Grimaldi, *An Arab American Charitable Connection That Might Be too Close for Comfort*, WASH. POST, Dec. 17, 2001.

57. *Id.*

58. Glenn R. Simpson, *Holy Land Foundation Allegedly Mixed Charity Money with Funds for Bombers*, WALL ST. J., Feb. 27, 2002, http://www.wsj.com/articles/SB1014760255597651120.

59. *Id.*

60. *Id.*

61. Glenn R. Simpson, *FBI Knew of Ties Between Hamas, Charity in U.S.*, WALL ST. J., Dec. 5, 2001.

62. Exec. Order No. 12947, Prohibiting Transactions with Terrorists Who Threaten to Disrupt the Middle East Peace Process, 60 Fed. Reg. 5079 (Jan. 25, 1995), http://www.treasury.gov/resource-center/sanctions/Documents/12947.pdf.

63. Barton Gellman, *Struggles Inside the Government Defined Campaign*, WASH. POST, Dec. 20, 2001.

64. Simpson, *supra* note 58.

65. Josh Meyer & Lisa Getter, *U.S. Islamic Charity's Assets Frozen*, L.A. TIMES, Dec. 5, 2001.

66. David Firestone, *After a Long, Slow Climb to Respectability, a Muslim Charity Experiences a Rapid Fall*, N.Y. TIMES, Dec. 10, 2001.

67. *White House Freezes Suspected Terror Assets*, WASH. POST, Dec. 4, 2001, http://www.washingtonpost.com/wp-srv/nation/specials/attacked/transcripts/bushtext_120401.html.

68. *Id.*

69. *Id.*

70. *Id.*

71. Noah Charney, *How I Write: Richard Posner*, THE DAILY BEAST, Nov. 7, 2013, http://www.thedailybeast.com/articles/2013/11/07/how-i-write-richard-posner.html.

72. Josh Gerstein, *Funding Terrorism is Issue in Chicago Case*, N.Y. SUN, Sept. 11, 2008, http://www.nysun.com/national/funding-terrorism-is-issue-in-chicago-case/85641/.

73. *Id.*

74. *Id.*

75. *Id.*

76. Boim v. Holy Land Found., 549 F.3d 685, 690 (7th Cir. 2008).

77. *Id.* at 690.

78. *Id.*

79. *Id.*

80. *Id.*

81. *Id.*

82. *Id.* at 691.

83. *Id.* at 698.

84. *Id.* at 702.

85. Author interview of Nathan and Alyza Lewin, *supra* note 23.

86. *Id.*

87. *Id.*

88. *Id.*

89. *Id.*

90. Michael Higgins, *21-Month Sentence For Salah*, CHICAGO TRIBUNE, July 12, 2007, http://articles.chicagotribune.com/2007-07-12/news/0707111436_1_muhammad-salah-hamas-prison-term.

91. *Id.*

92. Rudolph Bush, *Hamas-Case Trial Told of '96 Killing*, CHICAGO TRIBUNE, Dec. 8, 2006, http://articles.chicagotribune.com/2006-12-08/news/0612080314_1_muhammad-salah-hamas-david-boim.

93. Adam Dickter, *Terror Funders Take a Hit*, N.Y. JEWISH WEEK, June 14, 2002, http://www.thejewishweek.com:8080/features/terror_funders_take_hit.

94. Paul M. Barrett, *Can Banks Be Held Liable for Terrorism?*, BLOOMBERG BUSINESSWEEK, Mar. 18, 2015, http://businessweekme.com/Bloomberg/newsmid/190/newsid/479.

95. *Id.*

96. Joe Palazzolo, *Arab Bank Found Liable for Providing Assistance to Hamas*, WALL ST. J., Sept. 22, 2014, http://www.wsj.com/articles/arab-bank-found-liable-for-providing-assistance-to-hamas-1411419783.

97. *Id.*

98. Jonathan Stempel, *Arab Bank Fails to Void U.S. Liability Verdict Over Hamas Attacks*, REUTERS, Apr. 8, 2015, http://www.reuters.com/article/2015/04/08/us-arabbank-hamas-lawsuit-idUSKBN0MZ1RU20150408.

99. Palazzolo, *supra* note 96.

100. Stempel, *supra* note 98; Order, Linde v. Arab Bank, Case 1:04-cv-02799-BMC-VVP (filed May 7, 2015), available at http://www.motleyrice.com/sites/default/files/documents/AT_HR/Arab%20bank%20order%20august%202015.pdf.

101. Stephanie Clifford, *The Cost for Arab Bank is a Complex Calculation*, N.Y. TIMES, Sept. 23, 2014, http://www.nytimes.com/2014/09/24/nyregion/The-Cost-for-Arab-Bank-Is-a-Complex-Calculation.html.

102. Erik Larson & Christie Smythe, *Arab Bank Found Liable for Hamas Terrorist Attacks*, BLOOMBERG, Sept. 23, 2014, http://www.bloomberg.com/news/articles/2014-09-22/arab-bank-found-liable-for-hamas-terrorist-attacks.

103. For a list of the attacks, see Memorandum Opinion and Order, Linde v. Arab Bank, Case 1:05-cv-03738-BMC-VVP (filed Apr. 8, 2015), http://www.gpo.gov/fdsys/pkg/USCOURTS-nyed-1_05-cv-03738/pdf/USCOURTS-nyed-1_05-cv-03738-20.pdf; Palazzolo, *supra* note 96.

104. Larson & Smythe, *supra* note 102.

105. David L. Hall & Claire Coleman, *Banking and Bombs: What the "Linde" Verdict Portends*, N.Y. L.J., Oct. 15, 2014, http://www.newyorklawjournal.com/id=1202673331081/ Banking-and-Bombs-What-the-Linde-Verdict-Portends?slreturn=20150306202923.

106. Larson & Smythe, *supra* note 102.

107. Linde v. Arab Bank PLC, 269 F.R.D. 186, 191–92 (E.D.N.Y. 2010).

108. *Id.*

109. Larson & Smythe, *supra* note 102.

110. Memorandum Opinion and Order, *supra* note 103, at 43.

111. *Id.* at 43–44.

112. Hall & Coleman, *supra* note 105; Jury Charges, Linde v. Arab Bank, Case 1:04-cv-02799-BMC-VVP (filed 9/7/14) (available via Bloomberg Law as part of *Linde v. Arab Bank* docket).

113. Hall & Coleman, *supra* note 105; Jury Charges, Linde v. Arab Bank, *supra* note 112.

114. *See, e.g.*, [Corrected] Memorandum of Law of Defendant Arab Bank PLC in Support of Its Motion for a New Trial Pursuant to Fed. R. Civ. P. 59, Case No. CV-04-2799, pp. 3-6 (dated Oct. 10, 2014), http://www.arabbankfacts.com/wp-content/uploads/2014-10-10-Rule-59-Corrected-Memo-of-Law.pdf.

115. Jury Charges, Linde v. Arab Bank, *supra* note 112.

116. *Id.*

117. *Id.*

118. Memorandum Opinion and Order, *supra* note 103, at 44.

119. *Id.* at 45.

120. Holder v. Humanitarian Law Project, 561 U.S. 1, 7 (2010), quoted in Memorandum Opinion and Order, Linde v. Arab Bank, at 46.

121. Alison Frankel, *Why the Arab Bank Terror-Finance Trial Matters*, Reuters, Sept. 19, 2014, http://blogs.reuters.com/alison-frankel/2014/09/19/why-the-arab-bank-terror-finance-trial-matters/.

122. Barrett, *supra* note 94.

123. Arab Bank, Our Profile, http://www.arabbank.com/en/profile.aspx (last visited Apr. 6, 2015).

124. Arab Bank, Arab Bank Group Net Profits Grow by 15% to Reach USD 577.2 Million in 2014 and 24.5% Dividend Distribution, Feb. 1, 2015, http://www.arabbank.com/en/news/newsstory_598.aspx.

125. Daniel Fisher, *In Trial Starting Next Week, Terrorism Victims Seek Damages from Arab Bank*, Forbes, Aug. 8, 2014, http://www.forbes.com/sites/danielfisher/2014/08/08/arab-bank-trial-brings-tests-limits-of-u-s-law-in-palestinian-conflict/.

126. Edward Gnehm, *When Trial Lawyers Do Foreign Policy*, Wash. Times, June 24, 2014, http://www.washingtontimes.com/news/2014/jun/24/gnehm-when-trial-lawyers-do-foreign-policy/ (noting that Gnehm is "a consultant to Arab Bank").

127. Charlie Savage, *Terror Suit Against Jordanian Bank Tests U.S. Diplomacy and Secrecy Laws*, N.Y. Times, Apr. 1, 2014, http://www.nytimes.com/2014/04/02/us/terror-suit-against-jordanian-bank-tests-us-diplomacy-and-secrecy-laws.html?_r=0.

128. Nate Raymond & Jessica Dye, *Fallout from Dewey Collapse Hits Clients*, Reuters, May 28, 2012, http://www.reuters.com/article/2012/05/28/us-dewey-clients-idUSBRE84R0LC20120528.

129. *Id.*

130. Tom Moore, *Quality Not Quantity—Stalled Growth at DLA Piper But a Leaner Global Giant Boosts the Bottom Line*, Legal Business, Mar. 5, 2015, http://www.legalbusiness.co.uk/index.php/lb-blog-view/3777-quality-not-quantity-stalled-growth-at-dla-piper-but-a-leaner-global-giant-boosts-the-bottom-line.

131. Barrett, *supra* note 94.

132. Hall & Coleman, *supra* note 105.

133. Savage, *supra* note 127.

134. *Id.*

135. Roger Parloff, *Supreme Court Won't Save Arab Bank from Terror Trial*, FORTUNE, July 1, 2014, http://fortune.com/2014/07/01/supreme-court-wont-save-arab-bank-from-terror-trial/.

136. *Id.*

137. Edward Gnehm, *When Trial Lawyers Do Foreign Policy*, WASH. TIMES, June 24, 2014, http://www.washingtontimes.com/news/2014/jun/24/gnehm-when-trial-lawyers-do-foreign-policy/ (noting that Gnehm is "a consultant to Arab Bank").

138. *Id.*

139. *Id.*

140. Lawrence Hurley, *Obama Administration Asks Top Court to Turn Away Arab Bank Case*, REUTERS, May 27, 2014, http://www.reuters.com/article/2014/05/27/us-usa-court-banking-idUSKBN0E72MQ20140527.

141. Brent Kendall, *Supreme Court Declines to Review Sanctions Against Arab Bank in Records Case*, WALL ST. J., June 30, 2014, http://www.wsj.com/articles/supreme-court-declines-to-review-sanctions-against-arab-bank-in-records-case-1404138448; Greg Stohr & Christie Smythe, *U.S. Supreme Court on Terror Trial*, BLOOMBERG, June 30, 2014, http://www.bloomberg.com/news/articles/2014-06-30/arab-bank-rejected-by-u-s-supreme-court-on-terror-trial.

142. ARAB BANK, ARAB BANK GROUP NET PROFITS GROW BY 15% TO REACH USD 577.2 MILLION IN 2014 AND 24.5% DIVIDEND DISTRIBUTION, Feb. 1, 2015, http://www.arabbank.com/en/news/newsstory_598.aspx.

143. Barrett, *supra* note 94.

144. MCGEOUGH, *supra* note 30, at 304.

145. *Id.* at 392.

146. Nitsana Darshan-Leitner, *Starve Hamas of Money*, GLOBES, July 26, 2014.

147. *See, e.g.*, United States v. El-Mezain, 664 F.3d 467 (5th Cir. 2011), *cert. denied*, 133 S. Ct. 525 (2012).

148. U.S. DEP'T OF JUSTICE, FEDERAL JUDGE HANDS DOWN SENTENCES IN HOLY LAND FOUNDATION CASE, May 27, 2009, http://www.justice.gov/opa/pr/federal-judge-hands-downs-sentences-holy-land-foundation-case; Elizabeth J. Shapiro, *The Holy Land Foundation for Relief and Development: A Case Study*, U.S. ATTORNEYS' BULLETIN, Sept. 2014, *available at* http://law.huji.ac.il/upload/Shapiro.pdf.

149. *Statement of Steven R. Perles Before the Subcomm. on Terrorism, Nonproliferation, & Trade of the H. Comm. on Foreign Affairs* (Mar. 5, 2014), http://docs.house.gov/meetings/FA/FA18/20140305/101846/HHRG-113-FA18-Wstate-PerlesS-20140305.pdf.

150. Barrett, *supra* note 94.

151. Press Release, FinCEN & OCC, *FinCen and OCC Assess $24 Million Penalty Against Arab Bank Branch* (Aug. 17, 2005), http://www.fincen.gov/news_room/nr/pdf/20050817.pdf.

152. *Id.*

153. *Financial Services Regulatory Relief: The Regulators' Views: Hearing Before the Subcomm. on Financial Institutions & Consumer Credit of the H. Comm. on Financial Services*, 109th Cong. (June 9, 2005) (statement of Julie L. Williams, Acting Comptroller, Office of the Comptroller of the Currency), https://bulk.resource.org/gpo.gov/hearings/109h/24094.txt.

154. Hall & Coleman, *supra* note 105.

155. Frankel, *supra* note 121.

156. *Id.*

157. *Id.*

158. Barrett, *supra* note 94.

159. Barrett, *supra* note 94; Complaint, Freeman v. HSBC Holdings Plc, No. 14-cv-06601 (E.D.N.Y. Nov. 10, 2014), http://www.scribd.com/doc/246465188/Freeman-v-HSBC-Holdings#scribd.

160. Barrett, *supra* note 94; Complaint, Freeman v. HSBC, *supra* note 159.

161. Complaint, Freeman v. HSBC, *supra* note 159, at 167.

162. Barrett, *supra* note 94.

163. Order on Summary Judgment Motions, Sokolow v. PLO, No. 04 Civ. 397 (S.D.N.Y. Nov. 19, 2014), *available at* http://blogs.reuters.com/alison-frankel/files/2014/11/sokolowevpa-sjopinion.pdf.

164. Benjamin Weiser, *Palestinian Groups Are Found Liable at Manhattan Terror Trial*, N.Y. Times, Feb. 23, 2015, http://www.nytimes.com/2015/02/24/nyregion/damages-awarded-in-terror-case-against-palestinian-groups.html.

165. *Id.*

166. *Id.*

167. *Id.*

168. *Id.*

169. Jennifer Peltz & Tom Hays, *US Jury Finds Palestinian Groups Liable for Terror Attacks*, AP, Feb. 23, 2015, http://www.huffingtonpost.com/2015/02/23/plo-palestine-terror-attacks_n_6740670.html.

170. *See, e.g.*, Palestinian Authority Captured Documents: Main Implications (Apr. 7, 2002), submitted as Plaintiffs' Exhibit 631 in the *Sokolow* case on Dec. 30, 2014, *available at* http://www.investigativeproject.org/documents/case_docs/2581.pdf; Israel Ministry of Foreign Affairs, International Financial Aid to the Palestinian Authority Redirected to Terrorist Elements (June 4, 2002), submitted as Plaintiffs' Exhibit 632 in the *Sokolow* case on Dec. 30, 2014, *available at* http://www.investigativeproject.org/documents/case_docs/2590.pdf.

171. Itamar Marcus & Nan Jacques Zilberdik, *PA Responds to US Court Ruling that PA Must Pay $655 Million to Victims of Terror*, Palestinian Media Watch, Mar. 4, 2015, http://www.palwatch.org/main.aspx?fi=157&doc_id=14240.

172. Knox v. PLO, 248 F.R.D. 420 (S.D.N.Y. 2008).

173. Josh Gerstein, *Palestinians Reverse on Terror Victim*, Politico, Feb. 15, 2010, http://www.politico.com/news/stories/0210/33021.html.

174. Peltz & Hays, *supra* note 169.

175. Yonah Jeremy Bob, *Verdict Against Palestinian Authority Could Spell Trouble for Abbas at ICC*, Jerusalem Post, Feb. 24, 2015, http://www.jpost.com/Arab-Israeli-Conflict/Verdict-against-Palestinian-Authority-could-spell-trouble-for-Abbas-at-ICC-391974.

176. *Id.*

177. Shurat HaDin, Overview, http://israellawcenter.org/about/overview/ (last visited Apr. 7, 2015).

178. Bob, *supra* note 175.

179. Itamar Marcus & Nan Jacques Zilberdik, *PA Responds to US Court Ruling that PA Must Pay $655 Million to Victims of Terror*, Palestinian Media Watch, Mar. 4, 2015, http://www.palwatch.org/main.aspx?fi=157&doc_id=14240.

180. *Id.*

181. *Id.*

182. Herman Kahn, On Escalation: Metaphors and Scenarios 290 (1965).

183. Daniel Byman & Matthew Waxman, The Dynamics of Coercion: American Foreign Policy and the Limits of Military Might 40 (2002).

184. *Id.* at 38–44.

185. Yishai Schwartz, *Of Torts, Diplomacy, Israelis and Palestinians*, Lawfare Blog (Feb. 27, 2015, 10:00 AM), http://www.lawfareblog.com/torts-diplomacy-israelis-and-palestinians.

186. *Id.*

187. *Id.*

188. *Id.*

189. Stuart Winer, *After Synagogue Attack, Shin Bet Chief Says Abbas is Not Stoking Violence*, Times of Israel, Nov. 18, 2014, http://www.timesofisrael.com/security-chief-says-palestinian-leaders-not-stoking-violence/; Lahav Harkov, *Shin Bet Chief Says Abbas Does Not Encourage Terrorism, Contradicting Netanyahu*, Jerusalem Post, Nov. 18, 2014, http://www.jpost.com/Arab-Israeli-Conflict/Shin-Bet-chief-contradicts-Netanyahu-says-Abbas-not-responsible-for-inciting-terror-382145.

190. Jonathan Schanzer, *Huge Verdict is the Price the Palestinian Authority Pays for Not Controlling the P.L.O.*, N.Y. Times, Feb. 24, 2015, http://www.nytimes.com/roomfordebate/2015/02/24/terror-and-the-palestinian-authority/huge-verdict-is-the-price-the-palestinian-authority-pays-for-not-controlling-the-plo.

191. Isabel Kershner, *Israeli Releasing Impounded Palestinian Tax Revenue*, N.Y. Times, Mar. 27, 2015, http://www.nytimes.com/2015/03/28/world/middleeast/israel-netanyahu-palestinians-tax-revenue.html?_r=0; *Israel to Resume Tax Revenue Transfers to the Palestinian Authority*, Jerusalem Post, Mar. 27, 2015, http://www.jpost.com/Israel-News/Politics-And-Diplomacy/Israel-to-resume-tax-revenue-transfers-to-the-Palestinian-Authority-395338.

192. Kershner, *supra* note 191; Barak Ravid, *Israel Releases Withheld Tax Revenues to Palestinian Authority*, Haaretz, Mar. 27, 2015, http://www.haaretz.com/news/diplomacy-defense/.premium-1.649238; *Israel to Resume Tax Revenue Transfers, supra* note 191.

193. Jodi Rudoren, *Tensions Mount as Israel Freezes Revenue Meant for Palestinians*, N.Y. Times, Jan. 3, 2015, http://www.nytimes.com/2015/01/04/world/middleeast/tensions-mount-as-israel-freezes-revenue-meant-for-palestinians.html; *Israel to Resume Tax Revenue Transfers, supra* note 191.

194. Jim Zanotti, Cong. Research Serv., RS22967, U.S. Foreign Aid to the Palestinians (2014), https://fas.org/sgp/crs/mideast/RS22967.pdf.

195. Benjamin Weiser, *Palestinian Groups are Found Liable at Manhattan Terror Trial*, N.Y. Times, Feb. 23, 2015, http://www.nytimes.com/2015/02/24/nyregion/damages-awarded-in-terror-case-against-palestinian-groups.html.

196. Alison Frankel, *The Palestinian Authority Faces a Big Terror Trial*, Reuters, Nov. 20, 2014, http://blogs.reuters.com/alison-frankel/2014/11/20/the-palestinian-authority-faces-a-big-terror-trial-will-the-state-dept-help/.

197. Itamar Marcus & Nan Jacques Zilberdik, *PA Responds to US Court Ruling that PA Must Pay $655 Million to Victims of Terror*, Palestinian Media Watch, Mar. 4, 2015, http://www.palwatch.org/main.aspx?fi=157&doc_id=14240.

198. *See, e.g.*, Eric Tucker, *US Likely to Intervene in Palestinian Terror Case*, A.P., Aug. 4, 2015, http://bigstory.ap.org/article/484e67f459154e1cabaeee345926dcf5/us-likely-inter-vene-palestinian-terror-case; Beth Stephens, *Judicial Deference and the Unreasonable Views of the Bush Administration*, 33 Brooklyn J. Int'l L. 773 (2008).

199. Schwartz, *supra* note 185.

200. *Id.*

201. *Id.*

202. *Id.*
203. The Schooner Exchange v. M'Faddon, 11 U.S. (7 Cranch) 116 (1812).
204. AEDPA, Pub. L. No. 104-32, § 221, 110 Stat. 1214, 1241–43 (amending 28 U.S.C. § 1605, a part of FSIA).
205. 28 U.S.C. § 1605A.
206. *In re* Islamic Republic of Iran Terrorism Litig., 659 F. Supp. 2d 31 (D.D.C. 2009).
207. Flatow v. Islamic Republic of Iran, 999 F. Supp. 1, 7 (D.D.C. 1998).
208. *Id.* at 9.
209. *Id.*
210. Neely Tucker, *Pain and Suffering; Relatives of Terrorist Victims Race Each Other to Court, but Justice and Money are Both Hard to Find*, WASH. POST, Apr. 6, 2003.
211. *Id.*
212. Author interview of Steven Perles (May 2, 2015).
213. Douglas Martin, *Hugo Princz, 78, U.S. Winner of Holocaust Settlement, Dies*, N.Y. TIMES, July 31, 2001, http://www.nytimes.com/2001/07/31/nyregion/hugo-princz-78-us-winner-of-holocaust-settlement-dies.html.
214. Author interview of Perles, *supra* note 212.
215. *Id.*
216. MIKE KELLY, THE BUS ON JAFFA ROAD: A STORY OF MIDDLE EAST TERRORISM AND THE SEARCH FOR JUSTICE 163 (2014); e-mail to author from Edward Macallister of Perles Law Firm, Apr. 30, 2015.
217. Flatow v. Islamic Republic of Iran, 999 F. Supp. 1, 12 (D.D.C. 1998).
218. KELLY, *supra* note 216; e-mail to author from Macallister, *supra* note 216.
219. *Flatow*, 999 F. Supp. 1.
220. *Id.*
221. Stephen M. Flatow, *Use U.S. Law to Respond to Terrorism*, WIS. JEWISH CHRONICLE, Aug. 9, 2002, http://www.jewishchronicle.org/article.php?article_id=1531.
222. Author interview of Perles, *supra* note 212.
223. *Id.*
224. *Id.*
225. *Id.*
226. *Id.*
227. *Id.*
228. *Id.*
229. *Id.*
230. *Id.*
231. *Id.*
232. *Id.*
233. MIKE KELLY, THE BUS ON JAFFA ROAD: A STORY OF MIDDLE EAST TERRORISM AND THE SEARCH FOR JUSTICE 200 (2014).
234. Flatow v. Islamic Republic of Iran, 999 F. Supp. 1, 9 (D.D.C. 1998).
235. *Id.*
236. *Id.*
237. *Id* at 9.
238. Flatow v. Islamic Republic of Iran, 999 F. Supp. 1 (D.D.C. 1998).
239. *Id.* at 34.
240. *Id.*
241. Pub. L. No. 106-386, § 2002, 114 Stat. 1464, 1543.
242. Neely Tucker, *Pain and Suffering; Relatives of Terrorist Victims Race Each Other to Court, but Justice and Money are Both Hard to Find*, WASH. POST, Apr. 6, 2003.

243. *Id.*

244. *Id.*

245. *Id.*

246. Eisenfeld v. Islamic Republic of Iran, 172 F. Supp. 2d 1 (2000).

247. KELLY, *supra* note 233.

248. Author interview of Perles, *supra* note 212.

249. Jessica Silver-Greenberg & Ben Protess, *A Grieving Father Pulls a Thread That Unravels BNP's Illegal Deals*, N.Y. TIMES, June 30, 2014, http://dealbook.nytimes.com/2014/06/30/a-grieving-father-pulls-a-thread-that-unravels-illegal-bank-deals/?_r=0.

250. *Id.*

251. *Id.*

252. *Id.*

253. *Id.*

254. *Id.*

255. *Id.*

256. *Id.; see also* Press Release, U.S. Dep't of Justice, Southern District of New York, *Manhattan U.S. Attorney Announces Settlement Relating to Iranian-Owned Manhattan Office Tower That Will Provide Recovery to Terrorism Victims* (Apr. 17, 2014), http://www.justice.gov/usao/nys/pressreleases/April14/650FifthAvSettlementPR.php.

257. Julie Satow, *Seizing Iran's Slice of Fifth Avenue*, N.Y. TIMES, Sept. 24, 2013, http://www.nytimes.com/2013/09/25/realestate/commercial/with-judges-ruling-seizure-of-650-fifth-avenue-grinds-on.html?_r=0.

258. Author interview of Perles, *supra* note 212.

259. *In re* Islamic Republic of Iran Terrorism Litig., 659 F. Supp. 2d 31, 42 (D.D.C. 2009).

260. Glenn Kessler, *Libya's Final Payment to Victims' Fund Clears Way for Normal U.S. Ties*, WASH. POST, Nov. 1, 2008, http://www.washingtonpost.com/wp-dyn/content/article/2008/10/31/AR2008103103616.html; Kirit Radia & Maddy Sauer, *Pan Am 103 Families Finally Compensated*, ABC NEWS, Oct. 31, 2008, http://abcnews.go.com/Blotter/story?id=6158491; Jonathan B. Schwartz, *Dealing with a "Rogue State": The Libya Precedent*, 101 AM. J. INT'L L. 553, 568–72 (2007), http://archives.syr.edu/panam/pdf/103PUB0005.pdf.

261. Alejandre v. Republic of Cuba, 996 F. Supp. 1239 (S.D. Fla. 1997).

262. Christopher Marquis, *Families Win Cuban Money in Pilots' Case*, N.Y. TIMES, Feb. 14, 2001, http://www.nytimes.com/2001/02/14/us/families-win-cuban-money-in-pilots-case.html?ref=topics.

263. *Statement of Steven R. Perles Before the Subcomm. on Monetary Policy & Trade of the H. Comm. on Financial Services* (July 17, 2014), http://financialservices.house.gov/uploadedfiles/hhrg-113-ba19-wstate-sperles-20140717.pdf.

264. Gates v. Syrian Arab Republic, 2014 U.S. LEXIS 11811 (7th Cir. 2014); Gates v. Syrian Arab Republic, 646 F.3d 1 (D.C. Cir. 2011).

265. Terrorism Risk Insurance Act, Pub. L. 107-297 (2002).

266. *Statement of Steven R. Perles*, *supra* note 263.

267. Author interview of Perles, *supra* note 212.

268. *Id.*

269. Editorial, *Lawsuits and Terrorism*, WASH. POST, Dec. 26, 199, at B6.

270. Adam Liptak, *U.S. Courts' Role in Foreign Feuds Comes Under Fire*, N.Y. TIMES, Aug. 3, 2003, http://www.nytimes.com/2003/08/03/us/us-courts-role-in-foreign-feuds-comes-under-fire.html.

271. *In re* Islamic Republic of Iran Terrorism Litig., 659 F. Supp. 2d 38 (D.D.C. 2009).

272. *Id.* at 37.

273. *Id.*

274. *Id.*

275. *Id.*

276. Jay Solomon, *U.S. Freezes $2 Billion in Iran Case*, WALL ST. J., Dec. 12, 2009, http://online.wsj.com/article/SB126057864707988237.html.

277. Author interview of Perles, *supra* note 212.

278. Jennifer K. Elsea, CONG. RESEARCH SERV., MEMORANDUM TO THE HOUSE FINANCIAL SERVICES COMMITTEE, TERRORISM JUDGMENTS AGAINST IRAN (July 20, 2015). As of August 9, 2015, the memorandum had been shared with this book's author but had not been published.

279. *Id.*

280. Tucker, *supra* note 242.

281. Author interview of Perles, *supra* note 212.

282. *Id.*

283. KENNETH M. POLLACK, THE PERSIAN PUZZLE: THE CONFLICT BETWEEN IRAN AND AMERICA 203 (2005).

284. Mike Giglio, *Beirut: Echoes of 1983 Marine Barracks Bombing in Hassan Attack*, THE DAILY BEAST, Oct. 23, 2012, http://www.thedailybeast.com/articles/2012/10/23/beirut-echoes-of-1983-marine-barracks-bombing-in-hassan-attack.html.

285. DAVID CRIST, THE TWILIGHT WAR: THE SECRET HISTORY OF AMERICA'S THIRTY-YEAR CONFLICT WITH IRAN 148 (2012).

286. *Id.* at 140.

287. *Id.* at 134–35.

288. *Id.* at 142.

289. *Id.* at 141.

290. *Id.*

291. *Id.* at 142.

292. *Id.* at 148.

293. *Id.* at 146.

294. *Id.* at 142–46.

295. *Id.* at 142.

296. *Id.*

297. *Id.* at 146–48.

298. *Id.* at 148.

299. *Id.* at 152–53.

300. Peterson v. Islamic Republic of Iran, 264 F. Supp. 2d 46, 61 (D.D.C. 2003).

301. *Id.* at 54.

302. *Id.* at 60.

303. *"We Want to Hurt Iran,"* NEWSWEEK, Mar. 18, 2003, http://www.newsweek.com/we-want-hurt-iran-132447.

304. *Peterson*, 264 F. Supp. 2d at 60.

305. *Id.* at 61.

306. *Id.* at 54; *see also* author interview of Perles, *supra* note 212.

307. *Peterson*, 264 F. Supp. 2d at 54–56; *see also* author interview of Perles, *supra* note 212.

308. Author interview of Perles, *supra* note 212.

309. *Id.*

310. *Id.*

311. *Id.*

312. *Id.*

313. *Id.*

314. *Id.*

315. *Id.*

316. *Id.*

317. *Id.*

318. *"We Want to Hurt Iran,"* NEWSWEEK, Mar. 18, 2003, http://www.newsweek.com/we-want-hurt-iran-132447.

319. *Peterson,* 264 F. Supp. 2d at 54.

320. *Id.*

321. *Id.*

322. *Id.*

323. *Judge Fines Iran $2.65B Over 1983 Beirut Marine Barracks Bombing,* FOXNEWS.COM, Sept. 8, 2007, http://www.foxnews.com/story/0,2933,296141,00.html; *Peterson,* 515 F. Supp. 2d at 60.

324. *Peterson,* 515 F. Supp. 2d at 60.

325. *Id.*

326. Valore v. Islamic Republic of Iran, 700 F. Supp. 2d 52, 57–58 (D.D.C. 2010).

327. Memorandum Opinion, Brown v. Islamic Republic of Iran, No. 08-cv-531 (RCL) (D.D.C. 2012), http://legaltimes.typepad.com/files/brown-opinion.pdf.

328. Davis v. Islamic Republic of Iran, 882 F. Supp. 2d 7 (D.D.C. 2012).

329. Valore v. Islamic Republic of Iran, 700 F. Supp. 2d 52 (D.D.C. 2010).

330. Estate of Bland v. Islamic Republic of Iran, 831 F. Supp. 2d 150 (D.D.C. 2011).

331. Brown v. Islamic Republic of Iran, No. 08-cv-531 (RCL) (D.D.C. 2012), http://legaltimes.typepad.com/files/brown-opinion.pdf.

332. Spencer v. Islamic Republic of Iran, 2014 U.S. Dist. LEXIS 146081 (D.D.C. 2014).

333. Jay Solomon, *U.S. Freezes $2 Billion in Iran Case,* WALL ST. J., Dec. 12, 2009, http://online.wsj.com/article/SB126057864707988237.html.

334. *Id.*

335. *Id.*

336. Julie Triedman, *Can U.S. Lawyers Make Iran Pay for 1983 Bombing?,* AM. LAWYER, Oct. 28, 2013.

337. *Id.*

338. *Id.*

339. *Id.*

340. Author interview of Steven Perles, *supra* note 212.

341. Peterson v. Islamic Republic of Iran, 264 F. Supp. 2d 46, 63–64 (D.D.C. 2003).

342. *Id.* at 63.

343. Complaint, Fritz v. Islamic Republic of Iran, Case No. 1:15-cv-00456-RDM (Mar. 30, 2015) (accessed via PACER on May 2, 2015).

344. *Id.*

345. *Id.*

346. Martin Chulov, *Shia Cleric's Release by US Forces Provided Key to Peter Moore's Freedom,* THE GUARDIAN, Dec. 30, 2009, http://www.theguardian.com/world/2009/dec/30/iranian-shia-clerics-release.

347. Richard Lardner, *Lawsuit Alleges Iran Directed Killing of U.S. Soldiers in Iraq,* TELEGRAPH (UK), Mar. 31, 2015, http://telegraph.news.uk.com/article/3105179/lawsuit-alleges-iran-directed-killing-of-us-soldiers-in-iraq.

348. *Id.*

349. Joint Comprehensive Plan of Action, July 14, 2015, *available at* http://eeas.europa.eu/statements-eeas/docs/iran_agreement/iran_joint-comprehensive-plan-of-action_en.pdf.

350. Iran Nuclear Agreement Review Act of 2015, Pub. L. No. 114-17 (2015), *available at* https://www.congress.gov/114/plaws/publ17/PLAW-114publ17.pdf.

351. Kenneth Katzman & Paul K. Kerr, Cong. Research Serv., R43333, Iran Nuclear Agreement 15 (July 30, 2015), https://fas.org/sgp/crs/nuke/R43333.pdf.

352. *The Iran Nuclear Deal and Its Impact on Terrorism Financing: House Financial Services Committee Hearing on Task Force to Investigate Terrorism Financing* (July 22, 2015) (Federal News Service transcript available on Lexis).

353. *Statement of Steven R. Perles Before the Task Force to Investigate Terrorism Financing of the H. Comm. on Financial Services* (July 22, 2015), http://financialservices.house.gov/uploadedfiles/hhrg-114-ba00-wstate-sperles-20150722.pdf.

354. *See, e.g., Debts of the Ayatollah*, Wall St. J., Aug. 13, 2015, http://www.wsj.com/articles/debts-of-the-ayatollah-1439507940.

355. Complaint, Leibovitch v. United States, Case 1:15-cv-06133 (filed Aug. 5, 2015), http://www.investigativeproject.org/documents/case_docs/2798.pdf; Nicole Hong, *U.S. Terrorism Victims File Lawsuit Targeting Part of Iranian Nuclear Deal*, Wall St. J., Aug. 5, 2015, http://www.wsj.com/articles/u-s-terrorism-victims-file-lawsuit-targeting-part-of-iranian-nuclear-deal-1438788159.

356. Complaint, Leibovitch v. United States, *supra* note 355; Terrorism Risk Insurance Act of 2002, Pub. L. No. 107-297 (2002), http://www.gpo.gov/fdsys/pkg/PLAW-107publ297/html/PLAW-107publ297.htm.

357. *In re* Islamic Republic of Iran Terrorism Litig., 659 F. Supp. 2d 38, 37 (D.D.C. 2009).

358. Crosby v. Nat'l Foreign Trade Council, 530 U.S. 363, 381 (2000).

359. Richard F. Grimmett, Cong. Research Serv., Foreign Policy Roles of the President and Congress (June 1, 1999), http://fpc.state.gov/6172.htm.

360. U.S. Const. art. I, § 8, http://www.gpo.gov/fdsys/pkg/CDOC-110hdoc50/pdf/CDOC-110hdoc50.pdf.

361. *Id.*

362. *Id.*

363. *Id.*

364. *Id.*

365. *Id.*

366. *Id.*

367. *Id.*

368. U.S. Const. art. I, § 9, http://www.gpo.gov/fdsys/pkg/CDOC-110hdoc50/pdf/CDOC-110hdoc50.pdf.

369. U.S. Const. art. II, § 2, http://www.gpo.gov/fdsys/pkg/CDOC-110hdoc50/pdf/CDOC-110hdoc50.pdf.

370. Report of the Congressional Committees Investigating the Iran-Contra Affair 457 (Daniel K. Inouye & Lee H. Hamilton, chairs) (minority report) (1987), https://ia902205.us.archive.org/16/items/reportofcongress87unit/reportofcongress87unit.pdf.

371. Edward S. Corwin, The President: Office and Powers 171 (1957).

372. Alejandre v. Republic of Cuba, 996 F. Supp. 1239 (S.D. Fla. 1997).

373. Hill v. Republic of Iraq, 175 F. Supp. 2d 36 (D.D.C. 2001); *see also* Jennifer K. Elsea, Cong. Research Serv., RL31358, Suits Against Terrorist States by Victims of Terrorism 37, 39 (2008), http://www.fas.org/sgp/crs/terror/RL31258.pdf.

374. Glenn Kessler, *Libya's Final Payment to Victims' Fund Clears Way for Normal U.S. Ties*, Wash. Post, Nov. 1, 2008, http://www.washingtonpost.com/wp-dyn/content/article/2008/10/31/AR2008103103616.html; Kirit Radia & Maddy Sauer, *Pan Am 103 Families Finally Compensated*, ABC News, Oct. 31, 2008, http://abcnews.go.com/Blotter/story?id=6158491; Jonathan B. Schwartz, *Dealing with a "Rogue State": The*

Libya Precedent, 101 Am. J. Int'l L. 553, 568–72 (2007), http://archives.syr.edu/panam/pdf/103PUB0005.pdf.

375. Gates v. Syrian Arab Republic, 2014 U.S. App. LEXIS 11811 (7th Cir. June 18, 2014).

376. *See, e.g.*, Opinion and Order, Calderon-Corona v. DPRK, No. 08-1367 (D.P.R. July 16, 2010), http://freekorea.us/wp-content/uploads/2010/07/calderon-order.pdf.

377. *See, e.g.*, Perry S. Bechky, *The Politics of Divestment, in* The Politics of International Economic Law (2011), http://ssrn.com/abstract=1678208; Nat'l Conference of State Legislatures, *State Divestment Legislation* (Apr. 9, 2008), http://www.ncsl.org/print/standcomm/sclaborecon/statedivestmentlegislation040908.pdf.

378. Douglas F. Gansler, *Uniting States Against Iran*, Wall St. J., Mar. 8, 2013, http://www.wsj.com/articles/SB10001424127887324662404578332622153212746.

379. *See, e.g.*, Francis Njubi Nesbitt, *The People's Sanctions*, Foreign Policy in Focus, Dec. 6, 2013, http://fpif.org/peoples-sanctions/.

380. *See, e.g.*, John G. Dale, Free Burma: Transnational Legal Action and Corporate Accountability 108 (2011).

381. *See, e.g.*, Shira Schoenberg, *Pension Politics: The History of Divestment in Massachusetts*, MassLive.com, May 8, 2014, http://www.masslive.com/politics/index.ssf/2014/05/the_history_of_divestment_in_m.html (referencing a law enacted in Massachusetts).

382. *See, e.g.*, Matthew Porterfield, *State and Local Foreign Policy Initiatives and Free Speech: The First Amendment as an Instrument of Federalism*, 35 Stan. J. Int'l L. 1, 4 (1999).

383. *See, e.g., id.* at 5.

384. Press Release, U.S. Census Bureau, *State Government Revenues Exceed Expenditures in 2013, Census Bureau Reports* (Feb. 3, 2015), https://www.census.gov/newsroom/press-releases/2015/cb15-22.html; Hazel Bradford, *State Pension Funds' Combined Underfunding Rises to $4.7 Trillion—Report*, Pensions & Investments, Nov. 12, 2014, http://www.pionline.com/article/20141112/ONLINE/141119943/state-pension-funds-combined-underfunding-rises-to-47-trillion-8212-report.

385. Press Release, U.S. Census Bureau, *supra* note 384.

386. *See, e.g.*, UK Public Spending, Total Planned Public Spending, http://www.ukpublicspending.co.uk.

387. *See* Larry Oakes, *Essar Drops Plan with Iran: Steel Mill on Range Is a Go*, StarTribune.com, Oct. 31, 2007, http://www.startribune.com/business/11245206.html (discussing Minnesota Governor Tim Pawlenty's statement that Essar's plans with Iran, if carried out, would jeopardize Essar's subsidies to operate in Minnesota).

388. *See id.* (stating that Minnesota Governor Tim Pawlenty had threatened to pull construction permits if Essar followed through with its plans to build an oil refinery in Iran).

389. *See* Tim Pugmire, *Pawlenty Says Essar Concerns are Resolved*, MPR News, Oct. 31, 2007, http://minnesota.priprod.publicradio.org/display/web/2007/10/31/essargoesforward/.

390. Crosby v. Nat'l Foreign Trade Council, 530 U.S. 363 (2000).

391. USA Engage, *Supreme Court Rules Massachusetts Burma Law Unconstitutional*, June 19, 2000, *quoted in* Edward T. Swaine, *Crosby as Foreign Relations Law*, 41 Va. J. Int'l L. 101, 101 n.2 (2001), http://scholarship.law.gwu.edu/cgi/viewcontent.cgi?article=1009&context=faculty_publications.

392. *See, e.g.*, Perry Bechky, *Darfur, Divestment, and Dialogue*, 30 U. Pa. J. Int'l L. 823, 883–84 (2009).

393. *Crosby*, 530 U.S. at 381.

394. Zivotofsky v. Kerry, No. 13-628, slip op. at 1 (U.S. June 8, 2015), http://www.supremecourt.gov/opinions/14pdf/13-628_15gm.pdf.

395. *Id.* at 29.

396. *Id.* at 2–4.

397. *Id.* at 11.

398. *Id.*

399. Jack Goldsmith, *Why Zivotofsky Is a Significant Victory for the Executive Branch,* Lawfare Blog (June 8, 2015, 3:44 PM), http://www.lawfareblog.com/why-zivotofsky-significant-victory-executive-branch.

400. *Zivotofsky, supra* note 394, slip op. at 29.

401. Goldsmith, *supra* note 399.

402. *Convention on the Prevention and Punishment of the Crime of Genocide* art. II, Dec. 9, 1948, https://treaties.un.org/doc/Publication/UNTS/Volume%2078/volume-78-I-1021-English.pdf.

403. Genocide Convention arts. III and IV.

404. Louis Henkin, How Nations Behave: Law and Foreign Policy 228 (1979).

405. *Id.* at 229–31.

406. *Coining a Word and Championing a Cause: The Story of Raphael Lemkin,* Holocaust Encyclopedia (visited Apr. 17, 2015), http://www.ushmm.org/wlc/en/article.php?ModuleId=10007050.

407. *Id.*

408. Payam Akhavan, Reducing Genocide to Law: Definition, Meaning, and the Ultimate Crime 96 (2012).

409. *Id.*

410. Michael Ignatieff, *The Unsung Hero Who Coined the Term "Genocide,"* The New Republic, Sept. 21, 2013, http://www.newrepublic.com/article/114424/raphael-lemkin-unsung-hero-who-coined-genocide.

411. Samantha Power, "A Problem from Hell:" America and the Age of Genocide 55 (2002).

412. *See, e.g.,* PSJD, Careers in Federal Government, http://www.psjd.org/Careers_in_Federal_Government#_ftn1 (last visited Apr. 15, 2015).

413. www.Bakermckenzie.com (last visited Apr. 15, 2015).

414. *Id.*

415. Emily Cadei, *The Wonks Waging Financial War on Iran,* OZY, Jan. 22, 2014, http://www.ozy.com/rising-stars-and-provocateurs/the-wonks-waging-financial-war-on-iran/4912.

416. *Id.*

417. *Six Lives Transformed by Sept. 11,* NPR, Sept. 8, 2006, http://www.npr.org/templates/story/story.php?storyId=6041540.

418. Editorial, *Swift Sanctions on Iran,* Wall St. J., Feb. 1, 2012, http://www.wsj.com/articles/SB10001424052970203718504577178902535754464.

419. SWIFT, Company Information, http://www.swift.com/about_swift/company_information/company_information (last visited Apr. 22, 2015).

420. Editorial, *supra* note 418; Jay Solomon, *EU to Ban Iran Banks from Financial Network,* Wall St. J., Feb. 15, 2012, http://www.wsj.com/articles/SB10001424052970204795304577223900530203704.

421. *See, e.g.,* SWIFT, Annual Review 2010, at 29, http://www.swift.com/assets/swift_com/documents/about_swift/SWIFT_Annual_Report_2010.pdf (last visited Apr. 22, 2015).

422. Editorial, *supra* note 418.

423. *Id.*

424. *Id.*

425. *Id.*

426. *Id.*

427. Sen. Robert Menendez, Press Release, *Menendez Hails Banking Committee Passage of Iran Sanctions Legislation* (Feb. 2, 2012), http://www.menendez.senate.gov/news-and-events/press/menendez-hails-banking-committee-passage-of-iran-sanctions-legislation.

428. *Id.*

429. *Payments System SWIFT to Expel Iranian Banks Saturday*, REUTERS, Mar. 15, 2012, http://www.reuters.com/article/2012/03/15/us-nuclear-iran-idUSBRE82E15M20120315.

430. Rachelle Younglai & Roberta Rampton, *U.S. Pushes EU, SWIFT to Eject Iranian Banks*, REUTERS, Feb. 15, 2012, http://www.reuters.com/article/2012/02/16/us-iran-usa-swift-idUSTRE81F00I20120216.

431. Christopher Harress, *Iran's Rouhani Faces Music as Sanctions Bite Harder, Is There a SWIFT Solution in the Works?*, INT'L BUS. TIMES, Oct. 8, 2013, http://www.ibtimes.com/irans-rouhani-faces-music-sanctions-bite-harder-there-swift-solution-works-1417768.

432. *See, e.g.*, Thomas Erdbrink & Mark Landler, *Iran Said to Seek a Nuclear Accord to End Sanctions*, N.Y. TIMES, Sept. 19, 2013, http://www.nytimes.com/2013/09/20/world/middleeast/iran-said-to-seek-a-nuclear-accord-to-end-sanctions.html?_r=0.

433. Jonathan Schanzer & Mark Dubowitz, *It Just Got Easier for Iran to Fund Terrorism*, FOREIGN POLICY, July 17, 2015, https://foreignpolicy.com/2015/07/17/it-just-got-easier-for-iran-to-fund-terrorism-swift-bank/.

434. Claudia Rosett, *Obama's Iran Policy Is Lost at Sea*, WALL ST. J., Mar. 26, 2015, http://www.wsj.com/articles/claudia-rosett-obamas-iran-policy-is-lost-at-sea-1427410998; Claudia Rosett, *North Korean Ship Tests the Waters Near America's Shores*, FORBES, July 13, 2014, http://www.forbes.com/sites/claudiarosett/2014/07/13/north-korean-ship-tests-the-waters-near-americas-shores/.

435. *See, e.g.*, VESSEL FINDER, http://www.vesselfinder.com; MarineTraffic, MARINE TRAFFIC, https://www.marinetraffic.com.

436. UNITED AGAINST NUCLEAR IRAN, MARK WALLACE, http://www.unitedagainstnucleariran.com/about/leadership/mark-wallace (last visited Apr. 17, 2015).

437. Rick Gladstone, *Group Keeps Long-Distance Watch on Iran and Possible Sanctions Violations*, N.Y. TIMES, June 20, 2013, http://www.nytimes.com/2013/06/21/world/middleeast/group-keeps-watch-on-iran-and-possible-sanction-violations.html.

438. Matt Apuzzo, *Justice Dept. Moves to Shield Anti-Iran Group's Files*, N.Y. TIMES, July 27, 2014, http://www.nytimes.com/2014/07/28/us/politics/us-justice-dept-moves-to-shield-anti-iran-groups-files-united-against-nuclear-iran.html?_r=0.

439. *Id.*

440. *Id.*

441. *See, e.g.*, Jenara Nerenberg, *Satellites for Good: The NGO's Ultimate Tool*, FAST COMPANY, Dec. 29, 2010, http://www.fastcompany.com/1713015/satellites-good-ngos-ultimate-tool; Christoph Koettl, *Syria: New Satellite Images Document 12 Months of Deadly Conflict*, AMNESTY INT'L HUMAN RIGHTS NOW BLOG (Aug. 7, 2013, 9:13 AM), http://blog.amnestyusa.org/middle-east/syria-new-satellite-images-document-12-months-of-deadly-conflict/; Paul Brannan & David Albright, *ISIS Imagery Brief: New Activities at the Esfahan and Natanz Nuclear Sites in Iran*, INST. FOR SCI. & INT'L SEC., Apr. 14, 2006, http://isis-online.org/publications/iran/newactivities.pdf.

442. *See, e.g.*, Nerenberg, *supra* note 441.

443. *See, e.g., id.*; Koettl, *supra* note 441; David Albright & Robert Avagyan, *Further Activity at Suspected Parchin High Explosive Testing Site: Two Small Buildings Razed*, INST. FOR SCI. & INT'L SEC., May 30, 2012, http://www.isisnucleariran.org/assets/pdf/

Parchin_site_activity_May_30_2012.pdf; Fredrik Dahl, *U.S. Think-Tank Sees More Iran Site "Sanitization" Work*, REUTERS, June 20, 2012, http://www.reuters.com/article/2012/06/20/us-nuclear-iran-parchin-idUSBRE85J13G20120620.

444. *See, e.g.,* William A. Jacobson, *Huge BDS Loss—Greenstar Food Coop Rejects Israel Boycott*, LEGAL INSURRECTION, May 12, 2015, http://legalinsurrection.com/2015/05/huge-bds-loss-greenstar-food-coop-rejects-israel-boycott/; Heather Robinson, *36 Under 36: Benjamin Ryberg*, N.Y. JEWISH WEEK, June 4, 2013, http://www.thejewishweek.com/special-sections/36-under-36/benjamin-ryberg-28.

445. Sudan Divestment Task Force, *Sudan Divestment Resource Guide*, at 3 (Mar. 21, 2008), https://www.responsible-investor.com/images/uploads/resources/research/11209664579Resource_Guide.pdf.

446. *See, e.g.,* United to End Genocide, *Our History*, http://endgenocide.org/who-we-are/history/; Nick Timiraos, *Sudan-Divestment Activists Get Act Together*, WALL ST. J., July 19, 2006, http://www.wsj.com/articles/SB115327514737110704.

447. *Sudan Divestment Resource Guide, supra* note 445, at 3.

448. *Id.* at 5.

449. *Id.* at 8.

450. *Id.* at 4.

451. Floyd Norris, *S.E.C. Rethinks Lists Linking Companies and Terrorist States*, N.Y. TIMES, July 21, 2007, http://www.nytimes.com/2007/07/21/business/21sec.html.

452. *Id.*

453. *Id.*

454. *Id.;* Martha Graybow, *U.S. S.E.C.'s Country Watch List Draws Fire*, REUTERS, July 5, 2007, http://www.reuters.com/article/2007/07/05/sec-countrylist-idUSN0535227220070705.

455. Norris, *supra* note 451.

456. Sudan Accountability and Divestment Act of 2007, Pub. L. No. 110–74 (2007).

457. Sudan Accountability and Divestment Act of 2007, S. Rep. No. 110-213, at 6 (Oct. 31, 2007), http://www.gpo.gov/fdsys/pkg/CRPT-110srpt213/pdf/CRPT-110srpt213.pdf.

458. Laurence Norman, *EU Governments Approve Secret Evidence in Sanctions Cases*, WALL ST. J., Feb. 10, 2015, http://www.wsj.com/articles/eu-governments-approve-secret-evidence-in-sanctions-cases-1423583213.

459. *Id.*

460. *Id.*

461. RICHARD A. BEST, JR. & ALFRED CUMMING, CONG. RESEARCH SERV., RL34270, OPEN SOURCE INTELLIGENCE (OSINT): ISSUES FOR CONGRESS (Dec. 5, 2007), http://www.fas.org/sgp/crs/intel/RL34270.pdf.

462. Treasury's principal innovation can be described as follows: rather than asking, e.g., the Swiss government to order its banks to stop doing business with Iran, Treasury was going directly to the Swiss banks and advising them of the risks of doing even prima facie legal business with Iran. Treasury found that its unprecedented direct outreach to a country's key private financial institutions was yielding results much more quickly than did outreach to that same country's government, which often lacked political will or the necessary authority, or faced cumbersome bureaucratic procedures for exercising whatever relevant authorities it does have. And once one Swiss bank gets out, the others are under pressure not to be the last Swiss bank doing business with Iran, so they get out too.

463. *See, e.g.,* David E. Sanger, *U.S. Weighs Iran Sanctions if Talks Are Rejected*, N.Y. TIMES, Aug. 3, 2009, at A4, *available at* http://www.nytimes.com/2009/08/03/world/middleeast/03nuke.html.

464. *See, e.g., U.S. Exports to India for $6 Billion Refinery and Petrochemical Complex Are Backed by Ex-Im Bank $500 Million Loan Guarantee*, Export-Import Bank of the United States, May 16, 2007, http://www.exim.gov/news/us-exports-india-for-6-billion-refinery-and-petrochemical-complex-are-backed-ex-im-bank-500.

465. *See, e.g.*, Jerry Jackson, *Port Canaveral Greenlights Fuel Facility*, Nov. 17, 2006, http://articles.orlandosentinel.com/2006-11-17/business/TANKFARM17_1_fuel-pipeline-port-canaveral.

466. Orde F. Kittrie, *How to Put the Squeeze on Iran*, WALL ST. J., Nov. 13, 2008, at A19, http://online.wsj.com/article/SB122654026060023113.html.

467. *Id.*

468. *Id.*

469. *US Lawmakers Want RIL Assistance Stopped on Iran Ties*, INDIA TODAY, Dec. 20, 2008, http://indiatoday.intoday.in/story/US+lawmakers+want+RIL+assistance+stopped+on+Iran+ties/1/23180.html.

470. *See, e.g., Reliance's Iran Links Invite US Ire*, ECONOMIC TIMES, Dec. 21, 2008, http://articles.economictimes.indiatimes.com/2008-12-21/news/28381897_1_tehran-loan-guarantees-brad-sherman.

471. Michael Hirsh, *Obama's Enforcer*, NEWSWEEK, Dec. 12, 2009, *available at* http://www.newsweek.com/2009/12/11/obama-s-enforcer.html.

472. Asjylyn Loder, *Florida Senator Presses Firm to Stop Doing Business with Iran*, TAMPA BAY TIMES, Dec. 5, 2008, http://www.tampabay.com/news/business/energy/florida-senator-presses-firm-to-stop-doing-business-with-iran/927912.

473. *Id.*

474. Tom Doggett, *U.S. Lawmakers Vote to Punish Iran's Fuel Suppliers*, REUTERS, Oct. 1, 2009, http://uk.reuters.com/article/idUKTRE59072H20091001; Energy & Water Development and Related Agencies Appropriations Act of 2010, Pub. L. No. 111-85, § 313 (2009).

475. *Id.*

476. H.R. 2194, the Iran Refined Petroleum Sanctions Act of 2009, passed the House on December 15, 2009. S. 2799, the Comprehensive Iran Sanctions, Accountability, and Divestment Act of 2009, passed the Senate on January 28, 2010. The Senate named its Iran sanctions legislation conferees in early March 2010, and the House named its conferees in late April 2010. The bill that emerged from conference, H.R. 2194, the Comprehensive Iran Sanctions, Accountability, and Divestment Act of 2010, passed both the House and the Senate on June 24, 2010. For a complete bill summary and status, see http://thomas.loc.gov/cgi-bin/bdquery/z?d111:HR02194:@@@X. Swiss energy traders Vitol, Glencore, and Trafigura publicly committed in March 2010 not to supply refined petroleum to Iran. Press Release, U.S. Dep't of State, *Companies Reducing Energy-Related Business with Iran* (Sept. 30, 2010), http://www.state.gov/r/pa/prs/ps/2010/09/148458.htm (last visited Nov. 15, 2010). The French energy firm Total suspended gasoline shipments to Iran a few days after the conferenced legislation passed both houses of Congress. Paul Sampson, *Iran Sanctions Open Way for Chinese*, INT'L OIL DAILY, July 6, 2010. Lloyds of London announced on July 9, 2010, that it would not insure or reinsure petroleum shipments going into Iran. Press Release, *Companies Reducing Energy-Related Business, supra.*

477. Comprehensive Iran Sanctions, Accountability and Divestment Act of 2010, Pub. L. No. 111–95 (2010).

478. *Id.* § 102 (g).

479. As of November 2008, the top five suppliers of gasoline to Iran were the Swiss firm Vitol; the Swiss/Dutch firm Trafigura; the French firm Total; British Petroleum;

and the Indian firm Reliance Industries. Orde F. Kittrie, *How to Put the Squeeze on Iran*, WALL ST. J., Nov. 13, 2008, at A19, *available at* http://online.wsj.com/article/SB122654026060023113.html. As of September 30, 2010, all five firms had stopped supplying gasoline to Iran. Press Release, U.S. Dep't of State, *Companies Reducing Energy-Related Business with Iran* (Sept. 30, 2010), http://www.state.gov/r/pa/prs/ps/2010/09/148458.htm (last visited Nov. 27, 2010).

480. Reem Shamseddine & Luke Pachymuthu, *Iran Fuel Imports Dive in Sept on Sanctions-Trade*, REUTERS, Sept. 24, 2010, http://af.reuters.com/article/energyOilNews/idAFLDE68N0ZF20100924 (last visited Nov. 27, 2010); *Hearing on Iran Sanctions Before the H. Comm. on Foreign Affairs*, 111th Cong. (Dec. 1, 2010) (oral testimony of William Burns, Under Secretary of State for Political Affairs) (stating that Iran's imports of refined petroleum products were 85 percent less in October 2010 than they were before July 2010).

481. The White House, *National Security Strategy*, Feb. 2015, https://www.whitehouse.gov/sites/default/files/docs/2015_national_security_strategy.pdf.

482. *Id.*

483. *Id.*

484. *Id.*

485. *Thinking Over the Horizon: Michèle Flournoy on Prudential Foreign Policy in the World Today*, YALE J. INT'L AFF., Mar. 19, 2015, http://yalejournal.org/interview_post/thinking-over-the-horizon-michele-flournoy-on-prudential-foreign-policy-in-the-world-today/.

486. *Id.*

487. Karim Lakhani of Harvard Business School said his study of Innocentive found that solvers from adjacent fields were more likely to solve problems, often by applying specialized knowledge or instruments developed for another purpose. "The history of science is filled with such episodes, for example molecular biology was reportedly established by the movement of physicists into biology. They brought with them their tools and understandings of particles and applied it to biology." 5 *Questions with Dr. Karim Lakhani*, INNOCENTIVE (July 25, 2008), https://www.innocentive.com/5-questions-dr-karim-lakhani (last visited Apr. 18, 2015). "Problem solving requires the application of heuristics and perspectives. In many cases a problem that is difficult under one heuristic/perspective pair may be relatively easy … under a different heuristic/perspective pair. The key is the application of a variety of 'different' approaches to the problem—so that the 'home field' for the problem does not end up constraining the solution." *Id.*

488. Greg Miller & Scott Higham, *U.S. Struggles in Propaganda War Against ISIS*, WASH. POST, May 8, 2015, http://www.washingtonpost.com/world/national-security/in-a-propaganda-war-us-tried-to-play-by-the-enemys-rules/2015/05/08/6eb6b732-e52f-11e4-81ea-0649268f729e_story.html.

489. CSIS ANNUAL REPORT 2012, at 5, http://csis.org/files/publication/130305_annual-report_finalPDF-sm4.pdf.

490. Eric Pianin, *Why Government and Innovation Are Like Oil and Water*, FISCAL TIMES, Apr. 7, 2015, http://www.thefiscaltimes.com/2015/04/07/Why-Government-and-Innovation-Are-Oil-and-Water.

491. Partnership for Public Service and IDEO, *Innovation in Government*, http://www.ideo.com/images/uploads/news/pdfs/InnovationInGovernment.pdf.

492. Pianin, *supra* note 490.

493. Ellen Laipson, *Think Tanks: Supporting Cast Players in the National Security Enterprise*, *in* THE NATIONAL SECURITY ENTERPRISE: NAVIGATING THE LABYRINTH 289 (Roger Z. George & Harvey Rishikof eds., 2011).

494. Laipson, *id.* at 293.

495. *Id.*

496. Margaret E. Keck & Kathryn Sikkink, Activists Beyond Borders x (1998).

497. *Id.* at 2.

498. *Id.*

499. *Id.* at 3.

500. Abram Chayes, The Cuban Missile Crisis: International Crises and the Rule of Law 7 (1974).

501. Michael P. Scharf & Paul R. Williams, Shaping Foreign Policy in Times of Crisis: The Role of International Law and the State Department Legal Adviser (2010).

502. Harold Hongju Koh, *Foreword: America's Conscience On International Law, in* Scharf & Williams, Shaping Foreign Policy in Times of Crisis, *supra* note 501, at xv.

503. Scharf & Williams, Shaping Foreign Policy in Times of Crisis, *supra* note 501, at 206–07.

504. *Id.* at 211.

505. Koh, *supra* note 502.

506. Lee H. Hamilton, How Congress Works and Why You Should Care 113 (2004).

507. Scharf & Williams, supra note 501, at xx.

508. *The Role of International Law in U.S. Foreign Policymaking*, Proceedings of the Annual Meeting of the American Society of International Law (1992).

509. U.S. Army, *Army JAG Corps*, http://www.goarmy.com/jag/jag-reserve-component. html (last visited Apr. 24, 2015).

510. Author interview of Col. Guy Roberts, USMC (ret.) (Apr. 24, 2015).

511. Uriel Heilman, *Suing for Justice: Victims Take the War on Terrorism to the Courtroom*, Moment Magazine, June 2003, http://www.urielheilman.com/terrorlaw.html.

512. *Id.*

513. *Id.*

514. Rob Copeland, *Hedge Fund's $100 Million Bet: Iran Will Pay for Terror Attack*, Wall St. J., Mar. 23, 2014, http://www.wsj.com/articles/SB10001424052702304026304579451920304071640.

515. *Id.*

516. *Id.*

517. Author interview of Perles, *supra* note 212.

518. *Id.*

519. *Id.*

520. *Id.*

521. *Id.*

522. *Id.*

523. *Id.*

524. *Id.*

525. *Id.*

526. U.S. Department of Justice Asset Forfeiture Policy Manual 168 (2012).

527. Author interview of Perles, *supra* note 212.

528. *Id.*

529. United States v. BNP Paribas S.A., *Frequently Asked Questions*, http://www.usvbnpp. com/frequently-asked-questions.aspx (last visited May 3, 2015).

530. *Id.*

531. Author interview of Perles, *supra* note 212.
532. Jodi Rudoren, *Crusading for Israel in a Way Some Say Is Misguided*, N.Y. Times, Jan. 23, 2015, http://www.nytimes.com/2015/01/24/world/middleeast/crusading-for-israel-in-a-way-some-say-is-misguided.html.
533. Shurat HaDin Israel Law Center, *Donations*, http://israellawcenter.org/donations/.
534. *Id.*
535. PCHR, The Principle and Practice of Universal Jurisdiction: PCHR's Work in the Occupied Palestinian Territory 131 (Jan. 2010), http://www.fidh.org/IMG/pdf/PCHR_Work_Report_Web.pdf.
536. Palestinian Centre for Human Rights, *Funding*, http://www.pchrgaza.org/about/funding.html (last visited Apr. 20, 2105).
537. *See, e.g., Exploiting Justice: How the UK, EU & Norway Fund NGO Lawfare vs. Israel*, NGO Monitor, Feb. 20, 2014, http://www.ngo-monitor.org/article/exploiting_justice_how_the_uk_eu_norway_fund_ngo_lawfare_vs_israel; *European Governments Funding NGO "Documentation" for Lawfare Attacks*, NGO Monitor, Oct. 6, 2014, http://www.ngo-monitor.org/article/european_governments_funding_ngo_documentation_for_lawfare_attacks.
538. Human Rights & International Humanitarian Law Secretariat, *Secretariat Approves 9 CSO Proposals for Documentation Efforts in the Occupied Gaza Strip*, http://www.rightsecretariat.ps/events/112-secretariat-approves-9-cso-proposals-gaza-strip (last visited Apr. 20, 2015).
539. *Id.*
540. Human Rights & International Humanitarian Law Secretariat, *Donor Consortium*, http://www.rightsecretariat.ps/aboutus/donor-consortium (last visited Apr. 20, 2015).
541. Shurat HaDin Israel Law Ctr., *Overview*, http://israellawcenter.org/about/overview/ (last visited Apr. 20, 2015).
542. The Lawfare Project, *Mission Statement*, http://www.thelawfareproject.org/mission-statement.html (last visited Apr. 20, 2015).
543. The Lawfare Project, *Lawfare: The Use of the Law as a Weapon of War*, http://www.thelawfareproject.org/what-is-lawfare.html (last visited May 19, 2015).
544. Lawfare: Hard National Security Choices, http://www.lawfareblog.com/.
545. Just Security, http://justsecurity.org/.
546. Opinio Juris, http://opiniojuris.org/.
547. Yale Law School, *Lowenstein Clinic Past Project Highlights*, http://www.law.yale.edu/intellectuallife/pastlowensteinhighlights.htm (last visited Apr. 20, 2015).
548. *Id.*
549. *Id.*
550. Criminal Law Research Group, University of Pennsylvania Law School, *Legal Interdiction of Foreign Terrorist Fighters*, https://www.law.upenn.edu/institutes/clrg/legal-interdiction-of-foreign-terrorist-fighters.php.
551. University of Pennsylvania Law School, *Prof. Robinson and Criminal Law Research Group Use Foreign Prosecutions to Stop Terrorists*, Nov. 3, 2014, https://www.law.upenn.edu/live/news/5123-prof-robinson-and-criminal-law-research-group-use#.VTW21M5XmKz.
552. Case Western Reserve University School of Law, *Institute for Global Security Law and Policy*, http://law.cwru.edu/Academics/AcademicCenters/Cox/InstituteforGlobalSecurityLawandPolicy.aspx.
553. Jeffrey A. Lowe, Major, Lindsey & Africa, *2014 Partner Compensation Survey* at 48, http://www.mlaglobal.com/partner-compensation-survey/2014.

554. ABA MODEL RULE 6.1, http://www.americanbar.org/groups/probono_public_service/policy/aba_model_rule_6_1.html.

555. *Id.*

556. Debra Cassens Weiss, *The Cost of Wilmer Hale's Gitmo Victory: $17 M Worth of Pro Bono Hours*, ABA JOURNAL, June 25, 2008, http://www.abajournal.com/news/article/the_cost_of_wilmer_hales_gitmo_victory_17m_worth_of_pro_bono_hours.

557. *Id.*

CHAPTER 3

1. Annie Lowrey, *Aiming Financial Weapons from Treasury War Room*, N.Y. TIMES, June 3, 2014, http://www.nytimes.com/2014/06/04/business/aiming-financial-weapons-from-war-room-at-treasury.html?_r=0.

2. *Id.*

3. *Id.*

4. *Ahmadinejad: Hidden War on Global Scale Waged Against Iran's Oil Sector*, IRAN DAILY BRIEF, Oct. 8, 2012, http://www.irandailybrief.com/2012/10/08/ahmadinejad-hidden-war-on-global-scale-waged-against-irans-oil-sector/, quoted in part in JUAN ZARATE, TREASURY'S WAR: THE UNLEASHING OF A NEW ERA OF FINANCIAL WARFARE ix (2013).

5. David Ignatius, *Buying Time with Iran*, WASH. POST, Jan. 9, 2011, http://www.washingtonpost.com/wp-dyn/content/article/2011/01/07/AR2011010703149.html.

6. Leah McGrath Goodman & Lynnley Browning, *The Art of Financial Warfare: How the West Is Pushing Putin's Buttons*, NEWSWEEK, Apr. 24, 2012, http://www.newsweek.com/2014/05/02/art-financial-warfare-how-west-pushing-putins-buttons-248424.html.

7. *Id.*

8. *Id.*

9. Julie Hirschfeld Davis, *Enforcer at Treasury Is First Line of Attack Against ISIS*, N.Y. TIMES, Oct. 21, 2014, http://www.nytimes.com/2014/10/22/business/international/enforcer-at-treasury-is-first-line-of-attack-isis.html?_r=0.

10. McGrath Goodman & Browning, *supra* note 6.

11. *Id.*

12. In doing so, this chapter draws heavily on several previous works by the author, including especially Orde F. Kittrie, *Lawfare and U.S. National Security*, 43 CASE W. RES. J. INT'L L. 393–421 (2011), http://law.case.edu/journals/JIL/Documents/43_Kittrie.pdf; and Orde F. Kittrie, *New Sanctions for a New Century: Treasury's Innovative Use of Financial Sanctions*, 30 PA. J. INT'L L. 789–822 (2009), http://scholarship.law.upenn.edu/cgi/viewcontent.cgi?article=1149&context=jil.

13. Joint Comprehensive Plan of Action, July 14, 2015, *available at* http://eeas.europa.eu/statements-eeas/docs/iran_agreement/iran_joint-comprehensive-plan-of-action_en.pdf.

14. Iran Nuclear Agreement Review Act of 2015, Pub. L. No. 114-17 (2015), *available at* https://www.congress.gov/114/plaws/publ17/PLAW-114publ17.pdf.

15. KENNETH KATZMAN & PAUL K. KERR, CONG. RESEARCH SERV., R43333, IRAN NUCLEAR AGREEMENT 15 (July 30, 2015), https://fas.org/sgp/crs/nuke/R43333.pdf.

16. *The Implications of Sanctions Relief Under the Iran Agreement: Hearing Before the S. Comm. on Banking, Housing, and Urban Affairs* (Aug. 5, 2015) (written testimony of Adam Szubin, Acting Under Secretary of Treasury for Terrorism and Financial Intelligence), http://www.banking.senate.gov/public/index.cfm?FuseAction=Files.View&FileStore_id=267050cd-f198-4bbe-8f23-4b9aed9110e4.

17. *Statement of Steven R. Perles Before the Task Force to Investigate Terrorism Financing of the H. Comm. On Financial Services* (July 22, 2015), http://financialservices.house.gov/uploadedfiles/hhrg-114-ba00-wstate-sperles-20150722.pdf.

18. *See, e.g., The Implications of Sanctions Relief under the Iran Agreement: Hearing Before the S. Comm. On Banking, Housing, and Urban Affairs* (Aug. 5, 2015) (statement of Matthew Levitt), http://www.banking.senate.gov/public/index.cfm?FuseAction=Files.View&FileStore_id=f311b065-a725-442a-bb39-613d5c81ac0d; Jonathan Schanzer & Mark Dubowitz, *It Just Got Easier for Iran to Fund Terrorism*, FOREIGN POLICY, July 17, 2015, http://foreignpolicy.com/2015/07/17/it-just-got-easier-for-iran-to-fund-terrorism-swift-bank/.

19. KENNETH KATZMAN, CONG. RESEARCH SERV., RS20871, IRAN SANCTIONS 5 (June 17, 2015), https://www.hsdl.org/?view&did=767891.

20. Charles J. Dunlap, Jr., *Lawfare Today…and Tomorrow*, in INTERNATIONAL LAW AND THE CHANGING CHARACTER OF WAR 315–25 (Raul A. "Pete" Pedrozo & Daria P. Wollschlaeger eds., 2011), http://scholarship.law.duke.edu/faculty_scholarship/2465/.

21. Charles J. Dunlap, Jr., *Does Lawfare Need an Apologia?*, 43 CASE W. RES. J. INT'L L. 121, 124 n.16 (2010).

22. JUAN ZARATE, TREASURY'S WAR: THE UNLEASHING OF A NEW ERA OF FINANCIAL WARFARE (2013).

23. *Id.* at 287, 288.

24. DAVID L. ASHER, VICTOR D. COMRAS, & PATRICK M. CRONIN, PRESSURE: COERCIVE ECONOMIC STATECRAFT AND U.S. NATIONAL SECURITY 7 (2011), http://www.cnas.org/files/documents/publications/CNAS_Pressure_AsherComrasCronin_1.pdf.

25. *Id.* at 7,

26. *Id.* at 46.

27. *See, e.g.,* Paul Richter, *Obama Administration Keeps Bush Official Involved with Iran Sanctions*, L.A. TIMES, Feb. 3, 2009, http://articles.latimes.com/2009/feb/03/world/fg-usiran3.

28. Samuel Rubenfeld, *White House Nominates David Cohen as Sanctions Point Man*, WALL ST. J., Jan. 25, 2011, http://blogs.wsj.com/corruption-currents/2011/01/25/white-house-nominates-david-cohen-as-sanctions-point-man/.

29. Press Release, The White House, *President Obama Announces More Key Administration Posts* (Jan 9, 2015), https://www.whitehouse.gov/the-press-office/2015/01/09/president-obama-announces-more-key-administration-posts.

30. Press Release, The White House, *President Obama Announces More Key Administration Posts* (Apr. 16, 2015), https://www.whitehouse.gov/the-press-office/2015/04/16/president-obama-announces-more-key-administration-posts.

31. *Id.*

32. Press Release, The White House, *Remarks by the President at AIPAC Policy Conference* (Mar. 4, 2012), http://www.whitehouse.gov/the-press-office/2012/03/04/remarks-president-aipac-policy-conference-0.

33. U.S. DEP'T OF STATE, STATE SPONSORS OF TERRORISM, http://www.state.gov/j/ct/list/c14151.htm.

34. Press Release, U.S. Dep't of the Treasury, *Remarks of Under Secretary for Terrorism and Financial Intelligence David Cohen Before the Center for a New American Security on "Confronting New Threats in Terrorist Financing"* (Mar. 4, 2014), http://www.treasury.gov/press-center/press-releases/Pages/jl2308.aspx.

35. Press Release, U.S. Dep't of the Treasury, *Remarks at the Center for Strategic and International Studies by Treasury Under Secretary for Terrorism and Financial Intelligence Stuart Levey* (Sept. 20, 2010), http://www.ustreas.gov/press/releases/tg862.htm.
36. *Id.*
37. *Id.*
38. *Id.*
39. *See* Kimberly Ann Elliott, *Analyzing the Effects of Targeted Sanctions*, in SMART SANCTIONS: TARGETING ECONOMIC STATECRAFT 170, 171 (David Cortright & George A. Lopez eds., 2002). This paragraph draws heavily from Orde F. Kittrie, *Averting Catastrophe: Why the Nuclear Nonproliferation Treaty is Losing its Deterrence Capacity and How to Restore It*, 28 MICH. J. INT'L L. 337, 354–60 (2007), http://ssrn.com/abstract=996953.
40. S.C. Res. 1737, ¶ 2, U.N. Doc. S/RES/1737 (Dec. 27, 2006); *see also* S.C. Res. 1747, ¶¶ 12–13, U.N. Doc. S/RES/1747 (2007) (Mar. 24, 2007) (reaffirming resolution 1737); S.C. Res. 1803, ¶¶ 1, 14, 18–19, U.N. Doc. S/RES/1803 (2008) (Mar. 3, 2008) (reaffirming resolutions 1737 and 1747); S.C. Res. 1929, ¶¶ 1–2, 36–37, U.N. Doc. S/RES/1929 (2010) (June 9, 2010) (affirming Iran's noncompliance with resolutions 1737, 1747, and 1803 and reaffirming resolution 1737).
41. *See, e.g.*, Int'l Atomic Energy Agency [IAEA], *Implementation of the NPT Safeguards Agreement and Relevant Provisions of Security Council Resolutions in the Islamic Republic of Iran*, at 4, 8, IAEA Doc. GOV/2015/15 (Feb. 19, 2015), https://www.iaea.org/sites/default/files/gov2015-15.pdf; Int'l Atomic Energy Agency [IAEA], *Implementation of the NPT Safeguards Agreement and Relevant Provisions of Security Council Resolutions in the Islamic Republic of Iran*, at 4, IAEA Doc. GOV/2014/28 (May 23, 2014), http://www.iaea.org/Publications/Documents/Board/2014/gov2014-28.pdf; Int'l Atomic Energy Agency [IAEA], *Implementation of the NPT Safeguards Agreement and Relevant Provisions of Security Council Resolutions in the Islamic Republic of Iran*, at 11, IAEA Doc. GOV/2010/46 (Sept. 6, 2010), http://www.iaea.org/Publications/Documents/Board/2010/gov2010-46.pdf (similar language).
42. *See, e.g.*, U.S. DEP'T OF STATE, COUNTRY REPORTS ON TERRORISM 2013, http://www.state.gov/j/ct/rls/crt/2013/225328.htm (Iran "continued to provide arms" to the Assad regime, "assisted in rearming Hizballah," and "attempted to smuggle arms to Houthi separatists in Yemen and Shia oppositionists in Bahrain." Iran has also "provided weapons, training, and funding to Hamas and other Palestinian terrorist groups," and "has provided hundreds of millions of dollars in support of Hizballah.").
43. For example, Iranian arms transfers to Syria's Assad government and to Hamas violate U.N. Security Council Resolution 1747, which orders that "Iran shall not supply, sell or transfer directly or indirectly from its territory or by its nationals or using its flag vessels or aircraft any arms or related materiel." Jay Solomon, *U.S., Israel Fear Pickup in Iranian Support of Hamas*, WALL ST. J., July 30, 2014, http://blogs.wsj.com/washwire/2014/07/30/u-s-israel-fear-pickup-in-iranian-support-of-hamas/; Anne Barnard, Michael R. Gordon, & Jodi Rudoren, *Israel Targeted Iranian Missiles in Syria Attack*, N.Y. TIMES, May 4, 2013, http://www.nytimes.com/2013/05/05/world/middleeast/israel-syria.html?pagewanted=all; Joe Vaccarello, *Iran Sending Banned Weapons to Syria, UN Report Says*, CNN.COM, May 12, 2011, http://www.cnn.com/2011/WORLD/meast/05/12/un.syria.iran.weapons/; S.C. Res. 1747, *supra* note 40, at ¶ 5. Iranian arms transfers to Hezbollah violate Resolution 1747 as well as Resolution 1701, which ordered all States to "prevent ... the sale or supply to any entity or individual in Lebanon of arms and related materiel of all types." Adam Entous, Charles Levinson, & Julian E. Barnes, *Hezbollah Upgrades Missile Threat to*

Israel, Wall St. J., Jan. 2, 2014, http://online.wsj.com/news/articles/SB1000142405
2702304361604579290613920542386; S.C. Res. 1701, ¶ 15, U.N. Doc. S/RES/1701
(2006) (Aug. 11, 2006).

44. G.A. Res. 2200A (XXI), U.N. GAOR, 21st Sess., Supp. No. 16, U.N. Doc. A/6316, at
52–60, International Covenant on Civil and Political Rights (Dec. 16, 1966), *available
at* http://www.ohchr.org/Documents/ProfessionalInterest/ccpr.pdf; International
Covenant on Civil and Political Rights, Dec. 16, 1966, S. Treaty Doc. 95-20, 999
U.N.T.S. 171.

45. *Between Feckless and Reckless: U.S. Policy Options to Prevent a Nuclear Iran: Joint Hearing
Before the Subcomm. on the Middle East and South Asia, and the Subcomm. on Terrorism,
Nonproliferation and Trade of the H. Comm. on Foreign Affairs*, 110th Cong. 24 (2008)
(statement of Daniel Glaser, Deputy Assistant Secretary for Terrorist Financing and
Financial Crimes, U.S. Dep't of Treasury), http://www.gpo.gov/fdsys/pkg/CHRG-
110hhrg41849/pdf/CHRG-110hhrg41849.pdf.

46. This and the other paragraphs in this section draw heavily from Orde F. Kittrie, *New
Sanctions for a New Century: Treasury's Innovative Use of Financial Sanctions*, 30 Pa.
J. Int'l L. 789–822 (2009), http://ssrn.com/abstract=1402265.

47. *Between Feckless and Reckless, supra* note 45, at 24.

48. *Id.*

49. *Id.*

50. Press Release, U.S. Dep't of the Treasury, *Remarks by Treasury Secretary Paulson on
Targeted Financial Measures to Protect Our National Security* (June 14, 2007), http://
www.treasury.gov/press-center/press-releases/Pages/hp457.aspx.

51. *Id.*

52. *Between Feckless and Reckless, supra* note 45, at 24.

53. *See, e.g.*, Final Report of the Panel of Experts Established Pursuant to Resolution
1929 (2010), at 23, 26–27, June 5, 2014, U.N. Security Council, contained
in S/2014/394, June 11, 2014, http://www.un.org/ga/search/view_doc.
asp?symbol=S/2014/394.

54. *See, e.g.*, Deferred Prosecution Agreement, *U.S. v. Standard Chartered Bank*, U.S.
District Court for the District of Columbia, Dec. 10, 2012, p. 8, http://www.mainjus-
tice.com/wp-admin/documents-databases/114-1-Standard-Chartered-Bank-DPA.
pdf; *Between Feckless and Reckless, supra* note 45, at 28.

55. *Between Feckless and Reckless, supra* note 45, at 28.

56. Press Release, U.S. Dep't of the Treasury, *Remarks by Treasury Secretary Paulson, supra*
note 50.

57. *FATF Public Statement*, Financial Action Task Force, Feb. 27, 2015, http://www.fatf-
gafi.org/documents/documents/public-statement-february-2015.html.

58. McGrath Goodman & Browning, *supra* note 6; Juan Zarate, Treasury's War: The
Unleashing of a New Era of Financial Warfare 9 (2013).

59. Michael Jacobson, *Sanctions Against Iran: A Promising Struggle*, 31 Wash. Q. 69, 71
(2008).

60. Press Release, U.S. Dep't of the Treasury, *Remarks by Treasury Secretary Paulson, supra*
note 50.

61. FBI, *Famous Cases & Criminals: Al Capone*, http://www.fbi.gov/about-us/history/
famous-cases/al-capone; *In re* Alphonse Capone, Memorandum from the Internal
Revenue Service Intelligence Unit of Chicago, Illinois (July 8, 1931), http://www.
irs.gov/pub/irs-utl/file-1-letter-dated-07081931-in-re-alphonse-capone.pdf; Douglas
O. Linder, *Al Capone Trial (1931): An Account*, 2011, http://law2.umkc.edu/faculty/
projects/ftrials/capone/caponeaccount.html.

62. Bay Fang, *Treasury Wields Financial Sanctions: U.S. Strategy Straddles the Line Between Diplomacy, Military Might*, CHICAGO TRIBUNE, Apr. 23, 2007 (quoting Robert Einhorn).

63. Press Release, U.S. Dep't of the Treasury, *Remarks by Treasury Secretary Paulson*, *supra* note 50.

64. Steven R. Weisman, *The Ripples of Punishing One Bank*, N.Y. TIMES, July 3, 2007.

65. Press Release, U.S. Dep't of the Treasury, *Remarks by Treasury Secretary Paulson*, *supra* note 50.

66. *Id.*

67. *Id.*

68. *Id.*

69. *Id.*

70. *Id.*

71. ZARATE, *supra* note 58, at 9–10.

72. Press Release, U.S. Dep't of the Treasury, *Remarks by Treasury Secretary Paulson*, *supra* note 50.

73. *Id.*

74. ZARATE, *supra* note 58, at 329.

75. *Id.*

76. Leah McGrath Goodman & Lynnley Browning, *Sanctions Land Like a Bomb in Corporate Suites*, NEWSWEEK, May 2, 2014, http://www.newsweek.com/sanctions-land-bomb-corporate-suites-248608.

77. *Id.*

78. Sean M. Thornton, *"Iran, Non-U.S. Banks and Secondary Sanctions: Understanding the Trends,"* SKADDEN.COM, Oct. 24, 2012, http://www.skadden.com/insights/iran-non-us-banks-and-secondary-sanctions-understanding-trends.

79. *Id.*

80. *Id.*

81. This author has no knowledge that Treasury intentionally leaves their sanctions more confusing than necessary in order to increase their chilling effect. However, he has heard of other agencies having done so with regard to other sanctions.

82. Press Release, U.S. Dep't of the Treasury, *Remarks by Treasury Secretary Paulson*, *supra* note 50.

83. *See, e.g.*, Maria Tadeo, *Paying the Price for Sanctions: The Customers with Iranian Links Being Ditched by British Banks*, THE INDEPENDENT (UK), Aug. 19, 2014, http://www.independent.co.uk/news/business/analysis-and-features/paying-the-price-for-sanctions-the-customers-with-iranian-links-being-ditched-by-british-banks-9679692.html; Steve Slater & Michelle Price, *Bruised and Grumbling, Foreign Banks Bend to U.S. Rules*, CHICAGO TRIBUNE, July 13, 2014, http://articles.chicagotribune.com/2014-07-13/business/sns-rt-us-banks-sanctions-20140713_1_u-s-sanctions-foreign-banks-british-bankers.

84. *See, e.g., Bank Jitters Hit Iran Fuel Imports*, PETROLEUM ECONOMIST, Feb. 2008, at 28 (concluding that, due to U.S.-led sanctions, "Iran is starting to feel the effect of international sanctions on its domestic energy sector"); Paul Sampson, *Iran: Products in Flux*, ENERGY COMPASS, Feb. 8, 2008, at 1 (stating that due to the "US-led squeeze on Iran" many financial institutions have ceased to provide credit to Iranian companies); Mark Trevelyan, *More Companies Suspend Business with Iran*, INT'L HERALD TRIBUNE, Jan. 17, 2008, at 15 (discussing the effects of sanctions on "Iran's oil-based economy").

85. Trevelyan, *id.* at 15 (quoting a senior German banking and finance consultant as stating that "[i]t is today impossible more or less in Europe, with a couple of exceptions,

to get a letter of credit" for trade with Iran); *No Letters of Credit, No Steel for Iranian Importers, say Traders*, METAL BULLETIN WKLY., Sept. 13, 2010, http://www.metal-bulletin.co.uk/Article/2675316/No-letters-of-credit-no-steel-for-Iranian-importers-say-traders.html.

86. FORTUNE, GLOBAL 500 2014, RELIANCE INDUSTRIES, http://fortune.com/global500/reliance-industries-114/.

87. *Id.*

88. Trevelyan, *supra* note 84, at 15 ("Late last year, the Indian oil refiner Reliance halted sales of gasoline and diesel to Tehran after the French banks BNP Paribas and the Calyon unit of Crédit Agricole stopped offering letters of credit ....").

89. Robin Wright, *Stuart Levey's War*, N.Y. TIMES, Oct. 31, 2008, http://www.nytimes.com/2008/11/02/magazine/02IRAN-t.html?pagewanted=all.

90. Robin Wright, *Iran Feels Pinch as Major Banks Curtail Business: U.S. Campaign Urges Firms to Cut Ties*, WASH. POST, Mar. 26, 2007, at A10 (quoting Iranian Oil Minister Kazem Vaziri Hamaneh).

91. See David Blair, *Banks Recruited to Wage Financial War on Teheran*, DAILY TELEGRAPH (London), Sept. 18, 2007, at 17 ("One Teheran newspaper recently reported that Iranian companies had seen their import costs rise by 20 or 30 per cent because they had to employ middlemen to evade financial restrictions.").

92. Borzou Daragahi, *Economists in Iran Criticize Ahmadinejad*, L.A. TIMES, Nov. 10, 2008, at A3.

93. *Sixty Iranian Economists Write Open Letter to President*, BBC MONITORING WORLDWIDE, Nov. 14, 2008, at 3.

94. Press Release, U.S. Dep't of the Treasury, *Remarks of Under Secretary for Terrorism and Financial Intelligence David Cohen, supra* note 34.

95. Indira A.R. Lakshmanan, *Iran Is Seen Suffering Crippling Effect of Sanctions on Oil Trade, Banking*, BLOOMBERG NEWS, Feb. 29, 2012, http://www.bloomberg.com/news/2012-02-29/iran-is-seen-suffering-crippling-effect-of-sanctions-on-oil-trade-banking.html.

96. KENNETH KATZMAN, CONG. RESEARCH SERV., RS20871, IRAN SANCTIONS (Oct. 23, 2014), https://www.hsdl.org/?view&did=759207 (quoted language is in summary page).

97. *Id.* at 53.

98. U.S. GOV'T ACCOUNTABILITY OFFICE, GAO-13-326, U.S. AND INTERNATIONAL SANCTIONS HAVE ADVERSELY AFFECTED THE IRANIAN ECONOMY 13 (2013), http://gao.gov/assets/660/652314.pdf.

99. KATZMAN, *supra* note 96, at 50.

100. *Why the Oil Price is Falling*, THE ECONOMIST, Dec. 8, 2014, http://www.economist.com/blogs/economist-explains/2014/12/economist-explains-4; KATZMAN, *supra* note 96, at 50.

101. Juan Zarate, TREASURY'S WAR: THE UNLEASHING OF A NEW ERA OF FINANCIAL WARFARE 340 (2013).

102. *Id.* at 340.

103. KATZMAN, *supra* note 96, at 50.

104. *Id.*

105. *Id.* at 52.

106. *Id.*

107. *Id.* at 51.

108. *Id.* at 48.

109. *See, e.g.*, KATZMAN, *supra* note 96.

110. David E. Sanger, *C.I.A. Director Says Iran's Economic Peril Helped Drive Nuclear Deal*, N.Y. TIMES, Apr. 8, 2015, http://mobile.nytimes.com/2015/04/09/world/middleeast/cia-director-says-irans-economic-peril-helped-drive-nuclear-deal.html?_r=0&referrer=.

111. Joint Comprehensive Plan of Action, *supra* note 13.

112. Press Release, The White House, *Statement by the President on Iran* (July 14, 2015), https://www.whitehouse.gov/the-press-office/2015/07/14/statement-president-iran.

113. Press Release, The White House, *Remarks by the President on the Iran Nuclear Deal* (Aug. 5, 2015), https://www.whitehouse.gov/the-press-office/2015/08/05/remarks-president-iran-nuclear-deal.

114. *See, e.g.*, Press Release, Sen. Charles E. Schumer, *My Position on the Iran Deal* (Aug. 6, 2015), http://www.schumer.senate.gov/newsroom/press-releases/my-position-on-the-iran-deal (Schumer was at the time the third ranking Democrat in the Senate); Press Release, Congressman Eliot L. Engel, *Engel Statement on Iran Deal* (Aug. 6, 2015), http://engel.house.gov/latest-news1/engel-statement-on-iran-deal1/ (Engel was at the time the ranking Democrat on the House Committee on Foreign Affairs); Lauren Fox, *Sen. Bob Corker Rails Against the Iran Deal*, NAT'L J., July 23, 2015, http://www.nationaljournal.com/congress/sen-bob-corker-rails-against-the-iran-deal-20150723 (Corker, a Republican, was at the time the chairman of the Senate Foreign Relations Committee).

115. Press Release, Sen. Charles E. Schumer, *supra* note 114.

116. *See, e.g.*, William B. Caldwell, IV & Charles Wald, *Remind Iran of U.S. Military Option*, NEWSDAY, July 11, 2015, http://www.newsday.com/opinion/oped/remind-iran-of-u-s-military-option-1.10631791 (Caldwell and Ward are both retired generals in the U.S. armed forces); *Expert Opinions on the Extension of Negotiations*, Harvard Belfer Ctr., Juy 22, 2014, http://iranmatters.belfercenter.org/blog/expert-opinions-extension-negotiations (mini-essay by Orde Kittrie); DAVID ALBRIGHT, MARK DUBOWITZ, ORDE KITTRIE, LEONARD SPECTOR, & MICHAEL YAFFE, U.S. NONPROLIFERATION STRATEGY FOR THE CHANGING MIDDLE EAST 58–62 (2013), http://isis-online.org/uploads/isis-reports/documents/FinalReport.pdf.

117. International Emergency Economic Powers Act, 50 U.S.C. §§ 1701–1707 (2006).

118. *Id.* § 1702(a)(1)(A)(ii).

119. *Id.* § 1702(a)(1)(B).

120. Exec. Order No. 13,224, 66 Fed. Reg. 49,079 (Sept. 23, 2001).

121. *Id.* at 49,080.

122. U.S. GOV'T ACCOUNTABILITY OFFICE, GAO-13-326, *supra* note 98, at 20.

123. Press Release, U.S. Dep't. of the Treasury, *Fact Sheet: Designation of Iranian Entities and Individuals for Proliferation Activities and Support for Terrorism* (Oct. 25, 2007), http://www.treasury.gov/press-center/press-releases/Pages/hp644.aspx.

124. *Id.*

125. *Id.*

126. Exec. Order No. 13,382, 70 Fed. Reg. 38,567 (July 1, 2005).

127. Press Release, U.S. Dep't of the Treasury, *Fact Sheet*, *supra* note 123.

128. *Id.*

129. *Id.*

130. Benoit Faucon, *Oil Companies Facing Challenge in Iran*, WALL ST. J., May 26, 2014, http://online.wsj.com/news/articles/SB40001424052702303749904579579552501935932.

131. *Id.*

132. *Id.*

133. *Id.*

134. U.S. Dep't of the Treasury, *Fact Sheet: Overview of Iranian-Linked Financial Institutions Designated by the United States*, http://www.treasury.gov/press-center/press-releases/Documents/012312_Fact_Sheet_-_Designated_Iranian_Financial%20 Institutions.pdf (last visited May 10, 2015).

135. Press Release, U.S. Dep't of the Treasury, *Fact Sheet, supra* note 123.

136. *Id.*

137. *Id.*

138. Exec. Order No. 13,622 of July 30, 2012, 77 Fed. Reg. 45,897 (Aug. 2, 2012).

139. *Id.*

140. *Id.*

141. U.S. Gov't Accountability Office, GAO-13-326, *supra* note 98, at 20.

142. Iranian Transactions Regulations, 73 Fed. Reg. 66541 (Nov. 10, 2008) (to be codified at 13 C.F.R. pt. 560), http://www.treasury.gov/resource-center/sanctions/Documents/fr73_66541.pdf.

143. Juan Zarate, Treasury's War: The Unleashing of a New Era of Financial Warfare 308 (2013).

144. *Id.*

145. Press Release, U.S. Dep't of State, *New Sanctions on Iran: Fact Sheet* (Nov. 21, 2011), http://www.state.gov/r/pa/prs/ps/2011/11/177609.htm.

146. *Id.*

147. Zarate, *supra* note 143, at 333.

148. *Id.* at 336.

149. Comprehensive Iran Sanctions, Accountability, and Divestment Act of 2010, § 104, 22 U.S.C. § 8513 (2010), http://www.treasury.gov/resource-center/sanctions/Documents/hr2194.pdf.

150. Press Release, U.S. Dep't of the Treasury, *Remarks of Under Secretary for Terrorism and Financial Intelligence David Cohen Before the New York University School of Law on "The Law and Policy of Iran Sanctions"* (Sept. 12, 2012), http://www.treasury.gov/press-center/press-releases/Pages/tg1706.aspx.

151. *Id.*

152. Kenneth Katzman, Cong. Research Serv., RS20871, Iran Sanctions 27 (June 17, 2015), https://www.hsdl.org/?view&did=767891.

153. Press Release, U.S. Dep't of the Treasury, *Remarks of David Cohen, supra* note 139.

154. Michael Rothfeld, *Barclays to Pay $298 Million for Evading U.S. Economic Sanctions*, Wall St. J., Aug. 17, 2010, http://blogs.wsj.com/law/2010/08/17/barclays-to-pay-298-million-for-evading-us-economic-sanctions/.

155. Press Release, U.S. Dep't of the Treasury, *Remarks of David Cohen, supra* note 150.

156. *Id.*

157. *Id.*

158. U.S. Gov't Accountability Office, GAO-13-326, *supra* note 98, at 22.

159. *Id.*

160. Press Release, U.S. Dep't of the Treasury, *Treasury Removes Sanctions on Iraqi Bank*, (May 17, 2013), http://www.treasury.gov/press-center/press-releases/Pages/jl1949.aspx.

161. *Id.*

162. Juan Zarate, Treasury's War: The Unleashing of a New Era of Financial Warfare 336 (2013).

163. National Defense Authorization Act for Fiscal Year 2012 § 1245, 22 U.S.C. § 8513a (2011), http://www.treasury.gov/resource-center/sanctions/Programs/Documents/ndaa_publaw.pdf.

164. *Id.*
165. Press Release, U.S. Dep't of the Treasury, *Remarks of David Cohen, supra* note 150.
166. *Id.*
167. *Id.*
168. *Id.*
169. *Id.*
170. *Id.*
171. Kenneth Katzman, Cong. Research Serv., RS20871, Iran Sanctions 22 (June 17, 2015), .https://www.hsdl.org/?view&did=767891
172. *Id.*
173. *Id.* at 20.
174. Iran Threat Reduction and Syria Human Rights Act of 2012 § 302, 22 U.S.C. § 8742 (2012), https://beta.congress.gov/112/plaws/publ158/PLAW-112publ158.pdf.
175. Katzman, *supra* note 171, at 15.
176. Iran Threat Reduction and Syria Human Rights Act, *supra* note 174.
177. Katzman, *supra* note 171, at 21.
178. Press Release, U.S. Dep't of the Treasury, *Remarks of Under Secretary for Terrorism and Financial Intelligence David Cohen Before the New York University School of Law on "The Law and Policy of Iran Sanctions"* (Sept. 12, 2012), http://www.treasury.gov/press-center/press-releases/Pages/tg1706.aspx.
179. Katzman, *supra* note 171, at 21.
180. S.C. Res. 2231, U.N. Doc. S/RES/2231 (July 20, 2015).
181. *Id.* ¶¶ 5, 7.
182. *Id.* ¶¶ 11, 12.
183. S.C. Res. 1737, ¶ 12, U.N. Doc. S/RES/1737 (Dec. 23, 2006).
184. S.C. Res. 1737, ¶ 6, U.N. Doc. S/RES/1737 (Dec. 23, 2006).
185. S.C. Res. 1929, ¶ 22, U.N. Doc. S/RES/1929 (June 9, 2010).
186. S.C. Res. 1803, ¶ 10, U.N. Doc. S/RES/1803 (Mar. 3, 2008).
187. S.C. Res. 1929, preamble, U.N. Doc. S/RES/1929 (June 9, 2010).
188. S.C. Res. 1929, ¶ 21, U.N. Doc. S/RES/1929 (June 9, 2010).
189. *Id.* ¶ 23.
190. *Id.* ¶ 24.
191. *Between Feckless and Reckless, supra* note 45, at 33.
192. *FATF Members and Observers*, Financial Action Task Force, http://www.fatf-gafi.org/pages/aboutus/membersandobservers/ (last visited May 10, 2015).
193. *Who We Are*, Financial Action Task Force, http://www.fatf-gafi.org/pages/aboutus/ (last visited May 10, 2015).
194. *Id.*
195. *Between Feckless and Reckless, supra* note 45, at 32.
196. *FATF Recommendations 2012—Press Handout*, Financial Action Task Force, Feb. 16, 2012, http://www.fatf-gafi.org/media/fatf/documents/Press%20handout%20FATF%20Recommendations%202012.pdf.
197. *Id.*
198. *FATF Statement on Iran*, Financial Action Task Force, Oct. 11, 2007, http://www.fatf-gafi.org/dataoecd/1/2/39481684.pdf.
199. *Id.*
200. *Between Feckless and Reckless, supra* note 45, at 32.
201. *FATF Statement*, Financial Action Task Force, Feb. 28, 2008, http://www.fatf-gafi.org/topics/high-riskandnon-cooperativejurisdictions/documents/fatfstatement-28february2008.html; *FATF Statement*, Financial Action Task Force, Oct. 16, 2008, http://

www.fatf-gafi.org/topics/high-riskandnon-cooperativejurisdictions/documents/fatfstatement-16october2008.html.

202. *FATF Statement,* Financial Action Task Force, *id.*
203. *Id.*
204. *Id.*
205. *Between Feckless and Reckless, supra* note 45, at 32.
206. *FATF Public Statement,* Financial Action Task Force, Feb. 27, 2015, http://www.fatf-gafi.org/documents/documents/public-statement-february-2015.html.
207. *Id.*
208. *Id.*
209. *Guidance Regarding the Implementation of Financial Provisions of United Nations Security Council Resolutions to Counter the Proliferation of Weapons of Mass Destruction,* Financial Action Task Force, June 29, 2007, http://www.fatf-gafi.org/dataoecd/28/62/38902632.pdf. This June 2007 guidance addressed not only the financial measures contained in Resolutions 1737 and 1747 regarding Iran but also the financial measures contained in Resolutions 1695 and 1718 regarding North Korea's WMD and missile programs.
210. *Annex: Financial Sanctions Against a Financial Institution Designated Under United Nations Security Council Resolutions Relating to Prevention of WMD Proliferation,* Financial Action Task Force, Sept. 5, 2007, http://www.fatf-gafi.org/dataoecd/23/16/39318680.pdf.
211. *Guidance Regarding the Implementation of Activity-Based Financial Prohibitions of United Nations Security Council Resolution 1737,* Financial Action Task Force, Oct. 12, 2007, http://www.fatf-gafi.org/dataoecd/43/17/39494050.pdf.
212. *FATF Guidance: The Implementation of Financial Provisions of United Nations Security Council Resolutions to Counter the Proliferation of Weapons of Mass Destruction,* Financial Action Task Force, June 2013, http://www.fatf-gafi.org/media/fatf/documents/recommendations/Guidance-UNSCRS-Prolif-WMD.pdf.
213. Juan Zarate, Treasury's War: The Unleashing of a New Era of Financial Warfare 330 (2013).
214. *See, e.g.,* Neil MacFarquhar, *UN Approves New Sanctions to Deter Iran,* N.Y. Times, June 9, 2010, http://www.nytimes.com/2010/06/10/world/middleeast/10sanctions.html?pagewanted=print; Press Release, U.S. Dep't of the Treasury, *Remarks of Under Secretary for Terrorism and Financial Intelligence David Cohen Before the New York University School of Law on "The Law and Policy of Iran Sanctions"* (Sept. 12, 2012), http://www.treasury.gov/press-center/press-releases/Pages/tg1706.aspx.
215. *See, e.g.,* MacFarquhar, *supra* note 214.; Press Release, U.S. Dep't of the Treasury, *Remarks of Under Secretary for Terrorism and Financial Intelligence David Cohen, supra* note 214.
216. Press Release, U.S. Dep't of the Treasury, *Remarks of David Cohen, supra* note 214.
217. *Id.*
218. Council Decision 2012/35/CFSP, 2012 O.J. (L 19) 22.
219. Council Decision 2012/152/CFSP, 2012 O.J. (L77) 18.
220. *Between Feckless and Reckless, supra* note 45, at 34.
221. Press Release, U.S. Dep't of the Treasury, *Remarks by Treasury Secretary Paulson, supra* note 50.
222. Robin Wright, *Stuart Levey's War,* N.Y. Times, Oct. 31, 2008, http://www.nytimes.com/2008/11/02/magazine/02IRAN-t.html?pagewanted=all.
223. *Id.*
224. *Id.*

225. Press Release, U.S. Dep't of Justice, *ING Bank N.V. Agrees to Forfeit $619 Million for Illegal Transactions with Cuban and Iranian Entities* (June 12, 2012), http://www.justice.gov/opa/pr/2012/June/12-crm-742.html.

226. *HSBC to Pay $1.9bn in US Money Laundering Penalties*, BBC.COM, Dec. 11, 2012, http://www.bbc.com/news/business-20673466.

227. Press Release, U.S. Dep't of Justice, *HSBC Holdings PLC and HSBC Bank USA N.A. Admit to Anti-Money Laundering and Sanctions Violations, Forfeit $1.256 Billion in Deferred Prosecution Agreement* (Dec. 11, 2012), http://www.justice.gov/opa/pr/2012/December/12-crm-1478.html.

228. *Id.*

229. Press Release, U.S. Dep't of Justice, *BNP Paribas Agrees to Plead Guilty and to Pay $8.9 Billion for Illegally Processing Financial Transactions for Countries Subject to U.S. Economic Sanctions* (June 30, 2014), http://www.justice.gov/opa/pr/2014/June/14-ag-686.html.

230. Press Release, U.S. Dep't of Justice, *BNP Paribas Sentenced for Conspiring to Violate the International Emergency Economic Powers Act and the Trading with the Enemy Act* (May 1, 2015), http://www.justice.gov/opa/pr/bnp-paribas-sentenced-conspiring-violate-international-emergency-economic-powers-act-and; Press Release, U.S. Dep't of Justice, *BNP Paribas Agrees to Plead Guilty, supra* note 229.

231. *See, e.g.,* Tony Karon, *Stalemate: How Obama's Iran Outreach Failed*, TIME, Dec. 22, 2009, http://content.time.com/time/world/article/0,8599,1949265,00.html; JUAN ZARATE, TREASURY'S WAR: THE UNLEASHING OF A NEW ERA OF FINANCIAL WARFARE 322, 324 (2013) ("Levey was instructed to hold his powder dry while the administration attempted to reach out to the regime in Tehran. Meetings with bankers, designations of Iranian entities, and enlistment of partners to isolate Iranian financial activity stopped.")

232. U.S. GOV'T ACCOUNTABILITY OFFICE, GAO-13-326, *supra* note 98.

233. Press Release, U.S. Dep't of the Treasury, *Remarks by Treasury Secretary Paulson, supra* note 50.

234. *Id.*

235. *Id.*

236. *Between Feckless and Reckless, supra* note 45, at 28.

237. Bay Fang, *Treasury Wields Financial Sanctions: U.S. Strategy Straddles the Line Between Diplomacy, Military Might*, CHICAGO TRIBUNE, Apr. 23, 2007.

238. *Between Feckless and Reckless, supra* note 45, at 34.

239. *Id.*

240. Fang, *supra* note 237 (quoting Adam Szubin, director of Treasury's Office of Foreign Assets Control).

241. Press Release, U.S. Dep't of the Treasury, *Remarks by Treasury Secretary Paulson, supra* note 50.

242. Michael Hirsh, *Obama Prepares to Get Tough on Iran*, NEWSWEEK, Dec. 11, 2009, http://www.newsweek.com/obama-prepares-get-tough-iran-75581.

243. For example, Treasury Secretary Paulson accused the IRGC of being "directly involved in the planning and support of terrorist acts." Press Release, U.S. Dep't of the Treasury, *Remarks by Treasury Secretary Paulson, supra* note 50.

244. S.C. Res. 1929, ¶ 12, U.N. Doc. S/RES/1929 (June 9, 2010).

245. *Minimizing Potential Threats from Iran: Assessing the Effectiveness of Current US Sanctions on Iran: Hearing Before the Senate Committee on Banking, Housing and Urban Affairs*, 110th Congress (2007) (statement of Stuart Levey, Under Secretary for Terrorism and Financial Intelligence).

246. *Between Feckless and Reckless, supra* note 45, at 35.

247. Press Release, U.S. Dep't of the Treasury, *Remarks by Treasury Secretary Paulson, supra* note 50.

248. Sarah Butcher, *HSBC's Compliance Binge and How You Can Get a 6 Figure Compliance Job,* EFINANCIAL CAREERS, Nov. 3, 2014, http://news.efinancialcareers.com/us-en/189083/hsbcs-compliance-binge-can-get-6-figure-compliance-job/.

249. Sital S. Patel, *Citi Will Have Almost 30,000 Employees in Compliance by Year-End,* MARKETWATCH, July 14, 2014, http://blogs.marketwatch.com/thetell/2014/07/14/citi-will-have-almost-30000-employees-in-compliance-by-year-end/.

250. Press Release, U.S. Dep't of the Treasury, *Remarks by Treasury Secretary Paulson, supra* note 50.

251. Robin Wright, *Stuart Levey's War,* N.Y. TIMES, Oct. 31, 2008, http://www.nytimes.com/2008/11/02/magazine/02IRAN-t.html?pagewanted=all.

252. JUAN ZARATE, TREASURY'S WAR: THE UNLEASHING OF A NEW ERA OF FINANCIAL WARFARE 302 (2013).

253. Paul M. Barrett, *Can Banks Be Held Liable for Terrorism?,* BLOOMBERG BUSINESSWEEK, Mar. 18, 2015, http://businessweekme.com/Bloomberg/newsmid/190/newsid/479#cnttop.

254. John D. McKinnon & Marcus Walker, *Fed Fines UBS $100 Million for Money-Transfer Violations,* WALL ST. J., May 11, 2004, http://online.wsj.com/news/articles/SB108419978061306718.

255. *Id.*

256. Barnaby J. Feder, *ABN to Pay $80 Million for Violations,* N.Y. TIMES, Dec. 20, 2005, http://www.nytimes.com/2005/12/20/business/worldbusiness/20bank.html?_r=0.

257. Paul Blustein, *Dutch Bank Fined for Iran, Libya Transactions: $80 Million Levied for Foreign Dealings, Money Laundering,* WASH. POST, Dec. 20, 2005; U.S. DEP'T OF THE TREASURY, OFFICE OF FOREIGN ASSETS CONTROL, ENFORCEMENT INFORMATION FOR JANUARY 3, 2006 (Jan. 3, 2006).

258. Michael Jacobson, *Sanctions Against Iran: A Promising Struggle,* 31 WASH. Q. 73 (2008).

259. Press Release, U.S. Dep't of Justice, *Lloyds TSB Bank PLC Agrees to Forfeit $350 Million in Connection with Violations of the International Emergency Economic Powers Act* (Jan. 9, 2009), http://www.justice.gov/opa/pr/2009/January/09-crm-023.html.

260. Chad Bray, *Lloyds TSB Settles with U.S. Officials,* WALL ST. J., Jan. 9, 2009.

261. *Id.*

262. Press Release, U.S. Dep't of the Treasury, *U.S. Treasury Department Announces Joint $536 Million Settlement with Credit Suisse AG* (Dec. 16, 2009), http://www.treasury.gov/press-center/press-releases/Pages/tg452.aspx.

263. *Id.*

264. *Id.*

265. Joshua Gallu, Karen Freifeld, & Cary O'Reilly, *Credit Suisse to Pay $536 Million in U.S. Settlement,* BLOOMBERG, Dec. 16, 2009, http://www.bloomberg.com/apps/news?pid=newsarchive&sid=aG1wyIpbsqCU.

266. Press Release, U.S. Dep't of the Treasury, *U.S. Treasury Department Announces Joint $536 Million Settlement, supra* note 262.

267. Press Release, U.S. Dep't of Justice, *Credit Suisse Agrees to Forfeit $536 Million in Connection with Violations of the International Emergency Economic Powers Act and New York State Law* (Dec. 16, 2009), http://www.justice.gov/opa/pr/2009/December/09-ag-1358.html.

268. *Id.*

269. *Id.*

270. *Id.*

271. John Shiffman, *How Credit Suisse Helped Americans Avoid Taxes and Iran Dodge U.S. Sanctions*, Newsweek, July 2, 2014, http://www.newsweek.com/how-credit-suisse-helped-americans-avoid-taxes-and-iran-dodge-us-sanctions-256985 (excerpt from John Shiffman, Operation Shakespeare (2014)).

272. Press Release, U.S. Dep't of Justice, *Barclays Bank PLC Agrees to Forfeit $298 Million in Connection with Violations of the International Emergency Economic Powers Act and the Trading with the Enemy Act* (Aug. 18, 2010_, http://www.justice.gov/opa/pr/2010/August/10-crm-933.html.

273. *Id.*

274. *Id.*

275. *Id.*

276. Deferred Prosecution Agreement (Exhibit A), United States v. Barclays, No. 1:10-cr-00218-EGS (D.D.C., filed Aug. 16, 2010), http://online.wsj.com/public/resources/documents/081710barclaysruling.pdf.

277. Michael Rothfeld, *Barclays to Pay $298 Million for Evading U.S. Economic Sanctions*, Wall St. J., Aug. 17, 2010, http://blogs.wsj.com/law/2010/08/17/barclays-to-pay-298-million-for-evading-us-economic-sanctions/.

278. Deferred Prosecution Agreement, *supra* note 276; Michael Rothfeld, David Enrich, & Jay Solomon, *Barclays in Sanctions Bust*, Wall St. J., Aug. 17, 2010, http://online.wsj.com/news/articles/SB10001424052748703908704575433781894978828?mod=ITP_pageone_0&mg=reno64-wsj

279. Press Release, U.S. Dep't of Justice, *Barclays Bank PLC Agrees to Forfeit $298 Million*, *supra* note 272.

280. James Vicini & Jeremy Pelofsky, *U.S. Judge Approves Barclays $298 Million Settlement*, Reuters, Aug. 18, 2010, http://uk.reuters.com/article/2010/08/18/uk-barclays-settlement-idUKTRE67H3RM20100818.

281. *Id.*

282. Michael Rothfeld, *Barclays to Pay $298 Million for Evading U.S. Economic Sanctions*, Wall Street Journal, August 17, 2010, http://blogs.wsj.com/law/2010/08/17/barclays-to-pay-298-million-for-evading-us-economic-sanctions/.

283. Press Release, U.S. Dep't of Justice, *ING Bank N.V. Agrees to Forfeit $619 Million for Illegal Transactions with Cuban and Iranian Entities* (June 12, 2012), http://www.justice.gov/opa/pr/2012/June/12-crm-742.html.

284. *Id.*; *Settlement Agreement By and Between the U.S. Department of the Treasury's Office of Foreign Assets Control and ING Bank, N.V.*, June 11, 2012, http://www.treasury.gov/resource-center/sanctions/CivPen/Documents/06122012_ing_agreement.pdf.

285. Press Release, U.S. Dep't of Justice, *ING Bank N.V. Agrees to Forfeit $619 Million for Illegal Transactions with Cuban and Iranian Entities* (June 12, 2012), http://www.justice.gov/opa/pr/2012/June/12-crm-742.html.

286. *Id.*

287. Reed Albergotti, *ING Fined a Record Amount*, Wall St. J., June 12, 2012, http://online.wsj.com/news/articles/SB10001424052702303901504577462512713336378.

288. Press Release, U.S. Dep't of Justice, *ING Bank N.V. Agrees to Forfeit $619 Million for Illegal Transactions with Cuban and Iranian Entities*, U.S. Department of Justice, June 12, 2012, http://www.justice.gov/opa/pr/2012/June/12-crm-742.html

289. Albergotti, *supra* note 287.

290. Jessica Silver-Greenberg, *British Bank in $340 Million Settlement for Laundering*, N.Y. Times, Aug. 14, 2012, http://www.nytimes.com/2012/08/15/business/standard-chartered-settles-with-new-york-for-340-million.html?pagewanted=all.

291. Press Release, N.Y. Dep't of Fin. Servs., *Statement from Benjamin M. Lawsky, Superintendent of Financial Services, Regarding Signing of Final Agreement with Standard Chartered Bank* (Sept. 21, 2012), http://www.dfs.ny.gov/about/press/pr1209211. htm.

292. Silver-Greenberg, *supra* note 290; Press Release, *Statement from Benjamin M. Lawsky, supra* note 291.

293. Cyrus Sanati, *Why London Bankers Are Shrugging off Standard Chartered Threat,* FORTUNE MAGAZINE, Aug. 8, 2012, http://fortune.com/2012/08/08/why-london-bankers-are-shrugging-off-standard-chartered-threat/; Ben Rooney, *Standard Chartered's Stock Drops on Iran Allegations,* CNN.COM, Aug. 7, 2012, http://buzz. money.cnn.com/2012/08/07/standard-chartered-iran-sanctions/.

294. Sanati, *supra* note 293; Rooney, *supra* note 293.

295. Consent Order Under New York Banking Law § 44, In the Matter of Standard Chartered Bank, New York Branch, New York State Department of Financial Services, Sept. 21, 2012, http://www.dfs.ny.gov/about/ea/ea120921.pdf.

296. Jamie Grierson, *160-year-old Standard Chartered May Lose U.S. License over Iran Dealings,* IRISH EXAMINER, Aug. 8, 2012, http://www.irishexaminer.com/business/160-year-old-standard-chartered-may-lose-us-licence-over-iran-dealings-203400.html.

297. *Id.*

298. Jessica Silver-Greenberg & Ben Protess, *Accusations Against Bank on Iran Deals Surprised U.S. Regulators, Too,* N.Y. TIMES, Aug. 7, 2012, http://dealbook.nytimes. com/2012/08/07/iran-accusations-against-bank-surprised-regulators-too/.

299. Press Release, U.S. Dep't of Justice, *Standard Chartered Bank Agrees to Forfeit $227 Million for Illegal Transactions with Iran, Sudan, Libya, and Burma* (Dec. 10, 2012), http://www.justice.gov/opa/pr/2012/December/12-crm-1467.html.

300. *Id.*

301. *Id.*

302. Press Release, N.Y. Dep't of Fin. Servs., *NYDFS Announces Standard Chartered Bank to Suspend Dollar Clearing for High-Risk Clients in Hong Kong; Pay $300 Million Penalty; Take Other Remedial Steps After Anti-Money Laundering Compliance Failures* (Aug. 19, 2014), http://www.dfs.ny.gov/about/press/pr1408191.htm.

303. *Id.*

304. *Id.*

305. Ben Protess & Chad Bray, *Caught Backsliding, Standard Chartered Is Fined $300 Million,* N.Y. TIMES, Aug. 19, 2014, http://dealbook.nytimes.com/2014/08/19/ standard-chartered-in-deal-with-new-york-regulator/.

306. *HSBC to Pay $1.9bn in US Money Laundering Penalties,* BBC.COM, Dec. 11, 2012, http://www.bbc.com/news/business-20673466.

307. Press Release, U.S. Dep't of Justice, *HSBC Holdings PLC and HSBC Bank USA, supra* note 227.

308. *HSBC Exposed U.S. Financial System to Money Laundering, Drug, Terrorist Financing Risks,* Sen. Comm. on Homeland Security & Governmental Affairs, July 16, 2012, http://www.hsgac.senate.gov/subcommittees/investigations/media/hsbc-exposed-us-finacial-system-to-money-laundering-drug-terrorist-financing-risks; *U.S. Vulnerabilities to Money Laundering, Drugs, and Terrorist Financing: HSBC Case History,* Sen. Comm. on Homeland Security & Governmental Affairs, July 17, 2012, at 6, http://www.hsgac.senate.gov/subcommittees/investigations/hearings/us-vulnerabilities-to-money-laundering-drugs-and-terrorist-financing-hsbc-case-history.

309. Press Release, U.S. Dep't of Justice, *HSBC Holdings PLC and HSBC Bank USA, supra* note 227.

310. *Id.*

311. Isabella Steger, *Fine Times for Now at HSBC*, WALL ST. J., Dec. 11, 2012, http://online.wsj.com/articles/SB10001424127887324024004578172803564740238.

312. Press Release, U.S. Dep't of Justice, *HSBC Holdings PLC and HSBC Bank USA*, *supra* note 227.

313. Samuel Rubenfeld, *RBS Wrote a Manual for How to Evade Sanctions*, WALL ST. J., Dec. 12, 2013, http://blogs.wsj.com/riskandcompliance/2013/12/12/rbs-wrote-a-manual-for-how-to-evade-sanctions/.

314. Press Release, U.S. Dep't of the Treasury, *Treasury Department Reaches $33 Million Settlement with the Royal Bank of Scotland PLC* (Dec. 11, 2013), http://www.treasury.gov/press-center/press-releases/Pages/jl2239.aspx.

315. *Id.*

316. Kara Scannell, *RBS Settles US Sanctions Case with $100m Pact*, FINANCIAL TIMES, Dec. 11, 2013, http://www.ft.com/intl/cms/s/0/a28f9064-6291-11e3-bba5-00144feabdc0.html#axzz3BdefYtxM.

317. *Id.*

318. *Id.*

319. *Id.*

320. Press Release, U.S. Dep't of the Treasury, *Treasury Department Reaches Landmark $152 Million Settlement with Clearstream Banking, S.A.* (Jan. 23, 2014), http://www.treasury.gov/press-center/press-releases/Pages/jl2264.aspx.

321. *Id.*

322. *Id.*

323. *Id.*

324. Press Release, The White House, *Summary of Technical Understandings Related to the Implementation of the Joint Plan of Action on the Islamic Republic of Iran's Nuclear Program* (Jan. 16, 2014), http://www.whitehouse.gov/the-press-office/2014/01/16/summary-technical-understandings-related-implementation-joint-plan-actio (announcing the parties would begin implementing the Joint Plan of Action on January 20, 2014).

325. Rick Gladstone, *U.S. Warns Against Business with Iran*, N.Y. TIMES, Jan. 23, 2014, http://www.nytimes.com/2014/01/24/world/middleeast/us-warns-against-business-with-iran.html.

326. Press Release, U.S. Dep't of Justice, *BNP Paribas Agrees to Plead Guilty*, *supra* note 229.

327. Rob Blackwell, *Why the BNP Paribas Fine Matters to U.S. Banks*, AMERICAN BANKER, June 6, 2014, http://www.americanbanker.com/issues/179_109/why-the-bnp-paribas-fine-matters-to-us-banks-1067936-1.html.

328. Press Release, U.S. Dep't of Justice, *BNP Paribas Agrees to Plead Guilty*, *supra* note 229.

329. *Id.*

330. *Id.*

331. Blackwell, *supra* note 327.

332. Press Release, U.S. Dep't of Justice, *BNP Paribas Agrees to Plead Guilty*, *supra* note 229.

333. Blackwell, *supra* note 327.

334. Press Release, U.S. Dep't of Justice, *BNP Paribas Agrees to Plead Guilty*, *supra* note 229.

335. Lynnley Browning, *Regulator Benjamin Lawsky is the Man Banks Fear Most*, NEWSWEEK, June 30, 2014, http://www.newsweek.com/regulator-benjamin-lawsky-man-banks-fear-most-256626.

336. *Id.*

337. *Id.*

338. Remarks of Superintendent Lawsky on Financial Regulatory Enforcement at the Exchequer Club, Washington, D.C., Mar. 19, 2014, http://www.dfs.ny.gov/about/speeches/sp140319.pdf.

339. *Id.*

340. *Id.*

341. *Id.*

342. Leah McGrath Goodman & Browning, *supra* note 6.

343. *Id.*

344. Press Release, U.S. Dep't of Treasury, *Written Testimony of Adam J. Szubin, Acting Under Secretary of Treasury for Terrorism and Financial Intelligence: Before the S. Comm. on Banking, Housing, and Urban Affairs* (Aug. 5, 2015), http://www.treasury.gov/press-center/press-releases/Pages/jl0144.aspx.

345. *Id.*

346. *Id.*

347. *Id.*

348. *Id.*

349. *Id.*

350. Warren Strobel, *Iran's Sponsorship of Terrorism Sees "Marked Resurgence": US*, Reuters, May 30, 2013, http://www.reuters.com/article/2013/05/30/us-usa-terrorism-idUSBRE94T16Y20130530.

351. U.S. Dep't of State, Country Reports on Terrorism 2013, Chapter 3: State Sponsors of Terrorism Overview, http://www.state.gov/j/ct/rls/crt/2013/224826.htm; U.S. Dep't of State, Country Reports on Terrorism 2014, Chapter 3: State Sponsors of Terrorism Overview, http://www.state.gov/j/ct/rls/crt/2014/239410.htm.

352. Michael R. Gordon & Eric Schmitt, *Iran Still Aids Terrorism and Bolsters Syria's President, State Department Finds*, N.Y. Times, June 19, 2015, http://www.nytimes.com/2015/06/20/world/middleeast/state-department-terrorism-report-iran-syria.html.

353. David E. Sanger, *C.I.A. Director Says Iran's Economic Peril Helped Drive Nuclear Deal*, N.Y. Times, Apr. 8, 2015, http://mobile.nytimes.com/2015/04/09/world/middleeast/cia-director-says-irans-economic-peril-helped-drive-nuclear-deal.html?_r=0&referrer=.

354. Joint Comprehensive Plan of Action, *supra* note 13.

355. Press Release, U.S. Dep't of Treasury, *Written Testimony of Adam J. Szubin, supra* note 344.

356. *Id.*

357. *Id.*

358. Julian Hattem, *Ex-Sen. Lieberman Takes Reins of Anti-Iran Deal Group*, The Hill, August 11, 2015, http://thehill.com/policy/national-security/250808-ex-sen-lieberman-takes-reins-on-anti-iran-deal-group.

359. Joseph I. Lieberman, *Congress Should Step Up to Block the Terrible Iran Agreement*, Wash. Post, Aug. 14, 2015, https://www.washingtonpost.com/opinions/congress-should-step-up-to-block-the-terrible-iran-agreement/2015/08/14/57629e4c-41ce-11e5-8e7d-9c033e6745d8_story.html.

360. *See, e.g.*, Press Release, Sen. Charles E. Schumer, *supra* note 114; Press Release, Congressman Eliot L. Engel, *supra* note 114; Fox, *supra* note 114.

361. Press Release, Sen. Charles E. Schumer, *supra* note 114.

362. *See, e.g.*, Caldwell & Wald, *supra* note 116; *Expert Opinions on the Extension of Negotiations, supra* note 116; Albright, Dubowitz, Kittrie, Spector, & Yaffe, *supra* note 116.

363. Thomas Erdbrink, *Iranian President Is Hemmed in by Hard-Liners and New Western Sanctions*, N.Y. TIMES, Aug. 30, 2014, .http://www.nytimes.com/2014/08/31/world/middleeast/iran.html?ref=middleeast.

364. *Id.*

365. Jo Becker, *Web of Shell Companies Veils Trade by Iran's Ships*, N.Y. TIMES, June 7, 2010, http://www.nytimes.com/2010/06/08/world/middleeast/08sanctions.html?pagewanted=1&sq=becker%20iran&st=cse&scp=1.

366. Jo Becker, *Web of Shell Companies Veils Trade by Iran's Ships*, N.Y. TIMES, June 7, 2010, http://www.nytimes.com/2010/06/08/world/middleeast/08sanctions.html?pagewanted=1&sq=becker%20iran&st=cse&scp=1.

367. U.S. DEP'T OF THE TREASURY, THE HAWALA ALTERNATIVE REMITTANCE SYSTEM AND ITS ROLE IN MONEY LAUNDERING, http://www.treasury.gov/resource-center/terrorist-illicit-finance/Documents/FinCEN-Hawala-rpt.pdf.

368. *Id.*

369. *Id.*

370. Daniel Fineren, *Barter, Other Steps Help Iran Firms Beat Sanctions*, REUTERS, Feb. 29, 2012, http://www.reuters.com/article/2012/02/29/us-iran-trade-idUSTRE81S12G20120229.

371. *Id.*

372. Joe Parkinson & Emre Pekker, *Turkey Swaps Gold for Iranian Gas*, WALL ST. J., Nov. 23, 2012, http://www.wsj.com/news/articles/SB10001424127887324352004578136973602198776; Gary Clark, Rachel Ziemba, & Mark Dubowitz, *Iran's Golden Loophole*, FOUNDATION FOR DEFENSE OF DEMOCRACIES, May 13, 2013, http://www.defend-democracy.org/content/uploads/documents/FDD_RGE_Iran_Gol_Report__May_2013_FINAL_2.pdf.

373. *See, e.g.*, U.S. Dep't of State, *Fact Sheet: Iran Freedom and Counter-Proliferation Act of 2012*, http://www.state.gov/documents/organization/208111.pdf.

374. *See, e.g., id.*

375. Judgment of the Court, Cases C-584/10 P, C-593/10 P, and C-595/10 P (July 18, 2013), http://curia.europa.eu/juris/document/document.jsf?text=&docid=139745&pageIndex=0&doclang=en&mode=req&dir=&occ=first&part=1&cid=1914364.

376. *Id.*

377. *Id.*

378. *Id.*

379. *Id.*

380. Laurence Norman, *EU to Maintain Sanctions on Most Iran Firms*, WALL ST. J., Nov. 26, 2013, http://online.wsj.com/news/articles/SB1000142405270230401130457922220285227945 2.

381. *Id.*

382. Emanuele Ottolenghi & Saeed Ghasseminejad, *European Courts Are Gutting Iran Sanctions before a Nuclear Agreement Has Even Been Reached*, BUSINESS INSIDER, July 9, 2014, http://www.businessinsider.com/eu-gutting-iran-sanctions-2014-7; Sharif Univ. of Tech. v. Council of the European Union, Case T-181/13, July 3, 2014, http://curia.europa.eu/juris/document/document.jsf?text=&docid=154526&pageIndex=0&doclang=EN&mode=lst&dir=&occ=first&part=1&cid=521574.

383. *Iran (Nuclear Proliferation)*, Financial Sanctions Notice, HM Treasury, U.K. Gov't, Nov. 12, 2014, https://www.gov.uk/government/uploads/system/uploads/attachment_data/file/374510/Iran_1202_2014.pdf.

384. *See, e.g.*, Zachary Goldman, *A Door Half Open: Transparency, Secrecy, and the Future of EU Targeted Sanctions*, LAWFARE BLOG (June 16, 2014, 3:51 PM), http://www.

lawfareblog.com/door-half-open-transparency-secrecy-and-future-eu-targeted-sanctions; Laurence Norman, *EU To Maintain Sanctions on Most Iran Firms*, WALL ST. J., Nov. 26, 2013, http://online.wsj.com/news/articles/SB10001424052702304011304579222202852279452.

385. Laurence Norman, *EU Governments Approve Secret Evidence in Sanctions Cases*, WALL ST. J., Feb. 10, 2015, http://www.wsj.com/articles/eu-governments-approve-secret-evidence-in-sanctions-cases-1423583213.

386. *Id.*

387. *See, e.g.,* Nick Gillard & Dominic Williams, *What the Iran Deal Means for Blacklisted Entities*, BULL. OF ATOMIC SCIENTISTS, July 21, 2015, http://thebulletin.org/what-iran-deal-means-blacklisted-entities8540.

388. *See, e.g.,* Golnaz Esfandiari, *Iranian Media Say Sanctions Taking Toll on Seriously Ill Patients*, RADIO FREE EUROPE/RADIO LIBERTY, Oct. 15, 2012, http://www.rferl.org/content/iran-media-say-sanctions-taking-toll-seriously-ill-patients/24740542.html.

389. *See, e.g.,* Benoit Faucon, *EU Firms Join Debate over U.S. Sanctions on Iran*, WALL ST. J., Aug. 15, 2012, http://www.wsj.com/articles/SB10000872396390444233104577591311307733418.

390. The Trade Sanctions Reform and Export Enforcement Act of 2000, Title IX of Pub. L. 106-387 (Oct. 28, 2000).

391. *See, e.g.,* Arshad Mohammed, *U.S. Exports to Iran Rise Nearly One-Third Despite Sanctions*, REUTERS, Oct. 15, 2012, http://www.reuters.com/article/2012/10/15/us-iran-usa-exports-idUSBRE89E04L20121015. This issue is addressed in more detail in DAVID ALBRIGHT, MARK DUBOWITZ, ORDE KITTRIE, LEONARD SPECTOR, & MICHAEL YAFFE, U.S. NONPROLIFERATION STRATEGY FOR THE CHANGING MIDDLE EAST 43–44 (2013), http://isis-online.org/uploads/isis-reports/documents/FinalReport.pdf.

392. Press Release, U.S. Dep't of the Treasury, *Remarks by Treasury Secretary Paulson, supra* note 50.

393. Michael Pizzi, *Russia, China Sign Deal to Bypass US Dollar*, AL JAZEERA AMERICA, May 20, 2014, http://america.aljazeera.com/articles/2014/5/20/russia-china-bank-deal.html.

394. *See, e.g.,* STOP EXPLOSIVE INVESTMENTS, LEGISLATION, http://www.stopexplosive-investments.org/legislation (last visited Apr. 28, 2015).

395. *See, e.g., id.*

396. *See, e.g., Belgium Bans Investments in Depleted Uranium Weapons*, FAIRFIN, July 4, 2009, http://www.fairfin.be/en/whatsnew/news/2009/07/belgium-bans-investments-depleted-uranium-weapons (last visited Apr. 28, 2015).

397. *See, e.g., id.*

398. *See, e.g.,* INTERNATIONAL COALITION TO BAN URANIUM WEAPONS, PRODUCERS, http://www.bandepleteduranium.org/en/uranium-weapon-manufacturers (last visited Apr. 28, 2015).

399. *See, e.g., Worldwide Investments in Cluster Munitions: A Shared Responsibility*, PAX (Nov. 2014), http://www.stopexplosiveinvestments.org/uploads/pdf/Worldwide%20Investments%20in%20Cluster%20Munitions;%20a%20shared%20responsibility_2014.pdf (last visited Apr. 28, 2015).

400. Nicholas de Larrinaga, *Austria and Belgium Upgrade Their Pandur I APCs*, IHS JANE'S DEFENCE WKLY., Mar. 18, 2015, http://www.janes.com/article/50032/austria-and-belgium-upgrade-their-pandur-i-apcs.

401. *See, e.g.,* Matthijs van Wageningen's Photo Gallery, *Belgian Air Component—General Dynamics F-16AM* (Sept. 12, 2014), http://www.vanwageningen.net/

picture/1127-20140912_030_belgian_air_component_general_dynamics_f_ 16am_fighting_falcon_fa_110_ge_x_kleine_brogel_be.

402. *European SRI Study 2014*, EUROSIF (2014), http://www.eurosif.org/publication/view/european-sri-study-2014/.

403. *Company Exclusions: Responsible Investments*, The Government Pension Fund, GOVERNMENT.NO, https://www.regjeringen.no/en/topics/the-economy/the-government-pension-fund/internt-bruk/companies-excluded-from-the-investment-u/id447122/ (last updated Apr. 9, 2014; last visited May 31, 2015).

404. *Id.*

405. *Deterrence and Defence Posture Review*, NATO, May 20, 2012, http://www.nato.int/cps/en/natolive/official_texts_87597.htm.

406. Andrea Shalal-Esa, *Norway Says F-35 Jet on Track; Keeping Eye on Costs*, REUTERS, Jan. 9, 2014, http://www.reuters.com/article/2014/01/10/us-lockheed-fighter-norway-idUSBREA0903B20140110.

407. *Excluded Companies*, Danske Bank, https://www.danskebank.com/en-uk/CSR/business/SRI/Pages/exclusionlist.aspx (last visited May 31, 2015).

408. Mike Jacobson, *Cluster Munitions No More: What This Means for the U.S. Military*, EARMOR, Oct. 2014, http://www.benning.army.mil/armor/eARMOR/content/issues/2014/OCT_DEC/Jacobson.html.

409. *See, e.g., Royal Navy Phases Out DU Ammo*, BBC NEWS, Jan. 13, 2001, http://news.bbc.co.uk/2/hi/uk_news/1115771.stm.

410. Joseph Trevithick, *A-10s Battling ISIS Won't Use Depleted Uranium Ammo*, REAL CLEAR DEFENSE, Mar. 5, 2015, http://www.realcleardefense.com/articles/2015/03/05/a-10s_battling_isis_wont_use_depleted_uranium_ammo_107698.html.

411. William Branigin, *U.S. Declares It Will Not Produce Any More Antipersonnel Land Mines*, WASH. POST, June 27, 2014, http://www.washingtonpost.com/world/national-security/us-declares-it-will-not-produce-any-more-antipersonnel-land-mines/2014/06/27/f20f6f74-fdf5-11e3-932c-0a55b81f48ce_story.html.

412. EUROSIF, MISSION, http://www.eurosif.org/about/mission/.

413. EUROSIF, EUROPEAN SRI STUDY 2012, at 7, http://www.eurosif.org/publication/view/european-sri-study-2012/.

414. *Id.* at 17.

415. *Id. at* 7.

416. *Id.*

417. *Id.* at 25.

418. *The World's Biggest Companies: 2015 Ranking, #253 General Dynamics*, FORBES, http://www.forbes.com/companies/general-dynamics/.

419. *Id., #336 Northrup Grumman*, http://www.forbes.com/companies/northrop-grumman/.

420. *Id., #196 Lockheed Martin*, http://www.forbes.com/companies/lockheed-martin/.

421. JUAN ZARATE, TREASURY'S WAR: THE UNLEASHING OF A NEW ERA OF FINANCIAL WARFARE 324 (2013).

422. *See, e.g.,* Press Release, U.S. Dep't of Treasury, *Written Testimony of Adam J. Szubin*, *supra* note 344.

423. ZARATE, *supra* note 421, at 324.

424. *Id.*

425. JUAN ZARATE, TREASURY'S WAR: THE UNLEASHING OF A NEW ERA OF FINANCIAL WARFARE 356 (2013).

426. *See, e.g., Spider Web: The Making and Unmaking of Iran Sanctions*, INTERNATIONAL CRISIS GROUP, Feb. 25, 2013, http://www.crisisgroup.org/~/media/Files/

Middle%20East%20North%20Africa/Iran%20Gulf/Iran/138-spider-web-the-making-and-unmaking-of-iran-sanctions.pdf.

427. *See, e.g.,* Kenneth Katzman, *Easing U.S. Sanctions on Iran,* ATLANTIC COUNCIL, June 2014, http://www.atlanticcouncil.org/images/publications/Easing_US_Sanctions_on_Iran.pdf.

428. *See, e.g.,* Jonathan Schanzer & Mark Dubowitz, *It Just Got Easier for Iran to Fund Terrorism,* FOREIGN POLICY, July 17, 2015, http://foreignpolicy.com/2015/07/17/it-just-got-easier-for-iran-to-fund-terrorism-swift-bank/.

429. *Sanctions and the JCPOA: Hearing Before the S. Comm. on Foreign Relations* 12 (July 30, 2015) (statement of Juan Zarate), http://www.foreign.senate.gov/imo/media/doc/07-30-15%20ZarateTestimony.pdf.

430. *Id.* at 14.

431. *The Implications of Sanctions Relief Under the Iran Agreement: Hearing Before the S. Comm. On Banking, Housing, and Urban Affairs* (Aug. 5, 2015) (statement of Matthew Levitt), http://www.banking.senate.gov/public/index.cfm?FuseAction=Files.View&FileStore_id=f311b065-a725-442a-bb39-613d5c81ac0d.

432. *Id.*

433. *See, e.g.,* DAVID ALBRIGHT, MARK DUBOWITZ, ORDE KITTRIE, LEONARD SPECTOR, & MICHAEL YAFFE, U.S. NONPROLIFERATION STRATEGY FOR THE CHANGING MIDDLE EAST 58–62 (2013), http://isis-online.org/uploads/isis-reports/documents/FinalReport.pdf.

434. Leah McGrath Goodman & Browning, *supra* note 6.

435. Julie Hirschfeld Davis, *Enforcer at Treasury Is First Line of Attack Against ISIS,* N.Y. TIMES, Oct. 21, 2014, http://www.nytimes.com/2014/10/22/business/international/enforcer-at-treasury-is-first-line-of-attack-against-isis.html?_r=0.

436. Remarks of Superintendent Lawsky on Financial Regulatory Enforcement at the Exchequer Club, Washington, D.C., Mar. 19, 2014, http://www.dfs.ny.gov/about/speeches/sp140319.pdf.

437. Erika Eichelberger, *Elizabeth Warren Slams Federal Regulators over Bank Money Laundering,* MOTHER JONES, Mar. 7, 2013, http://www.motherjones.com/mojo/2013/03/elizabeth-warren-senate-banking-committee-hearing-money-laundering.

438. *Id.*

439. *Id.*

440. Press Release, U.S. Dep't of Justice, *"Karl Lee" Charged in Manhattan Federal Court with Using a Web of Front Companies to Evade U.S. Sanctions* (Apr. 29, 2014), http://www.fbi.gov/newyork/press-releases/2014/karl-lee-charged-in-manhattan-federal-court-with-using-a-web-of-front-companies-to-evade-u.s.-sanctions.

441. *Id.*

442. *Id.*

CHAPTER 4

1. Sun Tzu, THE ART OF WAR.

2. DONG WANG, CHINA'S UNEQUAL TREATIES: NARRATING NATIONAL HISTORY 128 (2005), quoted in Jonathan G. Odom, *A China in the Bull Shop? Comparing the Rhetoric of a Rising China with the Reality of the International Law of the Sea,* 17 OCEAN & COASTAL L.J. 224 (2012).

3. U.S. DEP'T OF DEFENSE, ANNUAL REPORT TO CONGRESS: MILITARY POWER OF THE PEOPLE'S REPUBLIC OF CHINA 2008, at 19 (Washington, D.C.: Office of the Secretary of Defense, Mar. 2008); Central Military Commission, People's Liberation Army of

China Regulation on Political Work, Article 14(18) (Dec. 2003) (setting forth the PLA's doctrine of "three warfares": public opinion, psychological, and legal), cited in Paul A. Stempel, Capt., USAF, Reading Lawfare in Chinese: The Meaning of the Term "Falu Zhan" ("Lawfare") in Chinese Military Literature (July 2011) (unpublished article).

4. Stempel, *id.* Stempel notes that when the Chinese government printed a translated version of an article titled *Lawfare: A Decisive Element of 21st-Century Conflicts?* by Major General Charles Dunlap, the former Deputy Judge Advocate General of the U.S. who coined the term "lawfare," the PRC's translators used the term *falu zhan* where Dunlap used the term "lawfare."

5. Cong Wensheng et al., Analysis of 100 Cases of lawfare 5 (PLA Publishing House 2004), quoted in Dean Cheng, *Winning without Fighting: Chinese Legal Warfare*, Heritage Foundation Backgrounder, May 18, 2012, http://www.heritage.org/research/reports/2012/05/winning-without-fighting-chinese-legal-warfare.

6. Wensheng et al., *supra* note 5, at 5.

7. Stempel, *supra* note 3.

8. *Id.*

9. *Id.*

10. Under Informatized Conditions: Legal Warfare 7 (Song Yunxia ed., 2007), quoted in Jonathan G. Odom, *A China in the Bull Shop? Comparing the Rhetoric of a Rising China with the Reality of the International Law of the Sea*, 17 Ocean & Coastal L.J. 224 (2012). Another leading Chinese book on lawfare, which has not been translated into English, is Xun Hengdong, Lawfare in Modern War (PLA Publishing House 2005).

11. Stempel, *supra* note 3.

12. Qiao Liang & Wang Xiangsui, Unrestricted Warfare (1999).

13. *Id.*

14. *See, e.g.,* U.S.-China Perception Monitor, The Inaugural Carter Center—Global Times Foundation Forum for Young Chinese and American Scholars, Sept. 6–7, 2014, Qiao Liang biographical paragraph, http://www.uscnpm.org/papers/.

15. *See, e.g.,* Stempel, *supra* note 3 (reporting several instances of PRC think tanks and media outlets citing to Dunlap's work).

16. *Id.*

17. Charles J. Dunlap, Jr., *Lawfare: A Decisive Element of 21st-Century Conflicts?*, 54 Joint Force Q. 34, 35 (2009), http://scholarship.law.duke.edu/faculty_scholarship/3347/.

18. Stempel, *supra* note 3.

19. U.S. Dep't of State, China's Strategic Modernization: Report from the ISAB Task Force, International Security Advisory Board (Washington D.C., 2008), www.fas.org/nuke/guide/china/ISAB2008.pdf.

20. William R. Kintner, Protracted Conflict: A Challenging Study of Communist Strategy (1959).

21. *See, e.g.,* Dean Cheng, *Winning without Fighting: Chinese Legal Warfare*, Heritage Foundation Backgrounder, May 18, 2012, http://www.heritage.org/research/reports/2012/05/winning-without-fighting-chinese-legal-warfare.

22. Eric W. Orts, *The Rule of Law in China*, 34 Vand. J. Transnat'l L. 43 (2001).

23. *Id.* at 58.

24. *Id.*

25. *Id.* at 59.

26. Benjamin L. Liebman, *Assessing China's Legal Reforms*, 23 Colum. J. Asian L. 17, 18 (2009).

27. *Id.* at 18–19.

28. *Id.* at 18.

29. *Id.* at 30.

30. Elizabeth M. Lynch, *China's Rule of Law Mirage: The Regression of the Legal Profession Since the Adoption of the 2007 Lawyers Law*, 42 Geo. Wash. Int'l L. Rev. 535 (2010).

31. *Id.*

32. Carl F. Minzner, *China's Turn Against Law*, 59 Am. J. Comp. Law 935 (Fall 2011).

33. Josh Chin, *"Rule of Law" or "Rule by Law"? In China, a Preposition Makes All the Difference*, Wall St. J., Oct. 20, 2014, http://blogs.wsj.com/chinarealtime/2014/10/20/rule-of-law-or-rule-by-law-in-china-a-preposition-makes-all-the-difference/.

34. Rachel Lu, *China's President Raises Eyebrows with Sharp Rhetoric on Rule of Law*, Foreign Policy, Feb. 3, 2015, http://foreignpolicy.com/2015/02/03/chinas-president-raises-eyebrows-with-sharp-rhetoric-on-rule-of-law/.

35. Carl Minzner, *What Does China Mean by "Rule of Law"?*, Foreign Policy, Oct. 20, 2014, http://foreignpolicy.com/2014/10/20/what-does-china-mean-by-rule-of-law/.

36. Benjamin Bissell, *A Sea Change for the Rule of Law in China*, Lawfare Blog (July 20, 2015, 10:30 AM), https://www.lawfareblog.com/sea-change-rule-law-china.

37. Chris Buckley, *Chinese Authorities Detain and Denounce Rights Lawyers*, N.Y. Times, July 11, 2015, http://www.nytimes.com/2015/07/12/world/asia/china-arrests-human-rights-lawyers-zhou-shifeng.html?ref=asia.

38. *Id.*

39. Dean Cheng, *Winning without Fighting: Chinese Legal Warfare*, Heritage Foundation Backgrounder, May 18, 2012, http://www.heritage.org/research/reports/2012/05/winning-without-fighting-chinese-legal-warfare.

40. Press Release, The White House, *Remarks by President Obama and Prime Minister Gillard of Australia in Joint Press Conference*, (Nov. 16, 2011), https://www.whitehouse.gov/the-press-office/2011/11/16/remarks-president-obama-and-prime-minister-gillard-australia-joint-press.

41. *Id.*

42. James Kraska & Brian Wilson, *China Wages Maritime "Lawfare,"* Mar. 12, 2009, http://foreignpolicy.com/2009/03/12/china-wages-maritime-lawfare/.

43. *Id.*

44. *Id.*

45. *Id.*

46. Raul Pedrozo, *The Building of China's Great Wall at Sea*, 17 Ocean & Coastal L.J. 253 (2012); Commander Robert C. De Tolve, JAGC, USN, *At What Cost? America's UNCLOS Allergy in the Time of "Lawfare,"* 61 Naval L. Rev. 1 (2012).

47. Pedrozo, *supra* note 46, at 287.

48. *Id.* at 257.

49. *Id.* at 285.

50. *Id.* at 284.

51. *Id.*

52. Lt. Commander Robert T. Kline, *The Pen and the Sword: The People's Republic of China's Effort to Redefine the Exclusive Economic Zone Through Maritime Lawfare and Military Enforcement*, 216 Mil. L. Rev. 122 (Summer 2013).

53. *See, e.g.*, I.C.J. Statute, art. 38, http://www.icj-cij.org/documents/index.php?p1=4&p2=2&p3=0.

54. Commander Robert C. De Tolve, JAGC, USN, *At What Cost? America's UNCLOS Allergy in the Time of "Lawfare,"* 61 Naval L. Rev. 1 (2012).

55. *Id.*

NOTES TO PAGES 164–167 **[399]**

56. U.S. Dep't of State, Limits in the Seas, No. 143, China: Maritime Claims in the South China Sea (Dec. 5, 2014), http://www.state.gov/documents/organization/234936.pdf.

57. *Id.*

58. *Id.*

59. *Id.*

60. Jerome A. Cohen, *Lawfare or Warfare? Let Impartial Tribunals Cool Asia's Maritime Disputes*, The Diplomat, May 29, 2014, http://thediplomat.com/2014/05/lawfare-or-warfare-let-impartial-tribunals-cool-asias-maritime-disputes/.

61. *Id.*

62. *U.N. Convention on the Law of the Sea*, art. 121 (Regime of Islands), http://www.un.org/depts/los/convention_agreements/texts/unclos/part8.htm.

63. *Id.*

64. *See, e.g.,* Jay Batongbacal, *Reclamation in the South China Sea: Legal Loopholes, Practical Impacts*, Ctr. for Strategic & Int'l Studies, Feb. 18, 2015, http://amti.csis.org/reclamation-in-the-south-china-sea-legal-loopholes-practical-impacts/.

65. Mira Rapp-Hooper, *Before and After: The South China Sea Transformed*, Ctr. for Strategic & Int'l Studies, Feb. 18, 2015, http://amti.csis.org/before-and-after-the-south-china-sea-transformed/.

66. Ingrid Wuerth, *U.S. Policy on the South China Sea*, Lawfare, Mar. 26, 2015, https://www.lawfareblog.com/us-policy-south-china-sea.

67. *China's Maritime Disputes in the East and South China Seas, Testimony of Peter Dutton*, U.S. Naval War College Rev., https://www.usnwc.edu/getattachment/9edbcea9-8425-4b96-aa14-aac1f81532c2/China-s-Maritime-Disputes-in-the-East-and-South-Ch.aspx (last visited May 6, 2015).

68. Lt. Commander Robert T. Kline, *The Pen and the Sword: The People's Republic of China's Effort to Redefine the Exclusive Economic Zone Through Maritime Lawfare and Military Enforcement*, 216 Mil. L. Rev. 122 (Summer 2013).

69. *Id.*

70. *Id.*

71. *Id.*

72. Letter from Senate Armed Services Committee Chair John McCain and Ranking Member Reed and Senate Foreign Relations Committee Chair Bob Corker and Ranking Member Bob Menendez to Secretary of Defense and Secretary of State (Mar. 19, 2015), http://breakingdefense.com/wp-content/uploads/sites/3/2015/03/03-19-15_Joint-letter-to-Kerry-and-Carter.pdf.

73. *Id.*

74. Larry Wortzel, *The Chinese People's Liberation Army and Space Warfare: Emerging United States-China Military Competition*, Am. Enterprise Inst., Oct. 17, 2007, http://www.aei.org/papers/foreign-and-defense-policy/regional/asia/the-chinese-peoples-liberation-army-and-space-warfare/.

75. U.S.-China Economic & Security Review Comm'n, 2008 Report to Congress 152 (Nov. 2008), http://origin.www.uscc.gov/sites/default/files/annual_reports/2008-Report-to-Congress-_0.pdf.

76. Bin Cheng, Studies in International Space Law 398 (1997), quoted in Major John W. Bellflower, *The Influence of Law on Command of Space*, 65 A.F. L. Rev. 107, 138 (2010).

77. William Blackstone, Blackstone's Commentaries on the Laws of England, Book II, ch. 2, p. 18, http://avalon.law.yale.edu/18th_century/black-stone_bk2ch2.asp; Yehudah Abramovitch, *The Maxim "Cujus Est Solum Ejus Usque Ad*

Coelum" as Applied in Aviation, 8 McGILL L.J. 247 (1961), http://lawjournal.mcgill. ca/userfiles/other/8509457-abramovitch.pdf. Special thanks to Jeremy Rabkin for bringing this to the author's attention.

78. Bellflower, *supra* note 76.
79. Fed'n of Am. Scientists, U.S. National Space Policy (Presidential Policy Directive 49, Aug. 31, 2006), *available at* http://www.fas.org/irp/offdocs/nspd/space.html.
80. White House, Office of Sci. & Tech. Pol'y, *U.S. National Space Policy*, Aug. 31, 2006.
81. Bellflower, *supra* note 76, at 141.
82. *Id.* at 141.
83. *Id.* at 144.
84. Zhang Hualiang & Song Huaren, "Luelun Xinxihua Zhanzheng Zhu Zhanchang Xiang Taikong Zhuanyi de Biranxing" 14–17, cited in Wortzel, *supra* note 74.
85. Wortzel, *supra* note 74.
86. *Id.*
87. *Id.*
88. Bellflower, *supra* note 76, at 133.
89. Wortzel, *supra* note 74; Bellflower, *supra* note 76, at 134.
90. Bellflower, *supra* note 76, at 133.
91. *See, e.g.,* OFFICE OF THE SECRETARY OF DEFENSE, MILITARY AND SECURITY DEVELOPMENTS INVOLVING THE PEOPLE'S REPUBLIC OF CHINA: 2011 ANNUAL REPORT, *available at* http://www.defense.gov/pubs/pdfs/2011_CMPR_Final. pdf ("China has not yet agreed with the U.S. position that existing mechanisms, such as International Humanitarian Law and the Law of Armed Conflict, apply in cyberspace."); Adam Segal, *China, International Law, and Cyberspace,* COUNCIL ON FOREIGN RELATIONS, Oct. 2, 2012, http://blogs.cfr.org/asia/2012/10/02/ china-international-law-and-cyberspace/.
92. U.N. General Assembly, Group of Governmental Experts on Developments in the Field of Information and Telecommunications in the Context of International Security, Rep. A/68/98 (June 24, 2013), http://www.un.org/ga/search/view_doc. asp?symbol=A/68/98 (in which a Chinese expert concurred in a report stating that international law is applicable to the cyber arena).
93. Kristen Eichensehr, *International Cyber Governance: Engagement without Agreement?,* JUST SECURITY, Feb. 2, 2015, http://justsecurity.org/19599/ international-cyber-governance-engagement-agreement/.
94. Joseph Marks, *U.S. Makes New Push for Global Rules in Cyberspace,* POLITICO, May 5, 2015, http://www.politico.com/story/2015/05/us-makes-new-push-for-global-rules-in-cyberspace-117632.html.
95. *See, e.g.,* Harold Hongju Koh, Legal Adviser of the U.S. Dep't of State, International Law in Cyberspace (speech at U.S. Cyber Command Inter-Agency Legal Conference, Sept. 18, 2012), *available at* http://opiniojuris.org/2012/09/19/ harold-koh-on-international-law-in-cyberspace/.
96. Wales Summit Declaration, Issued by the Heads of State and Government Participating in the Meeting of the North Atlantic Council in Wales, ¶ 72 (Sept. 5, 2014), http:// www.nato.int/cps/po/natohq/official_texts_112964.htm.
97. EUR. COMM'N, CYBERSECURITY STRATEGY OF THE EUROPEAN UNION (2013), http://eeas.europa.eu/policies/eu-cyber-security/cybsec_comm_en.pdf.
98. Qi Jianguo, "*Qian Suo Weiyou De Da Bianju: Dui Shijie Zhanlue Xingshi He Woguo Anquan Huanjing De Renshi Yu Sikao,*" QIUSHI LILUNWANG, Jan. 21, 2013, http://www. qstheory.cn/zywz/201301/t20130121_207019.htm (quoted in Nigel Inkster, *Conflict Foretold: America and China,* SURVIVAL: GLOBAL POLITICS AND STRATEGY, Oct. 1,

2013, https://www.iiss.org/en/publications/survival/sections/2013-94b0/survival-global-politics-and-strategy-october-november-2013-b1d0/55-5-02-inkster-8a63).

99. U.S.-China Economic & Security Review Comm'n, Report on the Capability of the People's Republic of China to Conduct Cyber Warfare and Computer Network Exploitation 24 (Oct. 2009).

100. Id.

101. James Mulvenon, The PLA and Information Warfare, in The People's Liberation Army in the Information Age 184–85 (1999), http://www.rand.org/content/dam/rand/pubs/conf_proceedings/CF145/CF145.chap9.pdf.

102. Id.

103. Protocol Additional to the Geneva Conventions of 12 August 1949, and Relating to the Protection of Victims of International Armed Conflicts (Protocol 1), art. 51(5)(b), June 8, 1977, 1125 U.N.T.S. 3, https://www.icrc.org/applic/ihl/ihl.nsf/7c4d08d9b28 7a42141256739003e636b/f6c8b9fee14a77fdc125641e0052b079.

104. Jean-Marie Henckaerts & Louise Doswald-Beck, Customary International Humanitarian Law 46, Rule 14 (2005), http://www.icrc.org/eng/assets/files/other/customary-international-humanitarian-law-i-icrc-eng.pdf.

105. Adam Segal, China, International Law, and Cyberspace, Council on Foreign Relations, Oct. 2, 2012, http://blogs.cfr.org/asia/2012/10/02/china-international-law-and-cyberspace/.

106. Protocol Additional to the Geneva Conventions of 12 August 1949, supra note 103, at art. 48.

107. Henckaerts & Doswald-Beck, Customary International Humanitarian Law, Rule 1, supra note 104, at 3–8.

108. Protocol Additional to the Geneva Conventions of 12 August 1949, supra note 103, at art. 51.

109. Henckaerts & Doswald-Beck, Customary International Humanitarian Law, Rules 11 and 12, supra note 104, at 37–43.

110. Adam Segal, China, International Law, and Cyberspace, Council on Foreign Relations, Oct. 2, 2012, http://blogs.cfr.org/asia/2012/10/02/china-international-law-and-cyberspace/.

111. Stephen Chen, Code Blue for China's Red Army, S. China Morning Post, Aug. 1, 2011, http://www.scmp.com/article/975063/code-blue-chinas-red-army.

112. Sun Tzu, The Art of War.

113. Basics of International Law for Modern Soldiers 3 (Zhao Peiying ed., 1996), quoted in Jonathan G. Odom, A China in the Bull Shop? Comparing the Rhetoric of a Rising China with the Reality of the International Law of the Sea, 17 Ocean & Coastal L.J. 224 (2012).

114. John Pomfret, China Ponders New Rules of "Unrestricted War," Wash. Post, Aug. 8, 1999.

115. Id.

116. See, e.g., Nuclear Control Institute, China's non-Proliferation Words vs. China's Nuclear Proliferation Deeds, http://www.nci.org/i/ib12997.htm.

117. See, e.g., Ron Synovitz, South Korea: Debate Heats Up over Seoul's Nuclear Admissions, Radio Free Europe, Sept. 9, 2004, http://www.rferl.org/content/article/1054764.html; Chen Kane, Stephanie C. Lieggi, & Miles A. Pomper, Time for Leadership; South Korea and Nuclear Nonproliferation, Arms Control Today, Mar. 3, 2011, https://www.armscontrol.org/act/2011_03/SouthKorea#4; Philip Iglauer, Nuclear Weapons for South Korea, The Diplomat, Aug. 14, 2014, http://thediplomat.com/2014/08/nuclear-weapons-for-south-korea/.

118. *See, e.g.,* John W. Garver, *Is China Playing a Dual Game in Iran?,* 34 WASH. Q. 75 (Winter 2011).

119. *Id.* at 83.

120. *Id.* at 76.

121. *Id.*

122. KENNETH KATZMAN, CONG. RESEARCH SERV., RS20871, IRAN SANCTIONS 36 (2015), https://fas.org/sgp/crs/mideast/RS20871.pdf.

123. Garver, *supra* note 118, at 77.

124. *Id.* at 79.

125. *Id.*

126. Michael Singh & Jacqueline Newmyer Deal, *China's Iranian Gambit,* FOREIGN POLICY, Oct. 31, 2011, http://www.washingtoninstitute.org/policy-analysis/view/chinas-iranian-gambit.

127. *See, e.g.,* Press Release, U.N. Security Council, *Security Council Imposes Sanctions on Iran for Failure to Halt Uranium Enrichment, Unanimously Adopting Resolution 1737* (Dec. 23, 2006), http://www.un.org/News/Press/docs/2006/sc8928.doc.htm.

128. *See, e.g.,* Press Release, U.N. Security Council, *Security Council Imposes Additional Sanctions on Iran* (June 9, 2010), http://www.un.org/News/Press/docs/2010/sc9948.doc.htm.

129. DAVID ALBRIGHT, MARK DUBOWITZ, ORDE KITTRIE, LEONARD SPECTOR, & MICHAEL YAFFE, U.S. NONPROLIFERATION STRATEGY FOR THE CHANGING MIDDLE EAST (2013), http://isis-online.org/uploads/isis-reports/documents/FinalReport.pdf. This and the following six paragraphs draw heavily from that book, of which this author was the principal coauthor.

130. Wyn Q. Bowen, Ian J. Stewart, & Daniel Salisbury, *Engaging China in Proliferation Prevention,* BULL. OF ATOMIC SCIENTISTS, Oct. 29, 2013, http://thebulletin.org/engaging-china-proliferation-prevention.

131. Ian J. Stewart, Andrea Stricker, & David Albright, *Chinese Citizen's Involvement in the Supply of MKS Pressure Transducers to Iran: Preventing a Reoccurrence,* INST. FOR SCI. & INT'L SEC., http://isis-online.org/uploads/isis-reports/documents/MKS_China_30Apr2014-final.pdf.

132. *Id.*

133. John Pomfret, *U.S. Says Chinese Businesses and Banks Are Bypassing U.N. Sanctions Against Iran,* WASH. POST, Oct. 18, 2010, http://www.washingtonpost.com/wp-dyn/content/article/2010/10/17/AR2010101703364_pf.html.

134. *Id.*

135. *Id.*

136. Joby Warrick, *Nuclear Ruse: Posing as Toymaker, Chinese Merchant Allegedly Sought U.S. Technology for Iran,* WASH. POST, Aug. 11, 2012, http://www.washingtonpost.com/world/national-security/nuclear-ruse-posing-as-toymaker-chinese-merchant-allegedly-sought-us-technology-for-iran/2012/08/11/f1c66d9a-e265-11e1-ae7f-d2a13e249eb2_story.html.

137. *Id.*

138. *Id.*

139. *Id.*

140. *Id.*

141. *Id.*

142. *Id.*

143. Press Release, U.S. Att'ys Office, Dist. of Mass., *Indicted Chinese National Lands at Boston's Logan Airport to Face Federal Prosecution for Supplying Iran with Nuclear*

Production Parts (Dec. 5, 2014), http://www.fbi.gov/boston/press-releases/2014/indicted-chinese-national-lands-at-bostons-logan-airport-to-face-federal-prosecution-for-supplying-iran-with-nuclear-production-parts.

144. Erik Larson, *Chinese Man Accepts U.S. Detention on Iran Export Charge*, BLOOMBERG.COM, Dec. 8, 2014, http://www.bloomberg.com/news/articles/2014-12-08/chinese-man-accepts-u-s-detention-on-iran-export-charge.

145. Press Release, U.S. Att'ys Office, *Indicted Chinese National*, *supra* note 143.

146. *Id.*

147. Indictment, *United States v. Sihai Cheng*, No. 13-CR-10332 (Dist. Mass., Nov. 21, 2013), available via www.pacer.gov and *available at* http://uschinatradewar.com/files/2014/04/CHENG-INDICTMENT.pdf.

148. Press Release, U.S. Att'y's Office, *Indicted Chinese National*, *supra* note 143.

149. Ian J. Stewart, Andrea Stricker, & David Albright, *Chinese Citizen's Involvement in the Supply of MKS Pressure Transducers to Iran: Preventing a Reoccurrence*, INST. FOR SCI. & INT'L SEC., http://isis-online.org/uploads/isis-reports/documents/MKS_China_30Apr2014-final.pdf.

150. *Id.*

151. *Id.*

152. Press Release, U.S. Att'ys Office, *Indicted Chinese National*, *supra* note 143; Stewart, Stricker, & Albright, *supra* note 149.

153. Press Release, U.S. Att'ys Office, *Indicted Chinese National*, *supra* note 143.

154. Stewart, Stricker, & Albright, *supra* note 149.

155. *Id.*

156. *Id.*

157. *Id.*

158. William Maclean & Ben Blanchard, *Chinese Trader Accused of Busting Iran Missile Embargo*, REUTERS, Mar. 1, 2013, http://www.reuters.com/article/2013/03/01/us-china-iran-trader-idUSBRE9200BI20130301.

159. Senate Foreign Relations Committee Hearing on The Civil Nuclear Agreement with China: Balancing the Potential Risks and Rewards, Fed. News Serv. transcript (May 12, 2015).

160. U.S. Dep't of State Bureau of Nonproliferation, Imposition of Nonproliferation Measures Against Fourteen Foreign Entities, Including Ban on U.S. Government Procurement, 69 Fed. Reg. 58,212–58,213 (Sept. 29, 2004), *available at* http://www.gpo.gov/fdsys/pkg/FR-2004-09-29/html/04-21790.htm.

161. Press Release, U.S. Dep't of the Treasury, *Treasury Designates Iranian Proliferation Network and Identifies New Aliases* (Apr. 7, 2009), http://www.treasury.gov/press-center/press-releases/Pages/tg84.aspx.

162. *Id.*; Additional Designation of Persons and Identification of New Aliases Pursuant to Executive Order 13382, 74 Fed. Reg. 19635–19636 (Apr. 29, 2009), http://www.gpo.gov/fdsys/pkg/FR-2009-04-29/html/E9-9771.htm.

163. Indictment, New York v. Li Fang Wei and LIMMT, N.Y. State Supreme Court, http://graphics8.nytimes.com/packages/pdf/nyregion/08INDICT.pdf.

164. John Eligon & William J. Broad, *Indictment Says Banned Materials Sold to Iran*, N.Y. TIMES, Apr. 8, 2009, http://www.nytimes.com/2009/04/08/nyregion/08indict.html?pagewanted=all&_r=0; indictment *available at* http://graphics8.nytimes.com/packages/pdf/nyregion/08INDICT.pdf.

165. Daniel Salisbury & Ian J. Stewart, *Li Fang Wei (Karl Lee) Proliferation Case Study Series*, at 22–23 (Project Alpha, Kings College London, May 19, 2014), http://npsglobal.org/eng/images/stories/pdf/karllee.pdf.

166. Eligon & Broad, *supra* note 164.

167. *Id.*

168. Inst. for Sci. & Int'l Sec., State Department Cables: United States Pressures China over Limmt, to No Avail (Feb. 3, 2011), http://www.isisnucleariran.org/assets/pdf/State_cables_limmit_3Feb2011.pdf.

169. Dep't of State, Public Notice 8183, Bureau of Int'l Sec. & Nonproliferation Imposition of Missile Sanctions on Two Chinese Foreign Persons, 78 Fed. Reg. 9768 (Feb. 11, 2013) (designations of Karl Lee and related entities), http://www.gpo.gov/fdsys/pkg/FR-2013-02-11/pdf/2013-03030.pdf.

170. Maclean & Blanchard, *supra* note 158.

171. Devlin Barrett & Jay Solomon, *U.S. Offers Bounty for Chinese Businessman Linked to Iran Missiles*, Wall St. J., Apr. 29, 2014, http://online.wsj.com/news/articles/SB10001424052702304163604579531543485420528.

172. Press Release, U.S. Dep't of Justice, *"Karl Lee" Charged in Manhattan Federal Court with Using a Web of Front Companies to Evade U.S. Sanctions* (Apr. 29, 2014), http://www.fbi.gov/newyork/press-releases/2014/karl-lee-charged-in-manhattan-federal-court-with-using-a-web-of-front-companies-to-evade-u.s.-sanctions.

173. Sealed Superseding Indictment, United States v. Li Fangwei (S.D.N.Y. Apr. 28, 2014), available via www.pacer.gov.

174. U.S. Dep't of State, *Transnational Organized Crime Rewards Program: Li Fangwei*, http://www.state.gov/j/inl/tocrewards/c62805.htm.

175. *Id.*

176. State Dep't Bureau of Int'l Sec. & Nonproliferation, Imposition of Nonproliferation Measures Against Foreign Persons, Including a Ban on U.S. Government Procurement, 79 Fed. Reg. 78,548–78,549 (Dec. 30, 2014), http://www.gpo.gov/fdsys/pkg/FR-2014-12-30/pdf/2014-30564.pdf.

177. Maclean & Blanchard, *supra* note 158.

178. *Id.*

179. Bowen, Stewart, & Salisbury, *supra* note 130.

180. *Id.*

181. Ben Blanchard, *China "Resolutely Opposes" U.S. Sanctions on Missile Parts Supplier*, Reuters, Apr. 30, 2014, http://www.reuters.com/article/2014/04/30/us-china-usa-iran-idUSBREA3T07720140430.

182. *Id.*

183. Basics of International Law for Modern Soldiers 3 (Zhao Peiying ed., 1996), quoted in Jonathan G. Odom, *A China in the Bull Shop? Comparing the Rhetoric of a Rising China with the Reality of the International Law of the Sea*, 17 Ocean & Coastal L.J. 224 (2012).

184. Bowen, Stewart, & Salisbury, *supra* note 130.

185. *See, e.g.*, Shirley A. Kan, Cong. Research. Serv., RL 31555, China and Proliferation of Weapons of Mass Destruction and Missiles: Policy Issues (2015), http://fas.org/sgp/crs/nuke/RL31555.pdf.

186. *See, e.g., id.*

187. Bowen, Stewart, & Salisbury, *supra* note 130.

188. *Id.*

189. Senate Foreign Relations Committee Hearing on The Civil Nuclear Agreement with China: Balancing the Potential Risks and Rewards, Fed. News Serv. transcript (May 12, 2015).

190. *Id.*

191. *Id.*

192. *Id.*

193. *Id.*

194. *Id.*

195. *Id.*

196. *Id.*

197. Jeff Stein, *How China Helped Iran Go Nuclear*, Newsweek, July 14, 2015, http://www.newsweek.com/2015/07/31/iran-nuclear-deal-china-karl-lee-353591.html.

198. Jeff Stein, *How China Helped Iran Go Nuclear*, Newsweek, July 14, 2015, http://www.newsweek.com/2015/07/31/iran-nuclear-deal-china-karl-lee-353591.html.

199. For example, the 2011 Report to Congress of the U.S.-China Economic and Security Review Commission, an arm of the U.S. government, stated that "China's government or military appeared to sponsor numerous computer network intrusions throughout 2011." U.S.-China Economic and Security Review Commission, 2011 Report to Congress 9 (Nov. 2011), http://www.uscc.gov/annual_report/2011/annual_report_full_11.pdf. Yet despite the Chinese government or military's apparent sponsorship, the IC was unable to actually attribute many of the breaches to a state sponsor. *See, e.g.*, Office of the Nat'l Counterintelligence Exec., Foreign Spies Stealing U.S. Economic Secrets in Cyberspace (Oct. 2011) ("US corporations and cyber security specialists also have reported an onslaught of computer network intrusions originating from Internet Protocol (IP) addresses in China ... but the IC has not been able to attribute many of these private sector data breaches to a state sponsor.").

200. Bowen, Stewart, & Salisbury, *supra* note 130.

201. *Military and Paramilitary Activities In and Against Nicaragua* (Nicaragua v. United States of America), 1986 I.C.J. 14 (June 27), http://www.icj-cij.org/docket/?p1=3&p2=3&case=70&code=nus&p3=90.

202. *Id.* The threshold was somewhat lower in the 1999 *Tadic* case opinion of the Appeals Chamber of the International Criminal Tribunal for the Former Yugoslavia. However, in its 2007 judgment on genocide in Bosnia, the International Court of Justice applied the "effective control" test enunciated in *Nicaragua* and rejected the test propounded in *Tadic*. Antonio Cassese, *The Nicaragua and Tadic Tests Revisited in Light of the ICJ Judgment on Genocide in Bosnia*, 18 Eur. J. Int'l L. 649 (2007), http://www.ejil.org/pdfs/18/4/233.pdf; Jens David Ohlin, *Control Matters: Ukraine & Russia and the Downing of Flight 17*, Opinio Juris, July 23, 2014, http://opiniojuris.org/2014/07/23/control-matters-ukraine-russia-downing-flight-17/.

203. David Albright, Mark Dubowitz, Orde Kittrie, Leonard Spector, & Michael Yaffe, U.S. Nonproliferation Strategy for the Changing Middle East (2013), http://isis-online.org/uploads/isis-reports/documents/FinalReport.pdf. This and the following four paragraphs draw heavily from that book, of which this author was the principal coauthor.

204. Comprehensive Iran Sanctions, Accountability, and Divestment Act of 2010, 22 U.S.C. §§ 8501 et seq. (2010), http://uscode.house.gov/view.xhtml?path=/prelim@title22/chapter92&edition=prelim.

205. Comprehensive Iran Sanctions, Accountability, and Divestment Act of 2010, § 303, 22 U.S.C. §§ 8543. (2010), http://uscode.house.gov/view.xhtml?path=/prelim@title22/chapter92&edition=prelim.

206. *Id.* § 301.

207. *Id.* § 303.

208. *Id.*

209. *Id.* § 301.

210. Ian J. Stewart & Daniel B. Salisbury, *Wanted: Karl Lee*, THE DIPLOMAT, May 22, 2014, http://thediplomat.com/2014/05/wanted-karl-lee/.

211. Michella Arrouas, *Wanted: Li Fangwei, Alias Karl Lee; Reward: $5 Million*, TIME, Apr. 30, 2014, http://time.com/82221/karl-lee-li-fangwei-wanted-reward/.

212. Press Release, U.S. Dep't of Justice, *"Karl Lee" Charged in Manhattan Federal Court*, *supra* note 172.

213. Aaron Arnold, *Big Banks and Their Game of Risk*, BULL. OF ATOMIC SCIENTISTS, Jan. 20, 2015, http://thebulletin.org/big-banks-and-their-game-risk7941.

214. Press Release, U.S. Dep't of Justice, *"Karl Lee" Charged in Manhattan Federal Court*, *supra* note 172.

215. *Id.*

216. *Id.*

217. *Id.*

218. *Id.*

219. Stefan Bergan, *Karl Lee—Too Much Trouble*, PROLIFERATION POST, June 4, 2014, http://theproliferationpost.blogspot.com/2014/06/karl-lee-too-much-trouble.html.

220. Eric W. Orts, *The Rule of Law in China*, 34 VAND. J. TRANSNAT'L L. 58 (2001).

221. Benjamin L. Liebman, *Assessing China's Legal Reforms*, 23 COLUM. J. ASIAN L. 18 (2009).

222. STEPHEN OLSON & CLYDE PRESTOWITZ, THE EVOLVING ROLE OF CHINA IN INTERNATIONAL INSTITUTIONS (report prepared for the U.S.-China Economic and Security Review Commission, Jan. 2011), http://origin.www.uscc.gov/sites/default/files/Research/TheEvolvingRoleofChinainInternationalInstitutions.pdf.

223. *Id.*

224. *Id.*

225. *See* INT'L LAW STUDENTS ASS'N, PHILIP C. JESSUP INTERNATIONAL LAW MOOT COURT COMPETITION, http://www.ilsa.org/jessuphome.

226. Author interview of Carol Kalinoski (Wash., D.C., Apr. 10, 2014).

227. *Id.*

228. *Id.*

229. *See* "Top 30 Team Memorial Scores," http://www.ilsa.org/jessup/jessup14/2014%20Top%2030%20Team%20Memorial%20Rankings.pdf.

230. WAYNE M. MORRISON, CONG. RESEARCH SERV., RL33536, CHINA-U.S. TRADE ISSUES (2015), https://fas.org/sgp/crs/row/RL33536.pdf.

231. *Id.*

232. *Id.*

233. JUAN C. ZARATE, TREASURY'S WAR 387 (2013).

234. *Id.*

235. MORRISON, *supra* note 230.

236. ZARATE, *supra* note 233, at 419.

237. *Id.* at 390.

238. Keith Bradsher, *Amid Tension, China Blocks Vital Exports to Japan*, N.Y. TIMES, Sept. 22, 2010, http://www.nytimes.com/2010/09/23/business/global/23rare.html?pagewanted=all.

239. *China Denies Japan Rare-Earth Ban Amid Diplomatic Row*, BLOOMBERG NEWS, Sept. 23, 2010, http://www.washingtonpost.com/wp-dyn/content/article/2010/09/23/AR2010092300277_pf.html.

240. Bradsher, *supra* note 238.

241. *Id.*

242. *China Denies Japan Rare-Earth Ban*, *supra* note 239.

243. Paul Krugman, *Rare and Foolish*, N.Y. Times, Oct. 17, 2010, http://www.nytimes.com/2010/10/18/opinion/18krugman.html.
244. Bradsher, *supra* note 238.
245. *China Blocked Exports of Rare Earth Metals to Japan, Traders Claim*, AFP, Sept. 24, 2010, http://www.telegraph.co.uk/finance/china-business/8022484/China-blocked-exports-of-rare-earth-metals-to-Japan-traders-claim.html.
246. WTO Dispute Settlement, *China—Measures Related to the Exportation of Rare Earths, Tungsten and Molybdenum*, Dispute DS431 (adopted Aug. 29, 2014), https://www.wto.org/english/tratop_e/dispu_e/cases_e/ds431_e.htm.
247. *See, e.g.*, Lesley Stahl, *Modern Life's Devices Under China's Grip?*, CBS News, Mar. 22, 2015, http://www.cbsnews.com/news/rare-earth-elements-china-monopoly-60-minutes-lesley-stahl/ (estimating 90 percent); Chuin-Wei Yap, *China Ends Rare-Earth Minerals Export Quotas*, Wall St. J., Jan. 5, 2015, http://www.wsj.com/articles/china-ends-rare-earth-minerals-export-quotas-1420441285 (estimating 86 percent); Brad Plumer, *China No Longer Has a Stranglehold on the World's Supply of Rare Earth Minerals*, Vox, Oct. 22, 2014, http://www.vox.com/2014/10/22/7031243/china-grip-rare-earth-metals-supply-weakening (estimating 70 percent).
248. Bradsher, *supra* note 238.
249. Inspector General, U.S. Dep't of Defense, Procedures to Ensure Sufficient Rare Earth Elements for the Defense Industrial Base Need Improvement (July 3, 2014), http://www.cbsnews.com/htdocs/pdf/00_2015/DODIG-2014-091.pdf.
250. The Science of Military Strategy 79 (Peng Guangqian & Yao Youzhi, eds., 2005), quoted in Larry M. Wortzel, *The Chinese People's Liberation Army and Information Warfare*, U.S. Army War College Strategic Studies Inst. 38 (2014), http://www.strategicstudiesinstitute.army.mil/pdffiles/PUB1191.pdf.
251. Dean Cheng, *Winning Without Fighting: Chinese Legal Warfare*, Heritage Foundation Backgrounder, May 18, 2012, http://www.heritage.org/research/reports/2012/05/winning-without-fighting-chinese-legal-warfare.
252. *Id.*
253. *Id.*
254. *Id.*
255. *Id.*
256. *Id.*
257. *Id.*
258. *Id.*
259. *See, e.g.*, Ewen MacAskill, *George Bush Calls Off Trip to Switzerland*, Guardian, Feb. 6, 2011.
260. Jack Goldsmith, The Terror Presidency: Law and Judgment Inside the Bush Administration 60–61 (2007).
261. *Id.*; Jim Yardley, *Spain Seeks to Curb Law Allowing Judges to Pursue Cases Globally*, N.Y. Times, Feb. 10, 2014, http://www.nytimes.com/2014/02/11/world/europe/spanish-legislators-seek-new-limits-on-universal-jurisdiction-law.html; Richard Bernstein, *Belgium Rethinks Its Prosecutorial Zeal*, N.Y. Times, Apr. 1, 2003, http://www.nytimes.com/2003/04/01/world/belgium-rethinks-its-prosecutorial-zeal.html.
262. The following paragraphs were informed in significant part by Dean Cheng's excellent and thought-provoking list of recommendations at Dean Cheng, *Winning Without Fighting: Chinese Legal Warfare*, Heritage Foundation Backgrounder, May 18, 2012, at 9–11, http://www.heritage.org/research/reports/2012/05/winning-without-fighting-chinese-legal-warfare.

263. Cheng, *id.*

264. *Id.* at 9.

265. *Id.* at 10.

266. *Id.*

267. *Id.*

268. *The Bull Run to China*, Businessweek, Dec. 13, 1992, http://www.bloomberg.com/bw/stories/1992-12-13/the-bull-run-to-china.

269. Sina Corporation, NASDAQ, http://www.nasdaq.com/symbol/sina/stock-report; Blaze Fabry, *Chinese Stocks in the World*, Chinavestor, Mar. 14, 2012, http://www.chinavestor.com/knowledge-base/adr-market/73653-chinese-stocks-in-the-world.html.

270. Minxin Pei, *Alibaba's IPO and the Hypocrisy in U.S.-China Economic Relations*, Fortune, Sept. 12, 2014, http://fortune.com/2014/09/12/alibaba-ipo-us-china/.

271. Organization for International Investment, Foreign Direct Investment in the United States: 2014 Report, at 9, http://www.ofii.org/sites/default/files/FDIUS2014.pdf.

272. Juro Osawa, *Lenovo Completes Motorola Acquisition*, Wall St. J., Oct. 30, 2014, http://www.wsj.com/articles/lenovo-completes-motorola-acquisition-1414665138.

273. Euan Rocha, *CNOOC Closes $15.1 Billion Acquisition of Canada's Nexen*, Reuters, Feb. 25, 2013, http://www.reuters.com/article/2013/02/25/us-nexen-cnooc-idUSBRE91O1A420130225.

274. Dean Cheng, *Winning Without Fighting: Chinese Legal Warfare*, Heritage Foundation Backgrounder, May 18, 2012, at http://www.heritage.org/research/reports/2012/05/winning-without-fighting-chinese-legal-warfare.

275. *Id.*

276. *Id.* at 10–11.

277. *See, e.g.,* Steven Lee Myers, *All in Favor of This Target, Say Yes, Si, Oui, Ja*, N.Y. Times, Apr. 25, 1999.

278. Philip Bobbitt, Terror and Consent 503–504 (2008).

CHAPTER 5

1. *See, e.g.,* Claude Bowers, My Mission to Spain: Watching the Rehearsal for World War II (1954) (Bowers was U.S. ambassador to Spain from 1933 to 1939; the Spanish Civil War was fought from 1936 to 1939).

2. Mahmoud Abbas, *The Long Overdue Palestinian State*, N.Y. Times, May 16, 2011, http://www.nytimes.com/2011/05/17/opinion/17abbas.html.

3. *Id.*

4. Penny L. Mellie, *Hamas and Hezbollah: A Comparison of Tactics*, in Back to Basics: A Study of the Second Lebanon War and Operation CAST LEAD (Lt. Col. Scott Farquhar ed., 2009).

5. Anne Barnard & Jodi Rudoren, *Israel Says That Hamas Uses Civilian Shields, Reviving Debate*, N.Y. Times, July 23, 2014, http://www.nytimes.com/2014/07/24/world/middleeast/israel-says-hamas-is-using-civilians-as-shields-in-gaza.html?_r=0.

6. The Palestinian Authority was established by the Agreement on the Gaza Strip and the Jericho Area, which was entered into on May 4, 1994, by the government of Israel and the Palestine Liberation Organization. Report of the S.C., U.N. Doc. A/49/180, S/1994/727 (1994), http://unispal.un.org/UNISPAL.NSF/0/15AF20B2F7F41905852560A7004AB2D5.

7. Jim Zanotti, Cong. Research Serv. RL34074, The Palestinians: Background and U.S. Relations (2014), http://fas.org/sgp/crs/mideast/RL34074.pdf.

8. *Id.*

9. *Id.*

10. *Id.*

11. *Palestinian Authority Officially Changes Name to 'State of Palestine,'* HAARETZ, Jan. 5, 2013, http://www.haaretz.com/news/middle-east/palestinian-authority-officially-changes-name-to-state-of-palestine.premium-1.492065.

12. G.A. Res. 67/19 (Dec. 4, 2012), http://www.un.org/ga/search/view_doc.asp?symbol=A/RES/67/19.

13. Abbas, *supra* note 2.

14. *Abbas to Act Against Israel at UN if Peace Talks Fail,* MA'AN NEWS AGENCY, May 12, 2013, http://www.maannews.net/eng/ViewDetails.aspx?ID=653791.

15. *Palestinian Authority Applies for Full UN Membership,* UNITED NATIONS, Sept. 23, 2011, http://www.unmultimedia.org/radio/english/2011/09/palestinian-authority-applies-for-full-un-membership/.

16. *See, e.g., U.S. Dep't of State, Foreign Operations, & Related Programs, Subcomm. of the House Appropriations Comm.: FY2015 Budget Hearing—Request for the United Nations and International Organizations* (testimony of Ambassador Samantha Power), Fed. News Serv. transcript (Apr. 2, 2014) (referencing "our firm opposition to any and all unilateral actions in the international arena, including on Palestinian statehood, that circumvent or prejudge the very outcomes that can only come about through a negotiated settlement" and asserting that "every time the Palestinians have sought to make a move on a U.N. agency, a treaty, et cetera, we have opposed it.").

17. Alan Baker, *Palestinian Deception and the Unwarranted Trust of the West: The Case of Palestinian Accession to International Conventions,* JERUSALEM CTR. FOR PUB. AFF., Apr. 17, 2014, http://jcpa.org/article/palestinian-deception/.

18. *Israeli-Palestinian Interim Agreement on the West Bank and the Gaza Strip* (Wash., D.C., Sept. 28, 1995), http://www.mfa.gov.il/mfa/foreignpolicy/peace/guide/pages/the%20israeli-palestinian%20interim%20agreement.aspx.

19. *See, e.g.,* Rick Richman, *"Palestine" Does Not Qualify as a "State,"* COMMENTARY, Nov. 13, 2012, http://www.commentarymagazine.com/2012/11/13/palestine-does-not-qualify-as-a-state/; Brett D. Schaefer, Steven Groves, & James Phillips, *Palestinian Intent to Accede to 15 Treaties and U.S. Response,* ISSUE BRIEF (Apr. 30, 2014), http://www.heritage.org/research/reports/2014/04/palestinian-intent-to-accede-to-15-treaties-and-us-response.

20. *See, e.g.,* Alex Spillius & Adrian Blomfield, *Barack Obama Tells Mahmoud Abbas US Will Veto Palestinian Statehood Bid,* THE TELEGRAPH (U.K.), Sept. 22, 2011, http://www.telegraph.co.uk/news/worldnews/barackobama/8780859/Barack-Obama-tells-Mahmoud-Abbas-US-will-veto-Palestinian-statehood-bid.html.

21. *General Assembly Grants Palestine Non-Member Observer State Status at UN,* U.N. NEWS CENTRE, Nov. 29, 2012, http://www.un.org/apps/news/story.asp?NewsID=43640#.UjZQDRYn8_s.

22. Ethan Bronner & Christine Hauser, *UN Assembly, in Blow to U.S., Elevates Status of Palestine,* N.Y. TIMES, Nov. 29, 2012, http://www.nytimes.com/2012/11/30/world/middleeast/Palestinian-Authority-United-Nations-Israel.html?pagewanted=all&_r=0.

23. G.A. Res. 67/19, U.N. Doc. A/RES/67/19 (Dec. 4, 2012), http://unispal.un.org/UNISPAL.NSF/0/19862D03C564FA2C85257ACB004EE69B.

24. For example, the PLO has had permanent observer status at the United Nations since 1974. JIM ZANOTTI, CONG. RESEARCH SERV., RS22967, U.S. FOREIGN AID TO THE PALESTINIANS 27 (2013), http://assets.opencrs.com/rpts/RS22967_20130930.pdf.

25. *General Conference Admits Palestine as UNESCO Member*, UNESCO MEDIA SERVS., Oct. 31, 2011, http://www.unesco.org/new/en/media-services/single-view/news/general_conference_admits_palestine_as_unesco_member_state/#.U4e9SF5ORY4.

26. *Id.*

27. Pub. L. 101-246, title IV, § 414, 104 Stat. 70 (Feb. 16, 1990), http://www.gpo.gov/fdsys/pkg/USCODE-2009-title22/html/USCODE-2009-title22-chap7-subchapXVI-sec287e.htm. In addition, Pub. L. 103-236, title IV, § 410, 108 Stat. 454 (Apr. 30, 1994), provides that: "The United States shall not make any voluntary or assessed contribution—

    (1). to any affiliated organization of the United Nations which grants full membership as a state to any organization or group that does not have the internationally recognized attributes of statehood, or

    (2). to the United Nations, if the United Nations grants full membership as a state in the United Nations to any organization or group that does not have the internationally recognized attributes of statehood, during any period in which such membership is effective." *See* 27 U.S.C. § 287e (2009), http://www.gpo.gov/fdsys/pkg/USCODE-2009-title22/html/USCODE-2009-title22-chap7-subchapXVI-sec287e.htm.

28. Caitlin Dewey, *Does It Matter That the U.S. Just Lost Its Vote in UNESCO?*, WASH. POST, Nov. 8, 2013, http://www.washingtonpost.com/blogs/worldviews/wp/2013/11/08/does-it-matter-that-the-u-s-just-lost-its-vote-in-unesco/.

29. *Id.*

30. *U.S. Dep't of State, Foreign Operations, & Related Programs, Subcomm. of the House Appropriations Comm.: FY2015 Budget Hearing—Request for the United Nations and International Organizations* (testimony of Ambassador Samantha Power), Fed. News Serv. transcript (Apr. 2, 2014).

31. *See, e.g.*, Edith M. Lederer, *Palestinians Hold Off on UN Agency Membership*, AP, May 20, 2013, http://bigstory.ap.org/article/palestinians-hold-un-agency-membership.

32. Joe Lauria, *PLO Official Says Palestinians Will Seek to Join International Court*, WALL ST. J., Apr. 29, 2014, http://www.wsj.com/news/articles/SB10001424052702304893404579532062791271786; UNITED NATIONS, FUNDS, PROGRAMMES, SPECIALIZED AGENCIES, AND OTHERS, http://www.un.org/en/sections/about-un/funds-programmes-specialized-agencies-and-others/index.html.

33. Joe Lauria, *PLO Official Says Palestinians Will Seek to Join International Court*, WALL ST. J., Apr. 29, 2014, http://www.wsj.com/news/articles/SB10001424052702304893404579532062791271786; UNITED NATIONS, FUNDS, PROGRAMMES, SPECIALIZED AGENCIES, AND OTHERS, *supra* note 32.

34. *See, e.g.*, Alex Spillius, *No UN Consensus Over Palestinian Bid for Statehood*, THE TELEGRAPH (U.K.), Nov. 8, 2011, http://www.telegraph.co.uk/news/worldnews/middleeast/palestinianauthority/8877650/No-UN-consensus-over-Palestinian-bid-for-statehood.html.

35. Brett D. Schaefer, Steven Groves, & James Phillips, *Palestinian Intent to Accede to 15 Treaties and U.S. Response*, HERITAGE FOUNDATION, Apr. 30, 2014, http://www.heritage.org/research/reports/2014/04/palestinian-intent-to-accede-to-15-treaties-and-us-response#_ftn6.

36. *Id.*

37. *Id.*

38. *Id.*

39. *See, e.g.*, *Abbas Moves for Palestine to Join 18 International Treaties*, MA'AN NEWS AGENCY, Jan. 1, 2015, http://www.maannews.com/eng/ViewDetails.aspx?id=751160 (listing the treaties to which the PA applied on Dec. 31, 2014).

40. *See, e.g., id.*
41. *See, e.g., id.*
42. UNITED NATIONS, FUNDS, PROGRAMMES, SPECIALIZED AGENCIES, AND OTHERS, *supra* note 32.
43. INT'L ATOMIC ENERGY AGENCY, PROCESS OF BECOMING A MEMBER STATE OF THE IAEA, https://www.iaea.org/about/policy/process-becoming-member-state-iaea (last visited Mar. 28, 2015).
44. *Id.*
45. JIM ZANOTTI, CONG. RESEARCH SERV., RS22967, U.S. FOREIGN AID TO THE PALESTINIANS (2014), https://fas.org/sgp/crs/mideast/RS22967.pdf.
46. *Cash-Strapped Palestinian Gov't Adopts Emergency Budget*, REUTERS, Mar. 17, 2015, http://www.reuters.com/article/2015/03/17/us-israel-palestinians-budget-idUSKBN0MD1U620150317.
47. *Palestinian PM Says Freed US Aid to Help Ease Crisis*, REUTERS, Mar. 24, 2012, http://www.trust.org/item/20120324123500-y9lw0?view=print.
48. ZANOTTI, *supra* note 45, at 29.
49. Sara Sorcher, *Clinton Overrules Republican Lawmakers' Hold on Palestinian Aid*, NAT'L J., Apr. 11, 2012, http://www.nationaljournal.com/nationalsecurity/clinton-overrules-republican-lawmaker-s-hold-on-palestinian-aid-20120411.
50. Letter from Rep. Ileana Ros-Lehtinen, Chair of the House Committee on Foreign Affairs, to Rajiv Shah, Administrator of the U.S. Agency for International Development (Mar. 23, 2012), http://assets.nationaljournal.com/pdf/MX-5111N_20120323_173148.pdf.
51. Department of State, Foreign Operations, and Related Programs Appropriations Act § 7086 (2012), (Pub. L. 112-74, Div. I), http://www.gpo.gov/fdsys/pkg/PLAW-112publ74/pdf/PLAW-112publ74.pdf.
52. ZANOTTI, *supra* note 45.
53. *Israel Withholds Palestinian Funds after UN Vote*, REUTERS, Dec. 2, 2012, http://www.reuters.com/article/2012/12/02/us-palestinians-israel-funds-idUSBRE8B104E20121202.
54. *Id.*; *Israel Vows to Withhold $400M in Tax Revenues from Palestinians over Statehood Drive*, REUTERS, Dec. 12, 2012, http://worldnews.nbcnews.com/_news/ 2012/ 12/12/15858391-israel-vows-to-withhold-400m-in-tax-revenues-from-palestinians-over-statehood-drive.
55. *Israel Withholds Palestinian Funds, supra* note 53.
56. Isabel Kershner, *Israel to Transfer Tax Funds to Palestinians*, N.Y. TIMES, Jan. 30, 2013, http://www.nytimes.com/2013/01/31/world/middleeast/israel-to-transfer-tax-funds-to-palestinians.html?_r=0.
57. *Cash-Strapped Palestinian Gov't Adopts Emergency Budget*, REUTERS, Mar. 17, 2015, http://www.reuters.com/article/2015/03/17/us-israel-palestinians-budget-idUSKBN0MD1U620150317.
58. Jodi Rudoren, *Tensions Mount as Israel Freezes Revenue Meant for Palestinians*, N.Y. TIMES, Jan. 3, 2015, http://www.nytimes.com/2015/01/04/world/middleeast/tensions-mount-as-israel-freezes-revenue-meant-for-palestinians.html.
59. *Israel to Resume Tax Revenue Transfers to the Palestinian Authority*, JERUSALEM POST, Mar. 27, 2015, http://www.jpost.com/Israel-News/Politics-And-Diplomacy/Israel-to-resume-tax-revenue-transfers-to-the-Palestinian-Authority-395338.
60. Isabel Kershner, *Israel Releasing Impounded Palestinian Tax Revenue*, N.Y. TIMES, Mar. 27, 2015, http://www.nytimes.com/2015/03/28/world/middleeast/israel-netan-yahu-palestinians-tax-revenue.html?_r=0.

61. *See, e.g.,* Saeb Erekat, Al Jazeera, Head to Head, Apr. 2, 2014, http://www.aljazeera.com/programmes/headtohead/2014/03/transcript-dr-saeb-erekat-201432611433441126.html ("I personally take the responsibility for delaying this accession nine months. I made the deal personally with John Kerry that if Netanyahu gives me the 104 prisoners before Oslo, we will refrain from going to these agencies for nine months. I made the deal. I know it's a heavy price. These 104 prisoners deserve this price."); *Palestinian Report: Israel to Release Fourth Group of Prisoners within 48 Hours,* Jerusalem Post, Mar. 30, 2014, http://www.jpost.com/Diplomacy-and-Politics/Palestinian-report-Deal-reached-for-fourth-prisoner-release-within-48-hours-346949 ("In order to move back to the negotiations table, Israel agreed in July to release 104 terrorists .... In return the Palestinians agreed not to pursue unilateral diplomatic actions in international forums, including taking Israel to the International Criminal Court."); Ben Birnbaum & Amir Tibon, *The Explosive, Inside Story of How John Kerry Built an Israel-Palestine Peace Plan—and Watched it Crumble,* New Republic, July 20, 2014, http://www.newrepublic.com/article/118751/how-israel-palestine-peace-deal-died (asserting that while Kerry and Abbas both understood the deal as "104 prisoners for no-UN," there had been an initial "miscommunication" as "Netanyahu told Kerry that he was prepared to release approximately 80 of them (excluding those with Israeli identity cards)." This initial misunderstanding was eventually resolved by the Israelis deciding "that the fourth tranche of prisoners, which included all the Israeli Arabs, would require a separate vote.").

62. *See, e.g.,* Saeb Erekat, *supra* note 61.

63. Isabel Kershner, *Netanyahu Agrees to Free 104 Palestinians,* N.Y. Times, July 27, 2013, http://www.nytimes.com/2013/07/28/world/middleeast/netanyahu-agrees-to-free-104-palestinians.html?_r=0.

64. *Palestinian Report, supra* note 61.

65. Ruth Eglash & William Booth, *Israel Frees More Palestinian Prisoners,* Wash. Post, Dec. 30, 2013, http://www.washingtonpost.com/world/israel-frees-more-palestinian-prisoners/2013/12/30/4c3bd7fc-7189-11e3-bc6b-712d770c3715_story.html; Liel Liebovitz, *The Lives They Lived,* Tablet Magazine, Dec. 31, 2013, http://www.tabletmag.com/scroll/157782/the-lives-they-lived.

66. *Israel Publishes List of Palestinian Inmates to be Freed,* Times of Israel, Dec. 29, 2013, http://www.timesofisrael.com/israel-published-list-of-palestinian-inmates-to-be-release/; Liebovitz, *supra* note 65.

67. *Israel Publishes List of Palestinian Inmates to be Freed, supra* note 66; Liebovitz, *supra* note 65.

68. *Israel Publishes List of Palestinian Inmates to be Freed, supra* note 66.

69. *Id.*

70. *Id.*

71. Eugene Kontorovich, *Politicizing the International Criminal Court,* Jeruselum Ctr. for Pub. Aff., Ap. 2014, http://jcpa.org/politicizing_the_international_criminal_court/.

72. *Id.*

73. *Id.*

74. Jodi Rudoren, Michael R. Gordon, & Mark Landler, *Abbas Takes Defiant Step, and Mideast Talks Falter,* N.Y. Times, Apr. 1, 2014, http://www.nytimes.com/2014/04/02/world/middleeast/jonathan-pollard.html.

75. *Id.*

76. *Id.*

77. *See, e.g.,* Edith M. Lederer, *Palestinians Hold Off on UN Agency Membership,* AP, May 20, 2013, http://bigstory.ap.org/article/palestinians-hold-un-agency-membership.

78. A complete list of the treaties and their depositaries is available at Brett D. Schaefer, Steven Groves, & James Phillips, *Palestinian Intent to Accede to 15 Treaties and U.S. Response*, Issue Brief, Apr. 30, 2014, http://www.heritage.org/research/reports/2014/04/palestinian-intent-to-accede-to-15-treaties-and-us-response.

79. *See, e.g.*, Rupert Colville, U.N. High Comm'r for Hum. Rts., *Press Briefing Notes on Palestine* (May 2, 2014), http://unispal.un.org/UNISPAL.NSF/0/262AC5B8C25 B364585257CCF006C010D; U.N. Office of the Spokesperson for the Sec'y-Gen., *Highlights of the Noon Briefing by Stephane Dujarric, Spokesman for Secretary-General Ban Ki-Moon* (Apr. 10, 2014), http://www.un.org/sg/spokesperson/highlights/index.asp?HighD=4/10/2014; Swiss Fed. Dep't of Foreign Aff., *Notification to the Governments of the States Parties to the Geneva Conventions of 12 August 1949 for the Protection of War Victims* (Apr. 10, 2014), http://unispal.un.org/UNISPAL.NSF/0/1FF93AEC8D3186CF85257CBC00682857.

80. *U.S. Dep't of State, Foreign Operations, & Related Programs, Subcomm. of the House Appropriations Comm.: FY2015 Budget Hearing—Request for the United Nations and International Organizations* (testimony of Ambassador Samantha Power), Fed. News Serv. transcript (Apr. 2, 2014).

81. Schaefer, Groves, & Phillips, *supra* note 78.

82. *See, e.g., U.N. Convention Against Corruption*, Oct. 31, 2003, https://treaties.un.org/doc/Publication/CN/2014/CN.264.2014-Eng.pdf.

83. *See, e.g., id.*

84. *See, e.g., id.*

85. *See, e.g., Ex-ICC Prosecutor Warns Palestinians on Anti-Israel War Crimes Effort*, Associated Press, May 7, 2014, http://www.timesofisrael.com/ex-icc-prosecutor-warns-palestinians-on-anti-israel-war-crimes-effort/.

86. Jonathan Schanzer & Grant Rumley, *Palestine's Plan for When Peace Talks Fail*, National Interest, Mar. 17, 2014, http://nationalinterest.org/commentary/palestines-plan-when-peace-talks-fail-10061.

87. *Id.*

88. Herb Keinon & Khaled Abu Toameh, *Abbas Signs Rome Statute, Paving Way for Possible War Crimes Probe Against Israel at ICC*, Jerusalem Post, Dec. 31, 2014, http://www.jpost.com/Arab-Israeli-Conflict/Abbas-signs-Rome-Statute-paving-way-for-possible-war-crimes-probe-against-Israel-at-ICC-386270.

89. Press Release, ICJ, *The State of Palestine Accedes to the Rome Statute*, International Criminal Court (Jan. 7, 2015), http://www.icc-cpi.int/en_menus/icc/press%20and%20media/press%20releases/Pages/pr1082_2.aspx.

90. *U.N. Confirms Palestinians Will Be ICC Member on April 1*, Reuters, Jan. 7, 2015, http://www.reuters.com/article/2015/01/07/us-palestinians-israel-un-idUSKBN0KG1JV20150107.

91. Press Release, ICJ, *The Prosecutor of the International Criminal Court, Fatou Bensouda, Opens a Preliminary Investigation of the Situation in Palestine* (Jan. 16, 2015), http://www.icc-cpi.int/en_menus/icc/press%20and%20media/press%20releases/Pages/pr1083.aspx.

92. *Id.*

93. Colum Lynch, *Should Israel Fear ICC War Crimes Prosecutions if Palestine Becomes a State?*, Foreign Policy, Sept. 12, 2011, http://foreignpolicy.com/2011/09/12/should-israel-fear-icc-war-crimes-prosecutions-if-palestine-becomes-a-state/.

94. *U.S. Dep't of State, Foreign Operations, & Related Programs, Subcomm. of the House Appropriations Comm.: FY2015 Budget Hearing—Request for the United Nations and International Organizations* (testimony of Ambassador Samantha Power), Fed. News Serv. transcript (Apr. 2, 2014).

95. Diaa Hadid & Marlise Simons, *Palestinians Join International Criminal Court, but Tread Cautiously at First*, N.Y. TIMES, Apr. 1, 2015, http://www.nytimes.com/2015/04/02/world/middleeast/palestinians-join-international-criminal-court-but-tread-cautiously-at-first.html?_r=0; Colum Lynch, *The Case Against the Prosecution*, FOREIGN POLICY, Aug. 5, 2014, http://thecable.foreignpolicy.com/posts/2014/08/05/palestinians_abbas_international_prosecution_of_israeli_soldiers_ICC_Hague.

96. Eugene Kontorovich, *Politicizing the International Criminal Court*, JERUSALEM CTR. FOR PUB.AFF.,Apr.2014,http://jcpa.org/politicizing_the_international_criminal_court/.

97. *Id.*

98. Michael R. Gordon & Somini Sengupta, *Resolution for Palestinian State Fails in United Nations Security Council*, N.Y. TIMES, Dec. 30, 2014, http://www.nytimes.com/2014/12/31/world/middleeast/resolution-for-palestinian-state-fails-in-security-council.html.

99. Jodi Rudoren, *Palestinians Set to Seek Redress in a World Court*, N.Y. TIMES, Dec. 31, 2014, http://www.nytimes.com/2015/01/01/world/middleeast/palestinians-to-join-international-criminal-court-defying-israeli-us-warnings.html.

100. Isabel Kershner, *Palestinian Officials Push for Delay in Elections*, N.Y. TIMES, Nov. 12, 2009, http://www.nytimes.com/2009/11/13/world/middleeast/13pals.html?_r=0.

101. Rudoren, *supra* note 99.

102. Not-for-attribution author interview with Israeli official (Mar. 2, 2015).

103. Author interview of Mostafa Elostaz (Feb. 21, 2015). Elostaz is project manager and coordinator of the Palestinian Peace Coalition.

104. Noam Dvir, *Netanyahu: Abbas Inciting Terror*, YNETNEWS, Nov. 5, 2014, http://www.ynetnews.com/articles/0,7340,L-4588572,00.html.

105. Stuart Winer, *After Synagogue Attack, Shin Bet Chief Says Abbas Is Not Stoking Violence*, TIMES OF ISRAEL, Nov. 18, 2014, http://www.timesofisrael.com/security-chief-says-palestinian-leaders-not-stoking-violence/; Lahav Harkov, *Shin Bet Chief Says Abbas Does Not Encourage Terrorism, Contradicting Netanyahu*, JERUSALEM POST, Nov. 18, 2014, http://www.jpost.com/Arab-Israeli-Conflict/Shin-Bet-chief-contradicts-Netanyahu-says-Abbas-not-responsible-for-inciting-terror-382145.

106. Jonathan Schanzer, *Huge Verdict Is the Price the Palestinian Authority Pays for Not Controlling the P.L.O.*, N.Y. TIMES, Feb. 24, 2015, http://www.nytimes.com/roomfordebate/2015/02/24/terror-and-the-palestinian-authority/huge-verdict-is-the-price-the-palestinian-authority-pays-for-not-controlling-the-plo.

107. John Hudson, *Israel, US Slam Palestinian Bid to Join International Criminal Court*, FOREIGN POLICY, Dec. 31, 2014, http://foreignpolicy.com/2014/12/31/israel-u-s-slam-palestinian-bid-to-join-international-criminal-court/.

108. *Id.*

109. *Id.*

110. Carol Morello & Ruth Eglash, *Palestinian-Backed Resolution Fails at UN Security Council*, WASH. POST, Dec. 30, 2014, http://www.washingtonpost.com/world/national-security/palestinian-backed-resolution-fails-at-un-security-council/2014/12/30/4aae230e-906e-11e4-ba53-a477d66580ed_story.html.

111. Author interview of Mkhaimar Abusada (Feb. 21, 2015). Abusada is a professor of political science at Al-Azhar University, Gaza.

112. Louis Charbonneau, *Palestinian Draft Resolution Fails in U.S. Council, U.S. Votes Against*, REUTERS, Dec. 30, 2014, http://www.reuters.com/article/2014/12/30/us-mideast-palestinians-un-idUSKBN0K81CR20141230.

113. *Id.*

114. *See, e.g.,* Rupert Colville, U.N. High Comm'r for Hum. Rts., *Press Briefing Notes on Palestine* (May 2, 2014), http://unispal.un.org/UNISPAL.NSF/0/262AC5B8C25 B364585257CCF006C010D; *Highlights of the Noon Briefing by Stephane Dujarric, Spokesman for Secretary-General Ban Ki-Moon* (Apr. 10, 2014), http://www.un.org/sg/ spokesperson/highlights/index.asp?HighD=4/10/2014; Swiss Fed. Dep't of Foreign Aff., *Notification to the Governments of the States Parties to the Geneva Conventions of 12 August 1949 for the Protection of War Victims* (Apr. 10, 2014), http://unispal.un.org/ UNISPAL.NSF/0/1FF93AEC8D3186CF85257CBC00682857.

115. Fatou Bensouda, *The Truth About the ICC and Gaza*, THE GUARDIAN, Aug. 29, 2014, http://www.theguardian.com/commentisfree/2014/aug/29/ icc-gaza-hague-court-investigate- war-crimes-palestine.

116. Joint Letter to President Abbas on the International Criminal Court (May 8, 2014), http://www.hrw.org/news/2014/05/08/joint-letter-president-abbas-international-criminal-court.

117. *Id.*

118. Author interview of Mostafa Elostaz (Feb. 21, 2015). Elostaz is project manager and coordinator of the Palestinian Peace Coalition.

119. *Id.*

120. Daoud Kuttab, *Will PA Focus on Settlements at ICC?*, AL-MONITOR, Apr. 2, 2015, http://almon.co/2eku.

121. Avi Issacharoff, *PA Says It'll Drop War Crimes Suit if Settlements Frozen*, TIMES OF ISRAEL, Jan. 18, 2015, http://www.timesofisrael.com/pa-says-itll-drop-war-crimes-suit-if-settlements-frozen/.

122. Author interview of Mkhaimar Abusada (Feb. 21, 2015). Abusada is a professor of political science at Al-Azhar University, Gaza.

123. *Id.*

124. *Id.*

125. Not-for-attribution author interview (Mar. 2, 2015).

126. Kevin Jon Heller, *Unfortunately, the ICC Doesn't Work the Way Palestine Wants It To*, OPINIO JURIS, Jan. 18, 2015, http://opiniojuris.org/2015/01/18/ palestine-really-no-idea-icc-works/.

127. *Id.*

128. *Id.*

129. Curriculum Vitae of Alex Whiting, Harvard Law School, http://hls.harvard.edu/ faculty/directory/10953/Whiting.

130. Alex Whiting, *On Palestine's Decision to "Hold Off" on Referring the Situation in Palestine to the ICC*, LAWFARE BLOG, (Apr. 2, 2015), https://www.lawfareblog.com/ palestines-decision-hold-referring-situation-palestine-icc.

131. *Id.*

132. Rome Statute of the International Criminal Court, art. 14, http://www.icc-cpi. int/NR/rdonlyres/ADD16852-AEE9-4757-ABE7-9CDC7CF02886/283503/ RomeStatutEngl.pdf.

133. Whiting, *supra* note 130.

134. *Id.*

135. *Id.*

136. *Id.*

137. *Id.*

138. *Id.*

139. Daoud Kuttab, *Will PA Focus on Settlements at ICC?*, AL-MONITOR, Apr. 2, 2015, http://almon.co/2eku.

140. Anthony Deutsch & Dan Williams, *Palestinian Shift Brings War Crimes Case Closer to Israel*, REUTERS, Aug. 7, 2014, http://www.reuters.com/article/2014/08/07/us-mideast-gaza-icc-analysis-idUSKBN0G723M20140807.

141. *Id.*

142. Thomas Escritt, *Palestinians Prepared to Trigger Case as They Join ICC*, REUTERS, Apr. 1, 2015, http://www.reuters.com/article/2015/04/01/us-israel-palestinians-icc-idUSKBN0MS41B20150401.

143. *Hamas Declares Support for Palestinian Bid to Join International Criminal Court*, THE GUARDIAN, Aug. 23, 2014, http://www.theguardian.com/world/2014/aug/23/hamas-back-palestinian-bid-international-criminal-court.

144. *Hamas Signs Palestinian Application for ICC Membership*, MA'AN NEWS AGENCY, Aug. 23, 2014, http://www.maannews.com/eng/ViewDetails.aspx?id=722727; *Hamas Declares Support for Palestinian Bid, supra* note 143.

145. *Hamas Welcomes ICC Inquiry into Israeli-Palestinian Conflict*, REUTERS, Jan. 17, 2015, http://www.reuters.com/article/2015/01/17/us-israel-palestinians-icc-idUSKBN0KQ0KG20150117.

146. *Id.*

147. *Id.*

148. Colum Lynch, *The Case Against the Prosecution*, FOREIGN POLICY, Aug. 5, 2014, http://thecable.foreignpolicy.com/posts/2014/08/05/palestinians_abbas_international_prosecution_of_israeli_soldiers_ICC_Hague.

149. *Id.*; EU @ UN, EU COUNCIL CONCLUSIONS ON THE MIDDLE EAST PEACE PROCESS (July 22, 2014), http://www.eu-un.europa.eu/articles/en/article_15300_en.htm ("the EU strongly condemns the indiscriminate firing of rockets into Israel by Hamas and militant groups in the Gaza Strip, directly harming civilians").

150. Kevin Jon Heller, *The ICC in Palestine: Be Careful What You Wish For*, JUSTICE IN CONFLICT, Apr. 2, 2015, http://justiceinconflict.org/2015/04/02/the-icc-in-palestine-be-careful-what-you-wish-for/.

151. JEAN-MARIE HENCKAERTS & LOUISE DOSWALD-BECK, CUSTOMARY INTERNATIONAL HUMANITARIAN LAW 3, Rule 1 (2005), http://www.icrc.org/eng/assets/files/other/customary-international-humanitarian-law-i-icrc-eng.pdf.

152. Protocol Additional to the Geneva Conventions of 12 August 1949, and Relating to the Protection of Victims of International Armed Conflicts (Protocol I), June 8, 1977, http://www.icrc.org/applic/ihl/ihl.nsf/Treaty.xsp?action=openDocument&documentId=D9E6B6264D7723C3C12563CD002D6CE4.

153. *Id.*

154. Statute of the International Criminal Court, art. 8, http://legal.un.org/icc/statute/romefra.htm.

155. *Envoy to UNHRC on Palestinian ICC Hopes: Israelis Warn Civilians Before Attacks, We Don't*, MEMRI, July 9, 2014, http://www.memri.org/clip_transcript/en/4343.htm (translation of Palestinian Authority TV interview with Palestinian Representative at the U.N. Human Rights Council Ibrahim Khreisheh, which aired on July 9, 2014).

156. *Id.*

157. Nidal al-Mughrabi, *Hamas Backs Palestinian Push for ICC War Crimes Probe*, REUTERS, Aug. 23, 2014, http://www.reuters.com/article/2014/08/23/us-mideast-gaza-icc-idUSKBN0GN09320140823.

158. Author interview of Mkhaimar Abusada (Feb. 21, 2015). Abusada is a professor of political science at Al-Azhar University, Gaza.

159. *Id.*

160. *Warrant Issued for Sudan's Leader*, BBC NEWS, Mar. 4, 2009, http://news.bbc.co.uk/2/hi/africa/7923102.stm.

161. Author interview of Mkhaimar Abusada, *supra* note 158.

162. *Id.*

163. Eugene Kontorovich, *Is the International Criminal Court Biased Against Israel?*, WASH. POST, Jan. 5, 2015, http://www.washingtonpost.com/news/volokh-conspiracy/wp/2015/01/05/is-the-international-criminal-court-biased-against-israel/.

164. *Security Council Inaction on Darfur "Can Only Embolden Perpetrators"—ICC Prosecutor*, U.N. NEWS CENTRE, Dec. 12, 2014, http://www.un.org/apps/news/story.asp?NewsID=49591#.VRhVqVxXmKw; Somini Sengupta, *Is the War Crimes Court Still Relevant?*, N.Y. TIMES, Jan. 10, 2015, http://www.nytimes.com/2015/01/11/sunday-review/is-the-war-crimes-court-still-relevant.html?_r=1.

165. Kontorovich, *supra* note 163.

166. Press Release, ICJ, *Statement of the Prosecutor of the International Criminal Court, Fatou Bensouda, on the Withdrawal of Charges Against Mr. Uhuru Muigai Kenyatta* (May 12, 2014), http://www.icc-cpi.int/en_menus/icc/press%20and%20media/press%20releases/Pages/otp-statement-05-12-2014-2.aspx.

167. Marlise Simons & Jeffrey Gettleman, *International Court Ends Case Against Kenyan President in Election Unrest*, N.Y. TIMES, Dec. 5, 2014, http://www.nytimes.com/2014/12/06/world/africa/uhuru-kenyatta-kenya-international-criminal-court-withdraws-charges-of-crimes-against-humanity.html.

168. Press Release, ICJ, *Statement of the Prosecutor of the International Criminal Court, supra* note 166.

169. *Id.*

170. Tristan McConnell, *How Kenya Took On the International Criminal Court*, GLOBALPOST, Mar. 25, 2014, http://www.globalpost.com/dispatch/news/regions/africa/kenya/140325/how-kenya-beat-the-international-criminal-court.

171. Press Release, ICJ, *Statement of the Prosecutor of the International Criminal Court, supra* note 166.

172. McConnell, *supra* note 170.

173. *Written testimony of Eugene Kontorovich, The Palestinian ICC Bid and U.S. Interests: Hearing of the Subcomm. on the Middle East and North Africa of the H. Comm. on Foreign Affairs* (Feb. 4, 2015), http://docs.house.gov/meetings/FA/FA13/20150204/102887/HHRG-114-FA13-Wstate-KontorovichE-20150204.pdf.

174. *Id.*

175. Author interview of Mostafa Elostaz, *supra* note 118.

176. *Id.*

177. Aeyal Gross, *If Palestinians Join ICC, Israel's Actions May Trigger Court's Jurisdiction*, HAARETZ, Jan. 3, 2015, http://www.haaretz.com/news/diplomacy-defense/.premium-1.635096.

178. *Id.*

179. *Id.*

180. Press Release, ICJ, *Palestine Declares Acceptance of ICC Jurisdiction Since 13 June 2014* (Jan. 5, 2015), http://www.icc-cpi.int/en_menus/icc/press%20and%20media/press%20releases/Pages/pr1080.aspx.

181. *Id.*

182. *Declaration Accepting the Jurisdiction of the International Criminal Court*, letter signed by Mahmoud Abbas, President of the State of Palestine (Dec. 31, 2014), http://www.icc-cpi.int/iccdocs/PIDS/press/Palestine_A_12-3.pdf.

183. Press Release, ICJ, *The Prosecutor of the International Criminal Court, Fatou Bensouda, Opens a Preliminary Investigation of the Situation in Palestine* (Jan. 16, 2015), http://www.icc-cpi.int/en_menus/icc/press%20and%20media/press%20releases/Pages/pr1083.aspx.

184. *Abduction of 3 Israeli Teens Cost NIS 220,000*, YNET NEWS, Sept. 4, 2014, http://www.ynetnews.com/articles/0,7340,L-4567528,00.html.

185. *Bodies of Three Kidnapped Teens Found*, TIMES OF ISRAEL, June 30, 2014, http://www.timesofisrael.com/bodies-of-three-kidnapped-teens-found/.

186. William Booth & Ruth Eglash, *Israeli Forces Kill Two Hamas Members Suspected in Kidnapping, Killing of 3 Teens*, WASH. POST, Sept. 23, 2014, http://www.washingtonpost.com/world/israeli-forces-kill-2-suspects-in-kidnap-murder-of-3-teens/2014/09/23/1e79414a-4304-11e4-b47c-f5889e061e5f_story.html.

187. *First Palestinian ICC Case to be Gaza War, Group Says*, TIMES OF ISRAEL (AFP), Jan. 4, 2015, http://www.timesofisrael.com/first-palestinian-icc-case-to-be-gaza-war-rights-group/.

188. *Council President Appoints Members of Commission of Inquiry Under HRC Resolution S-21/1*, Office of the High Comm'r for Hum. Rts., Aug. 11, 2014, http://www.ohchr.org/en/NewsEvents/Pages/DisplayNews.aspx?NewsID=14934&LangID=E.

189. Kifah Ziboun, *Palestinians Preparing ICC Cases Against Israel*, ASHARQ AL-AWSAT, Jan. 8, 2015, http://www.aawsat.net/2015/01/article55340216/palestinians-preparing-icc-cases-against-israel-chief-negotiator.

190. *Id.*

191. Ahmad Melhem, *Palestinians Preparing ICC Files*, AL-MONITOR, Jan. 29, 2015, http://www.al-monitor.com/pulse/originals/2015/01/palestinian-icc-gaza-war-crimes-west-bank-settlements.html#.

192. Ziboun, *supra* note 189.

193. Melhem, *supra* note 191.

194. *Id.*

195. *Id.*

196. Press Release, ICJ, *The Prosecutor of the International Criminal Court, Fatou Bensouda, Opens a Preliminary Investigation of the Situation in Palestine* (Jan. 16, 2015), http://www.icc-cpi.int/en_menus/icc/press%20and%20media/press%20releases/Pages/pr1083.aspx.

197. *Id.*

198. Adam Justice, *ICC Opens Preliminary Examination of Israeli-Palestinian Conflict*, INT'L BUS. TIMES, Jan. 19, 2015, http://www.ibtimes.co.uk/icc-opens-preliminary-examination-israeli-palestinian-conflict-1484151.

199. *Id.*

200. Kevin Jon Heller, *The ICC in Palestine: Be Careful What You Wish For*, JUSTICE IN CONFLICT, Apr. 2, 2015, http://justiceinconflict.org/2015/04/02/the-icc-in-palestine-be-careful-what-you-wish-for/ (response by Alex Whiting).

201. Alex Whiting, *Palestine and the ICC: An (Imagined) View from Inside the Court*, LAWFARE BLOG (Jan. 5, 2015), http://www.lawfareblog.com/2015/01/palestine-and-the-icc-an-imagined-view-from-inside-the-court/.

202. *Id.*

203. Heller, *supra* note 200.

204. *Report of the Detailed Findings of the Independent Commission of Inquiry Established Pursuant to Human Rights Council Resolution S-21/1*, June 24, 2015, http://www.ohchr.org/EN/HRBodies/HRC/CoIGazaConflict/Pages/ReportCoIGaza.aspx#report.

205. Benjamin Wittes & Yishai Schwartz, *What to Make of the UN's Special Commission Report on Gaza?*, LAWFARE BLOG (June 24, 2015), https://www.lawfareblog.com/what-make-uns-special-commission-report-gaza.

206. Alex Whiting, *How Israel Should Address the Gaza Report's Impact on the ICC*, LAWFARE BLOG (July 13, 2015), https://www.lawfareblog.com/how-israel-should-address-gaza-reports-impact-icc.

207. *Id.*

208. *Id.*

209. *Id.*

210. Marlise Simons, *Hague Court Sentences Congolese Warlord to 12 Years for Role in Tribal Massacre*, N.Y. TIMES, May 23, 2014, http://www.nytimes.com/2014/05/24/world/africa/hague-court-sentences-congolese-warlord-to-12-years.html?_r=0.

211. *Id.*

212. International Criminal Court, *The Court Today*, Mar. 13, 2015, http://www.icc-cpi.int/iccdocs/PIDS/publications/TheCourtTodayEng.pdf (the information sheet on this website states that "this information sheet is updated on a regular basis" and suggested that "for the latest update, please refer to the ICC website").

213. *Id.*

214. *Id.*

215. Jodi Rudoren, *Joining International Criminal Court Wouldn't Guarantee Palestinians a War Crimes Case*, N.Y. TIMES, Jan. 1, 2015, http://www.nytimes.com/2015/01/02/world/middleeast/court-membership-wouldnt-guarantee-palestinians-a-war-crimes-case.html.

216. *See, e.g.*, David Smith, *New Chief Prosecutor Defends International Criminal Court*, THE GUARDIAN, May 23, 2012, http://www.theguardian.com/law/2012/may/23/chief-prosecutor-international-criminal-court.

217. Rudoren, *supra* note 215.

218. *The Court Today, supra* note 212.

219. *Id.*

220. *Id.*

221. INTERNATIONAL CRIMINAL COURT, OFFICE OF THE PROSECUTOR, REPORT ON PRELIMINARY EXAMINATION ACTIVITIES 2014 (Dec. 2, 2014), http://www.icc-cpi.int/iccdocs/otp/OTP-Pre-Exam-2014.pdf.

222. *Id.*

223. *Id.*

224. *Id.*

225. *Id.*

226. *Id.*

227. *Id.*

228. *Id.*

229. *Id.*

230. *Id.*

231. David Bosco, *The War Over U.S. War Crimes in Afghanistan Is Heating Up*, FOREIGN POLICY, Dec. 3, 2014, http://foreignpolicy.com/2014/12/03/the-war-over-u-s-war-crimes-in-afghanistan-is-heating-up-icc-hague/.

232. David Bosco, *Is the ICC Investigating Crimes by U.S. Forces in Afghanistan?*, FOREIGN POLICY, May 15, 2014, http://foreignpolicy.com/2014/05/15/is-the-icc-investigating-crimes-by-u-s-forces-in-afghanistan/.

233. *Id.*

234. *Id.*

235. *Id.*

236. Bosco, *supra* note 232.

237. David Ignatius, *White House Considers Opening Breach in U.S.-Israel Relationship*, WASH. POST, Mar. 19, 2015, http://www.washingtonpost.com/opinions/white-house-considers-opening-breach-in-us-israel-alliance/2015/03/19/c9e93832-ce78-11e4-8c54-ffb5ba6f2f69_story.html?hpid=z5.

238. AMNESTY INT'L, FAMILIES UNDER THE RUBBLE: ISRAELI ATTACKS ON INHABITED HOMES (Nov. 5, 2014), https://www.amnesty.org/en/documents/MDE15/032/2014/en/.

239. *See, e.g., Statement of Dr. Riyad Mansour, Ambassador of Palestine to the United Nations Before the Assembly of States Parties to the Rome Statute of the International Criminal Court* (Dec. 15, 2014), http://www.icc-cpi.int/iccdocs/asp_docs/ASP13/GenDeba/ICC-ASP13-GenDeba-Palestine-ENG.pdf.

240. Human Rights Watch, *World Report 2015, Israel/Palestine*, http://www.hrw.org/world-report/2015/country-chapters/israel-and-palestine?page=2.

241. International Criminal Court, *Frequently Asked Questions: Is the ICC Meant to Replace National Courts?*, http://www.icc-cpi.int/en_menus/icc/about%20the%20court/frequently%20asked%20questions/pages/faq.aspx (last visited Mar. 21, 2015).

242. *Id.*

243. *Id.*

244. Rome Statute of the International Criminal Court, http://www.icc-cpi.int/NR/rdonlyres/ADD16852-AEE9-4757-ABE7-9CDC7CF02886/283503/RomeStatutEngl.pdf.

245. *Id.*

246. *Id.*

247. Fatou Bensouda, *Reflections from the International Criminal Court Prosecutor*, 45 CASE W. RES. J. INT'L L. 505, 507 (2012), http://law.case.edu/journals/jil/Documents/45CaseWResJIntlL1&2.24.Article.Bensouda.pdf.

248. *Id.*

249. *Id.* at 506.

250. *Id.*

251. Fatou Bensouda, *The International Criminal Court: A New Approach to International Relations*, transcript of presentation by ICC prosecutor Fatou Bensouda Before the Council on Foreign Relations (Sept. 21, 2012), http://www.cfr.org/courts-and-tribunals/international-criminal-court-new-approach-international-relations/p29351.

252. Bensouda, *supra* note 247, at 509.

253. *Id.*

254. *Id.* at 510.

255. Justin Jalil, *FM Calls to Dismantle ICC after Launch of "War Crimes" Probe*, TIMES OF ISRAEL, Jan. 16, 2015, http://www.timesofisrael.com/fm-calls-to-dismantle-icc-after-launch-of-war-crimes-probe/.

256. Jonathan Lis & The Associated Press, *ICC Opens Initial Probe into Possible War Crimes in Palestinian Territories*, HAARETZ, Jan. 16, 2015, http://www.haaretz.com/news/diplomacy-defense/1.637518.

257. Jodi Rudoren, *Tensions Mount as Israel Freezes Revenue Meant for Palestinians*, N.Y. TIMES, Jan. 3, 2015, http://www.nytimes.com/2015/01/04/world/middleeast/tensions-mount-as-israel-freezes-revenue-meant-for-palestinians.html.

258. Jalil, *supra* note 255.

259. Herb Keinon, *Exclusive: In Exchange for Freed Tax Funds, PA Won't Pursue Israel Over Settlements at ICC*, JERUSALEM POST, Mar. 29, 2015, http://www.jpost.com/

Arab-Israeli-Conflict/In-exchange-for-freed-tax-funds-PA-wont-pursue-Israel-over-settlements-at-ICC-395505.

260. Thomas Escritt & Anthony Deutsch, *Exclusive: ICC Backers Defy Israeli Call to Cut Funding to War Crimes Court*, YAHOO! NEWS, Jan. 27, 2015, http://news.yahoo.com/exclusive-icc-backers-defy-israeli-call-cut-funding-140637916.html.

261. *Id.*

262. *Id.*

263. *Id.*

264. *Written testimony of Eugene Kontorovich, The Palestinian ICC Bid and U.S. Interests: Hearing of the Subcomm. on the Middle East and North Africa of the H. Comm. on Foreign Affairs* (Feb. 4, 2015), http://docs.house.gov/meetings/FA/FA13/20150204/102887/HHRG-114-FA13-Wstate-KontorovichE-20150204.pdf.

265. Yonah Jeremy Bob, *18 Recommendations That Could Determine Israel's Fate Before the ICC*, JERUSALEM POST, Jan. 26, 2015, http://www.jpost.com/landedpages/printarticle.aspx?id=388955#; PUBLIC COMM'N TO EXAMINE THE MARITIME INCIDENT OF 31 MAY 2010, SECOND REPORT—THE TURKEL COMM'N, ISRAEL'S MECHANISMS FOR EXAMINING AND INVESTIGATING COMPLAINTS AND CLAIMS OF VIOLATIONS OF THE LAWS OF ARMED CONFLICT ACCORDING TO INTERNATIONAL LAW (Feb. 2013), http://www.turkel-committee.gov.il/files/newDoc3/The%20Turkel%20Report%20for%20website.pdf.

266. Bob, *supra* note 265.

267. *Id.*

268. *Id.*

269. *Id.*

270. *Id.*

271. *Id.*

272. *IDF Conducts Fact-Finding Assessment Following Operation Protective Edge*, ISRAEL DEFENCE FORCES, Sept. 12, 2014, http://www.idfblog.com/blog/2014/09/12/idf-conducts-fact-finding-assessment-following-operation-protective-edge/.

273. *Id.*

274. Yonah Jeremy Bob, *IDF Issues 3rd Report on Gaza War Probes*, JERUSALEM POST, Mar. 21, 2015, http://www.jpost.com/Arab-Israeli-Conflict/IDF-issues-3rd-report-on-Gaza-war-probes-394558.

275. *Id.*

276. THIS IS HOW WE FOUGHT IN GAZA: BREAKING THE SILENCE (2014), http://www.breakingthesilence.org.il/pdf/ProtectiveEdge.pdf.

277. William Booth, *Israeli Veterans Say Permissive Rules of Engagement Fueled Gaza Carnage*, WASH. POST, May 4, 2015.

278. Ido Rosenzweig, *Guest Post: The Palestinian Accession to the Rome Statute and the Question of Settlements*, OPINIO JURIS, Jan. 22, 2015, http://opiniojuris.org/2015/01/22/guest-post-palestinian-accession-rome-statue-question-settlements/.

279. Aeyal Gross, *Tiptoeing through the ICC Raindrops*, HAARETZ, Jan. 27, 2015, http://www.haaretz.com/opinion/.premium-1.639179.

280. *Id.*

281. Rosenzweig, *supra* note 278.

282. Aeyal Gross, *If Palestinians Join ICC, Israel's Actions May Trigger Court's Jurisdiction*, HAARETZ, Jan. 3, 2015, http://www.haaretz.com/news/diplomacy-defense/.premium-1.635096.

283. *Id.*

284. Yonah Jeremy Bob, *Does Abbas Signing Rome Statute Doom IDF to ICC War Crimes Trials?*, JERUSALEM POST, Jan. 2, 2015, http://www.jpost.com/Arab-Israeli-Conflict/ Does-Abbas-signing-Rome-Statute-doom-IDF-to-ICC-war-crimes-trials-386470.

285. *Id.*

286. Eugene Kontorovich, *Politicizing the International Criminal Court*, JERUSALEM CTR. FOR PUB. AFF., Apr. 2014, http://jcpa.org/politicizing_the_international_criminal_court/.

287. *Id.*

288. Rome Statute of the International Criminal Court, art. 8, http://www.icc-cpi.int/nr/ rdonlyres/ea9aeff7-5752-4f84-be94-0a655eb30e16/0/rome_statute_english.pdf.

289. Eugene Kontorovich, *Palestinians Seek to Take Advantage of ICC's Unique "Israel" Provision*, WASH. POST, Jan. 5, 2015, http://www.washingtonpost. com/news/volokh-conspiracy/wp/2015/01/05/palestinians-seek-to-take-advantage-of-iccs-unique-israel-provision/.

290. *Id.*

291. *Id.*

292. *Id.*

293. *Id.*

294. Anthony Deutsch & Dan Williams, *Palestinian Shift Brings War Crimes Case Closer to Israel*, REUTERS, Aug. 7, 2014, http://www.reuters.com/article/2014/08/07/ us-mideast-gaza-icc-analysis-idUSKBN0G723M20140807.

295. *Id.*

296. Ahmad Melhem, *Palestinians Preparing ICC Files*, AL-MONITOR, Jan. 29, 2015, http:// www.al-monitor.com/pulse/originals/2015/01/palestinian-icc-gaza-war-crimes-west-bank-settlements.html#.

297. Kevin Jon Heller, *Yes, Palestine Could Accept the ICC's Jurisdiction Retroactively*, OPINIO JURIS, Nov. 29, 2012, http://opiniojuris.org/2012/11/29/ yes-palestine-could-accept-the-iccs-jurisdiction-retroactively/.

298. *Id.*

299. John Hudson, *Israel, US Slam Palestinian Bid to Join International Criminal Court*, FOREIGN POLICY, Dec. 31, 2014, http://foreignpolicy.com/2014/12/31/ israel-u-s-slam-palestinian-bid-to-join-international-criminal-court/.

300. *Id.*

301. Quoted at § 2002(5) of the American Service-Members' Protection Act of 2002, 22 U.S.C. § 7401 note, http://legcounsel.house.gov/Comps/aspa02.pdf.

302. *Written testimony of Eugene Kontorovich, The Palestinian ICC Bid and U.S. Interests: Hearing of the Subcomm. on the Middle East and North Africa of the H. Comm. on Foreign Affairs* (Feb. 4, 2015), http://docs.house.gov/meetings/FA/ FA13/20150204/102887/HHRG-114-FA13-Wstate-KontorovichE-20150204.pdf

303. *Id.*

304. Michael Wilner, *Senate Warns "Strong Response" Prepared to Palestinian ICC Action*, JERUSALEM POST, Jan. 10, 2015, http://www.jpost.com/Arab-Israeli-Conflict/ Senate-warns-strong-response-prepared-to-Palestinian-ICC-action-387265.

305. *See, e.g.*, GEORGETOWN UNIV. LAW LIBRARY, INTERNATIONAL CRIMINAL COURT— ARTICLE 98 AGREEMENTS RESEARCH GUIDE, http://www.law.georgetown.edu/ library/research/guides/article_98.cfm.

306. Rome Statute of the International Criminal Court, http://www.icc-cpi.int/NR/rdon-lyres/ADD16852-AEE9-4757-ABE7-9CDC7CF02886/283503/RomeStatutEng1. pdf.

307. *See, e.g.*, GEORGETOWN UNIV. LAW LIBRARY, RESEARCH GUIDE, *supra* note 305.

308. *See, e.g., id.*

309. *See, e.g., id.*

310. *ICC Prosecutor Shelves Darfur War Crimes Inquiries,* BBC NEWS, Dec. 12, 2014, http://www.bbc.com/news/world-africa-30458347.

311. American Service-Members' Protection Act of 2002, § 2008, 22 U.S.C. § 7427 (2002).

312. *Id.* § 2008, 22 U.S.C. § 7427.

313. *Id.* § 2013, 22 U.S.C. § 7432.

314. *Written testimony of Eugene Kontorovich, The Palestinian ICC Bid and U.S. Interests: Hearing of the Subcomm. on the Middle East and North Africa of the H. Comm. on Foreign Affairs* (Feb. 4, 2015), http://docs.house.gov/meetings/FA/FA13/20150204/102887/HHRG-114-FA13-Wstate-KontorovichE-20150204.pdf.

315. Isabel Kershner, *UNESCO Adds Nativity Church in Bethlehem to Heritage List,* N.Y. TIMES, June 29, 2012, http://www.nytimes.com/2012/06/30/world/middleeast/unesco-grants-heritage-status-to-nativity-church-in-diplomatic-victory-to-palestinians.html?_r=0.

316. UNESCO, BIRTHPLACE OF JESUS: CHURCH OF THE NATIVITY AND THE PILGRIMAGE ROUTE, BETHLEHEM, http://whc.unesco.org/en/list/1433/documents/.

317. *Id.*

318. UNESCO, WORLD HERITAGE IN DANGER, http://whc.unesco.org/en/158/.

319. *Id.*

320. Kershner, *supra* note 315.

321. *Id.*

322. Tovah Lazaroff, *UNESCO: Nativity Church Heritage Site in "Palestine,"* JERUSALEM POST, June 29, 2012, http://www.jpost.com/Diplomacy-and-Politics/UNESCO-Nativity-Church-heritage-site-in-Palestine.

323. Kershner, *supra* note 315.

324. *Id.; see also* UNESCO, BIRTHPLACE OF JESUS, *supra* note 316.

325. Legal Consequences of the Construction of a Wall in the Occupied Palestinian Territory, Advisory Opinion, 2004 I.C.J. 136 (July 9), http://www.icj-cij.org/docket/files/131/1671.pdf.

326. *See, e.g., Israel's Security Fence; Questions and Answers,* Israel Ministry of Defense, Feb. 22, 2004, http://www.securityfence.mod.gov.il/Pages/ENG/questions.htm.

327. *See, e.g.,* Col. (Res.) Dr. Danny Tirza, *Israeli Security Fence Architect: Why the Barrier Had to be Built,* AL MONITOR, July 1, 2012, http://www.al-monitor.com/pulse/originals/2012/al-monitor/israeli-security-fence-architect.html; Emily Harris, *A Decade in the Making, West Bank Barrier Is Nearly Complete,* NPR, May 22, 2013, http://www.npr.org/blogs/parallels/2013/05/22/186017646/a-decade-in-the-making-west-bank-barrier-is-nearly-complete.

328. *Saving Lives: Israel's Anti-Terrorist Fence-Answers to Questions,* Israel Ministry of Foreign Affairs, Jan. 1, 2004, http://www.mfa.gov.il/mfa/foreignpolicy/terrorism/palestinian/pages/saving%20lives-%20israel-s%20anti-terrorist%20fence%20-%20answ.aspx.

329. *Israel's Security Fence, supra* note 326.

330. Statement by Ambassador Gillerman to the U.N. Security Council, Israel Ministry of Foreign Affairs, Oct. 14, 2003, http://mfa.gov.il/MFA/PressRoom/2003/Pages/Statement%20by%20Ambassador%20Dan%20Gillerman-%20Permanent%20R14Oct2003.aspx.

331. *See, e.g., Islamic Jihad Leader: Security Fence "Obstacle to the Resistance,"* Israel Ministry of Foreign Affairs, Nov. 20, 2006, http://www.mfa.gov.il/mfa/foreignpolicy/terrorism/palestinian/pages/islamic%20jihad%20leader%20says%20security%20fence%20obstacle%20to%20the%20resistance%2020-nov-2006.aspx; INTELLIGENCE &

TERRORISM INFORMATION CTR., THE LEADER OF THE PALESTINIAN ISLAMIC JIHAD AGAIN ADMITS THAT THE ISRAELI SECURITY FENCE BUILT BY ISRAEL IN JUDEA AND SAMARIA PREVENTS THE TERRORIST ORGANIZATIONS FROM REACHING THE HEART OF ISRAEL TO CARRY OUT SUICIDE BOMBING ATTACKS (Mar. 26, 2008), http://www.terrorism-info.org.il/data/pdf/PDF_08_089_2.pdf.

332. *The Security Barrier (Fence)*, IDF Military Advocate General Corps, http://www.law. idf.il/351-en/Patzar.aspx (last visited July 30, 2014.

333. *See, e.g.*, Written Statement of the League of Arab States, Request for Advisory Opinion: Legal Consequences of the Construction of a Wall in the Occupied Palestinian Territory, http://www.icj-cij.org/docket/files/131/1545.pdf.

334. Legal Consequences of the Construction of a Wall in the Occupied Palestinian Territory, Advisory Opinion, 2004 I.C.J. Reports 141 (July 9), http://www.icj-cij.org/docket/files/131/1671.pdf.

335. Press Release, United Nations, *General Assembly Adopts Text Requesting International Court of Justice to Issue Advisory Opinion on West Bank Separation Wall* (Dec. 8, 2003), http://www.un.org/press/en/2003/ga10216.doc.htm.

336. Statute of the International Court of Justice, art. 65, http://www.icj-cij.org/documents/index.php?p1=4&p2=2&p3=0#CHAPTER_IV.

337. Charter of the United Nations, art. 96, http://www.icj-cij.org/documents/index.php?p1=4&p2=1&p3=0#Chapter14.

338. Geoffrey R. Watson, *The "Wall" Decisions in Legal and Political Context*, 99 AM. J. INT'L L. 6, 6–7 (2005).

339. *Id.*

340. Legal Consequences of the Construction of a Wall, Advisory Opinion, 2004 I.C.J. Reports, *supra* note 334, at 184.

341. *Id.* at 193–94.

342. *Id.* at 201.

343. *Id.* at 201–202.

344. *Id.* at 198.

345. Declaration of Judge Buergenthal, Legal Consequences of the Construction of a Wall in the Occupied Palestinian Territory, Advisory Opinion, 2004 I.C.J. 242, http://www.icj-cij.org/docket/files/131/1687.pdf.

346. Beit Sourik Village Council v. Gov't of Israel, High Court of Justice 2056/04 (June 30, 2004), http://elyon1.court.gov.il/files_eng/04/560/020/a28/04020560.a28.pdf; Mara'abe v. Prime Minister of Israel, High Court of Justice 7957/04 (Sept. 15, 2005), http://elyon1.court.gov.il/files_eng/04/570/079/a14/04079570.a14.pdf.

347. *See, e.g.*, Lori Fisler Damrosch & Bernard H. Oxman, *Agora: ICJ Advisory Opinion on Construction of a Wall in the Occupied Palestinian Territory: Editors' Introduction*, 99 AM. J. INT'L L. 1 (2005) (summarizing views of contributors to the symposium).

348. *See, e.g., id.*

349. Tovah Lazaroff, *Netanyahu: Security barrier Saves Lives, Anti-Israel Incitement Makes It Necessary*, JERUSALEM POST, May 26, 2014, http://www.jpost.com/Diplomacy-and-Politics/Netanyahu-Security-barrier-saves-lives-anti-Israeli-incitement-makes-it-necessary-354388.

350. Secretary-General's Message to the Special Meeting of the Committee on the Exercise of the Inalienable Rights of the Palestinian People to Commemorate the 10th Anniversary of the Advisory Opinion of the International Court of Justice on the Legal Consequences of the Construction of a Wall in the Occupied Palestinian Territory (July 9, 2014), http://www.un.org/sg/statements/index.asp?nid=7849.

351. *Id.*

CHAPTER 6

1. BDS Movement, *Palestinian Civil Society Call for BDS*, July 9, 2005, http://www.bdsmovement.net/call.

2. *Id.*

3. *Id.*

4. *Id. See also* Civic Coalition for Palestinian Rights in Jerusalem & Birzeit Univ. Inst. of Law, Advocating for Palestinian Rights in Conformity with International Law (Feb. 2014), http://lawcenter.birzeit.edu/iol/en/project/outputfile/6/986afcc6c9.pdf.

5. BDS Movement, *Palestinian BDS National Committee*, http://www.bdsmovement.net/bnc (last visited Mar. 30, 2015).

6. RAND Corporation, *The Costs of the Israeli-Palestinian Conflict* 166 (2015), http://www.rand.org/content/dam/rand/pubs/research_reports/RR700/RR740/RAND_RR740.pdf.

7. John Reed, *Israel: A New Kind of War*, Financial Times, June 12, 2015, http://www.ft.com/intl/cms/s/0/f11c1e1c-0e13-11e5-8ce9-00144feabdc0.html?siteedition=intl#axzz3k4Ih9GiW.

8. *Id.*

9. *See, e.g.*, BDS Movement, *Cultural Boycott*, http://www.bdsmovement.net/active-camps/cultural-boycott (last visited July 31, 2014); Michele Chabin, *Anti-Israel Groups Push Product, Performers Boycott*, USA Today, Mar. 17, 2013, http://www.usatoday.com/story/news/world/2013/03/17/israeli-boycott/1930085/.

10. *Gregory Porter: Live Up to Your Words and Do Not Commit Musical Genocide*, Palestinian Campaign for the Academic & Cultural Boycott of Israel, Mar. 3, 2015, http://pacbi.org/etemplate.php?id=2684.

11. *Id.*

12. BDS Movement, *Freedom and Justice for Gaza: Boycott Action Against 7 Complicit Companies*, July 25, 2014, http://www.bdsmovement.net/2014/freedom-and-justice-for-gaza-boycott-action-against-7-complicit-companies-12386.

13. BDS Movement, *9 Ways to Effectively Support Gaza through Boycotts, Divestment and Sanctions* (last visited July 31, 1014), http://www.bdsmovement.net/get-involved.

14. Adam Reuter, *Who's Afraid of the Big, Bad Boycott?*, YNet, Aug. 28, 2014, http://www.ynetnews.com/articles/0,7340,L-4563597,00.html.

15. Civic Coalition for Palestinian Rights in Jerusalem & Birzeit Univ., *supra* note 4.

16. Anne Herzberg, *NGO "Lawfare": Exploitation of Courts in the Arab-Israeli Conflict*, NGO Monitor 26, Dec. 2010, http://www.ngo-monitor.org/data/images/File/lawfare-monograph.pdf.

17. *Id.*

18. *See, e.g.*, Peter Fabricius, *Palestinian Head Rejects Boycott of Israel*, The Star (South Africa), Dec. 11, 2013, *reprinted in Palestinian Officials Affirm "Respect" for BDS after Abbas Disavowal*, Ma'an, Dec. 23, 2013, http://www.maannews.net/eng/ViewDetails.aspx?ID=658870; Richard Perez-Pena & Jodi Rudoren, *Boycott by Academic Group Is a Symbolic Sting to Israel*, N.Y. Times, Dec. 16, 2013, http://www.nytimes.com/2013/12/17/education/scholars-group-endorses-an-academic-boycott-of-israel.html?_r=0.

19. *See, e.g., id.*

20. *Palestinian Officials Affirm "Respect" for BDS, supra* note 18.

21. Jake Wallis Simons, *Why Even the Palestinian Authority Opposes the Boycott of Israel*, The Telegraph (UK), June 9, 2014, http://blogs.telegraph.co.uk/

news/jakewallissimons/100275416/israels-enemies-are-dealt-a-heavy-blow-by-the-palestinian-authority/.

22. Khaled Abu Toameh, *Palestinians: BDS Activists Are Troublemakers, Criminals*, GATESTONE INST., May 30, 2014, http://www.gatestoneinstitute.org/4334/palestinians-bds-trial.

23. Simons, *supra* note 21.

24. *Id.*

25. Toameh, *supra* note 22.

26. Mohammed Daraghmeh, *Palestinians Call for Boycott of Israeli Goods*, AP, Feb. 11, 2015, http://news.yahoo.com/palestinians-call-boycott-israeli-goods-174638956.html.

27. *Id.*

28. *Id.*

29. *Palestinian Activist: Boycott of Israeli Products Begins*, AP, Mar. 1, 2015, http://www.nytimes.com/aponline/2015/03/01/world/middleeast/ap-ml-israel-palestinians.html.

30. *West Bank Boycott Takes Aim at Israeli Food Products*, AL JAZEERA, Mar. 22, 2015, https://en-maktoob.news.yahoo.com/west-bank-boycott-takes-aim-israeli-food-products-081556951.html.

31. *Id.*

32. Gill Plimmer, *G4S to End Israeli Jail Contracts Within Three Years*, FINANCIAL TIMES, June 5, 2014, http://www.ft.com/intl/cms/s/0/06e06252-ecc9-11e3-8963-00144fe-abdc0.html?siteedition=intl#axzz3Tq5RJna4.

33. BDS Movement, *Stop G4S*, http://www.bdsmovement.net/activecamps/g4s (last visited Mar. 30, 2015).

34. *Id.*

35. OECD GUIDELINES FOR MULTINATIONAL ENTERPRISES 31 (2011 ed.), http://www.oecd.org/daf/inv/mne/48004323.pdf.

36. Sec'y of State Hillary Rodham Clinton, U.S. Dep't of State, Remarks at the Commemoration of the 50th Anniversary of the OECD on Guidelines for Multinational Enterprises (May 25, 2011), http://www.state.gov/secretary/20092013clinton/rm/2011/05/164340.htm.

37. OECD GUIDELINES FOR MULTINATIONAL ENTERPRISES: RESPONSIBLE BUSINESS CONDUCT MATTERS 2 (2014), http://mneguidelines.oecd.org/MNEguidelines_RBCmatters.pdf.

38. *Id.* at 3.

39. *Id.* at 13.

40. *Id.* at 8 (emphasis added).

41. *Id.* at 13.

42. *Id.*

43. *Id.*

44. *Id.*

45. *Id.* at 14.

46. INITIAL ASSESSMENT BY THE UK NATIONAL CONTACT POINT FOR THE OECD GUIDELINES FOR MULTINATIONAL ENTERPRISES: COMPLAINT FROM LAWYERS FOR PALESTINIAN HUMAN RIGHTS (LPHR) AGAINST GS4 (May 2014), https://www.gov.uk/government/uploads/system/uploads/attachment_data/file/315104/bis-14-854-palestinian-lawyers-complaint-against-g4s-ncp-initial-assessment.pdf.

47. Gill Plimmer, *G4S to End Israeli Jail Contracts Within Three Years*, FINANCIAL TIMES, June 5, 2014, http://www.ft.com/intl/cms/s/0/06e06252-ecc9-11e3-8963-00144fe-abdc0.html?siteedition=intl#axzz3Tq5RJna4.

48. *See, e.g., Stop G4S, supra* note 33; Laurie Goodstein, *Methodist Church Pension Board Links Divestment to Firm's Role in Israeli Prisons*, N.Y. TIMES, June 15, 2014, http://www.nytimes.com/2014/06/16/us/methodist-church-group-links-divestment-move-to-israel-and-a-firms-prison-role.html?_r=0.

49. *UK Trade Body Investigation into G4S over Alleged Israeli Human Rights Abuses*, LEIGH DAY, June 3, 2014, http://www.leighday.co.uk/News/2014/June-2014/UK-Trade-body-investigation-into-G4S-over-alleged; Corporate Accountability for Alleged Human Rights Violations in Action: UK NCP Initial Assessment of LPHR's Complaint Against G4S, Lawyers for Palestinian Human Rights, June 2, 2014, http://lphr.org.uk/blog/corporate-accountability-for-alleged-human-rights-violations-in-action-uk-ncp-initial-assessment-of-lphrs-complaint-against-g4s/.

50. Corporate Accountability for Alleged Human Rights Violations in Action, *id.*

51. Gill Plimmer, *G4S Cleared of Human Rights Breach in Israel*, FINANCIAL TIMES, June 9, 2015, http://www.ft.com/cms/s/0/37f2581e-0eb0-11e5-8aca-00144feabdc0.html#axzz3k4Ih9GiW; LAWYERS FOR PALESTINIAN HUMAN RIGHTS (LPHR) & G4S PLC: FINAL STATEMENT AFTER EXAMINATION OF COMPLAINT (Mar. 2015), https://www.gov.uk/government/uploads/system/uploads/attachment_data/file/431972/bis-15-306-lawyers-for-palestinian-human-rights-final-statement-after-examination-of-complaint-uk-national-contact-point-for-the-oecd-guidelines-for-multinational-enterprises-r1.pdf.

52. *Id.*

53. *Id.*

54. *Id.*

55. *Id.*

56. Gill Plimmer, *G4S Cleared of Human Rights Breach in Israel*, FINANCIAL TIMES, June 9, 2015, http://www.ft.com/cms/s/0/37f2581e-0eb0-11e5-8aca-00144feabdc0.html#axzz3k4Ih9GiW.

57. *Id.*

58. OECD DECLARATION AND DECISIONS ON INTERNATIONAL INVESTMENT AND MULTINATIONAL ENTERPRISES, http://www.oecd.org/daf/inv/mne/oecddeclarationanddecisions.htm.

59. *Israel: Trade Statistics*, GLOBALEDGE, http://globaledge.msu.edu/countries/israel/tradestats (last visited Mar. 30, 2015).

60. OECD GUIDELINES FOR MULTINATIONAL ENTERPRISES: RESPONSIBLE BUSINESS CONDUCT MATTERS (2014), http://mneguidelines.oecd.org/MNEguidelines_RBCmatters.pdf.

61. *Id.* at 3.

62. *Guidelines on the Eligibility of Israeli Entities and Their Activities in the Territories Occupied by Israel Since June 1967 for Grants, Prizes and Financial Instruments Funded by the EU from 2014 Onwards*, 56 OFFICIAL J. EUR. UNION (C 205) 9 (2013), http://eeas.europa.eu/delegations/israel/documents/related-links/20130719_guidelines_on_eligibility_of_israeli_entities_en.pdf.

63. *Id.*

64. Barak Ravid, *Israel and EU Compromise on Terms of Joint Initiative, Following Rift Over Settlement Funding Ban*, HAARETZ, Nov. 26, 2013, http://www.haaretz.com/news/diplomacy-defense/.premium-1.560292; Joshua Mitnick, Israel, *EU Resolve Spat Over Settlements*, WALL ST. J., Nov. 27, 2013, http://www.wsj.com/articles/SB10001424052702303281504579222534127910404.

65. Ravid, *supra* note 64; Mitnick, *supra* note 64.

66. Press Release, BDS Movement, *EU Acknowledges Obligation to Not Recognize Israeli Annexation of Palestinian Territory* (July 18, 2013), http://www.bdsmovement. net/2013/eu-guidelines-press-release-11211.

67. *Id.*

68. *PLO Threatens Action over Israel Settlements*, MA'AN NEWS AGENCY (AFP), Aug. 23, 2013, http://www.maannews.com/eng/ViewDetails.aspx?id=623067.

69. *Id.*

70. *Guidelines on the Eligibility of Israeli Entities, supra* note 62.

71. Herb Keinon, *EU Officially Publishes Settlement Guidelines Despite Israeli Objections*, JERUSALEM POST, July 19, 2013, http://www.jpost.com/diplomacy-and-politics/ eu-officially-publishes-settlement-guidelines-despite-israeli-objections-320384.

72. Herb Keinon, *Netanyahu Working to Get EU to Freeze Publication of New Settlement Guidelines*, JERUSALEM POST, July 17, 2013, http://www.jpost.com/Diplomacy-and-Politics/Netanyahu-pushing-for-EU-freeze-on-publication-of-new-guidelines-320115.

73. Avi Bell & Eugene Kontorovich, *EU's Israel Grants Guidelines: A Legal and Policy Analysis* (Kohelet Policy Forum Research Paper, Oct. 2013), http://kohelet.org.il/ uploads/file/EUs%20Israel%20Grants%20Guidelines%20A%20Legal%20and%20 Policy%20Analysis%20-%20Kohelet%20Policy%20Forum%20-%20Final(1).pdf.

74. *Id.*

75. *Id.*

76. Press Summary, Richardson and Another v. Director of Public Prosecutions [2014] UKSC (Feb. 5, 2014), https://www.supremecourt.uk/decided-cases/docs/ UKSC_2012_0198_PressSummary.pdf.

77. *Id.*

78. *Id.*

79. *Id.*

80. *Id.*

81. *Id.* (emphasis added).

82. *Id.*

83. *Id.*

84. Judgment, Richardson and Another (Appellants) v. Director of Public Prosecutions (Respondent), 2014 UKSC 8 (Feb. 5, 2014), https://www.supremecourt.uk/decided-cases/docs/UKSC_2012_0198_Judgment.pdf.

85. *Id.*

86. *Id.*

87. *Id.*

88. *Supreme Court Rules Against Ahava Boycotters in Final Appeal*, BRITAIN ISRAEL COMMC'NS & RES. CTR., June 2, 2014, http://www.bicom.org.uk/ news-article/18648/.

89. *Activists Cleared over Brighton Weapons Factory Raid*, BBC NEWS, July 2, 2010, http://www.bbc.com/news/10489356.

90. Bibi van der Zee & Rob Evans, *Jury Clears Activists Who Broke into Brighton Arms Factory*, THE GUARDIAN, June 30, 2010, http://www.theguardian.com/world/2010/ jun/30/activists-arms-factory-acquitted.

91. Corporate Watch—Tracking Corporate Complicity in the Occupation of Palestine, *EDO Decommissioners Victorious*, July 29, 2010, https://corporateoccupation.word-press.com/2010/07/29/edo-decommissioners-victorious/.

92. *Id.*

93. *Judge Bathurst-Norman: The Full Summing-up*, JEWISH CHRONICLE, July 15, 2010, http://www.thejc.com/35771/judge-bathurst-norman-full-summing.

94. *Id.*

95. *Id.*

96. *Hove Trial Judge Reprimanded After Nazi Remarks*, BBC NEWS, Oct. 7, 2010, http://www.bbc.com/news/uk-england-sussex-11493124.

97. *Raytheon 6 Cleared*, DERRY JOURNAL, June 11, 2008, http://www.derryjournal.com/journal/Raytheon-6-cleared.4176443.jp.

98. *Id.*

99. *Nine Acquitted at Raytheon Trial*, BBC NEWS, June 4, 2010, http://www.bbc.co.uk/news/10241052.

100. *Id.*

101. *Defence Firm Protestors Arrested*, BBC NEWS, Aug. 9, 2006, http://news.bbc.co.uk/2/hi/uk_news/northern_ireland/4776051.stm.

102. *Raytheon to Pull out of Londonderry*, LONDONDERRY SENTINEL, Jan. 15, 2010, http://www.londonderrysentinel.co.uk/news/local-news/raytheon-to-pull-out-of-londonderry-1-2099755.

103. *Id.*

104. *Id.*

105. Tom Anderson & Therezie Cooper, *Ahava Blockaders Supreme Court Appeal Fails, but Campaign Remains Victorious*, CORPORATE WATCH, Feb. 7, 2014, http://corporateoc-cupation.org/ahava-blockaders-supreme-court-appeal-fails/.

106. French Penal Code, art. 132-76, http://www.legifrance.gouv.fr/Traductions/en-English/Legifrance-translations (French government translation of French legal texts) (last visited Mar. 15, 2015).

107. American Jewish Committee, *France*, http://www.ajc.org/atf/cf/%7B42d75369-d582-4380-8395-d25925b85eaf%7D/3_FRANCE.PDF (survey of French law pertaining to hate crimes, prepared by Hogan Lovells law firm) (last visited Mar. 15, 2015).

108. *Id.*

109. Bio of Pierre Lellouche, NTI, http://www.nti.org/about/leadership-staff/pierre-lellouche/ (last visited Mar. 15, 2015); *see also French Court Fines Boycott-Israel Activists for Discrimination*, JTA, Nov. 29, 2013, http://www.jta.org/2013/11/29/news-opinion/world/french-court-fines-boycott-israel-activists-for-discrimination.

110. William Safran, *Ethnoreligious Politics in France: Jews and Muslims*, 27 W. EUR. POL. 423, 435 (May 2004), http://dx.doi.org/10.1080/0140238042000228086; American Jewish Committee, *France, supra* note 107.

111. *Id.*

112. *BDS a Hate Crime? In France, Legal Vigilance Punishes Anti-Israel Activists*, HAARETZ, Feb. 15, 2014, http://www.haaretz.com/jewish-world/1.574361.

113. Peter Martino, *France Penalizes Boycott of Israeli Products*, GATESTONE INST., July 12, 2012, http://www.gatestoneinstitute.org/3164/france-penalizes-boycott-israeli-products.

114. *Id.*

115. *Id.*

116. *BDS a Hate Crime?, supra* note 112.

117. *Id.*

118. Martino, *supra* note 113.

119. Press Release Issued by the Registrar, Chamber Judgment, Willem v. France, Eur. Ct. H.R. (July 16, 2009), http://hudoc.echr.coe.int/eng?i=003-2803253-3069793.

120. Martino, *supra* note 13.

121. Press Release Issued by the Registrar, *supra* note 119.
122. *Id.*
123. Decision, S.A.S. OPM France v. Association France Palestine Solidarite, Tribunal de Grande Instance de Paris (Jan. 23, 2014), http://www.intjewishlawyers.org/main/files/Decision%20Sodastream%20(anglais).pdf (OPM France Decision).
124. *Id.*
125. Tzvi Ben-Gedalyahu, *SodaStream Wins Lawsuit Against French Boycott Israel Group*, JEWISH PRESS, Jan. 29, 2014, http://www.jewishpress.com/news/sodastream-wins-lawsuit-against-french-boycott-israel-group/2014/01/28/.
126. OPM France Decision, *supra* note 123.
127. *Id.*; *Paris Court Fines Pro-Palestinian Group for SodaStream Boycott Campaign*, JTA, Jan. 29, 2014, http://www.jta.org/2014/01/29/news-opinion/world/paris-court-fines-pro-palestinian-group-for-sodastream-boycott-campaign.
128. OPM France Decision, *supra* note 123.
129. *Id.*
130. Jodi Rudoren, *Israeli Firm, Target of Boycott, to Shut West Bank Plant*, N.Y. TIMES, Oct. 30, 2014, http://www.nytimes.com/2014/10/31/world/middleeast/sodastream-to-close-factory-in-west-bank.html?_r=0.
131. *Id.*
132. *Id.*
133. *Id.*
134. BDS Movement, *SodaStream to Close Illegal Settlement Factory in Response Growing Boycott Campaign*, Oct. 30, 2014, http://www.bdsmovement.net/2014/sodastream-closes-illegal-settlement-factory-in-response-growing-boycott-campaign-12782.
135. Pact of the League of Arab States [LAS] (Mar. 22, 1945), *available at* Avalon Project: Documents in Law, History & Diplomacy, Yale Law School, http://avalon.law.yale.edu/20th_century/arableag.asp#1.
136. MARTIN A. WEISS, CONG. RESEARCH SERV., RL33961, ARAB LEAGUE BOYCOTT OF ISRAEL (2013), https://fas.org/sgp/crs/mideast/RL33961.pdf.
137. *Id.*
138. *Id.*
139. *Id.*
140. *Id.*
141. 15 C.F.R. § 760.2(a).
142. 15 C.F.R. § 760.2(b).
143. 15 C.F.R. § 760.2(c).
144. 15 C.F.R. § 760.2(d).
145. 15 C.F.R. § 760.2(e).
146. 15 C.F.R. § 760.2(f).
147. U.S. DEP'T OF COMMERCE, OFFICE OF ANTIBOYCOTT COMPLIANCE, http://www.bis.doc.gov/index.php/enforcement/oac (last accessed Mar. 17, 2015).
148. *Id.*
149. *Id.*
150. *Id.*
151. *Id.*
152. WEISS, *supra* note 136.
153. The Export Administration Act of 1979, http://legcounsel.house.gov/Comps/eaa79.pdf (emphasis added) (last visited Mar. 17, 2015).
154. *See, e.g.,* 15 C.F.R. § 760.2(a)(10).
155. *See, e.g.,* 15 C.F.R. § 760.2(a)(1).

156. *Impact of Federal Anti-Boycott and Other Laws on BDS Campaigns*, Nat'l Lawyers Guild—Int'l Comm., Oct. 2009, http://palestinelegalsupport.org/download/bds/boycott/NLG_BDS_legal_memo.pdf.

157. *Id.*

158. *See, e.g.*, Memorandum from the Lawfare Project, The BDS Movement and Applicability of Federal and New York State Law to Challenge the Campaign, http://www.thelawfareproject.org/BDS_Analysis.pdf (last visited Apr. 1, 2015).

159. *See, e.g.*, MARC A. GREENDORFER, SCHOLARS FOR PEACE IN THE MIDDLE EAST, THE BDS MOVEMENT: THAT WHICH WE CALL A FOREIGN BOYCOTT, BY ANY OTHER NAME, IS STILL ILLEGAL 52, http://spme.org/files/2015/01/ssrn-id2531130.pdf.

160. *See, e.g., id.* at 59.

161. Pub. L. No. 114-26 (2015), https://www.congress.gov/114/plaws/publ26/PLAW-114publ26.pdf.

162. United States-Israel Trade Enhancement Act of 2015, S. 619, 114th Cong. (2015–2016), https://www.congress.gov/bill/114th-congress/senate-bill/619/text (last visited Apr. 1, 2015).

163. Press Release, Congressman Peter Roskam, *Roskam Anti-BDS Provisions Signed Into Law* (June 29, 2015), http://roskam.house.gov/media-center/press-releases/roskam-anti-bds-provisions-signed-into-law-0.

164. Pub. L. No. 114-26, § 102(b)(20).

165. *Transatlantic Trade and Investment Partnership*, U.S. Trade Representative, https://ustr.gov/ttip.

166. Pub. L. No. 114-26, § 102(b)(20).

167. *Id.*

168. Nahal Toosi, *Administration Objects to Israeli-Linked Provision in Trade Bill*, POLITICO, June 30, 2015, http://www.politico.com/story/2015/06/administration-objects-to-israeli-settlements-provision-in-trade-bill-119620.

169. United States-Israel Trade Enhancement Act of 2015, S. 619, 114th Cong. (2015–2016), https://www.congress.gov/bill/114th-congress/senate-bill/619/text (last visited Apr. 1, 2015).

170. United States-Israel Trade and Commercial Enhancement Act, H.R. 825, 114th Cong. (2015–2016), https://www.congress.gov/bill/114th-congress/house-bill/825/text (last visited Apr. 1, 2015).

171. *Id.*

172. *Id.*

173. *Id.*

174. AIPAC, *Bill Summary, The U.S.-Israel Trade & Commercial Enhancement Act (H.R. 825)* (Feb. 2015), http://www.aipac.org/~/media/Publications/Policy%20and%20Politics/AIPAC%20Analyses/Bill%20Summaries/2015/AIPAC%20Bill%20Summary%20-The%20US%20Israel%20Trade%20and%20Commercial%20Enhancement%20Act.pdf.

175. *Id.*

176. Illinois Public Act 099-0128, 99th General Assembly, July 23, 2015,http://www.ilga.gov/legislation/publicacts/fulltext.asp?Name=099-0128.

177. *Id.*

178. *Id.*

179. *Id.*

180. *Id.*

181. Stuart Winer, *Dutch Supermarkets Ban Settlement Products*, TIMES OF ISRAEL, July 22, 2013, http://www.timesofisrael.com/dutch-supermarkets-ban-settlement-products/.

182. Barak Ravid, *Denmark's Largest Bank Blacklists Israel's Hapoalim over Settlement Construction*, Haaretz, Feb. 1, 2014, http://www.haaretz.com/news/diplomacy-defense/1.571849.

183. *See, e.g., Letter: Over 100 Artists Announce a Cultural Boycott of Israel*, The Guardian, Feb. 13, 2015, http://www.theguardian.com/world/2015/feb/13/cultural-boycott-israel-starts-tomorrow.

184. *Guidance: Overseas Business Risk—Israel*, U.K. Foreign & Commonwealth Office, June 1, 2014, https://www.gov.uk/government/publications/overseas-business-risk-israel/overseas-business-risk-israel.

185. See, for example, this chapter's detailed discussion of the Dutch criminal investigation of Riwal/Lima.

186. Eugene Kontorovich, *Illinois Passes Historic Anti-BDS Bill, as Congress Mulls Similar Moves*, The Volokh Conspiracy, May 18, 2015, http://www.washingtonpost.com/news/volokh-conspiracy/wp/2015/05/18/illinois-passes-historic-anti-bds-bill-as-congress-mulls-similar-moves/.

187. Hazel Bradford, *State Pension Funds' Combined Underfunding Rises to $4.7 Trillion—Report*, Pensions & Investments, Nov. 12, 2014, http://www.pionline.com/article/20141112/ONLINE/141119943/state-pension-funds-combined-underfunding-rises-to-47-trillion-8212-report.

188. Press Release, U.S. Census Bureau, *State Government Revenues Exceed Expenditures in 2013*, Census Bureau Reports (Feb. 3, 2015), https://www.census.gov/newsroom/press-releases/2015/cb15-22.html; Bradford, *supra* note 189.

189. Douglas F. Gansler, *Uniting States Against Iran*, Wall St. J., Mar. 8, 2013, http://www.wsj.com/articles/SB10001424127887324662404578332622153212746; *Divestment: An Important Tool in Preventing Nuclear Iran*, AIPAC, Jan. 6, 2010, http://www.aipac.org/~/media/Publications-old/Policy%20and%20Politics/AIPAC%20Analyses/Issue%20Memos/2010/AIPAC_Memo_-_Divestment_-_An_Important_Tool_in_Preventing_Nuclear_Iran.pdf.

190. Alexander E.M. Hess, *The 10 Largest Employers in America*, USA Today, Aug. 22, 2013, http://www.usatoday.com/story/money/business/2013/08/22/ten-largest-employers/2680249/.

191. Company Exclusions: Responsible Investments, The Government Pension Fund, Government of Norway, https://www.regjeringen.no/en/topics/the-economy/the-government-pension-fund/internt-bruk/companies-excluded-from-the-investment-u/id447122/; Recommendation to the Ministry of Finance of November 15, 2005 from the Council on Ethics of the Norwegian Government Petroleum Fund regarding Wal-Mart Stores Inc., https://www.regjeringen.no/en/dokumenter/Recommendation-of-15-November-2005/id450120/; Two Companies—Wal-Mart and Freeport—Are Being Excluded from the Norwegian Government Pension-Fund Global's Investment Universe, Norway Ministry of Finance Press Release, June 6, 2006, https://www.regjeringen.no/en/aktuelt/two-companies---wal-mart-and-freeport---/id104396/.

192. Company Exclusions: Responsible Investments, The Government Pension Fund, Government of Norway, https://www.regjeringen.no/en/topics/the-economy/the-government-pension-fund/internt-bruk/companies-excluded-from-the-invest-ment-u/id447122/; Recommendation for Exclusion of Shikun & Binui Ltd. from the Government Pension Fund Global, memorandum from the Council on Ethics—The Government Pension Fund Global to the Ministry of Finance, December 11, 2011, https://www.regjeringen.no/contentassets/f65ed42d67ee49d29ee8d238ff53d61d/shikun_binui_eng.pdf; Recommendation to exclude the companies Africa Israel

Investments Ltd. and Danya Cebus Ltd. from the investment universe of the Government Pension Fund Global, memorandum from the Council on Ethics—The Government Pension Fund Global to the Ministry of Finance, November 1, 2013, https://www.regjeringen.no/contentassets/f65ed42d67ee49d29ee8d238ff53d61d/africa_israel_nov_2013.pdf.

193. Princeton Univ. Program in Law & Pub. Aff., The Princeton Principles on Universal Jurisdiction 23 (2001); https://lapa.princeton.edu/hosteddocs/unive_jur.pdf.

194. Mary Robinson, U.N. High Comm'r for Hum. Rts., *Foreword* to The Princeton Principles on Universal Jurisdiction, *supra* note 195, at 16; Luc Reydams, Universal Jurisdiction: International and Municipal Legal Perspectives 5 (2004).

195. Anne Herzberg, NGO "Lawfare": Exploitation of Courts in the Arab-Israeli Conflict 41 (2d ed. 2010), http://www.ngo-monitor.org/data/images/File/lawfare-monograph.pdf.

196. *Id.* at 41.

197. James Hider, *Hamas Using English Law to Demand Arrest of Israeli Leaders for War Crimes*, Times of London, Dec. 21, 2009.

198. *Id.*

199. *Id.; see also* Richard Ford, *Anyone Can Apply for a Warrant over Allegations of a Serious Offence*, Times of London, Dec. 21, 2009.

200. Soeren Kern, *New "War Crimes" Lawfare*, Hudson New York, Aug. 4, 2010, http://www.hudson-ny.org/1456/new-war-crimes-lawfare.

201. *Sayyed Nasrallah: Unite to Back Turkey, Egypt; Take Part in Freedom Flotilla 2*, Al Manar, April 6, 2010, http://www.almanar.com.lb/newssite/NewsDetails.aspx?id=140626&language=ar (note that Al Manar is a Lebanese media outlet affiliated with Hezbollah).

202. The Principle and Practice of Universal Jurisdiction: PCHR's Work in the Occupied Palestinian Territory (2010), http://www.fidh.org/IMG/pdf/PCHR_Work_Report_Web.pdf.

203. *Id.* at 111.

204. *Id.* at 117.

205. Chris McGreal, *Sharon's Ally Safe from Arrest in Britain*, The Guardian, Feb. 10, 2004, http://www.theguardian.com/world/2004/feb/11/israel.foreignpolicy.

206. *See, e.g.,* Associated Press, *British Police Cancel Almog Arrest Warrant*, Haaretz, Sept. 18, 2005, http://www.haaretz.com/print-edition/news/british-police-cancel-almog-arrest-warrant-1.170031; Human Rights Watch, *Universal Jurisdiction in Europe: The State of the Art* (June 2006), at 9, http://www.hrw.org/reports/2006/ij0606/2.htm.

207. Wolfgang Kaleck et al., International Prosecution of Human Rights Crimes 153 (2006).

208. Andy McSmith, *Keeping the Peace? The El Al Flight and the Israeli Army Officer*, The Independent (UK), Feb. 20, 2008, http://www.independent.co.uk/news/uk/home-news/keeping-the-peace-the-el-al-flight-and-the-israeli-army-officer-784407.html.

209. *Id.;* Human Rights Watch, *Universal Jurisdiction in Europe, supra* note 206, at 9.

210. McSmith, *supra* note 208.

211. Dominic Casciani, *Police Feared "Airport Stand-Off,"* BBC News, Feb. 19, 2008, http://news.bbc.co.uk/2/hi/uk_news/7251954.stm.

212. *Id.*

213. *Id.*

214. *Id.*

215. *See, e.g.,* McSmith, *supra* note 208.

216. The Principle and Practice of Universal Jurisdiction, *supra* note 202.

217. *See* Eugene Kontorovich, Lawfare Lessons from Israel: Universal Jurisdiction (2013) (unpublished manuscript).

218. The Principle and Practice of Universal Jurisdiction, *supra* note 202, at 131.

219. *See* Kontorovich, *supra* note 217.

220. John Goetz, *Public Prosecutors in Germany: German Members of Parliament File War Crimes Complaints Against Israel*, Spiegel Online, June 11, 2010, http://www.spiegel.de/international/world/aftermath-of-the-israel-flotilla-raid-german-activists-file-war-crimes-complaints-a-700127.html.

221. *Id.*; Benjamin Weinthal & Alex Feuerherdt, *Israel Praises German Prosecutor for Rejecting Mavi Marmara Complaint*, Jerusalem Post, Jan. 29, 2015, http://www.jpost.com/International/Israel-praises-German-prosecutor-for-rejecting-Mavi-Marmara-complaint-389390.

222. Goetz, *supra* note 220.

223. Weinthal & Feuerherdt, *supra* note 221.

224. Benjamin Weinthal, *Swedish Cabinet Minister Was On Board Gaza-bound Turkish Ship Mavi Marmara*, Jerusalem Post, June 10, 2014, http://www.jpost.com/Israel-News/Politics-And-Diplomacy/Swedish-cabinet-.member-was-on-board-Gaza-bound-Turkish-ship-Mavi-Marmara-378199.

225. *See* Kontorovich, *supra* note 217.

226. *See id.*

227. Jack Goldsmith, The Terror Presidency: Law and Judgment Inside the Bush Administration 60–61 (2007); Jim Yardley, *Spain Seeks to Curb Law Allowing Judges to Pursue Cases Globally*, N.Y. Times, Feb. 10, 2014, http://www.nytimes.com/2014/02/11/world/europe/spanish-legislators-seek-new-limits-on-universal-jurisdiction-law.html; Richard Bernstein, *Belgium Rethinks Its Prosecutorial Zeal*, N.Y. Times, Apr. 1, 2003, http://www.nytimes.com/2003/04/01/world/belgium-rethinks-its-prosecutorial-zeal.html.

228. *Spain High Court Dismissed China Rights Cases*, Reuters, June 23, 2014, http://uk.reuters.com/article/2014/06/23/uk-spain-china-idUKKBN0EY2IS20140623; Yardley, *supra* note 227.

229. *Spain High Court Dismissed China Rights Cases, supra* note 228; Yardley, *supra* note 227.

230. Yardley, *id*; Raphael Minder, *Argentine Judge Seeks to Put Franco Officials on Trial*, N.Y. Times, Sept. 30, 2013, http://www.nytimes.com/2013/10/01/world/europe/argentine-judge-seeks-to-put-franco-officials-on-trial.html.

231. Press Release, Ministry of Justice, *Universal Jurisdiction* (Sept. 15, 2011), https://www.gov.uk/government/news/universal-jurisdiction.

232. *Id.*

233. *William Hague Meets Israeli Tzipi Livni for Talks*, The Independent (UK), Oct. 6, 2011, http://www.independent.co.uk/news/world/middle-east/william-hague-meets-israeli-tzipi-livni-for-talks-2366301.html.

234. Anshel Pfeffer, *Fear of Arrest Still Prevents Israeli Officials from Visiting Britain*, Haaretz, May 30, 2012, http://www.haaretz.com/news/diplomacy-defense/fear-of-arrest-still-prevents-israeli-officials-from-visiting-britain.premium-1.433452.

235. Amnesty International, Universal Jurisdiction: A Preliminary Survey of Legislation Around the World 1–2 (Oct. 5, 2011), https://www.amnesty.org/en/documents/IOR53/004/2011/en/.

236. Stephanie Nebehay, *Bush's Swiss Visit Off after Complaints on Torture*, Reuters, Feb. 5, 2011, http://www.reuters.com/article/2011/02/05/us-bush-torture-idUSTRE7141CU20110205.

237. *Boycott Goes Prime-Time in Israel*, +972 Magazine, Jan. 19, 2014, http://972mag.com/boycott-goes-prime-time-in-israel/85974/.

238. *Id.*

239. Corrie v. Caterpillar, Inc., 403 F. Supp. 2d 1019, 1022 (W.D. Wash. 2005), *aff'd*, 503 F.3d 974 (9th Cir. 2007); Palestinian Ctr. for Hum. Rts., The Principle and Practice of Universal Jurisdiction: PCHR's Work in the Occupied Palestinian Territory 119 (2010), http://www.fidh.org/IMG/pdf/PCHR_Work_Report_Web.pdf.

240. Corrie v. Caterpillar, 503 F.3d 974, 979 (9th Cir. 2007).

241. *Id.*

242. *Id.*

243. *Id.*

244. *Corrie*, 403 F. Supp. 2d at 1024.

245. *Id.* at 1032.

246. *Corrie*, 503 F.3d 974.

247. David Gauthier-Villars, *French Court to Hear Israeli Tram Case*, Wall St. J., Apr. 17, 2009, http://online.wsj.com/news/articles/SB123992141785126493; Raphael Ahren, *French Court's Light Rail Ruling Breaks No Legal Ground, Scholars Say*, Apr. 29, 2013, http://www.timesofisrael.com/french-ruling-on-jerusalems-light-rail-adds-nothing-new-scholars-say/.

248. Ahren, *id.*

249. Gauthier-Villars, *supra* note 247.

250. France-Palestine Solidarite & Palestine Liberation Org. v. Societe Alstom Transp. SA, Societe Alstom SA, & SA Veolia Transp., Versailles Court of Appeal Decision (Mar. 22, 2013), http://blog.eur.nl/iss/hr/files/2012/02/Decision-Versailles-Appeal-Court-22-March-2013.pdf (unofficial translation).

251. *Id.*

252. Ahren, *supra* note 247; Press Release, Alstom, *Jerusalem Tramway: French Justice Rules out the Legal Action Against Alstom* (June 12, 2014), http://www.alstom.com/press-centre/2013/3/jerusalem-tramway-french-justice-rules-out-the-legal-action-against-alstom/.

253. *France-Palestine Solidarite & Palestine Liberation Org.*, *supra* note 250.

254. *Id.*

255. *See, e.g.*, Avi Bar-Eli & Itai Trilnick, *Not Afraid to Make Money in Israel*, Haaretz, Feb. 15, 2012, http://www.haaretz.com/business/not-afraid-to-make-money-in-israel-1.412966.

256. Harriet Sherwood, *Jerusalem's Long-Awaited Light Railway Splits Opinion*, The Guardian, Aug. 17, 2011, http://www.theguardian.com/world/2011/aug/17/jerusalem-light-railway-opinion.

257. *France-Palestine Solidarite & Palestine Liberation Organization*, *supra* note 250.

258. Sherwood, *supra* note 256.

259. *Id.*

260. Letter from Liesbeth Zegveld to National Public Prosecutors' Office, Re: Al-Haq/Report of War Crimes and Crimes Against Humanity by Riwal (Mar. 15, 2010) (certified translation), http://www.alhaq.org/images/stories/PDF/accoutability-files/Complaint%20-%20English.pdf.

261. *Id.*

262. *Id.*
263. *Id.*
264. *Id.*
265. *Id.*
266. *Id.*
267. *Id.*
268. Letter from A.R.E. Schram, National Public Prosecutor's Office, The Netherlands, to Van Eijck (May 13, 2013), (translation), http://www.alhaq.org/images/stories/Brief_Landelijk_Parket_13-05-2013_ENG__a_Sj_crona_Van_Stigt_Advocaten.pdf.
269. *See, e.g.,* Adri Nieuwhof, *Dutch Company Raided over Involvement in Occupation,* ELECTRONIC INTIFADA, Oct. 20, 2010, http://electronicintifada.net/content/dutch-company-raided-over-involvement-occupation/9076; *Lawfare Update: Al Haq Exploits the Dutch Legal System,* NGO MONITOR, Nov. 16, 2010, http://www.ngo-monitor.org/article.php?id=3112#lawfare.
270. Letter from Schram, *supra* note 268.
271. Mike Corder, *Dutch Won't Charge Company in Israeli Barrier Case,* ASSOCIATED PRESS, May 14, 2013, http://bigstory.ap.org/article/dutch-wont-charge-company-israeli-barrier-case.
272. Letter from Schram, *supra* note 268.
273. *Id.*
274. *Id.*
275. *Id.*
276. *Id.*
277. *Id.*
278. *Id.;* Corder, *supra* note 271.
279. Letter from Schram, *supra* note 268.
280. *Id.;* Corder, *supra* note 271.
281. Letter from Schram, *supra* note 268.
282. *Id.*
283. Corder, *supra* note 271.
284. *Id.*
285. On its website, Riwal describes itself as "the largest specialist in the area of working safely and efficiently at height." http://www.riwal.com/united-kingdom/en/about-riwal/profile. Its website also does not show Israel as a country in which it has a branch. http://www.riwal.com/united-kingdom/en/sitecore/content/riwal-kz/home/contact/branches%20international (last visited Aug. 6, 2014).
286. Ido Rosenzweig & Yuval Shany, *Establishment of a Legal Department by the Israeli Security Cabinet to Deal with Issues of International Jurisdiction,* TERRORISM & DEMOCRACY (2009), http://en.idi.org.il/analysis/terrorism-and-democracy/issue-no-12/establishment-of-a-legal-department-by-the-israeli-security-cabinet-to-deal-with-issues-of-international-jurisdiction/.
287. *Id.*
288. *Id.*
289. Yonah Jeremy Bob, *18 Recommendations That Could Determine Israel's Fate Before the ICC,* JERUSALEM POST, Jan. 26, 2015, http://www.jpost.com/Israel-News/Politics-And-Diplomacy/18-recommendations-that-could-determine-israels-fate-before-the-ICC-388955.
290. PUBLIC COMM'N TO EXAMINE THE MARITIME INCIDENT OF 31 MAY 2010, SECOND REPORT—THE TURKEL COMM'N, ISRAEL'S MECHANISMS FOR EXAMINING AND INVESTIGATING COMPLAINTS AND CLAIMS OF VIOLATIONS OF THE LAWS OF ARMED

Conflict According to International Law (Feb. 2013), http://www.turkel-committee.gov.il/files/newDoc3/The%20Turkel%20Report%20for%20website.pdf.

291. Bob, *supra* note 289.

292. Yonah Jeremy Bob, *New Deputy Attorney-General to Increase Country's Emphasis on International Law*, Jerusalem Post, Oct. 30, 2013, http://www.jpost.com/National-News/New-deputy-attorney-general-to-increase-countrys-emphasis-on-global-law-330134.

293. *Id.*

294. *Id.*

295. *Id.*

296. Ido Rosenzweig & Yuval Shany, *Establishment of a Legal Department by the Israeli Security Cabinet to Deal with Issues of International Jurisdiction*, Terrorism & Democracy, 2009, http://en.idi.org.il/analysis/terrorism-and-democracy/issue-no-12/establishment-of-a-legal-department-by-the-israeli-security-cabinet-to-deal-with-issues-of-international-jurisdiction/.

297. *Freedom in the World 2015: Gaza Strip*, Freedom House, https://freedomhouse.org/report/freedom-world/2015/gaza-strip#.VR3PCVxXmKw.

298. *Id.*

299. *Id.*

300. *Id.*

301. *Id.*

302. *Freedom in the World 2015: Israel*, Freedom House, https://freedomhouse.org/report/freedom-world/2015/israel#.VR3R9FxXmKw.

303. *Freedom in the World 2015: United States*, Freedom House, https://freedomhouse.org.

304. *Freedom in the World: West Bank 2013*, Freedom House, http://freedomhouse.org/report/freedom-world/2013/west-bank#.U-lUW1YsJY4.

305. *Freedom in the World 2015: West Bank*, Freedom House, https://freedomhouse.org/report/freedom-world/2015/west-bank#.VR3P7lxXmKw.

306. *Freedom in the World: Gaza Strip 2011*, Freedom House, https://freedomhouse.org/report/freedom-world/2011/gaza-strip#.VeCCr7RXmKw.

307. *Freedom in the World 2015: Gaza Strip*, Freedom House, https://freedomhouse.org/report/freedom-world/2015/gaza-strip#.VR3TEFxXmKw.

308. *See, e.g.*, David F. Chavkin, *Thinking/Practicing Clinical Legal Education from Within the Palestinian-Israeli Conflict: Lessons from the Al-Quds Human Rights Clinic*, 18 Hum. Rts. Brief 14 (2010), http://www.wcl.american.edu/hrbrief/18/1chavkin.pdf.

309. Chemonics Int'l, Fostering Respect for the Rule of Law: Final Report of the West Bank/Gaza Supporting Rule of Law Reform Project (Sept. 2007), http://pdf.usaid.gov/pdf_docs/pdack507.pdf.

310. *See, e.g.*, USAID, *Palestinian Justice Enhancement Program, Fact Sheet*, Dec. 2011, http://pdf.usaid.gov/pdf_docs/PDACT146.pdf.

311. *See, e.g.*, *Middle East Rule of Law Program*, Open Society Foundations, http://www.amideast.org/jordan/academic-and-cultural-exchange/middle-east-rule-law-program-merol.

312. *Freedom in the World: Palestinian Authority Administered Territories 1998*, Freedom House, http://www.freedomhouse.org/report/freedom-world/1998/palestinian-authority-administered-territories#.U-ppG1YsJY4.

313. Ireland Dep't of For. Aff. & Trade, Irish Aid: About Us, https://www.irishaid.ie/about-us/.

314. The Spanish Agency for International Development Cooperation, http://www.aecid.es/EN/aecid.

315. About Trocaire, http://www.trocaire.org/whatwedo/who-we-are.

316. Palestinian Ctr. for Hum. Rts., Annual Report: 2013, http://www.pchrgaza. org/files/2014/annual%20English%202013.pdf.

317. The Principle and Practice of Universal Jurisdiction: PCHR's Work in the Occupied Palestinian Territory 175 (2010), http://www.fidh.org/IMG/ pdf/PCHR_Work_Report_Web.pdf.

318. 2014's Partners, Al Haq, http://www.alhaq.org/about-al-haq/donors.

319. Orde F. Kittrie, *More Process Than Peace: Legitimacy, Compliance, and the Oslo Accords,* 101 Mich. L. Rev. 1661, 1705 (2003), *available at* http://ssrn.com/abstract=997485.

320. Mahmoud Abbas, Through Secret Channels 162 (1995).

321. *Id.* at 178–79.

322. *Id.* at 179.

323. *Id.* at 162.

324. Author interview of Mostafa Elostaz (Feb. 21, 2015). Elostaz is project manager and coordinator of the Palestinian Peace Coalition.

325. *Id.*

326. *See* Negotiations Affairs Dep't, PLO, http://www.nad-plo.org/etemplate.php?id=182.

327. *Id.*

328. *Saeb Erekat,* Al Jazeera, Head to Head (Apr. 2, 2014), http://www.aljazeera.com/ programmes/headtohead/2014/03/transcript-dr-saeb-erekat-201432611433441126. html.

329. Jodi Rudoren & Isabel Kershner, *Arc of a Failed Deal: How Nine Months of Mideast Talks Ended in Disarray,* N.Y. Times, Apr. 28, 2014, http://www.nytimes.com/2014/04/29/ world/middleeast/arc-of-a-failed-deal-how-nine-months-of-mideast-talks-ended-in- dissarray.html.

330. Elostaz Interview, *supra* note 324.

331. *See, e.g.,* Lee Hockstader, *A Dreamer Who Forced His Cause onto World Stage,* Wash. Post, Nov. 11, 2004, http://www.washingtonpost.com/wp-dyn/articles/A41509- 2004Nov10.html (obituary of Yasser Arafat).

332. *See, e.g.,* Mahmoud Abbas, *Palestine's Vision of Peace Is Clear,* Haaretz, July 7, 2014, http://www.haaretz.com/news/diplomacy-defense/israel-peace- conference/1.600293#!; Dennis Ross, *How to Break a Middle East Stalemate,* Wash. Post, Jan. 7, 2012, http://www.washingtonpost.com/opinions/how-to-unfreeze-a- middle-east-stalemate/2011/12/21/gIQAdhZdfP_print.html (referring to Abbas as among "those Palestinian leaders … who believe in nonviolence and coexistence"); Ben Birnbaum & Amir Tibon, *The Explosive, Inside Story of How John Kerry Built an Israel-Palestine Peace Plan—and Watched It Crumble,* New Republic, July 20, 2014, http://www.newrepublic.com/article/118751/how-israel-palestine-peace-deal-died ("Having ruled out a third intifada, Abbas believed the United Nations was his only leverage over Israel.").

333. Omar M. Dajani, *Shadow or Shade? The Roles of International Law in Palestinian-Israeli Peace Talks,* 32 Yale J. Int'l L. 61 (2007).

334. *See, e.g.,* Moran Azulay, *MKs to Discuss Bill Targeting "Anti-Israel" NGOs,* YnetNews, Feb. 26, 2014, http://www.ynetnews.com/articles/0,7340,L-4492814,00.html; Jonathan Lis, *Ministers Approve "Unconstitutional" Bill Penalizing Left-Wing NGOs,* Haaretz, Dec. 15, 2013, http://www.haaretz.com/news/national/. premium-1.563674.

335. Yonah Jeremy Bob, *High Court Upholds Part of Anti-Boycott Law, Strikes Part and Splits on "1967 Israel,"* Jerusalem Post, Apr. 15, 2015, http://www.jpost.com/Israel-News/ Politics-And-Diplomacy/High-Court-rules-on-boycott-law-398206.

336. Steven Scheer, *Israel Ramps Up Asia Trade Ties as Government Urges Shift from EU*, Reuters, Feb. 3, 2015, http://www.reuters.com/article/2015/02/04/israel-economy-trade-asia-idUSL6N0VD40E20150204.

CHAPTER 7

1. Charles J. Dunlap, Jr., Colonel, USAF, *Law and Military Interventions: Preserving Humanitarian Values in 21st Conflicts* (paper prepared for the Humanitarian Challenges in Military Intervention Conference, Carr Ctr. for Human Rights Policy, Kennedy Sch. of Gov't, Harvard Univ., Washington, D.C., Nov. 29, 2001), http://people.duke.edu/~pfeaver/dunlap.pdf.

2. Penny L. Mellie, *Hamas and Hezbollah: A Comparison of Tactics*, in Back to Basics: A Study of the Second Lebanon War and Operation CAST LEAD (Lt. Col. Scott Farquhar ed., 2009).

3. *Id.*

4. *Id.*

5. Yaakov Katz, *Haniyeh Hid in Hospital During Gaza Op*, Jerusalem Post, Apr., 22, 2009.

6. William Booth, *While Israel Held Its Fire, the Militant Group Hamas Did Not*, Wash. Post, July 15, 2014, http://www.washingtonpost.com/world/middle_east/while-israel-held-its-fire-the-militant-group-hamas-did-not/2014/07/15/116fd3d7-3c0f-4413-94a9-2ab16af1445d_story.html.

7. Anne Barnard & Jodi Rudoren, *Israel Says That Hamas Uses Civilian Shields, Reviving Debate*, N.Y. Times, July 23, 2014, http://www.nytimes.com/2014/07/24/world/middleeast/israel-says-hamas-is-using-civilians-as-shields-in-gaza.html?_r=0; *UNRWA Condemns Placement of Rockets, for a Second Time, in One of its Schools*, UNRWA, July 22, 2014, http://www.unrwa.org/newsroom/press-releases/unrwa-condemns-placement-rockets-second-time-one-its-schools; Terrence McCoy, *Why Hamas Stores Its Weapons Inside Hospitals, Mosques and Schools*, Wash. Post, July 31, 2014, http://www.washingtonpost.com/news/morning-mix/wp/2014/07/31/why-hamas-stores-its-weapons-inside-hospitals-mosques-and-schools/.

8. Barnard & Rudoren, *supra* note 7.

9. *See, e.g.*, *Photos: Hamas Holds Parade One Year after Battle with Israel*, Denver Post (AP photographs), Nov. 14, 2013, http://photos.denverpost.com/2013/11/14/photos-hamas-holds-parade-one-year-after-battle-with-israel/#8.

10. James Estrin, *Looking for the Enduring Photo in Gaza*, N.Y. Times, Aug. 5, 2014, http://lens.blogs.nytimes.com/2014/08/05/looking-for-the-enduring-photo-in-gaza/ (interview with *N.Y. Times* staff photographer Tyler Hicks).

11. *Exclusive: Hamas Rocket Launch Pad Lies Near Gaza Homes*, France 24 (last updated Aug. 7, 2014), http://www.france24.com/en/20140805-exclusive-video-hamas-rocket-launching-pad-near-gaza-homes-un-building/.

12. Patrick Martin, *Bad Food, Bad Smells at Refugee Shelter*, Globe & Mail, July 17, 2014, http://www.theglobeandmail.com/news/world/globe-in-gaza-bad-food-bad-smells-at-refugee-shelter/article19650579/.

13. George Thomas, *Gaza Bishop: Hamas Used Church to Fire Rockets*, Christian Broadcasting Network, Aug. 8, 2014, http://www.cbn.com/cbnnews/insideisrael/2014/August/Gaza-Bishop-Hamas-Used-Church-to-Fire-Rockets-/.

14. *Hamas Spokesman Encourages Gazans to Serve as Human Shields: It's Been Proven Effective*, MEMRI, July 8, 2014, http://www.memri.org/clip_transcript/en/4340.htm (translation of interview with Hamas spokesman Sami Abu Zuhri, which aired on Al-Aqsa TV on July 8, 2014).

15. *Id.*

16. *See also, e.g.,* Steven Erlanger & Fares Akram, *Israel Warns Gaza Targets by Phone and Leaflet*, N.Y. TIMES, July 8, 2014, http://www.nytimes.com/2014/07/09/world/middleeast/by-phone-and-leaflet-israeli-attackers-warn-gazans.html?_r=0.

17. *Hamas Tells Civilians to Ignore Warning Notices from the Israeli Army*, PALESTINIAN MEDIA WATCH, July 14, 2014, https://www.youtube.com/watch?v=Zm09uRDdzto&feature=youtu.be.

18. JEAN-MARIE HENCKAERTS & LOUISE DOSWALD-BECK, CUSTOMARY INTERNATIONAL HUMANITARIAN LAW 336, Rule 97 (2005), http://www.icrc.org/eng/assets/files/other/customary-international-humanitarian-law-i-icrc-eng.pdf.

19. Protocol Additional to the Geneva Conventions of 12 August 1949, and Relating to the Protection of Victims of International Armed Conflicts (Protocol I), art. 51, June 8, 1977, http://www.icrc.org/ihl/WebART/470-750065.

20. *Id.* Commentary, http://www.icrc.org/applic/ihl/ihl.nsf/Comment.xsp?viewComments=LookUpCOMART&articleUNID=4BEBD9920AE0AEAEC12563CD0051DC9E ("The term 'movements' ... is intended to cover cases where the civilian population moves of its own accord.").

21. Laurie R. Blank, *Taking Distinction to the Next Level: Accountability for Fighters' Failure to Distinguish Themselves from Civilians*, 46 VAL. U. L. REV. 765, 792 (2012) (citing *Kupreskic*, Case No. IT-95-16-T, Judgment, para. 524, http://www.icty.org/x/cases/kupreskic/tjug/en/kup-tj000114e.pdf).

22. Protocol Additional to the Geneva Conventions of 12 August 1949, and Relating to the Protection of Victims of International Armed Conflicts (Protocol I), art. 58, 8 June 1977, http://www.icrc.org/applic/ihl/ihl.nsf/Article.xsp?action=openDocument&documentId=C995BF5C5BCFB0E2C12563CD0051DDB2.

23. Press Release, The White House, *Remarks by the President at Press Conference after U.S.-Africa Leaders Summit* (Aug. 6, 2014), http://www.whitehouse.gov/the-press-office/2014/08/06/remarks-president-press-conference-after-us-africa-leaders-summit.

24. *EU Council Conclusions on the Middle East Peace Process*, July 22, 2014, http://www.eu-un.europa.eu/articles/en/article_15300_en.htm.

25. Secretary-General's Remarks at Press Conference with Prime Minister Benjamin Netanyahu of Israel (July 22, 1014), http://www.un.org/sg/offthecuff/index.asp?nid=3487.

26. Bassem Eid, *Hamas Needs the Palestinians' Deaths in Order to Claim Victory*, i24NEWS, Aug. 9, 2014, http://www.i24news.tv/en/opinion/39587-140808-hamas-needs-the-palestinians-deaths-in-order-to-claim-victory.

27. Anne Barnard & Jodi Rudoren, *Israel Says That Hamas Uses Civilian Shields, Reviving Debate*, N.Y. TIMES, July 23, 2014, http://www.nytimes.com/2014/07/24/world/middleeast/israel-says-hamas-is-using-civilians-as-shields-in-gaza.html?_r=0.

28. *Id.*

29. *Id.*

30. *Id.*

31. *Report of the Detailed Findings of the Independent Commission of Inquiry Established Pursuant to Human Rights Council Resolution S-21/1*, United Nations Human Rights Council, June 24, 2015, http://www.ohchr.org/EN/HRBodies/HRC/CoIGazaConflict/Pages/ReportCoIGaza.aspx#report.

32. *Id.* at 181.

33. *Id.*

34. Amnesty International, *UN: Gaza Conflict Report a Key Step Towards Justice for Victims on Both Sides*, June 22, 2015, https://www.amnesty.org/en/latest/news/2015/06/un-gaza-conflict-report-a-key-step-towards-justice-for-victims-on-both-sides/.

35. Jodi Rudoren & Somini Sengupta, *U.N. Report on Gaza Finds Evidence of War Crimes by Israel and by Palestinian Militants*, N.Y. TIMES, June 22, 2015, http://www.nytimes.com/2015/06/23/world/middleeast/israel-gaza-report.html.

36. Benjamin Wittes & Yishai Schwartz, *What to Make of the UN's Special Commission Report on Gaza?*, LAWFARE BLOG (June 24, 2015), https://www.lawfareblog.com/what-make-uns-special-commission-report-gaza.

37. Daniel Reisner, *Reflections on the UN Commission of Inquiry Gaza Report, Part I: The Historical Narrative*, LAWFARE BLOG (August 20, 2015), https://www.lawfareblog.com/reflections-un-commission-inquiry-gaza-report-part-i-historical-narrative.

38. Laurie R. Blank, *What the UN Report on Gaza Left Out*, THE HILL, July 7, 2015, http://thehill.com/blogs/pundits-blog/international/247041-what-the-un-report-on-gaza-left-out. The summary of the legal principles is at *Report of the Detailed Findings, supra* note 31, at 11.

39. Blank, *supra* note 38.

40. Professor Geoffrey Corn, *Analysis of the U.N. Report on the 2014 Gaza Conflict: The Distorting Effects of Flawed Foundations*, JINSA, June 2015, at 6, http://www.jinsa.org/files/AnalysisOfTheU.N.Report_ProfCorn.pdf.

41. Blank, *supra* note 38.

42. *Id.*

43. *Report of the Detailed Findings, supra* note 31, at 124.

44. *Id.* at 127.

45. *Id.*

46. *Id.*

47. *Id.* at 128.

48. *Id.* at 182–84.

49. Blank, *supra* note 38.

50. *Id.*

51. *Id.*

52. Wittes & Schwartz, *supra* note 36.

53. *Id.*

54. *Id.*

55. *Id.*

56. *Rocket Attacks on Israel from Gaza*, ISRAEL DEFENSE FORCES, http://www.idfblog.com/facts-figures/rocket-attacks-toward-israel/ (last visited Mar. 14, 2014).

57. Daniel Ben Simon, *Bomb Shelters Replace Summer Camps for Israeli Children*, AL-MONITOR, July 11, 2014, http://www.al-monitor.com/pulse/originals/2014/07/israel-sderot-south-north-rockets-children-shelter-summer.html#.

58. Charles Levinson, *Zahar Interview*, CONFLICT BLOTTER, Aug. 21, 2007, http://web.archive.org/web/20071224004555/http://conflictblotter.com/2007/08/21/zahar-interview/ (at the time of the interview, Levinson was Middle East correspondent for the *Sunday Telegraph*).

59. AMNESTY INTERNATIONAL, UNLAWFUL AND DEADLY: ROCKET AND MORTAR ATTACKS BY PALESTINIAN ARMED GROUPS DURING THE 2014 GAZA/ISRAEL CONFLICT (Mar. 2015), https://www.amnesty.org/en/documents/mde21/1178/2015/en/.

60. Human Rights Watch, *Gaza: Palestinian Rockets Unlawfully Targeted Israeli Civilians* (Dec. 24, 2012), http://www.hrw.org/news/2012/12/24/gaza-palestinian-rockets-unlawfully-targeted-israeli-civilians.

61. Human Rights Watch, *Gaza/Israel: Hamas Rocket Attacks on Civilians Unlawful* (Aug. 6, 2009), http://www.hrw.org/news/2009/08/06/gazaisrael-hamas-rocket-attacks-civilians-unlawful.

62. JEAN-MARIE HENCKAERTS & LOUISE DOSWALD-BECK, CUSTOMARY INTERNATIONAL HUMANITARIAN LAW 3, Rule 1 (2005), http://www.icrc.org/eng/assets/files/other/customary-international-humanitarian-law-i-icrc-eng.pdf.

63. Protocol Additional to the Geneva Conventions of 12 August 1949, and Relating to the Protection of Victims of International Armed Conflicts (Protocol I), June 8, 1977, http://www.icrc.org/applic/ihl/ihl.nsf/Treaty.xsp?action=openDocument&documentId=D9E6B6264D7723C3C12563CD002D6CE4.

64. Protocol Additional to the Geneva Conventions of 12 August 1949, and Relating to the Protection of Victims of Non-International Armed Conflicts (Protocol II), June 8, 1977, http://www.icrc.org/applic/ihl/ihl.nsf/Article.xsp?action=openDocument&documentId=A366465E238B1934C12563CD0051E8A0.

65. Protocol Additional to the Geneva Conventions of 12 August 1949, and Relating to the Protection of Victims of International Armed Conflicts (Protocol I), art. 48 June 8, 1977, https://www.icrc.org/applic/ihl/ihl.nsf/7c4d08d9b287a42141256739003e636b/f6c8b9fee14a77fdc125641e0052b079.

66. HENCKAERTS & DOSWALD-BECK, supra note 62, at 3–8.

67. Article 48, Protocol Additional to the Geneva Conventions of 12 August 1949, and relating to the Protection of Victims of International Armed Conflicts (Protocol I), 8 June 1977, https://www.icrc.org/applic/ihl/ihl.nsf/7c4d08d9b287a42141256739003e636b/f6c8b9fee14a77fdc125641e0052b079.

68. HENCKAERTS & DOSWALD-BECK, supra note 62, Rule 2, at 8–11.

69. Statute of the International Criminal Court, art. 8, http://legal.un.org/icc/statute/romefra.htm.

70. Hamas Responds to Goldstone Report—on PA's Behalf, Middle East Media Research Institute, Feb. 23, 2010, http://www.memri.org/report/en/print3990.htm.

71. Id.

72. Id.

73. Protocol Additional to the Geneva Conventions of 12 August 1949, and Relating to the Protection of Victims of International Armed Conflicts (Protocol I), art. 51, 8 June 1977, https://www.icrc.org/applic/ihl/ihl.nsf/Article.xsp?action=openDocument&documentId=4BEBD9920AE0AEAEC12563CD0051DC9E.

74. HENCKAERTS & DOSWALD-BECK, supra note 62, Rules 11 and 12, at 37–43.

75. Protocol Additional to the Geneva Conventions of 12 August 1949, and relating to the Protection of Victims of International Armed Conflicts (Protocol I), 8 June 1977, art. 85, https://www.icrc.org/applic/ihl/ihl.nsf/4e473c7bc8854f2ec12563f60039c738/73d05a98b6ceb566c12563cd0051e1a0.

76. Id.

77. Envoy to UNHRC on Palestinian ICC Hopes: Israelis Warn Civilians Before Attacks, We Don't, MEMRI, July 9, 2014, http://www.memri.org/clip_transcript/en/4343.htm (translation of Palestinian Authority TV interview with Palestinian Representative at the U.N. Human Rights Council Ibrahim Khreisheh, which aired on July 9, 2014).

78. Robbie Sabel, The Gaza Legal Battle, JERUSALEM REPORT, Sept. 8, 2014.

79. AMNESTY INTERNATIONAL, FAMILIES UNDER THE RUBBLE: ISRAELI ATTACKS ON INHABITED HOMES (Nov. 5, 2014), https://www.amnesty.org/en/documents/MDE15/032/2014/en/.

80. AMNESTY INTERNATIONAL, STATE OF THE WORLD 2014/15 (Feb. 25, 2015), http://www.amnestyusa.org/research/reports/state-of-the-world-20142015-0.

81. AMNESTY INTERNATIONAL, FAMILIES UNDER THE RUBBLE, supra note 79.

82. Id.

83. *See, e.g.,* Laurence Norman, *EU to Challenge Court Decision Striking Hamas Off Terror List,* Wall St. J., Jan. 19, 2015, http://www.wsj.com/articles/eu-to-challenge-court-decision-striking-hamas-off-terror-list-1421663087.

84. Paul Farhi, *Reporters Grapple with Politics, Erratic Sources in Reporting Israeli/Gaza Death Toll,* Wash. Post, Aug. 4, 2014, http://www.washingtonpost.com/lifestyle/style/reporters-grapple-with-politics-erratic-sources-in-reporting-israeligaza-death-toll/2014/08/04/c02ab282-1c10-11e4-ae54-0cfe1f974f8a_story.html.

85. Jodi Rudoren, *Civilian or Not? New Fight in Tallying the Dead from the Gaza Conflict,* N.Y. Times, Aug. 5, 2014, http://www.nytimes.com/2014/08/06/world/middleeast/civilian-or-not-new-fight-in-tallying-the-dead-from-the-gaza-conflict.html.

86. *Gaza Crisis Facts and Figures,* United Nations Office for the Coordination of Humanitarian Affairs, http://www.ochaopt.org/content.aspx?id=1010361 (for example, on August 20, 2014, the website stated that 1,999 Palestinians had been killed during the Gaza War up to that date, of whom 12 percent were women and 23 percent were children).

87. *Number of Women and Children Killed in Iraq Air Raids "Disproportionately High,"* The Telegraph (U.K.), Apr. 16, 2009, http://www.telegraph.co.uk/news/worldnews/middleeast/iraq/5161326/Number-of-women-and-children-killed-in-Iraq-air-raids-disproportionately-high.html (reporting on findings, published in the New England Journal of Medicine, that "46% of the victims of US air strikes whose gender could be determined were female and 39% were children."); Madelyn Hsiao-Rei Hicks et al., *The Weapons That Kill Civilians—Deaths of Children and Noncombatants in Iraq, 2003–2008,* 360 New Eng. J. Med. 1585 (Apr. 16, 2009), http://www.nejm.org/doi/pdf/10.1056/NEJMp0807240; Evelyn Gordon, Commentary, *Israel's Record on Civilian Casualties Compares Well to America's,* Aug. 19, 2014, http://www.commentarymagazine.com/2014/08/19/israels-record-on-civilian-casualties-compares-well-to-americas/.

88. W. Hays Parks, *Air Law and the Law of War,* 32 A.F. L. Rev. 1, 173 (1990).

89. Protocol Additional to the Geneva Conventions of 12 August 1949, and Relating to the Protection of Victims of International Armed Conflicts (Protocol I), art. 57(b), June 8, 1977, http://www.icrc.org/applic/ihl/ihl.nsf/Article.xsp?action=openDocument&documentId=50FB5579FB098FAAC12563CD0051DD7C.

90. Jean-Marie Henckaerts & Louise Doswald-Beck, Customary International Humanitarian Law 46, Rule 14 (2005), http://www.icrc.org/eng/assets/files/other/customary-international-humanitarian-law-i-icrc-eng.pdf.

91. Gary Solis, The Law of Armed Conflict 273 (2010).

92. Protocol Additional to the Geneva Conventions of 12 August 1949, and Relating to the Protection of Victims of International Armed Conflicts (Protocol I), art. 57, Commentary, June 8, 1977, http://www.icrc.org/applic/ihl/ihl.nsf/1a13044f3bbb5b8ec12563fb0066f226/d80d14d84bf36b92c12563cd00434fbd.

93. Howard S. Levie, The Code of International Armed Conflict 85 (1986).

94. Protocol Additional to the Geneva Conventions of 12 August 1949, and Relating to the Protection of Victims of International Armed Conflicts (Protocol I), 8 June 1977, http://www.icrc.org/applic/ihl/ihl.nsf/1a13044f3bbb5b8ec12563fb0066f226/d80d14d84bf36b92c12563cd00434fbd.

95. Protocol Additional to the Geneva Conventions of 12 August 1949, and Relating to the Protection of Victims of International Armed Conflicts (Protocol I), 8 June 1977, art. 52, Commentary, http://www.icrc.org/applic/ihl/ihl.nsf/1a13044f3bbb5b8ec12563fb0066f226/5f27276ce1bbb79dc12563cd00434969.

96. *Id.,* art. 57, Commentary.

97. *Id.*

98. Laurie R. Blank, *Asymmetries and Proportionalities*, THE HILL, July 29, 2014, http://thehill. com/blogs/pundits-blog/international/213546-asymmetries-and-proportionalities.

99. *Id.*

100. *Id.*

101. *Id.*

102. *Id.*

103. ALAN CRAIG, INTERNATIONAL LEGITIMACY AND THE POLITICS OF SECURITY: THE STRATEGIC DEPLOYMENT OF LAWYERS IN THE ISRAELI MILITARY 53 (2013).

104. Occupied Palestinian Territory: Gaza Emergency Situation Report (as of 16 July 2014, 1500 hours), U.N. Office for the Coordination of Humanitarian Affairs, *available at* http://reliefweb.int/sites/reliefweb.int/files/resources/ocha_opt_sitrep_ 17_07_2014.pdf.

105. William Booth, *While Israel Held Its Fire, the Militant Group Hamas Did Not*, WASH. POST, July 15, 2014, http://www.washingtonpost.com/world/middle_east/while- israel-held-its-fire-the-militant-group-hamas-did-not/2014/07/15/116fd3d7-3c0f- 4413-94a9-2ab16af1445d_story.html.

106. Steven Erlanger & Fares Akram, *Israel Warns Gaza Targets by Phone and Leaflet*, N.Y. TIMES, July 8, 2014, http://www.nytimes.com/2014/07/09/world/middleeast/by- phone-and-leaflet-israeli-attackers-warn-gazans.html?_r=0.

107. *Envoy to UNHRC on Palestinian ICC Hopes: Israelis Warn Civilians Before Attacks, We Don't*, MEMRI, July 9, 2014, http://www.memri.org/clip_transcript/en/4343.htm (translation of Palestinian Authority TV interview with Palestinian Representative at the U.N. Human Rights Council Ibrahim Khreisheh which aired on July 9, 2014).

108. *Id.*

109. Nechama Douek, *"It's a Nightmare, but I Just Don't See a Better Policy,"* YNETNEWS. COM, July 23, 2014, http://www.ynetnews.com/articles/0,7340,L-4548849,00.html.

110. Matti Friedman, *Ten Years after Passover Blast, Survivors Return to Park Hotel*, TIMES OF ISRAEL, Mar. 27, 2012, http://www.timesofisrael.com/ten-years-after-passover- bombing-survivors-return-to-netanyas-park-hotel/; James Bennet, *Bomber Strikes Jews and Arabs at Rare Refuge*, N.Y. TIMES, Apr. 1, 2002, http://www.nytimes. com/2002/04/01/world/mideast-turmoil-the-violence-bomber-strikes-jews-and- arabs-at-rare-refuge.html; Marcus Sheff, *A Decade Since the Battle of Jenin, "The Myth of Jeningrad,"* JERUSALEM POST, Apr. 19, 2012, http://www.jpost.com/Opinion/ Columnists/A-decade-since-the-battle-of-Jenin-the-myth-of-Jeningrad.

111. Bennet, *supra* note 110.

112. *Suicide Bombers from Jenin*, Israel Ministry of Foreign Affairs, July 2, 2002, http://mfa. gov.il/MFA/MFA-Archive/2002/Pages/Suicide%20Bombers%20from%20Jenin. aspx.

113. "UN Says No Massacre in Jenin," BBC, Aug. 1, 2002, http://news.bbc.co.uk/2/hi/ middle_east/2165272.stm.

114. Emily Amrousi, *"We Do Not Sanctify Death,"* ISRAEL HAYOM, June 22, 2012, http:// www.israelhayom.com/site/newsletter_article.php?id=4804 (interview with Professor Asa Kasher).

115. *Id.*

116. *Id.*

117. *See, e.g., The Jenin Refugee Camp Massacre*, AL JAZEERAH, April 2002, http://www. aljazeerah.info/Documents/jenin_refugee_camp_massacre.htm (claiming "a mas- sacre in which hundreds of Palestinians were killed" and stating that "initial estimates were more than 500 children, women, and men"); Dick Meyer, *What's a Massacre?*, CBS NEWS, Aug. 2, 2002, http://www.cbsnews.com/news/whats-a-massacre/.

118. James Bennet, *U.N. Report Rejects Claims of a Massacre of Refugees*, N.Y. Times, Aug. 2, 2002, http://www.nytimes.com/2002/08/02/international/middleeast/02JENI.html.

119. Steven Erlanger, *A Gaza War Full of Traps and Trickery*, N.Y. Times, Jan. 11, 2009, http://www.nytimes.com/2009/01/11/world/middleeast/11hamas.html?pagewanted=all.

120. *Id.; see also* Steven Erlanger & Fares Akram, *Israel Warns Gaza Targets by Phone and Leaflet*, N.Y. Times, July 8, 2014, http://www.nytimes.com/2014/07/09/world/middleeast/by-phone-and-leaflet-israeli-attackers-warn-gazans.html?_r=0; David Horovitz, *The Moralist*, Jerusalem Post, Aug. 9, 2014, http://www.jpost.com/Opinion/Columnists/Editors-Notes-The-moralist (interview with Professor Asa Kasher).

121. David Alexander, *Israel Tried to Limit Civilian Casualties in Gaza: U.S. Military Chief*, Reuters, Nov. 6, 2014, http://www.reuters.com/article/2014/11/06/us-israel-usa-gaza-idUSKBN0IQ2LH20141106.

122. *Id.*

123. *Id.*

124. Col. Richard Kemp, Submission to the United Nations Independent Commission of Inquiry on the 2014 Gaza Conflict, Feb. 20, 2015, http://richard-kemp.com/submission-to-the-united-nations-independent-commission-of-inquiry-on-the-2014-gaza-conflict/.

125. *Id.*

126. *Psaki: Israel Could and Should Have Done More to Prevent Civilian Casualties*, Real Clear Politics (video), Nov. 8, 2014, http://www.realclearpolitics.com/video/2014/11/08/psaki_israel_could_have_and_should_have_done_more_to_prevent_civilian_casualties.html.

127. Amnesty International, Families under the Rubble: Israeli Attacks on Inhabited Homes (Nov. 5, 2014), https://www.amnesty.org/en/documents/MDE15/032/2014/en/.

128. Craig, *supra* note 103, at 55.

129. *Id.* at 100.

130. *Id.*

131. *See, e.g.*, Yonah Jeremy Bob, *New Deputy Attorney-General to Increase Country's Emphasis on International Law*, Jerusalem Post, Oct. 30, 2013, http://www.jpost.com/National-News/New-deputy-attorney-general-to-increase-countrys-emphasis-on-global-law-330134.

132. U.N. Human Rights Council, Report of the United Nations Fact-Finding Mission on the Gaza Conflict, U.N. Doc. A/HRC/12/48, at 13 (Sept. 25, 2009), http://www2.ohchr.org/english/bodies/hrcouncil/docs/12session/A-HRC-12-48.pdf.

133. Ethan Bronner, *Israel Poised to Challenge a UN Report on Gaza*, N.Y. Times, Jan. 23, 2010, http://www.nytimes.com/2010/01/24/world/middleeast/24goldstone.html?pagewanted=all.

134. *Id.*

135. Richard Goldstone, *Reconsidering the Goldstone Report on Israel and War Crimes*, Wash. Post, Apr. 1, 2011, http://articles.washingtonpost.com/2011-04-01/opinions/35207016_1_drone-image-goldstone-report-israeli-evidence.

136. Craig, *supra* note 103, at 94.

137. U.S. Mission, Geneva, U.S. Response to the Report of the United Nations Fact-Finding Mission on the Gaza Conflict, Statement by Michael Posner, http://geneva.usmission.gov/2009/09/29/gaza-conflict/.

138. Report of the United Nations Fact-Finding Mission on the Gaza Conflict, *supra* note 132, at 13.

139. *Id.* at 15.

140. Goldstone, *supra* note 135.

141. *Id.*

142. Uriel Heilman, *Israel's Cooperation on UN Inquiry Signals Tactical Shift*, JTA, Aug. 3, 2010, http://www.jta.org/2010/08/03/news-opinion/israel-middle-east/ israels-cooperation-on-u-n-inquiry-signals-tactical-shift.

143. Gerald M. Steinberg & Gidon Shaviv, Palmer vs. Goldstone: *Lessons Learned*, JERUSALEM POST, Sept. 7, 2011, http://www.jpost.com/Opinion/Op-Ed-Contributors/Palmer-vs-Goldstone-lessons-learned.

144. REPORT OF THE SECRETARY-GENERAL'S PANEL OF INQUIRY ON THE 31 MAY 2010 FLOTILLA INCIDENT 4 (Sept. 2011), http://www.un.org/News/dh/infocus/middle_ east/Gaza_Flotilla_Panel_Report.pdf.

145. *Id.*

146. Steinberg & Shaviv, *supra* note 143.

147. PUBLIC COMM'N TO EXAMINE THE MARITIME INCIDENT OF 31 MAY 2010, PART I—THE TURKEL COMM'N (Jan. 2011), http://www.turkel-committee.gov.il/ files/wordocs/8808report-eng.pdf.

148. PUBLIC COMM'N TO EXAMINE THE MARITIME INCIDENT OF 31 MAY 2010, http:// www.turkel-committee.gov.il/index-eng.html (last visited Apr. 4, 2015).

149. Tovah Lazaroff, *UN Gaza War Probe to Also Investigate Palestinian Human Rights Violations*, JERUSALEM POST, Mar. 23, 2015, http://www.jpost.com/Arab-Israeli-Conflict/UN-Gaza-war-probe-to-also-investigate-Palestinian-human-rights-violations-394856.

150. *Israel Will Not Cooperate with UNHRC Investigative Committee*, Israel Ministry of Foreign Affairs, Nov. 13, 2014, http://mfa.gov.il/MFA/PressRoom/2014/Pages/ Israel-will-not-cooperate-with-UNHRC-investigative-committee-13-Nov-2014.aspx.

151. Lazaroff, *supra* note 149.

152. Author interview with Israeli official on not-for-attribution basis (Mar. 2, 2015).

153. Somini Sengupta, *Leader of War Crimes Inquiry into 2014 Gaza Conflict Resigns*, N.Y. TIMES, Feb. 2, 2015, http://www.nytimes.com/2015/02/03/world/mid-dleeast/leader-of-war-crimes-inquiry-into-14-gaza-conflict-resigns.html; Tovah Lazaroff, *Schabas to Quit UNHRC Gaza Probe over Israeli Bias Claims*, JERUSALEM POST, Feb. 3, 2015, http://www.jpost.com/Arab-Israeli-Conflict/ Schabas-to-quit-UNHRC-Gaza-probe-over-Israeli-bias-claims-389799.

154. *Report of the Detailed Findings*, *supra* note 31.

155. Curriculum Vitae of Alex Whiting, Harvard Law School, http://hls.harvard.edu/ faculty/directory/10953/Whiting.

156. Alex Whiting, *How Israel Should Address the Gaza Report's Impact on the ICC*, LAWFARE BLOG (July 13, 2015), https://www.lawfareblog.com/ how-israel-should-address-gaza-reports-impact-icc.

157. *Id.*

158. Author interview with Israeli official, *supra* note 152.

159. *Id.*

160. *Id.*

161. Matan Tzuri & Itamar Eichner, *Mother of 4-Year-Old Killed by Mortar During Gaza War Testifies in UN Inquiry*, YNET NEWS, Jan. 15, 2015, http://www.ynetnews.com/ articles/0,7340,L-4615351,00.html.

162. Herb Keinon & Tovah Lazaroff, *UNHRC Investigators Ask to Delay Gaza Report until June*, JERUSALEM POST, Mar. 9, 2015, http://www.jpost.com/Arab-Israeli-Conflict/ UNHRCs-investigators-ask-to-delay-Gaza-report-until-June-393402.

163. Wittes & Schwartz, *supra* note 36.

164. *Id.*

165. Craig, *supra* note 103, at 2.

166. *Id.* at 1 (paraphrasing presentation by Daniel Reisner, former head of the Int'l Law Dep't of the Israel Defense Forces).

167. *Id.* at 2.

168. *Id.*

169. *Id.* 2.

170. *See, e.g.*, Isabel Kershner, *Israel Braces for War Crimes Inquiries on Gaza*, N.Y. Times, Aug. 14, 2014, http://www.nytimes.com/2014/08/15/world/middleeast/israel-braces-for-war-crimes-inquiries-on-gaza.html?ref=world&_r=2.

171. Robbie Sabel, *Manipulating International Law as Part of Anti-Israeli "Lawfare,"* Jerusalem Ctr. for Pub. Aff. Issue Brief, June 2013, http://jcpa.org/article/manipulating-international-law-as-part-of-anti-israeli-lawfare/.

172. HCJ 5100/94 The Public Committee against Torture in Israel v. The State of Israel (1999) (Isr.), *quoted in* HCJ 769/02 The Public Committee Against Torture in Israel v. The Government of Israel (2005) (Isr.), http://elyon1.court.gov.il/Files_ENG/02/690/007/a34/02007690.a34.htm.

173. Sabel, *supra* note 171.

174. Craig, *supra* note 103, at 116.

175. *Id.* at 109.

176. Sabel, *supra* note 171.

177. *IDF Conducts Fact-Finding Assessment Following Operation Protective Edge*, Israel Defense Forces, Sept. 12, 2014, http://www.idfblog.com/blog/2014/09/12/idf-conducts-fact-finding-assessment-following-operation-protective-edge/.

178. Public Comm'n to Examine the Maritime Incident of 31 May 2010, Second Report—The Turkel Comm'n, Israel's Mechanisms for Examining and Investigating Complaints and Claims of Violations of the Laws of Armed Conflict According to International Law 383 (Feb. 2013), http://www.turkel-committee.gov.il/files/newDoc3/The%20Turkel%20Report%20for%20website.pdf.

179. Yonah Jeremy Bob, *18 Recommendations That Could Determine Israel's Fate Before the ICC*, Jerusalem Post, Jan. 26, 2015, http://www.jpost.com/Israel-News/Politics-And-Diplomacy/18-recommendations-that-could-determine-Israels-fate-before-the-ICC-388955.

180. *Id.*; Public Comm'n to Examine the Maritime Incident of 31 May 2010, Second Report, *supra* note 178, at 381.

181. Bob, *supra* note 179.

182. *IDF Conducts Fact-Finding Assessment Following Operation Protective Edge*, *supra* note 177; Bob, *supra* note 179.

183. David Horovitz, *"I'd Love to Tell Israelis How We Protect Them, But Then the Enemy Would Adapt,"* Jerusalem Post, June 30, 2006, http://www.jpost.com/Israel/Id-love-to-tell-Israelis-how-we-protect-them-but-then-the-enemy-would-adapt (interview with Eliezer Shkedy, then Israeli air force chief).

184. Ben Caspit, *Israel Prepares for an International Legal Assault*, Al-Monitor, Aug. 7, 2014, http://www.al-monitor.com/pulse/originals/2014/08/protective-edge-goldstone-hamas-yaalon-idf-1.html.

185. *Id.*

186. *Hamas Uses Hospitals and Ambulances for Military Purposes*, Israel Defense Forces, July 28, 2014, http://www.idfblog.com/blog/2014/07/28/hamas-uses-hospitals-ambulances-military-purposes/.

187. *Id.*

188. *Hamas War Tactics: Attacks from Civilian Centers*, MILITARY-STRATEGIC INFORMATION SECTION OF THE PLANNING DIRECTORATE OF THE ISRAEL DEFENSE FORCES, Aug. 2014, http://acdemocracy.org/wp-content/uploads/2014/08/Hamas-Urban-Warfare-Tactics.pdf?utm_source=Hamas+Urban+Warfare+Tactics&utm_campaign=Hamas+Urban+Warfare+Tactics&utm_medium=email.

189. Deroy Murdock, *IDF Details Hamas's Use of Civilian Areas as Missile Bases*, NAT'L REV., Aug. 11, 2014, http://www.nationalreview.com/corner/385139/idf-details-hamass-use-civilian-areas-missile-bases-deroy-murdock.

190. *Hamas War Tactics: Attacks from Civilian Centers, supra* note 188.

191. Caspit, *supra* note 184.

192. *Id.*

193. *Id.*

194. *Id.*

195. *See, e.g., Hamas Covenant 1988*, http://avalon.law.yale.edu/20th_century/hamas.asp; *Hamas Spokesman Fawzi Barhoum Calls to Carry Out Terrorist Attacks in Israel and the West Bank*, MEMRI, July 30, 2014, http://www.memritv.org/clip_transcript/en/4408.htm ("Anyone who has a knife, a club, a weapon, or a car, yet does not use it to run over a Jew or a settler, and does not use it to kill dozens of Zionists, does not belong to Palestine.")

196. *Freedom in the World 2015: Gaza Strip*, FREEDOM HOUSE, https://freedomhouse.org/report/freedom-world/2015/gaza-strip#.VUk4Nc5XmKw (last visited May 5, 2015).

197. U.S. DEP'T OF STATE, FOREIGN TERRORIST ORGANIZATIONS, http://www.state.gov/j/ct/rls/other/des/123085.htm.

198. *Profile: Hamas Palestinian Movement*, BBC News, July 11, 2014, http://www.bbc.com/news/world-middle-east-13331522.

199. *Id.*

200. *Id.*

201. AUSTRALIAN NATIONAL SECURITY, HAMAS'S IZZ AL-DIN AL-QASSAM BRIGADES, http://www.nationalsecurity.gov.au/Listedterroristorganisations/Pages/HamassIzzal-Dinal-QassamBrigades.aspx.

202. *Profile: Hamas Palestinian Movement*, BBC NEWS, July 11, 2014, http://www.bbc.com/news/world-middle-east-13331522.

203. Matthew Levitt, *EU Court Annuls Hamas Terrorist Designation*, WASH. INST. FOR NEAR EAST POL'Y, Dec. 16, 2014, http://www.washingtoninstitute.org/policy-analysis/view/eu-court-expected-to-annul-hamas-terrorist-designation.

204. *Statement by High Representative/Vice-President Federica Mogherini on the Decision to Appeal the Judgment Regarding Hamas*, European Union External Action Service (Jan. 19, 2015), http://eeas.europa.eu/statements-eeas/2015/150119_01_en.htm; Matthew Levitt & Neri Zilber, *The EU Still Has Issues with Hamas*, WASH. INST. FOR NEAR EAST POLICY (Apr. 2, 2015), http://www.washingtoninstitute.org/policy-analysis/view/the-eu-still-has-issues-with-hamas.

205. *Egypt Court Puts Hamas on Terrorist List*, BBC NEWS, Feb. 28, 2015, http://www.bbc.com/news/world-middle-east-31674458; Yasmine Saleh, *Court Bans Activities of Islamist Hamas in Egypt*, REUTERS, Mar. 4, 2014, http://www.reuters.com/article/2014/03/04/us-egypt-hamas-idUSBREA230F520140304.

206. David D. Kirkpatrick, *Arab Leaders, Viewing Hamas as Worse than Israel, Stay Silent*, N.Y. TIMES, July 30, 2014, http://www.nytimes.com/2014/07/31/world/middleeast/fighting-political-islam-arab-states-find-themselves-allied-with-israel.html.

207. Steven Erlanger, *Hamas Seizes Broad Control in Gaza Strip*, N.Y. TIMES, June 14, 2007, http://www.nytimes.com/2007/06/14/world/middleeast/14mideast.html.

208. *See, e.g., Rocket Attacks on Israel from Gaza*, ISRAEL DEFENSE FORCES, http://www. idfblog.com/facts-figures/rocket-attacks-toward-israel/; Josh Levs, *How Long Will It Last? Gaza Conflict by the Numbers*, CNN, July 30, 2014, http://www.cnn. com/2014/07/29/world/meast/gaza-conflict-numbers/.

209. *Israel Completes Gaza Withdrawal*, BBC NEWS, Sept. 12, 2005, http://news.bbc. co.uk/2/hi/middle_east/4235768.stm.

210. Colum Lynch, *The Case Against the Prosecution*, FOREIGN POLICY, Aug. 5, 2014, http://thecable.foreignpolicy.com/posts/2014/08/05/palestinians_abbas_ international_prosecution_of_israeli_soldiers_ICC_Hague.

211. Office of Tony Blair, *Tony Blair Welcomes Re-start of Direct Peace Talks During Herzliya Speech*, www.tonyblairoffice.org/news/entry/tony-blair-welcomes-re-start-of-direct-peace-talks-during-herzliya-speech/.

212. Press Release, Israel Ministry of Foreign Affairs, *PM Netanyahu Holds Press Conference* (transcript, Aug. 6, 2014), http://mfa.gov.il/MFA/PressRoom/2014/Pages/ PM-Netanyahu-holds-press-conference-6-Aug-2014.aspx.

213. *Id.*

214. Natan Sharansky, *Don't Set a Double Standard for Israel on Norms of War*, WASH. POST, Aug. 15, 2014, http://www.washingtonpost.com/opinions/natan-sharansky-dont-set-a-double-standard-for-israel-on-norms-of-war/2014/08/15/5ed74bb8-23c1-11e4-8593-da634b334390_story.html.

215. Laurie R. Blank, *Taking Distinction to the Next Level: Accountability for Fighters' Failure to Distinguish Themselves from Civilians*, 46 VAL. U. L. REV. 765, 766 (2012), http:// scholar.valpo.edu/cgi/viewcontent.cgi?article=2242&context=vulr.

216. *Id.* at 766–67.

217. *Id.* at 786–89.

218. *Id.* at 790; Blank, *supra* note 38.

CHAPTER 8

1. This chapter is informed in part by several interviews. The author interviewed Nitsana Darshan-Leitner on September 3, 2013, in her office in Ramat Gan, Israel. The author also interviewed several other prominent Israeli lawfare experts who were willing to discuss—only on a "deep background" basis—Shurat HaDin's work.

2. Charles J. Dunlap, Jr., *Lawfare Today … and Tomorrow, in* INTERNATIONAL LAW AND THE CHANGING CHARACTER OF WAR 315–25 (Raul A. "Pete" Pedrozo & Daria P. Wollschlaeger eds., 2011), http://scholarship.law.duke.edu/ faculty_scholarship/2465/.

3. Shurat HaDin–Israel Law Ctr., *About Us: Bankrupting Terror*, http://israellawcenter. org/about/our-mission/ (last visited May 5, 2015).

4. *Id.*

5. Yonah Jeremy Bob, *10 Years In, Shurat Hadin Fights Iranian Terrorism and BDS in International Courts*, JERUSALEM POST, Nov. 11, 2013.

6. Jodi Rudoren, *Crusading for Israel in a Way Some Say is Misguided*, N.Y. TIMES, Jan. 23, 2015, http://www.nytimes.com/2015/01/24/world/middleeast/crusading-for-israel-in-a-way-some-say-is-misguided.html.

7. Jennifer Hough, *Bankrupting the Terrorists*, NAT'L POST (Canada), May 31, 2014.

8. *Id.*

9. Rudoren, *supra* note 6.

10. *See, e.g.,* Yossi Gurvitz, *The Israeli Government's Official "Lawfare" Contractor*, 972 MAGAZINE, Oct. 19, 2013, http://972mag.com/the-israeli-governments-official-lawfare-contractor/80659/.

11. *See, e.g., id.; see also* John Reed, *Israeli Prime Minister Netanyahu Gets Flak for Yielding to China*, FINANCIAL TIMES, July 15, 2013, http://www.ft.com/intl/cms/s/0/c99b9938-ed56-11e2-8d7c-00144feabdc0.html#axzz3ggy7J0YT.

12. Sarah Hershenson, *A New Type of Warfare*, JERUSALEM POST, Sept. 21, 2012.

13. *Id.*

14. *See, e.g.,* Aviad Glickman, *High Court OKs 2nd Phase of Shalit Deal*, YNET NEWS, Dec. 16, 2011, http://www.ynetnews.com/articles/0,7340,L-4162634,00.html.

15. Rudoren, *supra* note 6.

16. Shurat HaDin–Israel Law Ctr., *Shurat HaDin Warns Government Against Increasing Egyptian Troops in Sinai*, Sept. 1, 2011, http://israellawcenter.org/pr/shurat-hadin-warns-government-against-increasing-egyptian-troops-in-sinai/; Rudoren, *supra* note 6.

17. *See, e.g.,* Michal Shmulovich, *Americans in Israel Sue United States for Funding Palestinian Terrorism*, TIMES OF ISRAEL, Nov. 27, 2012, http://www.timesofisrael.com/americans-in-israel-sue-united-states-for-funding-palestinian-terrorism/.

18. Isabel Kershner, *Deadly Israeli Raid Draws Condemnation*, N.Y. TIMES, May 31, 2010, http://www.nytimes.com/2010/06/01/world/middleeast/01flotilla.html.

19. UNITED NATIONS, REPORT OF THE SECRETARY-GENERAL'S PANEL OF INQUIRY ON THE 31 MAY 2010 FLOTILLA INCIDENT (Sept. 2011), http://www.un.org/News/dh/infocus/middle_east/Gaza_Flotilla_Panel_Report.pdf.

20. U.N. Human Rights Council, Report of the International Fact-Finding Mission to Investigate Violations of International Law, Including International Humanitarian and Human Rights Law, Resulting from the Israeli Attacks on the Flotilla of Ships Carrying Humanitarian Assistance, U.N. Doc. A/HRC/15/21 (Sept. 27, 2010), http://www2.ohchr.org/english/bodies/hrcouncil/docs/15session/A.HRC.15.21_en.pdf.

21. *Council adopts texts on follow-up on Report of Fact-Finding Mission on flotilla attack and on Committee of Independent Experts on Gaza conflict*, Office of the High Commissioner for Human Rights, Sept. 29, 2010, http://www.ohchr.org/EN/NewsEvents/Pages/DisplayNews.aspx?NewsID=10393&LangID=E.

22. REPORT OF THE SECRETARY-GENERAL'S PANEL OF INQUIRY ON THE 31 MAY 2010 FLOTILLA INCIDENT, *supra* note 19.

23. *Id.*

24. Ron Friedman, *Lawyers, Not IDF, at Forefront of Battle Against Flotilla*, JERUSALEM POST, June 6, 2011, http://www.jpost.com/Diplomacy-and-Politics/Lawyers-not-IDF-at-forefront-of-battle-against-flotilla.

25. *Id.*

26. Sarah Hershenson, *A New Type of Warfare*, JERUSALEM POST, Sept. 21, 2012 (stating that in stopping the flotilla, Shurat HaDin "worked with Israeli naval intelligence, the IDF and the Prime Minister's Office").

27. Alana Goodman, *Meet the Legal Wonks Who Brought Down the Flotilla*, COMMENTARY, Aug. 22, 2011, http://www.commentarymagazine.com/2011/08/22/shurat-hadin-flotilla/.

28. Author interview of Nitsana Darshan-Leitner & Avi Leitner in the Shurat HaDin office (Ramat Gan, Israel, Sept. 3, 2013).

29. *Id.*

30. *Id.*; Scott Sayare, *Israeli Advocacy Group Helps Delay Departure of Gaza-Bound Flotilla*, N.Y. Times, June 28, 2011, http://www.nytimes.com/2011/06/29/world/middleeast/29flotilla.html; Goodman, *supra* note 27.

31. Nitsana Darshan-Leitner, Shurat HaDin, Israel Law Ctr., *Sinking the Gaza Flotilla* (EMC Chair Conference Paper, Mar. 2014), https://www.usnwc.edu/Academics/Faculty/Derek-Reveron/Workshops/Maritime-Security,-Seapower,---Trade/Maritime-Working-Papers/nitsana.aspx.

32. Author interview of Darshan-Leitner & Leitner, *supra* note 28; Sayare, *supra* note 30; Goodman, *supra* note 27; Friedman, *supra* note 24.

33. Holder v. Humanitarian Law Project, 561 U.S. 1, 130 S. Ct. 2705 (2010), http://www.supremecourt.gov/opinions/09pdf/08-1498.pdf.

34. 18 U.S.C. § 2339B(a)(1).

35. 18 U.S.C. § 2339A(b)(1).

36. *Holder v. Humanitarian Law Project, supra* note 33.

37. *Id.*

38. *Id.*

39. *Id.*

40. Author interview of Darshan-Leitner & Leitner, *supra* note 28; Goodman, *supra* note 27.

41. Gil Ronen, *Maritime Lawfare Victory: Lloyd's Won't Insure Gaza Flotilla*, Arutz Sheva 7 (Israel National News), May 23, 2011, http://www.israelnationalnews.com/News/News.aspx/144423#.UkGizhYn8_s.

42. Miles Costello & James Hider, *Lloyd's Warned over Risks of Insurance for Hamas Aid Boats*, The Times (London), May 17, 2011, http://www.thetimes.co.uk/tto/news/world/middleeast/article3021568.ece.

43. Shurat HaDin–Israel Law Ctr., *Shurat HaDin Warns Satellite Communication Giant Inmarsat Over Gaza Flotilla*, June 6, 2011, http://www.israellawcenter.org/page.asp?id=341&show=photo&pn=1152&ref=report; Ron Friedman, "Lawyers, Not IDF, at Forefront of Battle Against Flotilla," Jerusalem Post, June 6, 2011, http://www.jpost.com/Diplomacy-and-Politics/Lawyers-not-IDF-at-forefront-of-battle-against-flotilla.

44. *Shurat HaDin Warns Satellite Communication Giant Inmarsat, supra* note 43; copies of the letters are available online at http://www.scribd.com/doc/101019445/Warning-Letters-Sent-to-Inmarsat-During-Flotilla (last visited May 5, 2015).

45. Letters from Shurat HaDin to Inmarsat and Inmarsat Officers (June 5, 2011), *available at* http://www.scribd.com/doc/101019445/Warning-Letters-Sent-to-Inmarsat-During-Flotilla (last visited May 5, 2015).

46. *Id.*

47. *Id.*

48. Boim v. Quranic Literacy Inst., No. 00 C 2905, 2012 U.S. Dist. LEXIS 126063 (N.D. Ill. Aug. 31, 2012).

49. *Id.*

50. Boim v. Holy Land Found., 549 F.3d 685, 698 (7th Cir. 2008) (citations omitted).

51. Complaint, Fendel v. Inmarsat, No. 11-19912CA15 (Fla. Miami-Dade County Ct. (filed June 27, 2011), *available at* http://www.investigativeproject.org/documents/case_docs/1594.pdf; Tim Elfrink, *Brickell Satellite Firm Inmarsat Accused of Aiding Hamas*, Miami New Times, July 14, 2011, http://www.miaminewtimes.com/2011-07-14/news/brickell-satellite-firm-inmarsat-accused-of-aiding-hamas/full/.

52. Complaint, Fendel v. Inmarsat, *supra* note 51.

53. *Id.*

54. *Id.*
55. *Id.*
56. *See, e.g.*, Press Release, U.S. Dep't of Justice, *Staten Island Satellite TV Operator Pleads Guilty to Providing Material Support to Hizballah TV Station* (Dec. 23, 2008), http://www.investigativeproject.org/documents/case_docs/756.pdf; Benjamin Weiser, *A Guilty Plea in Providing Satellite TV for Hezbollah*, N.Y. TIMES, Dec. 23, 2008, http://www.nytimes.com/2008/12/24/nyregion/24plea.html.
57. Complaint, Fendel v. Inmarsat, *supra* note 51.
58. *Id.*
59. *Id.*
60. Author interview of Darshan-Leitner & Leitner, *supra* note 28.
61. *Id.*
62. Joanna Paraszczuk, *US A-G Called On to Support Flotilla Lawsuit*, JERUSALEM POST, June 11, 2012, http://www.jpost.com/National-News/US-A-G-called-on-to-support-flotilla-lawsuit.
63. *Id.*
64. 18 U.S.C. § 962; Bauer v. Mavi Marmara, 774 F.3d 1026, 1030 (D.D.C. 2014).
65. Bauer v. Mavi Marmara, 942 F. Supp. 2d 31 (D.D.C. 2014), *aff'g* Bauer v. Mavi Marmara, 11-1267 (RC) (D.D.C. Apr. 18, 2013) (district court opinion *available at* http://www.gpo.gov/fdsys/pkg/USCOURTS-dcd-1_11-cv-01267/pdf/USCOURTS-dcd-1_11-cv-01267-0.pdf).
66. Bauer v. Mavi Marmara, 774 F.3d 1026, 1037 (D.C. Cir. 2014).
67. Scott Sayare, *Israeli Advocacy Group Helps Delay Departure of Gaza-Bound Flotilla*, N.Y. TIMES, June 28, 2011, http://www.nytimes.com/2011/06/29/world/middleeast/29flotilla.html; *Gaza-Bound Ships a Floating Flashpoint*, TORONTO STAR, June 29, 2011; Nitsana Darshan-Leitner, Shurat HaDin, Israel Law Ctr., *Sinking the Gaza Flotilla* (EMC Chair Conference Paper, Mar. 2014), https://www.usnwc.edu/Academics/Faculty/Derek-Reveron/Workshops/Maritime-Security,-Seapower,---Trade/Maritime-Working-Papers/nitsana.aspx.
68. Catrina Stewart, *Israeli Campaign Stops Gaza Flotilla Leaving Port*, THE INDEPENDENT (London), June 28, 2011.
69. Darshan-Leitner, Conference Paper, *supra* note 67.
70. Sayare, *supra* note 67.
71. Scott Sayare, *Stuck in Dock, Flotilla Activists See the Hand of Israel*, N.Y. TIMES, July 1, 2011, http://www.nytimes.com/2011/07/02/world/middleeast/02flotilla.html?pagewanted=1&_r=1.
72. Jack Shenker & Conal Urquhart, *"Sabotage" Sinks Plans for Gaza Flotilla*, THE GUARDIAN, July 6, 2011; Michael Jansen, *Greece Prohibits Gaza Flotilla Boats from Leaving Its Ports*, IRISH TIMES, July 4, 2011.
73. Shenker & Urquhart, *supra* note 72.
74. Jack Shenker & Conal Urquhart, *Activists' Plan to Break Gaza Blockade with Aid Flotilla Is Sunk*, THE GUARDIAN, July 5, 2011, http://www.theguardian.com/world/2011/jul/05/activists-gaza-blockade-aid-flotilla.
75. Jansen, *supra* note 72.
76. Sayare, *supra* note 67.
77. Yaakov Katz & Herb Keinon, *Navy Intercepts Ship Trying to Sail to Gaza*, JERUSALEM POST, July 20, 2011.
78. *Id.*
79. *See, e.g.*, Intervenor-Plaintiffs' Memorandum of Law in Opposition to Non-Party State of Israel's Motion to Quash Subpoena, Wultz v. Bank of China, No. 13-1282

(RBW) (D.D.C. Dec. 17, 2013), *available at* http://blogs.reuters.com/alison-frankel/
files/2014/08/wultvbankofchina-moriahoppositiontoquash1.pdf.

80. *See, e.g., id.*

81. John Reed & Jamil Anderlini, *Fresh Twist Emerges in Israelis' Case Against Chinese Bank*, FINANCIAL TIMES, Nov. 12, 2013.

82. Wultz v. Bank of China Ltd., 910 F. Supp. 2d 548, 554 (2012).

83. Charles Levinson, *U.S. Court Case Tests Israeli Resolve*, WALL ST. J., June 21, 2013, http://online.wsj.com/news/articles/SB100014241278873245779045785595310167 18160?mg=reno64-wsj.

84. Respondents' Memorandum of Law in Opposition to Petitioner's Motion to Quash, Wultz v. State of Israel, No. 13-1282 (D.D.C. Dec. 17, 2013), *available at* http://blogs. reuters.com/alison-frankel/files/2014/08/wultzvbankofchina-wultzquashoppos-brief1.pdf.

85. *Id.*

86. Sam Chester, *Netanyahu Favors Chinese Interests in Terror Case, Causing Dismay All Around*, TABLET, Aug. 20, 2013, http://www.tabletmag.com/jewish-news-and-politics/141261/netanyahu-chooses-china.

87. Alison Frankel, *Israel's Conflicted Role in Bank of China Terror Finance Case*, REUTERS, Aug. 11, 2014, http://blogs.reuters.com/alison-frankel/2014/08/11/israels-conflicted-role-in-bank-of-china-terror-finance-case/.

88. *Id.*

89. Yonah Jeremy Bob, *Israel Wins US Court Battle to Block Former Government Agent's "Smoking Gun" Testimony*, JERUSALEM POST, July 23, 2014; Declaration of Shlomo Matalon (from the case of Estate of Ungar v. Palestinian Auth., No. 1:04mc90 (D.D.C. May 16, 2009), in Wultz v. Iran, No. 13-1282 (RBW) (filed Dec. 17, 2013), *available at* http://blogs.reuters.com/alison-frankel/files/2014/08/wultzvbankofchina-ywultz-declaration.pdf (stating that "[d]espite the aforementioned information and requests BOC continued to carry out additional Funds Transfers for the PIJ and Hamas between April 2005 and early 2008 (and possibly later)."); Respondents' Memorandum of Law in Opposition to Petitioner's Motion to Quash in *Wultz, supra* note 84, at 9 ("the Chinese attendees informed Mr. Shaya and his GOI colleagues that BOC would not close the accounts ..., and PIJ and Hamas continued using BOC's services to launder money and deliver funds to Gaza and the West Bank.").

90. Bob, *supra* note 89; Declaration of Shlomo Matalon, *supra* note 89; Respondents' Memorandum of Law in Opposition to Petitioner's Motion to Quash in *Wultz, supra* note 84.

91. Chester, *supra* note 86.

92. Declaration of Yekutiel Wultz, Wultz v. State of Israel, No. 13-1282 (RBW) (filed Dec. 16, 2013), *available at* http://blogs.reuters.com/alison-frankel/files/2014/08/wultzvbankofchina-ywultzdeclaration.pdf; Ari Yashar, *US Family Accuses Israeli Gov't of "Sabotaging" Terror Lawsuit*, ARUTZ SHEVA ISRAEL NAT'L NEWS, Dec. 17, 2013, http://www.israelnationalnews.com/News/News.aspx/175254#.U-5bylYsJY4.

93. Yonah Jeremy Bob, *NGO Demands Answers from Ambassador to China Matan Vilna'i over Terror Funding Case*, JERUSALEM POST, Dec. 1, 2013.

94. John Reed, *Israeli PM Caught in Lawsuit Spat with Beijing*, FINANCIAL TIMES, July 16, 2013; Bob, *supra* note 89.

95. Charles Levinson, *U.S. Court Case Tests Israeli Resolve*, WALL ST. J., June 21, 2013, http://online.wsj.com/news/articles/SB100014241278873245779045785595310167 18160?mg=reno64-wsj.

96. Shimon Shiffer, *US Outraged after Israel Backs Out of Terror Suit*, YNetNews, July 15, 2013, http://www.ynetnews.com/articles/0,7340,L-4405213,00.html?utm; Reed, *supra* note 94; AFP & Gil Ronen, *Ex-NSA Boss Called to Testify in China Bank Terror Funding Case*, Nov. 28, 2013, http://www.israelnationalnews.com/News/News.aspx/174604#.VbBjDPmqGDk.

97. Respondents' Memorandum of Law in Opposition to Petitioner's Motion to Quash in *Wultz, supra* note 84.

98. Yonah Jeremy Bob, *Terror Victim's Family: PM Broke His Promise to Us*, Jerusalem Post, Dec. 18, 2013; Respondents' Memorandum of Law in Opposition to Petitioner's Motion to Quash in *Wultz, supra* note 84.

99. Bob, *supra* note 89.

100. Yashar, *supra* note 92.

101. *See, e.g.*, Intervenor-Plaintiffs' Memorandum of Law in Opposition to Non-Party State of Israel's Motion to Quash Subpoena, Wultz v. Bank of China, No. 13-1282 (RBW) (D.D.C. Dec. 17, 2013), *available at* http://blogs.reuters.com/alison-frankel/files/2014/08/wultvbankofchina-moriahoppositiontoquash1.pdf; Respondents' Memorandum of Law in Opposition to Petitioner's Motion to Quash in *Wultz, supra* note 84.

102. *Id.*

103. Intervenor-Plaintiffs' Memorandum of Law in Opposition to Non-Party State of Israel's Motion to Quash Subpoena in *Wultz, supra* note 101 (footnote omitted).

104. *See, e.g.*, Yossi Melman, *The Terrorist Kills, and the Bank Pays*, Haaretz, Feb. 14, 2007, http://www.haaretz.com/print-edition/features/the-terrorist-kills-and-the-bank-pays-1.212923.

105. Ronen Bergman, The Secret War with Iran: The 30-Year Clandestine Struggle Against the World's Most Dangerous Terrorist Power 284 (2008).

106. Yonah Jeremy Bob, *High Court Accepts NGO's Version of Events in Bank of China Dispute*, Jerusalem Post, Apr. 29, 2014.

107. Yonah Jeremy Bob, *Livni Given 7 Days by High Court to Respond to Petition over Bank of China Case*, Jerusalem Post, Jan. 15, 2014.

108. Bob, *supra* note 106.

109. Charles Levinson, *U.S. Court Case Tests Israeli Resolve*, Wall St. J., June 21, 2013, http://online.wsj.com/news/articles/SB10001424127887324577904578559531016718160?mg=reno64-wsj.

110. *Id.*

111. *Id.*

112. Sam Chester, *Netanyahu Favors Chinese Interests in Terror Case, Causing Dismay All Around*, Tablet, Aug. 20, 2013, http://www.tabletmag.com/jewish-news-and-politics/141261/netanyahu-chooses-china.

113. *The Chinese Conundrum*, Yedioth Ahronoth, July 12, 2013, http://www.dcwfoundation.org/yediot071213.htm (translation by Daniel Cantor Wultz Foundation).

114. Wultz v. Bank of China, 298 F.R.D. 91, 94 (S.D.N.Y. 2014).

115. *Id.* at 95.

116. *Id.*

117. *Id.*

118. *Id.* at 103.

119. Yonah Jeremy Bob, *Israel Wins US Court Battle to Block Former Government Agent's "Smoking Gun" Testimony*, Jerusalem Post, July 23, 2014.

120. Nitsana Darshan-Leitner, *Starve Hamas of Money*, Globes, July 26, 2014.

121. Ronen Bergman, The Secret War with Iran: The 30-Year Clandestine Struggle Against the World's Most Dangerous Terrorist Power 284 (2008).
122. *Id.*
123. Josh Meyer, *Influential Mideast Bank Accused of Funding Militants*, L.A. Times, Mar. 4, 2007, http://articles.latimes.com/2007/mar/04/world/fg-arabbank4/2.
124. *Id.*
125. Glenn R. Simpson, *Arab Bank's Link to Terrorism Poses Dilemma for U.S. Policy*, Wall St. J., Apr. 20, 2005, http://www.wsj.com/articles/SB111396116907311600.
126. Bergman, *supra* note 121, at 285 (2008). *See also, e.g.*, James Bennet, *Israelis, in Raid on Arab Banks, Seize Reputed Terrorist Funds*, N.Y. Times, Feb. 26, 2004, http://www.nytimes.com/2004/02/26/world/israelis-in-raid-on-arab-banks-seize-reputed-terrorist-funds.html.
127. Bergman, *supra* note 121, at 285.
128. Ilene R. Prusher & Ben Lynfield, *Israeli Bank Raid Breaks New Turf*, Christian Science Monitor, Feb. 27, 2004, http://www.csmonitor.com/2004/0227/p06s01-wome.html.
129. *Id.*
130. *Id.*
131. Bergman, *supra* note 121, at 285. *See also, e.g.*, Peter Hermann, *Israeli Troops Raid Arab Banks, Seize Cash Tied to Terror*, Baltimore Sun, Feb. 26, 2004, http://articles.baltimore-sun.com/2004-02-26/news/0402260008_1_west-bank-attacks-on-israelis-raid.
132. Bergman, *supra* note 121, at 285.
133. *Id.*
134. *Id.*
135. *See, e.g.*, United States v. El-Mezain, 664 F.3d 467 (5th Cir. 2011), *cert. denied*, 133 S. Ct. 525 (2012).
136. Press Release, U.S. Dep't of Justice, *Federal Judge Hands Down Sentences in Holy Land Foundation Case* (May 27, 2009), http://www.justice.gov/opa/pr/federal-judge-hands-downs-sentences-holy-land-foundation-case; Elizabeth J. Shapiro, *The Holy Land Foundation for Relief and Development: A Case Study*, 62 U.S. Attys' Bull. 23 (Sept. 2014), *available at* http://www.justice.gov/sites/default/files/usao/legacy/2014/09/23/usab6205.pdf.
137. United States v. El-Mezain, 664 F.3d 467, 488 (5th Cir. 2011).
138. *Id.* at 509.
139. *Id.* at 509–10.
140. *Id.* at 532.
141. *See* Jury Verdict, Linde v. Arab Bank, No. 04-CV-2799 (E.D.N.Y. Sept. 22, 2014). *See also* Joe Palazzolo, *Arab Bank Found Liable for Providing Assistance to Hamas*, Wall St. J., Sept. 22, 2014, http://www.wsj.com/articles/arab-bank-found-liable-for-providing-assistance-to-hamas-1411419783.
142. *Id.*
143. Glenn R. Simpson, *Arab Bank's Link to Terrorism Poses Dilemma for U.S. Policy*, Wall St. J., Apr. 20, 2005, http://www.wsj.com/articles/SB111396116907311600.
144. *Id.*
145. *Id.*
146. See, e.g., Yonah Jeremy Bob, *Will the Arab Bank Really Have to Pay Out a $1 Billion Settlement?*, Jerusalem Post, September 10, 2015.

147. Joint Press Release, *FinCEN and OCC Assess $24 Million Penalty Against Arab Bank Branch*, Financial Crimes Enforcement Network & Office of the Comptroller of the Currency (Aug. 17, 2005), http://www.fincen.gov/news_room/nr/pdf/20050817.pdf.

148. *See, e.g.,* INTELLIGENCE & TERRORISM INFORMATION CTR. AT THE CTR. FOR SPECIAL STUDIES, THE PALESTINIAN AUTHORITY'S SUPPORT OF HAMAS' SUICIDE TERRORISM (Oct. 2004), http://www.osenlaw.com/sites/default/files/uploaded/Counter-Terrorism/Arab_Bank/attacks/2001/said_al-hutari/MalamReport.pdf; Simpson, *supra* note 143.

149. *Sen. Hearing 109-253, Hearing Before the Senate Committee on Banking, Housing, & Urban Affairs, Nominations of: Christopher Cox, Roel C. Campos, Annette L. Nazareth, Martin J. Gruenberg, John C. Dugan and John M. Reich*, 109th Cong. (July 26, 2005).

150. *Id.*

151. *Id.*

152. Paul Alster, *Battling Islamic Terror in the Courts*, JERUSALEM REPORT, Feb. 22, 2015, http://israellawcenter.org/in-the-media-items/the-latest-from-nitsana-battling-islamic-terror-in-the-courts/.

153. *Id.*

154. *Sen. Hearing 109-253, supra* note 149; Glenn R. Simpson, *Arab Bank's Link to Terrorism Poses Dilemma for U.S. Policy*, WALL ST. J., Apr. 20, 2005, http://www.wsj.com/articles/SB111396116907311600.

155. Ethan Bronner & Christine Hauser, *UN Assembly, in Blow to U.S., Elevates Status of Palestine*, N.Y. TIMES, Nov. 29, 2012, http://www.nytimes.com/2012/11/30/world/middleeast/Palestinian-Authority-United-Nations-Israel.html?pagewanted=all&_r=0.

CONCLUSION

1. Interview of Gary Clyde Hufbauer, Sanctions Are Finally Hitting Iran Hard: Part II, Peterson Perspectives (Oct. 4, 2012), https://piie.com/publications/interviews/pp20121004hufbauer.pdf.

2. David A. Baldwin, *Success and Failure in Foreign Policy*, 3 ANN. REV. POL. SCI. 167, 180 (2000).

3. *See, e.g.,* GARY CLYDE HUFBAUER, JEFFREY J. SCHOTT, KIMBERLY ANN ELLIOTT & BARBARA OEGG, ECONOMIC SANCTIONS RECONSIDERED (3d ed. 2009); DANIEL W. DREZNER, THE SANCTIONS PARADOX: ECONOMIC STATECRAFT AND INTERNATIONAL RELATIONS (1999).

4. *See, e.g.,* Kimberly Ann Elliott, *The Sanctions Glass: Half Full or Completely Empty?*, 23 INT'L SEC. 50, 51–52 (Summer 1998); HUFBAUER ET AL., *supra* note 3.

5. Richard Locke & Kathleen Thelen, *Problems of Equivalence in Comparative Politics: Apples and Oranges, Again*, NEWSL. OF APSA ORGANIZED SEC. IN COMP. POL., Winter 1998, at 9–12.

6. Author interview of Mostafa Elostaz (Feb. 21, 2015).

7. David A. Baldwin, *Power and International Relations*, in HANDBOOK OF INTERNATIONAL RELATIONS 273 (Walter Carlsnaes, Thomas Risse, & Beth A. Simmons eds., 2013).

8. Robert A. Dahl, *The Concept of Power*, 2 BEHAVIORAL SCI. 201, 202–03 (1957).

9. JOSEPH S. NYE, JR., SOFT POWER 2 (2004).

10. José E. Alvarez, *Foreword: Why Nations Behave*, 19 MICH. J. INT'L L. 303, 305 (1998).

11. Beth A. Simmons, *Money and the Law: Why Comply with the Public International Law of Money?*, 25 YALE J. INT'L L. 323, 323–24 (2000), http://scholar.harvard.edu/files/bsimmons/files/Simmons2000Yale.pdf.

12. *See, e.g.*, Harold Hongju Koh, *Why Do Nations Obey International Law?*, 106 YALE L.J. 2599, 2648 (1997).

13. *See, e.g.*, Oona A. Hathaway, *Do Human Rights Treaties Make a Difference?*, 111 YALE L.J. 1935, 1952–55 (2002); Laurence R. Helfer & Anne-Marie Slaughter, *Toward a Theory of Effective Supranational Adjudication*, 107 YALE L.J. 273, 331–35 (1997).

14. *See, e.g.*, MARGARET E. KECK & KATHRYN SIKKINK, ACTIVISTS BEYOND BORDERS (1998); Eric Neumayer, *Do International Human Rights Treaties Improve Respect for Human Rights?*, 49 J. CONFLICT RESOL. 925, 930–32 (2005), http://www.lse.ac.uk/geographyandenvironment/whoswho/profiles/neumayer/pdf/article%20in%20journal%20of%20conflict%20resolution%20(human%20rights).pdf.

15. Neumayer, *supra* note 14, at 950.

16. Beth A. Simmons, *International Law and State Behavior: Commitment and Compliance in International Monetary Affairs*, 4 AM. POL. SCI. REV. 819 (2000).

17. Hathaway, *supra* note 13.

18. Neumayer, *supra* note 14, at 926.

19. Koh, *supra* note 12.

20. Hathaway, *supra* note 13.

21. STEPHEN G. BROOKS, PRODUCING SECURITY: MULTINATIONAL CORPORATIONS, GLOBALIZATION, AND THE CHANGING CALCULUS OF CONFLICT 1 (2005).

22. *Id.* at 5–6.

23. JOHN STUART MILL, PRINCIPLES OF POLITICAL ECONOMY WITH SOME OF THEIR APPLICATIONS TO SOCIAL PHILOSOPHY III.17.14 (1848), http://www.econlib.org/library/Mill/mlP46.html.

24. *See, e.g.*, Randall W. Stone, *Institutions, Power, and Interdependence*, in POWER, INTERDEPENDENCE, AND NONSTATE ACTORS IN WORLD POLITICS (Helen V. Milner & Andrew Moravcsik eds., 2009).

25. *See, e.g.*, THE POWER OF CITIES IN INTERNATIONAL RELATIONS (Simon Curtis ed., 2014).

26. *See, e.g.*, RETHINKING VIOLENCE: STATES AND NON-STATE ACTORS IN CONFLICT (Erica Chenoweth & Adria Lawrence eds., 2010).

27. *See, e.g.*, Margaret E. Keck & Kathryn Sikkink, ACTIVISTS BEYOND BORDERS (1998).

28. *See, e.g.*, Layna Mosley, *Private Governance for the Public Good?*, in POWER, INTERDEPENDENCE, AND NONSTATE ACTORS IN WORLD POLITICS (Helen V. Milner & Andrew Moravcsik eds., 2009).

29. Duncan B. Hollis, *Why State Consent Still Matters—Non-State Actors, Treaties, and the Changing Sources of International Law*, 23 Berkeley J. INT'L L. 137, 146 (2005), http://scholarship.law.berkeley.edu/cgi/viewcontent.cgi?article=1283&context=bjil.

30. *Id.*

31. *See, e.g.*, PAULINE VAILLANCOURT ROSENAU, PUBLIC-PRIVATE POLICY PARTNERSHIPS (2000); PUBLIC-PRIVATE PARTNERSHIPS: THEORY AND PRACTICE IN INTERNATIONAL PERSPECTIVE (Stephen P. Osborne ed., 2000); THE CHALLENGES OF PUBLIC-PRIVATE PARTNERSHIPS: LEARNING FROM INTERNATIONAL EXPERIENCE (Graeme A. Hodge and Carsten Greve eds., 2005).

32. Joe Palazzolo, *Arab Bank Found Liable for Providing Assistance to Hamas*, WALL ST. J., Sept. 22, 2014, http://www.wsj.com/articles/arab-bank-found-liable-for-providing-assistance-to-hamas-1411419783; Michael D. Goldhaber, *Arab Bank Settlement Said to Be More Than $1 Billion*, AMERICAN LAWYER, Aug. 21, 2015, http://www.americanlawyer.com/id=1202735394772/Arab-Bank-Settlement-Said-to-Be-More-Than-1-Billion-?slreturn=20150731164416.

33. Goldhaber, *id.*; Stephanie Clifford, *Arab Bank Reaches Settlement in Suit Accusing It of Financing Terrorism*, N.Y. TIMES, Aug. 14, 2015, http://www.nytimes.com/2015/08/15/nyregion/arab-bank-reaches-settlement-in-suit-accusing-it-of-financing-terrorism.html?_r=0.
34. Goldhaber, *supra* note 32.
35. *Id.*
36. *See, e.g.,* Rebecca J. Rosen, *"I've Created a Monster!" On the Regrets of Inventors*, THE ATLANTIC, Nov. 23, 2011, http://www.theatlantic.com/technology/archive/2011/11/ive-created-a-monster-on-the-regrets-of-inventors/249044/; *The Manhattan Project*, AM. MUSEUM OF NATURAL HISTORY, http://www.amnh.org/exhibitions/past-exhibitions/einstein/peace-and-war/the-manhattan-project (last visited June 5, 2015).
37. PHILIP BOBBITT, TERROR AND CONSENT 456–457 (2008).

INDEX

Arafat, Yasser, 68, 71, 274
Argentina, 232
Armstrong, Olin, 74
Arnaud-Khimoun, Saquina, 251
Arouri, Saleh, 218
"Article 98" agreements, 29, 231, 232, 280
Ashcroft, John, 57
Ashrawi, Hanan, 67, 234, 246
Ashton, Catherine, 246
Association for the Promotion of
     International Humanitarian Law
     (Israel), 228
Association France Palestine Solidarité
     (AFPS), 265
Asymmetric warfare, 40–43
Asymmetric Warfare (Thornton), 41
ATA. *See* Anti-Terrorism Act
Atomic Energy Organization of Iran,
     127, 133
Attorney fees, 24
Attorney General's remission authority, 104
Australia, 136, 209, 232
Averbach, Steve, 65
Aviation lawfare, China's use of, 165–168

Baker, Stewart, 21–22
Baker & McKenzie (law firm), 88–89
Baldwin, David, 333, 457n2, 457n7
Banco Delta Asia (Chinese bank), 115
Bank Hapoalim (Israel), 321
Ban Ki-moon, 36–37, 236, 287, 313
Bank Melli (Iran), 127, 133, 141
Bank of China case, 69, 318–322, 325
Bank of Kunlun (China), 129
Banks. *See also names of specific banks*
     civil lawsuits for providing financial
          services to terrorist groups, 16, 51,
          60–65. *See also* U.S. private civil
          litigation against terrorists, their
          material supporters, and their state
          sponsors
     enforcement actions by states against for
          providing financial services to rogue
          states or terrorist groups, 17, 143–144
     individual liability of bankers for
          violations of sanctions, 159–160
     seizure of Karl Lee (Li Fangwei) related
          accounts in U.S. banks, 185
Banks, William, 42
Bank Saderat (Iran), 126

Bank Sepah (Iran), 127
Barak, Aharon, 283, 303
Barclays PLC, 142
Barghouti, Omar, 242, 266
Al-Barghouti, Hafez, 67
Barhoum, Fawzi, 214
Barnidge, Robert, 42
al-Bashir, Omar, 216
Bathurst-Norman, George, 248
Battlefield lawfare. *See* Hamas battlefield
     lawfare
BDS (boycotts, divestment, and sanctions)
     movement, 13, 14, 83, 99–100, 239,
     240–259
     disruption of Israeli-affiliated
          businesses, 246–249
     EU guidelines used against Israel,
          245–246
     OECD guidelines used against Israel,
          243–245
     overview, 240–243
     responses by pro-Israel activists,
          249–259
BDS National Committee (BNC), 240,
     242, 243
Beirut attack on U.S. Marine barracks,
     liability for Iranian-sponsored
     bombing of, 16, 51–52. *See also* Iran,
     U.S. financial lawfare against
Belgium, 152, 153, 154, 273
     OECD guidelines and, 245
     universal jurisdiction laws in, 263
     "universal jurisdiction" repealed in, 262
Bell, Avi, 246
Bellflower, John W., 169
Bemba, Jean-Pierre, 225
Bensouda, Fatou, 208, 211, 213, 216, 219,
     221–222, 224–225, 229, 277
Benvenisti, Eyal, 42
Bergman, Ronen, 321, 322–323
Bilal, Damara Ibrahim Mustafa, 206
Bin Cheng, 168
bin Laden, Osama, 43
Birnbaum, Daniel, 252
Birzeit University Institute of Law, 242
"Black Hawk Down" incident (1993), 43
Blackstone, William, 168
Blair, Tony, 307
Blanchette, Richard, 18
Blank, Laurie, 288, 289, 309

Blum, Gabriella, 30

BNP Paribas, 17, 104–105, 137, 145–146, 159, 341, 383n88

Bob, Yonah Jeremy, 66, 227

Bobbitt, Philip, 195, 343

Boies, David, 318, 320

Boim v. Holy Land Foundation (7th Cir. 2008), 34, 54–60, 61, 103, 316, 323

Borch, Frederic L., III, 352n149

Bosco, David, 222

Breaking the Silence (NGO), 227

Brennan, John, 124, 148

Breuer, Lanny, 141–142

Brookings Institution, 106

Brooks, Stephen, 338

Brothers to the Rescue, 16, 74

Buergenthal, Thomas, 236

Burma-related Massachusetts law, 84

Bush, George H.W., 262

Bush, George W.
  "Article 98" agreements of, 29
  Executive Order 13224 (2001), 126
  Executive Order 13382 (2005), 126–127
  on Holy Land Foundation, 57
  ICC membership opposed by, 29, 32
  lawfare against Iran waged by, 115
  prosecution for war crimes, effect of threat of, 14, 47
  universal jurisdiction changing travel plans of, 263

Cairo-Amman Bank, 323

Canada, 136, 208, 209, 226

Cantor, Eric, 321

Carlin, John, 160

Carlson, John, 6

Carter, Phillip, 3

Case Western University School of Law, 107
  Lawfare! conference, 8–9

Casey, Lee, 5

Casualty aversion of Western nations, 43

Caterpillar Inc., 242, 264–265

Center for Constitutional Rights, 54

Center for Strategic Counterterrorism Communications (CSCC), 27

Central Bank of Iran (CBI), 130, 136, 145

Chayes, Abram, 100

Cheng, Dean, 189–190, 191, 408n262

Cheng, Sihai, 178, 184

China. *See also* China's use of lawfare
  acceding to international laws, 38
  arrest of human rights lawyers in, 164
  assertive and proactive stance in international organizations, 187
  Cultural Revolution (1966 to 1976), 163, 186
  economic interdependence of, 49
  Exclusive Economic Zone (EEZ) of, 166–168
  foreign direct investment in United States, 187–188, 192–193, 194
  Iran's energy sector, investment in, 175
  Israel-China relations, 320–322
  lawfare power of, 334
  legal system in, 164, 186–187
  nine-dash map and, 167
  nuclear weapons trade with Iran, 174–183
  responses to lawfare against, 281
  South China Sea islands and, 167–168
  U.S. commercial trade with, 187–188, 194
  U.S. foreign direct investment in, 187

China's use of lawfare, 10, 161–195
  agreements that may limit, 194–195
  compared to United States, 32, 161–162, 190
  compliance-leverage disparity lawfare, 12, 26, 172–186
  cyberspace lawfare, 169–172, 401n91, 406n199
  falu zhan (legal warfare), in Chinese literature, 8, 9, 162, 163, 348n66
  future of, 186–191
  instrumental lawfare, 13, 165–172
  against Japan, 188
  literature of lawfare in China, 9–10, 162–163
  maritime and aviation lawfare, 165–168
  nuclear nonproliferation obligations, Chinese failure to adhere to, 12, 26
  outer space lawfare, 168–169
  overview, 2
  strategic policy to use lawfare, 3
  U.S. options for responding, 183–186, 191–195

Chinese Central Military Commission, 162

Chinese Communist Party Central Committee, 162

Church of the Nativity, Bethlehem, 233, 234

CIA's detention and interrogation
program, 26
CISADA. *See* Comprehensive Iran
Sanctions, Accountability and
Divestment Act of 2010
Citigroup, 78–79, 139
Civilians
Hamas using. *See* Hamas battlefield
lawfare
international bodies ignoring violations
involving, 23
Taliban using. *See* Taliban's use of civilians
Clark, Phil, 217
Clarke, Ann Marie, 46
Clawson, Patrick, 72
Clearstream Banking, 145
Clement, Paul, 62
Clinton, Bill, 71
Clinton, Hillary, 204
Cluster munitions, ban on, 152–154
CNOOC (Chinese state-owned entity),
192–193
Cogan, Brian, 60–62
Cohen, David, 115, 116, 124, 129, 130,
131, 136
Cohen, Jerome, 167
Cole, David, 30
Cole, James, 146
Colombia, 221
Colombian Armed Revolutionary Forces
(FARC), 12, 27
Commerce Department (U.S.), 253, 254,
255, 257
Commission on the Limits of the
Continental Shelf, 166
Complementarity, 223, 225, 227, 280
Compliance-leverage disparity
lawfare, 18–25
benefits of compliance, 22
China's use of, 172–186
contributing factors, 20–25
cost of being subjected to
proceedings, 23–24
cost of penalties, 25
definition, 20
detainees alleging abuse, 26–27
differing ideologies regarding, 21–22
on kinetic battlefield, 11, 18–20, 198,
285–286. *See also* Hamas battlefield
lawfare

outside of battlefield, 25–28
probability of adverse judgment, 24–25
probability of being subjected to
proceedings, 23
recommended U.S. response to, 28
risks of actual or credibly alleged
violations, 22–25
rule of law and, 41
state vs. non-state actors and, 338
type of lawfare, 11
Compliance theory, 334–338
costs of noncompliance and, 335–338
Comprehensive Iran Sanctions,
Accountability and Divestment Act
of 2010 (CISADA), 95–96, 129–130,
183–184, 374n476
Congressional Research Service, 75, 82, 131
Cong Wensheng, 9, 162
Constitution, U.S., foreign policy powers
of President and Congress under,
82, 84–85
Convention Against Corruption
(U.N.), 207
Convention Against Torture (U.N.), 207
Convention on International Civil
Aviation, 168
Convention on the Rights of the Child
(U.N.), 207
Conventions on Cluster Munitions and
Anti-Personnel Mines, 154
Corn, Geoffrey, 288
Corrie, Rachel, 264
Cortright, David, 331
Corwin, Edward S., 82
Costs of adjudication, 23–24, 103, 333
costs of noncompliance and, 335–338
Council on Foreign Relations, 106
Countryman, Thomas, 179, 181–182
Cour de Cassation (France), 251
Craig, Alan, 298
Cramton, Roger C., 35
Credit Suisse, 141–142
Crimes against humanity, 212, 223
Crist, David, 76
Crosby v. National Foreign Trade Council
(U.S. 2000), 84
Cuba, 16, 83
Cultural Revolution of 1966 to 1976
(China), 163, 186
Customary international law, 19, 47, 166

Kosovo conflict (1999), 27
Kraska, James, 165–166
Kreczko, Alan, 102
Kuttab, Daoud, 212
Kuwait, 45

Lakhani, Karim, 98, 375n487
Lamberth, Royce, 72, 75, 77–78
Landes, Stephen, 55, 58, 59–60
Landmine treaty, 47
Law abidingness, 21–22
Law as a Means to an End: Threat to the Rule of Law (Tamanaha), 33
Lawfare, conceptual analysis of, 1–50
  benefits of, 3, 343
  compliance-leverage disparity lawfare, 17–28. *See also* Compliance-leverage disparity lawfare
  compliance theory and, 334–338
  data sets for study of lawfare, 332–333
  definition of, 2, 4–8
  derogative use of term "lawfare," 29
  economic sanctions scholarship, relationship to, 331–332
  examples of, 1–2, 12–19
  globalization and, 48–50
  increase in influence of, 40–50
  information technology revolution and, 48
  instrumental use of legal tools, 12–17. *See also* Instrumental lawfare
  introduction of term, 2, 4, 5–6
  legal and international relations scholarship, relationship to, 330, 333–334
  non-state actors and, 338–343
  overview of lawfare literature, 8–10
  power and, 333–334
  reasons for increasing influence of lawfare, 40–50
  typology of, 11–28
  U.S. approach to, 28–40. *See also* U.S. approach to lawfare
Lawfare: Hard National Security Choices (Lawfare Blog), 7, 106
Lawfare and U.S. National Security (Kittrie), 9
Lawfare Blog, 7, 106
Lawfare! conference (Case Western University School of Law), 8–9
Lawfare Project, 7, 91, 106

Law of armed conflict. *See* Geneva Conventions
Law of armed conflict (LOAC), 21–22. *See also* Geneva Conventions
Lawsky, Benjamin, 113, 143–144, 145, 146, 157, 159
Lawyers for Palestinian Human Rights, 243, 244
Lebanon War against Hezbollah (2006), 302
Lee, Judith, 112, 147
Lee, Karl (Li Fangwei), 160, 178–186
Legal & Policy Department of the PLO Negotiations Affairs Department, 274
Leigh Day (law firm), 244
Lellouche, Pierre, 250
Lellouche law (France), 250, 251
Lemkin, Raphael, 51, 52, 86–87, 343
Lenovo (Chinese computer company), 192
Levey, Stuart, 115, 116, 117, 122, 137, 139, 149, 388n231
Levitt, Matthew, 157
Lew, Jack (Jacob J.), 73, 111
Lewin, Nathan & Alyza, 55–59, 103
Liberation Tigers of Tamil Eelam (LTTE), 315
Libya, lawsuits against, 83
Lieberman, Avigdor, 226, 233
Lieberman, Joseph, 148
Li Fangwei (Lee, Karl), 160, 178–186
Lima Holding B.V, 266. *See also Riwal/Lima* case
LIMMT (Chinese company), 178, 180
Linde v. Arab Bank (E.D.N.Y. 2014), 60–65, 324
Livni, Tzipi, 260, 263
Lloyd's of London, 315
Lloyds TSB Bank, 141
LOAC (Law of armed conflict), 21–22. *See also* Geneva Conventions
Lockheed Martin, 153, 155, 259
London's Standard Club, 2
Lopez, George, 331
Lowenstein International Human Rights Law Clinic (Yale Law School), 107
LTTE (Liberation Tigers of Tamil Eelam), 315
Lubanga, Thomas, 220
Lyons, James, 76, 77–78

Machen, Ronald C., Jr., 144
Madhoun, Diya al-Din, 260
Mahmoud, Da'agna Nufal Mahmad, 206
Mahmoud, Muammar Ata Mahmoud, 206
Malka, Yosef, 206
al-Malki, Riyad, 214
Mandelblit, Avichai, 208
Mao Zedong, 163, 164
Mare Liberum (Grotius), 4–5
Maritime lawfare
    China's use of, 165–168
Markey, Edward, 182
Markowicz, Pascal, 251
Marxism, 163
al-Masri, Mushir, 215
Mavi Marmara flotilla raid, 261, 262, 270
McGeough, Paul, 63–64
Military Advocate General (MAG)
    (Israel), 227
Military commissions, 30, 352n164
Mill, John Stuart, 338
Missile Technology Control Regime
    guidelines, 181
Mofaz, Shaul, 260, 261
Mohtashemi, Ali Akbar, 76, 78
Money laundering, 119, 128, 134, 357n292
Morgenthau, Robert M., 180
Mouhlas, Sawafta Sudqi Abdel Razeq, 206
Muhammad, Afana Mustafa Ahmad, 206
Multinational companies
    civil lawsuits against for material
        support to Hamas, 16
    doing business with Iran, 127
    lawfare scholarship and, 341–342
Mulvenon, James, 170–171
Musawi, Hussein, 78

Nasrallah, Hassan, 260
National Bureau of Vigilance Against
    Anti-Semitism, 250
National Defense Authorization Act of
    2012 (NDAA), 130–131
National Defense Strategy (U.S.), 30
National Lawyers Guild, 255
National Security Council (U.S.), 31
NATO
    in Cold War, 96
    cyberspace and, 170
    Deterrence and Defense Posture
        Review, 153

differences among allies over what
    qualifies as legitimate military
    target, 194
ICC and, 232
Kosovo conflict (1999), 27
prosecutions against for alleged war
    crimes, averted, 28, 29
Rumsfeld and, 14
Taliban and. *See* Taliban's use of civilians
Netanyahu, Benjamin, 210, 214, 222,
    231, 281, 299, 307, 320, 321, 322,
    326, 413n61
Netherlands
    funding pro-Palestinian lawfare,
        105–106
    legal actions against companies "aiding
        and abetting" war crimes, 266–269
    OECD guidelines and, 245
    PA Legal & Policy Department funded
        by, 274
    Riwal/Lima case, 14, 266–269, 277, 279
Neumayer, Eric, 336
Neutrality Act, 317
*New Battlefields/Old Laws: Critical Debates
    on Asymmetric Warfare* (Banks), 42
New York Department of Financial
    Services (NYDFS), 17, 140, 143–144,
    146, 340
New York Times
    Abbas op-ed in, 197, 200
    on Hamas using civilian facilities, 199
    on PA joining ICC, 209
New Zealand, 232
NGO Monitor (Israeli NGO), 105
NGOs. *See* Non-governmental
    organizations
Nicaragua case (ICJ 1986), 183
Nigeria, 221
Nonaligned Movement, 37, 274, 275
Non-governmental organizations (NGOs),
    1, 10, 45–48, 92, 340–341. *See also*
    Palestinian NGOs, use of lawfare
    compliance theory and, 16–17, 335–336
    law of armed conflict and, 45–48
Nonproliferation. *See* Nuclear
    nonproliferation obligations
Non-state actors. *See also* Hamas; Hezbollah
    compliance-leverage disparity lawfare
        and, 338
    cost of penalties for, 25

Stein, Jeff, 182
Steinberg, Gerald, 300
Stempel, Paul A., 348n66
Stern, Menahem, 206
Stewart, Ian, 177, 178
Stewart, Lynne, 351–352n143
Stier, Max, 99
Strategic Petroleum Reserve, prohibition
on companies doing business with
Iran as suppliers to, 95
Straw, Jack, 261
Stricker, Andrea, 177, 178
Studies in International Space Law
(Bin), 168
Sub-state actors, role of, 339–340
Sudan
non-compliance with ICC
prosecutions, 226
Sudan Accountability and Divestment
Act of 2007, 92
Sudan Divestment Task Force, 91
Sullivan, Emmet, 142
Sun Tzu, 161, 163, 172
Sweden, 105–106, 274
SWIFT (Society for Worldwide
Interbank Financial
Telecommunications), 90–91
Switzerland, 263
funding pro-Palestinian lawfare,
105–106
OECD guidelines and, 245
restricting Iran's banking
activities, 136
Swiss banks, responsive to Treasury's
outreach, 138
Syria
Iranian arms transfer to Assad,
380nn42–43
lawsuits against, 83
U.S. financial lawfare against, 117
Szubin, Adam, 112, 115, 116, 142, 143, 145,
147, 148

Taft, William H., IV, 74
Taiwan, 186, 188, 232
Taliban
compliance-leverage disparity tactics,
use of, 12, 43, 285. *See also* Taliban's
use of civilians
as foreign terrorist organization, 7

Taliban's use of civilians
NATO forces dealing with,
18–19, 346n9
overview, 2
U.S. armed forces, self-imposed
restraints in response to, 19
Tamanaha, Brian, 33–35
Tamil Tigers (LTTE), 315
Tax Reform Act of 1976 (U.S.), 253
Terrorism Risk Insurance Act, 80
Terrorists. *See also specific names of terrorist
organizations*
compliance-leverage disparity tactics,
use of, 43, 308, 340
lawfare scholarship and, 340
private civil litigation against, 16, 53–80
rejection of law of armed conflict by, 43
*The Terror Presidency: Law and Judgment
Inside the Bush Administration*
(Goldsmith), 26, 29
Thornton, Rod, 41
Thornton, Sean, 122
Thrall, Nathan, 287
Through Secret Channels (Abbas), 273
Toameh, Khaled Abu, 243
Torture Convention (U.N.), 207
Torture memos, 26
Torture Victim Protection Act (U.S.), 264
Transatlantic Trade and Investment
Partnership, 256
Treasury Department (U.S.), 254
lawfare waged by, 28, 32, 111–160, 190,
341–342. *See also* Iran, U.S. financial
lawfare against
persuading foreign banks to stop
doing business with Iran, 119–123,
136–146, 373n462
*Treasury's War: The Unleashing of a New Era of
Financial Warfare* (Zarate), 9, 115, 121
Treaty on the Non-Proliferation of
Nuclear Weapons. *See* Nuclear
Nonproliferation Treaty (NPT)
Trocaire (NGO), 273
Tucker, Neely, 72, 75
Turkel, Jacob, 227, 300
Turkel Commission (Israel), 227, 270, 280,
300, 303
Turkey
OECD guidelines and, 245
settlers in Cyprus, 229

Turner, Tab, 62
The Twilight War (Crist), 76
Tyler, Tom, 21, 349nn102–103

UBS (Swiss bank), 141
Ukraine
    ICC preliminary examination, 221
    Russian invasion of (2014), 112
U.N. Convention on the Law of the Sea
        (UNCLOS), 166, 167
U.N. Educational, Scientific, and Cultural
        Organization (UNESCO), 339
    PA's membership in, 233–234
    PA's statehood recognition campaign
        and, 202–204, 205, 233, 277
U.N. Fact Finding Mission on the Gaza
        Conflict. *See* Goldstone Report
U.N. Human Rights Council (UNHRC),
        36–37, 218, 220, 284, 339
    fact-finding mission on Israel's handling
        of Gaza-bound flotilla, 313
    Independent Commission of Inquiry on
        the 2014 Gaza Conflict, 287–289, 298,
        300–301, 309
U.N. Office for the Coordination of
        Humanitarian Affairs, 295–296
U.N. Panel of Experts on Accountability in
        Sri Lanka, 309
UNCLOS International Law of the Sea
        Tribunal, 166
United Against Nuclear Iran (UANI),
        16–17, 91, 340–341, 343
United Kingdom
    Ahava case, 248, 249
    Crown Prosecution Service, 260
    ICC and, 221, 230
    as ICC donor, 226
    OECD guidelines and, 245
    Office for Judicial Complaints, 248
    restricting Iran's banking activities, 136
    Supreme Court, 247, 249
    universal jurisdiction laws in, 263
    use of lawfare to stop Russian ship
        bound for Syria, 2
United Nations. *See also headings starting
    with "U.N."*
    condemnations of Israel in, 284
    Genocide Convention, 52, 86–87
    instrumental lawfare in context of,
        35–38, 52

Palestine, non-member observer state
        status for, 13, 200–208, 328
    PRC membership, 186
United States. *See also* Iran, U.S. financial
        lawfare against; U.S. approach to
        lawfare
    Article 98 agreements by, 29, 231,
        232, 280
    bilateral aid to Palestinians,
        204–205, 280
    China's foreign direct investment in,
        187–188, 192–193
    China's use of lawfare, options for
        responding to, 183–186, 191–195
    Chinese investment in U.S. Treasury
        securities, 188
    cluster weapons, policy on, 154
    compared to China's use of lawfare, 32,
        161–162, 190
    detainees alleging abuse, 26–27
    ICC preliminary investigation in
        Afghanistan, 221
    instrumental lawfare, recommended
        approach for, 31
    lawfare power of, 334
    lawsuits against companies "aiding and
        abetting" war crimes, 264–265
    non-governmental attorneys and lawfare
        outside litigation arena, 80–102
    OECD guidelines and, 245
    PA's statehood campaign, response to,
        201, 202–207
    preeminence in international law, as
        advantage, 195, 343
    relationship with Israel, 69
    self-imposing restrictions in response to
        enemy using civilians, 18–20
    United States–Israel Trade
        Enhancement Act of 2015, 256, 257
Universal Declaration of Human Rights, 22
Universal jurisdiction prosecutions, 14, 29
    Chinese making possible use of, 193
    Palestinian NGOs use of, 198, 240, 241,
        259–263, 270, 278, 283
    U.S. opposition to, 14, 30, 262
Unrestricted Warfare, 5
U.S. approach to lawfare. *See also* Iran,
        U.S. financial lawfare against
    conceptual analysis of, 28–40
    in context of U.N. system, 35–38, 119

INDEX [479]

16x